PSYCHOPATHOLOGY
OF CHILDHOOD

Jane W. Kessler

PSYCHOPATHOLOGY
OF CHILDHOOD

Second Edition

PRENTICE HALL
Englewood Cliffs, New Jersey 07632

Library of Congress Cataloging-in-Publication Data

Kessler, Jane W.
Psychopathology of childhood.

Includes bibliographies and index.
1. Child psychiatry. I. Title. [DNLM: 1. Mental
Disorders—in infancy & childhood. WS 350 K42p]
RJ499.K44 1988   618.92'89   87-7192
ISBN 0-13-736778-3

Cover design: Photo Plus Art
Manufacturing buyer: Ray Keating

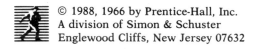 © 1988, 1966 by Prentice-Hall, Inc.
A division of Simon & Schuster
Englewood Cliffs, New Jersey 07632

Printed in the United States of America

10 9 8 7 6 5 4 3 2 1

ISBN 0-13-736778-3

Prentice-Hall International (UK) Limited, *London*
Prentice-Hall of Australia Pty. Limited, *Sydney*
Prentice-Hall Canada Inc., *Toronto*
Prentice-Hall Hispanoamericana, S.A., *Mexico*
Prentice-Hall of India Private Limited, *New Delhi*
Prentice-Hall of Japan, Inc., *Tokyo*
Simon & Schuster Asia Pte. Ltd., *Singapore*
Editora Prentice-Hall do Brasil, Ltda., *Rio de Janeiro*

CONTENTS

Chapter 4
PARENTS AND CHILDREN IN POVERTY   111

Chapter 5
PERSPECTIVES OF THE YOUNG CHILD   141

Chapter 6
BEHAVIOR PROBLEMS IN PRESCHOOL CHILDREN   171

Chapter 7
REFERRAL, ASSESSMENT, AND CHOICE OF TREATMENT   203

Chapter 8
ANXIETY DISORDERS   249

Chapter 9
DEPRESSION AND BEREAVEMENT   289

Chapter 10
CONDUCT DISORDERS   317

Chapter 11
LEARNING PROBLEMS IN SCHOOL-AGE CHILDREN   **355**

PREFACE

This book is the product of twenty years' continuing reflection on theory and practice in the field of child psychopathology. Beyond the astronomical increase of professional journal articles and books published since 1966, there have been new areas of investigation. The most dramatic change has been in the area of infancy and early childhood. What started as a social reform movement to counteract the effects of poverty, namely the Head Start program, gave birth to programs for early identification of and intervention with handicapped children. At the same time, new psychological information about infant capacities and the transactional nature of early relationships stimulated intervention efforts on behalf of infants at risk because of parental characteristics. This burgeoning of interest is reflected in the fact that almost half of this book is devoted to the age period from birth to 5 years.

With regard to the school-age child, there have been major changes in emphasis. Depression in childhood has emerged as a significant topic, partly as a consequence of the biological-genetic findings with regard to adult depression that suggest the same factors may be at work with children. Learning disability has become a relatively common diagnosis, partly as the result of the special services available to this group mandated by the Education for All Handicapped Children Act. Mental retardation has been redefined and cognitive psychology has introduced new ways of assessing and treating problems that have some cognitive learning defect in common. Because my clinical experience in the past twenty years has been mainly in this field, I have perhaps a disproportionate amount to say with regard to learning disabilities and developmental disabilities.

Some chapter headings have disappeared from the first edition, namely, psychosis, mind and body, and juvenile delinquency. Autism, formerly classified as a psychotic disorder, has been included in developmental disabilities following the revised explanations for this disorder. Juvenile delinquency has been omitted in its entirety because this edition does not attempt to cover problems of adolescence. "Psychoneurosis" is subsumed under "Anxiety Disorders" because it no longer exists as a diagnostic category in the official nomenclature.

The Diagnostic Statistical Manual (DSM-III), which was introduced in 1980, represents a systematic effort to use behavioral criteria for diagnosis and to avoid etiological inferences, which accounts for the disappearance of "psychoneurosis" as a diagnosis. Psychodynamic explanations, couched in terms of defense mechanisms against the arousal of anxiety, have faded, not because they were proven wrong but because of the greater interest in biological-genetic and learning-behavioral explanations. In theory, there is no reason why these various explanations cannot co-exist; however, in practice, most professionals adopt one or another frame of reference for studying and treating childhood behavior disorders.

One purpose of this book is the integration of both old and new theories. In my view, psychoanalytic theory is indispensable in understanding the impact of real-life experiences on the young child's development. It is all too easy to overlook the role of fantasy, or what

might be called "irrational beliefs" in cognitive behavioral terms, if one focuses narrowly on the overt behavior of child or parent. Psychoanalytic theory provides some order and predictability in what, to me, is insufficiently explained by other developmental theories. On the other hand, this approach does not dictate the preferred method of intervention. A child therapist needs to know and use the techniques developed by family, behavioral, and cognitive therapists, and at least have some familiarity with psychopharmacologic therapies. There is no simple one-to-one relationship between the kind of problem and the preferred treatment, but therapeutic flexibility and the ability to choose from and combine an array of options are imperative. However, the success of any intervention is still dependent on empathy and the ability to communicate effectively at different developmental levels.

The advent of new techniques is a sign of progress, but it is of concern that many of the new treatments are presented as superior because they are short term. Partly because of the economic concerns stemming from the reliance on third-party payment plans, treatment goals are likely to be constructed in relatively superficial terms with insufficient attention to maintenance or support over time. The crucial importance of relationships is neglected in favor of the "quick fix."

A second aim in writing this book was to integrate research and practice. A lot of research has been reported in the past twenty years, although it takes careful reading to understand the implications for practice. Most of the research has come from developmental psychologists or professionals working in academic or designated research centers; clinicians in "general practice" have contributed relatively little. The clinical practitioner has been a consumer rather than a producer. There are many reasons for this, but economic cost is probably a major deterrent. However, there seem to be some prospects for increasing clinically based research contributions by the use of the assessment measures included in the Appendix. These measures can provide uniform data and are useful in understanding the client with relative little added expense. The clinical practitioner needs to know the results of well-planned research studies but also needs to relate, in an organized way, something of the contradictions and perplexities encountered when working with children, their families, schools, and collateral professionals.

Many persons have helped in this ambitious undertaking and I want to express my gratitude to colleagues and graduate students who have patiently perused various versions. I am particu-larly indebted to Julia Krevans who not only prepared the Appendix but also assisted in the preparation of the text.

I would also like to express my appreciation to the following individuals for their review of and comments on the draft manuscript of the book:

- Alfred Kornfeld, Eastern Connecticut State University
- Karen Paulsen
- Elizabeth Robinson, University of Washington
- Margaret Appel, The Ohio State University, Athens
- Solomon A. Levin
- Linda Musun-Miller, University of Arkansas
- Thomas H. Ollendick, Virginia Polytechnic Institute and State University
- Phillip Harvey, State University of New York, Binghamton
- Andrew Newcomb, Michigan State University.

Jane W. Kessler

CHAPTER 1

DEVELOPMENT OF MENTAL HEALTH IN INFANCY

THE EMERGENCE OF DEVELOPMENTAL PSYCHOPATHOLOGY

In 1970 the Joint Commission on Mental Health of Children published the first of their several reports, calling for a general reorganization of the child mental health enterprise around prevention rather than the traditional treatment of mental disorders once they occur. In this spirit, the Commission's report advocated major societal reforms which did not materialize; however, the time was right to answer the Commission's plea for more attention to the very young.

Our mental health services are most deficient for the very young, yet there is general agreement among clinicians that the most important time for both remedial and preventive mental health services is during the mother's pregnancy and the very early years of the child's life. It has been estimated that 35 percent of apparently normal children of self-sustaining families show behavioral difficulties as early as age four. The prevalence of disorders is thought to be even higher among the poor children. The present tendency is to identify children in need and refer them for services after they have reached the age of six or more and are found to present problems in school adjustment. This is often too late for effective intervention.

The Commission believes that the highest priority should be given to the development of comprehensive mental health, pediatric, and supportive services for children under three, and that a major effort should be made to provide systematic care during the neonatal and postneonatal stage. (1970, p. 33)

It is unlikely that moral mandates or philosophical persuasion alone would have given birth to the fledgling now known as "developmental psychopathology" or "infant psychiatry." But good intentions combined with new experimental information regarding infant development brought together professional workers from many disciplines in a shared enterprise. Child clinicians and experimental developmentalists began an exchange of information seeking to identify the earliest points of departure from a "normal" course and to consider appropriate interventions.

This chapter starts with a presentation of what is now known about the capacities of the normal infant, the range of differences represented by characteristics of temperament, and the back-and-forth nature of parent-child interactions. This reciprocal interaction proceeds to the formation of attachments which provide a secure base for later development. The section on attachment compares major theories, describes stages, and offers empirical observations regarding attachment behaviors and responses to separation. The last section deals with clinical problems, namely, observations on children who have had atypical early experiences, e.g., institutional care, and infants who show "failure to thrive," also known as a "maternal deprivation syndrome." Reliable judgments can be made as to what constitutes mental health in infancy; although we have no "quick fix" to offer for the things which may go wrong, either on the side of the infant, or the parent, or both, an appreciation of the complexity of the first year gives some direction for early intervention efforts.

INFANT-CARETAKER INTERACTION

Infant Capacities

Since 1960, a steady outpouring of new information has toppled our old beliefs about infancy. To the casual observer, the newborn seems helpless, capable of little but eating, sleeping, and crying. But as Bower (1977), Brazelton (1973), and Fantz (1963), amongst others, have shown, the newborn is, in fact, an active, competent organism, preprogrammed to initiate social behaviors and respond to others. To mention some of these startling developments, Wertheimer demonstrated that within seconds after birth, infants can turn their eyes towards a source of sound (1961). Dayton, Jones, Steele, and Rose (1964) documented the newborn's ability to visually track a moving object. In a special apparatus where the mother is seen through a soundproof screen and sounds come in from a stereo system, infants as young as 3 weeks manifest surprise and upset if the heard voice and the mouth movements don't match (Aronson & Rosenbloom, 1971). Bower (1977) demonstrated that infants within the first week defend themselves against the approach of seen objects, suggesting very early development of depth perception. Fantz (1963) demonstrated that newborns discriminate and prefer patterned over plain stimuli. The origins of form perception were elaborated using infrared techniques for recording newborn eye movements (Haith, 1969).

Emde and Robinson stated that

These data suggest that the newborn is active and seeks to optimize exposure to informative aspects of his visual world (by scanning). . . . In effect, Haith has proposed a model, based on the principle of maximal cortical firing, in which the newborn comes preprogrammed to operate with an endogenous activity pattern resulting in a searching. (1979, p. 86)

With regard to hearing, Eisenberg (1969) provided data to support the contention that the newborn comes into the world especially tuned in to sound frequencies in the range of human speech.

Newborns are ready to learn, especially in the operant conditioning paradigm. Siqueland and Lipsitt (1966) put newborns in cribs with a special recording device to register their head movements. At the sound of a tone, if the baby turned his head to the right he received a sweet-tasting solution in his mouth. If a buzzer sounded, the baby had to turn his head to the left for the same result. Within a few trials, the newborns learned to turn their heads right or left according to the sound signal. Bower commented that "the fact that babies pick up connections between events so readily in the first few hours after birth should caution us against ready acceptance of any statement that such and such an ability is innate or unlearned unless we can rule out any opportunity the baby might have had to form the connections" (Bower, 1977, p. 17).

The fact that the newborn discriminates and prefers "person-related" visual and auditory stimuli predisposes him to respond to his caretakers; the fact that they also provide food intensifies the connections. The newborn demonstrates a primitive form of social behavior, formidably entitled "inter-actional synchrony," demonstrated by Condon and Sander (1974). They presented infants about 12 hours old with tape recordings of spoken English, isolated vowel sounds, regular tapping noises, spoken Chinese, and a straightforward adult speaker. The newborns showed body movements in synchrony with the structure of speech; the tapping sounds and isolated vowel sounds elicited no such synchronous response. Bower (1977) reported instances of babies less than a week old imitating other people. The imitated behaviors—sticking out the tongue, opening the mouth, fluttering the eyelashes—are spontaneous with the infant but increase in frequency when an adult model is present. However, recent efforts to replicate these findings failed to do so (Hayes & Watson, 1981).

Considering the abundance of evidence regarding the abilities of the newborn, one might well wonder how these abilities were overlooked for so many years! Indeed, they are not readily apparent or consistently demonstrated. The evidence can be elicited only during those times when the infant is in the "alert, inactive" state (about 10% of the usual day), when the baby is propped in a sitting position, and by means of the special recording equipment available in infant laboratories. Within the first 2 months, major changes occur that make the infant's capacities more obvious to the naked eye. There is a marked increase in conditionability. The "state" picture changes so that by 3 months, 70% of infants are sleeping through the night and have conspicuously longer periods of the "active awake" state.

The phenomena of infant memory

have been extensively studied by Fagan, who found that by 3 or 4 months, babies regularly prefer to look at a novel stimulus when it is paired with a familiar one and that this recognition memory persists at least for a number of days despite brief prior exposure—a matter of seconds (1973). Further, Fagan has some evidence that infant recognition ability, as measured by visual preferences for novel stimuli of varying degrees and kinds of differences, is related to later cognitive functioning. Fagan and Mc-Grath (1981) reported correlations in the range of .37 and .57 between previous infant recognition memory measures and vocabulary tests at age 4 and 7 years in 93 subjects. This is remarkable evidence of continuity, in view of the lack of correlation found for standard tests of infant intelligence and later IQ test results, and suggests some practical application in assessing infants considered to be at risk. Another remarkable long-term relationship was reported by Roe, McClure, and Roe (1982) for a small sample (12) of first-born male children. At age 3 months, infant vocalizations in response to a vocally interactive mother were compared with infant vocalizations in response to an interactive stranger. The amount of reduction with the stranger correlated highly (.79) with the Wechsler Verbal IQ at age 12 years! These data highlight the relationship between early infant-mother transactions and later development and present a hypothesis deserving further exploration.

Assessment of the Newborn

With a greater appreciation of the complexity of the newborn, more attention has been paid to early examination. To assess the immediate status of newborns while in the delivery room, Apgar (1953) devised a simple test, bearing her name and based on five signs—heart rate, respiratory effort, reflex irritability, muscle tone, and color. Scores range from 0 to 10, the higher the better; the test has become standard procedure in many obstetrical units. A much more involved procedure was developed by Brazelton (1973). The Brazelton Neonatal Behavioral Assessment Scale has 26 behavioral items to assess "the neonates' capacity to 1) organize their states of consciousness, 2) habituate reactions to disturbing events, 3) attend to and process simple and complex environmental events, 4) control motor tone and activity while attending to these events, and 5) perform integrated motor acts" (Tronick & Brazelton, 1975, p. 141). Brazelton stressed that the examiner should seek to achieve the newborn's best rather than his average performance and recommended repeated testings at the midfeeding interval over several days. If only one assessment is possible, the third day of life was chosen in order to ensure that the temporary but powerful effects of premedication given to the mother have worn off.

Rosenblith, working with the National Collaborative Perinatal Research Project, modified the Graham scales and developed measures of motor and tactile adaptive responses (General Maturation Scale) and responses to auditory and visual stimuli (1975). Ratings of irritability and muscle tonus were also included. Experience, both at the original site of Brown University and elsewhere, indicated good interscorer reliability.

By and large, prediction of later development from neonatal measures has not been impressive when differentiation in the broad range of "normal" is sought (St. Clair, 1978). Tronick and Brazelton (1975) compared the effectiveness of the Brazelton Scale and neurological examination for 53 "neurologically suspect" infants. Both procedures correctly identified about 80% of the 15 children who were judged to be "abnormal" at age 7 years, but the Brazelton misclassified only 9 neonates who were later judged "normal," compared with 30 such misclassifications from the neurological examination. The more comprehensive Brazelton examination resulted in more optimistic predictions. However, this is a fairly crude outcome study with simple dichotomies of "abnormal" versus "normal" in a preselected population with little relevance for individual prediction of normal infant outcomes.

From data on over 1,000 infants who participated in the longitudinal Collaborative Project, Rosenblith reported that neonatal muscle tonus score was related to attention span evaluation at age 4 years, and both tactile-adaptive responses and muscle tonus ratings were related to IQ classification at age 4 years (1975). Rosenblith concluded: "It is appropriate to say that the examination has a degree of prognostic validity ... The relations found between neonatal scores and follow-up criteria are not sufficiently strong to have much practical value except in the case of certain rather rare signs—hypersensitivity to light." (1975, p. 197). She goes on to say that combining behavioral measures with medical information leads to stronger relations to specific outcomes and that predictions would undoubtedly be even

more accurate if neonatal assessment measures and medical information were combined with measures of socioeconomic status.

Compared to the Rosenblith scale, the Brazelton places more emphasis on social behavior. Worobey and Belsky (1982) capitalized on this feature in an intervention project. Sixteen mothers received a verbal report of their newborn's performance; 16 watched the administration; and 16 were helped to administer the Brazelton scales with their own infants. In a follow-up a month later, the last group engaged in significantly more embellished involvement and contingent interaction with their babies than did the noninvolved mothers. The authors caution that they would not expect this neonatal "event" to have a long-lasting effect and talk about a "booster intervention" at a later age to sensitize the parent to the changing competencies of the infant. This is a wise caveat; we tend to expect too much from single-shot interventions and are let down by the later washout of immediate beneficial effects. The work reported by Worobey and Belsky stands as an example of a new way to use assessment, namely to sensitize the caretaker to certain important features of the child's current functioning and to give some expectations for the near future.

Interactional Behaviors

It is clear from the foregoing discussion that the newborn is especially responsive to the look, sound, feel, and smell of people; in addition, the newborn has a "calling system," the cry. Wolff (1969) identified types of cries by relating the circumstances which elicited the cry to the patterns produced on the sound spectrograph. Mothers have difficulty distinguishing their infant's cries in the first few days, but fortunately, within hours after birth most infants will be quiet when held and carried regardless of the specific stimulus for crying. Freedman (1977) found that only 3 out of 252 newborns could not be conforted in this way. Although they were few in number, one can readily empathize with the frustrations of those three mothers!

There are highly significant differences among newborns in how frequently and how long they cry (Korner, 1971), and these differences, in their extremes, may interfere with attachment. Robson and Moss (1970) described one mother whose original enthusiasm about having a baby changed to total rejection. Her infant fussed a great deal, was not responsive to holding, and was late in exhibiting smiling and eye-to-eye contact. The mother felt estranged and unloved. The infant was later found to have suffered relatively serious brain damage. Gil (1970) found that abused children often have a history of constant fussing and highly irritating crying that is different from other children in the family. He suggested that deviance in the child which exceeds the tolerance limits of the parents, combined with stressful circumstances, may result in child abuse.

Normally, during the first year the duration of crying drops from 7.7 minutes per hour (on the average) in the first 3 months to 4.4 minutes per hour in the last 3 months (Bell & Ainsworth, 1972). The "fussing" crying prominent in the first few months gradually fades, almost coincidentally with the appearance of the social smile. There are important neuro-maturational factors involved in this developmental "settling" (Emde & Robinson, 1979), but differences in caregiver responses also play a role. In a naturalistic, longitudinal study of 26 mother-infant pairs, Bell and Ainsworth (1972) found that consistency and promptness of maternal response was associated with a decline in frequency and duration of infant crying. By the end of the first year, individual differences in crying reflected the history of maternal responsiveness more than the original differences in infant irritability. They discussed this finding in the context of the ethological approach to attachment, contrasting this with a simple learning explanation that would predict an increase in crying behavior as the result of reinforcement (i.e., maternal responsiveness).

Using film and videotape recordings, several investigatiors have analyzed mother-infant interactions in detail. Brazelton, Koslowski, and Main (1974) filmed weekly sessions of five mother-infant pairs from 2 to 20 weeks of age and concluded that the most important rule for maintaining an interaction was the mother's sensitivity to her infant's alternating need for attention and withdrawal. Short cycles of attention and nonattention seemed to characterize all periods of prolonged interaction. Stern (1975) taped 3- to 4-month old infants (12 twins and 6 singletons) in a play situation with their mothers in their homes. He described the many adaptations adults make to communicate with infants—raised pitch and intonation in speech, exaggerated facial expression, prolonged visual gazing, and so on. Mothers who did not engage in these intensified social behaviors elicited less play behavior from their infants.

Like Brazelton, Stern noted that the infant turns back and forth from the mother's gaze. This is a reflection of the infant's general tendency to habituate, that is, to become accustomed and disinterested in any continuous stimulus pattern. By looking away, the infant turns off the stimulus of the mother's face; by looking back again, the infant turns on the stimulus, thus reactivating arousal. In Stern's words, "the goal of play activity is the mutual regulation of stimulation so as to maintain an optimal level of arousal which is affectively pleasant ... During the play activity both members are almost constantly making readjustments in their behavior so as to achieve the goal of the activity" (p. 210). It is truly amazing that mothers and infants regularly engage in such intricate behavior without "knowing it," so to speak!

There is more and more evidence to show that the important variable in the caregiving environment is not the overall level of stimulation provided by the caregiver but the extent to which the caregiver's responses are contingent on the infant's behaviors (Lewis & Coates, 1980). This has evoked a re-examination of early child care to look at maternal behavior as "cued" or "noncued." For example, Lewis and Wilson (1972) found no differences in the frequency of vocalization between mothers from middle-class and working-class backgrounds, but the former were more likely to respond to their infants' vocalization with a vocalization. Similar interactional differences have been found with regard to sex of infant and birth order (Lewis & Lee-Painter, 1974). It would be a serious

error to infer that all the interactional differences stem from the mother. Quoting Goldberg (1978)

It is important to note that the predictable, readable, responsive infant has the potential for "capturing" the initially unresponsive parent into cycles of effective interactions by generating parental feelings of efficacy. Similarly, the unpredictable, unreadable, unresponsive infant has the potential for "trapping" an initially responsive parent in cycles of ineffective interaction by generating parental feelings of failure and helplessness. (p. 260)

Temperament

The idea that infants are born with important differences, attributable both to genetic predispositions and intrauterine experiences, is by no means a new one. S. Freud discussed the relative roles of heredity and environment in the development and treatment of neuroses and wrote in 1937 that "each ego is endowed from the first with individual dispositions and trends" (p. 240). The first efforts to measure inborn characteristics were the infant intelligence tests which appeared on the scene in the late 1920's and 1930's (Cattell, 1940; Gesell, 1925; Stutsman, 1934). Even the more sophisticated infant intelligence tests of recent years have failed to predict later IQ (Honzik, 1976), either because they are sampling irrelevant behaviors or because intelligence is such a modifiable attribute. Our concern here, however, is the assessment of personality-related variables, particularly insofar as these variables affect early parent-infant relationships.

One of the first to describe early differences was Margaret Fries, a pediatrician who became a psychiatrist. In her original description of "congenital activity types," she proposed a standard method of observation (rather than measurement) and criteria by which to judge an infant to be "active," "moderately active," or "quiet." Children of different activity types require different kinds of maternal handling, according to Fries (Fries & Woolf, 1953).

A much more comprehensive, longitudinal study was carried out by Thomas, Chess, and Birch (1968) in New York City. They focused on the assessment of "temperament," a general term referring to the infant's style of responding. A 3-point scale was established for each of nine categories of temperamental characteristics: activity level, rhythmicity, approach or withdrawal, adaptability, intensity of reaction, threshold of responsiveness, quality of mood, distractibility, and attention span or persistence. They followed 133 children of middle-class backgrounds, predominantly of Jewish origin. The relatively homogeneous parent group expressed the permissive and child-centered attitudes that were the norm in 1956 when the study began. Parents were first interviewed when the child was between 2 and 3 months of age and then at regular intervals until the age of 7-8 years. Other data included measures of cognitive functioning at ages 3 and 6 years; measures of parental attitudes and child care practices when the child was 3 years old; information from teachers and direct observations of school behavior. Any other collateral information available from pediatric, neurologic, or psychiatric sources was also included.

Forty-two of the children developed behavioral disturbances. Although this percentage (over 30%) seems high, it must be noted that psychiatric resources were made freely available to the participating parents, who were a concerned group as a whole. Most of the cases were mild or moderate reactive behavior disorders, with a peak incidence at between 4 and 6 years of age. Only five were judged to be "moderately severe" and one as possibly psychotic. On the basis of earlier temperament scores, three clusters were identified and labeled "easy," "slow to warm up," and "difficult." (Roughly half of the total sample fit into one or another of these categories.) Approximately 70% of the 14 "difficult" children developed behavior problems; the 10% "difficult" children made up 23% of the behavior problem group. The authors pointed out that

Individual case analyses show clearly that there are children in the non-clinical group who had organizations of temperament highly similar to those of children in the clinical groups. Conversely, certain children in the clinical groups had characteristics of temperament that were identical with those typifying the non-clinical group as a whole. Therefore, to understand the etiology of behavior disorders it is insufficient to refer to temperamental organization alone. (1968, p. 70)

On the other hand, the authors felt that consideration of temperament or inborn factors is imporant if for no other reason than "to prevent the deep feelings of guilt and inadequacy with which innumerable mothers have been unjustly burdened as a result of being held entirely responsible for their children's problems" (p. 203).

Case 1.1 describes a longitudinal study of temperament in a "slow-to-warm-up" individual, Betty.

William Carey, a pediatrician, converted the original New York research interview protocol into the Infant Tem-

perament Questionnaire (1970), with obvious time-cost advantages. With the collaboration of a psychologist, Sean McDevitt, the questionnaire was extended and revised (1978) (see Appendix). Similar questionnaires for older children have followed (Carey, 1981; McDevitt & Carey, 1978). Hubert, Wachs,

CASE 1.1   Betty

As a participant in a longitudinal study of child rearing directed by Benjamin Spock at Case Western Reserve University, the author had the chance opportunity to observe an example of a "slow-to-warm-up" child from infancy to early adulthood. In early infancy, Betty was sensitive to sounds and startled easily. At the age of 11 months, she would not interact with strangers, even with her mother present. Her exploration of toys was tentative and delicate. When an object was positioned to drop into a box, she blinked in anticipation of the noise which would result. The mother tended to be silent, quietly encouraging, but very much respecting Betty's hesitation and uneasiness.

At her 2-year-old visit, Betty stood in a frozen position, with a miserable expression on her face, saying only two things, "no" and "go home." Although the mother was distressed, she was uniformly gentle with Betty. A year later was almost a repeat. Betty came in willingly but refused to sit down. She strung beads and made a block bridge but slowly and awkwardly, handling the objects in a gingerly fashion. She looked at the toys but did not play and said nothing. Then she began to refuse all suggestions and went to sit with her mother. The mother tried to cajole her into more activity but was pleasant and soothing. On other occasions, Betty was more cooperative but never outgoing. It was

necessary to proceed very slowly and to wait patiently for her to respond. Subsequent testing indicated superior intelligence.

This hesitant behavior was observable in school settings. She tended to hold back and watch what was going on for some time before she joined in. In the first grade, the teacher referred her for special study because she refused to talk in class. However, Betty grew up to be a very successful college student who had "all the friends that she really wanted," and many interests. The mother commented that she sometimes worried about Betty's solitary habits but decided that since Betty was not bothered, it should not be of concern to her. The mother was relieved by the fact that her later children did not show the same characteristics.

If Betty had been seen only at one point in time, one would have judged her to be "neurotic" and looked for special conflicts, perhaps with aggression, to explain her "withholding" behavior, or considered the mother's behavior as reinforcing Betty's social avoidance. However, noting the consistency of her temperamental style over the years modified this clinical judgment. The mother's total acceptance of her style, combined with Betty's high abilities, permitted her to grow up feeling good about herself and able to withstand the inevitable stresses from outside.

Peter-Martin, & Gandour (1982) reviewed these and other measures of temperament and concluded that most current temperament instruments approach high interjudge reliability and moderate internal consistency and test-retest reliability. They found that activity, approach, and mood most consistently attain relatively high retest reliability whereas persistence and intensity are relatively less consistent.

The inconsistent findings reported for the prediction of temperament (Hubert et al., 1982) are not surprising, as one would expect the stability to depend upon the interaction with the environment. In the case of Betty (Case 1.1), where the environment supported the infant's existing temperamental structure, there was a high stability. Some theorists have accorded less room for environmental modifiability (Buss & Plomin, 1975). The idea of "temperament" is clinically useful and assessment is appropriate for parent guidance. However, although one should be concerned about the reliability of such assessment, it is not necessary to engage in prognosticating the future. Teasing out the genetic component is of interest to theoreticians, but professionals working with the mothers and their infants are more concerned to facilitate a positive relationship than to prove a point.

There is evidence that the mother's perception of her infant has some predictive value. Broussard and Hartner (1971) followed 85 children whose mothers had completed the Neonatal Perception Inventories (NPI) 1 or 2 days after birth and again 1 month later. On the NPI, mothers rate both the "average baby" and their own baby in terms of the amount of difficulty experienced in six areas: crying, spitting up, feeding, elimination, sleeping, and predictability. Forty-nine mothers rated their babies as "better than average" and 36 indicated a "worse than average" rating. At around 4½ years of age, the children were examined and classified according to their need for therapeutic intervention. For the group rated at 1 month as "above average," 20% had identified problems compared to 66% of the babies rated as "below average." This does not mean that the mothers' negative judgments in infancy caused the later problems; it is equally possible that the mothers had an early awareness of the factors that were to develop into problems. But the findings do suggest that mothers who see their baby as difficult at an early age are more likely to have a child with problems 4 years later. It also indicates that mothers usually see their babies as "better than average," which is all to the good for the babies' future welfare.

ATTACHMENT

Psychoanalytic Theory

In this section we will discuss the two most developed theories of attachment, namely psychoanalytic and Bowlby's ethologically oriented approach. Psychoanalysis used the term "object relations" for significant interpersonal relationships, a somewhat awkward term stemming from psychoanalytic instinct theory. (The "object" of an instinct is the agent through which the instinctual aim is achieved; this agent is generally another person.) Sigmund Freud referred to early attachments in terms of "libidinal objects" and was first interested in the sexualized relationships involved in the Oedipal conflict. Later he recognized the enduring significance of the early mother-child relationships, and in his final summary of psychoanalytic principles (1940), he designated the mother's importance as "unique, without parallel, established unalterably for a whole life-time as the first and strongest love-object and as the prototype of all later love relations" (p. 188). Anna Freud (1965) described the developmental line in object relationships from the newborn's utter dependence on maternal care to the young adult's emotional and material self-reliance.

In this lifelong sequence, only the first four stages, which are of relevance to the first 2 years, will be identified. The first is "biological unity between the mother-infant couple"; the second, "anaclitic relationship" which fluctuates according to the child's body needs; the third, the stage of "object constancy" when the child is capable of retaining the memory of and emotional tie to the parents and to feel their nurturing, guiding presence even when they are sources of frustration or disappointment or when they are absent; and the fourth, "the ambivalent relationship of the preoedipal, anal-sadistic stage, characterized by the ego attitudes of clinging, torturing, dominating, and controlling the love objects" (Freud, 1933/1965, p. 65).

These stages were developed not only from observations of young children but also from therapeutic work with adult neurotic patients who continued to relate to people in infantile ways. For example, a person in the first stage has

difficulties in maintaining separate identity and ego boundaries, as does a psychotic person. In the next stage, the adult shows very dependent, needy behavior—loving or hating according to the other person's ability to satisfy immediate needs. In the next stage, the person has a better sense of the other person and can maintain attachment over separation and disappointment but is still unable to understand the other person's point of view. In the fourth stage, the person is manipulative, controlling, and excessively concerned with power issues.

There has been some significant dissension in the analytic field with regard to object relations theory about what happens when. Those emphasizing the importance of ego development, for instance Anna Freud and Margaret Mahler, felt that the baby "learns" important discriminations and distinctions, partly as the result of maturation of ego functions (like perception and memory) but mainly as the result of "reinforcement" or "need-gratification." The baby is perceived as aroused from a "resting state" of primary narcisissm only by physiological needs. The mother is connected with the pleasure associated with the relief from tension—relief of hunger by feeding being the prototype. Although the language is different, this is, in essence, a social learning theory.

The other analytic position is perhaps best represented by Melanie Klein. Klein endowed the baby with much more mental capacity from the beginning and advanced the Oedipus conflict to the age of about 1 year (Klein, 1928). She described the normal child of this age as caught in a conflict between wishing to devour the loved person and fearing retaliation in like manner. She saw this as an inevitable developmental event, frequently if not always needing psychoanalysis for complete resolution. The major differences in theory also lead to differences in therapeutic technique, with Kleinian analysts emphasizing direct interpretations of unconscious conflicts as inferred from symbols in play, where ego psychoanalysts are first concerned with the interpretation of defenses as manifested in behavior and much later interpret the unconscious anxiety-arousing conflicts which brought the defenses into being.

Although many of the attributions which Klein suggested for the very young child have been dismissed as fanciful, she drew attention to the complexity of the infant long before there was any general recognition of this fact. Psychoanalysts from the so-called Kleinian School took a second look at infant behavior and offered some valuable clinical contributions. For instance, Winnicott de-emphasized the importance of feeding per se and considered physical holding as a basic form of loving. He drew attention to an everyday observation, namely, that many infants adopt a soft object such as a blanket or teddy bear which they hold tightly, often in a special way. This "transitional object" (Winnicott, 1953) has a very comforting effect and is most used when the infant is fatigued or unhappy. Failure to find the object at such times heightens the already existing state of distress; reunion replaces anguish with joy and relief. The child may use this as a substitute for the mother, while going to sleep for instance, but may also want it even when the mother is present. When the baby

uses his blanket to soothe himself, he has created something, that is, he has given an inconsequential thing from the outside the potential to restore his good feelings. It seems probable that the object was originally connected with the mother's holding but then it was detached to "have a life of its own." This serves to spread the mother's comforting powers and give the child an auxiliary comforter—something that is within his control. This is a good illustration of replacing passivity with activity, a theme which runs throughout life.

Although it is common, a transitional object is not universal with "normal" infants. In a survey of 258 children, Litt (1981) found that 77% of the Private Pediatric group developed an attachment object compared with 46% of the Pediatric Clinic group. Tolpin (1971) suggested that some infants rely on other soothing transitional phenomena extracted from past comforting experiences, memories, making sounds, and, of course, finger or thumb sucking. Her major point is that these phenomena are very early examples of internalization which aid in the infant's developing autonomy.

Margaret Mahler has contributed greatly to our understanding of the early stages of developing independence. In her words, "Growing up entails a gradual growing away from the normal state of human symbiosis, of one-ness with the mother. This process is much slower in the emotional and psychic area than in the physical one. The transition from lap-babyhood to toddler-hood goes through gradual steps of a separation-individuation process, greatly facilitated on the one hand by the autonomous development of the ego and, on the other hand, by identificatory mechanisms of different sorts" (1972, p. 333).

Mahler's original interest in this period stemmed from her work with psychotic children who have not succeeded in separation and individuation and have obvious difficulties in ego boundaries. Later she tested out her developmental hypotheses with systematic observations of normal children (Mahler, Pine, & Bergman, 1975). The first subphase of separation-individuation, beginning around 4 months, is *differentiation*, where the infant leans back from the mother and "takes a good look."

Once the infant has become sufficiently individuated to recognize his mother, visually and tactilely, he then turns, with greater or less wonderment and apprehension . . . to a prolonged visual and tactile exploration and study of the faces of others, from afar or at close range. He appears to be comparing and checking the features—appearance, feel, contours and texture—of the stranger's face with his mother's face, as well as with whatever inner image he may have of her. He also seems to check back to her face in relation to other interesting new experiences. (1972, p 335)

This is closely followed by the *practicing period* from about 8 to 16 months.

At least three interrelated, yet discriminable, developments contribute to and/or, in circular fashion, interact with the child's first steps into awareness and into individuation. They are: the rapid body differentiation from the mother; the establishment of a specific bond with her; and the growth and functioning of the autonomous ego apparatuses in close proximity to the mother. (p. 335)

During the practicing period, the mother continues to be needed as a home base for refueling through physical contact. As the toddler enjoys the thrill of walking, he is often absorbed by his own activities and appears to be oblivious of the mother, but he keeps coming back!

The third phase, *rapprochement*, begins when the infant is accustomed to walking and beginning to talk. The naive confidence of the younger toddler is replaced by a growing awareness of his limitations in controlling his world. Paradoxically, he now seems to have an increased need and wish for his mother's presence. "Thus, in this subphase of renewed, active wooing, the toddler's demand for his mother's constant participation seems contradictory to the mother: while he is now not as dependent and helpless as he was six months before, and seems eager to become less and less so, nevertheless he even more insistently expects the mother to share every aspect of his life" (p. 337). Mahler's description of the behavior corresponds with Anna Freud's "ambivalent relationship" in stage 4, but their explanations differ. Freud related the behavior to the successive stages of libido development (i.e., oral, anal, phallic) whereas Mahler saw it as the result of feeling one's separateness. She referred to this period as the "mainspring of man's eternal struggle against both fusion and isolation." In either case, the resurgence of anxious dependent behavior illustrates the normal waxing and waning of behavior. A child does not proceed evenly and steadily on the path to maturity—a fact that is perplexing and disappointing to parents who expect that each month will be a "little better" from their point of view.

One important but elusive concept is

that of "object constancy." Anna Freud marked that as beginning towards the end of the first year but Mahler suggested a much later age, toward the end of the third year! In a thoughtful critique of this concept, Burgner and Edgcumbe (1972) pointed out that "object constancy" is easily confused with "object permanence," as proposed by Piaget. Piaget described a sequence of events starting with the baby's search for objects removed from her sight (around 5 months) and concluding with the toddler searching for a missing object that she recalls from past experience rather than immediate observation of its disappearance (around 16 to 18 months). Although this awareness of the permanence of objects (and persons) in reality seems to be a precondition for object constancy, it is not the same thing. Object constancy includes a steadiness of feeling: "the capacity to maintain a positive (loving) emotional attachment to a particular object regardless of frustration or satisfaction of needs, drive pressures and wishes; the capacity to tolerate ambivalent feelings toward the same object; the capacity to value the object for qualities not connected with its ability to satisfy needs and provide drive satisfaction" (Burgner & Edgcumbe, 1972, p. 320). (One is reminded here of the fact that children of abusing parents are still often firmly attached to them!)

These authors described the difficulties encountered in assessing object constancy, even in children with psychotic disturbances or organic defects where this is a matter of great concern. "We sometimes found it difficult to decide whether such children were in fact at all capable of a sustained and constant attachment to a specific object or whether the relationship was primarily based on the immediate satisfaction of their needs and the added security offered by the perceptual unchangeability of the object" (p. 327). The authors suggested that "object constancy" is not a single point in development and proposed that one think of it as the "capacity for constant relationships," acquired gradually by the child over a long period of time. "This capacity may, as we have seen, be subdivided into several main elements: perceptual object constancy (i.e., object permanence); the capacity to maintain drive investment in a specific object notwithstanding its presence or absence; the capacity to keep feelings centered on a specific object; and the capacity to value an object for attributes other than its function of satisfying needs" (p. 328). It is clear that this is a developmental line which extends into maturity; certainly it is difficult to think of the 1-year-old infant as so steadfast in her feelings. Mahler's concept of the 2- to 3-year-old child, after the separation-individuation period, as "on his way towards object constancy" seems to fit better.

Ethological Theory of Attachment

There is agreement about the evolving nature of early relationships but much controversy about the origins. John Bowlby, who has devoted his entire life to the study of parents and children and the effects of dislocations on their relationships, was one of the first to question the idea that the infant-mother tie was secondary to orality or to primary drive gratification. He felt that his early work on the adverse effects of maternal deprivation left out any description of the cause-and-effect mechanisms and proposed an "ethological approach to attachment," emphasizing the biological roots. The basic thesis (Bowlby, 1958) is that an infant's attachment to the mother originates in a number of species-characteristic behavior systems such as sucking, clinging, following, crying, and smiling. In the course of development, these behavior systems become integrated and bind child to mother and mother to child, serving a species-survival purpose. In 1969, Bowlby introduced a control systems model and suggested that between the ages of 9 and 18 months, these simpler behavioral systems are incorporated into far more sophisticated goal-corrected systems ". . . so organized and activated that the child tends to be maintained in proximity to the mother." Bowlby characterized attachment behavior as instinctive but pointed out that what is inherited is a potential, not specific behaviors (Bowlby, 1969).

Bowlby is concerned with the conditions—both internal and external—that activate and terminate behavioral systems. Internal activators include illness, hunger, pain, and cold; external activators include absence or distance from the attachment person, lack of responsiveness, unfamiliar situations, or alarming events of any kind (Ainsworth et al., 1978). Although the "set goal" is proximity to the mother, the degree of proximity required to terminate the attachment behavior system varies from time to time depending on circumstances. Ainsworth explains Bowlby's concept of "goal-corrected systems" as follows:

If in the course of his experience in interaction with his mother he has built up expectations that she is generally accessible to him and responsive to his signals and communications, this provides an important modifier to his proximity set-goal under ordinary circumstances. If his experience has led him to distrust her accessibility or responsiveness, his set-goal for proximity may well be set more narrowly. In either case, circumstances—her behavior or the situation in general—may make her seem less accessible or responsive than usual, with effects on the literal distance implicit in a proximity set-goal. (1978, p. 13)

As the inner representation of the attachment object advances, the child is capable of more distancing and separation (beginning of object constancy) although the desire to spend a substantial amount of time with attachment figures in reality remains.

Bowlby (1969) identified phases or stages of attachment on the basis of developmental differences in infant behavior. Three of these occur in the first year of life. Phase I was called "orientation and signals without discrimination of figure"; between 3 to 6 months, the baby orients and signals toward one or more discriminated figures (Phase II). Phase III introduces the behavioral system of locomotion. Bowlby then took a big jump to about 3 years of age for Phase IV, described as the "formation of a reciprocal relationship" or "goal-corrected partnership." Here the child is capable of seeing things from his mother's point of view, and thus of being able to infer what feelings and motives, set-goals, and plans might influence her behavior—all the better to engage her interest and involvement! Ainsworth emphasized the evolution of attachment in renaming the first three phases as follows: I. Initial preattachment phase; II. Attachment in the making; and III. Clear-cut attachment.

The choice of terms for these early developmental phases reflects in part the major interest of the labelers. Everyone agrees that initially the infant makes little distinction between caregivers and only gradually differentiates and responds accordingly. Where Bowlby and Ainsworth leave off—that is, with the formation of a clear-cut attachment— Anna Freud and Mahler continue to examine the vicissitudes of the relationship. The terms chosen reflect the theoretical explanations. All in all, there has been a clear movement away from simple need-gratification explanations and a move toward a greater appreciation of the infant's activity in promoting attachment, using a lot of biological "givens" in this endeavor. Before leaving Bowlby, the theoretician, and proceeding to Ainsworth, the researcher, it should be noted that Bowlby consistently adopted a family orientation in his psychiatric practice and is given credit for the first published paper on family therapy (1949).

Research in Attachment

Following the Bowlby model, Mary Ainsworth has been a major investigator in the field of mother-infant attachment, making use primarily of "the strange situation" as a way of eliciting and assessing attachment behavior. The strange situation was originally devised in 1964 as part of a longitudinal study of mother-infant attachment behavior observed in the home setting. The strange situation was then moved into the laboratory where the conditions were standardized. The carefully programmed episodes permit observation of (a) exploratory behavior both in the mother's presence and in her absence; (b) the infant's response to a stranger with the mother present or absent; (c) response to mother's absence alone or with a stranger; and (d) response to mother's return following different conditions. In 1978, Ainsworth, Blehar, Waters, and Wall carefully described the observational conditions, methods used for recording behavior, and the statistical analysis of the results. The technique was specifically designed to "activate attachment behavior at a high intensity" for the 1-year-old. There is some evidence that it is also appropriate for 18-month-olds and 2-year-olds, but not for older ages (Marvin, 1977; Waters, 1978).

Ainsworth et al. (1978) reported on 106 infants, all approximately 1 year of age, from white, middle-class Baltimore families who were originally contacted through pediatricians in private practice. Frequency counts were made of exploratory locomotion, exploratory manipulation, visual exploration, visual orientation, crying, smiling, vocalization, and oral behavior. Also, 7-point rating scales were developed to evaluate proximity and contact seeking; contact maintaining; resistance; avoidance; searching; and interaction over distance. For most infants, the strange situation initially activated exploratory behavior when the mother was present, which decreased markedly in subsequent conditions. The presence of the stranger elicited considerable visual examination of the stranger and an increase in smiling, especially when the stranger remained at some distance from the infant. Interestingly, vocalization, like exploration, was most evident in the mother's presence. Briefly, the infant was ready to look and smile at the stranger but not so inclined to play with or talk to a stranger. The amount of crying in each of the episodes indicated that being left alone was more distressing than being left with a stranger.

Patterns of behavior were identified for classification. Although the classifications reflect the behavior in all episodes, they are heavily weighted by the behavior in the two reunion episodes because of the greater differences in reunion behavior. Group A, labeled "avoidant," showed little distress during separation, ignored or avoided the mother in reunion and interacted with the stranger as much as with the mother. Group B, labeled "securely attached," sought contact with the mother, particularly in reunion; showed more interest in interacting with mother than with others; and was likely to have more manifest distress during separation. Group C, labeled "ambivalently attached," showed inconsistent behavior, on the one hand resisting interaction and on the other hand seeking proximity with considerable affect of anger and distress. In the original sample, there were 23 in Group A, 70 in Group B, and 13 in Group C; other studies with middle-class populations have reported similar percentages, that is, roughly 70% "securely attached," 20% "anxious-avoidant," and 10% "anxious-resistant or ambivalent."

Ainsworth et al. (1978) reviewed the observations of maternal behavior with 23 of the subjects who had been observed in their homes during the first quarter and again in the fourth quarter of life. From their data, the authors conclude that maternal behavior "is significantly associated with the security-anxiety dimension of an infant's attachment with his mother, and that this association is evident even in the first quarter of life" (p. 152). They describe differences in specific ways of dealing with babies but identify a common positive denominator, namely, "sensitive responsiveness to infant signals and communications" (p. 152). This ability to "read" and adapt to the behavioral cues of the baby is now widely accepted as the main ingredient in optimal caretaking for infants.

In a study using a variation of the strange situation, Sorce and Emde (1981) demonstrated that the physical presence of the mother is not enough to facilitate the exploratory behavior system. Forty 15-month-old infants and their mothers were introduced to four novel situations. Half of the mothers, although present, were engrossed in reading a newspaper whereas the other half watched and responded to their infants' explorations. Although they did not interrupt or seek maternal attention, the infants of the "reading" mothers stayed physically close and explored less. The authors cite Mahler's idea of the mother as a "home base for emotional refueling." To be available in this sense, the mother must respond to her infant's signals on an emotional level. "Such emotional involvement implies that the mother communicates to her infant that she is eager to share the infant's pleasure during positive experiences and ready to reassure and comfort the infant during negative experiences" (Sorce & Emde, p. 744). The attachment object is needed not only to relieve distress but also to share pleasure.

Numerous research studies have used the strange situation paradigm. The study of Matas, Arend, and Sroufe (1978) extends the concept to age 2 years. As the authors state, active exploration is a central task for the 12- to 18-month-old, but the 2-year-old has advanced to a different stage so a new dependent variable was selected, namely, working in a tool-using problem situation. Forty-eight white, middle-class infants were first assessed at age 18 months in the strange situation and then brought back at age 2 years for observations of free play, "clean-up," and problem-solving behavior. The mothers were present throughout. Some characteristics were common to all groups—for example, ignoring the great majority of suggestions from the caregivers! However, in the problem-solving situation, the securely attached children were more enthusiastic, complied with maternal requests more frequently, ignored the mother less, spent less time away from the task, and exhibited fewer frustration behaviors. These securely attached children were not more compliant in general, but they used their mothers as a source of assistance when they encountered difficulty. Thus, their behavior in a mildly stressful situation was more adaptive, or competent, to use the authors' term.

In discussing the theoretical importance of this finding of continuity in development, the authors state: "this relationship (i.e., attachment) is an important aspect of infant emotional develop-ment, the secure base serving as a context within which the infant develops its first sense of the emotional availability and sensitivity of others" (Sorce & Emde, 1981, p. 554). There is a growing body of evidence indicating that security of attachment at age 1 year affects later competence in adaptation, at least up to 2 and 3 years of age. Pastor (1981) found that securely attached infants were more sociable and positively oriented toward both mother and peers; Hazen and Durrett (1982) found that youngsters of 30-34 months who had been assessed as securely attached at age 1 year had less restricted patterns of exploration in a large-scale laboratory space and scored higher on tasks of spatial ability. Lewis, Feiring, McGuffog, and Jaskir (1984) reported a relationship, for boys but not for girls, between insecure attachments at age 1 year and "high" problem scores on the Achenbach and Edelbrock Child Behavior Profile at age 6 years.

The experimental studies to date confirm the importance and the manifestations of some time-honored ideas of Eric Erickson with regard to the need for a basic sense of trust (first year) paving the way for the second developmental task of developing autonomy (second year) (1950). Nonetheless, the data also show that secure attachment at age 1 year does not guarantee invulnerability and that many infants judged "insecurely attached" do well. It is better to be securely attached than not, but subsequent events make a difference. Somewhat curiously, the strange situation has not been used as a basis for early intervention so we do not know how readily the infant's response might be modified.

It should be noted that in the Ainsworth sample of 23 infants followed from the early months, there were some differences in scores on the Griffiths Scale of Infant Intelligence. Group B had a mean IQ of 118.7; Group A, 109.6; and Group C, 106.9. Again, in the Matas et al. study, the securely attached children scored higher on mental ability tests (Bayley MDI of 118 compared with 108 for the other two groups). Although in neither study were the differences sufficiently great to reach significance, one wonders if the relative superiority of the securely attached children gave them an advantage in communicating with their mothers. The investigators are of the belief that there is no "basic" difference in cognitive ability in the groups. Matas and associates attributed the score difference to the youngsters being more cooperative and involved in the testing tasks. This explanation receives some support from Stevenson and Lamb's finding that at age 1 year, sociable, friendly infants received higher scores on cognitive tests than the less sociable babies (1979). In the first 2 years of life, cognitive and affective development are so intertwined as to be almost inseparable; trying to determine which leads the way becomes a moot question.

Massie and Campbell (1983) published a scale to assess mother-infant interaction from birth to 10 months of age (see Appendix). This scale grew out of their earlier work analyzing home movies of infants who subsequently developed a childhood psychosis.

The critical finding of the Project was that the relationship between the mother and the infant who later became ill was often disturbed as early as the first weeks of life in terms of the rhythm, reciprocity, synchronicity, and force of the aforementioned parameters of mutual bonding. In some cases the primary contribution to the aberrant interaction seemed to come from the child, in some cases from the parent. (p. 396)

Although the scale requires practice to become attuned to the interactive behaviors to be rated, the Mother-Infant Attachment Indicators during Stress (AIDS Scale) looks promising as a practical tool for evaluating attachment behavior in ordinary real-life situations.

Bonding

Borrowing from the ethological concept of imprinting, Marshall Klaus and John Kennell, pediatrician at Case Western Reserve University, suggested that there is a "sensitive period" immediately after birth when the human mother is most susceptible to "bonding" with her infant. Their original concern was with the disproportionately high incidence of mothering disorders involving premature or low-weight babies who are customarily removed from their mothers for special neonatal care. They reported that in studies of failure-to-thrive infants, 24 to 41% were premature; in studies of battered children, the incidence of prematurity or serious neonatal illness ranged from 23 to 31% (Fanaroff, Kennell, & Klaus, 1972). They found significant differences in maternal feeding behavior 1 month after leaving the hospital in mothers who had been allowed to touch and hold their premature babies "early" (5 days after delivery) compared with those who had only visual contact until 20 days post partum (Klaus & Kennell, 1970). Linking data and observations from varied sources, Klaus and Kennell arrived at the hypothesis that the "entire range of mothering problems may be, in part, the end result of separation in the early newborn period" (1970, p. 1029).

To test the hypothesis of a special attachment period, Kennell et al. (1974) arranged for a group of mothers to be given their babies for a period of 1 hour within the first 3 hours after birth and also to have their babies 5 extra hours for each of the first 3 days. This added up to a total of 16 more contact hours than that allowed by routine hospital procedure. There were 14 months in both the "extended contact group" and the control group, mainly black, unmarried, and with an average age of 18 years. The babies and their mothers were seen about a month after delivery and again at 1 year. (The mothers were observed by investigators who did not know the earlier history.) At 1 year the mother-infant interactions during the development examination, interview, picture-taking, and free-play situations did not differ significantly. But the extended contact group were significantly different in responsiveness to crying, involvement during the physical examination, and verbal expression of concern about the baby on the part of those who had returned to work—about 50% of the total sample. Although these findings do not seem very powerful, it is impressive that any significant differences could be identified.

Klaus (1978) reviewed 11 studies that focused on whether additional time for close contact between mother and infant in the first minutes, hours, and days of life altered the quality of their attachment. He concluded that no matter when increased amounts of contact are added in the first 3 postpartum days, there appeared to be improved mothering behavior. He suggested that "Keeping the mother and baby together soon after birth is thus likely to initiate and enhance the operation of many behavioral, hormonal, physiological, and immunological mechanisms that probably lock the parent and infant together" (1978, p. 202). Later reviews were nowhere near as positive about the evidence. Herbert, Sluckin, and Sluckin (1982) reported findings of short-term differences that apparently disappeared within the first few weeks. Also, they cited retrospective studies which led them to conclude that there was little or no relationship between mother-neonate bonding and subsequent maltreatment. Other studies which failed to replicate the Klaus-Kennell findings used mothers who were somewhat older (average age 22 years rather than 18), married, and from middle-class backgrounds (Grossman, Thane, & Grossman, 1981; Svejda, Campos, & Emde, 1980).

There is growing skepticism about a biologically based sensitive period for bonding in the first hours after birth (Chess & Thomas, 1982). An alternative explanation for the Klaus and Kennell's findings stresses the special characteristics of their subjects. The special postpartum treatment of mother and infant gave these young mothers from low socioeconomic status positive contact with hospital staff with expressions of interest, encouragement, and reassurance. This affirmation that "you and your newborn infant are valuable" is probably less vital for the middle-class mother. It may very well be that lonely, young, poor, unmarried mothers are more sensitive to the earliest experiences than the mother with more internal and external supports. Despite the controversy, the work of Klaus and Kennell has had a positive impact in neonatal care, especially for the premature or sick newborn. The former isolation practices designed to prevent infection have been relaxed to afford more opportunities for parent-infant contact, not only to stimulate the infant's development but also to affirm the parents' caregiving potential.

Separations

"Separation response is the inescapable corollary of attachment behavior . . . the other side of the coin" (Bowlby, 1960, p. 102). In this section we will discuss the impact of two kinds of separation experiences: temporary living apart and repeated regular separation as in day care. We will not discuss separations associated with physical illness but look at experiences involving normal, healthy children under 3 years old.

Heinicke and Westheimer (1965) studied 20 young children, 10 of whom lived in a residential nursery for periods of from 12 to 148 days. The children ranged in age from 13 to 32 months. It is somewhat surprising that eight of the separated children had had previous separations lasting from 5 days to 4 weeks. Responses during separation were rather dramatic but changed over time. At first the children refused food but later became very greedy. Initially the children requested their parents' return often and loudly, but after a few days, the children became quiet and showed regression in language usage and toilet mastery.

After returning home, the separated children showed behavioral differences when compared with the nonseparated children; for instance, slower achievement of toilet mastery and more sleep problems. The differences are difficult to interpret because prior to separation, the mothers of the nonseparated children showed significantly more affection and pleasure in the company of the child. Those children who were separated for about 2 weeks were typically still in a phase of regression and minimal involvement with the nursery staff. These children more readily resumed the previous relationship with their parents. "The lack of affectionate response to the mother was short-lived, the emergence of ambivalent feelings related to the separation with minimal, and growth in such areas as sleep, sphincter control, language and identification with the parent was slowed down relatively little" (Heinicke & Westheimer, 1965, p. 354). The longer separations resulted in much more difficult readjustment. Although the material was viewed from the standpoint of the psychology of the child, one wonders if all the parents were equally emotionally responsive when the children returned! These observations strongly suggest that a separation of more than 2 weeks in the first 3 years presents a roadblock in the parent-child relationship.

James and Joyce Robertson looked at the effects of alternative care arrangements during separation. They studied 13 young children (17 to 29 months), four of whom were fostered by the Robertsons and nine who were looked after in their own homes by a familiar relative. Separations ranged from 10 to 27 days—usually because of a new baby. (Those were the days when new mothers were regularly hospitalized for 10 days.) After the first day or so, the children showed some sadness, lowered frustration tolerance, and some aggression, but the authors remarked that already they could be comforted by the foster mother. In contrast, the one child whom they observed in a residential nursery displayed the classic reactions of acute distress and despair. In brief, the Robertsons made a good case that if separation is necessary, the presence of a sensitive mother substitute can mitigate the negative effects (1971). We do not have residential nurseries, but some young children are placed in "detention homes" in times of family crises. If indeed they remain for 2 weeks or more and then return home, the family needs assistance to regroup. A much preferred alternative would be the provision of a temporary foster home.

Day Care

The provision of day-care facilities for children under 3 years has been on the increase. Bettye Caldwell was one of the first to question the assumption that the child under 3 is always best served by remaining at home.

One might infer that the optimal learning environment for the young child is that which exists when (a) a young child is cared for in his own home (b) in the context of a warm and nurturant emotional relationship (c) with his mother (or a reasonable facsimile

therefore) under conditions of (d) varied sensory and cognitive input." (1967, p. 19)

Caldwell suggested that alternative environments might be preferable if these conditions are not available in the home. She pointed out that the demand for new policies and facilities was largely from mothers rather than professional workers and that the need or desire for the mother to return to work was a powerful force. Like many others, she objected to extrapolating from the institutional literature to the issue of maternal separation in day care.

Caldwell was a partner in organizing a day-care program for infants at Syracuse University. At the age of about 2½ years, 18 of the children who had been enrolled in the Children's Center since about age 1 year were compared with 23 children who had received their primary care from their mothers. There was no significant difference in mental test scores (mean IQ 107.2 compared with 108.8 for the day-care group). The focus of the study, however, was on attachment. The data were obtained from an intensive interview with the mother and a 2-hour home visit for completing the Inventory of Home Stimulation. There were no differences on the ratings of mother-child or child-to-mother attachment. For both groups, there was a "definite suggestion that the better developed infants tend to be more strongly attached to their mothers" (Caldwell et al., 1970, p. 408), which confirms some of the earlier findings about "securely attached" children. For the Home sample, the authors found a significant association between low scores on the Home Stimulation Inventory and developmental level, which did not hold for the Day-Care sample. "Thus it appears that infant day care intrudes into the relationship between home stimulation and developmental level; it can, in effect, offer at least some of the resources and some of the influence of a 'second home.' It is clearly not the absence of a home" (Caldwell et al., 1970, p. 410).

Brookhart and Hock (1976) compared 18 home-reared infants with 15 who attended a day-care center for at least 2 consecutive months before exposure to the Ainsworth strange situation at age 11 months. These samples were from middle-class homes where the mothers were employed full time. Briefly, no differences were found. Blehar (1974) also used the strange situation to assess the effect of day care on older children. Attachment behavior was assessed about 5 months after starting day care, either at 2 or at 3 years. The total day-care group differed significantly from the home group in regard to a number of strange situation measures. In discussing the discrepancy between the results of these two studies, Ainsworth et al. (1978) suggests that

It is possible that an infant who begins day care in the first year, before he has become attached to the mother—or at least before attachment has become well consolidated—may accustom himself more readily than older preschoolers to long, daily separations and be less apt to experience them as implying rejection or abandonment by the mother. (p. 210)

Also, one should recall that the strange situation was designed as a specific assessment tool for the 1-year-old; it may be tapping a different facet of the mother-child relationship when applied to children of 2½ and 3½. One may then be eliciting responses of angry retaliation rather than separation anxiety per se. Finally, no mention is made of the quality of the day-care program; variations in the kind of day care probably go a long way to explain observed differences in children's responses.

Provence, Naylor, and Patterson (1977) described in detail a federally funded model day-care center at the Yale Child Study Center for inner-city children, age 6 months to 5 years. Although they noted "substantial gains" compared to those children not attending day care, the cost of such an ideal program looms large. They proposed a child-to-teacher ratio of two to one for the first years of life with no more than five children to a group. If the teachers were of the quality and training proposed by Caldwell (1967), the cost would be almost prohibitive. Writing in 1972, Caldwell reported that the Children's Bureau research and demonstration projects in infant day care ranged in cost from $2,400 to $8,000 per child per year. Although this included some cost for research and evaluation, that was probably offset by the free help provided by students, consultants, and volunteers drawn to innovative projects. It is doubtful that mothers and infants in need of day care will have ready access to "model" facilities; the unanswered question is how much less than ideal is tolerable? Recently, some quality day-care checklists have been developed (Endsley & Bradbard, 1981, see Appendix) which could be used first to differentiate among programs and then to look for differences in the children enrolled. One such study (McCartney, 1984) found that variations in overall quality of the day-care environment was predictive of all the measures the researcher used to assess intelligence and language development, even controlling for family background. It is not easy to get cooperation for such evaluative research and to control for all the factors which go into a parent's selection of a particular day-care facility.

MATERNAL DEPRIVATION

The idea that there is an important relationship between early maternal care and later mental health has been around for some time. Rene Spitz was an early contributor of direct observations of infants in institutions. He described two reactions frequently seen: "hospitalism," a vitiated condition of mind and body, generalized physical and mental retardation, and lack of responsiveness, which he felt resulted from prolonged institutional care (Spitz, 1945, 1946a) and "anaclitic depression" by which he meant a specific reaction to separation which tended to occur after the interruption of a good relationship between mother and infant. After an initial period of tearful woe, some infants became withdrawn, insomniac, ill, and emaciated. They assumed a far-away, dazed expression and screamed; their disturbance increased when an adult approached them. Spitz found this distinctive clinical picture in 19 of 123 infants. It occurred during a 3- to 4-month separation from the mother and disappeared after her return (Spitz, 1946b). Separation before the age of 6 months did not seem to evoke this "anaclitic depression."

J. Bowlby captured international attention with the publication of his analysis of maternal care and mental health in 1951. He sorted the evidence into three main sources: direct studies of the mental health and development of children living in institutions, hospitals, and foster homes; retrospective studies that investigated the childhood histories of adolescents or adults who developed psychological illness; and follow-up studies of children who suffered severe deprivation in their early years. From these varied sources, a strong case was made that deprivation of maternal care in the first years had lasting and measurable effects on personality and intellectual development. Although many kinds of deviations in maternal care have been subsumed under the label of "maternal deprivation" (Yarrow, 1962), the thrust of the research has been on the effects of long-term institutionalization.

A classic retrospective study is that of Goldfarb (1955), who compared 15 institutionalized children with 15 children who had lived in foster homes since infancy. The first group, supposedly of a similar genetic background, had entered the institution at about 5 months of age and were transferred to foster homes at an average age of 3 years, 11 months. The children were studied in early adolescence, mean age of 12 years. In summary, the institutionalized children were more retarded intellectually (mean IQ of 72.4 as compared with 94.5 on the WISC). There were also distinct emotional consequences, chiefly, the absence of a moral capacity for inhibition. The institutionalized group displayed extremely difficult behavior—hyperactivity, restlessness, inability to concentrate, and unmanageability. Furthermore, the institutionalized children seemed to have no genuine attachments, although they were indiscriminately and insatiably demanding of affection.

In a prospective study, Provence and Lipton made repeated examinations of 75 children who were placed in an institution when they were less than 3 weeks old comparing them with 75 children of similar backgrounds who were placed in foster homes in infancy and with 75 children who remained with their own families (1962). They concluded that the institutionalized children were significantly retarded, with developmental quotients dropping progressively during the first year. Provence and Lipton also compared the infants' motor, social, and language development, and their responses to inanimate objects. Motor development was the least retarded; language development was the first area to be depressed in early infancy and remained the sector of greatest retardation during institutionalization. Also, it required a longer period of family living for significant improvement in language to occur.

Provence and Lipton made some very interesting observations of the early interest in playthings. In the first few months, the infants' visual and acoustic responses to toys, as well as the approaches to them and their grasping of them, were very similar to those of the normal infants. From this point, however, the institutionalized infants displayed a decreasing interest in toys. They showed little displeasure when toys were lost, even toys they had appeared to enjoy, and rarely tried to recover them. In the second year, their discrimination was inferior and their capacity to exploit toys was poorly developed. Provence and Lipton suggested that the original source of interest in toys is the infants' personal relationship with the mother and that without this relationship, the toys are as interchangeable as the people around the infant. Provence and Lipton summarized their impression of the institutional environment as follows:

We believe that the poverty and the infrequency of the personal contact were the outstanding deficits in the experience of the institutionalized babies. It was a quantitative deficit in that there were not enough interchanges to promote development. It was also a qualitative deficit. While the attendants were pleasant to the babies and worked uncomplainingly and conscientiously, there was no relationship between nurse and infant that contained the variety and intensity of feelings a mother has for her own baby. The atmosphere as it appeared to the observer was mainly one of quiet, tranquility, and blandness. (1962, p. 47)

Fourteen of these infants were reexamined by Provence and Lipton after placement in foster homes. Cognitively, they made dramatic gains, but the authors felt that one could see concreteness of thought and intellectual rigidity. Mention was made of impoverished imagination observable in their play and conversation. Although the infants shed their lethargy, they were described as indiscriminately friendly, which was interpreted as reflecting a lack of depth and specificity in relations with people. Even after many months with the same foster mother, the institutional children did not turn to her for comfort; in stressful situations, they more commonly regressed to the solitary behavior of their first year.

The early work of Spitz, Bowlby, and Goldfarb had the immediate and salubrious effect of changing institutional practices, but the institutions did not disappear altogether. More recently, Barbara Tizard and her colleagues have published a number of reports on children in long-stay residential nurseries. The first of these (Tizard & Joseph, 1970) reported on 85 children aged 2–5 years placed in 13 different residential nurseries, usually before the age of 12 months. Contrary to the earlier studies, the mean test scores on both verbal and nonverbal tests were average. The authors suggested two reasons why the retardation reported elsewhere was not found.

First, the children in this study were all healthy and without a history of premature or difficult delivery; most had been admitted as infants and had not suffered from the early neglect or frequent environmental shifts of many children who come into residential care. Second, not only were the physical care and the provision of books and play equipment excellent in these nurseries, but the organization of the children into small mixed age groups with a relatively high staff ratio and few household duties for the staff resulted in a high frequency of adult talk. (p. 356)

These residential nurseries, obviously, did *not* offer an environment lacking sensory stimulation—an improvement over conditions prevailing in infant institutions studied in the 1940's.

These youngsters were followed over some time. At the age of 4½ years, a group of 64 children was observed (Tizard & Rees, 1974; Tizard & Rees, 1975). All had been admitted to a residential nursery before the age of 4 months and remained until at least 2 years of age. At this age, no important differences were detected, but in the final study, when the children were 8 years of age, the picture was quite different. At that time, only 8 remained in institutional care; the others had either been adopted or restored to their natural parents. It was possible to re-examine only 51 of the total number.

Again there was no retardation noted on standard IQ tests; the highest mean IQ (WISC IQ 115) was for those adopted between 2 and 4 years, which was explained on the basis of the higher socioeconomic status of the adoptive parents. The greatest differences were found in teacher reports. Table 1.1 shows the spread of scores on the Rutter Scale where a score of 9 or more is usually taken as a cutoff point for psychiatric screening (Rutter, Tizard, & Whitmore, 1970).

It is presumed that the teachers were unaware of the early life experiences of the children that they treated and were therefore "blind" judges. Looking at the scores in Table 1.1, it is apparent that the groups were differentiated mainly on the basis of the antisocial items. Additional questions about attention-seeking behavior also yielded major differences for both groups of the former institutionalized children (52% of the adopted and 69% of the restored, or returned, children) as compared with their classmates (7%). The children were also described as having poor peer relationships, probably secondary to their inordinate need for adult attention.

Cautiously, Tizard and Hodges (1978) concluded that "These findings appear to suggest that up to 6 years after leav-

TABLE 1.1 Teachers Scale Problem Scores for Different Groups of Children

Group	*Total Problem Score*			*"Neurotic" Items*		*"Antisocial" Items*	
	N	*Mean*	*SD*	*Mean*	*SD*	*Mean*	*SD*
London comparisons	27	5.4	5.4	1.7	2.1	0.9	1.6
Their classmates	27	4.1	5.5	1.3	1.7	0.5	1.2
All adopted	23	10.0	7.8	1.4	1.7	2.5	3.1
Their classmates	23	3.5	3.6	1.5	1.7	0.3	0.6
All restored	13	13.7	7.2	1.6	2.2	3.8	2.5
Their classmates	13	3.1	3.7	0.9	1.4	0.5	1.1
Institutional	7	9.9	9.8	1.4	1.1	2.4	2.4
Their classmates	7	4.1	4.5	2.1	2.3	0	0

ing the institution, some children still showed the effects of early institutional rearing" (p. 114). They discount alternative explanations such as genetic predisposition to emotional instability or maternal stress during pregnancy or childbirth.

It seems likely that the common difficulties of many of the restored and adopted children were due to their institutional experiences, perhaps in interaction with genetic or biological factors. The multiple and ever-changing caretaking which these children had experienced—on an average 50 different caretakers by the age of 4½—must be unique in the history of child-rearing, and it would be surprising if it had not at the time affected the children's social development." (p. 115)

Indeed, the more surprising finding is that so many of the children did so well!

An important observation was the finding that the adopted children fared generally better than those who were returned to their biological parents, probably as the consequence of the continuing ambivalence of many of these parents. In answer to a direct question, 84% of the adoptive parents felt the child was closely attached to them compared to only 54% of the mothers of the restored children. It was equally true that a much larger proportion of adoptive than restored mothers felt closely attached to their child. It would indeed be a mistake to conclude from the studies of maternal deprivation that "any home" is preferable to "any institution."

Institutional rearing is clearly a factor that increases the risk of adjustment difficulties even in adulthood. Quinton's long-term follow-up of women institutionalized in childhood (Quinton, Rutter, & Liddle, 1984) showed that they had significantly more difficulties compared with controls although some were functioning well. The outcome for 30% of the institutionalized women was rated "poor"; for the controls no outcomes were rated "poor." Some of the difficulties were teenage pregnancy (about 40%) and parenting problems that precipitated removal of the child in about 18%. The single most important factor associated with a good outcome was a harmonious marriage to a supportive, nondeviant man. It is not clear what succession of psychological experiences facilitated the postive marital choice, but some women with the early institutional background were capable of altering "the fate" of their early history. The continuity between early experience and later adjustment comes about in part because of its effect on the developing personality but also in part because of its influence in determining future environments.

Failure to Thrive

This syndrome, which includes symptoms of failure of physical growth, malnutrition, motor retardation, and affective-cognitive deficits, has been identified as a special case of "maternal deprivation." There are, of course, possible organic causes for failure to thrive, but the following discussion is limited to those for whom no organic basis has been determined. There are variations in the definition of "failure to thrive" so that sample descriptions vary accordingly. For instance, if developmental lag is used as a criterion for the diagnosis, retardation will appear as a concomitant condition. Drotar, Malone, and Negray (1980) reviewed 11 studies and found that of the total of 70 evaluated at the time of initial diagnosis, almost all showed some retardation. In a study using a matched control sample, the failure-to-thrive infants had a mean IQ of 87, compared, with 106 for the control subjects (Fitch et al., 1976). Thus, we see some apparent relationship between intellectual development and the malnutrition and deprivation in the failure-to-

thrive syndrome; however, the retardation is probably secondary to physical enervation.

Most of the research attention has been given to characteristics of the caregiver rather than to those of the child. In his review of the literature describing the mothers, Fischhoff (1975) reported consistent observations that they were depressed, angry, helpless, and desperate, and had problems in maintaining self-esteem. From the composite clinical picture of the mothers, Fischhoff concluded that, with rare exceptions, they had severe personality disorders and were best described as "unwilling mothers" who did not mean to be pregnant at a certain time or who felt that the role of motherhood had been forced upon them. As a group, the siblings of the infants manifested emotional, intellectual, and behavioral deviations to a disproportionate degree. In a study of 40 mothers (Evans, Reinhart, & Succop, 1972), three groups were differentiated. Fourteen women were extremely and acutely depressed. Fifteen mothers were also extremely depressed but in addition lived in very deprived conditions and had been poorly mothered themselves. The remaining 11 mothers were extremely hostile, antagonistic, and belittling of their children. Except for the first group, the prognosis was considered poor unless the child was placed out of the home. In a follow-up study of some 30 children, Hufton and Oates (1977) found that 3 were later victims of child abuse (with 2 deaths); of those who were seen 6 years later, all were normal in height and weight but showed other kinds of problems.

Drotar, Malone, and Negray (1980) expressed pessimism about the efficacy of intervention, of any sort, if it is limited to the period of hospitalization.

Close analysis of the preceding treatment studies suggested that the families were not sufficiently involved in the treatment to make significant or long-lasting differences in their children's development. In addition, many approaches have not provided sufficient treatment and follow-up after hospital discharge to insure transfer of the child's developmental gains to the home. (p. 238)

Drotar and Malone (1982) propose a family-oriented intervention in order to facilitate communication and support between the mother and another significant person in her life—husband, grandmother, or even great-grandmother. "We hypothesize that if one can facilitate positive change in one or more critical relationships within the family, the quality of the mother/child relationship might be enhanced" (p. 109). This approach is not aimed at providing the infant with alternative caretakers, but at providing the mother with nurturance so that she can assume the maternal role with more confidence and satisfaction.

A slightly different therapeutic approach has been taken by Fraiberg and her colleagues at the Infant Mental Health Program at the University of Michigan (Fraiberg, 1980). The focus of the work was directly with the mother and was a mix of emotional support, educational advice, and therapeutic interpretations of how past events were affecting the present. Some of this philosophy is explained further in Chapter 2. The cases fared very well, but the reader is impressed by the ingenuity and persistence required of the therapist as well as the amount of time. The

therapeutic relationship was maintained, at different levels, for periods of years. This is an instance of preventive intervention, but that does not mean that it is either brief or simple.

In failure-to-thrive situations, one is acutely aware of the danger when mother-infant difficulties result in unsuccessful feeding for the infant. Literally, it is a matter of life and death. However, there is a continuum, and there are undoubtedly instances of stressful or unsatisfactory feeding which do not eventuate in a medical emergency. Some years ago, Brody (1956) reported that mothers of infants from 1 to 7 months of age displayed a greater variety of attitudes and more individuality of behavior during feeding than during the other five situations observed in her research study. She pointed out that breast feeding versus bottle feedings, schedules of meals, and positions during feeding were not in and of themselves significant in the ratings of maternal behavior. Responsiveness to infant cues transcends any particular belief system about breast versus bottle feeding, scheduled versus demand feeding, or holding the baby during feeding rather than "propping" the bottle. This, unfortunately, complicates advice to new mothers but explains why little relationship has been found between any specific feeding practice and mental health outcome (Caldwell, 1964; Orlansky, 1949).

Diagnostic Considerations

In recent years there has been a growing awareness that there are psychological problems identifiable in infancy but that they are not classifiable by the parameters used for later childhood disorders. Formerly, professionals relied heavily on developmental test scores for general evaluation, but these are notoriously poor at prediction and are narrow in scope. In the official disgnostic system now in use, the *Diagnostic and Statistical Manual of Mental Disorders* (DSM-III) (American Psychiatric Association, 1980), much is subsumed under the category of "reactive attachment disorder of infancy," described as having its onset prior to age 8 months. Call (1983) proposed a more elaborated classification:

1. Healthy responses (transitory developmental responses or acute response to specific external events).
2. Reactive disorders (longer-lasting reactions to specific stress events).
3. Developmental deviations (behavior stemming from intrinsic differences in the infant).
4. Psychophysiological disturbances (such as bronchial asthma, eczema, colic, vomiting, etc.)
5. Attachment disorders (outlined in detail).
6. Disturbed parent-child relationships (mainly stemming from parents).
7. Behavioral disturbances of infancy (e.g., sleep problems).
8. Disturbances of the environment (overlaps with 6).
9. Genetic disturbance (overlaps with 3).
10. Communication disorders (also overlapping with 3 but less emphasis on organic causes).

Greenspan, Lourie, and Nover (1979) tried a different approach to diagnosis which is more theoretically based. The "structural developmental" model uses the idea of developmental tasks which can go awry for any number of reasons, resulting in various symptom formations. The developmental structural approach, in a sense, seeks a final common pathway for many kinds of lacks or distortions. These authors organized the following outline:

Disorders of homeostasis

Disorders of human attachment

Disorders of somato-psychological differentiation

Disorders of internalization

Disorders of organizing internal representations

Disorders of psychological differentiation

Disorders in the consolidation level of integration and flexibility of basic personality functions.

The underlying concepts are adapted from Freud, Mahler, Erickson, and Piaget; in the analysis of problems, particularly at older ages, the theoretical inferences are considerable. The virtues of the model, however, include the specification of caretaker responsibilities and typical anxieties that children experience at different stages, in addition to the tying together of normal and pathological developments.

SUMMARY

This chapter has addressed issues germane to the first years within the context of normal development. These considerations serve as general background against which to examine specific problems and intervention techniques for parents and children who are identified as being "at risk" for biological or psychosocial reasons.

New techniques of observation have radically altered the traditional view of the capabilities of the newborn. The infant is preprogrammed to respond specifically to the persons in the environment and has a repertoire of behaviors that elicit caregiving responses. However, there is also considerable variability amongst newborns, some of which is subsumed under the rubric of "temperament," which makes for relatively "easy" or "difficult" caretaking. In the words of Korner (1974):

We are just beginning to document the degree to which the child's characteristics affect the caregiver. . . . The place where the mutual dovetailing of response between parent and child is still insufficiently stressed, and where unilateral parent effect is still emphasized too much, is in the clinic . . . where the child effect is apt to be the strongest, and where, for the sake of therapy, recognition of this fact is apt to be most useful. (p. 118)

Theories and research on mother-infant attachment suggest good evidence that infants who are "securely attached" show more competent and adaptive behavior, at least in the preschool years. In this chapter, the notion that the hours immediately following birth represent a sensitive period for mother-infant bonding was explored pro and con. The possible impact of separation experiences was considered. In her summary of the implications of this research, Ainsworth (1973) stated that since major, prolonged maternal separations cause distress to the child, optional major separations should be avoided before 3 years of age. If separation is deemed necessary, the best alternative for the child is in a family care environment. With regard to minor, everyday separations as in day care, careful attention must be paid to the nature of the substitute caregiving. Infants form attachments to more than one person, as witness the extensive work reported by Lamb (1976, 1977) on the role of the father. However, there is some suggestion that the mother is usually preferred in stressful situations.

The historical material about the effect of maternal deprivation on child development was re-examined in the light of new evidence. The syndrome "failure to thrive" was reviewed as an illustration of a serious parent-infant disorder. Close examination of mother-infant interactions reveals complexities which go far beyond our earlier ideas of good maternal care based on physiological need gratification. A vital ingredient is the mother's responsivity to the baby's signals for varied kinds of attention. When the mother responds to the baby's cues, the baby develops a sense of control over the environment and this in turn has motivation consequences, leading to further efforts to gain mastery. Any action that can be taken to assist a mother to get in tune with her infant is truly in the service of primary prevention.

Although we are now sensitive to the fact that there can be psychologically determined problems of infancy which are of consequence, such disorders cannot be readily codified. As Call stated, "no definition of syndromes, no listing of symptoms, nor formal diagnostic scheme has yet been devised that deals with the complexity of the developmental process and the complexly organized and disorganized disturbances in the area of mutuality and reciprocity between infant and his environment" (1983, p. 122). Probably the general term "attachment disorder" is the best diagnosis that we can offer.

REFERENCES

AINSWORTH, MARY D. S. (1973). The development of infant-mother attachment. In B. M. Caldwell & H. N. Ricciuti (Eds.), *Child development and social policy. Review of child development research* (Vol. 3, pp. 1–94). Chicago: University of Chicago Press.

AINSWORTH, M., BLEHAR, M. C., WATERS, E., & WALL, S. (1978). *Patterns of attachment. A psychological study of the strange situation.* Hillsdale, NJ: Lawrence Erlbaum Associates.

American Psychiatric Association. (1980). *Diagnostic and statistical manual of mental disorders* (3rd ed.). Washington, DC: Author.

APGAR, V. (1953). A proposal for a new method of evaluation of the newborn infant. *Current Researches in Anesthesia and Analgesia, 32,* 260–267.

ARONSON, E., & ROSENBLOOM, S. (1971). Space perception in early infancy: Perception within a common auditory-visual space. *Science, 172,* 1161–1163.

BELL, S. M., & AINSWORTH, M. S. (1972). Infant crying and maternal responsiveness. *Child Development, 43,* 1171–1190.

BLEHAR, M. (1980). Anxious attachment and defensive reactions associated with day care. *Child Development, 45,* 683–692.

BOWER, T. G. R. (1977) *A primer of infant development.* San Francisco: W. H. Freeman.

BOWLBY, J. (1949). The study and reduction of group tensions in the family. *Human Relations, 2,* 123–128.

BOWLBY, J. (1951). *Maternal care and mental health* (2nd ed.). World Health Organization Monograph Series, No. 2. Geneva: World Health Organization.

BOWLBY, J. (1958). The nature of a child's tie to his mother. *International Journal of Psychoanalysis, 39,* 350–373.

BOWLBY, J. (1960). Separation anxiety. *International Journal of Psychoanalysis, 41,* 89–113.

BOWLBY, J. (1969). *Attachment and loss (Vol. 1): Attachment.* New York: Basic Books.

BRAZELTON, T. B. (1973). *Neonatal behavioral assessment scale.* (National Spastics Society Monograph). Philadelphia: Lippincott.

BRAZELTON, T. B., KOSLOWSKI, B., & MAIN, M. (1974). The origins of reciprocity: The early mother-infant interaction. In M. Lewis & L. A. Rosenblum (Eds.), *The effect of the infant on its caregiver* (pp. 49–76). New York: John Wiley.

BRODY, S. (1956). *Patterns of mothering.* New York: International Universities Press.

BROOKHART, J., & HOCK, E. (1976). The effects of experimental context and experiential background on infants' behavior toward their mothers and a stranger. *Child Development, 47,* 333–340.

BROUSSARD, E. R., & HARTNER, M. S. S. (1971). Further considerations regarding maternal perception of the newborn. In J. Hellmuth (Ed.), *Exceptional Infant* (Vol. 2, pp. 432–450). New York: Brunner/Mazel.

BURGNER, M., & EDGCUMBE, R. (1972). Some problems in the conceptualization of early object relationships: Part II: The concept of object constancy. In R. S. Eissler, A. Freud, M. Kris, & A. J. Solnit (Eds.), *The psychoanalytic study of the child* (Vol. 27, pp. 315–333). New York: Quadrangle Books.

BUSS, A. H., & PLOMIN, R. A. (1975). *A temper-*

ament theory of personality development. New York: Wiley Interscience.

CALDWELL, B. (1964). The effects of infant care. In M. L. Hoffman & L. W. Hoffman (Eds.), *Review of child development research* (Vol. 1, pp. 9–88). New York: Russell Sage Foundation.

CALDWELL, B. (1967). What is the optimal learning environment for the young child? *American Journal of Orthopsychiatry, 37*(1), 8–21.

CALDWELL, B. (1972). What does research teach us about day care: For children under three. *Children Today, 1*(1), 232–240.

CALDWELL, B., WRIGHT, C. M., HONIG, A. S., & TANNENBAUM, J. (1970). Infant day care and attachment. *American Journal of Orthopsychiatry, 40*(3), 397–413.

CALL, JUSTIN D. (1983). Toward a nosology of psychiatric disorders in infancy. In J. D. Call, E. Galenson, & R. L. Tyson (Eds.), *Frontiers of infant psychiatry* (pp. 117–129). New York: Basic Books.

CAREY, W. B. (1981). Clinical appraisal of temperament. *Developmental disabilities in preschool children.* New York: Spectrum.

CAREY, W. B., & McDEVITT, S. C. (1978). Revision of the infant temperament questionnaire. *Pediatrics, 61*, 735–739.

CATTELL, P. (1940). *The measurement of intelligence of infants and young children.* New York: Psychological Corporation.

CHESS, S., & THOMAS, A. (1982). Infant bonding: Mystique and reality. *American Journal of Orthopsychiatry, 52*(2), 213–223.

CONDON, W. S., & SANDER, L. (1974). Neonate movement is synchronized with adult speech: Interactional participation and language acquisition. *Science, 183*, 99–101.

DAYTON, G. O., JONES, M. H., STEELE, B., & ROSE, M. (1964). Developmental study of coordinated eye movements in the human infant. II. An electro-oculographic study of the fixation reflex in the newborn. *Archives of Ophthalmology, 1964, 71*, 871–875.

DROTAR, D., MALONE, C., & NEGRAY, J. (1980). Environmentally based failure to thrive and children's intellectual development. *Journal of Clinical Child Psychology, 8*, 236–239.

EISENBERG, R. B. (1969). Auditory behavior in the human neonate. *International Audiology, 8*, 34–45.

EMDE, R. N., & ROBINSON, J. (1979). The first two months: Recent research in developmental psychobiology and the changing review of the newborn. In J. D. Noshpitz (Ed.), *Basic handbook of child psychiatry* (Vol. 1, pp. 72–106). New York: Basic Books.

ENDSLEY, R. C., & BRADBARD, M. R. (1981). *Quality of day care: A handbook of choices for parents and caregivers.* Englewood Cliffs, NJ: Prentice-Hall.

ERIKSON, E. H. (1950). *Childhood and society.* New York: Norton.

EVANS, S. L., REINHART, J. B., & SUCCOP, R. A. (1972). Failure to thrive: A study of 45 children and their families. *Journal of the American Academy of Child Psychiatry, 11*, 440.

FAGAN, J. F. (1973). Infants' delayed recognition memory and forgetting. *Journal of Experimental Child Psychology, 16*, 424–450.

FAGAN, J. F., & McGRATH, S. K. (1981). Infant recognition memory and later intelligence. *Intelligence, 5*, 121–130.

FANAROFF, A., KENNELL, J., & KLAUS, M. (1972). Follow-up of low birth weight infants: The predictive value of maternal visiting patterns. *Pediatrics, 49*(2), 287–290.

FANTZ, R. L. (1963). Pattern vision in newborn infants. *Science, 140*, 296–297.

FISCHHOFF, J. (1975). Failure to thrive and maternal deprivation. In E. J. Anthony (Ed.), *Explorations in child psychiatry* (pp. 213–227). New York: Plenum.

FITCH, M. J., CADOL, R. V., GOLDSON, E., WENDEL, T., SWARTZ, D., & JACKSON, E. (1976). Cognitive development of abused and failure to thrive children. *Pediatric Psychology, 1*, 32–37.

FRAIBERG, S. (1980). *Clinical studies in infant mental health.* New York: Basic Books.

FREEDMAN, D. G. (1977). The social capacities of young infants. In E. M. Hetherington & R. D. Parke (Eds.), *Contemporary readings in child psychology* (pp. 66–76). New York: McGraw-Hill.

FREUD, A. (1965). *Normality and pathology in childhood: Assessments of development.* New York: International Universities Press.

FREUD, S. (1964). Analysis terminable and interminable. In J. Strachey (Ed.), *Standard Edition* (Vol. 23). London: Hogarth Press. (Originally published 1933.)

FREUD, S. (1964). An outline of psychoanalysis. In J. Strachey (Ed.), *Standard Edition* (Vol. 23). London: Hogarth Press. (Originally published 1933.)

FRIES, M. E., & WOOLF, P. J. (1953). Some hypotheses on the role of the congenital activity type in personality development. In R. S. Eissler, A. Freud, H. Hartmann, & E. Kris (Eds.), *Psychoanalytic study of the child* (Vol. 8, pp. 48–65). New York: International Universities Press.

GESELL, A. (1925). *The mental growth of the preschool child.* New York: Macmillan

GIL, D. (1970). *Violence against children.* Cambridge, MA: Harvard University Press.

GOLDBERG, S. (1978). Social competence in infancy: A model of parent-infant interaction. In S. Chess & A. Thomas (Eds.), *Annual progress in child psychiatry and child development* (pp. 247–264). New York: Brunner/Mazel.

GOLDFARB, W. (1955). Emotional and intellectual consequences of psychologic deprivation in infancy: A re-evaluation. In P. Hoch & J. Zubin (Eds.), *Psychopathology of childhood* (pp. 105–120). New York: Grune and Stratton.

GREENSPAN, S. I., LOURIE, R. S., & NOVER, R. A. (1979). A developmental approach to the classification of psychopathology in infancy and early childhood. In J. D. Noshpitz (Ed.), *Basic handbook of psychiatry* (Vol. 2, pp. 157–165). New York: Basic Books.

GROSSMAN, K., THANE, K., & GROSSMAN, K. E. (1981). Maternal tactual contact of the newborn after various postpartum conditions of mother-infant contact. *Developmental Psychology, 17*(2), 158–170.

HAITH, M. (1969). Infra-red television recording and measurement of ocular behavior in the human infant. *American Psychologist, 24*, 279–285.

HAYES, L. A., & WATSON, J. S. (1981). Neonatal imitation: Fact or artifact. *Developmental Psychology, 17*(5), 655–661.

HAZEN, N. L., & DURRETT, M. E. (1982). Relationship of security of attachment to exploration and cognitive mapping abilities in 2-year-olds. *Developmental Psychology, 18*(5), 751–760.

HEINICKE, C. M., & WESTHEIMER, I. (1965). *Brief separations.* New York: International Universities Press.

HERBERT, M., SLUCKIN, W., & SLUCKIN, A. (1982). Mother-to-infant bonding. *Journal of Child Psychology and Psychiatry, 23*(3), 205–221.

HONZIK, M. P. (1976). Value and limitations of infant tests: An overview. In M. Lewis (Ed.), *Origins of intelligence: Infancy and early childhood* (pp. 59–97). New York: Plenum.

HUBERT, N. C., WACHS, T. D., PETER-MARTIN, P., & GANDOUR, M. J. (1982). The study of early temperament: Measurement and conceptual issues. *Child Development, 53*, 571–600.

HUFTON, I. W., & OATES, R. K. (1977). Nonorganic failure to thrive: A long term follow up. *Pediatrics, 59*, 73–79.

Joint Commission on Mental Health of Children. (1970). *Crisis in Child Mental Health: Challenge for the 1970's.* New York: Harper and Row.

KENNELL, J. H., JERAULD, R., WOLFE, H., CHESLER, D., KREGER, N. C., MCALPHINE, W., STEFFA, M., & KLAUS, M. H. (1974). Maternal behavior one year after early and extended post-partum contact. *Developmental Medicine and Child Neurology, 16*(2), 172–179.

KLAUS, M. H. (1978). The biology of parent-to-infant attachment. *Birth and the Family Journal, 5*(4), 200–203.

KLAUS, M. H., & KENNELL, J. (1970). Mothers separated from their newborn infants. *Pediatrics Clinics of North America, 17*(4), 1015–1037.

KLAUS, M. H., KENNELL, J. H., PLUMB, N., & ZUEHLKE, A. (1970). Human maternal behavior at the first contact with her young. *Pediatrics, 46*(2), 187–192.

KLEIN, M. (1928). Early stages of the Oedipus conflict. *International Journal of Psychoanalysis, 9*, 167–332.

KORNER, A. F. (1971). Individual differences at birth: Implications for early experience and later development. *American Journal of Orthopsychiatry, 41*, 608–619.

KORNER, A. F. (1974). The effect of the infant's state, level of arousal, sex and ontogenetic stage on the caregiver. In M. Lewis & L. A. Rosenblum (Eds.), *The effect of the infant on its caregiver* (pp. 105–121). New York: John Wiley.

LAMB, M. E. (Ed.) (1976). *The role of the father in child development.* New York: Wiley.

LAMB, M. E. (1977). Father-infant and mother-infant interaction in the first year of life. *Child Development, 48*(1), 167–181.

LEWIS, M., & CHOATES, D. L. (1980). Mother-infant interaction and cognitive development in twelve-week-old infants. *Infant Behavior and Development, 3*, 95–105.

LEWIS, M., FEIRING, C., McGUFFOG, C., & JASKIR, J. (1984). Predicting psychopathology in six-year-olds from early social relations. *Child Development, 55*, 123–137.

LEWIS, M., & LEE-PAINTER, S. (1974). An interactional approach to the mother-infant dyad. In M. Lewis & L. A. Rosenblum (Eds.), *The effect of the infant on its caregiver* (pp. 21–48). New York: John Wiley.

LEWIS, M., & ROSENBLUM, L. A. (Eds.) (1974). *The effect of the infant on its caregiver.* New York: John Wiley.

LEWIS, M., & WILSON, C. D. (1972). Infant development in lower class American families. *Human Development, 15*, 112–117.

LITT, C. J. (1981). Children's attachment to transitional objects: a study of two pediatric populations. *American Journal of Orthopsychiatry, 51*, 131–139.

MAHLER, M. (1972). On the first three subphases of the separation-individuation process. *International Journal of Psychoanalysis, 53*, 333–338.

MAHLER, M., PINE, F., & BERGMAN, A. (1975). *Psychological birth of the human infant: Symbiosis and individuation.* New York: Basic Books.

MARVIN, R. S. (1977). An ethological-cognitive model for the attenuation of mother-child attachment behavior. In T. M. Alloway, L. Krames, & P. Pliner, (Eds.), *Advances in the study of communication and affect: Vol. 3. The development of social attachments.* New York: Plenum.

MASSIE, H. N., & CAMPBELL, B. K. (1983). The Massie-Campbell Scale of Mother-infant Attachment Indicators during Stress (AIDS Scale). In J. D. Call, E. Galenson, & R. L. Tyson (Eds.), *Frontiers of infant psychiatry* (pp. 394–413). New York: Basic Books.

MATAS, L., AREND, R. A., & SROUFE, L. A. (1978). Continuity of adaptation in the second year: The relationship between quality of attachment and later competence. *Child Development, 49*, 547–556.

McCARTNEY, K. (1984). Effect of quality of day care environment on children's language development. *Developmental Psychology, 20*, 244–261.

McDEVITT, S. C., & CAREY, W. B. (1978). The measurement of temperament in 3–7 year old children. *Journal of Child Psychology and Psychiatry, 19*, 245–253.

ORLANSKY, H. (1949). General review and summary: Infant care and personality. *Psychological Bulletin, 44*, 1–48.

PASTOR, D. L. (1981). The quality of mother-infant attachment and its relationship to toddlers' initial sociability with peers. *Developmental Psychology, 17*(3), 326–336.

PROVENCE, S., & LIPTON, R. C. (1962). *Infants in institutions.* New York: International Universities Press.

PROVENCE, S., NAYLOR, A., & PATTERSON, J. (1977). *The challenge of day care.* New Haven: Yale University Press.

QUINTON, D., RUTTER, M., & LIDDLE, C. (1984). Institutional rearing, parenting difficulties and marital support. *Psychological Medicine, 14*, p. 102–124.

ROBERTSON, J. & ROBERTSON, J. (1971). Young children in brief separation: A fresh look. In R. S. Eissler, A. Freud, M. Kris, L. M. Newman, & A. J. Solnit (Eds.), *Psychoanalytic study of the child* (Vol. 26, pp. 264–316). New York: Quadrangle Books.

ROBSON, K. S., & MOSS, H. A. (1970). Patterns and determinants of maternal attachment. *Journal of Pediatrics, 77*, 976–985.

ROE, K. V., MCCLURE, A., & ROE, A. (1982). Vocal interaction at 3 months and cognitive skills at 12 years. *Developmental Psychology, 18*(1), 15–16.

ROSENBLITH, J. F. (1975). Prognostic value of neonatal behavioral tests. In B. Z. Friedlander, G. M. Sterritt, & G. E. Kirk (Eds.), *Exceptional infant: Vol. 3. Assessment and intervention* (pp. 157–173). New York: Brunner/Mazel.

RUTTER, M. (1979). Maternal deprivation, 1972–1978: New findings, new concepts, new approaches. *Child Development, 50,* 283–305.

RUTTER, M., TIZARD, J., & WHITMORE, K. (1970). *Education, health and behavior.* London: Longman.

SIQUELAND, E. R., & LIPSITT, L. P. (1966). Conditioned head-turning in human newborns. *Journal of Experimental Child Psychology, 3,* 356–376.

SORCE, J. F., & EMDE, R. N. (1981). Mother's presence is not enough: Effect of emotional availability on infant exploration. *Developmental Psychology, 17*(6), 737–746.

SPITZ, R. A. (1945). Hospitalism: An inquiry into the genesis of psychiatric conditions in early childhood. In A. Freud, H. Hartmann, & E. Kris (Eds.), *The psychoanalytic study of the child* (Vol. 1, p. 53–75). New York: International University Press.

SPITZ, R. A. (1946a). Anaclitic Depression. In A. Freud, H. Hartmann, & E. Kris (Eds.), *The psychoanalytic study of the child* (Vol. 2., pp. 313–343). New York: International Universities Press.

SPITZ, R. A. (1946b). Hospitalism: A follow-up report. In A. Freud, H. Hartmann, & E. Kris (Eds.), *The psychoanalytic study of the child* (Vol. 2, pp. 115–117). New York: International Universities Press.

ST. CLAIR, K. (1978). Neonatal assessment procedures: A historical review. *Child Development, 49,* 280–292.

STERN, D. N. (1974). Mother and infant at play: The dyadic interaction involving facial, vocal, and gaze behaviors. In M. Lewis & L. A. Rosenblum (Eds.), *The effect of the infant on its caregiver* (pp. 187–213). New York: John Wiley.

STEVENSON, M. B., & LAMB, M. E. (1979). Effects of infant sociability and the caretaking environment on infant cognitive performance. *Child Development, 50*(1), 340–349.

STUTSMAN, R. (1934). *Mental measurement of preschool children.* Hudson, New York: World Book Co.

SVEJDA, M. J., CAMPOS, J. J., & EMDE, R. N. (1980). Mother-infant bonding: A failure to generalize. *Child Development, 51,* 775–779.

THOMAS, A., CHESS, S., & BIRCH, H. G. (1968). *Temperament and behavior disorders in children.* New York: New York University Press.

TIZARD, B., & HODGES, J. (1978). The effect of early institutional rearing on the development of eight-year-old children. *Journal of Child Psychology and Psychiatry, 19,* 99–118.

TIZARD, B., & JOSEPH, A. (1970). The cognitive

development of young children in residential care. *Journal of Child Psychology and Psychiatry, 11,* 177–186.

TIZARD, B., & REES, J. (1974). A comparison of the effects of adoption, restoration to the natural mother and continued institutionalization on the congitive development of four-year-old children. *Child Development, 45,* 92–99.

TIZARD, B., & REES, J. (1975). The effect of early institutional rearing on the behavior problems and affectional relationships of four-year-old children. *Journal of Child Psychology and Psychiatry, 16,* 61–73.

TOLPIN, M. (1971). On the beginnings of a cohesive self: An application of the concept of transmuting internalization to the study of the transitional object and signal anxiety. In R. S. Eissler, A. Freud, M. Kris, L. M. Newman, & A. J. Solnit (Eds.), *The psychoanalytic study of the child* (Vol. 26, pp. 316–355). New York: Quadrangle Books.

TRONICK, E., & BRAZELTON, T. B. (1975). Clinical uses of the Brazelton Neonatal Behavioral Assessment. In B. Z. Friedlander, G. M. Sterritt, & G. E. Kirk (Eds.), *Excep-*

tional infant: Vol. 3. Assessment and intervention (pp. 137–157). New York: Brunner/Mazel.

WATERS, E. (1978). The reliability and stability of individual differences in infant-mother attachment. *Child Development, 49,* 483–494.

WERTHEIMER, M. (1961). Psycho-motor coordination of auditory-visual space at birth. *Science, 134,* 1692.

WINNICOTT, D. W. (1953). Transitional objects and transitional phenomena. *International Journal of Psychoanalysis, 34,* 1–9.

WOLFF, P. H. (1969). The natural history of crying and other vocalizations in early infancy. In B. M. Foss (Ed.), *Determinants of infant behavior* (Vol. 4, pp. 81–109). London: Methuen.

WOROBEY, J., & BELSKY, J. (1982). Employing the Brazelton Scale to influence mothering: An experimental comparison of three strategies. *Developmental Psychology, 18*(5), 736–744.

YARROW, L. J. (1962). Maternal deprivation: Toward an empirical and conceptual reevaluation. In *Maternal deprivation.* New York: Child Welfare League of America.

CHAPTER 2

THE UNCOMMON PARENT

PARENTING DISORDERS AND THEIR TREATMENT

This chapter and the next deal with pathological problems in early development. Dividing these problems into those which originate with the parent versus those which originate with the infant is admittedly an artificial division. Winnicott (1958) remarked that "there is no such a thing as a baby, there is only a baby and a mother," and the converse is equally true. Infants elicit different responses from their parents, and parental behavior in turn shapes the baby's future behavior. When we are looking at the kinds, causes, and effects of parenting disorders, we must keep in mind that the infant is partner, if not an equal partner. Also, one must bear in mind that there are degrees of parental

ineptitude and that very few parents are totally consistent in their behavior—whether it be judged "good" or "bad."

This chapter is concerned first with groups of parents known to experience special problems, namely, psychotic, mentally retarded, and teenage parents. These are not mutually exclusive groups and poverty is likely to be a common feature. However, these populations have been reported separately in the literature with reference to their special difficulties and intervention programs which have been organized for their benefit. The fourth section of this chapter deals with child abuse, a parenting disorder which has received a great deal of attention since the 1960's. Although there is a significant minority to the contrary, most abusing parents are also poverty parents. (Chapter 4 deals with the multitude of problems and programs specifically relevant to parents and children in poverty circumstances.)

Both mentally retarded and mentally ill parents present a genetic risk factor for their offspring, but it is highly unlikely that this factor alone can account for the later problems presented by their children. Most of the intervention programs in this chapter are parent-centered rather than child-centered. Bromwich (1981) distinguished four models of early intervention: (a) the infant curriculum (to be discussed in Chapter 3); (b) the parent education model; (c) the parent-infant interaction model; and (d) the parent therapy model. In actual operation, programs are seldom "pure," but these categories are useful in describing differences in emphasis. The final section in this chapter, dealing with treatment approaches to all kinds of parenting disorders, emphasizes "parent therapy."

MENTALLY ILL PARENTS

Biological Risk Factors

Children of psychotic parents are an "at risk" population on two counts, genetic and psychosocial. The genetic data can be read in different ways. With regard to schizophrenia, for instance, 90% of those so diagnosed have parents who are not mentally ill, and vice versa, roughly 85% of children with one schizophrenic parent do not develop schizophrenia. On the other hand, the fact that 12 to 15% of the offspring of one schizophrenic parent and one healthy parent do develop a schizophrenic disorder is 10 times the 1% incidence of schizophrenia in the general population. The expectancy estimates for children of manic-depressive parents are almost identical, that is, a 15% risk of developing a similar illness if one parent has bipolar depression and 40 to 50% if both parents are ill (Targum & Gershon, 1979).

Follow-up information on children who have been adopted indicates a higher risk for those who have a schizophrenic biological mother. In a Danish adoptive study reported by Wender, Rosenthal, Kety, Schulsinger, & Welner (1974), nearly 20% of the children with a schizophrenic parent were judged as adults to be "seriously disturbed" despite "normal" adoptive parents, compared to about 10% of the "all normal parents" group and about 5% of those identified as having normal biological parents and one schizophrenic adoptive parent. This suggests that the biological component is stronger than the environmental component; however, sample populations are necessarily small because one is taking advantage of fortuitous circumstances that do not occur frequently.

Granted that a genetic factor operates in schizophrenia, the mode of inheritance remains obscure and there have been extensive efforts to identify genetic "markers," special characteristics that indicate increased vulnerability. Many kinds of psychophysiological characteristics have been implicated including disordered eye movements while following a swinging pendulum (Holzman, 1982; Holzman et al., 1974); dysfunction of sustained attention (Erlenmeyer-Kimling & Cornblatt, 1978; MacCrimmon, Cleghorn, Asarnow, & Steffey, 1980; Nuechterlein, Phipps-Yonas, Driscoll, &

Garmezy, 1982); and speed of skin conductance recovery rate (Mednick et al., 1978).

The possibility that genetic risk factors are increased by additional biological risk factors associated with prenatal and perinatal difficulties has been advanced by Zax, Sameroff, and Babigian (1977). Using the psychiatric register in Rochester, New York, the investigators identified psychiatric patients who were due to deliver at a local hospital. With the addition of matched controls, 337 mothers were interviewed in their final month of pregnancy; the course of the pregnancy and delivery and the condition of the infant at birth were monitored. Four out of the five infants who died were delivered by mothers diagnosed as depressed (4 out of 56), but the schizophrenic mothers (29) were more likely to have infants with low birthweight (under 2,500 grams). When the data were reanalyzed according to severity and chronicity of mental illness rather than formal diagnosis, the difference in birthweight was even more significant. Not surprisingly, those in the most chronic group were more likely to have been taking medication, especially tranquilizers, during pregnancy. The six infants given up for adoption all came from the 29 schizophrenic mothers. The six mothers were "most chronic," "most severe," in the lowest socioeconomic status, and unmarried, with one exception. Of special interest is the poor status of their infants; three were born prematurely and one had a cardiac problem requiring intensive care. The authors conclude that

The adoptive data from the current study, although derived from a small sample, suggest that the infant brings with him far more concrete evidence of his deviancy than his schizophrenic genes. He also may bring an underweight, tiny body which places extra caretaking demands on his new adoptive parents. These extra caretaking demands and deviant appearance have the potential of beginning a negative chain of transactions, which could produce a deviant outcome irrespective of whether the infant carried schizophrenic genes or not. (1977, p. 229)

Psychological Risk Factors

With the widespread use of the psychoactive drugs and shorter periods of hospitalization, the problems of living with a psychotic parent throughout childhood have become increasingly important. These have been examined by a number of investigators. Rice, Ekdahl, and Miller (1971) reported findings from these three studies completed between 1959 and 1967 under the auspices of the Department of Maternal and Child Health of the Harvard School of Public Health. The total number of families with mentally ill parents (mixed diagnoses) was 225, 199 of whom were mothers. Almost half of the children were found to have behavioral problems or neurotic difficulties. These investigators were particularly concerned about the substitute caretaking arrangements during the parents' hospitalization and urged that staff at admitting hospitals assist in finding such services on behalf of the total family. Landau, Harth, Othnay, and Scharfhertz (1972) reported on 63 psychotic parents and their 131 children in Israel. In almost all of the numerous comparisons, the research group fared worse than the control group even when matched for demographic characteristics. The authors were particularly impressed by the high incidence of psychopathology among the 70 children who comprised the third generation of mentally ill patients.

Cohler, Grunebaum, Weiss, Hartzman, and Gallant (1976) compared 47 discharged mental patients who had children under 5 years of age with a "well" group of mothers, using a self-administered maternal attitude scale and an interview rating of a Social Role Adaptation Instrument. In particular, those mothers who had had repeated hospitalizations indicated less concern about child-care questions, appeared to disregard the importance of fostering mother-child reciprocity, and tended to deny any feelings of ambivalence. They suggested that these attitudes, combined with genetic factors, increased disorganization in the home, and the factor of mother-child separation act together to affect the child's development adversely.

Early Intervention

The incidence of psychotic illness after childbirth is about 1 per 1,000 births for the general population but about 1 in 4 for women with previous psychotic episodes (McNeil & Kaij, 1977) so this represents one possible time for early intervention. McNeil and Kaij described the special problems in the wake of a postpartum psychosis as follows:

Separation of mother and baby for any reason during the early period is problematic for the relationship; but where the cause is mental illness, the mother is at a special disadvantage on two counts. The disturbance itself interferes with the emotional relationship; and she feels guilty because she cannot take care of the baby. Many of our subjects with postpartum psychoses have expressed the feeling of irreparable loss . . . Our own bias is toward separating mothers and babies as little as possible; hospitalizing the baby with the mother, supporting the mother substantially in the home, and intruding as little as possible on the mother-baby relationship. (1977, pp. 109–110)

The practice of joint admission for mother and infant started in Great Britain in 1948, and psychiatric mother and baby units appear to have flourished in that country (Brockington & Kumar, 1982). In the United States, the Massachusetts Mental Health Center has maintained the policy of carefully selected joint admissions, not only for the sake of the child but to aid the mother in returning to her family (Grunebaum, Weiss, Cohler, Hartman, & Gallant, 1982). Although their numbers were very small, these authors concluded that being with their mothers in the hospital had a facilitating effect on the cognitive development of the joint admission children, but both groups of children of psychotic mothers showed deficits in the capacity for close interpersonal relationships. The increased cost of mother-baby units is probably the major reason why they have not been widely adopted, and there is as yet no long-term follow-up to prove their value.

Continuing Intervention

In the early 1970's, there was a burgeoning of comprehensive, longitudinal studies focused on children identified as high risk for schizophrenia, usually because they were the offspring of schizophrenic parents (Garmezy, 1978). Two of the 20 or so such programs are the University of Rochester Child and Family Study (Wynne, Jones, Al-Khayyal, Cole, & Fisher, 1982) and the Edison Child Development Research Center in St. Louis (Anthony, 1977); these were selected for discussion because of the contrasting approaches to treatment.

The Rochester group selected 100 white subjects, predominantly middle class, married, initially with an intact family, and with male children aged 4, 7, or 10 years (Romano, 1978), a group that was admittedly not representative of schizophrenic populations as a whole. In the family-oriented treatment program, techniques were developed to assess communication deviance (including "double bind" messages); affective-relational domain (such as expressed emotion); structural-contextual domain (such as family roles and isolation from social support networks); and family subculture (e.g., beliefs about mental illness).

This group examined what might be called "the making of an exception" and related this to the parents' ability to communicate in a clearly focused, well-structured, and flexible task-appropriate manner (Wynne et al., 1982). With regard to intervention, Wynne wrote:

Family therapy was introduced to assist and guide families in drawing upon their capacities to rally and to grow despite liabilities that may co-exist in individual family members and in the family as a social unit. Unfortunately, some families, and even some poorly trained or uninformed psychiatrists, sometimes have construed or allowed family therapy to become a setting for continuation of blaming that often is associated with the onset of any poorly understood or frightening illness. In contrast, competent family therapists set as their first task the reduction of doubt and self-blame that many, if not most, families bring to the clinic or hospital. Guidance in restructuring family relationships and communications must be implemented through providing clear and feasible tasks for the family members to carry out with one another in a reciprocally supportive manner. (1978, p. 540)

In contrast, the St. Louis program emphasized direct intervention with the child. This group followed some 200 children with a psychotic parent. About 30% of the children seemed normally adjusted (10% being credited with superior adjustment), about 30% had minor adjustment problems, and about 40% manifested significant maladjustment (Anthony, 1977). Treatment services were made available for those who needed it. Various types of child intervention were used. *Compensatory interventions* included a special educational remedial program, group sessions concentrating on the parents' illnesses; and a big brother social program for children whose families lacked leadership and organization. *Classical interventions* were based on individual and group therapy without special focus on the parental illness. *Corrective interventions* were similar to "cognitive behavior" approaches and included courses on self-orientation and object differentiation; reality conversations emphasizing causal connections; demystification sessions regarding the nature of psychosis; and practice in organizational competence in small groups.

This is an interesting array of child-centered treatment approaches offering opportunities for comparison, bearing in mind that the treatment chosen was based on clinical assessment rather than random choice. Briefly, keeping the amount of treatment constant, the change generated by the classical intervention measures was greater than for any of the other procedures; keeping the kind of treatment constant, there was a significant association between the amount of intervention given and the amount of change produced in assessments of vulnerability and maladjustment (Anthony, 1977). Of greater concern is the long-range value of the interventions. In 1977, Anthony reported six breakdowns (12% of the treatment group of 50) in the 18- to 20-year-old group (not necessarily psychotic). He suggested that increased risk was associated with the age at the time of the parental psychosis (within the first 7 years), acute deterioration of the parent, and life stresses that had increased prior to onset. Anthony also noted the apparent paradox of an inverse relationship between the degree of parental disturbance and the degree of child disturbance. The probable explanation is that deeply psychotic individuals tend to be withdrawn and consequently do not enmesh their children in their illnesses.

Anthony pointed out that children have problems in the face of parental psychosis which must take precedence over research considerations.

First of all, the parent's psychosis is often experienced as psychic loss and followed by a period of bereavement during which the grief is generally masked. . . . Other disturbing affects include feelings of guilt (associated with the child's belief that his bad behavior has driven the parent crazy, or associated with experiencing relief at the parent's departure to a hospital), feelings of shame (when the parent's bizarre conduct becomes public knowledge, or when the parent misbehaves grossly in front of the child's peers), fear (of being attacked physically or sexually), anxiety (about becoming crazy oneself), and perplexity (at being subjected to contradictory and inconsistent demands). (Anthony, 1978, p. 482)

To this list, the author would add still another possible reaction noted in her clinical work, namely, a loyalty conflict with a feeling that the well parent has behaved badly toward the sick one. Any one, or all of these, is a heavy load for a child to carry.

Yet many children of psychotic parents show little or no adjustment difficulty (Grunebaum, Weiss, Cohler, Hartmann, & Gallant, 1982). Anthony described the "supernormal" children in his group as having the capacity "to develop an objective, realistic, somewhat distant and yet distinctly compassionate approach to the parental illness, neither retreating from it nor being intimidated by it, but viewing it as something needing to be fully understood" (1974, p. 540). Clearly, it would be difficult for a child under 7 years to use these coping devices, and even the older child needs external support, preferably from the adequately functioning other parent who may well need guidance to serve this function.

The foregoing discussion has stressed schizophrenia, but there is no doubt that severely and chronically depressed parents also cast a long shadow over their children's development. The group at the Massachusetts Mental Health Center, following 50 children from early infancy to 5 years of age who had psychotic mothers, reported that longer-term clinical follow-up data indicated that children of depressed mothers were more impaired than children of schizophrenic mothers (Garmezy, 1978). Parental unavailability, the common denominator in psychotic illness, is the noxious agent, not the formal diagnosis. (See Chapter 9 for further discussion of the depressed parent and depressed child.)

Some time ago, Goshen (1963) suggested that "neurotic maternal attitudes which are characterized by a failure to stimulate and evoke meaningful signals during critical periods of life can result in failure on the child's part in grasping the significance of language, thus proceeding to a state recognizable as mental retardation" (p. 174). He felt that a prime cause for such neglect was maternal depression. He no doubt exaggerated the significance of this factor when he estimated that perhaps 50% of the retarded population without organic findings was produced in this way. When this is reconsidered in a transactional context, however, it is more than likely that a child "born retarded" will evoke a depressive response which can exacerbate the degree of handicap.

It is high time that we regularly take a family point of view when a parent becomes mentally ill. There are many proven ways to be helpful, particularly for the older child. A family orientation has become standard for problems around alcoholism but there has been virtually no movement in this direction when the problem is mental illness. Following a medical model, those who treat the parent do not become involved with the children. About one-third of schizophrenic mothers are so diagnosed be-

fore or at the time of the birth of their first child (Mednick & Witkin-Lanoil, 1977), and a large number of these mothers probably need help in caring for their infants. This requires staff who are knowledgeable in adult psychopathology and infant development, as well as the financial resources to permit persistent outreach.

RETARDED PARENTS

Heritability of Intelligence

The fact that individual differences in intelligence are to some degree genetically determined is not in dispute. The controversy centers around the question: To what degree? This issue is discussed at greater length in Chapter 12. In reporting on the status of the offspring of retarded parents, it is readily apparent that one cannot satisfactorily separate the genetic and environmental components. The following discussion does not deal with parents whose retardation is part of a known genetic syndrome such as phenylketonuria or Down syndrome but is concerned mainly with parents in the so-called mild range of mental retardation, that is, the IQ's falling in the 50 to 70 range diagnosed as "familial-cultural" or "psychosocial" mental retardation.

Heber, Dever, and Conry (1968) surveyed a low socioeconomic area of Milwaukee and found that the mothers with IQ's less than 80 (45% of the sample) accounted for almost 80% of the children falling below 80 IQ. The mothers with IQ's below 67 were 14 times more likely to have children below 75 IQ. On the other hand, a review of studies not restricted to the very low socioeconomic level selected in the Milwaukee surveys indicated a general trend for the children to have higher IQ's than their parent (Haavik & Menninger, 1981). For example, Laxova, Gilderdale, and Ridler (1973) reported on 53 mothers with a mean IQ of 66 and found that 26% of the children had IQ's below 85, surpassing the maternal IQ average but skewed toward the low end of normal. All in all, the data suggest that children of retarded parents will be closer to average, that is, more intelligent than their parents, but nevertheless still below the general average. This trend, representing a regression toward the population mean, would be expected both from a genetic and statistical point of view.

Parenting Problems of Retarded Parents

Measured IQ of the offspring is not the only criterion that can be used to evaluate retarded persons' parenting success. Haavik and Menninger (1981) reviewed a number of studies attempting to evaluate the quality of child care, either by observers' ratings or incidence of referrals to child protective agencies. The reported incidences of removal from home ranged from 15 to 40%. There was agreement that extensive support from social service or health agencies was necessary, and evaluations of child care were generally negative.

Schilling, Schinke, Blythe, and Barth (1982) reviewed the literature to examine the possible relationship between child abuse/neglect and mental retardation in the parents. In addition to the previously cited studies, they looked at characteristics of neglecting/abusing parents and found a disproportionate number to be reported as mentally retarded. For example, Smith (1975) found almost half of 125 "battering" parents to be of "borderline subnormality or below," and Oliver (1977) reported nearly 30% of 67 abusing parents had "borderline or moderate mental subnormality."

All of the studies, however, suffer from two weaknesses. First, there are no comparisons adequately controlled for socioeconomic status. This is crucial because child maltreatment is negatively correlated with socioeconomic status, and lower-class families are disproportionately represented in child protective investigations of physical and emotional abuse and medical, physical, and emotional neglect (Pelton, 1978; 1981). There is little doubt that mentally retarded parents are also poor (Roth, 1982). "Thus, even without considering the special characteristics of mental retardation, mentally retarded parents are relegated to socioeconomic circumstances that foster child maltreatment" (Schilling et al., 1982, p. 205). The families are often described as at the "bottom of the social structure," lonely and isolated.

The second weakness has to do with the assessment of retardation in the parents; many times the judgment is made on the basis of historical information or partial testing and often persons with a wide range of mental abilities are treated together as representing "borderline and moderate mental subnormality." Looking at the problems of learning or teaching how to be a parent in supposedly "normal" populations, Harman and Brim (1980) commented that "the literature remains devoid of specific attempts to correlate intelligence with understanding of child development." In the early study of Mickelson (1947), mothers with IQ's from 30 to 50 tended to provide unsatisfactory child care, but above 50 IQ no relationship between IQ and adequacy of child care was noted! Outcomes reported in terms of percentages for the offspring of parents who share a recorded IQ "less than 80" are crude data which add little to our understanding of the phenomena involved.

Despite their reservations, however, both of the major reviews concluded with a negative judgment. "Although the question of incidence of child neglect involving developmentally disabled parents has not been thoroughly researched, the reported figures are disturbingly high" (Haavik & Menninger, 1981, p. 73). "Although the available research has many weaknesses, the preponderance of evidence points toward increased risk of maltreatment for children reared by mentally retarded parents" (Schilling et al., 1982, p. 206).

Legal Issues

In talking about their work with retarded parents, Kugel and Parsons (1967) described the families as difficult to motivate, suspicious, and constantly fearful of having their children taken away by court action. Their distrust was justified. Pessimism about the child rearing capacity of mildly retarded persons is widely shared and institutionalized in child neglect and custody laws. The enforcement of child neglect laws allows room for considerable discretion

for judges and court workers, so that "judgment" is liberally mixed with "evidence." There is evidence that some social welfare agencies assume that mental retardation equals poor parenting, and this assumption may well be the basis for numerous neglect and termination actions against retarded parents (Hertz, 1979).

Haavik and Menninger (1981) cite legal decisions where the judge acted on a presumption of parental incompetence by removing a child from retarded parents at the time of birth (*in re* Green, 1978); in Pennsylvania a trial court found the children "not undernourished, they receive ample food and have minimal clothing and are in good health" but nonetheless terminated the rights of the mother because of her mental retardation (*in re* Geiger, 1975). Other legal decisions have been cited where a presumption of incompetence was made on the basis of the parent's IQ rather than demonstrated proof of harm to the child (Steinbock et al., 1975).

The legal/ethical issues raised by these opinions concern the nature and limits of a state's right and obligation to separate a family "in the best interest of the child." The evidence clearly does not support an a priori judgment of parental incompetence as long as even 25% are rated "satisfactory" and another undetermined number are doing as well as others in the same economic circumstances. Equal protection demands that determination of parental fitness be based on the capabilities of an individual, not on assumptions about a group.

Sterilization is another issue which raises ethical/legal questions in reference to retarded persons. Involuntary sterilization has a complicated legal history; our concern is more with the dilemma of the mildly retarded person electing and giving informed consent. It seems ridiculous that in some situations, retarded persons are considered ipso facto incapable of giving informed consent and thus will be denied voluntary sterilization; by the same token, they may be involuntarily sterilized by court decree (Macklin & Gaylin, 1981). Clearly there are instances of abuse where the informed consent has been pro forma or there has been coercion in the form of contingencies, like making sterilization a condition for release from an institution.

It is a difficult task to counsel a retarded adult towards sterilization, first on intellectual grounds since there is so much room for misunderstanding. Even more important is the psychological impact. Removing the possibility of having children is one more obvious sign of inferiority to add to a long list. Many retarded adults cling to the whole picture of a job, a car, an apartment, marriage, and a family as proof that they are "normal"; to give up any part of this means they have to face their handicap. In addition to the injury to their self-esteem, many retarded persons feel comfortable with and have a genuine affection for babies and young children. Working with the young retarded adult to accept sterilization means that one has to work through lifelong disappointments. There may be alternatives to offer, such as babysitting for relatives or friends, working in child-care Head Start centers, or volunteering in hospitals, but giving up one's dreams is always painful. If it is not to be relinquished altogether, at least one can pursue the goal of limiting family size since families with fewer children have fewer problems.

A summary look at intervention programs designed for retarded parents indicates that without exception they follow an educational model, and usually short term at that. For example, at the University of Wisconsin-Milwaukee, nurses held once-weekly classes for a period of 5 weeks to cover (a) handling the small infant; (b) child growth and development; (c) food, recreation, and discipline, (d) hazards, emergencies and safety measures, and (e) use of health care and community resources (Madsen, 1979). This would be a tall order for any group of parents! Nowhere is the continuity between child and adult development more clear than with mental retardation. This is not to say that retarded parents should be treated like children, but it does mean that their childhood past is very real and oppressive to their adult functioning. Any successful intervention must be based on empathic understanding of the deprivations of their childhood experiences, particularly with regard to social gratification. Even though they may often need assistance in child rearing, and the child may require supplementary services like day care, the retarded parent must feel self-respect and appreciate the importance of loving and being loved. There is nothing to say that this could not be done.

TEENAGE PARENTS

Scope of the Problem

If childhood and adulthood problems are closely linked in retarded parents, the linkage is as close for teenage parents for chronological reasons! The problem has caused a great deal of public concern since the mid-1970's, for economic reasons if nothing else. *The Wall Street Journal* (Salamon, 1982) quoted an Urban Institute report indicating that many teenage mothers and their children are likely to live on public assistance indefinitely. In households receiving Aid to Families with Dependent Children payments, about 60% of the women were teenage mothers; in non-welfare households, only 35% of the mothers were teenagers when they had their first babies. In 1978 the 95th Congress passed Senate Bill 2910, the "Adolescent Health Services and Pregnancy and Care Act" which authorized appropriations of $60 million for fiscal year 1979, $70 million for 1980, and $80 million for 1981. However, by the end of 1979, only $1 million had been spent on new programs under this act.

Adolescent pregnancies are not technically an "epidemic" as described by Lincoln, Jaffe, and Ambrose (1976), despite the increasing numbers. The most recent census data show that there were 262,700 births in the United States to unwed teenage mothers in 1979, up 44% from 1969. Although these births account for a larger proportion of total births, this is in large part because of the increased numbers of teenagers. Like the birth rate in general, the teenage birth rate has also declined in the 17–19 age group. Birth rate has remained steady for the 14- to 17-year-olds and risen slightly for girls under 14 years (Robertson, 1981). It is unfortunate that reports often consider the age group from 13 to 19 as one, ignoring significant differences between the older and younger teens.

There have been other significant changes besides the increased number of births to young teenagers. First, a large number of children born to teenagers are illegitimate, 25% for the white mothers and 80% for the black mothers in 1978 (National Center of Health Statistics, 1980). Another change since the late 1960's is the tendency for young mothers to keep their out-of-wedlock children rather than giving them up for adoption. Over 80% of white adolescents relinquished their illegitimate children for adoption in 1965 compared to less than 10% of this group in 1980 (Chilman, 1982). There are some significant black-white differences in keeping the babies. In his discussion of the strength of kinship ties in black families, Hill (1972) pointed out that 90% of black children born out of wedlock in 1969 are cared for by parents or relatives, while only 7% of similarly born white children were cared for in this way. The election of abortion shows similar cultural differences. Zelnik, Kim, and Kantner (1979) reported that white teenagers showed an increased use of abortions from 1971 to 1976, causing the percentage of conceptions resulting in delivery to drop from 82 to 62%. On the other hand, there was little difference for black teenagers, and virtually 90% of pregnancies resulted in deliveries in both 1971 and 1976.

Causative Factors

The changing picture of teenage pregnancy reflects the shift in attitude towards sexuality in the past two or three decades. There is evidence that there has been a trend towards earlier sexual activity across all socioeconomic groups (Zelnik, Kim, & Kanther, 1979), and there is now much greater acceptance of illegitimacy and the single parent. Also, there has been some acceleration of physiological maturity, so that girls have their first menstruation at younger ages than formerly. The average age of first menstruation has dropped in the last 20 years from 13.5 years to about 12.7 years. The average age at which girls could conceive 20 years ago was 15.5; now it is 14.7. An increased length of time when it is possible to conceive could well explain the reported increased birth rate for girls under 14 years.

There have been efforts to identify special psychological characteristics of teenagers who become pregnant, but two recent reviews (Phipps-Yonas, 1980; Quay, 1981) concur in the conclusion that "few, if any differences can be demonstrated in either intelligence, personality, or psychopathology when unmarried pregnant girls are compared using appropriate methodologies to their nonpregnant peers. It appears that the more rigorous was the investigation, the fewer the differences which emerged" (Quay, 1981, p. 88). Although there is no single feature or unique psychological profile, certain combinations seem to increase the likelihood of pregnancy (Phipps-Yonas, 1980). In general, girls who become pregnant in adolescence are below average in their school performance, uninterested in school, low in educational and vocational aspirations, and likely to come from a home marked by poor familial relationships. It is surprising that no one seems to have specifically asked if pregnant teenagers are more likely to have mothers who first conceived in adolescence.

Still, many girls in similar circumstances do not become pregnant, in part because of effective use of contraception. Sex education has commonly been viewed as the major prevention technique for teenage pregnancy, but has not been proven successful, at least in the traditional "classroom" presentation. Looking at the motivational aspects of the problems, other than the few who conceived because of contraceptive failure or from sheer ignorance, some teenagers actively sought to have a baby and others conceived by default.

Phipps-Yonas (1980) describes the many reasons to want a baby, including rivalry with the mother, establishing a kind of adult status, having "something of your own," and so on. For a teenager who is unhappy and has little to look forward to, having a baby is an achievement well within her grasp. There are also guilt-related reasons for contraceptive default. Contraception requires planning ahead and "expecting" to have intercourse. Zelnik and Kantner (1979) found that adolescents' most common explanation for not taking precautions (23% of some 700 adolescents) was that they had not expected to have intercourse. Rains (1971), in her personal account, explained it as follows:

The problems of self-respect and moral ambivalence which are raised at each transition to a more permissive stage of sexual experience are handled by culturally derived evasions and techniques of neutralizing internal disapproval. Unconcern with contraception is such a technique for it allows a girl to evade recognition of what she is doing and to sustain a preferred view of herself. (p. 32)

Only recently have investigators begun to examine the attitudes of the adolescent males who are the usual partners. The reports are disheartening to say the least. For instance, in a survey of 421 black, white, and Hispanic youths ranging in age from 13 to 19, 72% had taken no precaution during their last sexual experience and the vast majority of these indicated that what might happen was of no concern to them (Finkel & Finkel, 1978). Planning ahead requires a mutual commitment within a relationship. "It is perhaps ironic and certainly unfortunate that those 'least involved' with one another, often the 'one-night-stands,' are the most likely to produce an unwanted pregnancy" (Phipps-Yonas, 1980, p. 411).

It is imperative to explore every possible avenue for intervention, even after the first delivery, because the teenager who has had one pregnancy is at high risk to repeat. Evans, Selstad, and Welcher (1976) found that more than 8% of 113 teenage mothers were pregnant again within 6 months after they delivered; Trussell and Menken (1978) concluded that the younger a female is at her first pregnancy, the more children she will have and the more closely spaced they will be, even when racial, educational, and religious differences are controlled. The work of Campbell and Barnlund (1977) with women (not necessarily teenagers) who had two or more unplanned pregnancies suggests a possible new direction. Twenty-eight pairs of women were matched by occupation, education, ethnic identity, marital status, and age and divided into two groups: effective versus noneffective users of contraception. Six measures of communicative style were used for comparison. The women who repeatedly failed to plan their pregnancies ranked significantly lower in their communicative skill in general. Specifically, they were lower in sensitivity, directness, control, empathy, and clarity. They disclosed verbally at a consistently lower level across all topics, including sex. They were more inclined to idealize interpersonal relationships and were more likely to inhibit hostile reactions. The authors concluded that the "problem of unplanned pregnancy and unwanted children is, in part, a consequence of a failure to maintain adequate communication with significant others" (p. 138).

A small pilot project (Schinke & Gilchrist, 1977) followed up on this idea using group sessions to work on interpersonal communication with roleplaying and the like. Improving communication, in the sense that it is used here, is not a simple educational task; it is possible that the techniques employed in cognitive behavioral therapy would be particularly useful. But again we would expect this to be much more efficacious in the context of an ongoing relationship, assuming that these teenagers are no less emotionally needy than the retarded parents discussed before.

Outcome Findings

The case for bringing to bear sophisticated and relatively expensive efforts to reduce the number of teenage pregnancies must be made on the basis of what is known about the outcomes. The relationships between early motherhood and lower educational attainment, higher probability of divorce among parents who marry, higher subsequent fertility, and later poverty are well documented. However, it is not clear if this is a causal relationship or if teenage pregnancy is just an incidental part of the total picture. In a 2-year research project, Moore, Hoferth, Wertheimer, Waite, and Caldwell (1981) attempted to isolate the consequences of teenage child-bearing from general background characteristics, using data from two large national surveys. In brief, after standardizing for numerous background factors other than age at first birth, these investigators concluded that the woman's age per se does make a difference, over and above these other factors:

The consequences of early childbearing appear to be sufficiently negative that we doubt it is a status normally entered by informed choice, characterized by equal opportunity, or beneficial to children. Our analysis suggests that it is in the mutual interest of government, individuals and families to help teenagers prevent unwanted pregnancies and to mitigate the consequences of early childbearing when preventive measures fail. (1981, p. 53)

It should be noted that a contemporary reviewer (Chilman, 1982) offers an opposite interpretation of the data:

Analyses of longitudinal data from a number of studies which statistically control for the adverse effects of poverty and racism indicate that parental age, as a factor by itself, is of little significance in life outcomes for teen-age parents and their children. For example, despite overly simplistic claims to the contrary, teen-age parenting, in and of itself, is a minimal cause of dropping out of high school, youth unemployment, and welfare dependency. (p. 429)

There is no debate about these associations in real life; the controversy centers on the question of statistical control for background factors in order to prove a causal chain. However, no one would recommend teenage pregnancy as helpful in breaking out of the poverty cycle!

Evaluating the outcomes for the infants of teenage parents is similarly confounded by socioeconomic and racial factors. With regard to prenatal effects, the best opinion seems to be that given adequate prenatal care, it is likely that the outcome will be satisfactory in purely physcial terms (Robertson, 1981). However, prenatal complications and low birth weight do seem to occur with more frequency in those mothers who conceive within 2 years after the onset of menstruation (Monkus & Bancalari, 1981). Maternal anemia has frequently been reported and is probably related to the poor dietary habits of the teenager. Teenagers from 13 to 16 years appear to be the most nutritionally vulnerable of any age group, and the risk of malnutrition appears to be even higher when pregnancy occurs close to the age of menarche (Kafatos, Christakis, & Fordyce, 1981).

Paralleling the attention to adolescent pregnancy has been a growing concern with the problem of child abuse, and many writers have suggested a link between the two. Bolton, Laner, and Kane (1980) found that over one-third of the substantiated cases of child maltreatment in one Arizona county involved a mother who was, or had been, an adolescent at the birth of one of her children. Kinard and Klerman (1980) analyzed survey data reported by Gil (1970), by the American Humane Association (1978), and by McCarthy (1978). Between 37 and 51% of the parents identified as abusing and/or neglectful were under 20 years of age at the birth of their first child, but the significance of the maternal age differences disappears when socioeconomic circumstances are controlled (Kinard & Klerman, 1980). In sum, it seems clear that if one becomes pregnant more than 2 years after the onset of menstruation, one's chronological age has little bearing on physical or psychological outcome—given comfortable economic circumstances! That, however, is the exception to the rule.

Intervention

Since 1960, there has been a phenomenal increase in services designed either to prevent adolescent pregnancy or to ameliorate its consequences. Amelioration has often focused on special school programs like the Webster School, which opened in 1963 in Washington, D.C. These programs, initially segregated, were later "mainstreamed" into regular public schools following the passage of the Education Amendments Act of 1976, which prohibits discrimination in a school's educational program because of pregnancy or childbirth.

The Johns Hopkins Adolescent Pregnancy Program is a good example of a federally funded demonstration model providing comprehensive medical, psycho-social, and health educational services from pregnancy until 4 weeks post

partum. A special feature of the program was that the same staff was involved with the teenagers before and after delivery. "The trust relationship that builds up between individual girls and individual staff members is an important factor in maintaining follow-up and in enhancing the socio-emotional growth of the adolescents, many of whom have never received adequate parenting" (Hardy, King, Shipp, & Welcher, 1981, p. 270). A follow-up component continuing for another 3 years included periodic assessment, nutritional services, referral and outreach, enrichment activities for teenagers, and individual and group educational services. The educational "curriculum" covered standard subjects of child care and family planning, but also the development of personal values and goals. The process of values clarification which stressed personal responsibility and responsible decision making was used to help the adolescents work through the identification of their immediate and longer range goals and to implement the decisions required to reach their objectives. Fathers and grandmothers (over 50% of whom were themselves adolescent parents) were encouraged to participate in the group meetings.

Preliminary outcome data suggested some effectiveness in the avoidance of pregnancy. Among the first 100 young mothers in follow-up, 7.5% became pregnant within a year as compared with 21% of the controls. For the infants, developmental evaluation at 12 months indicated that they were generally above average, except in language. At 24 months, development was generally average with indications of a more marked delay in language skills. However, those infants who had been in good day-care programs tended to maintain an advanced developmental level in all areas.

Field (1981) described an experimental model for preterm infants born to teenage mothers. The intervention focused on sensorimotor exercises for the infant and education on developmental milestones as well as interaction coaching for the adolescent mother. Home visits were made biweekly for a period of 4 months after birth. Field commented that the offspring were likely to be cared for by grandmothers, other relatives, or babysitters but "we were not concerned about the caretaking abilities of these adult caregivers" so the visits were scheduled after school hours. Comparisons were made for 30 preterm infants with no intervention, 30 full-term infants born to teenage parents, and 30 full-term infants born to older mothers—all of whom were black and low income. Many kinds of data were collected which, in brief, indicated many disadvantages for the teenagers' offspring, exaggerated if they were preterm. The most surprising result was the demonstration of positive effects for this short-term intervention program. The "treatment group" infants showed better physical growth and Denver scores at 4 months, and their mothers showed lower-state anxiety, more realistic assessments of developmental milestones, and more activity during face-to-face interactions with their infants. Field concluded with the suggestion that "even a minimal and relatively inexpensive intervention such as ours may help diminish the risk factors associated with teenage pregnancy and parenting, par-

ticularly in the case of parenting prematurely born infants" (p. 167).

A third intervention program is the Infant Stimulation/Mother Training Project at the Cincinnati General Hospital (Badger, 1981). This consisted of weekly classes during the first 6 months. There were large variations in class participation and attendance, with only 17% of the white mothers attending more than half of the classes and 52% of the black mothers. Badger offered several possible interpretations of the high attrition of the white mothers, but one possibility might be that they were clearly in the minority, and they may have felt threatened by the racial imbalance. Interpretation of the follow-up data reported by Badger is difficult because of the sizable differences between the "high attenders" and the "low attenders," which was in and of itself a measure of the mother's interest and motivation. However, for those who participated, the data suggest that "a mother training program seems to affect positively the ability of young mothers to realize educational and employment goals and to plan and limit family size" (Badger, 1981, p. 301).

Looking at these and other evaluative studies, one is impressed by the fact that positive effects have indeed been obtained with relatively simple and short-term intervention. However, one is also struck by the fact that what is good for the mother may conflict with what is optimum for the child. If she decides to continue her education or to become economically self-supporting with a job, she will inevitably encounter major difficulties with child care. Here indeed is the place of high-quality infant-day-care services.

ABUSING PARENTS

Emergence of Concern

The problem of child abuse was mentioned tangentially in the previous discussion of mentally retarded and teenage parents. Although the majority of child-abusing parents are of normal intelligence, average child-bearing age, and not psychotic, child abuse is a subject of such intense interest that it has been considered in relation to almost every imaginable parenting variable. The medical profession brought the problem to the front and center with the publication in 1962 of an article entitled "The Battered Child Syndrome" by Kempe and his colleagues at the University of Colorado Medical Center (Kempe, Silverman, & Steele, 1962). The prehistory of this landmark paper included several publications presenting radiological observations of multiple fractures from "unrecognized trauma," with the strong suggestion that parents might have willfully inflicted the injuries. Following these leads, Dr. Kempe and his staff studied all the different features of child abuse from 1951 to 1958 and in 1961 organized a multidisciplinary conference on the "battered child" at the annual meeting of the American Academy of Pediatrics. Radbill (1980) described this conference as "setting ablaze an impassioned outburst on behalf of abused children. A bandwagon effect was generated. The Children's Bureau climbed aboard with generous grants for study of the subject, and the American Humane Society carried out surveys, issued pertinent publications, and convened national symposia" (1980, p. 17). In 1974, the Federal Government enacted into law the Child Abuse Prevention and Treatment Act which, among other things, established the National Center on Child Abuse and Neglect. In 1977, the International Journal of Child Abuse and Neglect started publication. This chronology reflects a truly amazing response from professionals who had hitherto been indifferent.

One might well wonder about the reasons behind this explosion of concern. Child abuse was hardly a new problem; in the distant past, exposure and infanticide were universal forms of lethal child abuse, condoned particularly for deformed or unhealthy newborns. A New York girl named Mary Ellen, discovered savagely beaten by her parents in the year 1874, is often cited as the first recorded case of child abuse (Fontana, 1973). There were no laws directly relevant so she was "rescued" by the Society for the Prevention of Cruelty to Animals! In 1895, the Society for Prevention of Cruelty to Children summarized the many ways London children were battered (Burdett, 1895). If one goes back far enough in history, child abuse is less prevalent now than before. But in the short view, it does indeed seem to be an increasing problem. However, it was probably not the increased incidence which created the concern, but rather an increased sensitivity. The social climate of the 1960's was one of reform and attention to the rights of children vis-à-vis their parents. By 1975, all 50 states had child abuse reporting laws requiring certain professionals to report cases of child abuse or neglect. Most of these laws abrogate privileged communication and also have provisions for some penalty for failure to report. Having these laws on the books drastically changed the awareness of both the professional and the lay public regarding child abuse.

Definition and Incidence

The state laws vary in the definition of child abuse, ranging from Kempe's narrow 1962 definition of "inflicted injury" to Fontana's broad definition of "maltreatment syndrome" where the child "often presents itself without obvious signs of being battered but with the multiple minor evidences of emotional and, at times, nutritional deprivation, neglect and abuse" (1963). It seems probable that the choice of the term "battered child" helped to galvanize general public indignation at the onset. The broader definition introduces problems of cultural differences in values and beliefs about child rearing and would seem to have the potential of intruding on the family's right to privacy and autonomy. But no cultural difference is allowed to be physically injurious, hence the unanimity of opinion marshalled behind the concept of "the battered child." However, recent trends have been towards broadening the definition and including neglect issues together with physical abuse.

It is obvious that differences in definition will result in different counts of incidence. In addition, despite mandatory reporting laws, many instances are unknown and others go unreported, particularly in the private sector. This partially explains why estimate figures are a great deal higher than official reports. The Subcommittee on Select Education of the Committee on Education and Labor (House of Representatives) expressed considerable frustration about their inability to get incidence figures or trends during hearings on the proposed extension of the Child Abuse Prevention and Treatment Act (1977). At these hearings, the National Center reported that in 1975, 228,899 cases of reported abuse and neglect were investigated, of which about 60% were found to be valid. Of these, twice as many were neglect compared to abuse, but the reporter commented that many of the states did not include neglect in their mandatory reporting laws, so these would be underrepresented. The Center offered an estimate of approximately 1,000,000 abused and neglected children (as of 1977) and an estimate of some 2,000 resultant deaths per year. An interesting datum from this report was that natural parents accounted for almost 84% of the abuse-neglect, with more than twice as many mothers as fathers held accountable.

Parent Characteristics

In the search for the cause of what Fontana termed "parental delinquency," the first response was to view the parents as "psychologically sick" and to look for standard categories, but to little avail. Steele, one of the co-authors of the original 1962 article, studied over 100 abusive families, largely drawn from middle-socioeconomic status. He concluded that

There is no common psychiatric category into which even a majority of abusing parents can be placed. True sociopathy is rare. Moderately active psychotic states, either schizophrenic or depressive, are occasionally seen. Much more common are the various types of psychoneuroses and character disorders. Psychosomatic illnesses are frequent. There is the almost universal presence among abusing parents of some degree of depression, either overt or latent.... Child abuse cannot be considered an integral part of any of our usual psychiatric entities, but is best understood as a particular type of parent-child interaction which can exist in combination with any other psychologic state. (1970, p. 450)

In the following discussion of child-rearing attitudinal differences, Steele suggested that these parents expect too much and have a great investment in a child who performs to near-perfection. The parent needs the child to be consistently affectionate and promptly responsive to his or her wishes, almost a reversal of the usual parent-child roles (Morris & Gould, 1963) Like many other authors (Spinetta & Rigler, 1972), Steele stressed the idea that abusing parents were brought up in much the same manner as that employed in raising their own children. He suggested that if an investigator fails to find a history of abuse, neglect, or harsh treatment in the parent's childhood, it is because the parent is ashamed, defensive, or simply considers such treatment as "normal." Ten years later, Steele (1980) reiterated these observations. "The history of neglect and abuse in the early years of life of the abusive caretaker has been stressed because we believe that therein lies the source of the caretaker's later inability to provide empathic care for the infant" (p. 52). However, the converse does not follow, and no study has been reported that specifically examined those parents who were abused as children and did *not* become abusing parents (Friedrich

& Wheeler, 1982). The simple repetition hypothesis is not a sufficient explanation.

In a limited, but well controlled study, Melnick and Hurley (1969) compared two groups of lower-socioeconomic black mothers on 18 personality variables of which 6 reliably differentiated between the abusing mothers and the controls. The former demonstrated lower self-esteem, less family satisfaction, less need nurturance, higher frustration of need dependence, and a less openly rejecting stance toward children. The last finding was unexpected and could be interpreted as defensiveness for fear of criminal prosecution, or as a reflection of a more stable personality characteristic of rigid defenses against the open recognition of hostile feelings. Steele (1970) came to the same conclusions from clinical data: "Abusing parents are lonely people, yearning for love and understanding, yet plagued by a deep sense of inferiority and an inability to have any confidence in being lovable or in finding real understanding and help. Such feelings may be overt but often are covered by a superficial, defensive façade of social competence and protestations that 'everything is all right'" (p. 454).

Physical abuse often occurs as a "justified" action or deserved punishment when children fail to meet excessively high caretaker expectations; several writers (Fontana, 1973; Gil, 1975) have related this to the general acceptance of the use of corporal punishment which they perceive as giving cultural sanction to physical "attack" in child discipline. Zigler put the case succinctly: "I add my voice to those of many others and assert that so long as corporal punishment is accepted as a method of disciplining children, just so long will we have child abuse in our country" (1977, p. 104). This indeed treads on delicate ground because for many people, relinquishing the option of physical punishment is equal to "permissiveness" in child rearing. Prohibition of corporal punishment would be unanimously viewed as an intolerable invasion of parental rights—with visions of wild children running amok. The most one can do at this point is to stress realistic expectations and to urge restraint and caution in administering such punishment.

Environmental Stress

Most child abuse is episodic rather than constant, even in the parent who has the history, child rearing attitudes, and psychological characteristics described above. Also, many parents who share these attributes do well. The idea of stress has been introduced to explain the breakdown in the vulnerable parent. Egeland, Brietenbucher, and Rosenberg (1980) reported a prospective study of 267 primiparous women of low socioeconomic background, an average age of 20 years, and 60% unmarried. Parenthetically, they found no relationship between limited mother-infant contact at time of birth and later incidence of child abuse and neglect (Egeland & Vaughn, 1981). Comparing a group of 32 mothers judged to provide "inadequate care" with 33 mothers judged to give "excellent care" indicated a significant difference in stress index scores derived from the Cochrane and Robertson's Life Events Inventory (1973). (See Appendix.)

Straus (1980) used a different stress events scale (Holmes & Rahe, 1967) and interviewed 1,146 men and women (living together) who had at least one child between the ages of 3 and 17 years living at home. From parental reports with the Conflict Tactics Scale (Straus, 1979) he estimated that from 3 to 4% of the parents were "guilty" of abuse at least once. The higher the stress score, the higher the rate of child abuse, particularly for the fathers.

However, these investigators pointed out that stress does not inevitably lead to violent reaction, which led them to circle back to the issue of the psychological characteristics of the parents. Egeland, Breitenbucher, and Rosenberg, (1980) found that an important difference was that the stressed/abusing group had less support from family members and friends. Personality scores suggested that they were more suspicious, defensive, and rigid, qualities that would interfere with establishing helpful relationships. On the other hand, of course, their external reality circumstances might also have justified their suspiciousness. Straus reported similar differences, emphasizing accepted patterns of family violence and dominance structures and social isolation. Faced with overwhelming external stress, such unhappy, isolated persons, who have lived with patterns of violence, resort to violence.

The absence of support systems has been emphasized by many authors and has been related to socioeconomic status. Although child abuse and neglect occur in all economic strata, they are more frequent in the poverty groups. Gelles (1973) was one of the first to object to the "sickness model" for explaining child abuse and emphasized the importance of the social context. Pelton (1978) reviewed several studies to demonstrate the relationship between child abuse and poverty. He countered the argument that the disproportionate amount of child abuse in the lower socioeconomic classes is simply an artifact of public agency record-keeping by citing evidence that the highest incidence occurs in the most extreme poverty conditions. The neglecting and abusing families are the poorest of the poor, isolated even to the extent of often having no telephone. Also, the vast majority of the victims of fatal incidents of child abuse and neglect (which are of necessity more uniformly reported) are from poor families. He felt that the "myth of classlessness" was adopted by professionals in order to support the psychodynamic orientation toward etiology and treatment. However, there is no basic contradiction between Steele's interpretation (1980), for example, and acknowledging that poverty is a major contributory factor. The psychology of the poor parent is not of a different order than the psychology of a well-to-do parent. The latter has more options (access to baby sitters, for instance) and the same neglectful behavior (leaving a young child unattended, for example) does not expose the child to the same dangers in a safe neighborhood as it does in a crowded, rundown, poor neighborhood. From this point of view, one might say that parental feelings are not as different as they might appear, but the resultant behavior and the consequences depend in some measure on the socioeconomic circumstances.

The Abused Child

The last ingredient added to the complex of causative factors was the nature of the abused child (Friedrich & Boriskin, 1976). The majority of child-abuse victims are between 3 months and 3 years of age; a period well known to be taxing for parents. But it is obviously more than the usual wear and tear occasioned by infants and toddlers that evokes abuse, because generally, even in multi-child families, only one child has been abused. It is almost impossible to get a prospective view of the child's early development in order to assess special characteristics before the beginning of abuse or neglect, so much of the data on personality and cognitive characteristics are confounded by being obtained after the fact. Sandgrund, Gaines, and Green (1974) studied three groups of 30 children between the ages of 5 and 13 years. One-quarter of the abused children and one-fifth of the neglected children had IQ's below 70, compared with 3% of the control group. Since they had deliberately omitted those children with possible head trauma from abuse, these authors considered the possibility that the abused and neglected children were slow in development from the beginning.

Soeffing (1975) argued that abused children are often congenitally handicapped and cited unpublished statistics reported by 22 states on some 14,083 abused and neglected children. About 12% had "special" characteristics such as premature birth, mental retardation, physical handicap, chronic illness, etc. Without comparable data on nonabused children from similar socioeconomic backgrounds, it is hard to assess the causative role of these differences, but it is readily obvious that such problems could act as extra stress for the vulnerable parent. Particularly in the case of the slow-developing child, the discrepancy between performance and parental expectations, unrealistically high to start with, might well evoke parental frustration and angry retaliation.

It is even more difficult to determine the cause-and-effect sequence related to emotional development and abuse and neglect. Kinard (1980; 1982) investigated the emotional status of 30 physically abused children between the ages of 5 and 12 a year or more after the reported incident. Scores on standardized psychological measures indicated significant differences between the abused children and a control group in respect to self-concept, aggression, socialization with peers, establishment of trust in people, and separation from mother. These findings were interpreted as the result of the abuse experiences and led to a strong recommendation that abused children receive direct psychological help.

Other authors (Martin, 1980) have speculated on temperamental differences in children that increase difficulties in child care and might contribute to child abuse. There is some indirect confirmatory evidence; for example, in a comparison of 295 abused children and their 284 siblings, Herrenkohl and Herrenkohl (1979) found that parents remembered the abused children as less enjoyable in early life, listing behavior problems, trouble in eating and sleeping, etc. From a very young age, the interaction between the child and parent appears to be distorted and deviant (Gaensbauer & Sands, 1979), with both partners playing their part in its development and continuation.

Taking a different approach to the cause-and-effect problem, Burgess and Conger (1978) observed families at home for four visits. The median age of the "identified" children was 6.5 years. Standard tasks, games, verbal questions, and questionnaires were used to compare the interactions in 17 abusing, 17 neglectful, and 19 control families. Although this was an unusually intensive and well-controlled study, generalization is limited by the fact that the families were recruited from a generally rural environment and participated voluntarily; also, apparently they were all two-parent families. The abusing parents were distinguishable from controls because of lower rates of verbal and physical interactive behavior, but the neglecting parents were the most negative of the three groups. In only one regard was the abusing family most noteworthy, namely, the finding of more negative child-to-child interaction. This finding has been reported in other studies as well (Reidy, 1977).

With younger children (ages 1 to 3 years), observed outside of the home in daycare settings, greater behavioral differences were found. The abused toddlers (10 in number) more frequently physically assaulted their peers. They harassed their caregivers more both verbally and nonverbally and were the only infants who attacked or threatened to attack them. It is also noteworthy that the abused toddlers rejected friendly overtures whether from caregivers or from other children. This combination of aggressiveness and rejection of friendship offers has the consequence of social isolation even in neutral circumstances. Regardless of "first cause," George and Main (1979) also recommended that intervention efforts be directed to the child victim as well as the parents.

In some respects it is unfortunate that child abuse and child neglect have been treated together increasingly in the literature. Both can be equally grave but they seem to have different dynamics and consequences. With regard to child abuse specifically, the known causes are multiple: parental history and disposition, specific stresses including those presented by the particular child in his or her particular stage of development, lack of options or outside supports, and often a belief in the justification of physical means of correction which is culturally permissible. Child neglect, or "masked maternal deprivation," is more global and diffuse (see Failure to Thrive, Chapter 1).

Intervention

One of the special features of intervention in child abuse is the necessity to coordinate many agencies—protective services of county child welfare departments, pediatric clinics and hospitals, courts and police, and family and child treatment agencies. Handling child abuse not only presents all the usual problems of communication, sharing records, arranging appointments, and agreeing on responsibilities and priorities, but also it strains the emotional fortitude and objectivity of staff. The role of the concerned person trying to aid the abusive family is not a simple one. On one hand, there is a natural outrage on

behalf of the child, but one must see the parent as a person, not just a child beater. On the other hand, empathic work with the parents often leads to identification with them and the circumstances that led them to batter their child. Although the parent is in desperate need of nurturance and trust, a new experience, the child also needs protection.

Often the divided loyalties are solved by using a team approach. However,

not only the individual worker but the team as well must be able to tolerate these ambivalent feelings. Failure to tolerate ambivalence leads to value judgments, such as good or bad parents, parents' rights versus the child's, effective or ineffective worker, which in turn lead to the formation of rival factions within the team, drawn up on opposing sides like armies prepared to do battle. (Fletcher & Adler, 1980)

The danger is omnipresent that the person who began as a rescuer will end up feeling as helpless and furious as the parent. A review of failures resulting in the child's death after intervention attempts indicates the importance of full and open communication and the continuing need to pay attention to all signals of distress (Greenland, 1980).

Although the general intent is to keep the family together (partly because the alternatives are so limited), one must remember that past behavior is the best predictor of future behavior, and the helping team must be ready to take legal action when indicated. This may go beyond child placement to criminal prosecution of the parents. The typical mental health professional is very uncomfortable and likely to be inept on the witness stand as an adversary to the parent (Friedman, Cardiff, Sander, & Friedman, 1978; Rosenfeld & Newberger, 1977).

The majority of cases do not go to court but are treated with some combination of therapy for children and parents, foster care and crisis nursery placements, day care resources, homemaker services, volunteer programs, and concrete assistance in housing, food, transportation and the like. Derdeyn concluded from his review that

Small, well-organized demonstration-type programs may be quite effective in avoiding parent-child separations and in preventing subsequent abuse and neglect. For the majority of abused children and their families, however, available rehabilitative or treatment services are at a low level, and family disruption and long-term foster care too often follow intervention. (1977, p. 559)

One comprehensive study of treatment effectiveness looked at 11 federally funded demonstration programs and concluded that there was a reduced propensity for abuse and neglect in 42% of 1,208 families, although there was a severe recurrence in 20% of the families during treatment (Berkeley Planning Associates, 1977). A combination of parent aides and/or Parents Anonymous in conjunction with casework had a 53% success rate, which might be quite impressive if one knew what the spontaneous remission rate is in untreated cases. However, although this would speak well for the effectiveness of intervention, the consequences of a 50% failure rate are certainly unacceptable.

Preventive strategies have been considered (Starr, 1979), but there are ethical difficulties inherent in "labeling"

families as at risk as well as practical difficulties in trying to provide services to a greater number of potentially abusing parents. Parents Anonymous, a self-help group founded in 1969 by a child-abusing mother, has proven useful for many parents who have become concerned about their capacity for abusive behavior, in many instances not carried out in reality.[1] Another approach has been education for parenthood in the secondary schools. A specialized education-treatment curriculum has been proposed by Helfer (1980) in which he outlines interpersonal skills and graded experiential tasks that help parents to undo or repair the deficiencies of their own childhoods. In many ways, this program is one of "cognitive therapy," helping parents to become aware of their feelings and to make reasoned choices. There are indeed effective methods of assisting those parents who have anxiety or guilt about their behavior, but we are relatively helpless with those parents who are secretive, denying even to themselves what they are doing, or those who feel that they are completely in the right. Here, indeed, psychology fails and the law is the only recourse.

TREATMENT APPROACHES FOR PARENTING DISORDERS

A report published by the National Institute of Mental Health (1979) reviewed 24 clinical infant intervention research programs considered primarily preventive, that is, focused on children who

---

[1]Parents Anonymous Main Office, 1841 Broadway, New York, NY 10023.

present at least one risk factor but working with families and infants prior to the onset of any developmental problem. Historically, the focus of preschool intervention programs was on enhancing intellectual development, but new programs have appeared which emphasize the child's psychological development with a secondary interest in cognitive gains. The NIMH report identified seven programs which focused almost entirely on the psychological milieu and development of emotional and affective relationships between the infant and her/his family. Two of these, the Child Development Project at the University of Michigan, started by Selma Fraiberg, and the Clinical Infant Development Program at the Mental Health Study Center of the National Institute of Mental Health in Maryland, directed by Stanley Greenspan, have contributed a great deal to the literature and will be used to illustrate this approach.

Fraiberg was a pioneer in infant therapy. She began her work in early intervention with mothers of blind infants (Fraiberg, 1976; Fraiberg & Freedman, 1964) and in 1972 established the Child Development Project to serve infants referred for a variety of reasons such as failure to thrive, neglect, abuse, perinatal high risk, or mental illness of one or both parents. She did not make the usual distinctions between these groups in planning therapy but relied instead on an individual diagnostic assessment of the parents. The treatment sessions, typically once or twice weekly, were conducted in the parents' home, a technical point much stressed by Fraiberg and others (Buxbaum, 1983). In her summary of the work (1980), Fraiberg distinguished three treatment approaches.

"Brief crisis intervention" was chosen when the problem seemed largely reactive to a circumscribed set of external events. As an illustration, Gretchen, age 4 months, was referred because her parents were in constant fear that something would happen to her. In three sessions, their fears were related to unresolved grief over the loss of their firstborn child, and they were freed of the terror that they would lose Gretchen.

"Developmental guidance-supportive treatment" was used where the parents' capacities were strained by a chronically ill or handicapped infant and also for some disturbed parents who could not tolerate a more intensive, personal therapy. Fraiberg went to some length to describe developmental guidance in order to distinguish it from educational interventions which teach the infant, or teach the mother to teach the infant by providing information, materials, or models (the parent education approach mentioned by Bromwich, 1981). Briefly, in developmental guidance, much more attention is given to the parents' feelings and conflicts that block their ability to relate and respond to their infants. The professional worker is sensitive to the parent's feelings of worthlessness.

Many parents who fail as parents were once themselves children who were not valued, children who received at best obligatory parental care . . . For such parents, our affection for the baby and for them, our praise when merited, our sympathy and support through troubles were a form of nurture which they had rarely known. (Fraiberg, 1976, p. 282)

The worker must show caring for the mother as well as for the baby. Buxbaum (1983) cited the case of a mother who failed to medicate her baby's eczema according to instructions. Only when the therapist noted the mother's eczema and applied some ointment, did the mother begin to take care of the baby adequately.

In this kind of treatment, the worker acts as interpreter for the baby, "explaining" the infant actions as they occur and offering suggestions for parental response at that moment. Every opportunity is taken to point out the baby's attachment for the mother so that she will appreciate how special she is. The worker's role is to facilitate the parent-infant relationship by timely and consistent support, and care is taken to avoid rivalry. A worker who appears very knowledgeable or expert in handling and soothing the baby may increase the parents' sense of incompetence. This is not to say that giving information, advice, or demonstrations is never appropriate, but rather to stress that the worker must take into account the parents' ability to incorporate and make use of such material. Also, if the worker appears to be interested only in the infant's well-being, the parent may again feel excluded and superfluous.

"Infant-parent psychotherapy" includes some aspects of developmental guidance but goes beyond it "to identify those aspects of parental psychological conflict impeding the development of stable bonds between parents and baby or impeding development in the child in other specific areas, and to resolve those conflicts through a process in which the sources of parental conflict are illuminated and interpreted" (Fraiberg, Adelson, & Shapiro, 1980, p. 70). The problems are more involved and far-reaching than those dealt with in brief crisis intervention. To illustrate both the technique and the theory, Fraiberg et al. (1980) presented the case of Jane, the first baby referred to their project. The mother wanted to relinquish the baby for adoption, but the father did not agree. Jane's mother was severely depressed and had attempted suicide, and Jane mirrored the depressive affect in her listlessness and passivity. It was learned that Jane's mother had herself been cast out to unwilling relatives because of her own mother's postpartum depression. Many years later she was treating her baby as she herself had been treated. In once-weekly therapy over a period of about 4 months, with concurrent psychiatric treatment for the mother's depression, the mother formed a relationship and was able to respond to Jane. There continued to be some problems, particularly around issues of separation, and therapy went on for about a year longer, at which time mother and child seemed to be doing well together.

The treatment report is interesting, but the accompanying theoretical discussion is even more significant. Fraiberg described "visitors" from the unremembered past of the parents as taking possession and dictating the course of future events. She captured this problem in the term "ghosts in the nursery":

In our infant mental health program we have seen many of these families and their babies. The baby is already in peril by the time we meet him, showing the early signs of emotional starvation, or grave symptoms, or development impairment. In each of these cases the baby has become a silent actor in a family tragedy. The baby in these families is burdened by the oppressive past of his parents from the moment he enters the world. The parent, it seems, is condemned to repeat the tragedy of his own childhood with his own baby in terrible and exacting detail. (Fraiberg, 1980, p. 165)

She pointed out that the parents are unaware of what is happening and that the professional worker is likely to be viewed as the unwelcome intruder; it is by no means easy to establish a therapeutic alliance.

Fraiberg raised the question as to why some, but not all, parents who have experienced abuse and neglect in childhood repeat the experience. She proposed that these are the parents who identified with their "bad" parents and repressed their overwhelming feelings of rage and helplessness. The may remember what happened but they don't remember their feelings at the time. Because they don't remember the feelings, they have no empathy for their own baby's suffering. "There are many parents who have themselves lived tormented childhoods who do not inflict their pain upon their children . . . For these parents the pain and suffering have not undergone total repression. In remembering, they are saved from the blind repetition of that morbid past" (1980, p. 195).

The therapeutic task is to reconstruct the past events and to bring back the feelings of outrage. The therapist must have a significant relationship with the new mother which fosters trust and stability, so that the reactivation of old feelings is safe. The mother must see herself as undeservedly badly treated as a child and capable of doing something different for her own baby. She is no longer a powerless pawn but a person in control. At long last they can separate from the ghosts of their parents and can map out their own futures. Clearly one can expect blind spots in their ability to emphathize, but at least they are able to offer the love they never themselves received. It is not only the nurturance and interpretation of the therapists that help but also the evidence that the infant loves them which overcomes the hateful ghosts.

The Clinical Infant Development Program in Maryland actively recruited pregnant women who had had a history of difficulties in raising previous children, in many instances giving them up for placement. In the study sample of 47 multi-risk-factor families (with more than 200 children), two-thirds of the mothers had been exposed to sexual or physical abuse as children, even more had had a disruption in a significant relationship before the age of 12 years, and slightly more than one-third had experienced at least one hospitalization for psychiatric reasons (Wieder, Jasnow, Greenspan, & Strauss, 1983). There was a deliberate effort to reach the most pathological end of the caretaking casualty continuum, and extraordinary persistence in outreach was needed to hold these cases.

The key to recruitment and forming an alliance with these families was the staff's ability to deal with patterns of avoidance, rejection, anger, illogical and antisocial behavior and substance abuse. Experienced clinicians were selected in part on their ability not to be frightened by such behavior. . . . Sometimes it could take a year before a constant pattern of relatedness would evolve. (Weider, Jasnow, Greenspan, & Strauss, 1983)

In addition to the 47 high-risk mothers who became engaged, another 29 who signed initial consent forms refused to participate soon afterwards. The hopeful therapist often shares the baby's fate of being misunderstood and ignored.

Greenspan (1981) made several points with reference to clinical intervention. First, he emphasized the importance of the various community agencies concerned with housing, legal protection, economic support, and medical and mental health working together. Second, he stressed the therapeutic relationship and accessibility of the staff, often on a daily basis. Third, he distinguished the different kinds of demands made on the caretaker as the infant progresses in development, following the "structuralist developmental" diagnostic model described in Chapter 1. The caretaker may adapt to one stage and be thrown off as the child progresses to more autonomy. Each developmental change not only shifts family equilibrium but also revives new issues from the parents' childhoods. Although forming an attachment is an important base, it does not solve all caretaking conflicts.

Wieder et al. (1983) reported the following:

By carefully pinpointing the area in which a child's development first begins to go awry and by using organized and comprehensive clinical techniques and service system approaches, we have been able to effect significant reversals in the direction of more adaptive patterns. . . . In a number of these multi-risk factor families, we have observed that after they enter our program, a gradual improvement takes place in the mother and a modest but positive change in the first baby born thereafter. Then, if the family remains in the program and a second baby is born,

the change in the family is dramatic and is reflected in the new baby's more optimal development. (pp. 198–99)

Underlying the all-out commitment to working with these most difficult parents is the conviction that foster home placement is not a viable alternative. If foster home care were provided at an optimal level for the long-term welfare of the child, it would probably come close to the cost of infant mental health services offered by these programs!

SUMMARY

The shift in emphasis from educational to clinical, and from remediation to prevention, was epitomized in the establishment of the National Center for Clinical Infant Programs (Washington, D. C.) in 1979, bringing together the programs and professionals representing the "new look." Further evidence of the strength of this movement was the convening of the First World Congress on Infant Psychiatry in Portugal in 1980. Mental health professionals are now tackling problems at the point of emergence, but the numbers served are still very small. It is difficult to evaluate the results objectively with so few people being served by a very limited number of sophisticated therapists.

There is a real problem with the choice of outcome criteria. The early intervention programs with mentally ill, retarded, teenage, or abusing mothers have the traditional goals of preventing later psychopathology in the individual child. Most of the treatment programs discussed in this chapter used relatively gross criteria such as IQ test scores and absence of child abuse and neglect or major emotional disturbances as compared with the more subtle indicators of emotional health sought by others (Fineman & Boris, 1983). Finally, it is difficult to make a fair evaluation of the effectiveness of any approach to early intervention which has primary prevention goals. The outcomes must be compared with base rates, or behavior observations, which are drawn from the same kind of population.

Poverty has been a red thread running through this chapter from start to finish. To some degree, the psychological characteristics accompanying mental illness and mental retardation, or having a baby alone in one's teens, reduce one's income potential, but conversely, these problems are also likely to make their first appearance under poverty conditions. It is readily obvious that living on a bare subsistence income is worrisome and depressing, leading to feelings of frustration and futility which in turn may impair judgment and self-control. The crucial importance of socio-economic status was underscored by Sameroff (Sameroff, 1980; Sameroff & Chandler, 1975), who introduced the term "continuum of caretaking casualty" to match the earlier concept of "continuum of reproductive casualty" introduced by Pasamanich and Knobloch (1960). After reviewing main-effect studies attempting to link perinatal factors with later outcomes, Sameroff concluded that few causal chains were found when appropriate control populations were studied. "Where later deficits were associated with perinatal factors, it was generally in combination with an economically deprived environ-

ment. Where birth status showed little relation to later outcome, it was generally in combination with a better economic situation" (1980, p. 344). The same general statement can be made with regard to the outcomes of parental deviations. Sameroff proposed a "transactional model" of development which stresses the process of continuous interaction between parent and child. To illustrate this process, Sameroff described a complex transactional sequence for the etiology of mental disorder.

The sequence begins when a pregnant mentally-ill mother by her anxiety influences her obstetrician to use higher levels of medication and an instrumental delivery to speed her through the childbirth experience. A consequence of the complicated delivery could be a hyperactive and fussy child who lacks responsiveness. A consequence of the unresponsive infant could be anxiety and hostility in the mother. The mother's concerns with her own poor emotional status would prevent her from adequately adapting to the temperament of the child. A vicious cycle can then be produced in which the child becomes increasingly difficult in temperament as the mother becomes increasingly maladaptive in her caretaking, resulting in emotional disturbances for the child. (Sameroff, 1975, p. 284)

One can easily substitute other factors for the initial mental illness, for instance, the father has deserted, or the family has been evicted. It is only by putting many events in proper order with all the accompanying feelings that one can understand the result.

The parent therapies were designed for the hard-to-reach parent who would probably reject or drop out of an educational group program, or where circumstances require close surveillance. In terms of theory, the intervention programs of the 1980's stress relationships, particularly parent-child attachment. The importance of attachment for the development of coping skills, as described in Chapter 1, helps to explain the shift away from a straight cognitive intervention approach. The therapist-parent relationship is seen as a significant new developmental experience for the parent. In discussing their view of early intervention, Fineman and Boris commented that parenting involves a shift in narcissism from self to baby, and that the new mother's relationship with her own mother is crucial.

Particularly her identification, or failure thereof, with her own mother must be assessed. If this identification has been toward a mother who was disappointing or depriving or with whom she is still locked in conflicts over separation-individuation and identity, such remnants of the past will certainly be reevoked and threaten the mother-child pair with the possibility of repeating past unresolved conflicts. (1983, p. 232)

The clinical reports of parent therapy, arduous as it is, give us reason for optimism about the modifiability of the psychopathology of parents and a belief that new interpersonal experiences can change their patterns of interactions with their children and exorcise the ghosts of the past.

REFERENCES

American Humane Association. (1978). *National analysis of official child neglect and abuse reporting: An executive summary.* Englewood, CO: American Humane Association.

ANTHONY, E. J. (1974). The syndrome of the psychologically invulnerable child. In E. J. Anthony & C. Koupernik (Eds.), *The child in his family: Child at psychiatric risk* (pp. 529–544). New York: John Wiley.

ANTHONY, E. J. (1977). Preventive measures for children and adolescents at high risk for psychosis. In G. W. Albee & J. M. Joffee (Eds.), *The issues: An overview of primary prevention* (pp. 164–175). Hanover, NH: University Press of New England.

ANTHONY, E. J. (1978). Concluding comments on treatment implications. In L. C. Wynne, R. L. Cromwell, & W. Matthysse (Eds.) *The nature of schizophrenia* (pp. 481–483). New York: John Wiley.

BADGER, E. (1981). Effects of parent education program on teenage mothers and their offspring. In K. Scott, T. Field, & E. Robertson (Eds.), *Teenage parents and their offspring* (pp. 283–317). New York: Grune and Stratton.

Berkeley Planning Associates. (1977). *Evaluation of child abuse and neglect demonstration projects 1974–1977: Vol. 2. Final Report.* NTIS No. PB 278 439. Berkeley, CA: Author.

BOLTON, F. G., LANER, R. H., & KANE, S. P. (1980). Child maltreatment risk among adolescent mothers: A study of reported cases. *American Journal of Orthopsychiatry, 50*(3), 489–504.

BROCKINGTON, I. F., & KUMAR, R. (1982). *Motherhood and mental illness.* New York: Grune and Stratton.

BROMWICH, ROSE. (1981). *Working with parents and infants: An interactional approach.* Baltimore: University Park Press.

BURDETT, H. C. (1895). *Burdett's hospital and charities annual.* New York: Scribner.

BURGESS, R., & CONGER, R. (1978). Family interaction in abusive, neglectful, and normal families. *Child Development, 49,* 1163–1173.

BUXBAUM, E. (1983). Vulnerable mothers—vulnerable babies. In J. D. Call, E. Galenson, & R. L. Tyson (Eds.), *Frontiers of infant psychiatry* (pp. 86–95). New York: Basic Books.

CAMPBELL, B. K., & BARNLUND, D. C. (1977). Communication patterns and problems of pregnancy. *American Journal of Orthopsychiatry, 47*(1), 134–140.

CHILMAN, C. S. (1982). Adolescent childbearing in the United States. In T. M. Field, A. Huston, H. C. Quay, L. Troll, & G. E. Finley (Eds.), *Review of human development* (pp. 418–435). New York: John Wiley.

COCHRANE, R., & ROBERTSON, A. (1973). The life events inventory: A measure of the relative severity of psycho-social stressors. *Journal of Psychosomatic Research, 17,* 135–139.

COHLER, B., GRUNEBAUM, C., WEISS, C., HARTMAN, G., & GALLANT, C. (1976). Child care attitudes and adaption to the maternal role among mentally ill and well mothers. *American Journal of Orthopsychiatry, 46*(1), 123–134.

DERDEYN, A. P. (1977). Child abuse and neglect: The rights of parents and the needs of their children. *American Journal of Orthopsychiatry, 47*(3), 377–387.

EGELAND, B., BREITENBUCHER, M., & ROSENBERG, D. (1980). Prospective study of the significance of life stress in the etiology of child abuse. *Journal of Consulting and Clinical Psychology, 48*(2), 195–205.

EGELAND, B., & VAUGHN, B. (1981). Failure of "bond formation" as a cause of abuse, neglect and maltreatment. *American Journal of Orthopsychiatry, 51*(1), 78–85.

ERLENMEYER-KIMLING, L., & CORNBLATT, B. (1978). Attentional measures in a study of children at high-risk for schizophrenia. *Journal of Psychiatric Research, 14,* 93–98.

EVANS, J., SELSTAD, G., & WELCHER, W. (1976). Teenagers: fertility control behavior and attitudes before and after abortion, childbearing, or negative pregnancy test. *Family Planning Perspectives, 8*(4), 192–200.

FIELD, T. (1981). Early development of pre-term offspring of teenage mothers. In K. Scott, T. Field, & E. Robertson (Eds.), *Teenage parents and their offspring* (pp. 145–177). New York: Grune and Stratton.

FINEMAN, J. B., & BORIS, M. (1983). Outcomes of early intervention: a summary of an on-going follow-up study. In J. D. Call, E. Galenson, & R. L. Tyson (Eds.), *Frontiers of infant psychiatry* (pp. 231–235). New York: Basic Books.

FINKEL, M., & FINKEL, D. (1978). Male adolescent contraceptive utilization. *Adolescence, 13*(51), 443–451.

FLETCHER, L., & ADLER, R. (1980). The prevention of abuse by the child abuse team: The consultant's responsibility? In E. J. Anthony & C. Chiland (Eds.), *The child in his family: Preventive child psychiatry in an age of transition* (pp. 533–543). New York: John Wiley.

FONTANA, V. J. (1973). *Somewhere a child is crying: Maltreatment—its causes and prevention.* New York: Macmillan.

FONTANA, V. J., DONOVAN, D., & WONG, R. J. (1963). The "maltreatment syndrome" in children. *New England Journal of Medicine, 269,* 1389–1394.

FRAIBERG, S. (1976). Intervention in infancy: A program for blind infants. In E. N. Rexford, L. W. Sander, & T. Shapiro (Eds.), *Infant psychiatry* (pp. 264–285). New Haven, CT: Yale University Press.

FRAIBERG, S. (1980). Treatment modalities. In S. Fraiberg (Ed.), *Clinical studies in infant mental health: The first year of life* (pp. 49–78). New York: Basic Books.

FRAIBERG, S., ADELSON, E., & SHAPIRO, V. (1980). Ghosts in the nursery: A psychoanalytic approach to the problems of impaired infant-mother relationships. In S. Fraiberg (Ed.), *Clinical studies in infant mental health: the first year of life* (pp. 164–197). New York: Basic Books.

FRAIBERG, S., & FREEDMAN, D. A. (1964). Studies in ego development of the congenitally blind child. In R. S. Eissler, A. Freud, H. Hartmann, & E. Kris (Eds.), *The psychoanalytic study of the child* (pp. 113–

169). New York: International Universities Press.

FRIEDMAN, A. S., CARDIFF, M. F., SANDLER, A. P. & FRIEDMAN, D. B. (1978). Dilemmas in child abuse and neglect. In J. S. Mearig (Ed.), *Working for children* (pp. 262–296). San Francisco: Jossey-Bass.

FRIEDRICH, W. N., & BORISKIN, J. A. (1976). The role of the child in abuse: A review of the literature. *American Journal of Orthopsychiatry, 46*(4), 580–591.

FRIEDRICH, W. N., & WHEELER, K. K. (1982). The abusing parent revisited. *Journal of Nervous and Mental Diseases, 170,* 577–587.

GAENSBAUER, T. J., & SANDS, K. (1979). Distorted affective communications in abused infants and their potential impact on caretakers. *Journal of American Academy of Child Psychiatry, 18,* 236–250.

GARMEZY, N. (1978). Current status of a sample of other high-risk research programs. In L. C. Wynne, R. L. Cromwell, and S. Matthysse (Eds.), *The nature of schizophrenia* (pp. 473–481). New York: John Wiley.

In re GEIGER, 459 Pa. 636, 331 A. 2d 172 (175).

GELLES, R. J. (1973). Child abuse as psychopathology: A sociological critique and reformulation. *American Journal of Orthopsychiatry, 43*(4), 611–622.

GEORGE, C., & MAIN, M. (1979). Social interactions of young abused children: Approach, avoidance and aggression. *Child Development, 50,* 306–318.

GIL, D. (1970). *Violence against children.* Cambridge, MA: Harvard University Press.

GIL, D. (1975). Unraveling child abuse. *American Journal of Orthopsychiatry, 45,* 346–357.

GOSHEN, C. E. (1963). Mental retardation and neurotic maternal attitudes. *Archives of General Psychiatry, 9,* 168–174.

In re GREEN, Five Family law Reports (BNA) 2173 (New York Family Ct., 1978).

GREENLAND, C. (1980). Lethal family situations: An international comparison of deaths from child abuse. In E. J. Anthony & C. Chiland (Eds.), *The child in his family: Preventive child psychiatry in an age of transition* (pp. 389–409). New York: John Wiley.

GREENSPAN, S. I. (1981). *Psychopathology and adaptation in infancy and early childhood: Principles of clinical diagnosis and prevention intervention.* New York: International Universities Press.

GRUNEBAUM, H., WEISS, J. L., COHLER, B. J., HARTMANN, C. R., & GALLANT, D. H. (1982). *Mentally ill mothers and their children* (2nd ed). Chicago: University of Chicago Press.

HAAVIK, S. F., & MENNINGER, K. A. II. (1981). *Sexuality, law, and the developmentally disabled person.* Baltimore: Paul H. Brookes.

HARDY, J. B., KING, T. M., SHIPP, D. A., & WELCHER, D. W. (1981). A comprehensive approach to adolescent pregnancy. In K. Scott, T. Field, & E. Robertson (Eds.), *Teenage parents and their offspring* (pp. 265–283). New York: Grune and Stratton.

HARMAN, D., & BRIM, O. G. (1980). *Learning to be parents.* Beverly Hills, CA: Sage Publications.

HEBER, R., DEVER, R. B., & CONRY, J. (1968). The influence of environmental and genetic variables on intellectual development. In H. J. Prehm, L. A. Hamerlynck, & J. E. Crosson (Eds.), *Behavioral research in mental retardation* (pp. 1–22). Eugene, OR: University of Oregon.

HELFER, R. E. (1980). Retraining and relearning. In C. H. Kempe & R. E. Helfer (Eds.), *The battered child* (3rd ed., pp. 391–401). Chicago: University of Chicago Press.

HERRENKOHL, E. C., & HERRENKOHL, R. C. (1979). A comparison of abused children and their non-abused siblings. *Journal of American Academy of Child Psychiatry, 18,* 260–269.

HERTZ, R. A. (1979). Note. Retarded parents in neglect proceedings: The erroneous assumption of parental inadequacy. *Stanford Law Review, 31,* 785–805.

HILL, R. (1972). *The strengths of black families*. New York: Emerson Hall.

HOLMES, T. H., & RAHE, R. H. (1967). The social readjustment rating scale. *Journal of Psychosomatic Research, 11*, 213–218.

HOLZMAN, P. S. (1982). The search for a biological marker of the functional psychoses. In M. J. Goldstein (Ed.), *Preventive intervention in schizophrenia*. (Publication No. [ADM] 82-1111.) Rockville, MD: National Institute of Mental Health.

HOLZMAN, P. S., PROCTOR, L. R., LEVY, D. L., YASILLO, N. J., MELTZER, H. Y., & HURT, S. W. (1974). Eye-tracking dysfunctions in schizophrenic patients and their relatives. *Archives of General Psychiatry, 31*, 143–151.

KAFATOS, A. G., CHRISTAKIS, G., & FORDYCE, M. (1981). Nutrition and early teenage pregnancy. In K. Scott, T. Field, & Robertson (Eds.), *Teenage parents and their offspring* (pp. 103–131). New York: Grune and Stratton.

KEMPE, C. H., SILVERMAN, F. N., STEELE, B. F., DROEGEMUELLER, W., & SILVER, H. K. (1962). The battered-child syndrome. *Journal of American Medical Association, 181*, 17–24.

KINARD, E. M. (1980). Emotional development in physically abused children. *American Journal of Orthopsychiatry, 50*(4), 686–696.

KINARD, E. M. (1982). Experiencing child abuse: Effects on emotional adjustment. *American Journal of Orthopsychiatry, 52*(1), 82–92.

KINARD, E. M., & KLERMAN, L. V. (1980). Teenage parenting and child abuse: Are they related? *American Journal of Orthopsychiatry, 50*(3), 454–469.

KUGEL, R. B., & PARSONS, M. H. (1967). *Children of deprivation: Changing the course of familial retardation*. (Childrens's Bureau, Publication No. 440). Washington, DC: Superintendent of Documents.

LANDAU, R., HARTH, P., OTHNAY, N., & SCHARF-HERTZ, C. (1972). The influence of psychotic parents on their children's development. *American Journal of Psychiatry, 129*, 38–43.

LAXOVA, S., GILDERDALE, S., & RIDLER, M. A. C. (1973). An aetiological study of fifty-three female patients from a subnormality hospital and of their offspring. *Journal of Mental Deficiency Research, 17*, 193–226.

LINCOLN, R., JAFFE, F., & AMBROSE, A. (1976). *Eleven million teenagers*. New York: Alan Guttmacher Institute.

MacCRIMMON, D. J., CLEGHORN, J. M., ASARNOW, R. F., & STEFFEY, R. A. (1980). Children at risk for schizophrenia: Clinical and attentional characteristics. *Archives of General Psychiatry, 37*, 671–674.

MACKLIN, R., & GAYLIN, W. (1981). *Mental retardation and sterilization*. New York: Plenum Press.

MADSEN, M. L. (1979). Parenting classes for the mentally retarded. *Mental Retardation, 17*, 195–196.

MARTIN, H. P. (1980). The consequences of being abused and neglected: How the child fares. In C. H. Kempe & R. E. Helfer (Eds.), *The battered child* (3rd ed., pp. 347–367). Chicago: University of Chicago Press.

MATTINSON, J. (1971). *Marriage and mental handicap*. Pittsburgh: University of Pittsburgh Press.

McCARTHY, B. (1978). Unpublished data. Center for Disease Control, DHEW, Atlanta, GA.

McNEIL, T. F., & KAIJ, L. (1977). Prenatal, perinatal, and post-partum factors in primary prevention of psychopathology in offspring. In G. W. Albee & J. M. Joffee (Eds.), *The issues: An overview of primary prevention* (pp. 92–117). Hanover, NH: University Press of New England.

MEDNICK, S. A., SCHULSINGER, F., TEASDALE, T. W., SCHULSINGER, H., VENABLES, P. H., & ROCK, D. R. (1978). Schizophrenia in high risk children: Sex differences in predisposing factors. In G. Serban (Ed.), *Cognitive defects in the development of mental illness*. (pp. 169–187). New York: Brunner/Mazel.

MEDNICK, S. A., & WITKIN-LANOIL, G. H. (1977). Intervention in children at high risk for schizophrenia. In G. W. Albee & J. M. Joffee (Eds.), *The issues: An overview of primary prevention* (pp. 153–164). Hanover, NH: University Press of New England.

MELNICK, B., & HURLEY, J. (1969). Distinctive personality attributes of child abusing mothers. *Journal of Consulting and Clinical Psychology, 33,* 746–749.

MICKELSON, P. (1947). The feeble-minded parent: A study of 90 family cases. *American Journal of Mental Deficiency, 51,* 644–653.

MONKUS, E., & BANCALARI, E. (1981). Neonatal outcome. In K. Scott, T. Field, & E. Robertson (Eds.), *Teenage parents and their offspring* (pp. 131–145). New York: Grune and Stratton.

MOORE, K. A., HOFERTH, S. L., WERTHEIMER, R. F., WAITE, L. J., & CALDWELL, W. B. (1981). Teenage childbearing: Consequences for women, families and government welfare expenditures. In K. Scott, T. Field, & E. Robertson (Eds.), *Teenage parents and their offspring* (pp. 35–55). New York: Grune and Stratton.

MORRIS, M. G., & GOULD, R. W. (1963). Role reversal: A concept in dealing with the neglected/battered child syndrome. In *The neglected-battered child syndrome.* New York: Child Welfare League of America.

National Center for Health Statistics. (1980, April). *Monthly vital statistics report, 29,* 1, Supplement. Hyattsville, MD: Author.

National Institute of Mental Health (1979). *Clinical intervention research programs: Selected overview and discussion.* (DHEW Publication [ADM] 78-748.) Rockville, MD: Author.

NUECHTERLEIN, K. H., PHIPPS-YONAS, S., DRISCOLL, R. M., & GARMEZY, N. (1982). The role of different components of attention in children vulnerable to schizophrenia. In M. J. Goldstein (Eds.), *Preventive intervention in schizophrenia* (pp. 54–78). (Publication No. [ADM] 82-1111.) Rockville, MD: National Institute of Mental Health.

OLIVER, J. (1977). Some studies of families in which children suffer maltreatment. In A. W. Franklin (Ed.), *The challenge of child abuse* (pp. 16–38). New York: Grune and Stratton.

PASAMANICK, B., & KNOBLOCH, H. (1960). Brain damage and reproductive casuality. *American Journal of Orthopsychiatry, 30,* 298–305.

PELTON, L. H. (1978). Child abuse and neglect: The myth of classlessness. *American Journal of Orthopsychiatry, 48*(4), 608–618.

PELTON, L. H. (Ed.) (1981). *The social context of child abuse and neglect.* New York: Human Sciences Press.

PHIPPS-YONAS, S. (1980). Teenage pregnancy and motherhood: A review of the literature. *American Journal of Orthopsychiatry, 50,*(3), 403–432.

QUAY, H. C. (1981). Psychological factors in teenage pregnancy. In K. G. Scott, T. Field, & E. Robertson (Eds.), *Teenage parents and their offspring* (pp. 73–91). New York: Grune and Stratton.

RADBILL, S. X. (1980). Children in a world of violence: A history of child abuse. In C. H. Kempe & R. E. Helfer (Eds.), *The battered child* (3rd ed., pp. 3–21). Chicago: University of Chicago Press.

RAINS, P. (1971). *Becoming an unwed mother.* Chicago: Aldine.

REIDY, T. J. (1977). The aggressive characteristics of abused and neglected children. *Journal of Clinical Psychology, 33,* 1140–1145.

RICE, E. P., EKDAHL, M. C., & MILLER, L. (1971). *Children of mentally ill parents: Problems in child care.* New York: Behavioral Publications.

ROBERTSON, E. G. (1981). Adolescence, physiological maturity, and obstetric outcome. In K. G. Scott, T. Field, & E. Robertson (Eds.), *Teenage parents and their offspring* (pp. 91–103). New York: Grune and Stratton.

ROMANO, J. (1978). The central core of madness. In L. C. Wynne, R. L. Cromwell, & W. Matthysse (Eds.), *The nature of schizophrenia* (pp. 1–7). New York: John Wiley.

ROSENFELD, A. A., & NEWBERGER, E. H. (1977). Compassion vs. control. Conceptual and practical pitfalls in the broadened definition of child abuse. *Journal of the American Medical Association, 237,* 2086–2088.

ROTH, W. (1982). Poverty and the handicapped child. *Children and Youth Services Review, 4,* 67–75.

SALAMON, J., (1982, August 10). Poverty cycle. Welfare mother begets three welfare daughters, perpetuating life style. *The Wall Streeet Journal.*

SAMEROFF, A. J. (1975). Early influences on development: fact or fancy? *Merrill-Palmer Quarterly, 21,* p. 267–294.

SAMEROFF, A. J. (1980). Issues in early reproductive and caretaking risk: Review and current status. In B. Sawin, R. C. Hawkins, L. O. Walker, & J. H. Penticuff (Eds.), *Exceptional infant* (Vol. 4, pp. 343–359). New York: Brunner/Mazel.

SAMEROFF, A. J., & CHANDLER, M. J. (1975). Reproductive risk and the continuum of caretaking casuality. In F. D. Horowitz, M. Hetherington, S. Scarr-Salapatek, & G. Spiegel (Eds.), *Review of child development research* (Vol. 4, pp. 187–245). Chicago: University of Chicago Press.

SANDGRUND, A., GAINES, R. W., & GREEN, A. H. (1974). Child abuse and mental retardation: A problem of cause and effect. *American Journal of Mental Deficiency, 79*(3), 327–330.

SCHILLING, R. F., SCHINKE, S. P., BLYTHE, B. J., & BARTH, R. P. (1982). Child maltreatment and mentally retarded parents: Is there a relationship? *Mental Retardation, 20*(5), 201–210.

SCHINKE, S., & GILCHRIST, L. (1977). Adolescent pregnancy: An interpersonal skill training approach to prevention. *Social Work in Health Care, 3,* 158–167.

SMITH, S. M. (1975). *The battered child syndrome.* Reading, MA: Butterworth.

SOEFFING, M. (1975). Abused children are exceptional children. *Exceptional Children, 42*(3), 126–136.

SPINETTA, J. J., & RIGLER, D. (1972). The child-abusing parent: A psychological review. *Psychological Bulletin, 77*(4), 296–304.

STARR, R. H., Jr. (1979). Child abuse. *American Psychologists, 34*(10), 872–879.

STEELE, B. F. (1970). Parental abuse of infants and small children. In E. J. Anthony and T. Benedek (Eds.), *Parenthood: Its psychology and psychopathology* (pp. 449–479). Boston: Little, Brown.

STEELE, B. (1980). Psychodynamic factors in child abuse. In C. H. Kempe & R. E. Helfer (Eds.), *The battered child* (3rd ed., pp. 49–86). Chicago: University of Chicago Press.

STEINBOCK, E. A., BEERMANN, L. L., BELLAMY, G. T., DI ROCCO, P., ROSS, G., & FRIEDLAND, M. (1975). Civil rights of the mentally retarded: An overview. *Law and Psychology Review, 1,* 151–178.

STRAUS, M. A. (1979). Measuring intrafamily conflict and violence: The conflict tactics (CT) scales. *Journal of Marriage and Family, 41,* 75–88.

STRAUS, M. A. (1980). Stress and child abuse. In C. H. Kempe & R. E. Helfer (Eds.), *The battered child* (3rd ed.). Chicago: University of Chicago Press.

TARGUM, S., & GERSHON, E. (1979). Pregnancy, genetic counseling, and the major psychiatric disorders. In J. Schulman & Simpson (Eds.), *Genetic diseases and pregnancy.* New York: Academic Press.

TRUSSELL, J., & MENKEN, J. Early childbearing and subsequent fertility. *Family Planning Perspectives, 10*(4), 209–218.

WENDER, P. H., ROSENTHAL, D., KETY, S., SCHULSINGER, F., & WELNER, J. (1974). Cross-fostering: A research strategy for clarifying the role of genetic and experiential factors in schizophrenia. *Archives of General Psychiatry, 30,* 121–128.

WIEDER, S., JASNOW, M., GREENSPAN, S. T., &

STRAUSS, M. (1983). Identifying the multi-risk family prenatally: Antecedent psychosocial factors and infant developmental trends. *Infant Mental Health Journal, 4,* 165–202.

WINNICOTT, D. W. (1958). Anxiety associated with insecurity. In *Collected Papers* (pp. 97–101). New York: Basic Books.

WYNNE, L. C. (1978). Concluding Comments: Family relationships and communication. In C. Wynne, R. L. Cromwell, & S. Matthysse (Eds.), *The nature of schizophrenia* (pp. 534–542). New York: John Wiley.

WYNNE, L. C., JONES, J. E., AL-KHAYYAL, M., COLE, R. E., & FISHER, L. (1982). Familial risk factors in psychopathology. In M. J. Goldstein (Ed.), *Preventive intervention in schizophrenia* (pp. 136–156). (Publication No. [ADM] 80-1111.) Rockville MD: National Institute of Mental Health.

ZAX, M., SAMEROFF, A. J., & BABIGIAN, H. M. (1977). Birth outcomes in the offspring of mentally disordered women. *American Journal of Orthopsychiatry, 47*(2), 218–230.

ZELNIK, M., & KANTNER, J. (1979). Reasons for non-use of contraception by sexually active women aged 15–19. *Family Planning Perspectives, 11,* 289–296.

ZELNIK, M., KIM, Y. J., & KANTNER, J. F. (1979). Probabilities of intercourse and conception among U.S. teenage women, 1971 and 1976. *Family Planning Perspectives, 11,* 177–183.

ZIGLER, E. (1977). Statement. Hearings before the U.S. Senate Subcommittee on Select Education of the Committee of Education and Labor HR (95th Congress, 1st Session, February 25 and March 11, 1977) on the Proposed Extension of the Child Abuse Prevention and Treatment Act.

CHAPTER 3

THE UNCOMMON INFANT

This chapter shifts attention from parents to infants who have special problems because of biological circumstances, namely, the prematurely born, prelingually deaf, congenitally blind, and some mentally retarded. Usually these conditions, or situations, are referred to specialists in the respective areas. There is a danger in over-specialization, that is, that some of the knowledge regarding normal developmental needs will be neglected. Also, the biologically different child can contribute to our fuller understanding of normal developmental processes. It is, therefore, appropriate to bring the problems of biologically handicapped children into the mainstream of developmental psychopathology.

With regard to mental retardation, this chapter focuses on Down syndrome and intervention for retarded children

in the first 3 or 4 years of life. In Chapter 12, there is a fuller exposition of the broad range of mental retardation, emphasizing the psychology of the school-age child. Autism (See Chapter 13) is not included in this chapter because it is rarely diagnosed in the first year. Following a chronological developmental sequence forces some awkward organizational decisions, but early problems are grouped together in order to emphasize the commonalities of needs in early development.

In the 1960's, preschools were established to combat the deleterious effects of poverty, thereby setting the precedent of using early education for prevention. Early intervention programs specifically for mentally and physically handicapped children soon followed. Services for children 3 years and older were recommended in the Education for All

Handicapped Children Act of 1975 (PL 94-142) and virtually mandated in the Amendments to this act that were enacted in 1986 (PL 99-457). These Amendments also proposed that every state establish an agency to organize and coordinate programs for infants and toddlers identified as handicapped or "at risk." It is clear that the principle of early identification with provision of services has been generally accepted as part of public policy.

The move toward early intervention has highlighted the importance of parental involvement. Thus, many of the treatment programs to be considered in this chapter are either in the parent education or parent-infant interaction model described by Bromwich (1981). Although there is some overlap with Chapter 2 in the work with parents and young children, the presenting problem here is the developmental delay of the child rather than an attribute of the parents.

The work with prematurely born infants has a longer and different history, determined by the medical profession and advances in neonatal care rather than by social policy. Major changes in neonatal care came about because of medical technological advances but were also prompted by results of longitudinal studies with premature children. In this field, the importance of parent-child relationships has been consistently stressed. Relatively little attention has been given to direct intervention with the infant after hospital discharge. There are some indications that this may be an oversight, at least for a subset of prematurely born children who may need special attention beyond that provided by good parenting.

PREMATURELY BORN CHILDREN

Mortality and Morbidity

From the amount of outcome data which has been reported for prematurely born children, one might surmise that the subject has been exhausted. However, researchers continue to monitor the later development of such infants in order to determine the relationships between differences in newborn status, neonatal care practices, and subsequent results. The continuing dilemma for the neonatologist is the quality of life for those very low-birth-weight infants who survive as a result of "heroic" measures. One important innovation has been the successful application of mechanical ventilation to treat respiratory distress in the smallest babies. Stanford University Hospital, for example, reported that prior to 1967, no infant requiring mechanical ventilation survived, whereas 30% of those born after 1967 and requiring mechanical ventilation survived.

Life-and-death questions loom large in the intensive care units for prematurely born infants. Early in 1983 the Department of Health and Human Services issued a directive requiring that hospitals post a notice saying in part: "Any person having knowledge that a handicapped infant is being discriminatorily denied food or customary medical care should immediately contact the Handicapped Infant Hotline." It became obvious immediately that defining "handicapped infant" and "customary medical care" was very difficult and that the federal government could hardly improve on the combined wisdom and judgment of physicians and parents. The controversy aired in the public press ("Review and Outlook," 1983) and in professional publications soon resulted in major modification of this directive. Buck described the ethical issues involved as "more cogent than in other aspects of medical technology because the newborn infant is utterly incapable of giving informed consent to a lifesaving procedure. Only by careful longitudinal studies can we determine whether we have helped or harmed such babies. Therefore it is most encouraging to find that investigators are looking beyond the immediate results of neonatal intensive care" (1982, p. 265).

In their review of epidemiological factors associated with prematurity, Murphy, Nichter and Liden (1982) pointed out a number of factors that add to the risk for developmental problems. There are twice as many preterm babies among black mothers as among white mothers, and there is an inverse relationship with income, education, and adequate prenatal care. Maternal smoking and low maternal weight gain can serve to more than double the incidence of low birth weight. Thus, although prematurity and low birth weight are problems for the infant in and of themselves, the associated risk factors must be taken into account in follow-up studies. Also, there are different reasons for premature birth, including intrauterine growth failure, fetal alcohol syndrome, genetic anomalies, placenta previa, toxemia, and early induced deliveries because of such complications as maternal diabetes.

Investigators have differed on the birth weight used to define prematurity. The convention of denoting groups of infants as premature if they weighed less than 2,500 g (5½ lb.) was employed in early studies; since 1960, however, research has focused on infants weighing less than 1,500 g (3 lb., 4 oz.), termed Very Low Birth Weight (VLBW). Incidence figures for this birth weight figure range from .7% to 1% (Kitchen et al., 1982). Also, when birthweight is compared with gestational age, the infant's weight may be judged as appropriate, large, or small for gestation age (AGA, LGA, and SGA, respectively). Premature babies are far from a homogeneous group, so that at the outset research findings must be qualified by a detailed description of the subject sample.

Reports are consistent in indicating an increasing survival rate for very low birth weight infants. For example, Hunt, Tooley, and Halvin (1982), using data from the University of California, San Francisco Hospital, reported that half the babies born in the time period between 1976 and 1981 with birth weight under 1,000 grams survived, compared to about 20% of similar-birth-weight infants born between 1965 and 1969. In the same time period the survivor rate for infants between 1,000 and 1,500 grams went from approximately 57% to 90%. In 1958, Drillien, at the University of Edinburgh, predicted that "as the survivor rate of very small premature infants improves, increasing proportion of damaged infants will survive" (p. 18).

However, results of a longitudinal study of 261 children born between 1966 and 1970 led Drillien to a more optimistic conclusion. The overall incidence of handicap in children of birth weight under 1,500 grams was 14%, higher for the small-for-gestational age group. She compared the status at age 6–7 years for those of similar birth weights born in

1953–55 and 1966–70 and found a significant improvement for those under 3 pounds. She concluded that "there is general agreement that the incidence of major handicap in VLBW infants has declined in recent years, most likely as a result of improvements in prepartum and intrapartum care of mothers and of changing techniques of postnatal care of infants" (Drillien, Thomson, & Burgoyne, 1980, p. 42). Neonatal care practices in the 1940's and 1950's led to a number of serious iatrogenic handicaps—for example, the routine, and excessive, administration of oxygen in the premature incubators contributed to serious visual impairment and blindness from retrolental fibroplasia in a significant percentage, and delayed feeding of infants under 3 pounds had consequences for nutrition.

Kitchen et al. (1982) reported even better outcome for VLBW infants born in 1977–78 compared with 1966–70. There was a decrease in visual and hearing handicaps and significantly better IQ performance at age 2 years (mean Bayley IQ of 75 for the earlier-born group compared with 91 for the later-born group). However, there was an increase in incidence of cerebral palsy from 4.5% to 11.9%. These authors concluded that surviving VLBW infants are not adding significantly to the population of handicapped children and account for perhaps 1% of handicapping conditions in general.

Behavioral and Learning Problems

Attention has shifted from studies of morbidity (i.e., severe and obvious handicaps) to more subtle problems that do not become manifest until the child enters school. As a group, VLBW children are smaller in size, have a number of visual problems (particularly myopia), are clumsy in motor skills, show perceptual motor problems, and have difficulties in learning beyond what would be expected on the basis of IQ (Fitzhardinge, 1976). Since differences were derived from group means, it may well be that the same subset accounted for all these observations. From her review, Fitzhardinge (1976) stated that "in spite of near normal IQ scores, abstract verbal reasoning and perceptual motor integration were frequently impaired. Children so affected tended to have specific learning disabilities and to do poorly in school" (p. 511). Even when the comparisons are made with groups from the same socioeconomic population, the VLBW group show similar differences (Noble-Jamieson, Lukeman, Silverman, & Davies, 1982; Siegel, 1982).

In a follow-up study of 112 VLBW children born in Cleveland in 1976, 11% had a major handicap (defined as neurologic abnormality or IQ less than 70). The remaining "non-handicapped" children were compared with classmate controls matched by race, sex, and family background. The only significant test differences were on visual-motor tasks. Also, according to the teachers' ratings, the VLBW group had significantly more classroom problems in such areas as attending, following directions, making friends, gross and fine motor skills, and general classroom demeanor (Klein, Hack, Gallagher, & Fanaroff, 1985). Hunt, Topley and Halvin (1982) followed 102 VLBW children born between 1965 and 1975, mainly from middle-class families in the San Francisco area. They reported an average IQ difference of 14 points when compared with full-term siblings. On the basis of specific difficulties observed in visual-motor integration skills, language comprehension, and attention deficits, the authors estimated that 37% of the VLBW children were probably learning disabled, almost twice the highest estimate of learning disabilities in the population as a whole.

Thus it is apparent that the consequences of premature birth are now much more commonly psychological than physical and may not be obvious until the child reaches school age. An early study, rarely cited, forecast many of the more recent observations. Shirley (1939) followed 95 prematurely born children (defined as birthweight under 5 pounds and gestation periods under 8½ months) for varying periods of time up to 5 years of age. It should be noted that these children were less "premature" than present subject samples but received "old-time" care at birth. On the basis of incidental observations, she defined a behavior syndrome as characteristic of prematurely born children. Symptoms included auditory and visual hypersensitivity; lingual-motor, fine motor, and locomotor difficulties; hyperactivity or sluggishness; short attention span; high susceptibility to distraction; irascibility; and stubbornness. This corresponds closely to the current descriptions of learning disability, a subject discussed at length in Chapter 11. The fact that learning disability is much more prevalent in VLBW children supports the assumption that there is some "special" organic cause for these problems; however we do not know if there is a disproportionate number of VLBW children represented in the total population identified as learning disabled. Just what the underlying organic problem might be and how it mediates development is still a mystery. Looking more closely at the development of premature infants, one can identify many differences in life experiences, starting at birth, that probably have a cumulative effect on top of the neurological vulnerability.

Alterations in Experience: Intervention

For some weeks, or possibly months, very-low-birth-weight babies are confined to an intensive care unit that bears little resemblance to home! There is no day/night pattern in the activities, and there may be contact with as many as 70 different nurses in a 7-week period (Minde, Ford, Celhoffer, & Boukydis, 1975). Newman described "an auditory environment of high ground noise and intrusive sound of a disturbing nature and the filtering out of human sounds" (1981, p. 484), comparable to the noise levels typically found inside a motor bus (Lawson, Daum, & Turkewitz, 1977). The data about sound level are even more striking when one takes into account that preterm neonates are more hyperreactive to sounds than full-term newborns (Bench & Parker, 1971).

Many efforts have been made to provide "special" stimulation for the premature infant—either by stimulating the intrauterine environment, for example with oscillating water beds (Korner, Kraemer, Haffner, & Cosper, 1975) and the sound of the heart beat (Kramer & Pierpont, 1976), or by providing stimulation of a sort normally experienced by the full-term infant, e.g., a tape recording of the mother's voice (Katz, 1971). Other investigators have used tactile stimulation such as stroking and handling (Solkoff & Matuszak, 1975), or combinations of stimulative measures. Most of the outcome studies have noted short-term benefits in terms of weight gain, respiratory status, psychomotor development, or neonatal assessment scores (Meisels, Jones, & Stiefel, 1983; Schaefer, Hatcher, & Barglow, 1980).

One unique study began with talking, manual rocking, extra handling, and colored mobiles in the nursery and continued with a home program to promote behavioral "next steps" in hand-eye coordination, reaching, grasping, vocalizing, sitting up, and self-feeding (Scarr-Salapatek and Williams, 1973). Compared with controls, the experimental infants had better scores on the Brazelton at hospital discharge and a 10-point IQ difference at age 1 year. Unfortunately there was a much higher attrition rate for the control group, and it might be that the more healthy infants of the control group failed to return. Surprisingly, no one singled out visual pursuit and visual attention to a face to evaluate the intervention effects, although these early behaviors (at term and at 1 month) have been found to be significantly related to 1-year outcomes (Ross, Schecher, Frayer, & Auld, 1982), 4-year outcomes (Rosenblith, 1973), and 5-year outcomes (Sigman, 1983).

Rose (1980) used visual recognition memory to evaluate an intervention program which emphasized tactual, proprioceptive, and vestibular stimulation, incorporating auditory and visual components to a lesser extent. The daily 20-minute sessions started within 2 weeks after birth and continued until the in-

fant's discharge from the hospital. At age 6 months, the experimental preterm infants required less exposure time to differentiate the novel from the familiar stimulus. It is impressive that significant results in visual recognition memory, the best single predictor of later intelligence available in the infancy period (Fagan & Singer, 1982; Rose & Wallace, 1985), could be detected some months after relatively brief intervention.

It should be noted that stimulation effects may be achieved either by soothing or arousing the infant, and there may be a risk in over-stimulation. In an aberrant way, the environment of the neonatal intensive care unit is stimulating. The remedy is not simply to increase the amount but rather to alter the type and pattern of stimulation.

Help for Parents

It has been recognized for some time that the birth of a premature infant represents a crisis for the parents (Caplan, 1960; Kaplan & Mason, 1960). Interestingly, the women who were most upset at first survived the crisis best, while those mothers who had initially denied the danger of losing their babies were still in a state of emotional turmoil 2 months after the danger had passed. Minde et al. (1980) described an intervention program where mothers of very small premature infants were randomly assigned to treatment consisting of participation in self-help groups. The groups allowed parents to share their emotional reactions to the birth of their small infants and also provided instruction on parenting. One year later the "experimental" infants appeared more socially competent. The importance of early maternal contact has been widely accepted, and efforts are made to make parental visiting as easy and frequent as possible.

Although the importance of the caregiver-infant relationship in the recovery of infants at risk is well established (Cohen & Beckwith, 1979; Sigman, Cohen & Forsythe, 1981), a responsive synchronous relationship is not easily achieved. As the parent attempts to establish a relationship with a tiny infant full of tubes in an isolette, the high sound levels and medical apparatus may deflect sound, causing the infant to turn away from the face to seek the sound source elsewhere, a behavior that may be felt as rejection (Jones, 1982, p. 139). The best-intentioned parent is bewildered by a nonresponsive infant and either backs off or becomes over-eager. Als, Tronick, Adamson, and Brazelton (1976) found that a significant percentage of full-term but underweight newborns failed to muster an alert awake state for social interaction when tested over the first weeks of life, although later these same infants showed ceaseless, irritable, and disorganized activity spontaneously or when engaged socially. Gorski, Davison, and Brazelton (1979) discuss the importance of reassuring the parent that this disorganization is in the baby and is not the parent's fault; they offer specific, concrete techniques for taking advantage of the quiet, alert state and handling the baby without sensory overload. These authors are concerned about the danger of poorly timed stimulation.

Direct observations of infant-caregiver interactions confirm this warning. Brachfeld, Goldberg, and Sloman (1980) found that at age 8 months, preterm infants fussed more and smiled less in a play situation than their controls matched for post-conceptual age, although their parents were more active than those in the matched control group. The pattern of a high level of parent activity coupled with infant inattention and fussing was also observed by Field (1979) in face-to-face play of 3½-month-old preterm infants and their mothers; Bakeman and Brown (1980) made similar observations of greater maternal activity in the feeding situation. It seems clear that the parents of premature infants need support, at least in the first few months following hospital discharge, in order to establish normal and eventually routine adult-child interactions. The major task of intervention is to interpret the infant and to modify parental responses until the baby can "take over" and give her own messages.

A study by Boyle, Giffen, and Fitzhardinge (1977) suggests a second time for intervention, on a selective basis. They compared a group of 75 VLBW children with a control group of 55 when the children were between 3 and 5 years of age. The parents, of "average socioeconomic background," were interviewed regarding development, health, play, toilet training, feeding, sleeping, and discipline. In two areas, namely development and play, the parents of the VLBW children expressed significantly more concern than the parents of the control group. However, these differences came from the subgroup of 22 VLBW children with neurological deficits and/or IQ scores below 80 (about 30% of study group); there were no significant differences in parental concerns for the remaining 53 VLBW children and the control group. For purposes of secondary prevention (assuming that there is a "real" difference in the neurological status of some prematurely born children), it would be helpful to identify this subset before they enter school. Intervention would include special help with perceptual-motor activities; assistance in focusing attention both in play activities and in pre-academic learning tasks; and possibly delayed entrance into kindergarten. At this point, one would check that the parents are appropriate in their expectations and not overly protective, a natural after-effect of the arduous infancy and slow development. We must keep in mind that the later problems reported for prematurely born children are reflected in mean differences; most appear to be exempt from these sequelae.

Finally, it would be worthwhile to see how aware children are of being "special" by virtue of their unusual birth circumstances. For two adult patients known to the author, the fact of their premature birth was vitally important to them. They felt that in some way they were "different" but were uncertain as to whether they represented a "miracle" or an unfinished product. Although they were in their 20's and unaware of the literature, they described their special sensitivities and learning difficulties as ongoing problems. They seemed to be seeking some restitution for being born too soon and to be still waiting for a deliverance to join the mainstream of their contemporaries. Picking up these particular features, where they exist, might well have to wait until the child reaches adolescence, but one should be aware of the long shadow that may be cast by early birth circumstances.

MENTALLY RETARDED CHILDREN

Historical Background

Mental retardation is probably the most dreaded of all possible handicaps. Over the years, various definitions have been employed to indicate "significant subnormal intelligence," and one diagnostic label has replaced another in order to counteract the negative impact (see Chapter 12). Incurability was included as part of the traditional diagnosis (Doll, 1941), so it was understandable that professional workers delayed diagnosis as long as possible to ward off disappointment and discouragement for themselves as well as for parents. They could readily justify delayed diagnosis in most cases on the basis of the poor predictive validity of infant intelligence tests (McCall, 1979; Hatcher, 1976). The prevailing opinion in the 1950's was that early identification of mental retardation served no useful purpose except perhaps to protect the parents from becoming attached or "getting their hopes up." The impetus for early programs for young retarded children and infants came from educators who took a long view of the problem, rather than from psychologists or medical professionals.

Samuel Kirk, at the University of Illinois, was a pioneer in advancing the idea of early eduation in this domain. In 1949 he started a research-demonstration project that provided an "enriched nursery school environment" for 15 mildly retarded children, ages 3–6 years, who were residing in an institution and 28 mildly retarded children of like age who were living in the community. Three years later, these children were compared with community and institutional groups, matched for age and IQ, who had not been enrolled in the research preschool. The difference was greatest for the institutionalized children and least for those children, in both groups, whose retardation was associated with a definite diagnosis of organic defect. The message from this study was mixed. The authors concluded that for children from adequate homes, preschool experience was beneficial but not essential. On the other hand, preschool experience was deemed critical for those living in inadequate homes or institutional settings (Kirk, 1958). Because one would now never find preschool children with mild mental retardation in institutions, the study seems irrelevant in this respect, but the project was the first of its kind. Some years later, Connor and Talbot published an "experimental curriculum for young mentally retarded children" that was developed from a research preschool project at Teachers College (1964). In general, these early efforts drew attention to the problem of locating retarded children before school entry, the depressing effects of psychosocial deprivation, and the potential for learning at mental ages below the time-honored "readiness age" of 5 years.

Down Syndrome

Down syndrome is unique in that the mental retardation is predicted on the basis of physical signs apparent from the time of birth. The characteristic of "slanty" eyes accounts for the original name, "Mongolism," which erroneously suggested some sort of racial identifica-tion. Since Down was the first to describe the condition (1866), the present term was proposed as a substitute and is now universally used. A major breakthrough in understanding occurred when Lejeune, Gautier, and Turpin (1959) established that a chromosomal abnormality was present in all children with this syndrome. Although there are some cytogenetic variations, the 21st chromosome is always involved, usually as an extra chromosome because of failure of disjunction in the egg or sperm cell. The diagnosis can be made in utero by means of amniocentesis, which then permits elective abortion. Amniocentesis is particularly recommended for mothers over 35 years because incidence is positively related to maternal age.

The incidence of Down syndrome has decreased from previous estimates of 1 in 600–650 births to approximately 1 in 900 (Stein & Susser, 1977). The overall incidence (number of new cases) for older mothers has declined, perhaps because of elective abortion. At the same time, there has been a reduction of mortality, thereby increasing prevalence (total number of cases), perhaps reflecting changing attitudes and practices in medical care. Individuals with Down syndrome are subject to premature aging, including increased incidence of Alzheimer's disease at younger chronological ages than usual (Miniszek, 1983). Although the life span expectancy is shorter than normal, it is in the 40's, and some individuals live considerably longer. The previous idea that Down syndrome individuals do not live to become adult is far from true, and of course, the better the medical care, the longer the life expectancy.

Also, there is an increased incidence of other congenital physical problems, such as cardiac defect, intestinal obstruction, etc., which require surgical intervention in infancy. There have been many legal cases specifically involving the rights of Down syndrome infants and children to get necessary medical care (Hardman & Drew, 1978). The prediction of mental retardation has sometimes been used as justification for "letting nature take its course" both by parents and physicians. The attitude of physicians generally towards Down syndrome babies was tested in four studies in 1975, 1976, 1977, and 1982. The majority of physicians would not act to save the life of a Down syndrome child if the parents decided against a life-saving procedure; furthermore, a number would not recommend such action in the first place (President's Commission Report, 1983). Most of the legal decisions have supported the rights of Down syndrome infants and children, even when parents were opposed.

Because Down syndrome is such a distinguishable and sizable group (about a third of the moderately mentally retarded), there have been many longitudinal studies over the years. Recent studies show considerable individual variability contradicting, the very low expectations that many professionals have for a Down syndrome child. Connolly (1978) reported a mean IQ of 44, with about 40% having IQ levels above 50, that is, within the range of mild mental retardation. He pointed out that the outcome is probably determined by a combination of the normally inherited variables in potential, the specific effects of the chromosomal anomaly common to Down syndrome children, the

effect of cerebral insult if present, and the child's early environment. Rynders, Spiker, and Horrobin (1978) reviewed a number of studies and found that although no Down syndrome child scored in the average range, close to half were in the range of borderline or mild mental retardation.

Down syndrome children are often described as affectionate and agreeable "by nature," but systematic inquiry about temperament characteristics has revealed as much individual variation as in normal children (Baron, 1972; Gunn, Berry & Andrews, 1981; Gunn & Berry, 1985). There do seem, however, to be some general group differences in emotional expressiveness, with the Down syndrome children more subdued. Cicchetti and Sroufe (1976) found that Down syndrome infants not only showed a lag in the onset of laughter but also merely smiled when normal infants would laugh. Observation of responses in the strange situation (described in Chapter 1) indicated that Down syndrome infants evinced less intense separation distress, slower response time, and a quicker recovery in comparison with two normal groups, one matched for chronological age and one for mental age (Serafica & Cicchetti 1976; Thompson, Cicchetti, Lamb, & Malkin, 1985). The fact that normal children usually cry in the mother's absence and the Down syndrome children did not is open to several interpretations: less attachment, deficiencies in the sympathetic nervous system regulating emotional arousal, or less ability to express distress. All investigators underscore the variability of individual reactions, which, however, do not seem to relate to the variations in karyotype, that is, the common trisomy 21 versus the more unusual translocation or mosaic forms.

Early Intervention for Retarded Infants

Environmental variables have some effect on the developmental course even when a major biological factor is operative. For example, Down syndrome children do much better if they remain at home rather than growing up in an institution (Centerwall & Centerwall, 1960; Kugel & Reque, 1961; Shipe & Shotwell, 1965; Stedman & Eichorn, 1964). Numerous programs have been designed especially for Down syndrome infants and young children. All these programs start with infants, even as young as 4–5 weeks, and continue for varying periods of time. The Model Preschool Center at the University of Washington (Hayden & Dmitriev, 1975) is unique because it is "center-based," uses teachers for instruction, and includes a kindergarten-age program. The other programs train parents to work with their children in the home following the parent-education model.

The curricula in the Model Preschool Center and at the University of Oregon (Hanson, 1981) are highly structured, using behavioral techniques (e.g., prompting, fading, and systematic positive reinforcement) to teach specific tasks.

Goals were established based upon the assessed needs of infants and the parents' input. The Parent Advisor then wrote behavioral, step-by-step educational programs for the parents to follow on a daily basis. Parents performed four to five programs per week (10 trials per day for each program).

. . . by the end of the research program, parents were independently assessing their children, establishing goals, writing teaching programs, and modifying and/or advancing through programs based on the data they gathered. (Hanson, 1981, p. 99)

Project EDGE at the University of Minnesota (Rynders & Horrobin, 1975), on the other hand, identified "curricular principles," emphasizing communication with the infant by sensory-motor stimulation along with language, but allowing considerable flexibility in implementation. A lot of detail is provided with regard to choice of materials, vocabulary, and hierarchy of teaching strategies—not unlike the Montessori approach to early education.

With such differences in programming, one would wish that the reported results allowed direct comparison, but differences in selection of children and in the outcome measures used make that impossible. A great deal in a positive vein has been reported from the Model Preschool Center: "Children who did not attend the Model Preschool Program appear to be leveling off at 61 percent of normal development, while Model Preschool graduates appear to be leveling off at approximately 95 percent of normal development. While a behavioral program seems to be of value with any Down's child, therefore, it is apparently of greater value if begun during the early preschool years" (Hayden & Haring, 1977, p. 141). Reading was a particular area of emphasis, and all the children in the Preschool met the goal of learning 30 words by age 4½. Of the 35 children followed in Project EDGE, 20 had Binet IQ's above 52 at the age of 5 years, and those in the experimental program did somewhat better (Rynders, Spiker & Horrobin, 1978). Hanson's data are limited to children under 2½ years. Although a gradual decline in Bayley scores was noted over the 2-year period of the study, the means in the low 70's were about 20 points higher than those reported for a similar age group not in an intervention program (Carr, 1970). Hanson (1981) also commented on the individual variability, with some children performing within the average range.

Other studies have shown positive results for early intervention with Down syndrome infants (Bidder, Bryant, & Gray, 1975; Bricker & Bricker, 1976; Clunies-Ross, 1979) and for diverse populations of organically handicapped children. In a review of 27 intervention studies involving heterogeneous groups of biologically impaired infants, 93% reported positive results. However, only 16 studies included statistical comparisons, of which 13 were significantly positive (Simeonsson, Cooper, & Scheiner, 1982). Taken as a whole, the reports of early intervention are positive, at least in the short term. An exception to the rule was the no-difference finding reported by Piper and Pless (1980), but their intervention consisted only of 1 hour every other week for 6 months without clear specification of the program. It is not surprising that little intervention makes little difference. It is even possible that misdirected intervention could be harmful; one should recall the medical dictum: "First do no harm."

Assessment and Intervention

The initial efforts in the 1960's for early identification of retardation, even in the absence of physical diagnosis, were not based on an expectation of changing the course of mental development itself, but it was hoped that secondary complications arising from parental misunderstanding could be prevented (Oppenheimer, 1965). Major developments in direct intervention with the young retarded child followed the seed money support authorized by the Handicapped Children's Early Education Assistance Act (the First Chance Program), enacted in 1968.

A wide array of instructional materials and guides came on the market. The educational objectives were often derived directly from the assessment procedures; that is, the targets for teaching were the items failed in assessment. A distinction was made between "norm-referenced" assessment measures where a child's performance is compared with others of the same age and "criterion-referenced" assessments where a child's performance is compared against a standard of competence on a particular task. Bagnato and Neisworth (1981) analyzed the common tests and scales for young children in terms of their usefulness for developing individual teaching plans, emphasizing the importance of immediate utility over predictive validity.

Specifically, tasks that sample various functional abilities are arranged along a developmental task-analysis continuum according to age level or operational stage. The smaller the increments between each major task in the sequence and the next one, the more useful the measure is for fine-focus diagnosis and for individualized curriculum goal-planning, particularly for multihandicapped children. Developmental sequencing tends to provide a common and reliable underlying framework for assessment and intervention. In addition, it establishes functional, behavioral criteria for test, teaching and program evaluation. (Bagnato & Neisworth, 1981, p. 55)

One example of a criterion-referenced assessment scale to be used for curricular planning is the Learning Accomplishment Profile (LeMay, Griffin, & Sanford, 1978) developed at Chapel Hill in North Carolina for children from birth to 6 years. This approach assumes that all children follow the same sequence and that one needs to go from one step to another in each domain to achieve the final criteria of competence.

From another point of view, Keogh and Kopp (1978) described the relationship between assessment and intervention as an "elusive bridge." They questioned whether infant abilities are teachable in the sense that the older child is taught penmanship or the alphabet and suggest that generalization of such "tutored" skills would be limited. "Broadening the base of assessment information to include indicators of attention, social responsiveness, temperament, and affective and motivational characteristics seems promising" (p. 541). It may not be so important that a child can stack blocks, for instance, but rather that a child wants to stack blocks. Furthermore, once a skill has been acquired, the child needs plenty of opportunity to try it out in all kinds of settings and with all kinds of materials. Having learned a skill does not mean that the child will use it spontaneously and without assimilation; it may easily be lost. Highly structured prescriptive teaching does not take advantage of the child's active exploratory efforts.

Parent-Child Interaction

We have come a long way from the fatalistic expectations of 30–40 years ago; there is no longer any argument about the importance of psychosocial factors in modifying the effect of biological insults (Brassell, 1977). Further, there is now general acceptance of the key role played by parents but little consensus as to the best approach. The "parent-education model" is exemplified in The Portage Project in Wisconsin, a home-based program for a diverse population of handicapped children from birth to 6 years (Shearer & Shearer, 1976). Teachers visit the homes weekly to train the parents in "precision teaching" aimed at three target behaviors. The Portage Guide Kit, the Portage Parents Program, and the Parent Guide to Early Education are now commercially available. In follow-up, Shearer and Shearer (1972) reported greater gains for those in home training than for children in a Head-Start type of classroom program.

There is some concern that the prescriptive teaching in the parent-education model may be short-sighted. Stone (1975), for instance, made a plea for an "interaction model," suggesting that psycho-educational intervention be directed at the mother-child system itself rather than the child alone, with the goal of establishing "a mutually reinforcing mother-child system which can facilitate transactions between the child and his environment" (p. 17). Bromwich (1981) described the interaction model in detail in connection with her work with premature infants. With a background in educational psychology, Bromwich was in an excellent position to bridge the gap between special educators and mental health professionals. Essentially she tried to "normalize" the mother-infant interaction and to help the mother to respond to "the child behind the handicap." In this model one does not focus on the achievement of prescribed target behaviors but rather on the cues, signals, and strengths of the child.

In a well-designed study of the relationship of maternal behavior to the developmental status of organically impaired, retarded children ages 1, 2, and 3 years, Mahoney, Finger, and Powell (1985) found that the factor of child-oriented/maternal pleasure was related positively while the factor of quantity of stimulation and control were related negatively to Bayley scores. The authors suggest that their findings contrast considerably with the prevailing philosophy regarding early intervention, which tends to emphasize teaching strategies that are carefully structured to obtain preplanned behavior objectives. In contrast, their findings suggest that mothers would be better advised to support child-initiated activities and to seek opportunities for reciprocal interaction in mutual pleasure, following the pattern of maternal behavior associated with optimal development of normal children.

However, before any of this can come about, the mother must be ready to form an attachment to the child. One can readily imagine the difficulties encountered in caring for an infant who is not only a newcomer but also "strange." The professionals responsible for making the diagnosis are in the best position to support the parents through the period of shock (Drotar, Baskiewicz, Irvin, Kennell, & Klaus, 1975; Kessler, 1977). After

the shock, a common reaction is one of profound depression, described by Solnit and Stark (1961) as a kind of mourning process for the expected normal baby. This is often mixed with a feeling of disbelief or denial, used to ward off the depression. During this time, the parents may feel alienated from the baby, and caring for the infant may be a joyless process. The depresion is more than mourning for the lost normal baby; there is anger, resentment, and ambivalence. Parents may wonder if the baby would be better off somewhere else—or even dead. The death wishes may be conscious, they may appear as excessive solicitude and anxiety, or they may be inferred from expressions of irrational guilt.

During this period of anxious depression, there is a danger of parental apathy and withdrawal. Having accepted the diagnosis and reassurance as to their lack of responsibility, the parents may feel that they have no role to play in the upbringing of the child. They may conclude that nothing one does or does not do makes any difference; more likely, they cast around to find "the expert" who will direct them in every detail. Essentially they have lost confidence in their parenting ability.

The timing of referral is important in order to help the parents form an attachment to this unexpected infant. Affleck, McGrade, McQueeney, & Allen (1982) describe this as a "relationship-focused" intervention where the parent-professional partnership is used to enhance the parents' self-confidence, autonomy, and problem-solving behavior. The family consultants provide emotional support, encourage active coping, model realistically positive attitudes toward the infant, and limit their directive intervention to a few strategic suggestions adapted to the parents' own styles and goals. Changes in the parent and the development of attachment behavior become important outcome goals. Bromwich (1981) developed scales for evaluating Parent Behavior Progression that not only assess change but also give direction for ongoing intervention efforts (Allen, Affleck, McQueeney, & McGrade, 1982). We do not as yet have data to tell us if this approach is more effective in the long run; it may be that it is most appropriate in the first year of life and that more structured intervention can be introduced when there is a firm relationship basis.

This discussion reflects a growing sensitivity to the emotional needs of the handicapped child. Mordock (1979) suggested that handicapped children are likely to experience considerable difficulty in advancing through the separation-individuation phase to the phase of object constancy and therefore questioned the common practice of sending retarded children to infant or preschool programs which separate them from their mothers for long intervals during the day. Kessler, Ablon, and Smith (1969) discussed this same issue and suggested that some of the hyperactive or regressed behavior noted by teachers might be a form of disguised separation anxiety rather than a reflection of biological defect or lack of prior learning.

Ablon (1967) compared the level of play with or without the mother present in two groups of children with mental ages around 18 months (one normal and one mildly retarded) and found that both groups regressed in play. However, the normal toddler made it very clear

that he/she wanted the mother to return whereas the retarded child did not communicate this so plainly. It is reasonable to suppose that the retarded child has the same feelings but lacks the same communication skills; thus, the overt behavior looks different. In describing their intervention program for retarded children between 2 and 4 years of age, Kessler et al. commented that

We stress helping the child develop object relationships, to establish first an awareness of self with feelings, capacities and desires, and then a similar awareness of mother, teacher and peers. From this viewpoint, the total absence of any separation reaction in a child seems ominous. Therefore, we attempt to evoke the expected normal response from the children. We enlist the mother as an active collaborator, since we are trying to strengthen the mother-child relationship. (1969, p. 7)

It is most unfortunate if the normal reactions of distress are not recognized or accepted by the "early intervener" because of zeal to teach cognitive or self-help skills. This is not to say that the retarded child should not be separated from the mother but rather that one should help the child to communicate his/her feelings.

Measures of family or sibling adjustment are rarely included in evaluation studies of early intervention, although the family is invariably involved. One should indeed take note of the positive or negative impact on all members. An incidental finding in one intervention study (Sandler, Coren, & Thurman, 1983)—namely, that as the children improved, the fathers tended to express more negative attitudes—suggests the possibility that the mother's involvement with the handicapped child may strain other family relationships. This does not seem to be a necessary consequence of early intervention, but it does serve as a reminder that the handicapped infant is part of a family and that both parents should develop an increased sense of competence, confidence, and even enjoyment in their roles.

THE PRELINGUALLY DEAF CHILD

Incidence

For both vision and hearing there is a range of impairment from mild to total absence, and there is some arbitrariness in definitions. A hearing level at 70 decibels or more is generally classified as "deafness" although there may be some residual hearing at some frequencies. Severe hearing loss is usually not diagnosed in early infancy, but if it occurs in the first 2 years of life, the child is classified as "prelingually deaf." A national study conducted by Schein and Delk (1972) identified about 200,000 Americans as prelingually deaf; the incidence rate is between .001 and .002 (Downs, 1967; McFarland, Simmons, & Jones, 1980). About 73% of all deaf children are prelingually deaf. Inner ear problems usually cause the most severe hearing loss, as well as motor balance problems. Viral infections, bacterial infections, anoxia, and prenatal infections such as rubella are possible causes, resulting not only in severe hearing loss but also sometimes giving rise to associated neurological defects such as mental retardation. The epidemic of maternal rubella

in the early 1960's accounted for about a third of the prelingually deaf children in that period. It has been estimated that about one-third of deaf children have handicaps other than deafness (Gentile & McCarthy, 1973), so one can readily appreciate the problem of isolating deafness as a single factor in reporting outcomes. About 10% of prelingually deaf babies are born to deaf parents; these children have fewer additional handicaps as well as generally better adjustment.

Assessment of Hearing in Infancy

It is somewhat surprising that major hearing deficits are so difficult to diagnose in infancy. There is considerable evidence for the normal infant's discrimination and differential attention to auditory stimuli from birth onward (see Chapter 1), but in the first 6 months, the vocal behavior of the deaf child is much like that of the hearing child (Lenneberg, Rebelsky, & Nichols, 1965). A sophisticated observer might note that the deaf baby does not respond with body movements synchronized with speech patterns, and it seems more than likely that the rates of cooing and babbling would differ since the deaf baby only receives vibratory feedback and so has less reason to persist in making sounds. Downs (1967) screened some 10,000 newborns by simply observing reactions to a high, loud signal, but this simple method yielded an unacceptable number of "false positives," that is, response failures in hearing infants.

Special equipment has been devised which is useful but not widely available. McFarland at the Stanford University

Medical Center developed a "crib-o-gram" that records the infant's motion before, during, and after a sound stimulus (McFarland et al., 1980). The infant "passes" if he or she responds to 10% of the sound presentations. Friedlander's PLAYTEST (1975) procedure consists of a device placed in the older infant's crib. At his leisure, the baby can turn on the cassette players and thereby show a preference for different auditory input, or for none at all in the case of a totally deaf infant. An automated recording device is built in to the apparatus, which gives the listening time for recordings which differ in terms of loudness, frequency, speech patterns, etc. There are also electrophysiological tests, for example, the brainstem evoked-potential method, but these require highly trained personnel (Rapin & Rubin, 1982). At present, these elaborate procedures are reserved for those infants who are at risk for medical reasons or who show developmental delay. Rarely do hearing parents spontaneously think of their baby as possibly deaf until the baby fails to imitate sounds or to turn to find the source of sounds, behavioral responses expected to occur reliably around 6 months of age—the usual time of diagnosis.

There is consensus on the importance of early detection and intervention. Meadow (1980) commented on the consequences of degraded communication between the deaf infant and the mother in the light of the recent literature on attachment. Maternal sensitivity in interpreting and responding to an infant's signals is crucial in forming attachments; obviously, the more handicapped the infant is in communicating, the more likely that attachment formation will deviate from the norm. Greenberg and Marvin's study (1979) of 28 3- to 5-year-old deaf children and their hearing mothers indicated that the pattern and level of attachment behavior were more closely related to communicative competence than to chronological age, and the high and low communicators were differentiated on the basis of age of diagnosis and amount of time in the parent-infant program. Everything supports the value of early intervention.

Communication for the Deaf Child

Since the latter part of the 18th century, educators of the deaf have been divided into two camps, one favoring a manual system and the other espousing the oral method for speech and lip reading. This 200 year war has periodically heated up, with one or the other side winning a temporary victory. At the turn of the 20th century, oral methods became more and more the custom and manual methods were discouraged, or even outlawed, unless the child first failed to learn orally. In part, this coincided with the move toward educating deaf children in day-school programs rather than state residential institutions. In 1955, the opinion published in the Encyclopedia Britannica was unequivocally in support of oral communication: "In 1886 tension had modified sufficiently to permit the convention of Instructors of the Deaf to pass noteworthy resolutions urging endeavors in the schools to teach every pupil to speak and read from the lips." A regretful comment was added that "even in 1904 the World's Congress of the Deaf at St. Louis ruled that champions of the oral method were not friends of the deaf and that every teacher of the deaf ought to have a working command of the sign language" (Vol. 7, p. 103).

The reasoning behind the push for oral methods was to eliminate the barriers between the deaf and the hearing communities so that the deaf person could participate fully as a "mainstreamed" member of society. Although this objective was realized for some deaf children, by and large the long-term results were disappointing. Schlesinger (1978) reported that a "mere 4% (of the deaf) are proficient speech readers or speakers," and academic reports were discouraging. Of the 1,277 deaf pupils 16 years of age or older who left school in 1964, 30% were functionally illiterate, and only 5% achieved at the 10th grade level or better, most of these being either hard of hearing or postlingually deafened (Vernon & Mindel, 1978). The academic retardation was first explained on the basis of cognitive deficits, such as concreteness and rigidity of thought (McAndrew, 1962; Oleron, 1953), considered inextricably connected with lack of oral language. Later studies disproved this assumption that oral language skills were necessary for the development of abstract thinking and conceptualization.

Recently, sign language has regained favor as the "native language" of the deaf (Lane, 1984). "Gesture, particularly manual gesture, is an important element in early childhood language formation. Its attempted elimination from the early communicative experience of hearing impaired children raises serious ethical, and possibly legal, questions" (Siger, 1978, p. 149). Siger argued that children without hearing should be in the con-

stant company of other children and adults with an absolute two-way command of sign language, putting the responsibility on the hearing community to make the appropriate adaptation. Stokoe (1978) also asserted that the chief problem in communication arises because hearers reject the deaf child's gestural symbolization and fail to acknowledge that the deaf person has a valid language. American Sign Language is usually considered the "native" language of the deaf, something which deaf children in the past did not learn until their teens when they finally came into formal contact with deaf peers or adults. American Sign Language (ASL) is a separate language with a grammar distinct from the grammar of English. ASL differs from signed English, which keeps the syntactical order and all the word structures. Signed English in turn differs from finger spelling, which uses a hand sign for every letter.

Compared with signed English, ASL is shorter and more compact; ideas can be expressed less laboriously with the incorporation of facial expression and body language. Nonetheless, Meadow (1980) argued for signed English on the basis that this might be the language that hearing parents could learn most quickly and easily and feel most comfortable in using with their children. There is agreement that parents should start from the beginning so that their early efforts at signing, which will be simple, will be in tune with the child's readiness for input.

Another choice is total communication—the early, consistent, simultaneous use of spoken and manual language that enables the deaf child to use any and all of his or her capabilities in acquiring language and meaning. Total communication has also been used with young moderately and severely mentally retarded children and autistic children as a way of facilitating the acquisition of language. Total communication appears to be the "natural" choice, adding signs to the parents' spontaneous oral behavior and building on the gestural responses that are a natural part of mother-infant interaction. Oral English can later be learned as a second language after a solid base of mutual understanding is established. Television has familiarized the general public with sign language by often including signed translations, so one suspects that the stigma of deafness might be less than in the past. However, a changeover takes time for all concerned. As of 1976, only about half of the deaf preschool classes in the United States were using one of the manual sign languages for training (Jordan, Gustason, & Rosen, 1976). It is important in considering the reported observations on the deaf to take into account their early linguistic training experiences, which at present vary widely.

Evaluation of Communication Modes

Studies examining the comparative educational achievements and social/emotional adjustment of the deaf children of hearing parents and the deaf children of deaf parents consistently report that the latter show small but significantly higher levels of academic achievement and more positive social/emotional adjustment (Brasel & Quigley, 1977; Brill, 1970; Meadow, 1968, 1969; Schlesinger & Meadow, 1972; Stuckless & Birch, 1966; Vernon & Koh, 1970). One sug-

gested explanation is the greater ease of communication between the deaf infant and deaf parent, facilitating normal progression in object relations. In fact, Galenson, Kaplan, and Sherkow (1983) concluded that it is well-nigh impossible for a hearing mother to empathize sufficiently with her deaf infant. They felt that the mother's empathic difficulties contributed to the heightened and prolonged separation anxiety and attenuation of autonomous development which they described in an earlier report on 10 congenitally deaf infants at the Lexington School for the Deaf (Galenson, Kaplan, & Sherkow, 1979).

Meadow, Greenberg, Erting, and Carmichael (1981) at Gallaudet College analyzed the interactions between 7 deaf parents and their deaf preschool children, 14 hearing parents and their deaf children trained by oral-only methods, and 14 hearing parents and their hearing children. The most striking finding was the equivalence of the deaf mothers and their deaf children and the hearing mothers with their children. In contrast, the deaf children of hearing parents, who received oral-only input, spent significantly less time interacting with their mothers. The authors noted that about 40% of these mothers' behavior requests and attempts to command attention were ignored by their children, either because they were not understood or because the children were recalcitrant.

Greenberg (1980) also looked at the communication between hearing mothers and their deaf preschool children in relation to oral-only and total communication. Although only marginal differences in level of communicative competence were found, this might be explained by the current practice of changing promptly to total communication if a child is having any difficulty, so that those remaining in oral-only are superior. The assignment to one or the other communication mode was far from random. On the other hand, there were significant interactional differences: Total communication children showed less gaze aversion and greater touching; their mothers showed more frequent laughter; the mother-child dyads spent more total time in interactive play; the total communication children also used more spontaneous communication and showed more compliance with their mother's demands and requests. When these observations from the University of Washington are combined with those from Gallaudet College, it appears that at the least those mothers and children in total communication are having more fun together.

Social/Emotional Development

A review of many independent studies conducted over a period of 40 years led to the general conclusion that deaf children are less socially mature than hearing children, again with a relative advantage for deaf children of deaf parents. The negative evaluations are numerous. Levine (1956) described the deaf as egocentric, irritable, impulsive, and suggestible. Myklebust (1964) found that prelingually deaf individuals did not develop a sense of responsibility for others. Altshuler (1964) characterized the deaf as showing egocentricity, lack of empathy, coercive dependency, impulsivity, and an absence of thoughtful introspection! However, these character-

izations suffer from the weakness of generalization. Meadow (1980) pointed out the variability and argued that the negative observations result from a complex interplay of school and family environmental factors and the complications of institutional living for a significant number of the deaf children. Chess and Fernandez (1980) also argued against a "typical personality" for the deaf, from their longitudinal study of post-rubella children. At age 13 years, 75% of the deaf-only group were free of major behavioral problems as compared with only 32% of the group with multiple handicaps, including deafness.

The specific attribute of impulsivity was found to be the only symptom significantly higher in the deaf-only group of Chess and Fernandez (although it was characteristic of only 20%). It is of interest both theoretically and clinically. Inner language has been viewed as a major tool in achieving self-control (Katan, 1961; Meichenbaum & Goodman, 1971), so that it is interesting to consider this problem in particular reference to a group that may well be deficient in inner language. Clinically, poor impulse control is directly associated with behavioral and emotional problems.

Altshuler (1978) compared 100 Yugoslavian and American adolescents with early profound deafness with normal hearing controls on several measures of impulsivity including the Porteus Mazes and Draw-a-Line Slowly and found that the deaf scored higher for impulsivity on all measures, with no overlap between deaf and hearing subgroups on many of the measures. Somewhat surprisingly, a study looking for intragroup differences found no relationship between verbal skills and impulse control in deaf children (Binder, 1970). Harris (1978) using the Matching Familiar Figures Test with 324 6- to 10-year-old deaf children, found that the 50 deaf children of deaf parents obtained better impulse control scores on all measures and that less impulsivity was positively correlated with achievement test results. Again, the question was raised as to whether the advantage is ascribable to the early use of manual communication.

Surveys of the prevalence of identified emotional/behavioral problems in the deaf as a whole consistently indicate a disproportionate number, around 20% (Cohen, 1980; Freedman, Malkin & Hastings, 1975; Gentile & McCarthy, 1973; Vernon, 1969). This group of emotionally disturbed deaf youngsters represents a major challenge in treatment because the therapist must have fluency in communication and appreciation for the special life experiences of the deaf child, as well as a solid clinical background. Furthermore, in their discussion of clinical case material, Altshuler and Spady (1978) pointed out that many disturbed deaf children have associated organic problems (e.g. vestibular abnormalities, minimal cerebral dysfunction) that the therapist also must consider in the total treatment plan.

There seem to be many reasons for the generally better adjustment of the deaf child of deaf parents, of which the early use of a manual communication system is only one. Harris (1978) pointed out that the diagnosis is often made at a younger age; deaf parents are less shocked; and deaf parents tend to have higher expectations for the deaf child. Several writers have commented on the fact that hearing parents are more likely to resort to physical punishment and restraint, feeling that verbal discipline and explanation are futile (Mindel & Vernon, 1971; Schlesinger & Meadow, 1972).

As with so many other handicapping conditions, the stress put on parents to teach the child in his or her area of disability (for example, speech training for the deaf child) distorts the natural process of child rearing so that other developmental needs are ignored. A rapprochement between "normal" developmental issues and the difficulties faced by deaf children is reflected more and more in the literature. "All young children are engaged in comparable and primary basic tasks, namely, in identifying themselves in the world, in separating themselves from other objects, and in establishing relations with these other separate things and beings" (Altshuler & Spady, 1978, p. 194). There is consensus among all workers with the deaf—psychiatrists, psychologists, educators and speech therapists—that it is difficult but necessary to establish reciprocal interaction between mother and deaf infant and that the deaf child must then gradually proceed through the normal steps of separation and individuation.

THE CONGENITALLY BLIND CHILD

Incidence

The visually impaired population is diagnostically more diverse than the deaf population, with a continuum in both near and far visual acuity, as well as various visual field restrictions. Using the legal definition of less than 20/200 in the better eye (a far-visual acuity measure),

Robinson (1977) evaluated all children who became blind before the age of 20 years and who were born between 1944 and 1973 in British Columbia. The incidence of congenital blindness was approximately 3 per 10,000 in the latest year (1973), indicating that in numbers, prelingual deafness is the greater problem. In this population, totaling 454 blind children, 84% were considered congenitally blind but almost two-thirds of these had some useful vision or light perception. Compared to the prelingually deaf, a larger number (estimates range from 50% in Jan, Freeman, and Scott [1977] to 74% in Robinson [1977]) of congenitally blind persons have additional handicaps, in many cases related to the unmonitored use of oxygen for premature infants that causes blindness from retrolental fibroplasia as well as other neurological problems. With advances in medical care, the incidence of totally blind infants is decreasing.

Psychoanalytic Observations of Early Development

At the Hampstead Clinic in London, England, the child psychoanalysts started a Nursery Group for children blind from birth or with light perception only as a "laboratory" for studying their ego development in comparison with sighted infants (Burlingham, 1961), seeing this as an opportunity to better understand the role of vision in normal development. Sandler (1963) advanced the thesis that the development of blind and sighted infants follows a roughly parallel course for about 12 to 16 weeks after birth, which also coincides with the average age of the first diagnosis

(Jan, Freeman & Scott, 1977). Normally this is a point of transition from passive perceptual reception to active reaching and sensori-motor exploration. Sandler felt that all children blind from birth show a degree of fixation to this early transition point so that they are more or less prone to regression to a stage of primary body gratification. This, she felt, explained their later self-centeredness and passivity.

It appears that many of these children are abnormally content to be left alone and to indulge in repetitive self-stimulating movements or stereotyped nonadaptive activities. Strenuous efforts on the part of the teacher may often elicit the cooperation of these children, and they may even appear to enjoy such activities as group games, but this enjoyment is rather shallow, and the moment the teacher's efforts slacken, they appear to sink back into a state of lethargy. . . . Their progression as a reponse to the teacher's pressure is a temporary one, and what we see in most of these children is a constant and powerful pull back to self-centeredness, a limiting of their interest in the outside world, and a turning toward the experiencing of bodily sensations of one sort or another. (1963, p. 345)

Early reports on congenitally blind children described a high incidence of autistic behavior (around 25%) and stereotypic behavior such as swaying from one foot to the other, rocking, waving the arms, and twisting and turning the body which are so common that they are often referred to as "blindisms." Burlingham (1965) commented that these are generally offensive to the seeing world and contribute to the child's social isolation, but they are very difficult for the blind child to suppress. She explained them as serving a dual purpose, (a) autoerotic comfort and (b) an outlet replacing general motor activity. She also commented that some of the behavior of the young blind child that looks like withdrawal may represent "stillness" in order to catch all the variety of sounds in the environment. Obviously, sounds become crucial to the blind child—people and objects exist only when they are in touch or making a sound. With great sensitivity, Burlingham describes the panic occasioned by silence when a person departs, or seems to depart. The young blind child is much less sure of the permanence of the outside world and is therefore susceptible to major separation anxieties long after the sighted child has achieved object constancy. Again, the blind child's usual failure to search after a lost object is multiply determined; not only may he or she not be sure of its continued existence, but also he or she may realize that a sighted person can find it much more easily and his/her fumbling efforts serve as reminders of the defect. It is little wonder that the blind child "lets it go," asks for help, or regresses to a "blindism" when a desirable person or toy gets away.

Language assumes a major role in solidifying external reality for the young blind child. "Meaningful language may at least give the child without vision a chance to organize his understanding of the world that does not immediately impinge on his other senses, and helps him to differentiate between this outer world and his inner world of feelings" (Wills, 1965, p. 362). However, it is easy for the words to be disembodied sounds that the child repeats for the sake of repetition only. Many words of the seeing are meaningless for the blind child, except for her recollections as to when they were said, by whom, and in what context. One nursery child complained that the room was dark and requested the teacher to turn on the light. When the teacher asked what she meant by "dark," she replied, "You know, cold and horrible," indicating her recall of the circumstances when someone had remarked on "darkness." Other words, of course, are directly connected with the child's own sense experience. Burlingham (1965) noted that what often remains in the language of the adult blind person is a certain lack of individuality, some traces of borrowed experience, and in extreme cases some phrases creating the impression of insincerity.

In the United States, first in New Orleans and then in Ann Arbor, Fraiberg had the opportunity to observe a much larger number of congenitally blind children than the few enrolled in the nursery at Hampstead. Like others she remarked on the high incidence of major disturbances, including autistic behavior, and discussed the possibilities of additional neurological factors contributing to the disturbances. The large number of retrolental fibroplasia cases in the blind child population complicated the interpretation of developmental delays, but Norris, Spaulding, and Brodie (1957) found no difference in the performance of the 71% blind from retrolental fibroplasia and the 29% blind from other causes. Fraiberg and Freedman adopted a very positive attitude toward intervention: "It should be noted that we and others have found that if the pathological signs are detected in the early months or years, remedial measures can be employed which may bring about dramatic reversal of these tendencies and a favorable ego development" (1964, p. 121). She agreed with other writers that the blind baby who needs an extra amount of stimulation in infancy to make up for his lack of vision usually receives less than the sighted child, because of the mother's reaction to the handicap and the difficulty she experiences in making contact and eliciting feedback. However, Fraiberg started at the beginning to devise an infant intervention program to bring the blind baby along the normal developmental course.

Motor Development and Early Intervention

In a longitudinal study of "blind-only" infants, Adelson and Fraiberg (1974) observed that neuromuscular maturation and postural achievements were within the range of "normal" ages for sighted infants but that self-initiated mobility and locomotion were delayed. They attributed this to the fact that the blind infant was slow to substitute sound for sight as an incentive for mobility. The first demonstrations of "reaching on sound" did not appear until the last quarter of the first year, and this appeared to be a necessary prerequisite for self-initiated creeping or walking. In Fraiberg's words, they became "hand watchers," noting early failure to bring the hands together at the midline, and set about to be "hand educators." In their developmental guidance program, the parents were encouraged in every way to unite tactile-auditory experiences to develop a sound-touch identity for people and things. Through the de-

vices of a special play table and a play-pen, an "interesting space" was created in which a search or a sweep of the hand would guarantee an encounter and an interesting discovery. The parents were encouraged to play games and to employ strategies that would bring the hands together at midline to facilitate coordinate use of the hands. The first signs of success were activation of the hands by a sound cue which soon led to reaching and tracking. "When the hand must substitute for vision, it becomes the bridge between the body ego and the objective world. Without this bridge, the personality may remain frozen on the level of body centeredness and nondifferentiation of self-not-self" (Fraiberg, 1975, p. 50).

Comparing the 10 children in their Child Development Project with 66 blind children studied by Norris et al. (1957), Adelson and Fraiberg found that the former were ahead in all motor achievements, culminating in a wide spread of 13 months for "walks alone across room," giving support for their hypothesis that learning to reach by hand for things on sound cues promotes independent mobility. It should be noted, however, that the samples were not comparable in all respects, because although both excluded children with additional handicaps, 87% of Norris's sample was premature, in comparison with only 30% in the Child Development Project.

Social-Emotional Development

It has already been noted that a considerable number of congenitally blind children remain isolated or "autistic" with early bonding failures. In McGuire and Meyer's study of 27 "unselected" congenitally blind children (1971), they found that the majority exhibited hostility, passive aggression, compulsive solitary play, or other behavior disturbances so severe that half the mothers sought to place the child out of the home. In contrast, the blind infants whose mothers had elected to participate in Fraiberg's special project demonstrated normal attachment patterns. Fraiberg (1974) used observational procedures and variations of stranger and separation sequences and found that during their first year, blind infants seemed similar to sighted children in their discrimination, preference for, and valuation of mother. During their second year, the blind infants showed anxiety upon separation from mother and comfort upon reunion. However, there seemed to be an extra edge to their anxiety. Realistically, blind children are far more dependent on the sighted adult for protection, and it is no wonder that they are cautious in striking out for independence.

At some point in growing up, the blind child must deal directly with the fact of blindness. In a classic case report, Omwake and Solnit (1961) described the treatment of Ann, one of prematurely born twins who became blind because of retrolental fibroplasia. Her mother was depressed, and a good share of Ann's care was left to a nurse who considered her hopelessly retarded. By the age of 3, Ann had developed an inhibition against touching objects. She did nothing for herself—not even walk. She was not toilet trained, her vocabulary was meager, and she was described as both retarded and autistic. Over a period of 5 years in therapy, she proved to be of average intellectual ability and very creative. The authors give a vivid picture of the infantile anxieties that had been aroused by listening and touching and of the psychological conflicts that had forced her to retreat into autism. The report reveals her fantasy life, her expanding knowledge, and the increasing ability to cope, which she gained by acting out dramatic productions which she devised. Not until her fourth year of treatment did the subject of her blindness come up spontaneously. She wanted to know how the blindness started, why it started, and how long it would last. The title of the report "It Isn't Fair," is her statement when she was 6 years old. Discussion of her resentment was followed by further dramatic improvement.

Discussing the adjustment problems faced by the blind adolescent, Abel (1961) commented that very young blind children have been known to start their search early for the answer to the question, "Why am I blind?" They have talked with many who have evaded an answer or just said "We don't know," and thus dismissed the subject. "If we can help the blind adolescent want to raise questions about himself and then attempt to help him find the best possible answers, we can no doubt contribute much to his emotional and social growth" (Abel, p. 326). It is important in providing the best known factual answer to give the opportunity for discussing fantasies and angry feelings.

Development of Blind Children Compared with That of Deaf Children

There are many obvious problems in trying to compare the status of the blind population as a whole with that of the deaf population. The larger number of associated handicaps in the blind, almost 75% of the congenitally blind population surveyed by Robinson (1977), complicates such comparisons. It is hard to know how much of this retardation is secondary to the congenital blindness. The blind are more likely to be mainstreamed with sighted and the deaf are more likely to seek company of other deaf persons. Teachers' evaluations of moderate to severe behavior disorders favor the deaf somewhat; 20% for the deaf compared to 30% for the blind (Jan et al., 1977). The employment picture for the adult blind (a group that includes more than the congenitally blind) is rather bleak; 45% between ages 20 and 39 were reported to be gainfully employed by Josephson (1968). It is brighter for the deaf adult. As of 1972, deaf males had an unemployment rate of 2.9% versus 4.9% for the country as a whole; 10.2% of deaf females were unemployed compared to the overall population rate of 6.6% (Davis & Silverman, 1978). In casual encounters, the sighted and hearing person is more likely to be at ease with a blind rather than deaf individual because oral speech is the common social commodity. However, the deaf may be doing better with us than we are with them.

Freedman, who was an early collaborator with Fraiberg in working with the congenitally blind, went on to work with prelingually deaf children, taking the position that these are "natural experiments which serve as the basis for testing the validity of a number of generally held postulates concerning early maturation and development" (1982, p. 107). Briefly, he concluded that the state of

blindness has a more pervasive and uniform effect than that of deafness.

Congenital deafness modifies the forms of early internalizations but does not pose as massive an interference to the internalizing process as blindness does. The conditions of the practicing subphase are certainly different from those of the normally endowed, but again in contrast to the congenitally blind child, the youngster without hearing enters into the activities of this period and those that follow with an elan and enthusiasm which, if anything, exceeds that of his hearing peer. The effects of congenital deafness will therefore be idiosyncratic and reflect more closely the details of the specific mother-infant relation rather than the fact of the sensory deprivation per se. (1981, p. 113)

The deaf child develops a sense of self and not-self and awareness of the stability of other persons. Freedman quotes the study of Groce (1980) at Martha's Vineyard, where there was an unusually high incidence of deafness because of hereditary factors, to show that the deaf achieved a normal social life when the community made the necessary adaptations, i.e., using sign language. There is nothing equivalent to make up for the lack of sight. He was gloomy about early bonding for the blind infant because the "potent inducer" of eye contact is absent and "there is, therefore, simply no basis for maternal joy and gratification to complement the nurturance the infant receives" (Freedman, 1981, p. 111). This somewhat contradicts Fraiberg's optimism about early intervention, but even with intervention, Fraiberg noted that the congenitally blind child was usually close to 5 years of age before using the personal pronoun "I," an indicator of self-object differentiation (Fraiberg, 1968). In his summary, Freedman made an important distinction between speech and communication. Echolalia, or "parroting," was cited as an instance of speech in the absence of communication, whereas sign language provides an example of communication which does not depend on speech. The blind child, who can talk, is likely to remain echolalic because he has not established self-object differentiation or internalized self and object representations. The deaf child is more readily capable of establishing relations with external objects; he is motivated to communicate and will do so given the appropriate medium.

Nevertheless, many competent blind adult individuals have obviously escaped the mental retardation and/or autism characterizing a significant number of blind children. Writing from the perspective of the blind adult, Lambert and West (1980) described the ambivalence felt towards both the sighted and the nonsighted worlds: "Competent blind persons are angry at blind people who embarrass them, and they are angry at sighted persons who have refused to accept them despite their competence. Finally, competent blind individuals are angry at themselves because if they were not blind, they would not experience embarrassment and inequity" (p. 337). Again, it is risky to compare the deaf adult to the blind adult, but it seems that the blind have more shame about being blind and view the companionship of other blind persons as a "retreat to the ghetto," whereas deaf adults enjoy one another's company. Working with the parents of the blind or the deaf must continue beyond the stages of bonding and separation/individuation

into the school-age years where competencies are developed and tested in the milieu of the sighted and hearing world. As stated by Lambert and West, "Parents should equip the child with strategies for ensuring access to the world of activity and hypothesis testing and teach the child to alter hypotheses about his or her own competence only on the basis of success or failures, not on the basis of thwarted opportunities to test them" (1980, p. 337).

SUMMARY

The clinical problems which have been presented in this chapter are relatively rare and require specialized resources beyond those of a standard mental health agency or professional. Deafness, blindness, or retardation have lifelong consequences which need not be true for the vast majority of prematurely born children. Also, the focus here on children with early onset and near-total deprivation of sight or hearing does not mean that older children with lesser impairments are unaffected. But the work done with these special infant populations is of interest to any child psychologist because of what it can tell us about normal developmental processes.

Premature birth, retardation, prelingual deafness, and congenital blindness all obstruct the normal processes of development, although at different points along the line. With the premature infant, the challenge is to establish homeostasis for the infant and interactional synchrony with the parent. There may be a subset who need later assistance in integrating experiences and affects. For the retarded infant, the challenge is to being the parent into harmony with the unexpected child and to provide educational and social experiences that do not violate the development of autonomy and that assist in the recognition and expression of feelings. The special problems of interpersonal communication are highlighted with the prelingually deaf child, and the basic task of establishing a stable external world is a problem for the congenitally blind child. These special events provide "experiments in nature" for understanding the complexity of what goes on in normal early development.

The necessity of early intervention with these problems is not debated although the methods are diverse. Research findings to date do not allow any firm conclusions about "best ways," but there is a growing consensus that the parents play the key role. Outside support is vital for the parents struggling to find their way with a biologically handicapped infant. Every effort should be made to enhance the parents' feelings of competence and pleasure with the child. Meisels and Anastasiow (1982) succinctly stated a major point of this chapter: "For children who are biologically vulnerable, the most potent single predictive variable appears to be the characteristics of the family and the caretaking environment" (p. 268). No matter what the diagnosis may be, each child is an individual best known to the parents. The expert may cast a different light on what the parents report, shift priorities, or offer specific suggestions and additional experiences, but this must be incorporated by the parents since they represent the enduring aspects of the child's life. Finally, programs planned for the biologically different child should follow the principles of child rearing for the "normal child," carefully weighing the possible risks of any major deviation.

REFERENCES

ABEL, G. L. (1961). The blind adolescent and his needs. *Exceptional Children, 28,* 309–317.

ABLON, G. (1967). *Characteristics of the play of young mildly retarded and average children with mother present and absent.* Unpublished doctoral dissertation, Case Western Reserve University.

ADELSON, E., & FRAIBERG, S. (1974). Gross motor development in infants blind from birth. *Child Development, 45,* 114–126.

AFFLECK, G., MCGRADE, B. J., MCQUEENEY, M., & ALLEN, D. (1982). Relationship-focused early intervention in developmental disabilities, *Exceptional Children, 49*(3), 259–261.

ALLEN, D. A., AFFLECK, G., MCQUEENEY, M., & MCGRADE, B. J. (1982). Validation of the Parent Behavior Progression in an early intervention program. *Mental Retardation, 20,* 159–163.

ALS, H., TRONICK, E., ADAMSON, L., & BRAZELTON, T. B. (1976). The behavior of the full-term yet underweight newborn infant. *Developmental Medicine and Child Neurology, 18,* 590–602.

ALTSHULER, K. Z. (1964). Personality traits and depressive symptoms in the deaf. In J. Wortis (Ed.), *Recent advances in biological psychiatry* (Vol. 6, pp. 63–73). New York: Plenum Press.

ALTSHULER, K. Z. (1978). Toward a psychology of deafness. *Journal of Communication Disorders, 11,* 159–169.

ALTSHULER, K. Z., & SPADY, F. (1978). The emotionally disturbed deaf child: a first program of research and therapy. *Journal of Communication Disorders, 11,* 171–186.

BAGNATO, S. J., & NEISWORTH, J. T. (1981). *Linking developmental assessment and curricula: Prescriptions for early intervention.* Rockville, MD: Aspen.

BAKEMAN, R., & BROWN, J. V. (1980). Analyzing behavioral sequences: Differences between preterm and full-term infant-mother dyads during the first months of life. In D. B. Sawin, R. C. Hawkins, L. O. Walker, & J. H. Penticuff (Eds.), *Exceptional infant: Vol. 4. Psychosocial risks in infant-environment transactions* (pp. 271–299). New York: Brunner/Mazel.

BARON, J. (1972). Temperament profile of children with Down's syndrome. *Developmental Medicine and Child Neurology, 14,* 640–643.

BENCH, J., & PARKER, A. (1971). Hyper-responsivity to sounds in the short-gestation baby. *Developmental Medicine and Child Neurology, 13,* 15 19.

BIDDER, R. T., BRYANT, G., & GRAY, O. P. (1975). Benefits to Down's syndrome children through training their mothers. *Archives of Diseases in Childhood, 50,* 383–386.

BINDER, P. J. (1971). The relationship between verbal language and impulsivity in the deaf (Doctoral dissertation, Wayne State University, 1970). *Dissertation Abstracts International, 32,* 5614B–5615B. (University Microfilms No. 71–384).

BOYLE, M., GIFFEN, A., & FITZHARDINGE, P. (1977). The very low birthweight infant: Impact on parents during the preschool years. *Early Human Development, 1/2,* 191–201.

BRACHFELD, S., GOLDBERG, S., & SLOMAN, J. (1980). Parent-infant interaction in free play at 8 and 12 months: Effects of prematurity and immaturity. *Infant Behavior and Development, 3,* 289–305.

BRASEL, K. E., & QUIGLEY, S. P. (1977). Influence of certain language and communication environments in early childhood on the development of language in deaf individuals. *Journal of Speech and Hearing Research, 20,* 95–107.

BRASSELL, W. R. (1977). Intervention with handicapped infants: Correlates of progress. *Mental Retardation, 15,* 18–22.

BRICKER, W. A., & BRICKER, D. D. (1976). The infant, toddler and preschool research and intervention project. In T. D. Tjossem (Ed.), *Intervention Strategies for High Risk Infants and Young Children* (pp. 545–573). Baltimore, MD: University Park Press.

BRILL, R. G. (1970). The superior IQ's of deaf children of deaf parents. *Maryland Bulletin, 90,* 97–111.

BROMWICH, R. (1981). *Working with parents and infants: An interactional approach,* Baltimore, MD: University Park Press.

BUCK, C. (1982). Introduction. Low birth weight infants. In T. K. Oliver & T. H. Kirschbaum (Eds.), *Seminars in perinatology, 6,* 265.

BURLINGHAM, D. (1961). Some notes on the development of the blind. In K. Eissler, H. Hartmann, A. Freud, & M. Kris (Eds.), *Psychoanalytic study of the child, 16* (pp. 121–145). New York: International Universities Press.

BURLINGHAM, D. (1965). Some problems of ego development in blind children. In K. Eissler, H. Hartmann, A. Freud, & M. Kris (Eds.), *Psychoanalytic study of the child,* (pp. 194–209). New York: International Universities Press.

CAPLAN, G. (1960). Patterns of parental response to the crisis of premature birth: A preliminary approach to modifying mental health outcome. *Psychiatry, 23,* 365–74.

CARR, J. (1970). Mental and motor development in young mongol children. *Journal of Mental Deficiency Research, 14,* 205–220.

CENTERWALL, S. A., & CENTERWALL, W. R. (1960). A study of children with mongolism reared in the home compared to those reared away from home. *Pediatrics, 25,* 678–685.

CHESS, S., & FERNANDEZ, P. (1980). Do deaf

children have a typical personality? *Journal of the American Academy of Child Psychiatry, 19,* 654–664.

CICCHETTI, D., & SROUFE, L. A. (1976). The relationship between affective and cognitive development in Down's syndrome infants. *Child Development, 47,* 920–930.

CLUNIES-ROSS, G. G. (1979). Accelerating the development of Down's syndrome infants and young children. *Journal of Special Education, 13,* 171–176.

COHEN, B. K. (1980). Emotionally disturbed hearing-impaired children: a review of the literature. *American Annals of the Deaf, 125,* 1040–1048.

COHEN, S. E., & BECKWITH, L. (1979). Preterm infant interaction with the caregiver in the first year of life and competence at age two. *Child Development, 50,* 767–776.

CONNOLLY, J. A. (1978). Intelligence levels of Down's Syndrome children. *American Journal of Mental Deficiency, 83,* 193–196.

CONNOR, F. P., & TALBOT, M. (1964). *Experimental curriculum for young mentally retarded children.* New York: Teachers College Bureau of Publications.

DAVIS, H., & SILVERMAN, S. R. (1978). Hearing and Deafness. New York: Holt, Rinehart, and Winston.

DOLL, E. (1941). The essentials of an inclusive concept of mental deficiency. *American Journal of Mental Deficiency, 46,* 214–219.

DOWNS, M. D. (1967). Testing hearing in infancy and early childhood. In F. McConnell & P. H. Ward (Eds.) *Deafness in childhood* (pp. 25–334). Nashville, TN: Vanderbilt University Press.

DRILLIEN, C. M. (1958). Growth and development in a group of children of very low birth weight. *Archives Diseases of Childhood, 33,* 10–18.

DRILLIEN, C. M., THOMSON, A. J., & BURGOYNE, K. (1980). Low-birthweight children at early school-age: A longitudinal study. *Developmental Medicine and Child Neurology, 22,* 26–47.

DROTAR, D., BASKIEWICZ, A., IRVIN, N., KENNELL, J., & KLAUS, M. (1975). The adaptation of parents to the birth of an infant with a congenital malformation: A hypothetical model. *Pediatrics, 56,* 710–717.

Encyclopedia Britannica (Vol. 7). (1953). Deafness in children (pp. 101–104). Chicago, IL: Encyclopedia Britannica.

FAGAN, J. F., & SINGER, L. T. (1983). Infant recognition memory as a measure of intelligence. In L. P. Lipsitt (Ed.), *Advances in infancy research.* (Vol. 2, pp. 31–78). Norwood, NJ: Albex.

FIELD, T. (1979). Interaction patterns of preterm and term infants. In T. M. Field, A. M. Sostek, S. Goldberg, & H. H. Shuman (Eds.) *Infants born at risk: Behavior and development* (pp. 333–357). New York: Spectrum.

FITZHARDINGE, P. M. (1976). Follow-up studies on the low birth weight infant. *Clinics in Perinatology, 3,* 503–516.

FRAIBERG, S. (1968) Parallel and divergent patterns in blind and sighted infants. In K. Eissler, H. Hartmann, A. Freud, & M. Kris (Eds.) *Psychoanalytic study of the child.* (Vol. 23, pp. 264–300). New York: International Universities Press.

FRAIBERG, S. (1974). Blind infants and their mothers: An examination of the sign system. In M. Lewis & L. A. Rosenblum (Eds.), *The effect of the infant on its caregiver* (pp. 215–232). New York: John Wiley.

FRAIBERG, S. (1975). Intervention in infancy: a program for blind infants. In B. Z. Friedlander, G. M. Sterritt, & G. E. Kirk (Eds.), *Exceptional infant: assessment and intervention* (Vol. 3, pp. 40–62). New York: Brunner/Mazel.

FRAIBERG, S. (1977). *Insights from the blind.* New York: Basic Books.

FRAIBERG, S., & FREEDMAN, D. A. (1964). Studies in the ego development of the congenitally blind child. In K. Eissler, H. Hartmann, A. Freud, & M. Kris (Eds.) *Psychoanalytic study of the child* (Vol. 19, pp. 113–170). New York: International Universities Press.

FREEDMAN, D. A. (1981). Speech, language, and the vocal-auditory connection. In A. J.

Solnit, R. S. Eissler, A. Freud, M. Kris, & P. B. Neubauer (Eds.) *Psychoanalytic study of the child* (Vol. 36, pp. 105–128). New Haven, CT: Yale University Press.

FREEMAN, R. D., MALKIN, S. F., & HASTINGS, J. O. (1975). Psychosocial problems of deaf children and their families: A comparative study. *American Annals of the Deaf, 120*, 391–405.

FRIEDLANDER, B. Z. (1975). Automated evaluation of selective listening in language-impaired and normal infants and young children. In B. Z. Friedlander, G. M. Sterritt, & G. E. Kirk, (Eds.) *Exceptional infant: Assessment and intervention* Vol. 3, pp. 124–136. New York: Brunner/Mazel.

GALENSON, E., KAPLAN, E. H., & SHERKOW, S. (1983). The mother-child relationship and preverbal communication in the deaf child. In J. D. Call, E. Galenson, & R. L. Tyson (Eds.), *Frontiers of infant psychiatry* (pp. 136–149). New York: Basic Books.

GALENSON, E., MILLER, R., KAPLAN, E. H., & ROTHSTEIN, A. (1979). Assessment of development in the deaf child. *Journal of the American Academy of Child Psychiatry, 18*, 128–142.

GENTILE, D., & MCCARTHY, B. (1973). *Additional handicapping conditions among hearing impaired students, United States, 1971–1972.* (Gallaudet College Office of Demographic Studies, Series D, No. 14). Washington, DC: Gallaudet College Press.

GORSKI, P. A., DAVISON, M. F., & BRAZELTON, T. B. (1979). Stages of behavioral organization in the high-risk neonate: Theoretical and clinical considerations. *Seminars in Perinatology, 3*, 61–72.

GREENBERG, M. T. (1980). Social interaction between deaf preschoolers and their mothers: The effects of communication method and communication competence. *Developmental Psychology, 16*, 465–475.

GREENBERG, M. T., & MARVIN, R. S. (1979). Attachment patterns in profoundly deaf preschool children. *Merrill-Palmer Quarterly, 25*, 265–279.

GROCE, N. (1980). Everyone here spoke sign language. *Natural History, 89*, 10–19.

GUNN, P., & BERRY, P. (1985). Down Syndrome temperament and maternal response to descriptions of child behavior. *Developmental Psychology, 21*, 842–848.

GUNN, P., BERRY, P., & ANDREWS, R. J. (1981). The temperament of Down's syndrome infants: A research note. *Journal of Child Psychology and Psychiatry, 22*, 189–194.

HANSON, M. J. (1981). Down's syndrome children: characteristics and intervention research. In M. Lewis & L. A. Rosenblum (Eds.), *The uncommon child* (pp. 83–114). New York: Plenum Press.

HARDMAN, M., & DREW, C. (1978). Life management practices with the profoundly retarded: Issues of euthanasia and withholding treatment. *Mental Retardation, 16*, 390–397.

HARRIS, R. I. (1978). Impulse control in deaf children: Research and clinical issues. In L. S. Liben (Ed.), *Deaf children: developmental perspectives* (pp. 137–156). New York: Academic Press.

HATCHER, R. P. (1976). The predictability of infant intelligence scales: A critical review and evaluation. *Mental Retardation, 14*, 6–20.

HAYDEN, A. H., & DMITRIEV, V. (1975). The multidisciplinary preschool program for Down's syndrome children at the University of Washington Model Preschool Center. In B. Z. Friedlander, G. M. Sterritt, & G. E. Kirk (Eds.), *Exceptional infant: Assessment and intervention* (Vol. 3, pp. 193–221). New York: Brunner/Mazel.

HAYDEN, A., & HARING, N. (1977). The acceleration and maintenance of developmental gains in Down's syndrome and school age children. In P. Mittler, (Ed.), *Research to practice in mental retardation: Care and intervention* (Vol. 1, pp. 129–141). Baltimore: University Park Press.

HUNT, J. V., TOOLEY, W. H., & HALVIN, D. (1982). Learning disabilities in children with birth weights less than 1500 grams. *Seminars in Perinatology, 6*, 280–288.

JAN, J. E., FREEMAN, R. D., & SCOTT, E. P. (1977). *Visual impairment in children and adolescents*. New York: Grune and Stratton.

JONES, C. L. (1982). Environmental analysis of neonatal intensive care. *Journal of Nervous and Mental Diseases, 170*, 130–142.

JORDAN, I. K., GUSTASON, G., & ROSEN, R. (1976). Current communication trends at programs for the deaf. *American Annals of the Deaf, 121*, 527–532.

JOSEPHSON, E. (1968). *The social life of blind people*. New York: American Foundation for the Blind.

KAPLAN, D., & MASON, E. (1960). Maternal reactions to a premature birth viewed as an acute emotional disorder. *American Journal of Orthopsychiatry, 30*, 539–542.

KATAN, A. (1961). Some thoughts about the role of verbalization in early childhood. In R. S. Eissler, H. Hartmann, A. Freud, & M. Kris (Eds.), *Psychoanalytic study of the child* (Vol. 16, pp. 184–188). New York: International Universities Press.

KATZ, V. (1971). Auditory stimulation and developmental behavior of the premature infant. *Nursing Research, 20*, 196–201.

KEOGH, B. K., & KOPP, C. B. (1978). From assessment to intervention: an elusive bridge. In F. D. Minifie & L. L. Lloyd (Eds.), *Communicative and cognitive abilities: Early behavioral assessment* (pp. 523–549). Baltimore, MD: University Park Press.

KESSLER, J. W. (1977). Parenting the handicapped child. *Pediatrics Annals, 6*(10), 654–661.

KESSLER, J. W., ABLON, G., & SMITH, E. (1969). Separation reactions in young, mildly retarded children. *Children, 16*(1), 2–8.

KIRK, S. A. (1958). *Early education of the mentally retarded: An experimental study*. Urbana, IL: University of Illinois Press.

KITCHEN, W. H., RYAN, M. M., RICKARDS, A., ASBURY, J., FORD, G., LISSENDEN, C. G., & KEIR, E. H. (1982). Changing outcome over 13 years of very low birthweight infants. In T. K. Oliver, Jr., & T. H. Kirschbaum (Eds.), *Seminars in Perinatology, 6*, 373–390.

KLEIN, N., HACK, M., GALLAGHER, J., & FANAROFF, A. A. (1985). Preschool performance of children with normal intelligence who were very low-birth-weight infants. *Pediatrics, 75*, 531–537.

KORNER, A., KRAEMER, H., HAFFNER, E., & COSPER, L. (1975). Effects of waterbed flotation on premature infants: A pilot study. *Pediatrics, 56*, 361–367.

KRAMER, L. I., & PIERPONT, M. E. (1976). Rocking waterbeds and auditory stimuli to enhance growth of preterm infants. *Journal of Pediatrics, 88*, 297–299.

KUGEL, R. B., & REQUE, D. A. (1961). A comparison of mongoloid children. *Journal of the American Medical Association, 175*, 959–961.

LAMBERT, R., & WEST, M. (1980). Parenting styles and the depressive syndrome in congenitally blind individuals. *Visual Impairment and Blindness, 74*, 333–337.

LANE, H. (1984). *When the mind hears*. New York: Random House.

LAWSON, K., DAUM, C., & TURKEWITZ, G. (1977). Environmental characteristics of a neonatal intensive care unit. *Child Development, 48*, 1633–1639.

LEJEUNE, J., GAUTIER, M., & TURPIN, R. (1959). Etudes des chromosomes somatique de neuf enfants mongoliens. *Comptes Rendus de l'Academie des Sciences, 248*, 1721–1722.

LeMAY, D. W., GRIFFIN, P. M., & SANFORD, A. R. (1978). *Learning Accomplishment Profile: Diagnostic edition* (Rev.). Winston-Salem, NC: Kaplan School Supply.

LENNEBERG, E. H., REBELSKY, F. G., & NICHOLS, I. A. (1965). The vocalizations of infants born to deaf and to hearing parents. *Human Development, 8*, 23–37.

LEVINE, E. S. (1956). *Youth in a soundless world: a search for personality*. New York: New York University Press.

MAHONEY, G., FINGER, I., & POWELL, A. (1985). The relationship of maternal behavioral style to the developmental status of mentally retarded infants. *American Journal of Mental Deficiency, 90,* 296–302.

McANDREW, H. (1962). Rigidity and isolation: A study of the deaf and blind. In E. P. Trapp & P. Himelstein (Eds.), *Readings on the exceptional child* (pp. 368–386). New York: Appleton-Century-Crofts.

McCALL, R. B. (1979). The development of intellectual functioning in infancy and the prediction of later IQ. In J. D. Osofsky (Ed.), *Handbook of infant development* (pp. 707–741). New York: John Wiley.

McFARLAND, W. H., SIMMONS, F. B., & JONES, F. R. (1980). An automated hearing screening technique for newborns. *Journal of Speech and Hearing Disorders, 45,* 495–503.

McGUIRE, L. L., & MEYERS, C. E. (1971, May). Early personality in the congenitally blind child. *The New Outlook,* pp. 137–143.

MEADOW, K. P. (1968). Early manual communication in relation to the deaf child's intellectual, social, and communicative functioning. *American Annals of the Deaf, 113,* 29–41.

MEADOW, K. P. (1969). Self-image, family climate, and deafness. *Social Forces, 47,* 428–438.

MEADOW, K. P. (1980). *Deafness and child development.* Berkeley, CA: University of California Press.

MEADOW, K. P., GREENBERG, M. T., ERTING, C., & CARMICHAEL, H. (1981). Interactions of deaf mothers and deaf preschool children: Comparisons with three other groups of deaf and hearing dyads. *American Annals of the Deaf, 126,* 454–468.

MEICHENBAUM, D., & GOODMAN, J. (1971). Training impulsive children to talk to themselves: A means of developing self-control. *Journal of Abnormal Psychology, 77,* 115–126.

MEISELS, S. J., & ANASTASIOW, N. J. (1982). The risks of prediction: Relationships between etiology, handicapping conditions and developmental outcomes. In S. Moore & C. Cooper (Eds.), *The Young Child: Re-*

views of research (Vol. 3, pp. 259–280). Washington, DC: National Association for the Education of Young Children.

MEISELS, S. J., JONES, S. N., & STIEFEL, G. S. (1983). Neonatal intervention: Problem, purpose and prospects. *Topics in Early Childhood Special Education, 3,* 1–13.

MINDE, K., FORD, L., CELHOFFER, L., & BOUKYDIS, C. (1975). Interactions of mothers and nurses with premature infants. *Canadian Medical Association Journal, 113,* 741–745.

MINDE, K., SCHOSENBERG, N., MARTON, P., THOMPSON, J., RIPLEY, J., & BURNS, S. (1980). Self-help groups in a premature nursery. *Journal of Pediatrics, 96,* 933–940.

MINDEL, E. D., & VERNON, M. (1971). *They grow in silence: The deaf child and his family.* Silver Spring, MD: National Association of the Deaf.

MINISZEK, N. A. (1983). Development of Alzheimers disease in Down Syndrome individuals. *American Journal of Mental Deficiency, 87,* 377–385.

MORDOCK, J. B. (1979). The separation-individuation process and developmental disabilities. *Exceptional Children, 46,* 176–184.

MURPHY, T. F., NICHTER, C. A., & LIDEN, C. B. (1982). Developmental outcome of the high-risk infant: A review of methodological issues. In K. Oliver, Jr., & T. H. Kirschbaum (Eds.), *Seminars in Perinatology, 6*(4), 353–365.

MYKLEBUST, H. R. (1964). *The psychology of deafness: Sensory deprivation, learning and adjustment* (2nd ed.). New York: Grune and Stratton.

NEWMAN, L. F. (1981). Social and sensory environment of low birth weight infants in a special care nursery: An anthropological investigation. *Journal of Nervous and Mental Diseases, 169,* 448–455.

NOBLE-JAMIESON, C. M., LUKEMAN, D., SILVERMAN, M., & DAVIES, P. A. (1981). Low birth weight children at school age: Neurological, psychological and pulmonary function. In T. K. Oliver, Jr. & T. H. Kirschbaum (Eds.), *Seminars in Perinatology, 6*(4), 266–274.

NORRIS, M., SPAULDING, P., & BRODIE, F. (1957). *Blindness in children.* Chicago: University of Chicago Press.

OLERON, P. (1953). Conceptual thinking of the deaf. *American Annals of the Deaf, 98,* 304–310.

OMWAKE, E. G., & SOLNIT, A. J. (1961). "It Isn't Fair": The treatment of a blind child. In *Psychoanalytic Study of the Child* (Vol. 16). New York: International Universities Press.

OPPENHEIMER, S. (1965). Early identification of mildly retarded children. *American Journal of Orthopsychiatry, 35,* 845–851.

PIPER, M. C., & PLESS, I. B. (1980). Early intervention for infants with Down's syndrome: A controlled trial. *Pediatrics, 65,* 463–468.

President's Commission for the Study of Ethical Problems in Medicine and Biomedical and Behavioral Research. Decisions to forego treatment (1983). (p. 208, fns. 46, 47, 48, 49).

RAPIN, I., & RUBIN, R. J. (1982). Appraisal of auditory function in children. In M. Lewis & L. T. Taft (Eds.), *Developmental disabilities, theory, assessment and intervention* (pp. 79–101). Jamaica, NY: MTP Press Limited.

Review and outlook: Infants. (1983, August 30). *The Wall Street Journal.*

ROBINSON, G. C. (1977). Causes, ocular disorders, associated handicaps, and incidence and prevalence of blindness in children. In J. E. Jan, R. D. Freeman, & E. P. Scott (Eds.), *Visual impairment in children and adolescents* (pp. 27–52). New York: Grune and Stratton.

ROSE, S. A. (1980). Enhancing visual recognition memory in preterm infants. *Developmental Psychology, 16,* 85–93.

ROSE, S. A., & WALLACE, I. F. (1985). Visual recognition memory: A predictor of later cognitive functioning in preterms. *Child Development, 56,* 843–853.

ROSENBLITH, J. F. (1973). Prognostic value of neonatal behavioral tests. *Early Child Development and Care, 3,* 31–50.

ROSS, G., SCHECHNER, S., FRAYER, W. W., & AULD, P. A. M. (1982). Perinatal and neurobehavioral predictors on one-year outcome in infants less than 1500 grams. In T. K. Oliver, Jr., & Kirschbaum, T. H. (Eds.), *Seminars in Perinatology, 6*(4), 317–327.

RYNDERS, J., & HORROBIN, J. (1975). Project EDGE: The University of Minnesota's communication stimulation program for Down's syndrome infants. In B. Z. Friedlander, G. Sterritt, & G. Kirk (Eds.) *Exceptional infant: Assessment and intervention* (Vol. 3, pp. 173–192). New York: Brunner/Mazel.

RYNDERS, J. E., SPIKER, D., & HORROBIN, J. M. (1978). Underestimating the educability of Down's syndrome children: Examination of methodological problems in recent literature. *American Journal of Mental Deficiency, 82,* 440–448.

SANDLER, A. M. (1963). Aspects of passivity and ego development in the blind infant. In R. S. Eissler, H. Hartmann, A. Freud, & M. Kris (Eds.), *Psychoanalytic study of the child* (Vol. 18, pp. 343–360). New York: International Universities Press.

SANDLER, A., COREN, A., & THURMAN, S. K. (1983). A training program for parents of handicapped preschool children: Effects upon mother, father, and child. *Exceptional Children, 49*(4), 355–358.

SCARR-SALAPATEK, S., & WILLIAMS, M. L. (1973). The effects of early stimulation on low-birth weight infants. *Child Development, 44,* 94–101.

SCHAEFER, M., HATCHER, R. P., & BARGLOW, P. D. (1980). Prematurity and infant stimulation: A review of research. *Child Psychiatry and Human Development, 10*(4), 199–212.

SCHEIN, J., & DELK, M. (1974). *The deaf population of the United States.* Silver Spring, MD: National Association of the Deaf.

SCHLESINGER, H. S., & MEADOW, K. P. (1972).

Sound and sign: Childhood deafness and mental health. Berkeley: University of California Press.

SCHLESINGER, H. S. (1978). The acquisition of signs and spoken language. In L. S. Liben (Ed.), *Deaf children: Developmental perspectives* (pp. 69–86). New York: Academic Press.

SERAFICA, F. C., & CICCHETTI, D. (1976). Down's syndrome children in a strange situation: Attachment and exploration behaviors. *Merrill-Palmer Quarterly, 22,* 137–150.

SHEARER, D. E., & SHEARER, M. S. (1976). The Portage Project: A model of early childhood intervention. In T. D. Tjossem (Ed.), *Intervention strategies for high risk infants and young children* (pp. 335–351). Baltimore, MD: University Park Press.

SHEARER, M. S., & SHEARER, D. E. (1972). The Portage Project: A model for early childhood education. *Exceptional Children, 39,* 210–217.

SHIPE, D., & SHOTWELL, A. M. (1965). Effect of out-of-home care on mongoloid children: A continuation study. *American Journal of Mental Deficiency, 69,* 649–652.

SHIRLEY, M. (1939). A behavior syndrome characterizing prematurely-born children. *Child Development, 10,* 115–128.

SIEGEL, L. S. (1982). Reproductive, perinatal, and environmental variables as predictors of development of preterm and full-term children at 5 years. In T. K. Oliver, Jr., & T. H. Kirschbaum, (Eds.), *Seminars in Perinatology, 6*(4), 274–280.

SIGER, L. P. (1978). That deaf child and you: A forensic approach to the problems of hearing and speech. *Journal of Communication Disorders, 11,* 149–158.

SIGMAN, M. (1983). Individual differences in infant attention: Relations to birth status and intelligence at 5 years. In T. Field & A. Sostek (Eds.), *Infants born at risk: Physiological, perceptual and cognitive processes* (pp. 271–293). New York: Grune and Stratton.

SIGMAN, M., COHEN, S. L., & FORSYTHE, A. B.

(1981). The relation of early infant measures to later development. In S. L. Friedman & M. Sigman (Eds.), *Preterm birth and psychological development* (pp. 313–328). New York: Academic Press.

SIMEONSSON, R. J., COOPER, D. H., & SCHEINER, A. P. (1982). A review and analysis of the effectiveness of early intervention programs. *Pediatrics, 69*(5), 635–641.

SOLKOFF, N., & MATUSZAK, D. (1975). Tactile stimulation and behavioral development among low birth weight infants. *Child Psychiatry and Human Development, 6,* 33–37.

SOLNIT, A. J., & STARK, M. H. (1961). Mourning and the birth of a defective child. In R. S. Eissler, H. Hartmann, A. Freud, & M. Kris (Eds.), *Psychoanalytic Study of the Child,* (Vol. 16, pp. 523–537). New York: International Universities Press.

STEDMAN, D. J., & EICHORN, D. H. (1964). A comparison of the growth and development of institutionalized and home-reared mongoloids during infancy and early childhood. *American Journal of Mental Deficiency, 69,* 391–401.

STEIN, Z. A., & SUSSER, M. (1977). Recent trends in Down's syndrome. In P. Mittler (Ed.), *Research to practice in mental retardation: Biomedical aspects* (Vol. 3, pp. 45–54). Baltimore: University Park Press.

STOKOE, W. C. (1978). Sign codes and sign language: Two orders of communication. *Journal of Communication Disorders, 11,* 187–192.

STONE, N. W. (1975) A plea for early intervention. *Mental Retardation, 13*(5), 16–18.

STUCKLESS, E. R., & BIRCH, J. W. (1966). The influence of early manual communication on the linguistic development of deaf children: II. *American Annals of the Deaf, 111,* 499–504.

THOMPSON, R. A., CICCHETTI, D., LAMB, M. E., & MALKIN, C. (1985). Emotional responses of Down syndrome and normal infants in the strange situation: The organization of affective behavior in infants. *Developmental Psychology, 21,* 828–842.

VERNON, M. (1969). *Multiply handicapped deaf children: Medical, educational and psychological considerations.* Reston, VA: The Council for Exceptional Children.

VERNON, M., & KOH, S. D. (1970). Early manual communication and deaf children's achievement. *American Annals of the Deaf, 115,* 527–536.

VERNON, M., & MINDEL, E. (1978). Psychological and psychiatric aspects of profound hearing loss. In E. E. Rose (Ed.), *Audiological assessment* (pp. 87–132). Englewood Cliffs, NJ: Prentice-Hall.

WILLS, D. M. (1965). Some observations on blind nursery school children's understanding of their world. In R. S. Eissler, H. Hartmann, A. Freud, & M. Kris (Eds.), *Psychoanalytic study of the child* (Vol. 20, pp. 344–366). New York: International Universities Press.

CHAPTER 4

PARENTS AND CHILDREN
IN POVERTY

POLITICS AND PSYCHOLOGY

In one sense this chapter is history because it chronicles the great experiments of the 1960's War on Poverty. Most of the programs were aimed at young children and their families in a valiant effort to break the intergenerational cycle of poverty. But poverty did not go away. Bronfenbrenner (1986) suggested that the most rapid, and perhaps the most consequential, change taking place in American family life in the 1980's has been the widening gap between poor families and the rest of society. As of March, 1985 (U.S. Bureau of Census) nearly 25% of the nation's children under 6 years of age were living in families below the "poverty line," compared to 15% for the population as a whole. The child-family programs of the 1960's did not have a major economic ef-

fect, but they did have a long-lasting impact in shifting attention to the developmental needs of the preschool child. In the 1980's, political winds shifted from economic class definitions of children at risk to definitions based on individual handicap, either readily identifiable in the present or predictable in the future.

The 1960's also marked the rise of the community mental health movement. From both inside and outside the professional field, questions were raised about the restricted population served by child guidance clinics and mental health clinics. For example, in 1965, Gordon wrote:

A review of the literature concerned with the description of patients seen in treatment suggests that for a variety of reasons clinics are not serving the needs of children from low income areas or from the areas which are representative of depressed minority

111

groups. Such areas tend to produce the bulk of social pathology, delinquency, narcotic addiction, mental illness, and school failure. In general, it appears that the more disturbed the child, the less likely the child will be seen in a child guidance clinic. (Gordon, 1965, p. 136)

Not only was there a strong push for "outreach" services that would attract the hard-to-reach populations, but also, in the spirit of the community mental health movement, professional workers were obliged to consider community conditions and the environmental context of behavior. "Community psychologists were characterized as change agents, social systems analysts, consultants in community affairs, and students generally of the whole man in relation to all his environments" (Bennett, 1965, p. 832). This was by no means the unanimous position of psychology, and there were many heated arguments regarding the scientific basis for psychology in social activism.

The enactment of the Community Mental Health Centers Act in 1963 (P.L. 88-164) revamped the system of delivery of mental health services. In part, this act was designed to offer community services in place of institutional services for the severely mentally ill, but it was also intended to broaden the scope of traditional services. Community representatives served on the center boards and were also employed as "paraprofessionals." New modalities of treatment were tried, and consultation and education were mandated as part of the "comprehensive services plan." Some referred to this "retooling" as a changeover from a professional-elitist position to a democratic position in which the community could plan its own destiny.

The success of the "community takeover" varied from one location to another. As federal support faded and finally disappeared, community mental health agencies were driven to depend more and more on fees for services and reimbursements from Medicaid, Title XX, and insurance plans. To collect third-party payments, the client needed a diagnosis, the service needed definition, and the service provider needed professional identification. This brought us right back to the medical model that had been so decried in the community mental health movement. As briefly stated by Hersch, "Individual modes of help will thrive in times of social conservatism. Situational modes of help will flourish in times of social reform" (1972, p. 749). It is difficult to look at the 1980's as part of history, but there is no doubt that many professional practices are determined more by an outside funding agency than by individual professional conviction. There is probably a bimodal distribution where two groups get services—the very poor and those with good insurance plans. Professional training is still inadequate to prepare individuals to work with persons who are the product of traumatic and impoverished circumstances.

POVERTY AND PREVENTION

One cannot make psychological attributions to parents on the basis of income level, but general influences often associated with "growing up poor" are detrimental to the child (Chilman, 1966). Further, there can be a kind of psychological habituation to poverty which results in outward passivity and perpetuates an intergenerational cycle. The Report of the Joint Commission on Mental Health of Children (1970) discussed the child rearing patterns more prevalent among the very poor, including harsh and inconsistent punishment, magical thinking, orientation to the immediate present, limited verbal communication; and a push for premature child independence. The Commission reflected the spirit of the 1960's in urging the eradication of poverty and racism as primary prevention measures. The hopes for prevention worked in two directions—elimination of poverty would improve mental health and improved child rearing conditions would reduce later poverty. Promoting one particular early intervention program, Hunt expressed the hope that "It is conceivable that by gradually deploying the kind of parental involvement depicted in these demonstrations through the Parent and Child Centers, we of these United States of America could bring a major share of the children of the persistently poor into the mainstream of our society within a generation" (1969, p. 233).

This chapter reviews the array of early intervention programs mustered for low-income groups. The realization that poor children were behind from the beginning of school, and therefore slated for failure, combined with a faith in the modifiability of intelligence, provided a powerful impetus for early intervention that rescued the nursery school from professional oblivion. What started in 1965 as preparatory programs for 4-year-olds was soon extended downward to younger ages and finally to infants. These programs had a heavy cognitive emphasis, and results were measured largely in terms of IQ changes or academic achievement.

With the commitment to early intervention came a strong push for early identification. In an Amendment to Title XIX of the Social Security Act, early periodic screening, diagnosis, and treatment (EPSDT) for Medicaid-eligible children became public policy in 1967 as a specific effort in prevention. Never before has the preschool child been the focus of so much concerted attention. Although more was promised than was delivered, the results of these experiences have much to tell us. As a corrective to a possible overemphasis on early identification and intervention, the issue of constancy versus change throughout development is addressed in the final section of this chapter.

Theoretical Background

Some key publications provided a theoretical rationale for early education. Using correlations from test-retests and other approaches to graphing mental growth curves, Bloom concluded that "in terms of intelligence measured at age 17 years, at least 20 percent is developed by age 1, 50 percent by about age 4, 80 percent by about age 8 and 92 percent by age 13. . . . This would suggest the very rapid growth of intelligence in the early years and the possible great influence of the early environment on this development" (1964, p. 68). It is of interest to note that Bloom's conclusion was virtually identical with an earlier statement made by Goodenough to the effect that "one-half of an individual's ultimate mental stature had been attained by the age of 3 years" (1946), but this failed to instigate any social action because of the prevailing doubts about the modifiability of intelligence. Goodenough's conclusion was of academic interest only, whereas Bloom became almost the standard citation for justifying early intervention.

Although the depressing effects of early deprivation were well known, it was not until the 1950's and early 1960's that there were systematic efforts to look at the other side of the coin, namely, the accelerating effects of early stimulation. The research published in 1964 by White and Held is but one example of the new zeitgeist. In a series of studies systematically varying aspects of institutional life for infants from 1 to 6 months of age, these investigators examined the development of visually directed reaching for objects. In the first study, from day 6 to day 36, nurses administered 20 minutes of extra handling each day to each of the infants without significant effects. On the basis of considerations put forward in Chapter 1, no effects would really be expected, as the extra handling was in no way contingent or responsive to the infants' cues. The second modification consisted of "enriching" the visual environment by changing the infants' positions in the cribs and providing mobiles, figured sheets, and crib bumpers. In a third study, pacifiers were mounted on the crib rails. These relatively simple changes in the infants' environments accelerated the appearance of reaching responses to an average age of about 3 months for the experimental group compared to almost 5 months for the control infants.

These results were frequently cited to illustrate the modifiability of early development. In the relatively depersonalized environment of the institution, apparently objects could be used to stimulate and reinforce early eye-hand coordination skill development. In White's opinion, "these studies show clearly that enrichment procedures can produce remarkable effects on the course of early development" (1968). This study attracted considerable attention at the time and it was all too easily forgotten that the results were obtained for infants in a very unusual situation, namely, a foundling home which seemed to be rather backward in the kind of care provided.

Hunt (1964) drew on research of this kind, as well as the contributions of Piaget and Montessori, for an important theoretical paper that reconciled earlier experimental findings of the importance of maturation in child development with newer evidence of its modifiability. He described the need for stimulation, spontaneous action, and encounters with circumstances that provide the proper level of incongruity—what he termed "the problem of the match between incoming information and that already stored" (1964).

Renaissance of the "Nursery School"

The status of nursery schools and day nurseries has always been particularly vulnerable to social needs. The first nursery schools were under private, voluntary agencies in the 1880's for children of working mothers and stressed physical hygiene and morality. In the 1920's a number of schools, organized for purposes of child study and research, appeared on university campuses. There was some interest in the effects on intellectual development of these university-based nurseries; for example, Wellman at the University of Iowa (1943) reported an average IQ gain of 10 points after 2 years of school attendance compared to no change for the nonattenders. Since the populations were above average in any case, this was not considered socially significant. Also, psychologists at the time were theoretically committed to a belief in the predetermination of intelligence, so that nearly 20 years passed before psychologists took up where the Iowa studies left off.

Public funds were used in the 1930's to support nursery schools (and unemployed teachers) to offset the devastating effects of the Great Depression. During World War II, the Lanham Act funded some 2,000 nursery schools and daycare centers for children of mothers in wartime employment (Educational Policies Commission, 1945; Forest, 1935). In the 1950's, nursery schools were generally viewed as luxuries for the middle-class mother, and the professional training and pay scale for nursery teachers fell far behind general educational standards. In 1949, the National Association for the Education of Young Children stressed the importance of the young child learning to live in a democratic culture and the importance of working with others. In addition to the social goals of adjusting to a group, considerable importance was given to the opportunity for physical manipulation, exploration, and creative expression. Teacher acceptance of individual differences was stressed, and the teacher's role was perceived as providing protection and opportunity rather than formal instruction (Gans, Stendler, & Almy,

1952). This has been described as an "enrichment model" (which might even increase individual differences). The concept of maturational readiness was a pervasive concept in the "traditional" nursery school. It was presumed that the child arrived from a "normal expectable environment"; differences in readiness were attributable to individual growth patterns rather than deprivations in experience (Elkind, 1969). The War on Poverty shed a whole new light on the purposes of nursery education.

PRESCHOOL: AN ANTIDOTE FOR CULTURAL DISADVANTAGE

The term "culturally disadvantaged" was coined to refer to a group of minority populations which have in common such characteristics as low economic status, low social status, low educational achievement, marginal employment record, and little, if any, social power. In school, on the average, these children show disproportionately high rates of social maladjustment, behavioral disturbance, physical disability, academic retardation, and mental subnormality. The 1954 Supreme Court school desegregation decision and the momentum of the civil rights struggle prompted many efforts at compensatory education within the public school system (Gordon & Wilkerson, 1966). Looking behind the problems in academic performance, researchers pinpointed differences in linguistic skills (Bernstein, 1961; Deutsch, 1965; Loban, 1963) and differences in motivation (Zigler & Butterfield, 1968). Such differences are expressed in IQ test differences that appear first in the second year of life and increase in size throughout the school years (Deutsch, 1967; Klineberg, 1963).

One of the first efforts to combat cultural disadvantage was initiated in 1962 by Susan Gray in Murfreesbro, Tennessee under the aegis of George Peabody College. The Early Training Project was designed to determine the timing and minimum duration of a program of intervention for offsetting the "progressive retardation in school achievement and general cognitive development that is the usual fate of the culturally deprived child as he passes through the elementary school" (Gray & Klaus, 1968, p. 63). Three equal groups were randomly selected from a total of 60 black children born in 1958 of families with an income below $3,000 (poverty level at that time), limited educational background, and in poor housing.

Beginning at age 4 years, the two treatment groups attended preschool for either two or three summers with weekly home visits during the remainder of the year, and the third group served as control. The summer programs stressed (a) reinforcement for behavior related to achievement (e.g., persistence, waiting, interest in school-type activities, etc.) and (b) work on perceptual development, development of concepts, and use of language. Although there was a 13-point IQ difference on first testing in favor of those who had attended the three summer programs, follow-up testing when the children were 10 years of age indicated no significant difference between the groups. The problems of interpreting this "washout" phenomenon and findings in even later follow-up will be discussed in the section on evaluation.

Also beginning in 1962, Deutsch at the Institute for Developmental Studies instituted an enrichment program for 4-year-olds in Harlem, which continued through grade 3 under the auspices of the public schools. These two programs were the prototypes of the national effort known as Operation Head Start.

CURRICULUM APPROACHES

The 1960's provided golden opportunities to test innovative approaches to the education of young children, mainly directed toward the culturally disadvantaged but also influencing private preschool programs. The rediscovery of Montessori, who after all started her work at the turn of the century with mentally retarded children and then organized "infant schools" in slum tenements of Rome, was particularly attractive to the middle class parents, although there were also Head Start Montessori programs (Banta, 1969; Kohlberg, 1968). Piaget's detailed descriptions of the evolution of reasoning in the young child also gave direction to curriculum planners. In 1962, the Ypsilanti-Perry Preschool Project, under the direction of David Weikart, began a 5-year study comparing 3-year-old, black, economically disadvantaged children enrolled in a Piagetian, cognitively oriented preschool with a control group. In addition to the preschool, there were weekly home teaching visits and parent group meetings. There were significant differences in IQ through the end of kindergarten which then disappeared, although achievement test scores collected in grades 1, 2, and 3 showed the experimental children to be superior to the controls. Weikart (1978) noted particularly the differences in grade placement. By the end of the fourth grade, significantly more children in the experimental group were on grade in regular classrooms (83% compared to 62% of the control group children).

A radically different approach was taken by Bereiter and Engelmann at the University of Illinois. Stressing the language deficiencies of the culturally disadvantaged child and the need for fast-paced intensive instruction to close the gap, these investigators developed an academically oriented, highly structured curriculum that later evolved into the DISTAR reading program for use in elementary schools. The teaching style was repetitive drill with unison responding by the pupils in rhythmic sing-song and clapping out the beat of language patterns. Little was left to the child's discovery or initiative and no special notice was taken of "individual growth patterns." Without doubt, this was the most extreme model mobilized to attack the deficits of cultural deprivation. After one year, the 4-year-olds had achieved first grade levels in academic achievement and advanced from a mean IQ of 93 to 100 (Bereiter & Engelmann, 1966).

Other approaches that were systematically developed included planned social reinforcement procedures, particularly for language stimulation (Risley, 1972), and the "responsive environments model" (Moore & Anderson, 1968) which also stressed the importance of reinforcement but utilized intrinsic rather than extrinsic motivational factors. The latter resembled the Montessori approach in emphasizing a prepared environment to encourage exploration and discovery with immediate feedback from the materials. A prime example was the talking typewriter which spoke the letter sound when the child pressed the key. The activities were self-rewarding or "autotelic," and the adult's behavior was responsive to the child's initiative. Meier, Nimnicht, and McAfee (1968), who developed the program for Chicano children in Greeley, Colorado, borrowed from Deutsch's early work, stressing the deficiencies in the sense of self and belongingness. In the responsive model program, the teacher's social responses are aimed at building a positive self-image and positive expectancies of others. Like Montessori, this requires considerable advance preparation on the part of the teacher and quick but flexible responses during school time to prevent disorder or disinterest. This is in marked contrast with the prescription manuals offered by other models.

With so many potential child subjects and such an array of choices, the possibilities for comparative research were many. In Ypsilanti, Weikart randomly assigned 3-year-olds to one of three programs: Cognitively oriented curriculum (Piagetian), language training curriculum (Bereiter & Engelmann, 1966) and unit-based curriculum (emphasizing the social-emotional goals and teaching methods of the "traditional" nursery school). To his surprise, each of the three programs did unusually well on all criteria, but the initial positive and equal findings were modified in subsequent groups. By the third year of replication, the unit-based program was out of the running, but Weikart's analysis of the reasons are very interesting. Using notes from the teachers, he demonstrated the demoralization of the teachers in this program and their growing sense of being forgotten and overlooked. Apparently, "the operational conditions of an experimental project are far more potent in outcome than the particular curriculum employed. The curriculum is more important for the demands it places upon the project staff in terms of operation than for what it gives the child in terms of content" (1972, p. 40).

Spicker (1971) quoted other studies to the same effect and commented

It is important to note that these studies had one major element in common—the traditional preschool classes under investigation were directly controlled by the investigators. This meant that teachers were assisted by a research staff in planning the details of the curriculum. Short and long-term goals were established; daily lesson plans were constructed; teachers were convinced that their approach would produce positive results . . . whenever the traditional curriculum has been evaluated in the absence of such an experimental structure, it has been found to be signficantly less effective with disadvantaged children than curriculum models that were designed specifically for such children." (p. 631)

These observations highlight some factors often neglected in evaluation studies, namely, the idiosyncratic skills and enthusiasm (or the opposite) of the teaching staff, and the time and support system available.

Miller and Dyer (1975) conducted the most comprehensive study of different curricula for 4-year-olds considered to be representative of "moderately" disadvantaged children throughout the country. There were 14 experimental classes in all: 4 in the Bereiter-Engel-mann model, 4 in the DARCEE model, described in *Before First Grade* (Gray, Klaus, Miller & Forrester, 1966); 4 traditional, and 2 Montessori. There were 214 children in experimental programs and 34 control children. Care was taken to offer the teachers equal training and support and to monitor the operations. In the final follow-up at the end of the second grade, there were no longer any significant differences in IQ for any group. Also, the control group children did as well in reading achievement, although all groups were below grade level expectancies. In brief, there was no finding of lasting significance attributable to different programs except possibly some interaction effects on noncognitive measures that were complex, small in magnitude, and difficult to interpret.

It is rash to suggest that these very careful investigators might have overlooked something, but if they used the 1972 Binet norms in their final follow-up in 1972, it would make quite a difference in the interpretation of findings. The Binet norms in use from 1960 to 1972 provided deviation IQ's based largely on the performance of the original 1937 standardization sample, and the renorming which took place in 1972 resulted in a major shift in IQ's, as illustrated in Table 4.1.

This table tells us two things. First, young children are more proficient with Binet tasks now than they were in the 1930's, and second, the historical change has been more pronounced for children under 5 years. If indeed Miller and Dyer stayed current and switched to the 1972 norms, the resultant pre and post IQ's would not be directly comparable, and the apparent decline in IQ would be arti-

TABLE 4.1 Comparison of 1960 and 1972 Binet Norms

Mental Age	Chronological Age	1960 IQ	1972 IQ
3–0	3–0	96	86
4–0	4–0	98	88
5–0	5–0	100	91
8–0	8–0	98	95

factual rather than real. That, however, would not change the basic fact that no final differences between the various groups and the control children were found.

FROM HEAD START TO HOME START

One of the consequences of the "wash-out" phenomenon so often reported was to direct attention to disadvantaged children under 3 years of age. At the same time programs were designed to "train" the parents to "train" their children. The projects varied in age-of-starting, duration, intensity of programming, and staffing pattern. Karnes (1969), at the University of Illinois, offered a 15-month training program of weekly group sessions for mothers of children between 13 and 27 months. Lambie and Weikart (1970), in Ypsilanti, Michigan, used trained teachers for once-weekly home tutoring sessions with a Piagetian-derived infant curriculum. Schaefer used "trained" college graduates for daily home tutoring (Schaefer, 1969, 1972; Schaefer & Aronson, 1977). The Florida Parent Education Program, directed by Gordon (1969), employed disadvantaged women to train other mothers in a series of "exercises" designed to stimulate infants' perceptual, motor, and verbal activities.

In Nassau County, New York, Levenstein and Sunley (1968) started a unique program in low-income housing projects. They derived their rationale for "Project Verbal Interaction" from the experimental work of Hess and Shipman (1968), who observed that the linguistic input provided by socially disadvantaged mothers oriented the child to "imperatives" and failed to offer opportunities for using language as a tool for labeling, ordering, and manipulating stimuli in the environment. "Toy Demonstrators" visited the home for half-hour semiweekly sessions spread over 2 school years. The toy demonstrators were drawn from a variety of backgrounds and trained to model verbal interaction with the child for the mother, rather than to directly teach it. The interaction materials (books and toys) were then given to the parents. The program was designed for children from 21 to 48 months of age. The structured cognitive curriculum is spelled out in a set of guide sheets, one of which is presented for each "Verbal Interaction Stimulus Material." The curriculum consists of a list of concepts and behaviors that remain the same on every guide sheet but are illustrated and elaborated differently by each new toy or book. This is a particularly interesting program because it is relatively simple and economical, estimated to cost about $700 per year per child (Levenstein, 1983).

From his review of intervention programs for children under 3 years of age, Beller (1979) concluded optimistically that "the first returns of the longitudinal investigations of infant intervention have yielded amazing results of persistent effects that have lasted close to a decade from infancy into the school years," with no evidence for "differential effectiveness of focusing on the child or the parents at home or outside the home once length of intervention is controlled" (p. 890). The persistent effects to which he had reference are not IQ changes but improved academic performance. As in the Head Start reports, at the conclusion of formal programs experimental children compared with controls showed a significant difference in IQ. For example, Guinagh and Gordon (1976) reported that 1 year after the program's end, and again 2 years later when the children were 6, there were significant effects on three tests of intelligence (Binet, Peabody Picture Vocabulary, and Leiter Performance Scale). At age 8 years, comparison of school achievement test data yielded significant differences for the experimental groups in reading, math concepts, and math problem solving with no significant IQ difference. Levenstein, O'Hara, and Madden (1983) also reported that the experimental groups were significantly superior in reading and arithmetic achievement tests at the third grade, although no statistically significant treatment effects were observed for IQ at that point.

The observations regarding the mother's participation in these programs are most interesting. First, there is the simple point of recruiting and preventing dropout. In Schaefer's program, 25% failed to complete the 15 months of training. This introduces a self-selection factor that makes it difficult to pinpoint the crucial factors in success.

Lambie and Weikart (1970) emphasized the diversity in their mothers and described four general groups: (a) those doing well and needing encouragement, (b) those who were ignorant but receptive to suggestions, (c) uninvolved mothers, and (d) mothers who were negatively related, either punitive or inappropriately protective. In a way, echoing the opinions expressed in previous chapters, Lambie and Weikart described the human relationship as the essential condition for any educational growth. Their primary focus was on the vicissitudes of the teacher-parent relationship, and they stressed the need for the teacher to be persistent, intuitive, and flexible in meeting the mother halfway to help her focus on her child.

Lambie and Weikart, as well as Gordon (1969), found that the mothers of children with relatively high intelligence offered more positive verbal reinforcement to their children for learning behavior. The ability to do this was strongly affected by the number of children in the home. Schaefer found significant correlations between maternal attitudes and measures of children's cognitive and emotional functioning. For example, negative maternal attitudes, such as withdrawal, punishment, irritability, hostile involvement, detachment, and low verbal epressiveness assessed when the child was 36 months correlated $-.40$ with the concurrent Binet IQ. Gordon reported very similar correlations.

The relationship between maternal behavior and child functioning seems to be very strong and more influential on the future course of development than the particular early intervention strategy employed. Bronfenbrenner analyzed reported results in terms of program categories and concluded that the involvement of the child's family as an active participant is critical. "Without family involvement, intervention is likely to be unsuccessful and what few effects are achieved are likely to disappear once the intervention is discontinued" (1975, p. 470). Some of the ramifications of this statement are discussed later in this chapter under the heading of "Home environment and early cognitive development."

FURTHER PROGRAM DEVELOPMENTS

Other variants were introduced for parents and children in poverty circumstances. In 1967, Hunt, as Chairman of the White House Task Force on Early Childhood Education, proposed the concept of Parent and Child Centers which were subsequently authorized by Congress as a function of the Office of Economic Opportunity. Expounding on the purpose of these centers, Hunt (1971) stressed both the potential of teaching mothers of poverty to become effective teachers of their young and the expectation that the lives of the parents would be enriched in the process. The improvement in the quality of life for the parents was expected as an indirect result of the "cooperation fostered among neighbors in slum neighborhoods and in highly impersonal public housing projects toward the care and education of their children" (p. 14).

Three of the 36 Parent and Child Centers were selected for evaluation in a major federally funded research program launched in 1970 (Andrews et al., 1982). Although all three programs continued until the child reached the age of 3 years, the Birmingham and New Orleans programs started with the mother when the child was 2–3 months of age, and the Houston program began when the child was 1 year old. In all, 326 "treated" children were compared with 267 controls.

The attrition rate of about 45% over the 2 or 3 years involved in program intervention confounds the interpretation of the results. The first consistent pattern of significant differences between the program and control children appeared at age 3 years. However, although significant, the Binet IQ difference was small (104.7 for program children and 98.5 for control groups). The average yearly cost of $5,000 per mother-child pair included health services for target children and siblings, care for siblings during the program hours, transportation, snacks or meals at the Center, and a stipend for the mothers ranging from $3 to $14 per day. This can be compared with the estimated cost of $1,900 per child per year in Head Start (1981) or $700 in the Mother-Child Home Program!

The final innovation in the Head Start context was the Child and Family Resources Program funded in 1973. CFRP programs used the Head Start Center as a base to develop a community-wide system linking a variety of programs and services to families with children through the age of 8 years. It represented an extension of the Parent-Child Centers concept, but family functioning as a whole was the focus, rather than the mother-infant dyad. All in all, there was a clear movement away from teaching the child specific skills in a classroom setting towards work with families in a larger context.

OVERALL ASSESSMENT

As of the 1980's, this 15-year period of massive social action and experimentation with early intervention has left a mixed legacy. As indicated, evaluations of methods have not provided a blueprint of specifically what to do for disadvantaged infants and preschoolers. With good planning, support, and enthusiasm, various curriculum models, whether center based or home based, do equally well in short-term effects. The reports of long-term effects on intelligence, academic, and school performance measures have been variously interpreted. In 1969, the results of a national study were released and generally understood to be negative. This study, known as the Westinghouse Report, followed the graduates of 104 Head Start Centers. Of these, 70% were summer programs only, and all had been initiated in the early halcyon days of the program. No positive effect from the summer sessions was discernible; however, in the first and second grades, the full-year graduates were significantly superior on achievement tests. The difference though (less than one standard deviation), was not considered to be educationally significant. This led a well-known educational psychologist, Arthur Jensen, to proclaim that compensatory education had failed and to rekin-

dle the controversy regarding the heritability of intelligence (1969). Others criticized the methodology of the study (Smith & Bissell, 1970) and the problems of judging from start-up programs (White, 1970). A more recent review of the research (Caruso, Taylor, & Detterman, 1982) also suggested that Head Start had failed in its goal to modify intelligence, although about half of the studies showed some gain in intellectual development. There has been considerable objection voiced to the notion that changing IQ was a primary mission of Head Start (Zigler & Trickett, 1978), despite the constant use of this measure for evaluation.

A report emphasizing the positive was presented by the members of the Consortium for Longitudinal Studies who collaborated by pooling their shared data and designing a common follow-up study (Lazar & Darlington, 1982). Looking at IQ scores on the Wechsler Intelligence Scale for Children, no treatment/control differences were found for children 13 years and over, which confirms previous findings. However, there was an impressive difference in school performance as reflected in special education placement. Although statistically significant differences were found only for mathematical achievement tests, they found that twice as many control children were placed in special classes; there was also evidence of reduced incidence of grade failure in the "treated" groups.

Some members of the Consortium have reported separately as well. In an analysis of the economic impact of the Perry Project, Weber, Foster, and Weikart (1978) concluded that there was more than complete recovery of the total cost of the preschool project from savings which accrued because the experimental group children required less costly forms of education during their school years and because of better educational progress by the experimental group children, predicting slightly higher lifetime earnings. Weikart also reported twice as many control as experimental children arrested by the age of 19 years and almost twice as many employed in the experimental group (Schweinhart & Weikart, 1981). It is not clear how these later effects came about; it is possible that the participants in the Perry Project had a concept of themselves as "privileged" and that this self-image had something to do with their expectations and later behavior.

Gray, Ramsey, and Klaus (1982) also followed their children into adulthood. They figured the total input from their early intervention program occupied less than 1% of the waking hours of the participants from birth to 18 years. On that basis, the finding of long-lasting, although modest, gains seemed a strong statement as to the value of early intervention. In their study, the major differences were found for the female participants. For example, three-fourths of the experimental girls had graduated from high school as compared to one-fourth of the local control girls. The authors suggested an explanation: "It is our guess that the motivational aspects of the program may be somewhat differentiated between the two sexes in the experimental group. It is perhaps easier, because of socialization and school practices, to arouse motivation in school-type activities among small girls than among small boys" (p. 255).

Evaluators have also examined other aspects of the Head Start program, particularly the meaning for parents. From the outset, parents were given several important roles. First, it was conceived of as providing employment opportunities and a "career ladder" with specially designed opportunities leading to certification as Child Development Associate or a 2-year degree in early education (Trickett, 1979). Also, parents were given an important part in operational decisions, including selection of the Head Teacher. The political power of the parents has been effective in ensuring the continuance of Head Start, despite changes in the political climate. As of 1979, there were approximately 1,200 full-year programs, enrolling about 15% of eligible children (that is, those between 3 and 5 years of age, with 90% from families whose income is less than the poverty line set annually by the U.S. Office of Management and Budget). Despite some increase in funding, however, the number enrolled in 1977 was less than half of the peak number enrolled in 1966 (Richmond, Stipek, & Zigler, 1979).

Some leaders in the early education field (Hymes, 1979; Omwake, 1979) have suggested that the actual operation of many programs has become routinized.

The impression of the writer from visits to centers, conversations with other professionals familiar with Head Start, and discussions at professional meetings and workshops for staff is that despite training programs, increased parental involvement and close supervision by monitoring teams, the model has reached a standstill. Descriptions of classrooms suggest a picture of thousands of children spending half or full days in a relentless round of identifying shapes, matching colors, repeating the alphabet and counting to ten. Such activities as dramatic play, block building, painting, and water play tend to be viewed by many teachers as special rewards for good behavior instead of important learning experiences. (Omwake, 1979, p. 225)

There is no doubt that many parents and some teachers perceive learning letters and numbers as the "real business" of preschool and attach little importance to expressive language development, reasoning processes, or independent discovery.

In brief, Operation Head Start did not prove to be corrective surgery for poverty. It was naive to expect that 1 or 2 years of preschool intervention could so change the child's intelligence that a chain of competitive success experiences would persist through 12 years of later schooling and into the labor market. Not only was this naive with regard to the effects of later environment on child development but also with regard to the origins of poverty. In the rosy glow of the 1960's, it might have been legitimate to overlook the role of the general economy, but in the "hi-tech" society of the 1980's, one cannot fail to see how the system itself creates unemployment and income deficiencies for part of the population.

Calculating the cost-effectiveness of early intervention is a tricky business when one considers the small numbers who have been followed into adulthood—and these few from very good programs. But even stronger positive evidence on a larger scale might not prevail to influence distribution of public funds. Mental health services, particularly for the "underclass" (Auletta, 1983), are always dependent on the political priorities of the moment. It has been noted that individual modes of help thrive in times of social conservatism and situational-environmental modes of help flourish in times of social reform (Hersch, 1972; Levine & Levine, 1970).

Preschool programming, in some form, for young children in disadvantaged areas is probably here to stay, not as a prevention for future poverty nor to elevate IQ but to assist families in providing good comprehensive care in health, education, and emotional well-being. Preschools for middle-class children are even more firmly entrenched, as a by-product of the increase in maternal employment if nothing else. It is to be hoped that these programs are neither traditional kindergarten moved down a year nor supervised playrooms. The experience of the past 20 years has demonstrated the critical role of the teacher in creating an effective preschool experience. There are hidden costs in teacher preparation and educational planning that might appear expendable in times of tight budgets, but it would be unfortunate indeed if we were to regress to the lackluster programs of the 1950's. The parents' involvement and their ability to choose and control at least some aspects of their child's preschool experience is an important and unique feature of this educational period that should be safeguarded.

THE FEDERAL PROGRAM: EPSDT

Repeatedly, with regard to every type of handicap or high risk factor, the importance of early intervention has been stressed. Clearly this is not possible without early identification. The Early and Periodic Screening, Diagnosis, and Treatment Program (EPSDT) originated as part of the national effort to improve the health and welfare of the children of the poor. In 1967, Congress amended the Social Security Act to set up a preventive program for all Medicaid-eligible children that includes not only welfare recipients but others who are considered "medically indigent," estimated to be nearly 15% of the American population. This went through various stages of rule-setting with penalty regulations put in force as of 1975. In 1979, the regulations were expanded to require extensive screening services including developmental assessment (effective as of January 1, 1981).

In his review of the program, Meisels described EPSDT as the most ambitious program of medical and psychosocial prevention ever launched:

Yet from its inception it failed to ignite the interest of professionals, to capture the attention of parents, or most importantly, to provide comprehensive services to children. Moreover, in its first fifteen years of existence virtually no systematic evaluation or research was conducted on EPSDT; no data exist that measure its impact, demonstrate its effectiveness, or determine its ratio of cost to benefit." (1984 p. 268)

The EPSDT program perhaps foundered because of the sheer size of the target population, or more likely because of the implication that poverty equals child neglect. The major issues of screening, how, who, and when, regained importance with the mandates for early identification and appropriate services in the 1986 Amendments to the Education for All Handicapped Act. The name changed but the essentials remain the same.

Theoretically, the three major functions of the EPSDT program—screening, diagnosis, and treatment—occur in sequence. In some instances, screening and diagnosis are simultaneous events (for instance Down syndrome, congenital blindness or deafness), and intervention has the function of preventing secondary complications. In other instances, screening is supposed to identify children in the "presymptomatic" phase where intervention would serve a primary preventive function. Screening a child for dental care, amblyopia, or dangerous lead levels in the blood are good examples. Frankenburg and North (1974) described the criteria to be used in the selection of health problems for screening as follows:

1. Is the problem or disease important to the affected individual?

2. Is the problem or disease important to the community because of contagion or cost of future care?

3. Is the problem or disease treatable?

4. Does early detection and treatment improve the effectiveness or reduce the cost of treatment?

5. Is there a substantial "lead time" between the time that the problem can first be discovered through screening and the time that it would ordinarily be detected without screening?

6. Are adequate resources available to diagnose and treat persons discovered through screening, or is there potential for their development?

7. Are the total costs of screening, diagnosis, and treatment for the problem

justified by the benefits of early detection?

8. Is there a safe, economical, reliable, accurate, and valid screening test for the problem in question?

Screening for medical conditions is comparatively straightforward; as long as treatment facilities are readily available, there is little controversy. The discussion that follows is restricted to developmental assessment. The objectives of the EPSDT program in the areas of developmental assessment and treatment were described as implementing measures directed toward detection of emotional, mental, and learning disability problems to permit identification, evaluation, and plans for treatment. This proved to be a very tall order.

DEVELOPMENTAL SCREENING AND ASSESSMENT

From the beginning there was a major emphasis on cognitive development, partly because the target population was by definition low income, with a disproportionately high incidence of mental retardation. Also, the early developmental milestones are fairly well established and there is an abundance of infant intelligence tests for item selection. To be efficiently used with relatively large populations, screening measures must be short, simple to administer, and widely available. The first, both in time of origin and frequency of use, is the Denver Developmental Screening Test (Frankenburg & Dodds, 1967). Although there is a way of calculating mental age (Frankenburg, Camp, & Van Natta, 1971), the Denver is usually scored as "normal," "questionable," or "abnormal" on the basis of a prescribed number of "delays" in the various sectors (see Appendix).

Frankenburg, Goldstein, and Camp (1971) reported that the Denver identified all children with IQ's below 70 on other tests as "abnormal" or "questionable," but Applebaum (1978) found that the Denver missed 62% of children aged 2 to 30 months with Bayley scores less than 70. Longitudinal studies have also suggested that the Denver is too "easy" (Camp, Van Doorninck, Frankenburg, & Lampe, 1977). An "abnormal" or "questionable" Denver seems to be clinically significant but it tends to yield a high proportion of "normals" or false negatives. In part, this may be because the Denver has many more test items for the child under 2 years of age, with only 30% of the 105 items appropriate for the age group between 2 and 6 years. In recognition of this discrepancy, Boyd (1969) proposed the CCD Developmental Progress Scale, which has the same format but with an equal distribution of items (15) at every age level through 7 years.

Frankenburg, Van Doorninck, Liddell and Dick (1976) developed a Denver Prescreening Developmental Questionnaire (PDQ) to be answered by a parent or caregiver, and in 1981, Frankenburg, Fandal, Sciarillo, and Burgess presented an abbreviated Denver that reduced the time from 15–20 minutes to 5–7 minutes. This put the full Denver almost in the category of an infant intelligence test, with the major difference that the Denver is generally administered by pediatricians or health personnel and the intelligence scales are restricted to psychologists.

In addition to the Denver prescreening questionnaire, a number of other brief screening questionnaires were offered (Knobloch, Stevens, Malone, Ellison, & Risemberg, 1979; Giannini, 1972). The Minnesota Child Development Inventory (MCDI, see appendix) is longer and more complete, providing a general developmental index as well as specific scale scores (Ireton & Thwing, 1972a, 1972b). In a comparison of 4-year-olds in nursery schools, Ullman and Kausch (1979) found that on most dimensions the MCDI indicated potential developmental problems in from one-third to one-half of the Head Start children in contrast to less than 8% of the regular nursery school children. Only on the self-help dimension were the Head Start and nursery school groups classified similarly. This finding is particularly interesting when one recalls that it is obtained from parents' reports; possibly the "middle-class" parents are over-rating their children! In checking with the teachers' ratings, Ullman and Kausch found satisfactory correspondence on most scales but not all, but they did not compare degree of agreement between parents' and teachers' ratings in the two groups.

Other screening measures use direct observation of behavior, sometimes in combination with parents' reports. For children under 2 or 3 years, the Denver still seems to be pre-eminent, but there are many contenders for the age group between 3 and 5 years. These include the Thorpe Developmental Inventory (Thorpe, 1972); Developmental Indicators for the Assessment of Learning (DIAL) (Mardell & Goldenberg, 1975); the

Minneapolis Preschool Screening Instrument (MPSI) (Lichtenstein, 1980, 1982); and the Early Screening Inventory (Meisels & Wiske, 1983). The last two provide some data regarding predictive validity. The MPSI consists of 50 items, requiring about 15 minutes. Scores are totalled in order to achieve a result of "pass" or "refer." In a 1-year later follow-up of 428 children, the MPSI proved to be highly sensitive to later problems (few false negatives) as well as specific (few false positives). The ESI consists of 32 items for children between 4 and 6 years of age and proved to be both sensitive and specific in follow-up studies of performance through the fourth grade. However, the predictive utility decreased as the interval between the predictor and the criterion measure increased.

Some of the tests used for screening preschool-age children are modifications of standard IQ tests; for instance, the McCarthy Screening Test (MST) (McCarthy, 1978), consists of 6 of the 18 subtests of the full McCarthy Scales of Children's Abilities (McCarthy, 1972). The Peabody Picture Vocabulary Test (PPVT) (Dunn, 1965) is a well-standardized test of receptive vocabulary that has been used for screening because it is brief and easy to administer. Tests designed to measure school readiness specifically include the Head Start Developmental Screening Test and Behavior Rating Scale (Dodds, 1967); the School Readiness survey (Jordan & Massey, 1967); and the Cooperative Preschool Inventory (CPI) (Caldwell, 1970). The CPI has been used most extensively by teachers in Head Start programs, sometimes using pre and post scores as a measure of the effectiveness of preschool instruction. The CPI Handbook (1970) makes a special point that the CPI is a measure of achievements which suggest "preparedness" rather than "readiness": "The readiness concept is a tricky one which makes too many assumptions about the experience for which one is presumably measuring. A child might be ready for one type of kindergarten and definitely not ready for another type" (p. 6). And herein lies "the rub" with the use of early screening measures to predict difficulties that may emerge at a later time.

CONTROVERSIAL ISSUES

Developmental screening programs did not meet with unqualified acceptance. The position paper of the American Orthopsychiatric Association (1978) criticized the reliance on cognitive measures and the neglect of social-emotional assessment. It was felt that this was a particularly sensitive issue in screening a low-income population because "standard tests typically make no provision for distinguishing between cultural differences and deficiencies" (p. 16). The paper also commented on the importance of searching for strengths as well as weaknesses: "focusing on coping strengths, rather than screening primarily for defects, would have the added benefit of forcing tests and other personnel to deal with the children as individuals" (p. 17). Their counter-proposals, however, far exceeded the intended purposes of population screening.

Many expressed the concern that effective treatment would not be available and that identification alone might do more harm than good. In the 1970's

there was a growing awareness of the negative effects of labeling and the dangers of the self-fulfilling prophecy (Mercer, 1973).

Screening is a seductive business because it gives the impression of concisely stating something about a child. . . . Screening results are often used to label a child "mentally retarded," "learning disabled," or "hyperactive," and with these labels come a set of assumptions and expectations. The label becomes a shorthand for the whole child. Despite the best intentions of professionals, many programs and institutions, particularly schools, make and justify far-reaching decisions about children on the basis of the labels, not the child's abilities. (Children's Defense Fund, 1977, p. 177)

The Children's Defense Fund recommended that identification of developmental problems should be considered a part of a comprehensive pediatric assessment rather than a special component of the EPSDT program.

In practice, developmental "screeners," at least in the traditional medical and agency settings, have been very cautious and the fears about labeling effects have not been borne out. This conservatism has been questioned in other circles. With the Amendments to the Education for all Handicapped Children enacted in P.L. 99-457, there will be renewed interest in screening for early identification and the definition of "handicapped" or "at serious risk" will come under close scrutiny. One project used a comprehensive identification process (CIP) to screen 3- to 5-year-olds in the neighborhood of the University of Illinois (Zehrbach, 1975) and reported that of 762 children, only 71.5% "passed" on the first screening; 13.7% were identified in the final assessment as needing some type of special service. When this population was compared with children referred by "traditional" sources, "The children referred by CIP tended to be brighter and shyer, possess learning (or prelearning) disability, and exhibit both enuresis and immature speech" (1975, p. 82). When one widens net to include mild degrees of delay, it is imperative to carry out controlled studies in order to justify the need and costs of special services. Many of these children showing immaturity (for instance, enuresis or tantrums at age 3 to 5 years) would in fact "outgrow" the problem on their own, or with minimal supportive help for the parents. It is doubtful that they should be included in a definition of a preschool "handicapped" population.

HOME ENVIRONMENT AND EARLY COGNITIVE DEVELOPMENT

A major conceptual problem with developmental screening is the assumption that the difficulty lies within the child. Prediction validity decreases over time because the child changes, for better or for worse, in response to environmental situations. This suggests "screening the environment" (Bradley & Caldwell, 1978). Ramey, Stedman, Borders-Batterson, and Mengel, (1978) demonstrated that using only information available from birth certificates, children who were likely to need special services before or during elementary school could be identified: "The children who appeared to be the most severely at risk for retarded development were third or later born siblings whose mother had a

tenth grade or less educational level and who, herself, had a previous live birth now dead and who began care for the target child in the third or later month of pregnancy" (p. 533).

Data from many studies using the Home Observation for Measurement of the Environment (HOME) Inventory (Caldwell & Bradley, 1978) show that lower (compared to middle) socioeconomic groups have lower scores on Emotional and Verbal Responsivity of Mother, Provision of Appropriate Play Materials, Maternal Involvement with Child, Opportunities for Variety in Daily Stimulation, and total scores (Gottfried, 1984). Crowding and number of children in the family were found to be consistently related to HOME scores; in general, the first-born fares better. For many reasons (e.g., less crowding, smaller families, more resources, and higher parental education), children from relatively higher socioeconomic families receive an intellectually more advantageous environment, independent of ethnic origin. Reviewing a number of studies, Gottfried (1984) found an average correlation of .50 between HOME scores recorded at 2 years of age and the child's measured intelligence between 3 and 5 years, which means that the HOME total score accounted for an average of 25% of the intellectual variance in the children. The most important factors seem to be maternal involvement, maternal responsivity, and play materials.

A specific issue of theoretical interest is whether the correlation between home environment on the one hand and children's cognitive development on the other is accounted for by the fact that both are related to maternal intelligence. Statistically it is possible to partial out maternal intelligence or education, and when this has been done there is evidence that home environment is significantly and independently related to children's cognitive development (Barnard, Bee, & Hammond, 1984; Gottfried & Gottfried, 1984). This has implications for intervention because it suggests that one can analyze what the more intelligent mother does "naturally" and help the less intelligent mother to find her way to the same end. Two factors are selected for illustration. One of the best general predictors of cognitive development is the presence of age-appropriate play material (Elardo, Bradley & Caldwell, 1975), and this could be facilitated by toy-lending libraries and programs like the Verbal Interaction Project (Levenstein, 1983). The finding that contingent verbal responsiveness to the child, in contrast to labeling or demonstration, is perhaps the greatest single influence on early cognitive development (MacPhee, Ramey, & Yeates, 1984) could be used to redirect mothers who try to "pour" information into their child by drill.

Screening with environmental measures is scientifically appropriate but fraught with difficulties. It takes time to obtain permission and make arrangements for a home visit, and it is not easy to interpret the results to the parents in a way that leads to effective intervention. The medical visit ordinarily does not allow sufficient time to make such arrangements, but with a captive group enrolled in ongoing day care or Head Start, there should be enough opportunity to establish the necessary working relationship with the parents.

MAINSTREAMING HANDICAPPED CHILDREN IN PRESCHOOL PROGRAMS

Concern about possible negative consequences of early identification and labeling was an important factor in the push to include handicapped children in "normal" preschool programs, also known as "mainstreaming." This represented an interesting reversal of previous opinion. In 1971, Hirsch, Borowitz and Costello, reporting on individual differences in "ghetto" 4-year-olds, criticized the policy of mixed ability grouping: "The children at the lower end of the functioning continuum did not sustain the teacher's attention, except through disruptive behavior. These children did not profit from the examples set by their better-functioning classmates. They tended to withdraw into nonconstructive activity. This neither enhanced their already fragile self-esteem, nor led to their greater accessibility for learning" (p. 348). This probably corresponds closely to the opinion of many, if not most, teachers.

Nonetheless, for many reasons, there was a growing sentiment to integrate educational programs, and the 1972 Amendments to the Economic Opportunities Act mandated that not less than 10% of the Head Start enrollment consist of handicapped children. In part, this was seen as a way to influence public opinion: "The Head Start movement is the most promising force available today to reverse the trend in the U.S. toward greater and greater segregation of the weak, the elderly and people with special needs" (Nazzaro, p. 106, 1974). In practice, the handicapped children enrolled in Head Start are likely to have handicaps so minimal as to be imperceptible, with mental retardation the least represented (Ensher, Blatt, & Winschel, 1977). Head Start staff are torn between the need to meet the mandate and the reluctance to label young children, especially as mentally retarded.

The psycho-educational reasons for encouraging integration include the potential value of normal peers for interactional partners and role models. But, as suggested by the earlier quotation, experience has proved that these goals do not come about by simply placing retarded and nonretarded children together in the same classroom (Guralnick, 1978; Snyder, Apolloni, & Cook, 1977). Most of the serious efforts to integrate retarded and normal preschoolers have been experimental demonstration projects (Bricker & Bricker, 1976). Several studies have programmed social interactions, using verbal praise and physical contact for reinforcement. Other studies have programmed the nonhandicapped child to model appropriate language or to provide reinforcement for the handicapped child's efforts at communication. Karnes and Lee (1979) reported on the judicious use of material and space to facilitate interaction, and some toys lend themselves more readily to interactive play (Quillitch & Risley, 1973). However, children must first have the skills to use the play materials before peer interaction can occur.

It is clear that meaningful integration involves extra effort on the part of the teacher. The mentally retarded child needs more preparation in order to start and more assistance to finish. Perhaps the biggest challenge, however, is in talking with the other children. Any child who is conspicuously different either by reason of physical or mental handicap will arouse questions which must be answered. Children will ask "Why does he talk funny?" or comment "He's just scribbling, he's not doing it right." It is easier to explain a physical handicap than one which is manifest only in behavior, and it is somewhat easier to explain a moderately or severely retarded child than one who is only mildly handicapped.

The usual explanation is in terms of slowness or need for special help to learn. Following that idea, one can involve the normal child as a "helper" and thus promote the goal of increased understanding and sensitivity. But this requires that the teacher feel comfortable talking about the "special" child with other parents as well as the children. The parent of the special child must understand that this will, and should, come up and agree with the teacher about the nature of the explanation. If the parent has placed the child in a "normal" nursery school as part of denial, it is indeed difficult.

The same issues arise with integration for physically handicapped preschoolers. Although this may be an easier situation for the teacher, it is likely to arouse anxiety in the nonhandicapped child. Three- and 4-year-olds are often concerned about body injury and fearful that they will "catch" or otherwise acquire the physical handicap. Reassurance requires explanation about the cause of the physical problem and reassurances that it was "no one's fault." Again there will be some open conversation and the handicapped child must bear with the curiosity. When the anxieties are put to rest, preschool children usually relish the helping role and one must then take care that the handicapped child does not become the "baby" of the school. Although it is extra work to include a handicapped child, it also presents an educational opportunity for the teacher and for handicapped and nonhandicapped children alike.

CONSTANCY AND CHANGE IN HUMAN DEVELOPMENT

The idea of prevention through early identification and intervention has a strong hold despite the difficulties in implementation. However, there are frequent reminders of the need for continued services for children and families at biological or environmental risk. There is no way of immunizing a child against all further deprivations or deleterious circumstances. Fortunately, with children we do not seem to be locked into a timetable or "critical periods" which, if missed, seal their fate. Extrapolation from animal research on the effects of early experiences is limited, not only because of species differences, but also because it is rare to have truly parallel conditions in human life circumstances. Even the worst circumstances for a human infant have some redeeming features when compared to the laboratory conditions used in animal deprivation experiments.

Kagan and Klein (1973) advanced a "discontinuity theory" of early development from their work with Guatemalan Indian infants. The early infant environment was extremely limited in sensory stimulation (although not in social interaction), which explained the marked developmental retardation observed when

the infants were brought from their huts at 1 year of age. Testing at various ages indicated a steady developmental acceleration, and by age 11 years, there was no longer any difference when compared to an urban Guatemalan group and an American sample on some nonverbal cognitive measures selected to be "culturally relevant." Since U.S. culture demands other skills in addition to those included in this cross-cultural comparison, one cannot assume that severe sensory deprivation in the first year of life would not show up in comparisons of two sets of American children at age 11 years. Nonetheless, these Indian children were able to "catch up" in many important ways with exposure to a more stimulating environment, and they were far from retarded.

What looks like the long-term result of early environmental circumstances may be more the result of the fact that environments usually remain relatively constant over time and thereby continue their effect. The Clarkes (1976) brought together a number of reports documenting the fact that later positive changes in care and overall environment can counteract the effects of poor care in early life. For example, Kadushin (1970) evaluated the success of placement for a group of 91 children in their teens who had been 5 to 12 years of age at the time of adoptive placement. Despite the fact that the early lives of these children were often insecure, inconsistent, harsh, and abusive, 78% of the adoptive placements were successful. Major factors for success were acceptance of the child as a member of the family and lack of self-consciousness on the part of the parents concerning their adoptive status. The age of child at time of placement, number of previous placements, and degree of child pathology were found to be negatively related reflecting some effect of the past.

Children show an amazing resiliency and for most, the influence of their present environment considerably offsets the influence of their past environment. Thomas (1981) commented that

Overall, it should be no surprise that early life experience does not determine later psychological development and functioning. The unique capacity of the human brain for learning and for plasticity in developmental pathways would be wasted if the individual's potential for mastery and adaptation were frozen, or even severely limited, by his early life experiences. (p. 595)

Of course, a healthy start in life is better than a sickly childhood, both psychologically and physically, but it is seldom too late for change, either for better or worse.

In contrast, what has been called the "strong early experience position" (Goldhaber, 1979) gives the parents a unique and all-important role. Some parents, usually middle-class parents who try to follow what they read, may take this responsibility very seriously. White (1975) warned parents that if they have not provided the proper environment for their child by age 3, they may have so handicapped their child that subsequent intervention may be virtually useless; conversely, if they have done a good job, a few years of a mediocre school system will have little impact. Bijou takes a somewhat similar view when he predicts that future educators will view "preschool as the most important educational experiences in a person's life" (1976, p. 164). Although the

professional workers who urge early identification and intervention for handicapped children or those at biological and/or environmental risk are not directly addressing the majority of parents and teachers of young children, there is a natural "spill-over," so that one might infer that if too little stimulation is deleterious, the more stimulation the better.

SUMMARY

This chapter has reviewed the work of two decades, during which time the parent and young child in poverty circumstances have been the focus of much attention. It is impossible to ignore the influence of government policies that tried to convert psychological observations into national programs. Interventions were designed to compensate for the perceived deficiencies in the young child's experience. They met with some success, although less than was desired. All suffered from a lack of follow-through, partly at least because of a belief that the first 5 years represent a "sensitive period" and that a child entering school with an appropriate "stock" of skills and knowledge could carry on independently. Our renewed appreciation of the plasticity in development not only gives hope for later intervention but also implies a responsibility to continue early efforts.

The intervention programs described in this chapter have been largely of an educational nature, although psychologists were very much involved in both curricular development and evaluation. There was a natural tendency to depend on those tools that were readily at hand, namely, the IQ and achievement tests. These measures do not by themselves determine success or failure in later life, and recent reports on other parameters such as delinquency and unemployment have been more positive. Regrettably, there is little information regarding the emotional development of these children and their families during their participation in special programs. It was a period when we seemed to divorce affective/motivational development from cognitive development.

Parent programs followed the "parent-educator" model with the parents trained to implement carefully structured curricular plans. In Bond's words, "parents continued to be treated as actors reading someone else's script; they are encouraged to depend upon the recipes of experts with little thought toward the process of creating their own" (1982, p. 29). This model is a long way from the parent therapy model discussed in Chapter 2, which focuses rather narrowly on parent-child interactions in the first 2 years, perhaps taking it for granted that the happy, healthy child will later learn what he or she needs to know. Hopefully, in the future, there will be some wedding of these points of view. Then, one would first work on the obstacles in the way of attachment and reciprocal interaction, moving to effective language exchange and finally to mastery of perceptual and conceptual problems. The key is to encourage the development of problem-solving skills of both parents and their children so that they can take the credit for success. It is not a question of feeding facts onto an empty diskette but of showing others how to write their personal programs. Laboring with the gigantic "rescue fantasy" of the War on Poverty, the professionals tried to do too much *for* rather than *with* those they wanted to help.

It is important to retain the information provided by years of experience with intervention programs for infants and young children and apply it judiciously in the new thrust prompted by PL 99-457. This law requires an individualized "family service plan" and hopefully, this will take cognizance of relationships as well as educational needs.

REFERENCES

American Orthopsychiatric Association. (1978). Developmental assessment in EPSDT. *American Journal of Orthopsychiatry, 48,* 7–22.

ANDREWS, S. R., BLUMENTHAL, J. B., JOHNSON, D. L., KAHN, A. J., FERGUSON, C. J., LASATER, T. M., MALONE, P. E., & WALLACE, D. B. (1982). The skills of mothering: A study of Parent Child Development Centers. *Monographs of the Society for Research in Child Development, 47*(6), 1–83.

APPELBAUM, A. (1978). Validity of the revised Denver Developmental Screening Test for referred and non-referred samples. *Psychological Reports, 43,* 227–233.

AULETTA, KEN. (1983). *The underclass.* New York: Vintage Books.

BANTA, T. J. (1969). Research on Montessori and the disadvantaged. In R. C. Orem (Ed.), *Montessori and the special child* (pp. 171–176). New York: G. P. Putnam's Sons.

BARNARD, K. E., BEE, H. L., & HAMMON, M. A. (1984). Home environment and cognitive development in a healthy, low-risk sample: The Seattle study. In A. W. Gottfried (Ed.), *Home environment and early cognitive development* (pp. 117–149). New York: The Academic Press.

BELLER, E. K. (1979). Early intervention programs. In J. Osofsky (Ed.), *Handbook of infant development* (pp. 852–894). New York: John Wiley & Sons.

BENNETT, C. C. (1965). Community psychology: Impressions of the Boston conference on the education of psychologists for community mental health. *American Psychologist, 20,* 832–836.

BEREITER, C., & ENGELMANN, S. (1966). *Teaching disadvantaged children in the preschool.* Englewood Cliffs, NJ: Prentice-Hall.

BERNSTEIN, B. (1961). Social structure, language, and learning. *Educational Research, 3,* 163–176.

BIJOU, S. W. (1976). *Child development: The basic state of early childhood.* Englewood Cliffs, NJ: Prentice-Hall.

BLOOM, B. S. (1964). *Stability and change in human characteristics.* New York: John Wiley & Sons.

BOND, L. A. (1982). From prevention to promotion: optimizing infant development. In L. A. Bond & J. M. Joffe (Eds.), *Facilitating infant and early childhood development* (pp. 5–39). Hanover, NH: University Press of New England.

BOYD, R. D. (1969). *CCD Developmental Progress Scale* (Experimental form, manual and directions). Portland: University of Oregon Medical Center, Dept. of Clinical Psychology.

BRADLEY, R. H., & CALDWELL, B. M. (1978). Screening the environment. *American Journal of Orthopsychiatry, 48*(1), 114–131.

BRICKER, W. A., & BRICKER, D. D. (1976). The infant, toddler and preschool research and intervention project. In T. D. Tjossem (Ed.), *Intervention strategies for high risk infants and young children* (pp. 545–573). Baltimore, MD: University Park Press.

BRONFENBRENNER, U. (1975). Is early intervention effective? In B. Z. Friedlander, G. M. Sterritt, & G. E. Kirk (Eds.), *Exceptional infant: Vol. 3. Assessment and intervention* (pp. 449–475). New York: Brunner/Mazel.

BRONFENBRENNER, U. (1986). Ecology of the family as a context for human development: Research perspectives. *Developmental Psychology, 22,* 723–742.

CALDWELL, B. (1970). *Preschool inventory (rev. ed.) handbook.* Princeton, NJ: Educational Testing Service.

CALDWELL, B. M., & BRADLEY, R. H. (1978). *Home observation for measurement of the environment.* Little Rock: Center for Child Development and Education, University of Arkansas at Little Rock.

CAMP, B., VAN DOORNINCK, W., FRANKENBURG, W., & LAMPE, J. (1977). Preschool developmental testing in prediction of school problems: Studies of 55 children in Denver. *Clinical Pediatrics, 16,* 257–263.

CARUSO, D. R., TAYLOR, J. J., & DETTERMAN, D. K. (1982). Intelligence research and intelligent policy. In D. K. Detterman & R. J. Sternberg (Eds.), *How and how much can intelligence be increased?* (pp. 45–66). Norwood, NJ: Ablex.

Children's Defense Fund. (1977). *EPSDT: Does it spell health care for poor children?* Washington, DC: Washington Research Project.

Children's Defense Fund. (1978). EPSDT in Practice: What's happening in the field? *American Journal of Orthopsychiatry, 48* (1), 77–95.

CHILMAN, C. (1966). *Growing up poor* (U.S. Department of Health, Education and Welfare). Washington, DC: U.S. Government Printing Office.

CLARKE, A. M., & CLARKE, A. D. B. (1976). *Early experience: Myth and evidence.* New York: The Free Press.

DEUTSCH, M. (1965). The role of social class in language development and cognition. *American Journal of Orthopsychiatry, 35,* 78–88.

DEUTSCH, M. (1967). *The disadvantaged child.* New York: Basic Books.

DODDS, J. (1967). The Head Start developmental screening test and behavior rating scale, CAP-HS Form 56, GSA DC 68.

DUNN, L. M. (1965). *Peabody Picture Vocabu-*

lary Test manual. Minneapolis, MN: American Guidance Service.

Educational Policies Commission. (1945). *Educational services for young children.* Washington, DC: National Education Association and American Association of School Administrators.

ELARDO, R., BRADLEY, R., & CALDWELL, B. (1975). The relation of infants' home environment to mental test performance from six to thirty-six months: A longitudinal analysis. *Child Development, 46,* 71–76.

ELKIND, D. (1969). Preschool education: Enrichment or instruction? *Childhood Education, 37,* 321–326.

ENSHER, G. L., BLATT, B., & WINSCHEL, J. F. (1977). Head Start for the handicapped: An audit of the congressional mandate. *Exceptional Children, 43*(4), 202–214.

FOREST, I. (1935). *The school for the child from two to eight.* Boston: Ginn.

FRANKENBURG, W. K., CAMP, B. W., & VAN NATTA, P. A. (1971). Validity of the Denver Developmental Screening Test. *Child Development, 42,* 475–481.

FRANKENBURG, W. K., & DODDS, J. B. (1967). The Denver Developmental Screening Test. *Journal of Pediatrics, 71,* 181–191.

FRANKENBURG, W. K., FANDAL, A. W., SCIARILLO, W., & BURGESS, D. (1981). The newly abbreviated and revised Denver Developmental Screening Test. *Journal of Pediatrics, 99,* 995–999.

FRANKENBURG, W. K., GOLDSTEIN, A., & CAMP, B. W. (1971). The revised Denver Developmental Screening Test: Its accuracy as a screening instrument. *Journal of Pediatrics, 79,* 988–995.

FRANKENBURG, W. K., & NORTH, A. F. (1974). A Guide to Screening for the EPSDT under Medicaid. Social and Rehabilitation Service, U.S. Dept. HEW (SRS) 74-24516. Washington, DC: U.S. Government Printing Office.

FRANKENBURG, W. K., VAN DOORNINCK, W. J., LIDDELL, T. N., & DICK, N. P. (1976). The Denver Prescreening Developmental Questionnaire (PDQ), *Pediatrics, 57,* 744–753.

GANS, R., STENDLER, C. B., & ALMY, M. (1952). *Teaching young children.* Yonkers-on-Hudson, NY: World Book.

GIANNINI, M. J., & Committee on Children with Handicaps, American Academy of Pediatrics. (1972) The Rapid Developmental Screening Checklist. Valhalla, NY: Mental Retardation Institute, New York Medical College.

GOLDHABER, D. (1979). Does the changing view of early experience imply a changing view of early development? In L. G. Katz (Ed.), *Current topics in early childhood education* (Vol. 2, pp. 117–140). Norwood, NJ: Ablex.

GOODENOUGH, F. L. (1946). The measurement of mental growth in childhood. In L. Carmichael (Ed.), *Manual of child psychology* (pp. 450–475). New York: John Wiley.

GORDON, E., & WILKERSON, D. A. (1966). *Compensatory education for the disadvantaged.* New York: College Entrance Examination Board.

GORDON, I. J. (1969). *Early child stimulation through parent education. Final Report to the Children's Bureau, Social and Rehabilitation Seminars, HEW.* Washington, DC: U.S. Government Printing Office, June 30, 1969.

GORDON, S. (1965). Are we seeing the right patients? Child guidance intake: The sacred cow. *American Journal of Orthopsychiatry, 35,* 131–137.

GOTTFRIED, A. W. (1984). Home environment and early cognitive development: Integration, meta-analyses and conclusions. In A. W. Gottfried (Ed.), *Home environment and early cognitive development* (pp. 329–342). New York: Academic Press.

GOTTFRIED, A. W., & GOTTFRIED, A. E. (1984). Home environment and cognitive development in young children of middle-socioeconomic status families. In A. W. Gottfried (Ed.), *Home environment and early cognitive development* (pp. 57–115). New York: Academic Press.

GRAY, S., & KLAUS, R. A. (1968). The early training project and its general rationale. In R. D. Hess & R. M. Baer (Eds.), *Early education* (pp. 63–70). Chicago, IL: Aldine.

GRAY, S. W., KLAUS, R. A., MILLER, J. O., & FORRESTER, B. J. (1966). *Before first grade.* New York: Teachers College Press.

GRAY, S. W., RAMSEY, B., & KLAUS, R. A. (1982). *From 3 to 20: The early training project.* Baltimore, MD: University Park Press.

GUINAGH, B. J., & GORDON, I. J. (1976). School performance as a function of early stimulation. Final Report to Office of Child Development. (Cited by Beller).

GURALNICK, M. J. (1978). *Early intervention and the integration of handicapped and nonhandicapped children.* Baltimore, MD: University Park Press.

HERSCH, CHARLES. (1972). Social history, mental health, and community control. *American Psychologist, 27,* 749–754.

HESS, R. D., & SHIPMAN, V. C. (1968). Maternal influences upon early learning: The cognitive environments of urban pre-school children. In R. D. Hess & R. M. Baer (Eds.), *Early education* (pp. 91–104). Chicago, IL: Aldine.

HIRSCH, J. G., BOROWITZ, G. H., & COSTELLO, J. (1971). Individual differences in ghetto 4-year-olds. In S. Chess & A. Thomas (Eds.), *Annual progress in child psychiatry and child development* (pp. 335–349). New York: Brunner/Mazel.

HUNT, J. McV. (1964). The psychological basis for using preschool enrichment as an antidote for cultural deprivation. *Merrill-Palmer Quarterly, 10,* 209–248.

HUNT, J. McV. (1969). *The challenge of incompetence and poverty: Papers on the role of early education.* Urbana: University of Illinois Press.

HUNT, J. M.cV. (1971). Parent and child centers: Their basis in the behavioral and educational sciences. *American Journal of Orthopsychiatry, 41,* 13–38.

HYMES, L., JR. (1979). Head Start, a retrospective view: The founders. In E. Zigler & J. Valentine (Eds.), *Project Head Start* (pp. 43–134). New York: Free Press.

IRETON, H., & THWING, E. (1972a). *The Minnesota Child Development Inventory.* Minneapolis, MN: Interpretive Scoring Systems, National Computer Systems.

IRETON, H. & THWING, E. (1972b). The Minnesota Child Development Inventory in the psychiatric developmental evaluation of the preschool-age child. *Child Psychiatry and Human Development, 3,* 102–114.

JENSEN, A. R. (1969). How much can we boost IQ and scholastic achievement? *Harvard Educational Review, 39*(1), 1–124.

Joint Commission on Mental Health of Children (1970). *Crisis in child mental health: Challenge for the 1980's.* New York: Harper and Row.

JORDAN, F. L., & MASSEY, J. (1967). *School Readiness Survey: Ages 4–6.* Palo Alto, CA: Consulting Psychologists Press.

KADUSHIN, A. (1970). *Adopting older children.* New York: Columbia University Press.

KAGAN, J., & KLEIN, R. E. (1973). Cross-cultural perspectives on early development. *American Psychologist, 28,* 947–962.

KARNES, M. B. (1969). *Investigation of classroom and at-home intervention: Research and development program of preschool disadvantaged children.* (Final Report, Bureau No. 5-1181). Washington, DC: Bureau of Research, Office of Education, US Department of Health, Education and Welfare.

KARNES, M. B., & LEE, R. C. (1979). Mainstreaming the preschool. In L. G. Katz (Ed.), *Current topics in early childhood education* (Vol. 2, pp. 13–42). Norwood, NJ: Ablex.

KLINEBERG, O. (1963). Negro-white differences in intelligence test performance: A new look at an old problem. *American Psychologist, 18,* 198–203.

KNOBLOCH, H., STEVENS, F., MALONE, A., ELLISON, P., & RISEMBERG, H. (1979). The validity of parental reporting of infant development. *Pediatrics, 63,* 872–878.

KOHLBERG, L. (1968). Montessori with the culturally disadvantaged: A cognitive developmental interpretation and some research findings. In R. D. Hess & R. M. Baer (Eds.), *Early education* (pp. 105–118). Chicago, IL: Aldine.

LAMBIE, D. Z., & WEIKART, D. P. (1970). Ypsilanti Carnegie infant education project. In J. Hellmuth (Ed.), *Disadvantaged Child* (Vol. 3). *Compensatory eduction: A national debate* (pp. 362–404). New York: Brunner/Mazel.

LAZAR, I., & DARLINGTON, R. (1982). Lasting effects of early education: a report from the consortium for longitudinal studies. *Monographs Society for Research in Child Development, 47* (Nos. 2–3). Chicago, IL: University of Chicago Press.

LEVENSTEIN, P. (1983). Implications of the transition period for early intervention. In R. Golinkoff (Ed.), *The transition from prelinguistic to linguistic communication* (pp. 203–218). Hillsdale, NJ: Lawrence Earlbaum Associates.

LEVENSTEIN, P., O'HARA, J., & MADDEN, J. (1983). The mother-child program of the verbal interaction project. In Consortium for Longitudinal Studies (Ed.), *As the twig is bent* (pp. 237–263). Hillsdale, NJ: Lawrence Erlbaum Associates.

LEVENSTEIN, P., & SUNLEY, R. (1968). Stimulation of verbal interaction between disadvantaged mothers and children. *American Journal of Orthopsychiatry, 38,* 116–121.

LEVINE, M., & LEVINE, A. (1970). *A social history of helping services: Clinic court, school and community.* New York: Appleton-Century-Crofts.

LICHTENSTEIN, R. (1980). *Minneapolis Preschool Screening Instrument.* Minneapolis, MN: Minneapolis Public Schools.

LICHTENSTEIN, R. (1982). New instrument, old problem for early identification. *Exceptional Children, 49,* 70–73.

LOBAN, W. D. (1963). *The language of elementary school children.* Champaign, IL: National Council of Teachers of English.

MACPHEE, D., RAMEY, C. T., & YEATES, K. O. (1984). Home environment and early cognitive development: Implications for early intervention. In A. W. Gottfried (Ed.), *Home environment and early cognitive development* (pp. 343–369). New York: Academic Press.

MARDELL, C. D., & GOLDENBERG, D. S. (1975). *DIAL—Developmental Indicators for the Assessment of Learning.* Edison, NJ: Childcraft Education Corporation.

MCCARTHY, D. (1972). *McCarthy Scales of Children's Abilities.* New York: Psychological Corporation.

MCCARTHY, D. (1978). *McCarthy Screening Test.* New York: Psychological Corporation.

MEIER, J. H., NIMNICHT, G., & MCAFEE, O. (1968). An autotelic responsive environment nursery school for deprived children. In J. Hellmuth (Ed.), *The disadvantaged child: Vol. 2. Head Start and early intervention,* (pp. 299–398). New York: Brunner/Mazel.

MEISELS, S. J. (1984). Prediction, prevention and developmental screening in the EPSDT program. In H. W. Stevenson & A. E. Siegel (Eds.), *Child development and social policy* (pp. 267–317). Chicago: University of Chicago Press.

MEISELS, S. J., & WISKE, M. S. (1983). *The Early Screening Inventory.* New York: Teachers College Press.

MERCER, J. R. (1973). *Labeling the mentally retarded.* Berkeley, CA: University of California Press.

MILLER, L. B., & DYER, J. L. (1975). Four preschool programs: their dimensions and effects. *Monographs Society of Research in Child Development, 40* (Nos. 5–6).

MOORE, O. K., & ANDERSON, A. R. (1968). The Responsive Environments Project. In R. D. Hess & R. M. Baer (Eds.), *Early education* (pp. 171–190). Chicago, IL: Aldine.

National Association for Education of Young Children (1949). *Essentials of nursery education.* New York: Author.

NAZZARO, J. (1974). Head Start for the handicapped—What's been accomplished? *Exceptional Children, 41,* 103–109.

O'KEEFE, R. A. (1979). What Head Start means to families. In L. G. Katz (Ed.), *Current topics in early childhood education* (Vol. 2, pp. 43–68). Norwood, NJ: Ablex.

OMWAKE, E. B. (1979). Assessment of the Head Start preschool education effort. In E. Zigler & J. Valentine (Eds.), *Project Head Start* (pp. 221–228). New York: The Free Press.

QUILLITCH, H. R., & RISLEY, T. R. (1973). The effects of play materials on social play. *Journal of Applied Behavior Analysis, 6,* 573–578.

RAMEY, C. T., STEDMAN, D. J., BORDERS-BATTERSON, A., & MENGEL, W. (1978). Predicting school failure from information available at birth. *American Journal of Mental Deficiency, 82,* 525–534.

RICHMOND, J. B., STIPEK, D. J., & ZIGLER, E. (1979). A decade of Head Start. In E. Zigler & J. Valentine (Eds.), *Project Head Start,* (pp. 135–152). New York: Free Press.

RISLEY, T. (1972). Spontaneous language and the preschool environment. In J. C. Stanley (Ed.), *Preschool programs for the disadvantaged* (pp. 92–110). Baltimore, MD: Johns Hopkins University Press.

SCHAEFER, E. S. (1969). A home tutoring program. *Children, 16,* 59–61.

SCHAEFER, E. S. (1972). Parents as educators: Evidence from cross-sectional longitudinal and intervention research. *Young Children, 27,* 222–239.

SCHAEFER, E. S., & AARONSON, M. (1977). Infant education research project: Implementation and implications of the home-tutoring program. In R. K. Parker (Ed.), *The preschool in action* (2nd ed.) (pp. 51–72). Boston, MA: Allyn & Bacon.

SCHWEINHART, L. J., & WEIKART, D. P. (1981). *Young children grow up: The effects of the Perry Preschool Program on youths through age 15.* Ypsilanti, MI: High/Scope Press.

SMITH, M. S., & BISSELL, J. S. (1970). Report analysis: The impact of Head Start. *Harvard Educational Review, 40,* 51–104.

SNYDER, L., APOLLONI, T., & COOKE, T. P. (1977). Integrated settings at the early childhood level: the role of nonretarded peers. *Exceptional Children, 43,* 262–266.

SPICKER, H. H. (1971). Intellectual development through early childhood education. *Exceptional Children, 37*(9), 629–642.

THOMAS, A. (1981). Current trends in developmental theory. *American Journal of Orthopsychiatry, 51,* 580–610.

THORPE, H. S. (1972). *The Thorpe Developmental Inventory: Ages three to six years, instructional manual.* Davis: Office of Medical Education, University of California at Davis, School of Medicine.

TRICKETT, P. K. (1979). Career development in Head Start. In E. Zigler & J. Valentine (Eds.), *Project Head Start* (pp. 315–336). New York: The Free Press.

ULLMAN, D. G., & KAUSCH, D. F. (1979). Early identification of developmental strengths and weaknesses in preschool children. *Exceptional Children, 46,* 8–13.

WEBER, D. U., FOSTER, P. P., & WEIKART, D. P. (1978). *An economic analysis of the Ypsilanti Perry Preschool Project* (Monographs of the High/Scope Educational Research Foundation, Number 5). Ypsilanti, MI: High/Scope Research Foundation.

WEIKART, D. P. (1972). Relationship of curriculum, teaching, and learning in preschool education. In J. C. Stanley (Ed.), *Preschool programs for the disadvantaged* (pp. 22–66). Baltimore, MD: Johns Hopkins University Press.

WEIKART, D. P., BOND, J. T., & McNEIL, J. T. (1978). *The Ypsilanti Perry Preschool Project: Preschool years and longitudinal results through the fourth grade* (Monographs of the High/Scope Educational Research Foundation, Number 3). Ypsilanti, MI: High/Scope Research Foundation.

WELLMAN, B. L. (1943). The effects of preschool attendance upon intellectual development. In R. G. Barker, J. S. Kounin, & H. F. Wright (Eds.) *Child behavior and de-*

velopment (pp. 229–244). New York: Mc-Graw-Hill.

Westinghouse Learning Corporation/Ohio University. (1969). *The Impact of Head Start: An evaluation of the effects of Head Start on children's cognitive and affective development* (Vols. 1 & 2). Springfield, VA: Clearinghouse for Federal Scientific and Technical Information, U.S. Department of Commerce.

WHITE, B. L. (1968). Informal education during the first months of life. In R. D. Hess & R. M. Baer (Eds.), *Early education* (pp. 143–170). Chicago, Aldine.

WHITE, B. L. (1975). *The first three years of life.* Englewood Cliffs, NJ: Prentice-Hall.

WHITE, B. L., & HELD, R. (1964). Plasticity of sensory-motor development in the young infant. In J. F. Rosenblith & W. Allinsmith (Eds.), *The causes of behavior: Readings in child development and educational psychology* (2nd ed.) (pp. 60–70). New York: Allyn and Bacon.

WHITE, S. H. (1970). The National Impact Study of Head Start. In J. Hellmuth (Ed.), *The disadvantaged child: Vol. 3. Compensatory education: A national debate* (pp. 163–184). New York: Brunner/Mazel.

ZEHRBACH, R. R. (1975). Determining a preschool handicapped population. *Exceptional Children, 42,* 76–83.

ZIGLER, E., & BUTTERFIELD, E. (1968). Motivational aspects of changes in IQ test performance of culturally deprived nursery school children. *Child Development, 39,* 1–14.

ZIGLER, E., & TRICKETT, P. K. (1978). Social competence and evaluation of early childhood intervention programs. *American Psychologist, 33,* 789–797.

CHAPTER 5

PERSPECTIVES
OF THE YOUNG CHILD

This chapter is a review of certain aspects of early development that are important in evaluating and understanding clinical problems. With very few exceptions, abnormal psychological processes are drawn from psychological processes that are appropriate at younger ages. Abnormal behavior may appear as an inability to master the next level or as a regression to an earlier stage. Emotional conflicts in the older child may produce the illogical thinking and fantasies commonplace in the young child. In the case of the psychotic person, primitive mental processes invade the total personality. A full appreciation of normal psychological development is crucial for the assessment of individual children, and effective intervention requires empathy for both the parents' and the child's viewpoints. The importance of understanding the past is not

simply to pinpoint possible causes but to facilitate therapeutic communication in the present.

In this chapter we consider the perspectives of the young child. Writing about developmental factors in child behavior therapy, Harris and Ferrari commented that

We make a gross error if we assume that because a youngster was standing next to us, heard what we heard, saw what we saw, and used our words, that we share a commonly understood experience. It behooves us as therapists and researchers to understand these differences in perception, so that we can translate our therapeutic intent into terms that will effect change in the child. (1983, p. 56)

Although young children are very observant and have a good memory for what they have seen or heard, their understanding of events is distorted by their characteristic ways of thinking as well as by their limited life experience. The differences in their understanding of reality legitimize anxiety and anger responses for them, however illogical these responses may seem to adult observers.

Relatively speaking, there is more description and theory than research to report. We owe a debt of gratitude to Jean Piaget for providing some insight into the thought processes of the very young child. His chronological age references sometimes miss the mark but he never attempted to provide "norms" by which to judge children. His goal was rather to explicate the evolution of logical reason from its roots in sensorimotor experiences to its culmination in formal operations. Like the child psychoanalysts, he used observation of infants and patient questioning of young children to reconstruct what we as adults cannot remember. The value of these observations is timeless, and it would be a serious error to dismiss them either on the basis of questions about the value of psychoanalysis as a method of treatment, or debates about the exact beginnings and ends of the cognitive stages described by Piaget.

CONSTRUCTION OF REALITY

Discovery of the Physical Self

While the observer sees the infant as a separate entity, the infant has no conception of where she ends and the environment begins. The first distinction between "self" and "not-self" is made on the basis of physical boundaries. One of the first parts of self which the baby recognizes as such is the hands. Many times during the early months, the infant catches sight of her hands as they move across her field of vision; she follows their movement just as she follows any moving object that comes into sight. Touch provides another source of information. The fingers of one hand discover the fingers of the other, so that she touches herself and is touched simultaneously. Gradually she learns to do this in front of her eyes and can watch, feel, and be felt. Sometime around the third month, she learns that her hands are always with her, in contrast to other things that come and go, and derives a sense of the permanence and predictability of her hands. From this evolves the notion that these are part of oneself. This is a first lesson in self-discovery, crucial to the task of differentiating between the inner and outer worlds. One can observe children with profound ego retardation or regression, playing with their fingers in front of their eyes with the same absorption and fascination of a baby in this early stage of discovery. In normal development, it is a quick step from viewing the hands as playthings to using them as tools. The growing ability to grasp things and examine them at leisure provides yet another opportunity to learn what belongs to the self and what does not.

Object Permanence

Piaget introduced the concept of "object permanence," a major step in differentiating self from not-self, as the infant comes to realize that objects exist even when out of sight or hearing. This is easily demonstrated by the purposive searching efforts the baby makes when something is hidden from view or rolls out of sight. At about the same time, around 7 or 8 months, many infants show a definite anxiety reaction at the mere sight of a stranger, particularly if the stranger resembles the mother. This is not a response learned from prior frightening experiences but rather a developmental anxiety that emerges with the realization that this is not the mother and that the mother (as object) still exists somewhere. This is a good illustration of the reciprocal relationship between cognitive and emotional development. Progress in the perception of reality permits the baby to form more meaningful attachments to specific persons; the converse is also true—the attachment to familiar persons prompts the baby to think about them, remember them, search for them, reject substitutes, and wait for their return.

Although some anxiety with a stranger persists for some time, particularly in the absence of the mother (see discussion of Strange Situation in Chapter 1), the 1-year-old is much less immobilized than the infant. Also, as discussed in connection with the congenitally blind child, the realization that things exist even when out of sight gives rise to the curiosity for which the toddler is famous and serves as an incentive for mobility and active exploration.

Repetition and Imitation

Piaget described the early pleasure in repetition that offers some predictability in a world of shifting sights and sounds. Much of the baby's activity—staring, listening, and reaching—helps to hold onto objects, to preserve images for longer periods of time, and to postpone the helplessness of losing them. The infant's obvious pleasure in recognition and repetition conveys the strong impression that they are highly rewarding. This evidence of infant activity and pleasure in the absence of primary need satisfaction or social reinforcement has led theoreticians to postulate motivations such as "urge to mastery" (Hendrick, 1943), "competence motivation" (White, 1959), and "motivation inherent in information processing and action" (Hunt, 1963). Although the infant's orienting system selects novel stimuli for attention from the first few days of life (see Chapter 1), it is not long before he shows obvious pleasure in the reappearance of familiar sights and sounds which, of course, confirms the permanence of their existence.

Around 8 months, imitation begins, prolonging interesting sights and sounds. Initially, the baby is limited to the sounds and gestures already in his or her repertoire of behavior; the baby cannot learn to play pattycake before clapping the hands at the midline, for instance. The mother makes something out of the self-initiated behavior and gives it social meaning. The child learns to please the mother by clapping in response to her signals. Failure to respond to this kind of social stimulation is often a first sign of the developmental disorder known as "autism." In his description of the stages of imitative behavior, Piaget noted that when the child is capable of repeating movements he or she has already made but which he or she cannot see (e.g., sticking out the tongue), there are efforts to copy sounds and gestures to which the baby has been indifferent. The baby's urgent wish to do as others do fosters a tremendous amount of self-instruction.

Imitation is as much a cornerstone of personality as of intellect. The new skills the toddler acquires through imitation are obvious ones. Bandura (1974) described this as learning by observation. "The capacity to represent modeled activities symbolically enables man to acquire new patterns of behavior observationally without reinforced enactment. From observing others, one forms an idea of how certain behavior is performed, and on later occasions the coded information serves as a guide for action" (p. 863). The stored memories, acting as templates for future behavior, encompass more than bits of specific action. Imitation is a copying of another's specific actions; identification is based on a deferred and more comprehensive imitation that includes the feelings as well as the behavior. Over time, the baby develops a comprehensive gestalt of beloved and well-known persons, which remains as an "internal representation" when the person is absent. The older child uses these representations as a guide for behavior both in terms of what to do and what not to do. It is an interesting question when considering caretaking arrangements as to how many such internal representations can be formed in the developing mind of the young child. The completeness of the image will depend on the attachment and extent of familiarization; there is some relationship with the sheer amount of time spent in caring for the baby. The long-lasting nature of these early identifications makes it imperative to know the characteristics of the significant caretakers if one is to have a complete understanding of the older child's personality.

Comprehension of Language

As mentioned in Chapter 3, language is not simply the articulation of sounds. The primary purpose of language is communication with other people; language includes facial expression and gestures as well as sounds. The hearing child, however, early discovers the advantages of sounds for making things happen, particularly for making the mother reappear. (It would be valuable to have more information than we do about the "calling" system of deaf infants in the first year.) Since the child must have some language comprehension before he or she speaks, the receptive side of speech development merits consideration before we look at expressive speech.

Spoken words first become significant because of the accompanying tone or gesture and the familiarity of their context. Toddlers quickly learn to recognize "no, no," or "hot" said in a special way, but they will ignore the words if the negative command voice is not used. Babies recognize the cue words that precede routine activities such as eating, going outside, or going to bed, but the cue words are recognized only in association with sights that remind them of what is about to happen. By the end of the first years, the baby shows some response to words such as "give me" or "show me," but there is little understanding of the words per se. Initially, the baby is not far different from the well-trained dog that, signaled by cue words, can go through a repertoire of tricks. The child has learned an auditory discrimination and paired this stimulus with a predictable outcome. Soon the child learns to connect certain sounds with objects rather than with actions.

At the same time that the child is learning to differentiate sounds and their meanings, he or she learns to make a similar differentiation between objects and their uses. In the first year, the child treats all objects as if they were the same, handling them in accordance with the latest motor achievement—mouthing, banging, throwing, or whatever. Early in the second year, object uses are discriminated. Food or eating utensils go to the mouth; the ball is thrown; blocks are stacked; the pencil is used for marking. The recognition of objects and their specific uses is a process parallel to the discrimination between words and the recollection of the associations between them and activities or objects.

The first meaningful words that refer to objects are frequently the parts of the body. At first, the child must point these out in a certain order, and a familiar person must do the asking. Then he makes a transfer of this knowledge and can point out the same parts of the body on a person other than himself, and in any order. At around 18 months, he takes another step in generalization and can point out the parts of a doll's body. At about 2, he takes a truly giant step and can identify parts of the body on a two-dimensional representation, a drawing of a person. The child's understanding of these words is now as abstract as that of an adult.

Development of Spoken Language

In the first year, two processes that later coalesce into spoken speech go on concomitantly. One is the child's play with sounds; the other, his prelinguistic signals, cries, and gestures. In babbling, the child is experimenting with the kinesthetic and tactile sensations of the oral apparatus. Simply for the pleasure of feeling, his lips and tongue move into different positions. In addition, the infant learns that his sounds produce an effect on his environment; also, when he realizes that the sounds are produced by himself, he listens and tries to make the auditory perceptions persist by self-imitation. Additional insight into this early phase of speech development was provided by the circumstances of World War II. Anna Freud and her co-workers observed a number of infants who were reared in residential nurseries because their homes had been destroyed (1944). They observed that the vocalizations of children under 1 year were normal in extent and kind but that these same children were verbally backward by their second birthday. This suggested that vocalization in the first year is stimulated by different influences than in the second year.

Snow (1984) identified two principles of language acquisition as especially obvious during the first year: (a) adults interpret child behaviors as attempts to communicate, even in situations where it is quite obvious that no explicit intention to communicate exists; and (b) children search for contingencies between salient objects, persons, and events in the world and the behavior of their caregivers. "These two principles, operating together, create a situation in which maximum correspondence is attained between the child's focus of attention and the caretaker's communicative behaviors" (1984, p. 72). Game playing (e.g., pat-a-cake and peek-a-boo) and social routines (e.g., "hi" and "bye-bye") are highlights of social-linguistic interaction for the infant and parent.

It is not easy to determine exactly when the child begins to talk. It is traditionally thought that the child's first word is usually "mama" or "dada," but this is probably more in the ear of the parent than in the mind of the child. Many toddlers use a syllabic combination to convey all kinds of feelings and intentions. One child, of 15 months, could ask questions, say "no," express delight, and announce his hunger, by modifying the tone and inflection with which he said "gaga." The "word" at this juncture is a tool to get the adult to do something, similar in structure to the child's use of a stick to pull something closer.

Dale (1972) commented that "Disentangling emotional expression from denotative meaning is a major achievement in language learning. 'Mama' originally meant 'food' or 'delicious' or 'hungry' to Hildegard; undoubtedly all were said to her mother, who was either feeding her or desired to do so. For Hildegard, the meaning of mama was a combination of emotion, desire, and name. Only after several months did 'mama' come to refer to a person" (p. 39).

A gigantic step is taken in the second year when the child starts to name things for the sake of naming. The child will name an object, person, or animal simply to indicate that she or he knows the object and to communicate the mere fact of observation. In emphasizing the importance of this step, Terrace (1985) contrasted animal and human learning.

In many instances, the child refers to the object in question spontaneously and shows no interest in obtaining it. The child not only appears to enjoy sharing information with his or her parent but also appears to derive intrinsic pleasure from the sheer act of naming. . . . these aspects of uttering a name have not been observed in apes, and there is reason to doubt whether the most intensive training program imaginable could produce an ape that would approximate a child's natural ability to refer to objects as an end in itself. (1985, p. 1017)

Many years ago, Church also discussed the intrinsic pleasure in naming:

Sometimes the child names objects as a way of communicating with adults; he enjoys the adult's pleasure and approval, and he enjoys the very fact of communication. Some of the child's naming activity seems to be a request for verification: 'Is this a. . . . ?' rather than 'This is a. . . '. Finally, the child names things to himself, just as though exercising a skill. (1961, p. 62)

He added that "it seems likely that the toddler's insatiable hunger for names reflects the sense of possession and domination of the object that knowing its name gives him" (1961, p. 74).

When the child has the general idea that everything has a name, he or she either asks the adult for this label by pointing or saying "whatzat," or picks it up silently by hearing words used in context. This was termed the "Original Word Game" by Roger Brown: "In simple concrete terms the tutor says 'dog' whenever a dog appears. The player (i.e., the child who is learning) notes the equivalence of these utterances, forms a hypothesis about the nonlinguistic category (i.e., the external object or activity) that elicits this kind of utterance, and then tries naming a few dogs himself" (1956, p. 285). The child is by no means a passive learner who must be spoon-fed each name by deliberate effort on his parents' part; he is active in making the connections between word and object or word and activity.

There is no single explanation for the acquisition of language, but there has been heated debate on the relative importance of contributing factors (Piattelli-Palmarini, 1980). Behaviorist explanations in terms of reinforcement by approval or specific outcomes will not account for the development of language comprehension nor the tremendous acceleration of language in the second year. Imitation clearly plays a part but again does not explain comprehension, and many of the very earliest utterances of children cannot be viewed as imitations or even reduced imitations of adult speech.

The species-specific character of language development and the similar course followed by young children in all kinds of cultures requires some kind of biological basis. Chomsky minimized the significance of the environment in his emphasis on the role of innate language structures (1968). In his view, the environment serves only to provide the raw data, the forms of the particular language that a child will learn. In the Piagetian framework, language acquisition is a matter of the child's figuring out which linguistic devices will express what he already knows nonlinguistically. Meanings are allegedly used to decipher language, an interpretation that has become known as the "strong cognition hypothesis" (Macnamara, 1972). This may explain the initial stages of language acquisition but it seems insufficient to explain the later acceleration. Clearly, a biological predisposition, reinforcement, modeling, and cognition are all involved to varying degrees at various stages.

Although the vast majority of children "pick up" language without special help, probably reflecting biological readiness, there are significant differences in the skill and sophistication of language usage which reflect environmental as well as constitutional differences. In her succinct review of the current issues, Rice (1982) cited recent research showing the facilitative effects of adult responses which are "semantically contingent" with the child's utterance; for example, a repetition, expansion, clarification, comment, or affirmation. This kind of response takes advantage of the child's attention and is yet another example of the importance of following up on the initiatitve of the child.

Studies in the 1930's and 1940's provided consistent evidence that girls talk earlier (McCarthy, 1954), but recent research suggested that there were no sex differences (Maccoby & Jacklin, 1974). The discrepancy in findings may be explained by the particular measures used. Schachter, Shore, Hodapp, Chalfin, and Bundy (1978) used the "old" measures and found that girls at 24 months did indeed surpass same-aged boys in mean length of utterance (close to two words) and length of longest utterance (4.7 words). It would be more accurate to say that girls talk more rather than that they talk earlier.

There is a snowball effect in learning language; after a slow start, verbal development accelerates rapidly in the second half of the second year. Vocabulary increases sevenfold between 12 and 18 months and twelvefold between 18 and 24 months (Smith, 1926). There is a corresponding increase in loquacity; the child of 2 years uses words much more frequently and reliably than the 18-month-old. Also in this period words are combined into sentences, many of which represent novel combinations rather than repetitions of adult speech. Cross-cultural studies of early child syntax have shown a uniformity supporting the biological position. The child generates grammatical rules for making plurals or past tense which often do not fit what they have heard. Not only are new combinations created, but new words. One 3-year-old decided against taking her favorite doll to nursery school because "it was too fightable," a very sensible decision. On the other hand, the young child also begins to detect linguistic carelessness, as witness a 4-year-old who corrected her mother for buying "grass seed" instead of "grass seeds."

We should consider what speech might mean to the child. It is easier to see what the ability to walk means because it is a relatively sudden acquisition and the child shows obvious pleasure in it by wanting to walk all the time. Talking appears more gradually and in the beginning the child uses speech almost frugally. These sounds seem to have the magic power of making something happen. The toddler is something like the traveler in a foreign country. The sounds of a foreign language are

mysterious, and the stranger usually hesitates to experiment with the few words he may know. There is the danger of being misunderstood and of setting something undesirable in motion.

Freud was one of the first to call attention to the tremendous power that the very young child ascribes to speech. "The child's earliest speech is a charm directed toward forcing the external world and fate to do those things that have been conjured up in words" (Fenichel, 1945, p. 46). Church spoke of "word realism": "Word realism is sometimes interpreted narrowly to mean the child thinks of the name as somehow inherent in the thing named, but this is only one of its manifestations. Its central manifestation is in the power that words have over us, and the sense of power over reality that words give us" (1961, p. 74).

The child's first words are usually so effective that some "unlearning" must take place before he or she realizes that words, per se, do not reshape reality. The toddler will try to change things by verbal fiat. The author reviewed a clinical record in which a 3-year-old child was diagnosed as schizophrenic because she described seeing and talking with her mother, who had been deceased for some time. The unfortunate consequence of this diagnosis was placement in a residential institution where she remained until adolescence. Although this might be considered evidence of delusional thinking in an adult person, a mental health professional sensitive to the magic power that young children give to the spoken word would appreciate the child's strong wish to bring her mother back alive.

Vestiges of this period of development can be seen in normal people as well as in disturbed or psychotic persons. Many people are superstitious about voicing an unpleasant possibility; they fear that to express a possible misfortune may make it more likely. If they happen to use an unlucky word referring to death, accidents, or illness, they promptly knock on wood in order to undo the damage that the words might cause. The primitive belief in the magic of thought and word is closely allied to denial, a psychological mechanism whereby painful sensations and facts are said not to exist. If denial is applied wholesale to large segments of the outside world, the falsification of reality that follows reduces the person's competence, perhaps even to the extent of a psychosis.

Distortions in the use of words are frequently observed in obsessive-compulsive disorders and in schizophrenics. The obsessive-compulsive individual, like the young child, overvalues words. Certain words become taboo and others become talismans. Yet the obsessive-compulsive person remains aware of the usual meanings and has some insight into his idiosyncracies. The schizophrenic patient lacks this insight, however, and may restructure his language so that it loses its value as a form of communication.

Characteristics of Early Thought

Crucial differences appear between 2 and 5 years in the nature of reasoning processes. It is difficult to converse with a 2- or 3-year-old. Although the language sounds like that of the adult, it is not being used in what one would call a logical way. An example is the following verbatim conversation with a 3-year-old:

SARAH: (very pleased). I found my purse (which had been lost for several months.)

MOTHER: Where did you find it?

SARAH: On the floor in John's room.

MOTHER: How did it get there?

SARAH: (with great conviction). The sun put it there.

MOTHER: How did the sun put it there?

SARAH: With his prindles.

MOTHER: I'm not sure I understand what prindles are.

SARAH: You know, like the pine cones.

MOTHER: You mean the sun puts the pine cones on the ground too?

SARAH: No, just purses. You know, the sun has a face.

MOTHER: But where was the purse before it was on the floor in John's room?

SARAH: I don't know.

An important principle in understanding the vagaries of child thought is that of "egocentrism," initially described by Piaget. Briefly, the idea is that the child's view of the world depends on his own activity. This does not imply selfishness, or even self-consciousness; egocentrism is the absence of both self-perception and objectivity. The child cannot conceive of anything beyond his own experiences and his own feelings. He assumes that everyone and everything shares the identical experiences with him and at the same moment; he cannot detach himself from his particular vantage point and put himself in the position of another person. For example, Alice, age 18 months, was drinking from a dark cup with a high glaze. She saw herself in the bottom of the cup and said, "Hi, Ayah!" to herself, then handed the cup around to the others present and told them to say "Hi" to Ayah. Clearly, she did not appreciate the fact that they would see a different reflection. A familiar example can be observed when a 2-year-old plays hide-and-go-seek by closing his eyes, saying, in effect, "I can't see you; therefore I know you can't see me."

Egocentrism is not outgrown all at once. The child may become conscious of himself and aware of the relativity of his own point of view in one area, yet remain subjective (i.e., egocentric) in another. Piaget and Inhelder (1956) demonstrated this with children of 4 to 6. Each child was presented with a model representing three mountains in relief. He was then asked which of a number of colored pictures showed the mountains from the point of view of a doll that was placed in successive positions in the mountains in the model. The younger ones considered their own perspective absolute, the same no matter where the doll was placed. As an example of the "revisionist movement" Borke (1975) repeated this experiment and found that 67% of the 4-year-olds gave correct responses and also that they were uniformly more successful when asked to find the correct three-dimensional display rather than to select a pictorial representation. This does not change the validity of the concept, particularly for 2-year-olds, but it does indicate that egocentrism is not an all-or-none phenomenon.

The phenomena of perspective-taking have been studied extensively, not only from the standpoint of perceptual perspectives but also in reference to role-taking and "referential communication," that is, the ability to explain events to someone who is not or was not an eye-witness to the scene (Glucksberg, Krauss, & Weisberg, 1966). As the child learns to distinguish between his own viewpoint and that of others, he takes less for granted and can adjust his speech to what the listener needs to know. Everyone is familiar with the difficulties of communicating with young children via the telephone. For example, the author called her daughter's home and when a voice said "Hello," she asked "Who is this?" The reply "It's you, Nana" gave a good clue that it was the 3-year-old and not the 8-year-old who had answered.

Egocentrism is closely linked with animistic, or anthropomorphic thinking. Animism is the belief that objects are alive and endowed with will; it ascribes to objects and animals the same feelings and intentions as a person. A little girl of 2, having poked a hole in a piece of paper with her pencil, started to cry because the paper felt hurt. A little boy cried out, "Poor zweiback!" when the biscuit was broken into halves. Sometimes parents subscribe to this way of thinking as a way of offering reassurance but achieve the opposite result. For instance, a little girl of 2, who had a great fear of vacuum cleaners, visited her grandmother and immediately asked where the vacuum cleaner was. The grandmother replied that she need not worry because "It is in the closet taking a nap." After a moment's silent reflection, the child began to cry in terror. The fanciful explanation had not allayed her fears, because anything which can sleep, can also wake up, can walk around, and anything which can walk around can get very angry and be very dangerous!

As a mode of thinking, egocentrism is related to projection. Piaget remarked that egocentrism has two sides: suggestibility, which is a kind of identification with the behavior or feelings of someone else; and a projection of the ego into someone or something outside (1945, 1951). Psychoanalysts reserve the term "projection" to describe a particular defense mechanism whereby unpleasant feelings or wishes are attributed to someone other than the self, so that the individual feels, "It is not I who thinks or feels in such and such a way; it is the other person." The paranoid patient, whose ability to test reality is severely distorted, produces the most extreme projective misinterpretation of reality. Paranoid narcissism, like the narcissism of the young child, sees the universe as revolving around the person, either to hurt or help (i.e., megalomania), and all happenings are personified in terms of projected wishes and fears. But the adult's thinking, unlike that of the young child, is not open to correction by subsequent experience with reality.

Progression from egocentrism requires that the child become aware that he or she thinks, feels, sees, and hears from a point of view unique to him or her self. The child needs a dual perspective, so that he or she not only perceives reality but is aware of him or herself perceiving. This awareness of self is achieved by the process of socialization. Thoughts and experiences must be socially shared before the differences in viewpoints are exposed. Discussing the functions of language, Piaget described the central role of socialization:

Intelligence, just because it undergoes a gradual process of socialization, is enabled through the bond established by language between thoughts and words to make an increasing use of concepts; whereas autism, just because it remains individual, is still tied to imagery, to organic activity and even to organic movements. The mere fact, then, of telling one's thought, of telling it to others, or of keeping silence and telling it only to oneself must be of enormous importance to the fundamental structure and functioning of thought in general, and of child logic in particular. (1955, p. 26)

In another context, the construction of reality in the child, Piaget commented:

It is by cooperation with another person that the mind arrives at verifying judgments, verification implying a presentation or an exchange and having in itself no meaning as regards individual activity. Whether conceptual thought is rational because it is social or vice versa, the interdependence of the search for truth and of socialization seems to us undeniable. (1954, pp. 360–361)

Normally, by listening and talking, the child discovers his mental self. In the first year of life, he or she learned to distinguish body boundaries; a similar differentiation has to be made in respect to mental boundaries. When the child relinquishes the naive assumption of the identity of his perceptions and feelings and those of other people and objects, he or she begins to wonder about the true nature of this outside world. The mental curiosity of the intelligent 3- and 4-year-old parallels the investigative curiosity of the toddler. As long as he or she operates solely on egocentric assumptions, there is no need to ask questions.

For the very young child, anything is possible. All things imaginable are equally possible; the thought is father to the reality. The child takes no cognizance of differences between animate and inanimate objects nor of differences in size. Young children cannot see, upon inspection, that one object may be much too large to be contained within another. The child who stuffs things into the toilet has to do it over and over, exploring the possibility of flushing down every kind of household object, before he or she is satisfied that some things, including him or herself, are simply too large to disappear down the toilet. One experience does not immediately convince a 2-year-old of any general fact—if this white shoe won't go down, maybe a red one will. The same process can be observed as the child plays with toys. The 2-year-old, hard at work trying to put a round peg into a square hole, turns the peg upside down, turns the square hole around, takes the peg in the other hand and pushes harder. There is no appreciation that the causes of failure rests in the physical properties of the objects, so the child attempts to accomplish the impossible by sheer determination. By the time the child is 3, he or she can perceive gross differences in size and shape at a glance and adjust accordingly.

The Impact of Television

The 2-year-old accords to dreams, make-believe, stories, or television programs the same respect he accords to reality. And, if one considers the whimsies of television, one can get a feel for the child's conception of the world. It is reported that preschoolers watch television on the average of 4 hours a day (Singer & Singer, 1981). We have yet to understand the full impact on development. Television provides verbal and visual stimulation to the smallest child in a way that has never before been a part of human experience. Singer (1983) asked: "Is it possible that our daily reliance on the television medium . . . has led to a change in how we think, what we think about, and how hard we are willing to work to extract information from other communication media?" (p. 815). It is surprising that mental health professionals seem to have a blind spot for this aspect of a child's home life; at least it is rare to make any inquiry about the child's viewing habits. It is assumed that all children watch TV, but when, what, how much and with whom?

Investigators distinguish between the form and the content of television programming. Most of the research has had to do with the latter, particularly the effects of viewing television violence. A 1982 update of the 1972 Surgeon General's Report on Television and Social Behavior in general confirmed the evidence of a significant, although weak, causal relationship between television viewing and later aggressive behavior (Rubinstein, 1983). Alternative explanations such as aggressive children preferring violent programs, or imitating aggressive parents who prefer violent programs, have not explained away the findings (Singer & Singer, 1981). Despite the evidence, the 10-year update report indicated that no significant reduction in violence levels in programming took place in the interim.

The formal features are the auditory and visual production and editing techniques characterizing the medium. "Information is organized and represented by visual features, such as cuts, pans, dissolves, and special effects; auditory features such as music, sound effects, dialogue, and laugh tracks; and more molar characteristics such as pacing (rates of scene and character change), physical movement (action), and variation" (Wright & Huston, 1983, p. 836). Wright and Huston commented that at a perceptual level, the forms of children's programs appear even to the casual observer to involve intense sensory bombardment and a rapidly changing set of images. Educational programs, however, are different not only in content but also in form, with considerably lower levels of pacing, frenetic activity, loud music, and sound effects—and considerably more dialogue.

Singer and Singer (1983) summarized the findings on 84 children studied over a period from ages 4 through 9 years as follows:

The following combination of television and family variables puts a child at risk for problematic behavior by early elementary school age: (a) a home in which television viewing of an uncontrolled type is emphasized; (b) heavy viewing of television in the preschool years; (c) more recent heavy viewing of violent programming; (d) parents who themselves emphasize physical force as a means of discipline; and (e) parents whose self-descriptions or values do not stress imagination, curiosity, or creativity, traits that might offer alternatives to the direct imitation of the television content or to reliance on television as major source of entertainment. (p. 831)

The fact that heavy viewing, and some associated family variables, predicted difficulties in the ability to sit quietly in a simulated astronaut test and during a natural waiting situation (amongst other outcomes) suggests a link with the "attention disorder" so often reported in school-age children and commonly ascribed to a vague neurological deficit (see Chapter 10). Clearly, monitoring television viewing in the preschool years has preventive potential.

Compared to books, television is far more realistic, but parents are likely to be more casual about what the child sees on the screen than what he might see on the printed page. With a full appreciation of the reality accorded to television, one might take greater care. The positive value of television as a teaching medium is well documented by the research of Ball and Bogatz (1972) on the effects of viewing "Sesame Street," but this is not the only program watched by preschoolers! Singer and Singer (1983) commented that on the whole, direct intervention with parents built primarily around cutting down the viewing patterns of their children are largely unavailing. "Instead we have been forced to recognize that the baby-sitting function of television is so attractive and pervasive for parents, both in middle and lower socioeconomic groups, that we have had to turn our attention in other directions to intervene" (p. 830). These intervention efforts have been designed to encourage the parents to explain what the children are seeing and to practice "co-viewing" as often as possible. In addition, lesson plans have been developed to learn how television works. There is much to learn from and about television.

Causal Thinking

At the same time that the preschool child is learning to discriminate the "possible" from the "impossible," the child is formulating some cause-and-effect relationships. The first causal explanations are in terms of the child's over-valuation of his own words and thoughts. When a child's efforts result in repeated disappointments, he or she is forced to conclude that his or her powers are limited and that everything cannot be controlled by words or wishes.

The next step is attributing the magic properties and powers to another person, usually the parent. One 3-year-old was infuriated by the refusal of his blocks to remain standing. Suddenly he turned to his mother and said, "Say 'stand up'!" It takes more time for the child to forego the belief in the parent's omnipotence. It is, after all, a great comfort to believe that even if one personally is helpless, there is someone else who can control what happens. Some of the irritation that children express against their parents probably stems from a mistaken belief in their parents' responsibility for disappointments and frustrations. Other characters too may be endowed with great power; for instance, many preschoolers consider the weather man to be responsible for making the weather.

Another causal explanation is in terms of temporal connections. Many times it is correct to explain a later event on the basis of an earlier one, but the young child overdoes it. He applies this *post hoc, ergo propter hoc* reasoning to all situations and makes no discrimination between chance circumstances and essential causes. This leads to the rigid conservatism typical of the 2- or 3-year-old. Custom becomes law, and any departure from the usual routines is regarded with suspicion. Rituals are developed where nothing is irrelevant— the whole sequence stands or falls as one piece. The child who insists on a glass of milk, one cookie, and one scraped carrot at his bedside is not necessarily hungry. It is as if he says, "When I had these things before and went to sleep, everything was all right. If I have these things again and go to sleep, everything will be all right again." The child's passion for sameness is more than a simple error in judgment; the determination behind it stems from the feeling of helplessness. It is an effort to make life predictable, and it involves a method which will be used until the child can predict on the basis of more advanced comprehension. This mode of causal thinking is not entirely discarded by adult persons; it reappears in states of emotional distress or ignorance. The obsessive-compulsive individual is often as rigid as the young child, although with the insight to consider the habits as "superstitions."

The 4-year-old is famous for his persistent "why" questions, many of which are unanswerable. He believes that everything must have a reason and that his omniscient parents know all the answers. The idea of chance is absent from the child's thought. "Every event can be accounted for by its surroundings," or "Everything is connected with everything else," might be the tenets of this creed. The child will find a justification at any price. As he or she expects an answer from others, so the child, if asked why, will invent an answer. Freud stated the universal problem thus:

There is an intellectual function in us which demands unity, connection, and intelligibility from any material, whether of perception or thought, that comes within its grasp; and if, as a result of special circumstance it is unable to establish a true connection, it does not hesitate to fabricate a false one. (1913, 1955, p. 95)

The younger, the less logical, the more primitive, or the more disturbed the person, the more easily will he or she find causes. Acceptance of the answer "One cannot know" requires a lot of sophistication.

At 4 years, or thereabouts, the child stands at the threshold of adult modes of thought. He or she accepts the fact that there is an important difference between reality and imagination, although the two will be confused from time to time. In this respect, he or she is no worse off than the adult who substitutes thoughts and feelings for facts, especially in areas of ignorance or emotional involvement. At least, the child now knows the difference and can make some separation between the two. He or she can now appreciate the fanciful, the make-believe, and the humorous as belonging to the exaggerations and unrealities afforded by the world of play. On the other hand, he or she can appreciate the importance of information, the relatedness of facts, and the communication of ideas for verification. He or she is interested in the acquisition of knowledge as well as in pretending.

DEVELOPMENTAL ASPECTS OF ANXIETY

Some authors make a distinction between fear and anxiety on the basis that the former is "real," that is, justified by the external circumstances. However, the response feelings are identical and it is very difficult to say what is "justified" by reality, particularly for young children. No such distinction will be attempted in the following discussion.

Some fears arise from direct association with a terrifying or unpleasant event following the classical conditioning paradigm first described by Pavlov (1928). The classic case of "little Albert" who was conditioned to fear a white rat by linking it with a loud, unpleasant noise is often cited (Watson & Rayner, 1920). The original data on this case has been carefully reviewed by Harris (1979) and Samelson (1980) who not only pointed out inconsistencies in reporting of the data but also described some little-known facts. The conditioning experiments were carried out over a 4-month period between the ages of 9 and 13 months, and at least for some of this time, Albert was in a hospital for undefined reasons. Apparently he was not ill since his mother gave a month's notice for his returning home. Another incidental observation quoted by Samelson was that whenever Albert was emotionally upset, he would "continually thrust his thumb into his mouth . . . (thus becoming) impervious to the stimuli producing fear. Again and again . . . (while making the movie) we had to remove the thumb from his mouth before the conditioned response could be obtained" (Watson & Rayner, 1920, p. 13). Over the span of years, this poignant observation of little

Albert's remarkable ability to comfort himself under the most trying circumstances is truly remarkable and shows that even an infant has some self-protective devices.

However, infants and young children are vulnerable to fears on this basis because there is no intervening mediation. That is, the very young child cannot think through the event and appreciate its happenstance nature. Another source of fear for the young child is the observation of someone else's fear although the child may not be able to surmise the cause accurately. This reflects the suggestibility mentioned by Piaget; again, as the child becomes more mature, the identification is less automatic. However, Bandura, Grusec and Menlove (1967) demonstrated the value of using "courageous" role models to eleminate specific fears (e.g., fear of dogs) in children as old as 4 years. It should be pointed out, however, that the way in which a child conquers a fear may not be the same as the way in which the child originally acquired the fear.

The vignette described in Case 5.1 (provided by his mother) illustrates anxiety arising from a mixture of a reality experience and fantasy.

Although few children undergo EEG examination at age 3 years, it is generally considered a minor experience since there is no pain involved. In later life the parents would not recall this as a traumatic event. But looking at it from Peter's viewpoint, the experience of helplessness was overwhelming. One should add that his perceptions were probably colored by his awareness that the parents were anxious—not about the EEG per se but about the seizure episode—so that he got the definite impression that

there was something scary going on. The importance of this example is simply to illustrate the frightening possibilities of a world where "anything imaginable is possible."

Some topics of concern are virtually universal to young children. Even with object permanence, there is some anxiety about the phenomenon of disappearance. The toddler feels an acute sense of loss and helplessness when the mother "takes off" despite the child's protestations. Even with people much less important, the toddler is often upset if someone departs without going through the "bye-bye" ritual that seems to give the toddler a feeling of being in control. And there are some objects in the modern world, such as the vacuum cleaner, the toilet, or bathtub drains, which have the special function of making things disappear. Lacking a concept of relative size, it is understandable that a toddler might entertain the thought that he or she could disappear in one of these contrivances. Some of the anxieties in the early stages of achieving toilet mastery may well relate to the toddler's thought that it is not only the bowel movement that will disappear! Because of a unique experience, one 2-year-old connected this fear of disappearance with a snake. She was present at an enthusiastic lecture given by a teenager at a local natural history museum. With a somnolent boa constrictor wrapped around her, the teenager described how the snake could open his mouth very wide and swallow very big things. Following this, the two-year-old "saw" snakes everywhere and talked about them frequently with obvious fear. When she was reintroduced to the teenager—alive and well and without

CASE 5.1 Peter

Peter was close to 3 when he had an EEG after a seizure episode. To prepare for this experience, he visited the laboratory ahead of time and it was explained that the electrodes were simply stuck on the skin with adhesive and carried a message from him to the machine. The parents found a book about EEG's with pictures of the machine and the recordings made by the pens on a roll of paper. He was told that it was like a photograph of the brain and did not hurt any more than it hurts to have a photo taken with a camera. Peter was reassured but alarmed that he had a brain. Should he have a brain, he wondered. It was explained that everyone has a brain; it is inside the head.

At the time of the EEG, he was terrified and screamed, "Let me up, please. Please, let me up." He finally fell asleep hugging his stuffed dog while the technician rocked him and sang to him. When he awakened, he was relieved to have the electrodes removed. They then examined the recording machine and its many buttons in anticipation of future tests.

Subsequent to the EEG he developed severe sleep problems. It was necessary to review the experience with him many times and to prepare him for a repeat EEG several months later. He then clearly expressed the fear that the wires going from the machine to his head would light him up like a light bulb, just as happens when a lamp is plugged in. Further, he said, if you pressed the brown button on the machine, the machine would blow up. He also expressed the fear that the pens which record the impulses would write on his body (something which he had done himself in play and for which he had been mildly rebuked).

Close to the age of 6 he had a dissociative state during a temper tantrum when he clearly relived the EEG experience. He lay down on the floor and screamed, "Let me up, please. Please, let me up," when no one was restraining him. Usually he has little recollection of the experience except for a memory of a "flashing light which was like the sun coming down into my eyes." This memory is remarkable because he was ostensibly asleep during the photic stimulation.

the snake—she forgot about snakes. Her immediate recovery from this incipient phobia suggests that she had concluded that the girl had been swallowed up.

A special kind of disappearance is involved with the puzzle of the genital sex difference. In accordance with the principle of egocentrism, the child assumes that all bodies are identical. The first discovery of the difference between boys and girls is bound to come as a surprise. Many parents feel that the emotional impact of this discovery has been overrated by child psychoanalysts, because their own child did not ask any questions regarding the sex difference. In such a case, it is probable that the child did not ask because he or she believed that he or she knew the answer. The egocentric child is unaware of his ignorance and cannot imagine any explanation other than the one which spontaneously occurs to him.

The spontaneous explanation of a 2-year-old would have to be in terms of his or her very limited experience. In the life of most 2-year-olds, there has been considerable emphasis on destruction.

Favorite toys wear out, many household objects are taboo because of their fragility, and so forth. In view of this, we can deduce that a frequent spontaneous explanation for the absent penis would be that there has been a particularly unfortunate breakage. And the unhappy part of this notion is that what has happened once to one person can happen again to another. This particular misconception has a unique position in child psychology, because it is not one which can be dismissed lightly. Nor is it easy to correct, unless it comes out in the open. One might argue that a child would not think of such a thing unless he has been told something of this sort, or been threatened. But ideas are not formed passively; the normal child is not an inert being who registers only what people say to him. From the age of 2, and perhaps even younger, he or she puts together one bit of experience with another bit, and out of these combinations the child conceives original ideas. Other possibilities include the notion that the parents were negligent in "checking things out," perhaps that the penis will "grow" and appear when one is older. Castration anxiety can take many forms and have many causes but the fear has its genesis partly in the discrepancy between the knowledge of the young child and direct observations.

The child is also vitally interested in matters of life and death. As he or she learns to distinguish between animate and inanimate, there is an awareness of the distinction between living and dead. It will not be long before the child realizes that there was a time when he or she did not exist. Where was he? This is not a casual question; underlying the curiosity is a concern lest one disappear back into the void.

It is even easier to understand the curiosity of the youngster into whose family a new baby is born. There is the intellectual problem of reconciling the observations of the mother and the coincidence of the baby's appearance, but the curiosity is further piqued by jealously. There is always the possibility that if one knew how this new baby arrived, one could effect a convenient disappearance, or at least prevent a recurrence. Freud was particularly impressed by the young child's concern with the birth of babies and suggested that this was the prototype of many of the child's questions (1908/1959). When a child persistently asks about the origin of things, it may represent displaced curiosity about the origin of babies. In view of parental difficulties in explaining just where babies come from, many children give up asking direct questions and express their anxiety in other forms of curiosity, never finding the answer they are seeking.

Death is only the other side of the birth question, but again the question is simple and the answer difficult. The child wants to know why it happens, in order to forestall it both for himself and his parents. The young child, observing a dead animal or plant, will ask plaintively, "Why did it die?" or "What made it dead?" This might seem like a great surge of sympathy, but basically the child is trying to find the guilty party. Organic life is, for the young child, a sort of story, well-regulated according to the wishes and intentions of its inventor.

Two approaches have been taken to the systematic study of anxiety in young children: one in terms of underlying causes (Freud, 1926/1959) and the other in terms of outward behavior. In psychoanalytic theory, the common denominator is the fear of helplessness (Waelder, 1960), aroused by "dangers" that appear in a rather typical developmental sequence, namely, fear of loss of object (i.e., significant person), fear of loss of the love of object (i.e., fear of disapproval), fear of bodily harm (i.e., castration or death), and fear of loss of self-love (i.e., guilt or shame). To this phasic sequence of danger situations, Anna Freud added the fear of the strength of one's own drives, i.e., fear of losing self-control or "falling apart" (1936). These can be thought of as special sensitivities that will influence the child's perception and interpretation of events.

The external manifestations of childish anxiety were extensively studied by Jersild and Holmes (1935). The studies included direct observation of preschool children in experimental situations and reports of parents and teachers on preschool children. In normal preschool children, fears of concrete and tangible stimuli declined between 1 and 6 years. On the other hand, fears of imaginary, anticipated, and supernatural dangers (e.g., dreams, robbers, imaginary creations, the possibility of accidents and events associated with the dark) increased over the same age span. "Fear scores" correlated positively with the intelligence quotient, the relationship being most marked (.53) in those between 2 and 3 years old. With regard to this finding, Jersild remarked, "As the child matures, new things affect him by virtue of his keener perceptions and fear is likely to arise when the individual knows enough to recognize the potential danger in a situation but has not advanced to the point of a complete comprehension and control of the changing situation" (1960, p. 257).

Gaining mastery over these early anxieties is achieved by (a) further life experience which minimizes the potential dangers, (b) clarification by the child's own progress in reasoning and timely explanations by observant and empathic parents, and (c) assimilation through play. In play, the child restructures reality to suit his or her wishes and, in most cases, it is easy to see how and why. The child reenacts events that were fun, assumes grown-up roles, bosses his toys and imaginary helpers, etc. But it is somewhat surprising that young children will also reenact scary experiences where the pleasure is not so apparent. Waelder described the paradox as follows:

... a child was taken to a dentist. It had been very apprehensive concerning the dentist, from whom it had previously suffered tormenting pain. According to the pleasure principle, we should offhand suppose that the highly disagreeable situation, once it was fortunately in the past, would have been set aside, and that the child would be only too glad to let the matter drop. The pleasure principle hardly prepares us to expect the return of the situation in play. Nevertheless, in reality, this often occurs. (1933, p. 210)

The explanation is in the change of role from passive to active. In the original situation, the child was done to; in play, he or she is the doer. Not only does the child take the part of the powerful, dangerous grown-up, but also he or she can start and stop the game at will. Play can be a method of constantly working over and assimilating piecemeal an experience that was too big to be assimilated at one swoop. A painful experience is repeated in play while it is still unmastered, and the playful repetition helps to gain mastery over the experience. Then the matter can be safely forgotten and the child loses zest for the game. Observing the child's distortions in the "re-play" can often provide leads as to the child's perception and understanding of the experience. Like frustration, anxiety is unavoidable in the process of growing up, although of course one would hope that anxiety-provoking experiences would be well-outnumbered by reassuring experiences. It is important to remember that true reassurance comes from the workings of the mind of the participant, not simply from an external reality presentation.

DEVELOPMENTAL ASPECTS OF ANGER

The word "anger" has been chosen to sidestep a comprehensive discussion of the ambiguous concept of "aggression," and also because it is a "feeling" word like "anxious." Anger and fear are closely related. Similar factors are involved in their instigation, and either emotion may accompany or give rise to the other. The effects of anger on the body chemistry are not as clear-cut as those of anxiety, but the physiology is close. In anxiety, the body is prepared for fight or flight. The sharpest difference between the response of anger and the response of anxiety is the way that the person feels. If the person wants to attack, it is anger; if he or she wants to run, it is anxiety. On the other hand, a

child who feels "pushed into a corner" and unable to escape will "attack" out of fear.

The healthy infant demonstrates assertive behavior from the beginning, that is, behavior that demands a reaction from the environment. In Chapter 1 it was pointed out that it is important for these early efforts to meet with some success. The infant's calls for attention, indications of preference for one food or toy over another, or protestations over physical discomfort are not seen as aggressive except in the very broadest sense of the word, and it is unlikely that they are accompanied by a feeling of anger. But the picture changes during the second year as the toddler has a more clear and stable goal in mind. Assertive efforts are bound to meet with frustration as the toddler's world widens.

In 1939, Dollard, Doob, Miller, Mowrer, and Sears put forth the idea that there is a one-to-one relationship between frustration and aggression, that is, that frustration always leads to aggression and that aggression is always the result of frustration. Even with a modifiction by Miller (1941) suggesting that the aggression might not be obvious, but that frustration might lead to an "instigation to aggression outweighed by other behavioral habits," the frustration-aggression hypothesis was severely criticized on the basis that some aggression seems to occur without frustration and that frustration sometimes leads to withdrawal rather than aggression (Bandura & Walters, 1963; Kaufman, 1970). However, it would be foolish to discard the relationship between frustration and aggression, or anger, in toto. The toddler clearly displays displeasure, which we can call anger, when people or things do not respond to his or her demands. And we must remember that the toddler can see no reason for their noncompliance!

The common problems around separation which often peak between 18 and 24 months serve to illustrate the frustration-aggression-anxiety sequence. The first part of this is signal anxiety, the child's distress in seeing the parents get ready to leave, and the toddler goes to great lengths to stop them. As he or she gets worked up, it is difficult to tell whether he or she is only frightened, or angry as well, but often, in the midst of tears and clinging, there is a scream, "I hate you, Mommy!" Ire is aroused by the pain the mother is about to cause, but the hostility exposes the toddler to a new set of anxieties. With magical thinking, the child is deeply afraid that his destructive wishes might actually come true, and that the mother might permanently disappear. And even should that not happen, she might be so angry that she would retaliate by not returning.

If a parent attempts to handle this by spanking or scolding, the punishment seems to the child to justify his apprehensions. His fantasies are further confirmed if in the past there have been threats of separation for bad behavior, a not uncommon threat because parents find it brings children into line so quickly. Sometimes, when the parent returns, the child treats her with studied neglect, as if the separation had meant nothing whatsoever. The child is giving her the treatment that he or she found most devastating, namely, to be ignored, and in this way expressing resentment. Sufficiently reassured by her physical presence, the child can afford to express the anger. If the separation was lengthy, e.g., the mother's hospitalization for a new baby, or the child's own hospitalization for some reason, the reactions may be quite intense and lead to a serious estrangement between the bewildered mother and the angry, unhappy child.

There are countless frustrations less powerful than that of separation; most toddlers are very demanding and bossy, easily aroused to both anger and joy. As observed by the little girl with her favorite doll, things can be very "fightable." Dawe's (1934) study of 200 quarrels occurring in a nursery school indicated that 78 percent of the youngest children's quarrels were instigated over possessions. The same study indicated, however, that the average preschool quarrel lasted only 15–36 seconds. Parenting tasks are not easy in the toddler period. On one hand, parents should be respectful of so-called "instrumental aggression" or anger directly related to frustration, but clearly they cannot be intimidated. There are many alternatives between "giving in," which would simply reinforce the angry responses, and simply ignoring the response. Parents become adept at distraction and substitution to turn away the toddler's wrath. It is unfortunate when an angry response on the child's part is met with an angry rejoinder by the parents because this reinforces the egocentric assumptions. Also, the parents are constant models; the ways in which they handle their own frustration serve as behavioral examples for the young child.

Complicating the frustration picture is the fact that the toddler shows destructive or pain-inflicting behavior independent of specific frustration and quite separate from angry feelings. There is some "power play" or sheer pleasure in making the predictable happen—the cat will squeal when the tail is pulled; glasses will break when hurled on the floor; and mother will dash around when food is dumped. Usually this kind of aggression is tempered by the child's anxiety about loss of love. Discomfort about parental disapproval wins out if there is a strong parent-child bond and if parental approval is readily forthcoming when the child behaves in a kindly, careful fashion.

As the child grows older, there are changes in what makes him or her angry. There is less sense of immediacy, and the 3- or 4-year-old can wait—for a little while at least. With a surer sense of the future, separation is much less threatening. On the other hand, there are new sources of anger in violations to self-esteem. Many a parent has been surprised by the 4-year-old's anger at being "looked at" or "laughed at," failing to appreciate the child's new sensitivities to opinion. The child at this age takes himself or herself very seriously and feels humiliated by any response suggesting that he or she is "funny" or unimportant. Jealousy rears its ugly head, even without a sibling. Positive comments about another child are seen as detracting from the child's worth as if there were a limited amount of beauty or intelligence to go around. At this point it is very helpful if the child has learned to put his anger into words so that he or she can make a direct statement about the anger and the reason, because usually the misunderstanding can be corrected. If, on the other hand, the child sulks or looks for ways to get even,

relatively simple disappointments or hurts can escalate into running battles.

An Experiment in Intervention

In his discussion of "behavior theory and the models of man" Bandura (1974) pointed out that "People learn and retain much better by using cognitive aids that they generate than by repetitive reinforced performance (Anderson & Bower, 1973; Bandura, 1971). With growing evidence that cognition has causal influence in behavior, the arguments against cognitive determinants are losing their force" (p. 865). This concept has been utilized in what is known as "cognitive behavior therapy." This is a hybrid concept which brings education and treatment close together. The work of Shure to be described in the following section is an example of "special" education designed to help children resolve their conflicts with other people. Although the formal experiment was done with inner city black children, they were not selected because of special aggressive characteristics, nor were the principles modified because of demographic attributes.

As a clinician, Shure first noted that maladjusted older children showed an absence of planning and a reliance on impulsive action. Moving to younger children, she observed that as early as age 4 years, both adjusted and nonadjusted expressed forceful ways to obtain a toy from another child. While most 4-year-olds thought of some form of "ask," the adjusted youngsters were more ingenious and thought of a greater variety of range of nonforceful ways to achieve their end. She developed the

Preschool Interpersonal Problem-Solving (PIPS) test (Shure & Spivack, 1974), which distinguished 4- and 5-year-olds' ability to think of ways to: (a) get a chance to play with a toy in another child's possession, and (b) to avert mother's anger after damaging some property. Consistent throughout seven studies (Spivack, Platt, & Shure, 1976), well-adjusted children could offer three or four solutions to each problem while those displaying characteristics of impulsivity or inhibition more typically thought of only one or two. Following these observations, she and her co-workers developed problem-solving training programs and tried them out to determine if interpersonal cognitive problem-solving skills could be taught successfully.

The experimental program involved 113 4-year-olds in a federally funded day-care program and 106 controls. The training program consisted of 3 months of daily 20-minute small group lessons (Spivak & Shure, 1974) and teacher-guided dialogues during the day when children were having real problems with one another. Pre and post measures included the PIPS test, another measure called "What Happens Next Game," and the Hahnemann Pre-School Behavior Rating Scale completed by teachers. The "trained" youngsters improved significantly more than controls on all measures, independent of sex, general verbal skills, and Stanford-Binet IQ. In follow-up in kindergarten, the data indicated that the trained youngsters maintained adjusted behaviors significantly more than controls over time. (Shure, 1981). There were also reports where the mothers were "trained" to "train" their children in interpersonal cognitive prob-

lem-solving and improved child behavior was observed at school (Shure, 1982). Further studies indicated that a 1-year intervention, either at age 4 or age 5, seemed to be as beneficial as a 2-year intervention.

In discussing the findings, Shure emphasized the importance of helping the child to think of alternative actions, as opposed to the adult giving direct advice. The goal is to teach the child "how" to think rather than "what" to think, thus increasing the child's sense of mastery over the situation. Also, the time spent in thinking is time saved from action. The second specific skill that was both modifiable and related to the positive results was "consequential thinking" or anticipating consequences. The linkage between improved consequential thinking and behavior change was stronger in the kindergarten than in the nursery year (Shure & Spivack, 1980), suggesting that this skill may be developmentally more suitable for 5-year-olds than 4-year-olds. As an interesting sidelight, causal thinking—that is, asking why a child does something—did not prove a mediator of socially adaptive behavior. In role-taking, these children could learn how another child was likely to respond, and how this would affect them, but they were apparently less likely to appreciate the original motivation on the part of another child. The 4- or 5-year-old is still a pragmatist, interested mainly in "what's in it for me."

Shure (1982) gave the following example of a dialogue planned to foster interpersonal cognitive problem-solving:

TEACHER: Steven, what happened?

STEVEN: He won't give me the bike.

TEACHER: What happened when you pushed Robert off?

STEVEN: He started fighting.

TEACHER: How did that make you feel?

STEVEN: Mad.

TEACHER: How do you think Robert felt when you pushed him?

STEVEN: Mad.

TEACHER: Pushing him off is one way to get to ride the bike. Can you think of a different way so he won't fight and so you won't both be mad?

Here one sees that in addition to identifying the point of conflict (i.e., riding the bike) and encouraging Steven to consider alternative solutions, feelings have been identified. Some time ago, Katan (1961) wrote about the importance of verbalization in achieving self-control, and particularly the need for parents to help children to disciminate and put their feelings into words.

It now becomes clear that verbalization of feelings leads to an increase of mastery by the ego. The young ego shows its strength by not acting upon its feelings immediately, but by delaying such action and expressing its feelings in words instead ... This delayed action, as a result of the verbalization, enables the ego to judge the situation. The verbalization as such is a part of the intellectual process, which, according to Freud's formulations (1911), is a trial acting. (pp. 186–187)

Although this suggestion came from psychoanalytic theory, it also fits cognitive behavior modification. The various and assorted aspects of problem solving described by Shure would be seen as ego activities by the child analyst and very much to be desired. What is not stressed in the cognitive approach is the role of fantasy or ego defenses. To illustrate how complicated the conflict might be, we will rewrite the Steven-Robert scenario.

TEACHER: Steven, what happened?

STEVEN: Robert ran into me on purpose.

TEACHER: Robert, what happened?

ROBERT: He was going to take my bike away from me.

TEACHER: How did that make you feel?

ROBERT: Scared—I was going to fall off.

In this scene, Robert demonstrates "identification with the aggressor," an imagined aggressor, and the switching from anxiety to aggression. Some of the same techniques could be used to help Robert think through his unjustified assumptions, but without appreciating the role of his anxiety, they would probably not suffice.

Oedipal Fantasies

The Oedipal complex has been a much-maligned part of psychoanalytic theory, perhaps because of Freud's insistence on its universality and biological base. Allowing that it is not universal (although common) and that it is determined by social-cognitive rather than biological factors does not lessen its importance. As the result of social learning, the child identifies with the same-sex parent and wants to be everything that the parent is—including married. The 4- or 5-year-old can see the problem in this, namely, the desired marriage partner is already taken! In a classical love-triangle situation, the child would like to replace the same-sex parent. At first, the child tries such solutions as suggesting new roles for the parent who is in the way, for instance, a grandparent or a sibling, but even child logic rules this out.

The child is then caught on the horns of a dilemma, on one hand wishing to be rid of the rival, but on the other hand very much attached to this same person. Feeling both anger and love for the same person is most uncomfortable. In this situation the child is likely to be quite inconsistent in relationship to the rival parent, sometimes irritable and disagreeable and sometimes very loving, perhaps to undo the damage of the angry feelings. The aggressive component of the Oedipal fantasies engenders anxiety for three related, but slightly different, reasons. The child fears (a) that the wishes will come true, (b) that the rival parent will cease to love the child if he or she detects the child's hostility, and (c) that there will be retaliation. The 4- or 5-year-old child tends to be silent about the Oedipal fantasies because of the associated discomfort. Barring seductive circumstances that keep hope alive, or accidental circumstances that seem to prove the potency of aggressive wishes, the Oedipal fantasies fade because of frustration and also because of the child's broadened social horizons and alternative attachments.

A reformulation of the Oedipus complex in social-cognitive terms omits one important feature included in the original psychoanalytic formulation, namely, the importance of sexual feelings accompanying the fantasies. In the words of Brenner:

The most important single fact to bear in mind about the Oedipus complex is the strength and force of the feelings which are involved. It is a real love affair. For many people it is the most intense affair of their entire lives, but it is in any case as intense as any which the individual will ever experience. (Any) description ... cannot begin to convey what the reader must keep in mind as he reads it; the intensity of the tempest of passions of love and hate, of yearning and jealousy, of fury and fear that rages within the child. This is what we are talking about when we try to describe the Oedipus complex. (1955, p. 121)

Interest in infantile sexuality has waned since Freud's original contributions (1905/1953). There is general acceptance of the fact that young children play with their genitals but little recognition of the accompanying sexual excitement. It is assumed that sexual feelings would cause no conflicts if childish masturbation is treated with benign neglect. However, clinical work with children reveals that many have frightening fantasies about parental intercourse which get very much mixed up in their Oedipal fantasies.

All-or-none Assumptions

In quite a different context, Susan Harter (1982) noted the special problems that young children have with ambivalence, which is so prominent in the Oedipal situation. She commented that young children have difficulty acknowledging that two seemingly conflicting emotions or personal attributes can co-exist simultaneously. In her therapeutic work with children she noted that they thought in dichotomous terms, viewing themselves as "all dumb" or "all bad" and accepting a very one-sided view of their own feelings or those of others.

They vehemently deny alternative emotions and experience great difficulty in accepting the possibility that seemingly contradictory feelings might simultaneously exist. Another related manifestation is the tendency for some young children to vacillate from one extreme to the other. While today they may feel "all happy," tomorrow some event may cause a dramatic shift toward the opposite pole where they can only express their strong feelings of anger. (pp. 29–30)

She interpreted these difficulties as a function of age-specific conceptual limitations and suggested that the most difficult conceptual task is to realize that one can have two opposing feelings, say, love and anger, toward the same person at the same time. This is the very essence of the Oedipal conflict.

The dichotomous thinking characteristic of the preschool child can be interpreted in Piagetian terms. He categorized the period between 2 and 6 years as the "preoperational" stage of cognitive development. The preoperational child is able to take account of only one dimension at a time. With regard to the perceptual world, the child forms conclusions on the basis of a single factor and does not comprehend the principles of conservation. There are various demonstrations of this phenomenon, but in the classic water beaker experiment the child is instructed to judge the amount of water poured from one glass into a second taller but narrower glass. In his/her insistence that there is now more water in the taller glass, the preoperational child's judgment is determined by the perception of the most salient physical dimension or attributed, namely,

height. Harter drew an analogy between the one-sidedness in perceptual processing and the difficulty in focusing on more than one emotional dimension at a time.

It takes time for the young child to be convinced that his anger will not destroy the parent nor will it destroy the parent's love. Conversely, the child learns that the parents' anger at him/her does not mean that they don't love him/her. At the same time the child develops a more complex self-concept that is not just positive or negative but which contains a mix of strong points and weak points. The recent efforts to coordinate social-cognitive and affective development are exciting because they narrow the gap between the emotionally disturbed and the "normal" child and offer some specificity for therapeutic intervention (Harter, 1982). The fact that it also brings about a collegial relationship between experimental and clinical psychologists is a further fringe benefit.

SUMMARY

In this chapter we have tried to look at the first 5 years as experienced by the child. The cognitive characteristics of the under-5 child lead him to erroneous conclusions which in turn give rise to rather typical developmental anxieties and aggressions. His or her understanding of reality is imperfect, and the child needs the active mediation of adults to get it straight. The digression into the subject of television was to stress the fact that this too is part of the young child's world and also feeding in much information, some of it wrong or at least not well understood.

General opinion would have us believe that the later problems of children are caused either by constitutional differences (including neurological variations), identification with parents, or misguided teaching on the part of the parents. What is left out in this conceptualization is the fact that early life experiences are absorbed as through a glass darkly, so that what the child takes in is not a faithful reproduction of what the external world intended. The preschool child enters school age with a mix of "true" and "wrong" ideas, but hopefully with a mind open to correction. The child who has learned to share his thoughts and feelings with others, who feels he can be in error without being "stupid," and who has faith in the capacity of adults to be honest in giving information and forthcoming in their support is ready to tackle the problems of school life.

REFERENCES

ANDERSON, J. R., & BOWER, G. H. (1973). *Human associative memory.* New York: Wiley.

BALL, S., & BOGATZ, G. A. (1972). Summative research on SESAME STREET: Implications for the study of preschool children. In A. D. Pick (Ed.), *Minnesota Symposia on Child Psychology* (Vol. 6, pp. 3–18). Minneapolis: University of Minnesota Press.

BANDURA, A. (Ed.). (1971). *Psychological modeling: Conflicting theories.* Chicago, IL: Aldine-Atherton.

BANDURA, A. (1974). Behavior theory and the models of man. *American Psychologist, 29,* 859–869.

BANDURA, A., GRUSEC, J. E., & MENLOVE, F. L. (1967). Vicarious extinction of avoidance behavior. *Journal of Personality and Social Psychology, 5,* 16–23.

BANDURA, A., & WALTERS, R. H. (1963). *Social learning and personality development.* New York: Holt, Rinehart and Winston.

BORKE, H. (1975). Piaget's mountains revisited: Changes in the egocentric landscape. *Developmental Psychology, 11,* 240–244.

BRENNER, C. (1955). *An elementary textbook of psychoanalysis.* New York: International Universities Press.

BROWN, R. W. (1956). Language and categories. In J. S. Bruner, J. L. Goodnow, & G. A. Austin (Eds.), *A study of thinking* (pp. 247–312). New York: Wiley.

CHOMSKY, N. (1968). *Language and mind.* New York: Harcourt Brace Jovanovich.

CHURCH, J. (1961). *Language and the discovery of reality.* New York: Random House.

DALE, P. S. (1972). *Language development. Structure and function.* Hinsdale, IL: The Dryden Press.

DAWE, H. C. (1934). An analysis of two hundred quarrels of preschool children. *Child Development, 5,* 139–157.

DOLLARD, J., DOOB, L., MILLER, N., MOWRER, O., & SEARS, R. (1939). *Frustration and aggression.* New Haven: Yale University Press.

FENICHEL, O. (1945). *The psychoanalytic theory of neurosis.* New York: W. W. Norton.

FREUD, A. (1936). *The ego and the mechanisms of defense.* New York: International Universities Press.

FREUD, A., & BURLINGHAM, D. (1944). *Infants without families.* New York: International Universities Press.

FREUD, S. (1905, 1953). Three essays on the theory of sexuality. In J. Strachey (Ed.), *Standard Edition* (Vol. 7, pp. 125–231). London: Hogarth Press.

FREUD, S. (1908, 1959). On the sexual theories of children. In J. Strachey (Ed.), *Standard Edition* (Vol. 9, pp. 205–226). London: Hogarth Press.

FREUD, S. (1913, 1955). Totem and taboo. In J.

Strachey (Ed.), *Standard Edition*, Vol. 13. London: The Hogarth Press.

FREUD, S. (1926, 1959). *Inhibitions, symptoms and anxiety*. In J. Strachey (Ed.), *Standard Edition*, Vol. 20. London: The Hogarth Press.

GLUCKSBERG, S., KRAUSS, R. M., & WEISBERG, R. (1966). Referential communication in nursery school children: Method and some preliminary findings. *Journal of Experimental Child Psychology, 3*, 333–342.

HARRIS, B. (1979). Whatever happened to Little Albert? *American Psychologist, 34*, 151–160.

HARRIS, S. L., & FERRARI, M. (1983). Developmental factors in child behavior therapy. *Behavior Therapy, 14*, 54–72.

HARTER, S. (1982). A cognitive-developmental approach to children's understanding of affect and trait labels. In F. C. Serafica (Ed.), *Social-cognitive development in context* (pp. 27–60). New York: The Guilford Press.

HENDRICK, I. (1943). The discussion of the instinct to master. *Psychoanalytic Quarterly, 12*, 561–65.

HUNT, J. McV. (1963). Motivation inherent in information processing and action. In O.J. Harvey (Ed.), *Motivation and social interaction* (pp. 35–94). New York: The Ronald Press.

JERSILD, A. T. (1960). *Child psychology* (5th ed.). Englewood Cliffs, NJ: Prentice-Hall.

JERSILD, A. T., & HOLMES, F. B. (1935). Children's fears. *Child Development Monographs, 20*. New York: Bureau of Publications, Teachers College, Columbia University.

KATAN, A. (1961). Some thoughts about the role of verbalization in early childhood. In R. S. Eissler, H. Hartmann, A. Freud, & M. Kris (Eds.), *The psychoanalytic study of the child* (Vol. 16, pp. 184–188). New York: International Universities Press.

KAUFMANN, H. (1970). *Aggression and altruism*. New York: Holt, Rinehart, and Winston.

MACCOBY, E. F., & JACKLIN, C. N. (1974). *The psychology of sex differences*. Stanford, CA: Stanford University Press.

MACNAMARA, J. (1972). Cognitive basis of language learning in infants. *Psychological Review, 79*, 1–13.

MCCARTHY, D. (1954). Language development in children. In L. Carmichael (Ed.), *Manual of child psychology* (2nd ed., pp. 476–581). New York: Wiley.

MILLER, N. E. (1941). The frustration-aggression hypothesis. *Psychological Review, 48*, 337–342.

PAVLOV, I. P. (1928). *Lectures on conditioned reflexes*. New York: Liveright.

PIAGET, J. (1926, 1955). *The language and thought of the child*. (Marjorie Gabain, Trans.). New York: Meridian Books.

PIAGET, J. (1937, 1954). *The construction of reality in the child*. (Margaret Cook, Trans.). New York: Basic Books.

PIAGET, J. (1945, 1951). *Play, dreams and imitation in childhood*. (C. Gattegno & F. M. Hodgson, Trans.). New York: W. W. Norton.

PIAGET, J., & INHELDER, B. (1956). *The child's conception of space*. London: Routledge and Kegan Paul.

PIATTELLI-PALMARINI, M. (Ed.). (1980). *Language and learning: The debate between Jean Piaget and Noam Chomsky*. Cambridge, MA: Harvard University Press.

RICE, M. B. (1982). *Child language. What children know and how*. In T. M. Field, A. Huston, H. C. Quay, L. Troll, & G. E. Finley (Eds.), *Review of human development* (pp. 253–268). New York: John Wiley.

RUBINSTEIN, E. A. (1983). Television and behavior: Research conclusions of the 1982 NIMH report and their policy implications. *American Psychologist, 38*, 820–826.

SAMELSON, F. B. (1980). Watson's Little Albert, Cyril Burt's twins, and the need for a critical science. *American Psychologist, 35*, 619–625.

SCHACHTER, F. F., SHORE, E., HODAPP, R., CHALFIN, S., & BUNDY, C. (1980). Do girls talk earlier?: Mean length of utterance in toddlers. *Developmental Psychology, 14,* 388–393.

SHURE, M. B. (1981). Social competence as a problem-solving skill. In J. D. Wine & M. D. Smye (Eds.), *Social competence* (pp. 158–188). New York: Guilford Press.

SHURE, M. B. (1982). Interpersonal problem solving: A cog in the wheel of social cognition. In F. C. Serafica (Ed.), *Social-cognitive development in context* (pp. 133–162). New York: Guilford Press.

SHURE, M. B., & SPIVACK, G. (1980). Interpersonal problem solving as a mediator of behavior adjustment in preschool and kindergarten children. *Journal of Applied Developmental Psychology, 1,* 29–43.

SINGER, J. L., & SINGER, D. G. (1981). *Television, imagination and aggression: A study of preschoolers.* Hillsdale, NJ: Erlbaum.

SINGER, J. L., & SINGER, D. G. (1983). Psychologists look at television: Cognitive, developmental, personality, and social policy implications. *American Psychologist, 38,* 826–835.

SMITH, M. E. (1926). An investigation of the development of the sentence and the extent of vocabulary in young children. *University of Iowa Studies in Child Welfare* (Vol. 3, No. 5).

SNOW, C. E. (1984). Parent-child interaction and the development of communicative ability. In R. L. Schiefelbusch & J. Pickar (Eds.), *Communicative competence: Acquisition and intervention* (pp. 69–108). Baltimore, MD: University Park Press.

SPIVACK, G., PLATT, J. J., & SHURE, M. B. (1976). *The problems solving approach to adjustment.* San Francisco: Jossey-Bass.

SPIVACK, G., & SHURE, M. B. (1974). *Social adjustment of young children.* San Francisco: Jossey-Bass.

TERRACE, H. S. (1985). In the beginning was the "Name." *American Psychologist, 40,* 1011–1028.

WAELDER, R. (1933). The psychoanalytic theory of play. *The Psychoanalytic Quarterly, 2,* 208–224.

WAELDER, R. (1960). *Basic theory of psychoanalysis.* New York: International Universities Press.

WATSON, J. B., & RAYNER, R. (1920). Conditioned emotional reactions. *Journal of Experimental Psychology, 3,* 1–14.

WHITE, R. W. (1959). The concept of competence. *Psychological Review, 66,* 297–333.

WRIGHT, J. C., & HUSTON, A. C. (1983). A matter of form: Potentials of television for young viewers. *American Psychologist, 38,* 835–844.

CHAPTER 6

BEHAVIOR PROBLEMS
IN PRESCHOOL CHILDREN

This chapter considers everyday problems of "normal" children, ages 1 to 5 years, from the adult perspective. The assumption is made throughout that neither child nor parent is exceptional in terms of innate characteristics, environmental circumstances, or mental stability. Those conditions classified as "developmental disabilities," such as autism, language disorder, and mental retardation, are discussed in Chapters 12 and 13, primarily because they have lifetime significance and therefore are not strictly speaking "preschool" problems. Another assumption is that the affectional ties between parents and child are within the wide range of expectable and that the parents are the major caregivers. However, in contrast with times past, it is necessary to keep in mind the

50–50 probability that the mother is employed outside the home.

First we look at the common concerns of parents and the prevalence of clinically identified problems with an eye toward their long-range significance. The particular problems discussed at length are sleep difficulties, toilet mastery or failure thereof, and noncompliance. Some practical suggestions for managing these problems are offered on the assumption that a person who is called upon to diagnose and treat persistent difficulties may well be called upon to advise in much less serious situations. It should be noted that pediatricians play a major role in advising parents of preschool-age children and have contributed much of the relevant literature. The final section reviews general approaches and effectiveness of parent education generally offered by nonmedical professional workers.

PARENTAL CONCERNS

Various surveys indicate that preschool children display a wide variety of behaviors that concern parents. Whether or not such behavior becomes labeled a "problem" depends on the type, frequency, duration, and severity of the problem as well as the tolerance and expectations of the parents. There is a progression starting with "parental concern" to "behavior problem" to a clinically diagnosed "behavior disorder," with fuzzy boundaries between each category.

In 1954, MacFarlane, Allen, and Honzik reported on a longitudinal study of mothers' reports of problem behaviors. The children were selected on a random basis from the birth certificate registry in Berkeley, California, and the mothers were interviewed at regular intervals from age 21 months to 14 years. A somewhat similar study of "normal" preschool children was reported by Chamberlin in 1974. Parents recruited from private pediatric practice in suburban Rochester, New York, were asked to describe their child's behavior on a descriptive checklist near the child's second, third, and fourth birthdays. It is interesting to compare parental reports in these studies because there is at least 40 years' difference in the birth years of the children involved, and many changes in child rearing attitudes occurred between 1929 and 1969. Table 6.1 presents the percentages for those be-

havioral items investigated in both surveys.

By and large, the parents in the later sample reported more problem behaviors, although this might reflect in part the way the questions were worded. For example, in 1974 approximately half of the parents reported that their children "rubbed or played with sex organs" compared with an average 10% of the 1954 mothers reporting "masturbation." The practice of starting toilet training at earlier ages in the 1930's is reflected in the comparative figures for soiling and wetting at the youngest ages. Although at age 4 years, the differences are much less, they favor the early-trained group.

Changing Views of Thumb Sucking

There also seems to be a greater acceptance of thumb sucking. In the 1930's and 1940's, there was considerable debate about whether sucking was an innate drive requiring fulfillment (Levy, 1934; Ribble, 1944) or learned behavior (Sears & Wise, 1950). In this argument, the absence of thumb-sucking was used almost as a criterion of successful infant feeding. There was an implicit assumption that all thumb sucking was undesirable and that anything which prevented it was good. There is now so little concern about it that persistent sucking was not even included in the Chamberlin survey. It is properly viewed as a behavior that is normally relinquished as part of growing up, although not always. Lapouse and Monk (1959) and MacFarlane (1954) reported about 2% of "normal" children of school age to be still thumb sucking.

The reasons for persistence beyond

TABLE 6.1   Percentages Reported in Parent Surveys (MacFarlane et al., 1954 & Chamberlin, 1974)

	Age of Child		
Behavior	21 months 24 months	3 years	4 years
1954 Insufficient Appetite	7/10%[1]	2/6%	31/29%
1974 Eats Too Little	50%[2]	26%	37%
1954 Diurnal Enuresis	62/43%	6/2%	0/2%
1974 Wets Self During Day	75%	14%	7%
1954 Nocturnal Enuresis	75/73%	18/31%	13/20%
1974 Wets Bed at Night	82%	49%	26%
1954 Soiling	32/20%	4/0%	0/2%
1974 Has b.m. in pants	71%	17%	1%
1954 Masturbation	9/8%	8/4%	16/8%
1974 Rubs or plays with sex organs	56%	49%	51%
1954 Disturbing Dreams	16/13%	29/29%	24/22%
1974 Nightmares	17%	18%	36%
1954 Temper Tantrums	59/43%	69/63%	53/47%
1974 Temper Outbursts	83%	72%	70%
1954 Lying	0/0%	14/12%	33/49%
1974 Tells fibs	2%	26%	63%

[1] Percentage girls/percentage boys

[2] Sexes combined in one percentage

the normal age are probably quite different than the reasons for the appearance of thumb sucking in infancy. Those children who were still thumb sucking at the ages of 11 and 16 years were described by their mothers as moody, depressed, and high-strung compared to those who had desisted (Newson, Newson, & Mahalski, 1982). With regard to other "infant comfort habits" such as clinging to a blanket, these authors found that all children had relinquished them by 11 years. The child who continues to suck fingers or thumb into later childhood does so more because of the tensions belonging to that period rather than frustration or over-gratification in early childhood. What remains from early childhood is the form of comfort learned at that time; the reasons for needing comfort change.

Living with the Preschool Child

Present-day parents reported a higher percentage of temper outbursts and "telling fibs," which might reflect less parental tolerance, more undisciplined children, or the fact that Chamberlin's survey provided the alternatives of "present" or "not at all," whereas the earlier study provided more graded choices. Temper tantrums ranked highest in the parent-identified problems (Chamberlin, 1974). In both surveys, however, there was a high number of behaviors causing concern or conflict. In the

Chamberlin study, at both 2 and 4 years, almost half of the parents identified at least one area of conflict, and 38% identified at least one area of concern. Coleman, Wolkind, and Ashley (1977) reported that over 40% of a 3-year-old sample of London preschoolers were described as difficult to manage, wakeful at night, fearful, showing nervous habits, and having problems relating to playmates. In their words, "This is a formidable list of problems and underlines in no uncertain manner the mothers' perceptions of what they have to cope with" (p. 207).

In another study of London preschoolers, Jenkins, Bax, and Hart (1980) compared parental impressions with those of staff physicians. The most frequent problems complained of by parents were difficulty in management, demanding too much attention, and, again, temper tantrums. The percentage of mothers worried about their child's behavior peaked at age 3 years (23%). Professional judgment tends to be more benign than that of the parents because the professional perspective is a long-range view of the child's adaptive capacities, whereas the parent judges more by the immediate experience of mutual distress and conflict. As an interesting sidelight, Brown (1975) found a remarkably high degree of depression in working-class mothers with children under 5 years, and Richman (1976) discussed the interactional aspects of maternal depression and living with preschool children. With or without daycare centers, nursery schools, maternal employment, or television, living with a preschool child qualifies as a "life stress."

IDENTIFICATION AND PREVALENCE OF CLINICALLY DEFINED PROBLEMS

Measures have been developed to identify "behavior disorders" by comparing reports from nonidentified preschool populations with preschoolers attending a psychiatric treatment clinic (Richman & Graham, 1971) or enrolled in a special nursery school for the emotionally disturbed (Behar & Stringfield, 1974). (See Appendix for description of measures.) There are some problems with using a "referred" group as the differential criterion because the reasons for referring a child for psychological help are complex. The differences between a "referred" and a "normal" population may be as much in the receptivity of the parents and the availability of resources as in the child (Shepherd, Oppenheim, & Mitchell, 1971).

Using a comprehensive 45-minute interview (the Behavioral Screening Questionnaire), 7% of all 3-year-olds in a North London borough were identified as having a moderate or severe behavior problem (Richman, Stevenson, & Graham, 1975). Boys were significantly more likely to be overactive and to have soiling and wetting problems. Girls were more likely to be fearful.

There is some argument about the long-term significance of early problems. Graham, Richman and Stevenson (1982) located over 90% of their original sample when they were 8 years of age. On a parent questionnaire, 43% of the problem group were deviant at age 8 compared with 20% of the control group. This might be attributed to continuity in parental attitude but for the fact that there was a similar difference in teachers' ratings. Although this indicates some continuity, the authors pointed out that only about one-third were disturbed at both points of time and almost two-thirds of those rated as disturbed at age 8 showed no previous signs at age 3. They concluded that "even though behavioral continuity may be relatively high, for efficient detection of disturbance one needs to rely on a process of continuous surveillance rather than on a once-for-all assessment with follow-up of a group thought to be particularly at risk" (1982, p. 87). The factors in the original problem group that seemed to be associated with persistent disturbance included sex of the child (boys more vulnerable than girls). Somewhat surprisingly, they found no relationship between social class, maternal employment, and external stress operating on the family in the *persistence* of disturbance from age 3 to age 8 although these same factors seemed to play a role in the *development* of disturbance between 3 and 8 years.

There seems to be little relationship between preschool home reports and teacher judgments in kindergarten and the first grade (Chamberlin, 1977; Coleman, Wolkind, & Ashley, 1977). The question arises as to whether the children are indeed behaving differently in different settings or whether the teacher and parents take different views of the same behavior. The fact that a better relationship was found when the children were rated by teachers at age 8 years suggests that kindergarten and first grade teachers may be relatively tolerant of individual differences so that they underestimate the significance of negative behaviors.

Acknowledging the high rate of parental concerns and the prevalence of be-havior disorders in preschool children raises the question as to what services should be provided. Richman, Stevenson, and Graham (1975) remarked that "The presence of a 'problem' within a child should not be equated with the presence of a mental disorder or illness, and in our view attempts to produce medical solutions are less likely to be effective than re-examination of the role young mothers play in society together with the esteem (or lack of it) ascribed to their child-rearing activities" (1975, p. 285). Coleman et al. (1977) and Chamberlin (1977) also imply that intervention efforts should be directed towards helping the parents.

SLEEP DISTURBANCES

A survey of children ages 12 to 18 months (Jenkins et al., 1980) and another survey of 3-year-olds (Earls, 1980) indicated that a "sleep problem" was identified in one-fourth of both age groups. This is not a new phenomenon. Gesell, in his behavior profiles based on large-scale studies of infants and small children at the Yale Clinic, included night waking and reluctance to go to sleep as one of the developmental features of the period from 15 to 30 months (Gesell & Ilg, 1943). It is a problem which is a great trial to parents, however "normal" it might be in a statistical sense.

There has been some investigation of factors other than age associated with sleep problems. Carey (1974, 1975) suggested that infants with night waking were characterized temperamentally by significantly lower than average sensory thresholds, and also reported that infants breast-fed beyond 6 months of age awakened significantly more often than bottle-fed babies. In a well-controlled study of preschool-age children, Lozoff, Wolf, and Davis (1985) found that roughly 30% had sleep problems, mainly difficulties in going to sleep rather than night waking, and that the problems persisted well over a year. There were significantly more occurrences of such stresses as new pregnancy, family accident or illness, unaccustomed maternal absence during the day, and maternal depressed mood or marked psychological upset in the sleep-disturbed group.

The importance of the mother's absence during the day in this study suggests that sleep problems are a possible "side effect" of day care. In the relatively extensive research in early day care (Belsky & Steinberg, 1978) and in surveys of prevalence of behavior disorders among preschoolers in day care (Crowther, Bond, & Rolf, 1981), no mention is made of sleep habits, partly because respondents were often teachers rather than parents. One could hypothesize a number of possible relationships between the daytime and nighttime separation involved in sleep that would warrant exploration; however, this connection has not been explored.

Infant Sleep Patterns

The observation by Aserinsky and Kleitman in 1953 of a relationship between rapid eye movement (REM) sleep and dreaming led to an explosion of research into the ontogenic development of the human waking sleeping cycles. Two distinct states of sleep have been differenti-

ated: REM sleep and non-REM sleep, and these sleep states alternate during the night, recurring about every 90 minutes in adults. By age age of 3 months, most infants have settled to a diurnal pattern of sleep and wakefulness. Sleeping through the night is not related to weight gain or changes in infant feeding but reflects maturation of the nervous system which enables the infant to suppress arousal (Zuckerman & Blitzer, 1981).

However, most infants continue to wake regularly. Anders (1979) found that 84% of 9-month-old infants wakened one or more times during the night. Of those that woke, half quietly fell back to sleep without parental attention. Even for those who cry on waking a parent is well advised to wait a few minutes before assuming that the baby is "really awake." In addition to the aggravation of being awakened from one's own sleep, parents are uncertain as to what they should do. Most parents feel that there must be something amiss when their infant cries, but any nighttime visit should be brief and low-key. If the night attention is highly pleasurable and stimulating, any infant can become a "trained night crier" (Schmitt, 1981).

The standard treatment for night waking in infancy is allowing the infant to "cry it out" (Spock, 1976) but this cannot always be followed to the letter. If the crying goes on for more than 10 or 15 minutes, it can become an escalating crescendo that in itself arouses the baby. When the infant is thoroughly aroused, he or she needs the reassurance of seeing the parent. By the age of 8 or 9 months, the infant will have a clear image of the mother and "know" exactly what he or she wants. The failure of her reappearance is too frightening to bear. But this is not a time for feeding, playing, holding, or rocking; a pat and soothing words will prove that the mother is still there. It is indeed a fine line between reinforcement and reassurance, and subsequent events tell the story. If the infant starts to wake on a nightly basis, then the reinforcement aspects have taken hold, and one needs to plan a strategy of withdrawal. This would include such mundane issues as reducing day naptime and over-stimulation at bedtime. But basically the parents need moral support in "waiting out" the usual two or three nights. Parents can be enraged by an infant who won't stop crying, and this can carry over into the normal waking hours and further complicate the situation, or they capitulate because they feel so guilty.

Co-Sleeping

It is generally assumed that children should fall asleep alone and that one of the developmental tasks in infancy is to learn to put oneself to sleep. Schmitt (1981) suggested that infants who are consistently held and rocked to sleep at bedtime expect their mothers to appear and help them go back to sleep when they awaken normally during the night. The connection between sleeping alone and independence was made explicit by Brazelton: "I view learning to sleep alone at night as intimately tied to the job of learning independence . . . Being able to manage alone at night helps a child develop a positive self-image and gains for him a real feeling of strength in the day" (1978).

However, cross-cultural comparisons indicate that this view is almost unique to the American middle class (Burton & Whiting, 1961). For instance, in Japan the infant often shares the mother's bed until a new baby arrives; this goes along with general encouragement of close body contact between family members. Here one can see a connection between child-rearing practices and ultimate cultural values. "A value sign of maturity in Japan is the capacity for *ittaikan*—a feeling of merger or oneness with persons other than self which in turn leads to vicarious experiencing of others' feelings" (Weisz, Rothbaum, & Blackburn, 1984, p. 959). In our culture, separateness and autonomy are more highly valued.

The possible connection between co-sleeping and sleep problems was investigated by Lozoff, Wolf, and Davis (1984) in a sample of 126 children between 6 months and 4 years of age. Children who slept with their parents only in an isolated or extraordinary circumstance were not identified as "co-sleepers." Sleeping in the parental bed was common in these Cleveland children, particularly for the black families (35% of the white and 70% of the black children). Breast-feeding and available physical space were not significant variables. More than half of the co-sleeping white children were rated as having a disruptive overall sleep problem with an average duration of 16 months. But for the black children there was no association between co-sleeping and sleep problems.

Black parents slept with their young children most nights, apparently as an accepted sub-cultural pattern. . . . Even if co-sleeping in some cultural settings proves to be benign with respect to sleep problems, rigorous assessment of concerns about other ill effects, such as its interference with independence, its addictive quality, the potential trauma of witnessing intercourse, and overstimulation of the child will continue to present challenges for future research. (Lozoff et al., 1984)

Since the large majority of white co-sleepers began after 1 year of age, it would appear that co-sleeping was a response to sleep difficulties, but it did not lead to their resolution.

Bedtime Anxieties

Toddlers are characteristically uninterested in going to bed. Devices to postpone bedtime are familiar to every parent, and bedtime rituals can take hours if parents are unwary. Up to a point, the problem may simply be one of parental indulgence. After the parents have set reasonable limits on the child's procrastination, however, it may become clear that he or she is genuinely afraid of being left alone and has real difficulty falling asleep. For the very young child, sleep is like a separation and sleep disturbances are linked with separation anxiety. The child is afraid to leave the mother; something might happen to her as a result of mean thoughts or perhaps the child might get into trouble in her absence. Sleep is a special danger because of the abandonment of control.

At this stage, the child is comforted by the physical presence of the mother or father, or substitutes such as leaving the bedroom door open so the child feels less alone, leaving a night-light on, etc. The child may find comfort in a bed toy, a stuffed animal, a pillow, blanket or transitional object which has become a magic talisman against danger. It is the author's opinion that parents are well advised to remain neutral with regard to such comforters. If the child spontaneously elects to give a stuffed animal this value, fine. It is his own idea, and he can give it up later. If the idea comes from the parents, it has the additional weight of adult authority, which prolongs magical thinking and reliance on objects and rituals (see Chapter 5).

Separation anxiety usually abates by the age of 2 years to 3 years, but reluctance to go to sleep may reappear for new reasons. Some children are afraid of dreams and not only of bad dreams. Dreams seem very real to children, who have an incomplete understanding of the nature of dreams. One child described a dream of being on Roy Roger's ranch and added plaintively, "But how would I get back?" As the child lets down his guard to go to sleep, all kinds of scary thoughts come to mind. There are mental replays of things that happened during the day, including the ever-present television. The dark shadows turn into wild animals or supernatural creatures lying in wait. These "wild things" are a mix of projected angry thoughts and figures of retribution. Efforts to prove that they are not really there are not convincing because they are still seen in the "mind's eye." Giving in to sleep seems to expose the child to innumerable dangers. If sleep has in any way been linked to death, the picture is further compounded. "Talking through" bedtime thoughts can help a child to see things more clearly and feel more safe, but one must keep the objective of going to sleep in mind. Otherwise, these conversations can become endless and a technique of postponement. The child still faces the task of falling asleep alone.

Nightmares and Night Terrors

Night terrors, or pavor nocturnus, are characterized by intense anxiety and piercing screams, and usually no memory of the event. Ablon and Mack (1979) reported that they occur in approximately 3% of all children and are most common between the ages of 5 and 7 years. Night terrors occur during arousal from slow wave Stage 4 sleep, while the more common nightmares or anxiety dreams occur during REM periods. They may be brought on by traumatic events but since they lack any mental content and are followed by amnesia, it is hard to establish the psychological connections. Fortunately they occur infrequently and children usually outgrow them without special assistance.

In contrast, nightmares are common, mainly in the preschool years although Lapouse and Monk reported that 28% of the 6- to 12-year-olds they studied were still having nightmares (1959). In many respects, they represent a fulfillment of the bedtime fears previously described. Usually a child goes back to sleep without much difficulty after waking from a dream, but may be fearful of a recurrence on subsequent nights. Jersild, Markey, and Jersild (1933) concluded that children's dreams are a reflection of their fears, since a large number of dreams contain the same themes that children report when they tell about their fears. Often, children are unclear about whether they are recounting a

fantasy, a so-called daydream, or a dream they had while asleep. It is rare to have a child referred for the single symptom of nightmares, but nightmares frequently accompany other problems of anxiety which are apparent during the day, and the dreams may be useful in the process of treatment for understanding what is going on in the child's mind (see Chapter 8). Some bad dreams seem to be almost a straight repetition of a frightening experience, but most dreams bear little resemblance to real events.

Oedipal conflicts may in part account for the reported peak in sleep disturbances and nightmares around 5 years of age. Case 6.1 illustrates the connection between these anxieties and the eruption of a night fear which was much like a waking nightmare.

In this situation, an Oedipal anxiety was transformed into fear of a skeleton—which could just as easily have been a ghost, robber, Martian, lion, tiger, or, especially for girls, a witch or a snake. The child's aggressive wishes are repressed because he or she fears retaliation or fulfillment. The repression is only partial, however. The aggressive feelings remain extant, although the true source and object are replaced by something dangerous which will do to the child what he wanted to do to someone else. This projection still causes anxiety but it is more acceptable to be afraid of a skeleton than to acknowledge confused feelings about the parent. The amount of anxiety may be very little less, but it is at least contained and restricted to a time and place; thus, there it is at least contained and restricted to a time and place; thus, there is less sense of inner conflict, confusion, and guilt.

Case 6.1 Ben

An intelligent 5-year-old boy, Ben, complained miserably of a skeleton in his bedroom. He did not fight going to bed but lay awake for long periods, talking to himself and keeping his mind occupied, actually becoming more wakeful, and finally fleeing from his room. This was the boy's only symptom and it was decided to help him through his mother rather than to start psychotherapy.

The first step was his explanation that he thought the skeleton was that of his father. There is only one way to become a skeleton, or a ghost, and that is by dying. The second step was that the dead father was going to attack him. The boy was both frightened and sad in relating these facts. At this point, the mother took the initiative. She recalled to Ben a recent suggestion he had made that

his father should "join the Marines." At the time, this had been treated humorously by the parents, but now the mother remarked that perhaps Ben wished that his father really would go away and stay away. The boy said nothing, did not even appear to be listening.

Another night she went one step further, suggesting that he might be afraid his father knew some of these secret bad wishes. She assured him that nothing would happen to the father and also that he would not be angry. At this point, Ben objected, indicating that he had followed her every step—and rejoined that of course his father would be mad if he knew. Who wouldn't? The mother was able to convince him that this would not be the case, and that was the end of the skeletons.

When this child had the opportunity to share his secret bad wishes, he learned that they were not so dangerous or reprehensible, which greatly diminished the anxiety and the resultant fantasies of imminent dangers.

PROBLEMS IN TOILET TRAINING

Changing Views of Toilet Training

There have been major changes in the recommendations offered on the subject of toilet training, particularly when to start. The studies reported by Gesell in the 1930's compared the effectiveness of "early" training (before 3 months) and "late" training (around 1 year) and con-

cluded that a child was easier to train when maturationally ready as judged by independent walking. In 1942, the Children's Bureau publication on Infant Care stated firmly:

When a baby can sit up by himself, when he begins to pay attention to what is said to him—usually at 8 to 10 months—is a good time to start training him to have a bowel movements when he is on a chamber or a toilet seat. It is possible to start training much earlier, but, regardless of when training is started, babies as a rule do not learn to control their bowel movements much before they are 10 to 12 months of age. (p. 58)

Pediatric advice gradually shifted toward older ages. For instance, in *Parents* magazine, Fontana (1979) recommended that "Only when your child has reached the age of being aware of wetting and is able to anticipate urination can you begin to toilet train him. This stage of recognition usually occurs between 1 year and 18 months of age, although it may occur later" (p. 84).

There are now wide variations in practice and significant differences related to educational and economic status of the parents. Carlson and Asnes (1974) found that mothers made no distinction between bladder and bowel training and that over half of the clinic mothers thought training should begin by 16 months compared to about 20% of the private practice mothers. Most "sophisticated" mothers at present elect to wait until the child is around 30 months of age. There seems to be general consensus that training should be accomplished by age 3 years, so clearly the middle-class mothers expect the late training to be promptly accomplished. To some extent the changes of the past 40 years may reflect the availability of disposable diapers and diaper service, but there are also changes in psychological expectations.

Choosing a Time to Start

Three considerations are relevant in choosing the "best" time: later breakdowns, length of time for training, and parent-child conflicts. Although there are many "belief" statements, there are little empirical data relating later regression to time of starting training. Brazelton (1962) argued for the benefits of later training (around 2 years) on the basis of the high rate of enuresis (15%) in British Army inductees whose toilet training presumably had been initiated

according to custom before the age of 1 year, but other factors could have been involved and there have been no other such comparisons.

Book titles such as *Toilet Training in Less than a Day* (Azrin & Fox, 1974) hold out the promise that toilet training can be quick and easy if the timing is right. This is in marked contrast to Fraiberg's statement that "Many parents do not know that normally the process of toilet training, including bladder control, can take many months and we can expect occasional relapses until well into the fourth year" (1959, p. 99). Present-day parents feel that this is just too long a process and are convinced that if one waits for the child's active cooperation, he will "train himself" in a few days, or weeks at most. In effect, they are asking the child to decide when he or she wants to be clean "like a big boy, or big girl" (as long as it is before 3 years) and then making it possible to achieve that goal, usually by changing from diapers to training pants.

Again more by general impression than reported facts, many parents are fearful of the psychological consequences of "too early" toilet training. Freud's description of the "anal character" (1908/1955) as stubborn, miserly, compulsive, and depressive left a surprisingly lasting impression (Bernstein, 1979), although toilet training in that period was very early and often associated with coercive measures such as enemas and suppositories which also acted to eroticize anal activities. The message that filtered down, however, was that early training could lead to very neurotic behavior, and parents were duly impressed. Parents feel that toilet training should be free of conflict so that the child will have no anxiety. This hope leads parents to retreat quickly if the child shows any reluctance. Spock and Bergen (1964) ascribed the hesitancy observed in well-educated middle-class mothers to a "fear of conflict." "What they feared, some said directly and others indirectly, was that they would arouse antagonism in their children and become angry themselves" (p. 113).

Every age has its perils. In the first year, the child is a passive partner in a conditioning process which entails a lot of effort for the parents. The child can be more actively involved by 18 months, but at this age there may be some anxiety connected with the toilet or disappearing bowel movement (see Chapter 5). At age 2 years, these fears have probably subsided, but one encounters the "maybe I will, maybe I won't" character of the age so that training may proceed by fits and starts. There are some problems with later ages as well, however. Some children still find it difficult to change their habits and are not so eager to give up their infantile life as one might expect. The child may conclude that getting "bigger" is full of new responsibilities not to his or her liking.

Generally, between 18 and 24 months seems appropriate from the standpoints of both physiological and cognitive readiness. Children, of course, will vary, but usually by 2 years they have periods of 2–3 hours of dryness and some regularity in bowel habits. Also they have the ability to understand what is expected and to communicate their bathroom needs. Timing also depends on the mother's readiness, most preferring to start in warm weather and when they have the time to give training their full attention. Once started, the parents are at the mercy of their child's signals and there will be some messy accidents and many a trip to the bathroom to no avail. A parent who is going to be repulsed or angered by these events might do well to delay until well after age 2 years.

Psychological Aspects of Toilet Mastery

One can look at toilet training as simply getting the child out of diapers, or one can consider this achievement as a mastery and a prototype of doing something to please others. Spock (1976) remarked that it is "from their toilet training that children get some of their feeling that one way of doing things is right and another is not; this helps them develop a sense of obligation, to become systematic people" (p. 286). Learning to wait, ask for help, and then perform at the right time and place is a major accomplishment which can bring parents as teachers and children as learners considerable satisfaction. If training for mastery is postponed until the child is socially shamed into compliance, there is little pride to be found in the accomplishment.

Except in extreme cases, there is little evidence connecting child rearing practices per se with adult personality characteristics (Yarrow, Campbell, & Burton, 1968). An unusual follow-up study found a significant positive relationship between "need achievement" in a group of 26-year-old adults (measured by the Thematic Apperception Test, see Chapter 7) and mothers' reports of scheduled feeding and "severe" toilet training obtained from interviews when these adults were 5 years of age (McClelland

& Pilon, 1983). (It is interesting to note that nearly half of these white, suburban mothers whose children were born in 1946 or 1947 began bowel training before the child was 9 months of age; at age 5 years, 20% were still bed-wetting at least occasionally.) McClelland and Pilon interpreted their findings cautiously:

Although it is theoretically interesting to know the mothers' attitudes toward early child training practices have apparently influenced the development of the children's social motives, practically speaking, these early learnings account for at most 10–30% of the variance in adult motive scores. Obviously, later experiences in school or adult life are also important sources of individual differences in need achievement. (p. 573)

Encopresis (Soiling)

Continued soiling after the age of 4 years, even as infrequently as once monthly, is the criterion for the diagnosis of "encopresis" according to the DSM III. Roughly half of encopretic children failed to achieve toilet mastery, whereas half regressed after a period of bowel control. Bellman (1966) surveyed the 7-year-old population in Stockholm (9,591 first graders) and reported that 1.5% still had frequent soiling episodes, with more than 3 times as many boys as girls and no differences in different socioeconomic groups. Although there were no differences in the time of starting training, coercive measures were used by 31% of the mothers of encopretics and by only 5% of the control mothers (Bellman, 1966). Many more of the mothers of encopretics beat their chil-

dren after accidents during the training period and described extreme loathing and disgust at such times. Also, fear of the toilet was reported in 13% of the encopretics and in none of the controls.

An important distinction is made between "retentive encopresis" associated with persistent constipation, which presents many secondary complications, and "nonretentive encopresis" where bowel habits are regular. Chronic constipation leads to painful defecation which in turn increases the withholding and diminishes the defecatory reflex. There are possible medical complications secondary to fecal impaction or psychophysiologic megacolon. Physicians are faced with the problem of differential diagnosis between congenital megacolon (perhaps requiring surgical intervention) and functional encopresis (Prugh, 1983). It is possible for these diagnostic procedures to be quite traumatic in and of themselves, so an initial presumption of psychogenic origin is usually made.

In Bellman's study, the encopretic children differed from matched controls in personality (more anxious, unassertive, and passive-aggressive), social skills (less peer contact), and family background (more punitive-authoritarian parents and more separations from mothers). In two-thirds of the "regressive" encopretics, the symptom began after a major separation from the mother. Although there are exceptions, most encopretic children are unhappy and oppositional in relation to other people. Particularly the retentive encopretics function in a kind of constant anxiety, fearing both having a bowel movement and not having a bowel movement. It is almost impossible for a parent to avoid becoming equally anxious.

Treatment. Behavioral and psychodynamic approaches differ radically in the treatment of encopresis. Parker and Whitehead (1982) summarized studies of behavioral approaches, all of which involved some combination of positive and negative reinforcements. One "comprehensive training procedure" used to treat retentive encopresis involved enemas and suppositories.

All unsuccessful attempts to evacuate are followed immediately by an enema or suppository which then results in a stimulated bowel movement. By pairing the meal and evacuation, the meal becomes a conditioned stimulus which sets the occasion for a bowel movement . . . Daily suppositories or enemas can be faced after continence is demonstrated. (p. 167)

Unfortunately the authors describe the methods in some detail but say nothing about the children. The possible effect of this "cure" on personality functioning was not considered. One would surely reserve this technique for those who failed to respond to other treatments and where physical health was endangered by the symptom.

Prugh (1983), taking a very different pediatric approach, emphasized enlisting the child's participation in reestablishing bowel routines and controls. He was particularly concerned with modification of parental attitudes and described "bowel-oriented families, in which a history of constipation or diarrhea may reflect a combination of autonomic patterns of inheritance and a psychic inheritance regarding the importance of bowel regularity and stool consistency" (1983, p. 600).

Looking at the family dynamics from a broader perspective, Baird (1974) described three pathological interaction patterns in families of encopretic children: (a) withholding of information or miscommunication about essential family affairs; (b) infantilization of the patient; and (c) mishandling of anger through repression and denial. These observations suggest a family therapy approach, strongly endorsed by Bemporad:

The soiling mysteriously disappears with an amelioration of the family atmosphere and interrelationships. The prime task of the therapist, in my opinion, is to determine what is lacking in the child's everyday life, what is causing him to feel frustrated and angry, what is blocking an appropriate expression of his feelings—in short, the causes of his having to resort to soiling as a method of expression—and then to attempt to rectify these sources of discontent. (1978, p. 167)

There are times when a family refuses to engage in family therapy and one offers psychotherapy for the child, working with the parents in an adjunct supportive role rather than trying to change family dynamics. Most encopretics can give no reason for their symptom and seem remarkably indifferent to it. They become adept in hiding the dirty clothes and denying that they have soiled, or even that they are in the act of soiling! Many times their denial confuses others so that indeed they "get away with it." Such children are often stoical about their symptom, treating it as an unfortunate handicap and hiding their anxiety and depression about it with the same intensity as they hide other emotional reactions. As one boy of 8 said, "I push the feelings back inside," which is exactly what he tried to do with his excretory products. With all these defenses, psychotherapy is usually a lengthy process.

Case 6.2, a partial case report, is offered to illustrate the personality dynamics involved.

In Bellman's 2-year follow-up study of 200 encopretic children, about half had stopped spontaneously and none had continued beyond 16 years of age. With this relatively high rate of spontaneous remission, it is hard to compare the effectiveness of the various treatments which have been used, all of which report a good measure of success (Levine & Bakow, 1976). The treatments de-

Case 6.2   Sarah

Sarah had never achieved dryness and had been subjected to numerous medical examinations and treatments, all unsuccessful. At age 4, when she started nursery school, she started to soil as well. Her parents were earnest, well-educated people but with serious problems which only gradually came to light. The mother's regular (but secret) drug use finally led to a divorce. Because the mother was ill at the time, the father had taken the initiative in training the daughter. At 7, she was bright, articulate, imaginative, and a model of deportment at school. She was favored by her teachers, who felt sorry for her, but she was heartily disliked by the other children. Sarah hated school and complained of stomachaches and headaches almost daily. On the surface, however, she was determinedly cheerful and constantly made up jokes and riddles to make people laugh.

For a long time she convinced herself that no one would know of her problem if she herself ignored it. Thus, she could carry on a sprightly conversation without any change of expression, while urinating or defecating. She was quite far along in treatment before she could admit that it was not a well-kept secret. Later, she admitted that she had little

control over her urination or defecation. Her wishes to be a boy were exceptionally strong, and she entirely disassociated herself from that part of her body which reminded her that she was only a girl.

The following anecdote illustrates the relationship between her character and her symptom. Sarah was helpless to defend herself against the merciless teasing of the other children. One day, a classmate passed out treats to everyone except Sarah. She was incensed, but when it was suggested that she retaliate in kind, she could not bring herself to spend the money to buy candy to give away. She held back gifts in the same way that she held back urine and feces and feelings. This was yet another reason for her lack of friends.

Sarah came to appreciate the extent of her obstinacy and the fact that it often led her to act against her own better judgment. She explained that once she had started something, she didn't know how to stop, even though she had a bad conscience about it. "Once I start, I just can't stop like that. I just have to go anyhow." Treatment was long and arduous, weaving through attitudes and feelings which finally led to the soiling symptom itself.

scribed show how great the gap can be between behavioral and dynamic approaches. Part of the difference may come from the nature of their cases—the dynamic therapists are usually discussing normally intelligent children whereas the behaviorists include retarded or organically impaired children. Conditioning for bowel control may be necessary if there is no possibility of treatment collaboration, but if the child is "normal," it is preferable to treat soiling with the same considerations that one gives to the initial task of toilet training.

Enuresis: Definition and Prevalence

Wetting is a far more common problem than soiling. The DSM III requires at least 1 event per month for children over 6 years of age, and even with this rather strict criterion, the prevalence rates stated in the Manual (e.g., 3% for boys and 2% for girls aged 10 years) are considerably lower than those reported in various surveys (Lapouse & Monk, 1958; Oppel, Harper, & Rider, 1968). Day wetting is less common than bed-wetting and the sex difference is reversed, with about twice as many girls as boys (Bloomfield & Douglas, 1956).

Oppel et al. (1968) reported a highly significant racial difference at age 12 years, with 5% of white males bedwetting compared with 15% of the black males. These investigators also pointed out the importance of regression; over half of the children who were bedwetting at age 12 were "relapsers" and had had dry periods lasting 6 months or more. In general, the percentage of bedwetters decreases regularly with age to

about 2% of the 12- to 14-year-olds, which is about the same as that reported for military enlistees (Sours, 1978).

Prevalence figures in clinical populations vary according to reporting source. Psychiatric clinics in hospitals report the highest rate, as much as 26% in the Child Psychiatry Service at Johns Hopkins (Kanner, 1957). A rate of 12% was reported for two community clinics compared with 1% in school mental health services (Gilbert, 1957). Somewhat surprisingly, there have been no contemporary reports of prevalence, perhaps because enuresis is not considered an "important" symptom.

In contrast to the personality difficulties frequently associated with encopresis, there is no personality pattern uniquely associated with enuresis. There is considerable disagreement as to whether enuretic children in general are more disturbed than non-enuretic (Rutter, Yule, & Graham, 1973). Even if they were, it would be hard to determine which came first, the enuresis or the personality problem. Quite aside from the question of whether enuresis is itself a sign of an emotional problems, it presents problems to the child. The parents may adopt a tolerant attitude, but the child knows that it is "babyish" to wet the bed and suffers a certain amount of shame and embarrassment with relationship to his peers. This is obvious in the great reluctance to even mention the problem; children want to keep it a family secret. Wetting interferes with the child's freedom to sleep away from home, so it becomes a social handicap. Finally, with regard to self-concept, the child who has not mastered this aspect of toilet training, apparently so simple for most people, feels a measure of helplessness which may be associated with fantasies that "something is really wrong." If only for the imposed restrictions and the loss of self-esteem, it is a problem deserving attention.

Causes. There is no direct evidence linking nighttime wetting to specifics of toilet training. Even early training started in the first year seems to have no bearing on later incidence of enuresis (Largo & Stutzle, 1977). There is a familial pattern. If one or both parents were enuretic, the child is about 3 to 5 times more likely to be enuretic (Doleys & Doce, 1982) although how much of this is genetic and how much environmental has not been studied. Despite lip service to the goal of dryness, in some families one can easily detect a permissiveness toward wetting which may well perpetuate the problem.

Anders and Weinstein (1972) viewed bed-wetting as a *sleep* disorder. Sleep studies have suggested that most episodes take place 1 to 3 hours after falling asleep in the transition from NREM to REM sleep. These children are characteristically difficult to awaken, have no recollection of wetting, and are not dreaming at the time. This observation leads to the impression that enuretics are characteristically "deep sleepers," but the relationship between enuresis, sleep arousal, and depth of sleep is not yet clear. From the practical standpoint, if one wants to prevent wetting, the child should probably be taken to the bathroom in the early part of the night's sleep. Some enuretics are more nearly conscious of the event and can associate the wetting with dreams or partial waking. Although one would expect that the latter group would be more amenable to

psychotherapy, these distinctions are rarely made for the purpose of choosing the form of treatment.

It seems doubtful that constitutional factors alone can explain enuresis although they may explain the choice of symptom. Whatever the cause, wetting can easily be entangled with interpersonal or internal conflicts. The symptom may be used to express aggression against the parents; it may be used to express infantile wishes; or it may become part of a sexual conflict. Katan (1946) and Sperling (1965) stressed the importance of fantasies of genital damage, an explanation that a child might reasonably generate. In some instances, bed-wetting may express not only the fear of damage but a boy's wish to be a girl. Occasionally it is linked with sexual excitement and the wetting is a symbolic way of "putting out the fire."

Treatment. The diversity of treatment approaches parallels the array of possible cause. Tricyclics (e.g., imipramine or Tofranil) are the only group of drugs shown to be more effective than placebos in double-blind studies, but there is a 70–90% relapse rate when drugs are discontinued (Parker & Whitehead, 1982). Looking at bladder control as something to be learned, behavior therapies have been extensively used, starting with the bell-and-pad procedure originally proposed by Mowrer and Mowrer (1938). The basic premise is that by pairing bladder fullness (UCS) with the alarm, the UCS becomes a conditioned stimulus (CS) for the conditioned response (CR) of awakening. The review of 12 studies using this paradigm indicated that bed-wetting was arrested in 75% of the children in treatment lasting from 5 to 12 weeks. However, a 41% relapse rate was noted, which leaves about one-third "successfully treated" (Doleys, 1977). To some degree the success of this treatment depends on the child's cooperation. If the child is not motivated to work on the problem, the alarm can be turned off or "slept through" so that the apparatus is inoperative.

Retention control training was introduced by Kimmel and Kimmel (1970) following the observation that enuretics urinate more frequently and seem to have smaller bladder capacities. Increasing fluid intake and encouraging the child to hold back urination is included as one component of the rather complex procedure known as the "Dry Bed Training" program (Azrin, Sneed, & Fox, 1974). This procedure employs the standard urine-alarm device but adds nighttime awakenings, massed practice to teach nighttime toileting, positive reinforcement for dry bed or nighttime toileting, negative consequences for wetting (i.e., changing sheets and making bed), and retention control training. It appears to be highly effective in the short term but in a 2-year follow-up, Bollard (1982) found that 39% of the enuretics treated by DBT had relapsed. There are other problems in that dry bed training involves the active participation of the parents and many fall by the wayside, preferring their own sleep to the nighttime vigilance required in this treatment program. Also, the requirements for "massed practice" of 20 rehearsal trips to the bathroom is tiring for child and parent alike. Bollard and Nettelbeck (1982) compared a number of modifications and concluded that the waking schedule combined with the urine-alarm was almost as effective as

the complete DBT program, and certainly simpler. It is not clear how many children become dry because they refrain from urination altogether during the night as opposed to the number who wake and go to the bathroom. It is certainly easier for those who can stay asleep and remain dry.

It is doubtful that one would recommend psychotherapy for the single symptom of enuresis, but since it often appears in association with other problems (particularly learning problems), many enuretic children are in psychotherapy. Psychotherapy does not focus on the symptom of enuresis but is directed more to the other daytime problems. It is presumed that when other conflicts are relieved, the enuresis will diminish. The problem is discussed in terms of its significance to the child (real or imagined), and the therapist seeks to support the child's effort to achieve control. When it becomes clear that the child is aware of the act of wetting, psychotherapy is helpful in elucidating the reasons for making this choice, such as fear of the dark, enjoying the sensation of wetness, and so on. Also, when bed-wetting is an occasional event, it may be linked with specific occurrences or feelings of the day, or even with a particular dream. It is hard to judge the relative effectiveness of psychotherapy because it is a much longer treatment than the behavioral methods described above, and spontaneous remissions might well occur.

In the author's experience, the most important feature is to start with an open family discussion of the bed-wetting as a significant problem, even when the child is as young as 4 or 5 years. Without some anxiety engendered in the child, there is little motivation to exert the extra effort to get up at night. The mere act of keeping careful track of the wet beds may be effective. Also, it is important not to let the child become discouraged by a wet bed after a string of dry nights—the successes should reassure the child that nothing is "broken" or out of order. Enuresis is a symptom with so many secondary consequences that the focus on prompt elimination of the symptom which characterizes the behavioral approach has considerable merit. However, in choosing the treatment, the child should be an active partner and have some stake in its success. Passive sufferance on the child's part may explain the high relapse rate. Although most enuretics who come for treatment are of school age, the solution of the problem rests on many of the considerations involved in toilet training. The goal is not simply a dry bed, but for the child to gain a sense of mastery and to feel on a par with others of his age.

NONCOMPLIANCE

"Normal" Negativism

Parents of both "normal" and clinic-referred children frequently complain that their child "does not listen," ignores requests or commands, or is generally disobedient. Many observers have commented on the "terrible two's" who seem to say "no" on general principle. Erickson (1950) related this phenomenon to the child's effort to be more independent and establish autonomy. Generally, after the initial resistance, the child comes around to adopting the par-

ent's suggestion as his or her idea, but it takes time. Occasionally the child does not accept the parent's directive voluntarily and there is no recourse but to assert one's greater power as a parent.

Recently there has been a shift from permissiveness or democratic parental styles to an increased emphasis on the importance of setting limits for child behavior. For instance, Baumrind concluded from her studies that "In the preschool years, authoritative control, by comparison with authoritarian control or permissive non-control, is associated with social responsibility (achievement orientation, friendliness toward peers, and cooperativeness toward adults) and social dominance, nonconforming behavior, and purposiveness" (1973, pp. 30–31). It is very difficult to isolate a single aspect of parental practices because the effect depends so much on the total family context. Lewis (1981) pointed out that the children whose parents were identified by Baumrind as "harmonious" demonstrated similar positive characteristics and suggested that the single factor of disciplinary style was an insufficient explanation. In her rejoinder, Baumrind (1983) defended the importance of "firm control" but added that it would not be effective in the absence of affection and "induction" (that is, offering explanations for the rules and requests). Although permissiveness has faded and power assertion returned to favor, it must be judiciously employed.

Negativism does not magically disappear when the child becomes 3 years old. In a home observation study of 33 "normal" children between the ages of 4 and 6 years, Johnson, Wahl, Martin, and Johansson (1973) found a compliance ratio of 76%, indicating a probability of 1 in 4 that a child will not obey a command which his parents give him. This is an improvement over the 65% compliance ratio calculated by Lytton (1976) for 2½-year-old boys. Lytton's data indicated that compliance behavior scores correlated positively with the child's independence and maturity of speech, and consistently enforced discipline, encouragment of independence, psychological rewards, and maternal play were predictive of the child's compliance. On the other hand, the amount of physical punishment used by the mother was a negative predictor. As an interesting sidelight, Lytton (1977) reported that the mother's compliance ratio also contributed to the prediction of the child's compliance. Apparently to the child of 30 months, the mother's willingness to do as the child requests increases the child's willingness to reciprocate in kind.

Principles of Discipline

It is difficult to interpret the data on the effects of various forms of parental discipline in child rearing because of subject selection, the role played by the child in evoking particular parental responses, and the place of discipline in the total context of parental behavior and expectations. Disciplinary practices are often considered without regard to the appropriateness of parental demands, so that the methods may not be harsh but the expectations may be unrealistic in terms of kind or quantity.

The author has suggested that parents consider the issues of clarity, consistency, and contrast in discipline (Kes-

sler, 1968). Clarity requires that parents be specific in their demands and that the child be able to comprehend what is expected. Consistency involves thinking ahead so that parents focus on what is important and do not vary according to their mood, fatigue, or external circumstances. It is all too easy to issue directions which are really hopeful suggestions, but with the linguistic form of "orders." It is little wonder then that children ignore these remarks until the parents underscore them with repetition, raised voices, or threats. Above all, parents should eschew threats which they cannot or will not carry out.

Contrast has to do with consequences; approval or disapproval should be promptly communicated with a contrast which is readily apparent to the young child. The attempt made by some parents to explain that "I love you but not what you are doing" is probably lost on most preschool-aged children. But at the same time that the young child feels the "withdrawal of love," he should feel that it is within his power to regain that love in short order. With all the firmness, there should be nothing catastrophic or irrevocable about the disapproval. If the child is not sure she can please, she won't bother to try. Overall, the parents' goal should be to help the child "stay in favor." In one of his few statements regarding child rearing, Piaget commented:

How can one fail to be struck by the psychological inanity of what goes on in the efforts which parents make to catch their children in wrong-doing instead of anticipating consequences and preventing the child by some little artifice or other from taking up a line of conduct which his pride is sure to make him stick to; the multiplicity of orders that are given by the average parent is like an unintelligent government that is content to accumulate laws in spite of the contradictions and the every-increasing mental confusion which this accumulation leads to. (1932, p. 190)

Treatment via Parent Training

There are instances where the parents are unable to set limits for their young child and general guidance does not suffice. The frequent result is tremendous inconsistency, with the parents alternating between a kind of impatient helplessness of "letting things go" and sudden attacks of firmness, often expressed in physical punishment. Forehand and McMahon (1981) described a parent training program which involves didactic instruction, modeling, role playing, and practicing with the child in the clinic. In the first phase of treatment, the parent is taught to be a more effective reinforcing agent, in part using a device of "The Child's Game," where the child determines the nature and rules of the interaction. When the criteria for positive parenting skills are reached, they move to the second phase of training the parent to use appropriate commands and a time-out procedure to decrease noncompliance. In "The Parent's Game," the parents are taught to avoid chaining or vague commands, or commands which are in question form ("Wouldn't you like to. . . ."). The time-out procedure is carefully outlined and rehearsed. Evaluation data indicate that the program is effective in relatively short order (less than 10 sessions), generalizes from the clinic to the home, and

is relatively long-lasting (Forehand & McMahon, 1981).

The authors warn that parent training is not uniformly effective and cite evidence that parent depression, low socioeconomic status, and referral by authority sources in contrast to self-referral are associated with poor therapy outcome and/or high dropout rates. The common denominator is that these parents are unable or unwilling to make the necessary commitment of effort and time. Forehand and McMahon also point out a limitation, namely, that there seems to be no generalization to school settings. Apparently, the parents have learned a good deal in the program and the child has learned appropriate responses to their behavior, which is all to the good. However, the situational specificity suggests that the child has not internalized the general norm of compliance to authority or has not developed the self-control to act accordingly. This program is essentially a sophisticated operant conditioning treatment which is useful in bringing order out of chaos; at a later point, though, the child must operate with internal reinforcements.

The ultimate sources of such internal reinforcements are the child's ego ideal and conscience, discussed further in the context of conduct disorders (Chapter 10). The goal of discipline is the development of an internal set of standards which the child will follow autonomously. External reward and punishment give the "lessons" affective significance, but they are a means to an end and perhaps of less importance than the modeling offered by parents and significant other adults and the attachment bond between child and parents.

PARENT EDUCATION

In general, parent education is aimed at "normal" parents with "normal" children and appeals predominantly to a white, middle-class clientele with above-average education and income, despite efforts to reach other groups (Harman & Brim, 1980). Clarke-Stewart (1978) found that young women with relatively high levels of formal education, expecting their first child or engaged in raising their first child during infancy, formed the bulk of library users of child-care literature. It appears that parental participation is highest during infancy, begins to decline when children are about 2 or 3, declines further during the primary school years, and then increases again during early and mid-adolescence. The subject of parent education is reviewed in the context of the preschool age period because that is the time when parental behavior has the greatest directed impact on child behavior. At later ages, the influence of parents is diluted by the influence of teachers, peers, and the child's own personality structure. Again, it is assumed that the child therapist may be asked to make recommendations or lead discussion groups for parents who want to avail themselves of "expert" knowledge.

Written Materials

Since the beginning of written history there have been commentators on the subject of parental duties. For instance, the Talmud contains considerable advice to parents on the subject of child rearing and clearly assigns parents the primary responsibility to educate their children. On the subject of noncompliance, the Jewish Zohar (c. 1230) tells in a teaching parable of a father who was grieved because his son was disobedient. He mulled over his problem thus in his mind: "What if I were to punish him—what would I accomplish thereby? If I were to inflict pain on him, it would cause me pain also, and if I were to rebuke him publicly, it would only humiliate him. What then shall I do? I know—I shall plead with him to mind me!" A Talmudic maxim is "If you must strike your child, do it with a shoestring." In contemporary times, the most widespread form of parent education in terms of coverage is still the printed word: books, pamphlets, journals, and magazines. Dr. Spock's *The Common Sense Book of Baby and Child Care* (1946/1963) has sold more than 28,000,000 copies. While no other book has approached this figure, it has been calculated that the average annual sales for a recognized book on child care is 44,000 copies (Clarke-Stewart, 1978).

Harman and Brim (1980) suggested that there are two central foci regarding content of parent education, the first emphasizing knowledge of child development and the second offering specific advice. An early example of the former is Gesell and Ilg's *Infant and Child in the Culture of Today* (1943), which described typical behavior at different ages. Suggestions were made about play equipment and daily routines, but little advice was offered regarding education or training. For example, referring to the difficult behavior of the normal 2-year-old, Gesell and Ilg wrote, "He needs developmental time; he deserves discerning patience" (p. 180). A later version (Ilg & Ames, 1955) still emphasized the importance of inner determinants: "The more you know about the normal changes which ordinarily take place in behavior as a child grows, the more successful you can be in guiding your child along the complicated path which leads to maturity" ... through "remarkably patterned and largely predictable stages" (1955, p. 3). Selma Fraiberg's *The Magic Years* (1959) drew on Piagetian and psychoanalytic concepts to give the young child's point of view. Although there are management suggestions, they are embedded in descriptive and theoretical narrative. Books of this genre are outnumbered by those which offer specific advice.

Dr. Spock's book stands foremost in the field, partly because its appearance coincided with the postwar baby boom but also because it covers a wide variety of facts, medical as well as psychological, which can be quickly located by the index. Although he is generally accused of promulgating permissiveness, a careful reading does not justify this interpretation. His permissiveness had more to do with his efforts to increase parents' self-confidence, so he expressed tolerance of many different child-rearing practices. In an address to parent educators, he stated that the "only question you have to ask yourself is 'Will this make them (i.e., parents) more comfortable or will it make them more guilty?' My impression is that you rarely help them by making them guilty and that you always get a reflection of better management of the child by making them more comfortable" (Spock, 1955). Nonetheless, he gave as one reason for revising his book "a need to counteract a growing tendency toward overpermissiveness among certain parents, to buck

up their self-assurance and authority, to help them to give firmer guidance to their children" (1963). Reviews of child-rearing advice reveal frequent cycles between rigidity and permissiveness (Stendler, 1950; Vincent, 1951; Wolfenstein, 1953), so that these publications are as much a reflection of the times as they are trend-setters.

It is difficult to rival Spock for comprehensiveness. Brazelton (1974) and White (1975) concentrate on infants and toddlers. Weisberger's *When Your Child Needs You* (1987) discusses management problems in the years from 1 to 5 with considerable attention to parental feelings. Three books which are more oriented to the school-age and adolescent years and share a common theme of parent-child communication are Haim Ginott's *Between Parent And Child* (1965), Dreikurs' *Children: The Challenge* (1964); and Gordon's *Parent Effectiveness Training* (1970).

The California-based P.E.T. has become almost a "movement," with a prescribed course curriculum and a training program for instructors. In Gordon's words, "The P.E.T. program has also thrown new light on punishment in child-rearing. Many of our P.E.T. parents have proven to us that punishment can be discarded forever in disciplining children—and I mean all kinds of punishment, not just the physical kind" (p. 3). "This book—as does the P.E.T. course—teaches parents a rather easy-to-learn method of encouraging kids to accept responsibility for finding their own solutions to their own problems" (p. 7). The book, in many ways exemplifying an application of client-centered techniques of counseling, presents many illustrations of "active listening" and persuasive means of talking to children.

Almost diametrically opposed to this approach is Gerald Patterson's *Living with Children* (1976), which presents detailed instructions for the rewards and punishments parents should use to change behavior. For instance, in the section on noncompliance, the child gets a star each time he minds and a special reward when he reaches a certain number. For failure to mind, he is to have 2 minutes alone in the bathroom with the door closed. If he is noisy when the timer rings, he remains in Time Out for an additional minute, and so on. These approaches are so different that they do not allow for reconciliation. It would be instructive to know what parents are drawn to which and how much they find they can apply the advice.

Following almost any of these books, however, would take a great deal of parental attentiveness, much more than is probably realistic under contemporary circumstances. The limited time and many demands on the mother employed outside the home are generally overlooked. Even those remaining at home spend less time exclusively with their young children, at most perhaps one-third of waking hours (Bane, 1973, 1976). Parent education should be thought of as "child care education" and made readily available to alternate caregivers, including day-care staff and teachers.

Influence of Television Programming

A few "public service" spots are allocated to advice for parents, but these are so brief that they probably have little impact. The greater impact probably comes by incidental learning from viewing programs intended for entertainment. There are a number of family situation comedies or serials which depict parents and their children, often in everyday conflicts. Casual observation suggests that these contain quite enlightened views of child rearing even when they are cloaked by humor. It would be worthwhile to test viewing audiences for their recall of what was shown and their judgment of its relevance for "real life." The potential of this medium has hardly been considered to date.

Oral Techniques

Other approaches include the time-honored lecture, discussion groups, special need groups, and responses to individual requests to telephone services or inquiries made of professionals like pediatricians, clergymen, teachers, and psychologists. A 1983 Parent Education Directory published by the Family Health Association in Cleveland listed a total of 276 programs, some ongoing and some lasting as long as 10 weeks. Of these 43% were childbirth classes. Some of these had a special focus such as single parenting, children of divorce, handicapped children, teenage parents, adoptive parenting, and so on. It is hard to imagine any topic that was not covered. The fact that the 1983 listing indicated a 30% overall increase from 1981 suggests that these offerings are fully utilized. Parent education is a very robust and thriving enterprise!

Evaluation

In 1959, Brim summarized the results of nearly two dozen studies evaluating effectiveness of parent education as "leaving little doubt that their results are inconclusive," a comment that was interpreted by the Carnegie Council on Children in a discouraging statement that "research on parent education in past decades does not provide grounds for much optimism about the power of this approach to make significant changes in the family life of large numbers of people" (Keniston, 1977, p. 8). In their later review, however, Harman and Brim (1980) took pains to state that the inconclusive evaluation results partly reflect the inadequacy of available research methods and cited positive results from the group programs serving disadvantaged parents (See Chapter 4). They concluded that effects on parents appeared to correlate with extent of program participation.

Overall, the programs that appeared in evaluation studies to have had the most distinct effects were those that engaged parents from between a year and a half to at least two years, indicating that length of program and sustained participation are significant aspects of program impact. (1980, p. 251)

This leaves wide open the question of the impact of reading materials, lectures, or short-term group discussions for the middle-class parent. Even if it does not result in measurable change in the participants, parent education seems to be here to stay. Five functions can be identified as having positive value, however limited in scope. First, the mere fact that there are study groups and literature on this subject affirms the importance of child rearing and calls attention to the parental role. Second, there is the sharing of experiences in study groups or the vicarious sharing obtained by reading articles about children. Even to know that other parents have the same questions or problems reduces the sense of isolation. Third, factual information about behavior usual at different ages helps the parents to know what to expect. There is no reason to expect that the biological fact of parenthood makes people immediately comfortable with, or knowledgeable about, infants and children. Fourth, interpretive information tries to get under the surface and explain some of the whys of child behavior. If nothing else, this may quicken the parents' interest in observing and thinking about their child. It may also improve their empathy and ability to communicate. The fifth function is to offer recommendations in child management. This is perhaps the most hazardous aspect of parent education because the best prescription can be misused, but generally parents are not so much in awe of so-called experts that they fail to use their common sense.

Education for Alternate Care-Givers

As mentioned earlier, an increasing number of mothers of preschool children are employed outside the home and must perforce arrange for alternate child care. The fact is that a small minority are enrolled in child-care centers; most preschoolers are cared for in homes of relatives, neighbors, friends, or in day-care homes. Nothing is known about the impact of educational materials on these care-givers, and surprisingly few discussion groups are identified for this population. It is tacitly assumed that if they "like" children and are willing to assume the responsibility of care, they are qualified.

In a survey of a diversified, representative sample of San Francisco parents with children in day-care centers or homes, Auerbach-Fink (1974) found that most mothers encountered difficulties in balancing the needs of the employers with those of their children. Three out of four reported difficulty locating day-care programs; transportation represented an awesome burden, with mothers typically spending at least an hour on buses each morning and evening. Approximately two out of three mothers stated that the programs in which their children were enrolled did not meet their expectations. The most frequent criticisms were lack of outdoor play opportunities, overcrowding, and limited individual attention. Many mothers expressed their feelings of loneliness and isolation in different ways. Few could afford baby-sitters, and as a consequence their social lives suffered. The working mother has little time to spare for parent education discussion groups. Very few day-care centers offer parent programs (which include serving an evening meal) in which both parents and staff participate.

Observations of working mothers and their children suggest that the mother's employment status makes little difference in the quality of interaction (Hoffman, 1984). There is some evidence that daughters of working mothers fare better than sons over a period of time, but the reasons are not clear. Also, the mother's motivations for working outside the home are important. If her work provides personal satisfaction, her relationships at home are usually positive (Stuckey, McGhee, & Bell, 1982). Although there is nothing automatically deleterious for the child about maternal employment per se, the realities of locating and paying for convenient child care are often overlooked. Ideally, there should be a requirement of some kind of "child care education" for those who go into the business.

SUMMARY

In this chapter we have examined the stresses in development from ages 1 to 5, reviewing common parental concerns and some of the historical changes. The identification and distribution of "behavior problems" as seen by professional judges have been discussed. This is a period of rapid change, constantly challenging parents' patience, flexibility, and ingenuity.

Particular problems selected for more comprehensive discussion were sleep difficulties, toilet training, and noncompliance. The problems of enuresis and encopresis, which by definition are problems of older children, were included on the basis that treating these problems in the school-age child draws on the principles of early training. Handling noncompliant behavior reaches deep into the philosophy of child rearing, and in this domain one sees sharply divergent views.

The final section on techniques and content of parent education further illustrates divergence of expert opinions. The prescriptions offered by behavior therapists are invaluable in those chaotic situations where the parents have lost all control. The general principles of modeling, clear and consistent communication, and appropriate reinforcement, positive as well as negative, apply across the board. The implementation of these principles is facilitated by a knowledge of what to expect at different ages and an understanding of the feelings and misunderstandings common to the young child. It is essential that both parent and child feel good about themselves and achieve a sense of partnership rather than operating in an adversary relationship.

In spite of, or perhaps partially because of, the differences in "expert" advice, parents of young children still seek out reading material and opportunities to discuss their concerns. Any professional person working with this age group should be well acquainted with the opportunities available, because discussion groups help to relieve the sense of isolation and desperation sometimes experienced by parents of young children. Parents gain perspective and derive considerable support from one another. By sharing experiences, they may also come to recognize those relatively few situations where the child is in "real trouble" and in need of individual help.

REFERENCES

ABLON, S. L., & MACK, J. E. (1979). Sleep disorders. In J. D. Noshpitz (Ed.), *Basic handbook of child psychiatry* (Vol. 2, pp. 643–660). New York: Basic Books.

ANDERS, T. F. (1973). Night-waking in infants during the first year of life. *Pediatrics, 63,* 860–864.

ANDERS, T. F., & WEINSTEIN, P. (1972). Sleep and its disorders in infants and children: A review. *Journal of Pediatrics, 50,* 311–324.

ASERINSKY, E., & KLEITMAN, N. (1953). Regularly occurring periods of eye motility and concomitant phenomena during sleep. *Science, 118,* 273–274.

AUERBACH-FINK, S. (1974). *Parents and child care: A report on child care consumers in San Francisco.* San Francisco: Far West Laboratory.

AZRIN, H. H., & FOXX, R. M. (1974). *Toilet training in less than a day.* New York: Simon and Schuster.

AZRIN, N. H., SNEED, T. J., & FOXX, R. M. (1974). Dry-bed training: rapid elimination of childhood enuresis. *Behaviour Research and Therapy, 12,* 147–156.

BAIRD, M. (1974). Characteristic interaction patterns of encopretic children. *Bulletin of the Menninger Clinic, 38,* 144–153.

BANE, M. J. (1973). A review of child care books. *Harvard Education Review, 43,* 669–680.

BANE, M. J. (1976). *Here to stay. American families in the twentieth century.* New York: Basic Books.

BAUMRIND, D. (1973). The development of instrumental competence through socialization. In A. D. Pick (Ed.), *Minnesota symposia on child psychology* (Vol. 7, pp. 3–47). Minneapolis: University of Minnesota Press.

BAUMRIND, D. (1983). Rejoinder to Lewis' reinterpretation of parental firm control effects: Are authoritative families really harmonious? *Psychological Bulletin, 94,* 132–142.

BEHAR, L., & STRINGFIELD, S. (1974). A behavior rating scale for the preschool child. *Developmental Psychology, 10,* 601–610.

BELLMAN, M. (1966). Studies on encopresis. *Acta Paediatrica Scandinavica, 170,* 1–151.

BELSKY, J., & STEINBERG, L. D. (1978). The effects of day care: A critical review. *Child Development, 49*, 929–949.

BEMPORAD, J. R. (1978). Encopresis. In B. B. Wolman, J. Egan, & A. O. Ross (Eds.), *Handbook of treatment of mental disorders in childhood and adolescence* (pp. 161–178). Englewood Cliffs, NJ: Prentice-Hall.

BERNSTEIN, A. C. (1979). Toilet training without tears. *Parents Magazine*, pp. 5ff.

BLOOMFIELD, J. M., & DOUGLAS, J. (1956). Enuresis: Prevalence among children aged 4–7 years. *Lancet, 1*, 850–852.

BOLLARD, J. (1982). A 2-year follow-up of bed-wetters treated by dry-bed training and standard conditioning. *Behaviour Research and Therapy, 20*, 571–580.

BOLLARD, J., & NETTELBECK, T. (1982). A component analysis of dry-bed training for treatment of bedwetting. *Behaviour Research and Therapy, 20*, 383–392.

BRAZELTON, T. B. (1962). A child-oriented approach to toilet training. *Pediatrics, 29*, 121–128.

BRAZELTON, T. B. (1974). *Toddlers and parents: A declaration of independence.* New York: Dell.

BRAZELTON, T. B. (1978, October). Why your baby won't sleep. *Redbook Magazine*, pp. 82ff.

BRIM, O. G. (1959). *Education for child rearing.* New York: Russell Sage.

BROWN, G. W. (1975). Social class and psychiatric disturbance among women in an urban population. *Sociology, 9*, 225–254.

BURTON, R. V., & WHITING, J. W. M. (1961). The absent father and cross-sex identity. *Merrill-Palmer Quarterly, 7*, 85–95.

CAREY, W. (1974). Night waking and temperament in infancy. *Journal of Pediatrics, 84*, 756–758.

CAREY, W. (1975). Breast feeding and night waking. *Journal of Pediatrics, 87*, 327–329.

CARLSON, S. S., & ASNES, R. S. (1974). Maternal expectations and attitudes toward toilet training: A comparison between clinic mothers and private practice mothers. *Journal of Pediatrics, 84*, 148–151.

CHAMBERLIN, R. W. (1974). Management of preschool behavior problems. *Pediatric Clinics of North America, 21*, 33–47.

CHAMBERLIN, R. W. (1977). Can we identify a group of children at age 2 who are at high risk for the development of behavior or emotional problems in kindergarten and first grade? *Pediatrics, 59*, Supple. 6, 971–81.

Children's Bureau. (1942). *Infant care.* (U.S. Department of Labor, Publ. No. 8.) Washington, DC: Superintendent of Documents.

CLARKE-STEWART, A. (1978). Popular primers for parents. *American Psychologist, 33*, 359–369.

COLEMAN, J., WOLKIND, S., & ASHLEY, L. (1977). Symptoms of behaviour disturbance and adjustment to school. *Journal of Child Psychology and Psychiatry, 18*, 201–209.

CROWTHER, J. H., BOND, L. A., & ROLF, J. E. (1981). The incidence, prevalence, and severity of behavior disorders among preschool-aged children in day care. *Journal of Abnormal Child Psychology, 9*, 23–42.

DOLEYS, D. M. (1977). Behavioral treatments for nocturnal enuresis in children: A review of the recent literature. *Psychological Bulletin, 84*, 30–54.

DOLEYS, D. M., & DOLCE, J. J. (1982). Toilet training and enuresis. *Pediatric Clinics of North America, 29*(2), 297–313.

DREIKURS, R. (1964). *Children: The challenge.* Des Moines, Iowa: Meredith Press.

EARLS, F. (1980). Prevalence of behavior problems in 3-year-old children. *Archives of General Psychiatry, 37*, 1153–1157.

ERIKSON, E. (1950). *Childhood and society.* New York: W.W. Norton.

Family Health Association, Inc. (1983). *Parent education newsletter/directory.* Cleveland, OH: Author.

FONTANA, V. J. (1979, March). Toilet training. *Parents*, p. 84.

FOREHAND, R. L., & MCMAHON, R. J. (1981). *Helping the noncompliant child. A clini-*

cian's guide to parent training. New York: The Guilford Press.

FRAIBERG, S. H. (1959). *The magic years.* New York: Charles Scribner's Sons.

FREUD, S. (1953). The interpretation of dreams. In J. Strachey (Ed.), *Standard Edition* (Vol. 4, 5). London: Hogarth Press. (Original work published 1900.)

FREUD, S. (1955). Character and anal erotism. In J. Strachey (Ed.), *Standard Edition* (Vol. 10). London: Hogarth Press. (Original work published 1908.)

GESELL, A., & ILG, F. L. (1943). *Infant and child in the culture of today.* New York: Harper.

GILBERT, G. M. (1957). A survey of referral problems in metropolitan child guidance centers. *Journal of Clinical Psychology, 13,* 37–42.

GINOTT, H. G. (1965). *Between parent and child.* New York: Macmillan.

GORDON, T. (1970). *Parent effectiveness training.* New York: Peter H. Wyden.

GRAHAM, P. J., RICHMAN, N., & STEVENSON, J. E. (1982). Family factors and outcome of preschool behavior problems. In J. de Wit & A. L. Benton (Eds.), *Perspectives in child study* (pp. 77–93). Lisse: Swets and Zeitlinger.

HARMAN, D., & BRIM, O. G. (1980). *Learning to be parents.* Beverly Hills, CA: SAGE.

HOFFMAN, L. W. (1984). Maternal employment and the young child. In M. Perlmutter (Ed.), Parent-child interaction and parent-child relations in child development. *The Minnesota Symposia on Child Psychology* (Vol. 17, pp. 101–128). Hillsdale, NJ: Lawrence Erlbaum.

ILG, F. L., & AMES, L. B. (1955). *Child behavior from birth to ten.* New York: Harper and Row.

JENKINS, S., BAX, M., & HART, H. (1980). Behavior problems in pre-school children. *Journal of Child Psychology and Psychiatry, 21,* 5–19.

JERSILD, A., MARKEY, F. V., & JERSILD, C. L. (1933). Children's fears, dreams, wishes, daydreams, likes, dislikes, pleasant and unpleasant memories. *Child Development Monographs, 12,* New York: Columbia University Press.

JOHNSON, S. M., WAHL, G., MARTIN, S., & JOHANSSON, S. (1973). How deviant is the normal child? A behavioral analysis of the preschool child and his family. In R. D. Rubin, J. P. Brady, & J. D. Henderson (Eds.), *Advances in Behavior Therapy* (Vol. 4, pp. 37–54). New York: Academic Press.

KANNER, LEO. (1957). *Child psychiatry* (3rd ed.). Springfield, IL: Charles C Thomas.

KATAN, A. (1946). Experiences with enuretics. In A. Freud, H. Hartmann, & E. Kris (Eds.), *The psychoanalytic study of the child* (Vol. 2, pp. 241–256). New York: International University Press.

KENISTON, K. (1977). *All our children: The American family under pressure.* New York: Harcourt Brace Jovanovich.

KESSLER, J. W. (1968, October). Taking the "mis" out of misbehavior. *Parent-Teachers Magazine.*

KIMMEL, H. D., & KIMMEL, E. (1970). An instrumental conditioning method for the treatment of enuresis. *Journal of Behavior Therapy and Experimental Psychology, 1,* 121–123.

LAPOUSE, R., & MONK, M. (1958). An epidemiologic study of behavior characteristics in children. *American Journal of Public Health, 48,* 1134–1144.

LARGO, R. H., & STUTZLE, W. (1977). Longitudinal study of bowel and bladder control by day and at night in the first six years of life. II. *Developmental Medicine and Child Neurology, 19,* 607–613.

LEVINE, M. D., & BAKOW, H. (1976). Children with encopresis: A study of treatment outcomes. *Pediatrics, 58,* 845–852.

LEVY, D. M. (1934). Experiment of the sucking reflex and social behavior of dogs. *American Journal of Orthopsychiatry, 4,* 203–24.

LEWIS, C. C. (1981). The effects of parental firm control: A reinterpretation of findings. *Psychological Bulletin, 90,* 547–563.

LOZOFF, B., WOLF, A. W., & DAVIS, N. S. (1984). Co-sleeping in urban families with young children in the United States. *Pediatrics, 74,* 171–182.

LOZOFF, B., WOLF, A. W., & DAVIS, N. (1985). Sleep problems seen in pediatric practice. *Pediatrics, 75,* 477–483.

LYTTON, H. (1976). The socialization of 2-year-old boys: Ecological findings. *Journal of Child Psychology and Psychiatry, 17,* 287–304.

LYTTON, H. (1977). Correlates of compliance and the rudiments of conscience. *Canadian Journal of Behavioral Science, 9,* 242–251.

MACFARLANE, J. W., ALLEN, L., & HONZIK, M. P. (1954). *A developmental study of the behavior problems of normal children between 21 months and 14 years.* Berkeley: University of California Press.

MCCLELLAND, D. C., & PILON, D. A. (1983). Sources of adult motives in patterns of parent behavior in early childhood. *Journal of Personality and Social Psychology, 44,* 564–574.

MOWRER, O. H., & MOWRER, W. M. (1938). Enuresis: A method for its study and treatment. *American Journal of Orthopsychiatry, 8,* 436–459.

NEWSON, J., NEWSON, E., & MAHALSKI, P. A. (1982). Persistent infant comfort habits and their sequelae at 11 and 16 years. *Journal of Child Psychology and Psychiatry, 23,* 421–437.

OPPEL, W. C., HARPER, P. A., & RIDER, R. V. (1968). The age of attaining bladder control. *Pediatrics, 42*(4), 614–626.

PARKER, L., & WHITEHEAD, W. (1982). Treatment of urinary and fecal incontinence in children. In D. C. Russo & J. W. Varni (Eds.), *Behavioral pediatrics* (pp. 143–175). New York: Plenum Press.

PATTERSON, G. R. (1976). *Living with children* (Rev. ed.). Champaign, IL: Research Press.

PIAGET, J. (1932). *The moral judgment of the child.* London: Kegan Paul, Trench, Trubner.

PRUGH, D. G. (1983). *The psychosocial aspects of pediatrics.* Philadelphia: Lea & Febiger.

RIBBLE, M. (1944). Infantile experience in re-lation to personality development. In J. McV. Hunt (Ed.), *Personality and behavior disorders.* (Vol. 2, pp. 621–652). New York: The Ronald Press.

RICHMAN, N. (1976). Depression in mothers of preschool children. *Journal of Child Psychology and Psychiatry, 17,* 75–78.

RICHMAN, N., & GRAHAM, P. J. (1971). A behavioral screening questionnaire for use with 3-year-old children: Preliminary findings. *Journal of Child Psychology and Psychiatry, 12,* 5–35.

RICHMAN, N., STEVENSON, J. E., & GRAHAM, P. J. (1975). Prevalence of behavior problems in 3-year-old children: An epidemiological study in a London borough. *Journal of Child Psychology and Psychiatry, 16,* 277–287.

RICHMAN, N., STEVENSON, J. E., & GRAHAM, P. J. (1982). *Preschool to school: A behavioral study.* London: Academic Press.

RUTTER, M., YULE, W., & GRAHAM, P. (1973). Enuresis and behavioural deviance: Some epidemiological considerations. In I. Kolvin, R. C. MacKeith, & S. R. Meadow (Eds.), *Bladder control and enuresis* (pp. 137–172). Philadelphia: W. C. Saunders.

SCHMITT, B. D. (1981). Infants who do not sleep through the night. *Developmental and Behavioral Pediatrics, 2,* 20–23.

SEARS, R. R., & WISE, G. W. (1950). Relation of cup feeding in infancy to thumb sucking and the oral drive. *American Journal of Orthopsychiatry, 20,* 123–139.

SHEPHERD, M., OPPENHEIM, A. N., & MITCHELL, S. (1971). *Childhood behavior and mental health.* London: University of London Press.

SOURS, J. A. (1978). Enuresis. In B. B. Wolman, J. Egan, & A. O. Ross (Eds.), *Handbook of treatment of mental disorders in childhood and adolescence* (pp. 153–160). Englewood Cliffs, NJ: Prentice-Hall.

SPERLING, M. (1965). Dynamic considerations and treatment of enuresis. *Journal of the American Academy of Child Psychiatry, 4,* 19–31.

SPOCK, B. (1955). Values and limits of parent

education. In *Communication in parent education: Proceedings of the Ninth Annual Institute for Workers in Parent Education.* New York: Child Study Association.

SPOCK, B. *Baby and child care* (Rev. Giant Cardinal ed.). New York: Pocket Books, Inc., 1963. (A new version of the *Pocket book of baby and child care,* originally published as the *Common sense book of baby and child care.* New York: Duell, Sloan and Pearce, 1946.)

SPOCK, B. (1976). *Baby and child care* (3rd Revision). New York: Pocketbooks.

SPOCK, B., & BERGEN, M. (1964). Parents' fear of conflict in toilet training. *Pediatrics, 34,* 112–116.

STENDLER, C. B. (1950). Sixty years of child training practices: Revolution in the nursery. *Journal of Pediatrics, 36,* 122–34.

STUCKEY, M. F., McGEE, P. E., & BELL, N. J. (1982). Parent-child interaction: The influ-

ence of maternal employment. *Developmental Psychology, 18,* 635–644.

VINCENT, C. E. (1951). Trends in infant care ideas. *Child Development, 22,* 199–210.

WEISBERGER, E. (1987). *When your child needs you.* Bethesda, MD: Adler & Adler.

WEISZ, J. R., ROTHBAUM, F. M., & BLACKBURN, T. C. (1984). Standing out and standing in. The psychology of control in America and Japan. *American Psychologist, 39,* 955–970.

WHITE, B. L. (1975). *The first three years of life.* Englewood Cliffs, NJ: Prentice-Hall.

WOLFENSTEIN, M. (1953). Trends in infant care. *American Journal of Orthopsychiatry, 23,* 120–130.

YARROW, M. R., CAMPBELL, J. D., & BURTON, R. V. (1968). *Child rearing.* San Francisco: Jossey-Bass.

ZUCKERMAN, B. S., & BLITZER, E. C. (1981). Sleep disorders. In S. Gabel (Ed.), *Behavioral problems in children: A primary care approach* (pp. 257–272). New York: Grune and Stratton.

CHAPTER 7

REFERRAL, ASSESSMENT, AND CHOICE OF TREATMENT

We now move to consider the age group between 5 and 12 years, which still represents the major source of referrals. The discussion of referral and initial screening is followed by a presentation of assessment methods and diagnostic classification. The concluding section is concerned with choosing the mode of treatment from the great array of possibilities. The focus of this chapter throughout is on the decision-making process as one moves from the first inquiry to the formulation of recommendations. The process is viewed in general terms, because features of diagnosis and treatment specific to particular clinical problems are examined in later chapters.

REFERRAL

It is not always easy to answer what looks like a simple question when a parent or teacher asks "Should we worry about this child who tells lies, or another child who is afraid of walking to school alone," or whatever. Experts have wrestled with the definition of "normal" and one can rarely offer a simple yes-or-no reply. Seldom do children themselves ask for help. Invariably some significant adult, usually parent or teacher, raises a question and asks for an opinion. The first person involved is frequently the pediatrician, but it may well be a psychologist employed in a school or agency or in private practice.

The following criteria are suggested as guidelines for consideration of referral for specialized help.

1. The behavior should be unusual for the age. With a solid knowledge of normal development, one knows the ages by which most children have outgrown particular habits and behaviors and assesses the presenting problem accordingly.

2. Frequency of occurrence of the symptom must be considered. No one would be concerned if a child occasionally wet his bed, even after the age of 5 or 6. Under special emotional or physical stress, any child will regress to previous patterns of behavior, and isolated regressions are not pathological as long as the child can recover quickly. One should be concerned when the symptomatic behavior is aroused under minimal stress, which means that it occurs very often.

3. The number of symptoms is an obvious consideration. The more symptoms, the more the child is disabled. However, one cannot rely exclusively on the criterion of multiplicity of symptoms to judge the extent of psychopathology. It is possible for a single symptom to work so efficiently that all the child's anxieties are taken care of at once. A good example is that of school phobia. Such a child may appear completely happy and well-adjusted if he is allowed to remain home. All the problems may be bound up in the one phobic situation so that there is no spillage to other areas.

4. The degree of social disadvantage is an inevitable determinant of parental concern about children's symptoms. School phobia is obviously serious because it prevents the child from receiving an education. Behavior, such as aggressiveness or day wetting and soiling, which alienates the child from others, has real secondary consequences. It is easy to see a vicious cycle at work where the effects of symptoms tend to perpetuate the symptom. After a while, the school-phobic child will be even more fearful of returning to school because she will be so far behind in her school work. The aggressive child will make so many enemies that he has no choice but to continue to fight.

5. The child's affects are often overlooked. Low self-esteem or feelings of discouragement and depression may hide behind the behavioral symptoms which give concern to the adult observer. Children form their own opinions and may feel ashamed and inferior because of unspoken thoughts and fantasies or "secret" habits. Inner distress may be revealed only to someone who knows the child well or on careful inquiry. The obvious pride in the occasional dry night demonstrated by a chronic bed-wetter, for example, also reveals the hidden shame about wetting.

6. Intractability of behavior is implied, in part, in the criterion of frequency. It is conceivable that a child persists in behavior which is abnormal for the age simply because no one has suggested that he or she change. But usually, common sense efforts to discourage the behavior have proven

futile. The persistence of symptoms, despite the efforts of the child and others to change them, is the hallmark of so-called behavior disorders.

7. General personality appraisal is the most important criterion and the most difficult. The first six criteria have to do with the behavior as such, but this criterion has to do with the child's general adjustment rather than with isolated symptoms.

Freud defined emotional adjustment in adulthood in terms of the ability to love and to work (Lieben & Arbeiten), and this applies equally well to children. The child's relationships with family members, with outside authority, and with peers should contain affection and give pleasure. Mere compliance is not enough. Also important, particularly in relation to the adult love life to come, the school-age child should be reasonably content with his or her sex gender. This is not meant to imply a narrow stereotype of what is deemed sexually appropriate behavior. The boy who feels he must be always strong and brave, or the girl who assumes that she should be modest and dependent, is in as much psychological trouble as the young child who wants to be the opposite sex.

The child's work is his schooling and here one would like to see the flowering of ambition, responsibility, and gratification in work well done. Whether such attitudes result in academic excellence depends on other factors, which are irrelevant. To judge a child's mental health by school grades would be like judging the parents' mental health by their income.

Preparing the Parents

If someone other than the parent is the first to raise questions, the parents must be prepared for referral. This customarily involves three steps. The first is the explanation of why the child needs help. The referring person must describe the difficulties that have been observed and explain in what ways the child differs from others. Presumably this person knows the child and has significant information to offer. However, this information must be presented tactfully and empathically so that the parents do not feel that the person is merely criticizing and rejecting their child.

During this process, it is important to communicate a feeling of genuine concern for the child's welfare. For instance, if a school officer wanting to refer a hyperactive, aggressive child stresses the disruptive effect on the group, the parent might think, "Oh, you just want to get rid of him somehow, because he is a nuisance to your school." It is preferable to talk about the effect on the child of lack of friends and social isolation, for example. If a doctor who can find no organic reason for persistent stomachaches tries to initiate a referral by saying, "There's nothing really wrong; it's all in her head," this conveys the impression that the child is malingering. Again, it is better to discuss the symptom in terms of the child's suffering, to say that the stomachaches are an expression of painful feelings which are hard to see. An approach that emphasizes the child's inner feelings is apt to convince the parent that the referring person is not simply trying to avoid responsibility.

The second step in preparing the parents is to deal with their resistances and objections to referral. Some of these arise from ignorance, but even some sophisticated people believe that psychiatric or psychological services are reserved for the crazy or the obviously handicapped. They need to know that basically normal children may have emotional problems at some time. Some parents fear that the child will be stigmatized if he or she has a record with a child guidance clinic and may need reassurance about the confidentiality of such records.

Another source of resistance is the parents' sense of guilt. They commonly feel that they are entirely responsible for their child's personality and behavior and that if there are problems, it is a reflection on them. Often they feel that it must mean that the child is insecure because they did not give him enough love, or else that they have made some serious mistake. It is vitally important that the referring person realize that children can develop emotional problems from traumatic events that were fortuitous or completely unintended by the parents, and the referring person must be familiar with the part played by fantasy. If indeed there has been parental mismanagement, the parents need reassurance as to the difficulties of child rearing and how easy it is to become bewildered and confused in responding to special problems.

The third step in the preparation of the parents is to convey a realistic understanding of what a referral can accomplish. Sometimes in the zeal to sell parents, the referring person endows a visit to an agency or clinic with almost magical powers. The parents get the idea that you just walk in to the office and come out cured. A referral for diagnostic study should be described in some such way as, "These specially trained people can give you some ideas of what to do next." The referring person should avoid promising that the clinic, or whoever, will "fix the child up." Equally, dire predictions about what will happen if they do not go should be avoided. The objective is not to get the parents to the agency no matter what, but to start them thinking along certain lines so that they will want to study their problem with someone.

Preparing the Child

It is equally important to prepare the child. The child has a right to know where he or she is going and why. As to why, the child should know what is meant by the "problem." Sometimes this has never been identified or discussed frankly for fear of shaming. On the other hand, perhaps it has been talked about too much and always negatively: "I don't know what will become of you." or "I don't know what we will do with you," or "Why don't you just quit that baby stuff?" The child assumes that the psychologist will say more of the same, and the parents will have a difficult time convincing him or her that the therapist will be for the child, not another critic.

It is impossible for a child to visit a mental health professional without knowing that something is up. Subterfuges never work. He or she soon realizes that this is no "old friend of mother's." The explanation has to be tailored to age and level of understanding, but it should be completely honest. The child should know whom he or she is going to see, and what interviews, tests, and procedures to expect. Right from the beginning, even with a young child, one sets a pattern of honest communication, hoping that the child can respond with equal honesty.

Although it is common practice to insist that a parent call to make the initial appointment, it is helpful if one has checked ahead to make sure that the referral is appropriate and that the agency or person can accept the case in a reasonable period of time. The very process of referral is the beginning of treatment, and it should be carried out in a respectful, careful manner.

ASSESSMENT

The Intake Interview

If at all possible, it should be arranged that both parents attend the intake interview. The interviewer of course starts with the nature of the referral, why the parents have come for help, how they chose the time and place, where they have been before, what has been suggested to them, what they have tried on their own, and what they now expect. As one moves into a deeper discussion of the presenting problems, the interviewer must get the parents' opinions, as opposed to their quotation of others, and also determine how they feel—sad, guilty, anxious, irritated, etc. What do they see as the chief locus of the problem—the unsympathetic teacher, unkind playmates, something wrong with the child such as a learning disability,

something wrong with them such as overindulgence or neglect or marital conflicts? It is important to record their exact words as they state the problem. In this inquiry one is trying to learn their style. Do they remember well? Do they connect things? Are they focused on their own needs and problems? Are they consistent in what they say? Are they open-minded or do they have some fixed notions about what is going wrong and why? Even at intake, parents expect some feedback, at the very least some confirmation that they made the right decision to come for help.

Current Functioning of the Child. A complete history includes the history of the problem behavior, the history of the child, and the family's history, but this usually evolves over a number of parental contacts. Initially one tries to determine the details about the presenting problem in terms of specific behavior, frequency, and duration. Sometimes the onset has been insidious: "He was always this way, but I didn't worry until this year." Or, "She was always sensitive, but it seems to be getting worse." There are some symptoms, particularly phobias or anxiety reactions, which may have a sudden onset, and the circumstances may be important to an understanding of the symptom. It is useful to inquire about other common symptoms of childhood psychopathology. It is remarkable how often parents come to a clinic because a child is failing in school and never volunteer the information that he is also an enuretic, suffers from recurrent nightmares, and has chronic constipation or severe feeding problems! Because they are unaware of the possible connections, they fail to mention problems which do not bother them.

Although there are still major differences in treatment between the behaviorally oriented therapist and the psychodynamic therapist, there is relatively little difference in the initial assessment process between the two. Historically, the behavior therapy approach to assessment was almost exclusively concerned with the specification of target problems in terms of frequency counts, rate, and duration measures. Careful attention was given to the consequences which followed such behaviors because it was thought that they provided the reinforcement necessary to maintain the behavior. Therefore, treatment consisted mainly of changing the usual response patterns of the people in the environment. It soon became apparent that instigating factors played an important contributory role. Werry and Wollersheim (1967) described the process of problem analysis as follows:

Having isolated the symptoms which are both deserving of and amenable to therapy, the therapist then attempts to determine the factors or stimuli which elicit the behavior, such as the feared situation in a phobia, and/or the factors which are perpetuating or reinforcing the problem behavior. This kind of information frequently requires some kind of observation of the child in a real-life situation such as at school or in the mother-child interaction. In respondent or emotional behavior, the therapist is likely to spend more time with stimuli; and in operant behavior, he is more likely to be concerned with determining the response-reinforcement contingencies in the child's natural environment. (p. 360)

Behavior therapy continued to widen its horizons.

As behavior therapy with children evolved, greater emphasis was placed on viewing the child as part of a larger network of interacting social systems ... and on the important role of cognition and affect in mediating child behavior change ... These developments have changed the quality of behavioral assessment from target behavior measurement to a more general problem-solving strategy based upon ongoing functional analysis and encompassing a greater range of independent and dependent variables. (Mash & Terdal, 1981, p. 7)

The behavior therapists made a very important contribution in forcing closer examination of surrounding environmental circumstances.

In the assessment interviews, the psychodynamic therapist, perhaps more than the behavior therapist, looks for habitual patterns of behavior and ways of responding to situations in order to get a total personality picture. This includes the child's role in the family, social behaviors, likes and dislikes, and so on. In general character, some children are overly conscientious, but the referred child is more likely to be passive about responsibilities. He or she dawdles and procrastinates until forced to dress, make the bed, finish homework, go to bed, etc. The child's reaction to competitive situations is also interesting. Some are afraid of success and scrupulously avoid achieving a top rating, but more fear failure and avoid situations where success is not a sure thing. The child's reaction to physical risk can be revealing. No child likes to be hurt, but some go to extraordinary lengths to keep out of harm's way whereas others seem to fear nothing.

One inquires of the parents what the child does when angry or frightened.

Their replies are of interest not only because they contain information about the child, but also because they reveal something about parental perceptiveness. These questions may draw a blank because the parents can't remember when their child was ever angry or frightened. Since one can be sure that the child has experienced both emotions, either the child is extraordinarily inhibited or the parents are extraordinarily good at forgetting. This context provides a natural opportunity to discuss how to prepare the child for his or her visit and to speculate on possible misapprehensions.

Structured Parent Report Measures. Although the above data are usually assembled from unstructured interviews, a number of standardized methods provide a common data base for all children. There are simple behavior checklists requiring a yes or no answer (Louisville Behavior Check List, Miller, 1967; the Missouri Children's Behavior Checklist, Sines, Pauker, Sines, & Owen, 1969). The most complicated example of this genre is the Personality Inventory for Children (Lachar & Gdowski, 1979; Wirt, Lakar, Klinedinst, & Seat, 1977). Following the model of the Minnesota Multiphasic Personality Inventory, the parent responses to 600 items are scored in a profile form with 12 clinical scales: Achievement; Intellectual Screening; Developmental; Somatic Concern; Depression; Family Relations; Delinquency; Withdrawal; Anxiety; Psychosis; Hyperactivity; and Social Skills.

The most widely used scale is the Child Behavior Checklist (Achenbach & Edelbrock, 1983, see Appendix). By factor analysis of the item responses, nine behavior problem scales were identified and labeled: Schizoid or Anxious; Depressed; Uncommunicative; Obsessive-compulsive; Somatic complaints; Social withdrawal; Hyperactive; Aggressive; Delinquent. There are still others from which to choose (Parent Questionnaire, Conners, 1973; Revised Behavior Problem Checklist, Quay & Peterson, 1983), all of which discriminate between referred and nonreferred populations and have reasonably high intercorrelations.

In their review of parent report measures, Humphreys and Ciminero (1979) suggested that a major problem is the failure of parent reports to correlate highly with direct observations, indicating that parents are far from unbiased. Lobitz and Johnson (1975) found considerable overlap in actual behavior between a clinic group and a control group and negligible correlations between observed child behavior and parent questionnaires. Similar results were reported by Peed, Roberts, and Forehand (1977), but it should be noted that the child observational data were based on brief periods of time, often under somewhat unusual conditions which might well not elicit typical behavior. When parent report measures are used for diagnostic assessment or for the evaluation of therapy, the scores are properly seen as parents' "perceptions" rather than objective facts about the child, but this does not mean that they are of no significance.

There has been some work on a structured interview for parents which is basically an oral questionnaire. The Diagnostic Interview Schedule for Children-Parents (DISC-P) was developed at the request of the National Institute of Mental Health for use as an epidemiological research tool (Edelbrock, Costello, Dulcan, Kalas, & Conover, 1985). It is lengthy, requiring about an hour for administration, and focuses on symptom behaviors for purposes of formal diagnostic classification. In all probability, it will not be generally used in clinical practice.

Questionnaires are a worthwhile supplement in assessment, but they do not replace the personal inquiry where one goes beyond the parental complaints. It is usually poor strategy to start the assessment by asking the parent to fill out a questionnaire, first because the answers may be confounded by positive or negative attitudes about the referral and second because some parents might have difficulty in doing it. It seems preferable to delay the request until after the intake interview.

The potential value of the standardized measures is that they provide a description of the population served, allowing for comparisons which cannot be done as well using simple diagnostic labels or individual clinical records. Quoting Achenbach, "Even if investigators prefer a different approach to diagnostic classification, the generalizability of their work will be greatly enhanced by scoring subjects on at least one well-validated checklist" (1978, p. 763).

Factorial Analysis of Presenting Problems. A major use of questionnaires has been the identification of "clusters" of simultaneous behaviors or factors. It is expected that disorders sharing a cluster of characteristics will be similar in etiology, amenability to treatment, prognosis, etc. One of the most interesting findings of the factor analytic studies is the regularity with which two major factors emerge. Peterson (1961) distinguished between two factors labeled "conduct problems" and "personality problems," the first representing a tendency to express impulses against society and the second containing a variety of elements suggesting low self-esteem, social withdrawal, and dysphoric mood. Achenbach (1966) factor-analyzed the symptoms from the case histories of 300 male and 300 female child psychiatric patients between the ages of 4 and 16 years and identified a bipolar first principal factor given the label of Internalizing versus Externalizing. Briefly, the symptoms at the externalizing end describe conflict with the environment while those at the other end describe problems within the self. The Internalizing-Externalizing factor has been replicated with new samples of children in different clinical settings (Achenbach & Lewis, 1971; Schechtman, 1970).

Further examination showed that externalizers of both sexes had poorer school performance, more previous problems with authorities, parents with more overt social problems, and parents who were less concerned about their child's problems. Twice as many girls were internalizers, while the ratio of internalizers to externalizers among boys was almost the opposite. Other associations were found for secondary factors. For example, children classified by the "Obsessions, Compulsions and Phobias" factor had higher social class status and mean IQs than did children classified by any other specific factor.

Quay (1979) mentioned a third pattern frequently found in multivariate statistical analyses, namely, "immaturity," which includes attention problems. This factor was especially prominent in public school populations. This highlights the fact that the behavioral factors which appear are dependent on the nature of the population providing the data. Usually children of limited intelligence and those who have severe emotional problems are not included. The infrequency with which psychotic children are found in most population samples precludes the appearance of a "psychotic" dimension, which does not mean it does not exist. For diagnostic purposes, the classifications provided by factor analysis are too broad and too few to be clinically discriminating, but the structured measures are useful for obtaining normative data on large samples, in addition to providing a standard base of comparison for clinical samples.

Child's Past History. There used to be a great deal of emphasis on the child's history, and one systematically covered such items as the age and manner of weaning, age and method of toilet training, early development, and perhaps the parents' attitude toward the pregnancy. However, typically these details are poorly recalled by the parents when asked directly. It is more productive to ask open-ended questions such as: "How was this child as an infant—easy or hard to feed, put down to sleep, to keep entertained, and so on? Did toilet training go easily? Were separations a problem? How did the child respond to your discipline? Did he or she play well with other children?" Factual data, such as separations from home, serious parental illnesses or separations, hospitalization or illness of the child, and subsequent births are usually recalled accurately and can be specifically asked for.

By both direct and indirect means, one tries to reconstruct the child's life experiences to date, putting them in proper sequence and arriving at some preliminary judgments as to temperament, areas of conflict, areas of strength and parental satisfaction, and special stress events. With regard to stresses, both usual and unusual, one tries to determine the child's manner of coping and the degree of parental responsivity to the needs of the child. The presenting problem is not the whole child and one needs to learn about the child's strengths as well as weaknesses.

Family History. There has been a similar shift from formal inquiry regarding the parents' early history toward more interest in current family functioning. It is important to ascertain the degree of harmony between the parents regarding the child's problems; if the parents disagree radically, not only does the child experience inconsistency but also the problem may be a manifestation of marital disagreement as much as anything else. In addition, it is useful to learn about the parents' relationships to their own parents who may be an important support system or may be continuing sources of tension. With care and tact, one may deduce that the child is perceived as "just like" someone—a parent, or perhaps a brother or sister of the parents—and this perception may lead the parents to overreact or possibly to deny some difficulties.

Through all of this inquiry one gleans a picture of the family style of life, prevailing values, dominant concerns, and capacity for change. The parents are going to be the mainstay of the child's treatment, whatever form it takes, and the process of getting the history should engage their active participation. If they feel threatened in this process, either by probing questions or demands that they cannot fulfil, one risks a premature termination as soon as they get the courage or find an excuse. The expected cost or difficulties in finding appointment times in their schedule (considering transportation, school, and work times) can provide a ready reason. Usually initial costs are covered by some third-party payment such as insurance, but nonetheless there are hidden costs and inconveniences which must be counterbalanced by their concern for the child and trust in the therapist.

Child Interview. Since Rutter and Graham (1968) first suggested standardizing the child psychiatric interview, a number of structured interview schedules have been developed for children (*Diagnostic Interview for Children and Adolescents*, Herjanic & Campbell, 1977; *Child Assessment Schedule*, Hodges, McKnew, Cytryn, Stern, & Kline, 1982; *Interview Schedule for Children*, Kovacs, 1985). Some of these were developed specifically to assess childhood depression where it is particularly important to get the child's statements of feelings (see Chapter 9). Although the degree of concordance between information given separately by the child and the mother suggests that children are reliable reporters (Herjanic, Herjanic, Brown, & Wheatt, 1975), there are significant differences on specific questions. Not surprisingly, mothers report more behavioral symptoms and children report more subjective, or feeling, problems (Herjanic & Reich, 1982).

Under the aegis of the National Institute of Mental Health, Costello and his colleagues (Costello, Edelbrock, Dulcan, & Kalas, 1984) developed the *Diagnostic Interview Schedule for Children* (DISC) which parallels the DISC-P mentioned earlier. In its present form, the DISC is formidable. There are some 250 questions to be asked, many of which are couched in negative terms. One would seriously question young children's capacity to be "honest" in such a series of self-critical statements. In some cases, even asking the question might be frightening, for example, to ask a young boy, "Do you feel like a girl inside a boy's body?" Young children assume that adults have a particular reason for asking a question and interpret the question as the adults' way of voicing their suspicions (which is frequently the case). Also, the interview is audiotaped, which adds to the formality of the interrogation, and little is said about explaining the purpose to the child or guaranteeing confidentiality. Comparing the results on two interviews about two weeks apart (Edelbrock, Costello, Dulcan, Kalas, & Conover, 1985), the children reported substantially fewer and less severe symptoms during the second interview, perhaps hoping to forestall still another interview. These authors cautioned about the use of the DISC with children under 10 years because of the low test-retest reliabilities in this age group.

The DISC has been programmed more for the computer than for establishing rapport, and it is doubtful that clinicians will be comfortable using it except perhaps with adolescent patients. A more practical approach to standardization, if it is deemed necessary, would seem to be to retain the unstructured child interview but to require the interviewer to summarize the data in a standard form with full recognition that there will be some areas not covered in the interview.

The unavoidable fact that the child interview will be incomplete is not the fault of the interviewer. One can cover only so much ground and maintain a dialogue with the child. Also, young children do not come prepared to "open up," in fact, quite the contrary. Anna Freud described the initial resistance of the young child as follows:

Whoever has dealt with school children will tell you they betray very little. They are resentful usually of being brought to the clinic. They are suspicious, the more normal they are, the less they like strangers prying into the intimacies of their lives. (1954, p. 5)

The child is less able to verbalize his feelings and his complaints, partly because he lacks the skill and experience to do so and partly because he rarely seeks help of his own accord. There are still other reasons for the child's lack of verbalization. There is an understandable reluctance to confide anything which might get back to the parents. Even without fear of reproach, a child is hesitant to become intimate with a stranger. Another inhibiting factor is a dread of verbalizing something painful or frightening. As mentioned in Chapter 5, putting something into words gives it added reality, makes it seem more likely to be true. Children are likely to be silent about the very things which cause them the greatest anxiety.

Most clinicians start the first interview by mentioning the problems that have been reported to them and indicating a wish to understand better so that they can be helpful. It is also appropriate to review any recent events of probable relevance, such as a divorce, previous visits to a psychologist, hospitalization, accident, move, etc. It is important to empathize with the child's fears or resentment and offer appropriate reassurance. Occasionally the simple Sentence Completion Test (Rotter & Willerman, 1947) is used; it is relatively nonthreatening because the child has many options in completing the sentences and can choose to be entirely neutral and conventional.

Some clinicians avoid any formal verbal inquiry and try to circumvent the communication obstacles by encouraging the child to explore, play, or draw "whatever they want." This may provide an opportunity to make behavioral observations, but the situation is sufficiently unusual that it is hard to generalize to school or home. Sometimes, however, the child gives a lot of information unintentionally, perhaps because the anxiety of the situation provokes some core reactions. Anna Freud described one such interview:

I saw a boy of ten who was most restless, he fidgeted, touched everything, did not say a thing. I asked him about the semi-delinquent symptoms for which he had been sent, the circumstances of his family, and so on, but all he said was, 'I would not like to give you wrong impressions' by which he gave me no impression at all. Finally he found a tape measure (spring type) and he began to play with it and did not stop until he broke it. Then he changed completely. He became most cooperative, nearly cringing in his appeals, asking me over and over whether I could not mend it again. (1954, p. 5)

Freud suggested that his basic fears centered around fears of damaging himself, although it is also possible that he was afraid of damaging others with his aggression. In any case, this boy displayed real anxiety about the consequences of his behavior—possibly the beginning of a therapeutic alliance.

Winnicott (1971) proposed an interview technique which he called the "Squiggle Game." As he explains it to the child, "I shut my eyes and go like this on the paper and you turn it into something, and then it is your turn and you do the same thing and I turn it into something" (p. 12). This provides a means of interaction which is not entirely verbal but still allows for some direction from the interviewer—direction which the child may ignore or redirect. It is clearly a "game" with no right or wrong answers and therefore less threatening to a young child than direct questions or "tests," but at the same time it is more focused than "free" play.

Psychological Testing

The use of intelligence tests and specialized assessment techniques for particular cognitive skills are presented in some detail in the later chapters dealing with learning problems and developmental disorders. There is no doubt that in the hands of a skillful clinician, intelligence tests may yield useful information regarding a child's personality and even perhaps some hint regarding particular conflicts, but they are too time-consuming if the child is known to be of at least average mental ability and has no academic difficulties. Techniques used to assess particular problems such as depression, anxiety, and hyperactivity are presented in later contexts so the

discussion here is concerned with multi-purpose tests.

The Rorschach Test. In the 1940's and '50's, the projective tests seemed to offer great promise for revealing underlying personality patterns and psychodynamic conflicts. The Rorschach Inkblot test was historically the first (Rorschach, 1921, 1951) and has continued to be number one in its field. The test materials and methods of administration and scoring are similar for children and adults, but of course, the normative standards are different.

Many early studies showed that disturbed children could be reliably differentiated from so-called normal children on the basis of their Rorschach responses (Beck, 1931; Krugman, 1942) and that diagnoses based on the Rorschach agreed closely with final diagnoses formulated after a period of therapy (Seigel, 1948). Kessler and Wolfenstein (1953) found that Rorschach test-and-retest results in a group of emotionally disturbed children in residential treatment corresponded very closely to the actual change observed by the treatment staff. It should be noted, however, that much of this early validation research indicated that the Rorschach confirmed what was already well-known about the child.

In their discussion of the increasing use of the Rorschach technique in child guidance clinics, Anderson and Higham (1956) explained the aims of testing as follows:

When we test a child in a clinic, it is less important to describe his unconscious conflicts than it is to understand how he deals with these conflicts. We are interested to know in any given case which areas of ego functioning are intact, which are impaired, and how much they are impaired. We are concerned with the child's ability to tolerate tension, to test reality, to differentiate and organize his experience. We want to know the nature of his ego defenses and how rigidly or flexibly he uses them. We want to gauge his ego strength and his potential for treatment. (p. 187)

In the 1950's, a basic tenet of professional practice was that identical symptomatic behavior might be manifest for any number of underlying reasons and that treatment planning depended on these reasons rather than on the specific overt behavior.

Ross (1959), in the first book describing the "practice" of clinical child psychology, commented that few psychologists would dispense with the Rorschach "which, in skilled hands, has proved to be a valuable clinical instrument" (p. 180). But in his next book (Ross, 1974), there is no mention of the Rorschach or any other projective technique. Like many others, he shifted attention to observable behavior and current environmental conditions. In this zeitgeist, the relevance of Rorschach data for diagnostic decisions or treatment planning was questioned and serious doubts raised about the time and cost involvement (Gittelman-Klein, 1978; O'Leary & Johnson, 1979). The recent move toward subtyping various diagnostic categories defined by behavior may well restore the clinical usefulness of the Rorschach technique.

Exner and Weiner, who provided extensive norms from a large sample of nonpatient children, suggested that the Rorschach presents both a perceptual-cognitive task as well as a stimulus to fantasy.

These conceptions have substantially different implications for (a) which aspects of a Rorschach protocol are selected for interpretation, (b) which aspects of personality functioning are addressed by these interpretations, (c) whether Rorschach behavior is taken as representative of or as symbolic of behavior, and (d) the degree of certainty that accompanies the interpretative process. (Exner & Weiner, 1982, p. 3)

They argue that structurally based interpretations have an extensive base of validating evidence. Using the Rorschach as a perceptual-cognitive task, Friedman (1952) and Goldfried, Stricker, and Weiner (1971) developed a structurally based system of scoring responses as either "developmentally high" or "developmentally low" according to location, specificity, accuracy, and integration of detail. The resultant developmental level score has been shown to differentiate children of different ages and to discriminate between different clinical groups.

The ability of the Rorschach to distinguish between various groups of children or individuals gives it considerable utility in research situations, but the overlap between groups reduces its value for individual prediction. It is not uncommon with children to obtain a very sparse record (Bergman & Schubert, 1974), which does not allow fine-tuned interpretation. Relatively few mental health professionals currently use the Rorschach with children on a routine basis, but there are occasions when it is helpful in organizing a confusing clinical picture. Particularly when there are no clear-cut symptoms but rather an aggregate of characterological traits which are giving trouble, the Rorschach serves to organize one's impressions, or suspicions. If nothing else, the Rorschach situation illuminates the degree of deviance from the "norm" in regard to organizational ability, regard for external reality, integration of external and internal stimuli, and dominant thought content. It also may provide an opportunity to focus in on a particular aspect of personality functioning such as developmental level or primary process thinking as operationalized by Holt and Havel (1977).

Picture Tests. There are many projective techniques which use pictures rather than inkblots as the presenting stimuli. The first of these was the Thematic Apperception Test (TAT) first introduced by Morgan and Murray in 1935. The development of different picture sets using animal characters (Children's Apperception Test) and child-adult scenes (CAT-Human) is described by Bellak (1986). Various adaptations have been published for very young children and children from different cultures (Haworth, 1986). The Michigan Picture Test-Revised (Hutt, 1980) is unique in providing detailed instructions for administering, scoring, and both quantitative and qualitative analysis, which makes it potentially useful for research. From this array, a clinician usually chooses a favorite on the basis of personal experience rather than empirical data. For instance, Palmer (1983) expressed a preference for Shneidman's Make-A-Picture Story (1952) because children enjoy the figures which they use to make up a play, an easier task particularly for the relatively nonverbal child.

Schneidman listed five general approaches to the analysis of thematic-test interpretation: (a) the normative approach; (b) the hero-oriented approach where one looks for identifications; (c) the intuitive approach, emphasizing needs, defenses, and affects; (d) the interpersonal approach in which the interaction between characters is emphasized; and (e) the formal approach where cognitive style is considered. It is important to keep in mind that these picture story tests are reaching for fantasies and that the child's productions cannot be taken at face value to indicate actual relationships, past or present. As Mundy (1972) stated, "While it is possible that the content reflects real life, other possibilities are equally likely. The relationships may be wished for, feared, defensively presented to cover significant issues, pointed to a polar opposite, or based on perceptions of others" (p. 802). Any attempt to use the TAT or similar projective measures to get at the "real facts" would be in serious error.

An area of particular interest has been the relationship of fantasy aggression and overt aggressive behavior. Davids (1973) reported little or no relationship between TAT "aggression scores" and observed behavior in a group of emotionally disturbed boys. The Hand Test, where the child is asked to interpret nine different drawings of hand gestures plus a blank card on which the child is to imagine a "hand" doing something, was especially designed to predict aggressive acting-out behavior (Bricklin, Piotrowski, & Wagner, 1970). Wagner

(1986) cited studies that demonstrated a significant relationship between Hand Test variables and overt behavior, but others did not confirm this prediction (Breidenbaugh, Brozovich, & Matheson, 1974). There does not seem to be a direct connection between amount of fantasied aggression and overt aggressive behavior. For some children, fantasied aggression remains just that, i.e., thoughts, which, of course, may cause them anxiety and/or guilt.

Rosenzweig developed the Picture-Frustration test specifically to explore suggested responses to frustration. (Rosensweig, 1978; Rosensweig, Fleming, & Rosensweig, 1948). The material is a series of cartoon-like pictures of frustrating situations and the subject is requested to fill in the "balloon" for the aggrieved character. Responses are scored according to direction and type of aggression. The test results

may contribute knowledge of the subject's characteristic modes of response to frustration and the nature of his recourse to aggression. Deviations from the percentage norms for the various P-F categories aid in such interpretations . . . However, the most telling interpretations are those which are derived from the interrelationships of the various scoring components, which, among other things, throw light upon the subject's frustration tolerance. (Rosenzweig, 1978, p. 14)

There have been some interesting research findings; for instance, child guidance patients show a greater tendency to externalize blame and to expect solutions from outside than do nonreferred children (Rosenzweig & Rosenzweig, 1952). However, the connection with behavior is mediated by other factors, and

some children with these expectations withdraw into passivity rather than demonstrate overt aggression.

Other materials have been employed as projective tests, for example three-dimensional figures (Allen, 1948), wooden mosaic pieces, and a set of 360 toys and figures for constructing three "Worlds" (Buhler, 1951). Although these materials attest to the ingenuity of psychologists, none has remained in the usual clinical battery, probably because they are expensive and recording responses is difficult.

Another semi-projective test was devised by Anthony and Bene (1957) to investigate family relations. In the Family Relations Test, the child selects figures to represent himself, the members of his family, and a "Mr. Nobody." The child then "delivers" to the proper figures "postcards," which contain emotional statements indicating varying degrees of affection, hostility, etc. Norms for different age groups have been published by Frost (1969).

Drawing Tests. Drawing tests remain popular, for cost reasons if nothing else. The Draw-a-Person Test also uses a list of 33 questions to be asked about the child's drawing (Machover, 1949, 1960); another variation is the House-Tree-Person (Buck, 1948). There is nonetheless considerable disagreement as to the validity of personality interpretations. Koppitz (1968) identified 30 Emotional Indicators which differentiated clinic patients and well-adjusted children. She concluded that "human figure drawings and family portraits can be used for the evaluation and understanding of children's self-concepts and of their interpersonal relationships" (p. 145) and further remarked that drawings are quite sensitive to changes in a child's attitudes toward himself and others. Much less optimistic views have been expressed by Harris (1963), who felt that there was little evidence that the human figure drawing is in fact a drawing of the self, and by Palmer who, although a staunch supporter of the use of tests in child assessment, remarked that "Children's drawings as presently used often provide dramatic illustrations to the case histories, but the generalizations made on the basis of them are among the most tenuous and specious of all clinical predictions" (1983, p. 166).

In Palmer's extensive discussion of the use of tests in psychological assessment, he pointed out that frequently one critical aspect of a child's emotional adjustment is the ability to differentiate affects, or feelings. This can be assessed through interview ("How did that make you feel?"), parental reports, the effect of the color stimulus in the Rorschach, attribution of feelings to picture-story characters, answers to Sentence Completion items which start with an expression of feeling, and "last but not least, the child's drawings of human figures often illustrate very dramatically affective discriminations" (1983, p. 257). The overall amount of expression in the drawings may be one measure of the child's awareness of feelings and ability to make affective discriminations. Although it is fairly easy for a receptive and empathic adult to recognize how a child is feeling, many disturbed children are living in relatively insensitive environments where their feelings are not recognized, and projective testing techniques may well provide an opportunity to explore the feeling aspect of the child's life.

If the child's productions are viewed as a reflection of how he or she feels about life, rather than for prediction or diagnostic categorization, the projective materials are for the school-age child what the play materials are for the preschooler. In the final written report, the psychologist must avoid the temptation to report findings test by test, which usually yields a potpourri of apparently unrelated facts. The material from many sources, i.e., history, observations, and tests, must be integrated into a cohesive whole that reflects the child in a comprehensive way, strengths as well as weaknesses.

Developmental Profile

One model for a comprehensive assessment is the Developmental Profile proposed by Anna Freud (1965). It is essentially a detailed case study outline, requiring a lot of inferences to be made by the clinician regarding assessments of drive development (libidinal and aggressive), ego and superego development, regression and fixation points, dynamic assessment regarding the specific nature of internal conflicts, and evaluation of ego strength in coping with frustration, anxiety, or delay of gratification. There are two problems immediately obvious in the practical utilization of this guide. First, it is very difficult to get the information needed to make such assessments, and second, it requires a commitment to, and thorough understanding of, psychoanalytic theory.

The most valuable contribution to nonanalytic workers is the concept of developmental lines. Examples described by Anna Freud include the progressive steps from dependency to self-reliance and adult object relationships; from sucking to self-regulating eating; from wetting and soiling to bladder and bowel control; from dependency to self-care in body management; from egocentricity to companionship; and from play to work. The lines which are most carefully detailed are largely relevant to the first 5 years of life. A noteworthy exception is the progression from play with the body, play with toys, social games, hobbies, to work, or task orientation in educational parlance. The metapsychological explanations for progress or failure to achieve the developmental steps are based on psychoanalytic premises regarding drive development, but it would be possible to describe these, and many other developmental lines, in operational terms without using concepts from any one personality theory. If behavioral assessments along the developmental lines were combined with assessments of mental development (using mental age levels from intelligence tests and Piagetian categories) and assessments of motor, perceptual, and social development, the resultant composite would provide an excellent basis for diagnosis and treatment. To move in this direction, however, we would need more complete and detailed descriptions of normal stages in all these developmental areas, better methods of behavior observations, more eclecticism, and a better sense of connection between presenting problems and other aspects of development.

DIAGNOSTIC CLASSIFICATION

Clinical Prevalence of "Emotional Disorder"

Public planning officials ask for a global estimate of the number of "disturbed children," and many answers have been given. Gould, Wunsch-Witzik, and Dohrenwend (1981) reported a median prevalence rate of childhood psychiatric disorder of 11.8% in 25 surveys done in the United States between 1928 and 1975. However, it is disconcerting to examine these studies more carefully. In the British studies of all 10- to 11-year-olds on the Isle of Wight, Rutter and Graham (1966) found very little overlap between those children identified by their parents and those identified by their teachers. It is essential to make a distinction between surveys of specific symptoms as isolated bits of behavior (like the "parental concerns" discussed in Chapter 6) and surveys that utilize an additive or evaluative approach to determine deviance. Follow-up clinical evaluation of the relatively large numbers indicated "at risk" by the Behavioral Screening Questionnaire yielded a prevalence rate of 6–7%. Four years later, more than half of these were still identified as disturbed at age 14–15 years (Graham & Rutter, 1973); on the other hand, a significant number were not so identified. Obviously the frequency of individual symptoms is much higher than the prevalence of confirmed chronic disorders.

Reported prevalence rates of emotional disorders in childhood range from a minimum of 6% to a maximum of about 20% (Graham, 1969). After a painstaking review of the methodological problems inherent in community surveys, Links concluded that

estimations of true prevalence of child psychiatric disorders have not been made any easier as a result of the various community surveys. Because each of the surveys has differed in terms of the definitions of disorders studied, the age groups investigated, and the instruments used, few definitive conclusions can be drawn. (1983, p. 541)

Considering the variability in children's behavior according to the immediate situation, prevalence figures should be derived from "double counts," that is, identification by teacher and parent alike or by teacher or parent on successive rather than single occasions. When this has been done, the prevalence estimates fall somewhat below the 10% figure customarily cited.

Conceptual Problems in Classification

Our methods of classifying children's problems are so unsatisfactory that one would wish we could do without any labels. Unfortunately there are many reporting requirements, mainly for insurance reimbursement or other funding sources; also, categories are necessary to briefly describe clinical populations for epidemiological counts and for evaluating treatment approaches. "Diagnosis," derived from the Greek, means "thorough understanding," but that cannot be captured in a diagnostic label; it is important not to be beguiled by words into thinking we know more than we do when we call a child "autistic," "borderline," "retarded," or whatever. Ideally, diagnosis should be based on cause, or

etiology, but in fact, we are far from this, divided as we are with allegiance to the disease model in the Kraepelinan tradition, dynamic explanations borrowing psychoanalytic concepts, psychobiologic and constitutional explanations based on neurophysiology, learning propositions relying on histories of reinforcement and role models, and broad-based environmental explanations in terms of failures of social systems. The conflicts are not so much between professions as between theoretical positions with adversary rather than complementary points of view. The parts and pieces are still greater than any whole that has been constructed.

Kessler (1971) reviewed seven classification systems proposed between 1955 and 1968 and found that the differences were chiefly in the relative emphasis on one or another of the following questions as a principle of grouping:

1. Etiology: Is the behavior organic or functional in origin?
2. Etiology: Is the disturbance the result of inner conflict or of conflict between the child and the environment?
3. Effect: Does the disturbance result in suffering for the child or in suffering for others?
4. Effect: How seriously is the individual's functioning disturbed?
5. Effect: What specific functions are retarded or deviant?

The system proposed by a task force organized by the Group for the Advancement of Psychiatry (GAP) is presented as a prototype of "traditional" classification. The GAP Report (1966) suggested 10 major diagnostic categories:

1. Healthy Responses
2. Reactive Disorders
3. Developmental Deviations
4. Psychoneurotic Disorders
5. Personality Disorders
6. Psychotic Disorders
7. Physiologic Disorders
8. Brain Syndromes
9. Mental Retardation
10. Other

The evaluation of a problem as "reactive" involved two determinations: first, that the behavior is appropriate to the external circumstances, and second, that the reaction is transient and reversible; thus the etiology would be mainly environmental. "Developmental deviations" covered a wide sweep of delays or aberrations in body functions such as sleeping, eating, speech, bowel or bladder control, problems in motor coordination, sensory development, speech development, and deviations in cognitive functions. From the etiological standpoint, biological (hereditary, constitutional, maturational) factors were conceived of as contributing prominently to developmental deviations.

Psychoneurosis was defined in psychoanalytic terms: "Those disorders based on unconscious conflicts over the handling of sexual and aggressive impulses which, though removed from awareness by the mechanism of repression, remain active and unresolved" (p. 229). Personality disorder was reserved for chronic problems that have become ingrained in the personality structure and are generally acceptable or ego-syntonic to the child, however disagreeable to others. Most of the symptoms listed for psychosis could as well be included under developmental deviations except for the "severe and continued impairment of emotional relationships with persons, associated with an aloofness and a tendency toward preoccupation with inanimate objects" (p. 251). The other categories are more or less self-explanatory.

The GAP system follows the medical model in identifying groups of disorders primarily on the basis of etiology and only secondarily on the basis of presenting symptoms. The distinction between reactive and neurotic disorders proved particularly controversial. Behavior therapists objected on the basis that so-called internalized or neurotic disorders were also modified by environmental factors such as reinforcement contingencies, role modeling, etc., and saw the difference as one of degree rather than of kind. And indeed the term "neurotic" was eliminated in the nomenclature adopted as "official" in 1980 (DSM-III) as part of a classification system which would be equally acceptable to mental health professionals of all theoretical persuasions. Other groups also parted company with the medical model; for instance, those concerned with children's learning disabilities tried to replace etiologic statements with diagnostic statements describing the specific deficits without specification of probable cause.

Clinical Bias in Diagnosis

As Clements and Peters (1965) pointed out, diagnosis in child guidance is as much influenced by the setting and the orientation of the diagnostician as it is by the particular characteristics of the child under study. Innumerable anecdotes can be told of different labels being given to the same child as his parents made their odyssey through specialized clinics. The controversy over organic versus functional explanations almost divided child guidance workers into two camps, and in the absence of indisputable evidence, workers relied on their personal judgment to decide whether organic or functional factors were most important.

Kal (1969) suggested some personal reasons why a practitioner would align himself with one side or the other:

Does the clinician label a condition organic in order to absolve himself from blame if he fails to cure it—or because he dislikes the patient and doesn't want to bother with psychotherapy—or because prescribing medication gives him a sense of control which the nebulousness of psychogenicity does not provide him with? Or does he prefer a psychological and social etiologic explanation because admitting an organic defect would leave him much too hopeless—or again because he can criticize the schizophrenogenic mother? (p. 164)

Clinicians seem to prefer an organic explanation when they like the parents and lean toward a psychogenic explanation when they do not, as if an issue of fault were at stake, either to absolve or blame the parents (Aaronson & Kessler, 1968).

After reporting the surprising finding that diagnoses of mental retardation and organic brain syndrome were made less frequently in the children from the lower end of the socioeconomic scale, workers from the University of Michigan Children's Psychiatric Hospital commented on the practical purpose of diagnostic labels and how these influence the decisions of diagnosticians.

In our work, the placing of a label often has less to do with etiology than with the intention and goals one has for the individual. We are not suggesting that we, or other clinics, consistently and consciously manipulate diagnoses in order to make the diagnosis fit the hoped-for environmental response, but we do suggest that our own particular backgrounds and orientation may tend to make us err in this direction and if so, we must be aware of this. (McDermott et al., 1968, p. 309)

The great difficulty with etiologic diagnostic statements is that several causes may co-exist and behavior outcome does not reveal which one came first.

Bias plays a part in the educational diagnosis field as well. Looking for the particular disability in need of remediation, psychologists turned to tests for objective evidence, but no one can give all possible tests and bias appears in the matter of test selection. To illustrate, if a child is referred to an occupational therapist trained in the Ayres method (see Chapter 11), there is a strong possibility that many of the referred learning disabled children will show deficiencies in sensory-motor integration. If, on the other hand, the child is referred to a clinic that focuses upon language development, measures of language development will often show deficit patterns. With or without tests, clinicians tend to find what they are looking for. Like the blind men describing an elephant, different people see different aspects of the situation and report their view as the total picture.

DSM-III

The task forces charged by the American Psychiatric Association with the responsibility for developing an official diagnostic nomenclature deliberately chose a descriptive, atheoretical approach. As mentioned earlier, "neurotic" conditions were reclassified according to presenting symptoms and history. In order to achieve better reliability (consistency) in diagnostic classification, the DSM-III offers comprehensive descriptions and specific criteria as diagnostic guides. It is impossible to achieve total objectivity, but the goal of developing a diagnostic system which could be used by clinicians of many persuasions was clear and reasonably well realized.

The *Diagnostic and Statistical Manual of Mental Disorders*, Third Edition, (DSM-III) was published by the American Psychiatric Association in 1980 and is the generally accepted nomenclature at present, replacing the earlier editions published in 1952 and 1968. The DSM-III was developed over a period of 5 years with field trials and professional critiques of successive drafts. This revision introduced the feature of "multiaxial evaluation." Axis I labels the presenting "illness" or problem; Axis II identifies underlying, chronic personality disorders; and Axis III includes physical problems which may co-exist with the psychiatric disorder. Axis IV assesses severity of psychosocial stressors and Axis V rates the highest level of adaptive functioning during the preceding year. For children, Axis V usually has little meaning but the identification of life stress events is clearly important. However, the following discussion is limited to the diagnostic classifications contained in Axis I and II.

In the section identified as "Disorders usually first evident in infancy, childhood, or adolescence," some 43 disorders are presented in five major groups:

1. Intellectual Retardation
2. Behavioral Problems (Attention Deficit Disorder and Conduct Disorder)
3. Emotional Problems (Anxiety Disorders and "Other" which includes Reactive Attachment Disorder of Infancy, Schizoid Disorder, Elective Mutism, Oppositional Disorder, and Identity Disorder
4. Physical Disorders (Eating Disorders, Stereotyped Movement Disorders, and other disorders with physical manifestations such as stuttering, enuresis, encopresis, and sleep terror)
5. Developmental Disorders such as Infantile Autism

Specific developmental disorders in language, reading, arithmetic, articulation, etc. are coded on Axis II. Adult diagnostic categories, for instance, depression, are used when the essential features in childhood are the same as those seen in adult persons.

Categories 2 and 3 are reminiscent of the familiar conduct/personality or externalizing-internalizing distinction which has already been discussed. Category 4 is a mix of "habit" problems which can have a significant constitutional, genetic, or physiological basis. Categories 1 and 5 are presumed to be organically based cognitive deficits which impinge on development. These are all descriptive categories which differ greatly in size, scope, and specificity.

In an NIMH-sponsored field trial reported in the Manual, involving 84 clinicians and 126 patients of whom approximately half were below the age of 11 years, the overall reliability was considered "fair" with a Kappa coefficient of agreement close to .7. Nearly a third of the cases were diagnosed in the Adjustment Disorder category, which emphasizes the importance clinicians give to psychosocial stressors in causing childhood problems. The DSM-III Manual points out that the reliability was higher than that obtained using the GAP system (Beitchman, Dielman, Landis, Benson, & Kemp, 1978). The overall result of most of the reliability studies is that there is reasonably good interrater agreement with the major categories which differentiate between psychoses, emotional, and conduct disorders, but far less agreement with the subcategories (Mattison, Cantwell, Russell, & Will, 1979). The problem of reliability in diagnostic classification may have been improved but it has not been resolved. We are still a long way from the desiderata expressed by Cromwell, Blashfield, and Strauss that "Classification systems should have clear definitions and a coherent logical structure" (1975, p. 14). Despite its weaknesses and inconsistencies, however, the DSM-III is the basis for extensive record keeping used for all manner of purposes including justification for third-party payments.

The Value of Diagnosis

It was mentioned at the outset that some form of classification is a necessary evil, but one would hope that it would serve more than bureaucratic purposes. One should carefully consider the impact of the diagnostic process on the participants. Wolfensberger (1965) warned that diagnosis can be an intellectual exercise in which "the professional can find many rewards and a good deal of security—just the opposite of what the parent typically finds in it." On the other hand, the potential value of the diagnostic evaluation is at least suggested in a follow-up study of 49 children studied in an outpatient clinic in which 80% of the parents reported definite improvement following evaluation only (Perez-Reyes & Lansing, 1967). About three-fourths of the parents recalled the diagnostic study as helpful, of value for them and the child, and as a nonpainful experience; they felt understood, and thought the doctor spent enough time with them; they understood the suggestions and usually found them useful. In many instances, the diagnostic study is the only contact between children with emotional disturbances and psychological services; therefore it should be given serious consideration as a potential therapeutic tool.

Diagnostic labeling with children is particularly treacherous because of their growing, changing nature, disturbed or otherwise. The major portion of diagnostic disagreement with adult patients has been attributed to inadequate guidelines while the variance attributable to inconstancy in the patient's behavior is relatively negligible (Zubin, 1969). This factor is infinitely more important with children because they present themselves differently in different situations and change over relatively short periods of time. When an adult person is diagnosed as hysterical, obsessive-compulsive, or whatever, there is a silent prediction that without treatment, the condition will continue. Prediction with children is much more hazardous; not only are they changing as the result of maturation but they are much more susceptible to environmental influences, and it is difficult to forecast the events that lie in store for a child. In child diagnosis it is important to gauge the probabilities that the child will outgrow this problem in the expectable course of events. The clinician may need to adopt the role of a facilitator rather than a therapist.

The link between formal diagnosis and choice of treatment is weak at best. Goodman (1987) criticized both the DSM-III and multivariate systems (e.g., Achenbach) for "enshrining complaints" without regard for context or causes. She commented that the modern effort to eliminate theoretical bias in diagnosis by using "skin level descriptors" offers little direction for treatment. There are two important principles to keep in mind. One is the *principle of over-determination;* that is, overt behavior is the result of multiple causes acting in concert. The second principle is that of *overlapping categories.* More often than not, a given child shows characteristics of multiple diagnoses and no single label fully describes the situation. The heterogeneity that results is one reason for the constant search for subtypes within the diagnostic categories.

If one took seriously the multi-axial approach of the DSM-III, more consideration would be given to the description of the underlying personality of the child including temperament and cognitive styles (Axis II) and the identification of stressors in the family, school, and neighborhood as they impact on a child

(Axis 4). In actual practice, formal diagnosis is largely irrelevant to the choice of treatment. More weight is given to collateral factors such as family circumstances, motivation, scheduling problems, external pressures, and last but not least, the clinician's preference.

With children, diagnosis should merge with treatment and be a sequential process over a period of time. In mapping a strategy of intervention, the first features needing attention are often not the first factors in causing the presenting problem. For instance, if a child with a receptive aphasia is negativistic, one will have to establish a relationship before working directly on the primary language disorder. As one works first with one problem and then the next, the etiology becomes increasingly clear. Present-day diagnosis is based on the classification of behavior— not the classification of children—so one would expect that the "working diagnosis" would change over time, admittedly a problem for the record-keepers. Ideally there should be no separation of diagnostic and treatment functions, but unfortunately, in this era of specialization, professionals tend not only to "partialize" their diagnoses but also to "partialize" their treatments so that a child may bounce around in a field of pediatricians, neurologists, speech therapists, special education teachers, family therapists, behavior therapists, guidance counselors, psychologists, psychiatrists, optometrists, and still others. Hopefully, if we are faithful to the operational definitions in DSM-III, put the diagnosis in a psychosocial context, and constantly update the diagnosis, interprofessional communication will be improved so that we can achieve a better understanding of child problem behaviors and the effectiveness of treatments.

APPROACHES TO TREATMENT

The list of categories for possible intervention is extensive. In this section, 10 psychological approaches are presented in general terms; further specific discussions are presented in the context of the particular disorders for which they have proved most useful. Ideally the persons involved in the assessment and diagnostic formulation have all these possibilities under consideration and are moving toward a choice of one or a combination of the following.

Environmental Manipulation/ Parent Advice

This is a "one-shot" intervention consisting of recommendations offered in the assessment interpretation interview. Such recommendations would be based on both general principles of child development and specific features of the individual child and family. Obviously it can take many forms, but examples would include changes in television viewing, bedtime, mealtime, visitations with divorced parents, helping with homework, explanations regarding family affairs, setting responsibilities, offering more or less freedom, changing schools, locating a tutor, facilitating peer friendships, etc. The advice must be both specific and feasible within the family structure. General recommendations such as "spend more time with so-and-so" are more useful if parents and

therapist consider when and what might be done. This intervention is usually most appropriate for relatively well-adjusted children and families. One is well-advised to follow up such cases to see if one's tacit assumption of a good prognosis was justified.

Occasionally this intervention is appropriate for more disturbed cases, either because there is no treatment time available or the parents are reluctant to proceed with treatment. The importance of the follow-up is even greater. If the parent tried the suggestion and it worked, the parent may be receptive to further ideas. If the parents did not carry out the recommendation, or if they say they did and it did not work, there are three possibilities: (a) it was a poor recommendation; (b) the parents had difficulties mobilizing themselves to act; or (c) the problem is internalized and not amenable to environmental manipulation. Understanding the operative factors assists the diagnostic formulation and suggests new directions for further intervention.

Parent Counseling

We are using the term "counseling" in a generic sense to include all methods of treating the child via the parents. As mentioned earlier, this is particularly effective for children under 5 years. There are discussion groups for parents of preschoolers, Parents Without Partners, and Parents Anonymous (see Chapter 2) which provide both educational suggestions and support for parents who feel isolated. For parents of children with problems, counseling may be psychodynamically or behaviorally oriented and offered either in small groups or individually. Arnold's book, *Helping Parents Help their Children* (1978), illustrates the wide range of techniques and applications for parent guidance.

In the following chapters, there are many discussions of parent counseling related to specific problems. In some instances, counseling emphasizes support in understanding and adapting to a "different" child—for instance, one with mental retardation or autism. In other instances, it is highly structured and teaches the parents new techniques of child management. With some problems, it is appropriate to open new channels of parent-child communication and to initiate new opportunities for the child to grow. But in all cases, the parent counselor aims to increase the parents' feelings of competence and the effectiveness of their relationship with their child.

There is no hard evidence to support one orientation in parent counseling over another (Bernal, Klinnert, & Schultz, 1980). Behaviorally oriented "parent training" is often employed with conduct-disordered children and usually results in short-term gains but with limited generalization to other settings and over time. Very optimistic statements have been made for behavioral counseling, for example, "you can guarantee parents and their children 100% success in meeting their behavioral goals if they learn to pinpoint, chart, change, and try, try again" (Lindsley, 1978, p. 90). But even Lindsley cautioned that the behavioral goals must be realistic, the rewards appropriate, and the parents persistent. If the child is seriously disturbed or if the parents are overwhelmed with their own difficul-

ties, the promise of behavioral counseling cannot be fulfilled. On the other hand, the results of psychodynamic or client-centered counseling tend to be amorphous and not clearly related to the techniques or content of the counseling sessions. Apparently there are many roads to the common goal of increasing parental competence.

The term "filial therapy" has been used to describe techniques of using parents as therapists. Guerney (1964), who introduced the term, followed the reflective model by training parents to conduct client-centered play therapy with their own children. Hornsby and Appelbaum (1978) expanded on this method and recommended its use with adjustment reactions, children in active conflict with one or both parents, and borderline psychotic or retarded children. They found that it did not work so well with severely neurotic or psychotic children.

Filial therapy has been used in a very different theoretical context by Furman (1979), who pointed out that the first recorded treatment of a young child by his parent was that of Little Hans described by Freud (1955). This is a strictly individual approach that involves an extension of psychoanalytic understanding and technique. In Furman's words:

The parent presents a weekly account of observations of the child. This material is used to help in recognizing and resolving existing external struggles between the parent and the child. In the case of internalized conflicts, the parent is helped to proceed gradually, first to an understanding of the child's defenses against emerging anxiety and the uncovering of heretofore unconscious struggles, and then to their interpretation.... At the same time, the parent is helped to give the child age-appropriate support of ego functions and to provide guidance toward healthy mastery. (1979, p. 154)

This treatment requires highly trained staff who are not available in many parts of the country, and Furman urged caution in using this method with school-age children because it might distort the parent-child relationship normal for this age by encouraging dependency and an inappropriate intimacy.

In Furman's opinion, the parent's personal difficulties are outside the reach of filial therapy, but Chethik (1976) suggested that there might be exceptions to that rule. Psychodynamic psychotherapy may be limited to treatment of the parent-child relationships, bringing in the past only insofar as it bears on the present difficulties with the child. But there are other instances where the parent is so disturbed or so deprived that one has to address his or her personal problems directly and not always in direct reference to the child. Many child therapists are uncomfortable when they are drawn into "parent therapy," and, indeed, if the parents will accept referral, it is preferable to find the parent another therapist. However, when this is not feasible, addressing the parents' personal difficulties may be a necessary part of helping their child.

Behavior Therapy

Mary Cover Jones's treatment of the fears of 3-year-old Peter (1924) is usually cited as the beginning of behavior therapy with children, but there was a long latency. It was the success of operant conditioning methods with institutionalized children where all else had previously failed (Ferster & DeMyer, 1962) that attracted wide attention to the possibilities of behavior therapy for children. It seemed particularly appropriate for children because environmental control is relatively easy in homes and schools when compared with the complex environments in which adults operate. In addition, children are often referred for well-defined behaviors such as bed-wetting, phobia, or temper tantrums, that are amenable to behavior therapy techniques (Gelfand & Hartmann, 1968).

The techniques are derived from learning principles of respondent conditioning (previously called classical or Pavlovian conditioning), operant learning (also known as instrumental conditioning), and observational learning from models. Systematic desensitization illustrates the first model and is particularly used for fears and phobias (see Chapter 8). Operant methods involve manipulation of environmental consequences by token economies, contingency contracting, or time-out procedures to decrease undesirable behaviors and increase desired alternatives. The underlying principle is relatively straightforward, but considerable skill is involved in targeting and analyzing the behavioral components and in engineering the schedule for carefully selected positive and negative reinforcements.

Behavior therapists recognize that children learn not only specific actions but also attitudes vicariously, by watching what others do and what happens as a result (Rachman, 1972). Clearly, models in the natural environment are not easy to control but pre-arranged situations in preschools with child collaborators and also prepared films with child subjects to prepare others for traumatic events such as surgery have been used (Melamed & Siegel, 1975).

At first sight, behavior modification looks much like "common sense" and indeed Stolz, Wienckowski, and Brown (1975) described behavior modification as "codifying and organizing" common sense, showing under what conditions and in what circumstances each aspect of "common sense" should be applied. These learning principles are relevant in any therapy, even if there are expanded elements. In many cases, a behavioral program represents a necessary "first step" in bringing some order and consistency into a situation and is similar to what the psychodynamic therapist calls "setting limits." A behavioral therapy approach should not shut off one's ability to empathize. Ross's statement stressing the difference between psychotherapy and behavior therapy suggests a potential danger of constriction:

Parents must be convinced that the therapist is interested in what is happening now, not in what happened years ago; that they are to relate what they saw the child do, not what they thought the child was feeling. Observed behaviors, not inferences about inner states, are the data with which the behavior therapist seeks to deal. (1980, p. 45)

This credo must be tempered with the realization that a child's behavior may be a direct and appropriate expression of feeling and a legitimate request for needed attention.

Cognitive Behavior Therapy

In 1981, Di Guiseppe described this as the "new kid on the block" in the field of child psychotherapy. Rational emotive therapy (Ellis, 1962) is the forerunner in emphasizing cognitive components.

It particularly shows people that they practically never get disturbed by external experiences, events, or conditions but that they make themselves disturbed by their own thoughts, attitudes, or interpretations about these conditions. (Ellis, 1978, p. 92)

It represents a major break from "traditional" behavior therapy as shown by Di Guiseppe's remarks about assessment:

During assessment therapists should also be watchful for distorted perceptions of reality, statements the child makes about him or herself or others that reflect unrealistic or incorrect views of the world. Errors in logic such as arbitrary inference, selective abstraction, or overgeneralization are quite common in a child's thinking. This category of cognitive distortions would include statements that are contradicted by available data—for example, "My mother doesn't love me," "I'm stupid," "None of the other children play with me." (1981, p. 53)

This opens up the whole vista of the inner life of the child, including fantasies and feelings.

Cognitive behavior therapy strives to change the child's beliefs, attitudes, and perceptions by experience, modeling, or instruction. The work by Shure and Spivack in interpersonal problem solving, described as an "experiment in intervention" (see Chapter 5), is one example of the application of this approach.

Meichenbaum and Goodman's 1971 work in training impulsive children to talk to themselves is another early example (see Chapter 10). Although the intervention programs vary in the details, there is uniformly a high degree of structure and use of role playing (behavioral rehearsal), self-instruction, and self-evaluation as well as training "exercises" in perspective taking, consequential thinking, and generating alternative solutions. It lends itself readily to group approaches and has been adopted for use in schools and institutions (Urbain & Kendall, 1980). Urbain and Kendall's review of social-cognitive problem-solving interventions with children (1980) led them to be cautiously optimistic about their therapeutic effectiveness. The programs have been developed mainly for conduct problems, and there is still much to learn regarding what facet is effective with what kind of child, under what circumstances, and for how long.

Cognitive behavior therapy partially bridges the gap between "traditional" behavior therapy and "traditional" psychotherapy. The problem-solving approach leaves room for the consideration of children's feelings as part of the "problem" to be resolved. Kendall (1981) stressed the importance of a positive child-therapist relationship in cognitive behavioral interventions and commented on the apparent differences in therapists' abilities to establish such a relationship. His plea for additional research in "a more direct and programmatic evaluation of the components of an efficacious relationship, the processes included in the development of such a relationship, and the strategies for either selecting those therapists skilled in relationship making or teaching the skills to those less adept" (p. 85) resonates with concerns of experienced child therapists. In contrast to the adult client who usually seeks help of his own accord, the child comes to treatment unwillingly, and the task of creating trust is a necessary first step for treatment of any kind.

Psychotherapy

In psychotherapy there is no set system of techniques and procedures, in part because different processes are involved at different points in the treatment and also because major modifications are made according to the assessment of the child. Recognizing that there is overlap, Freedheim and Russ (1983) distinguished three major types of psychotherapy. In *supportive* therapy, the therapist is an empathic listener and helps the child to think about real events and people in his or her life. Sometimes the therapist needs to assume an active advocacy role, for instance, in situations where sexual or physical abuse is suspected. Although this may seem like the "purchase of friendship," when one considers how rarely a child can command an hour of an adult's undivided attention, the worth of this approach becomes more apparent.

Freedheim and Russ identified the second form as *"the development of new psychological structures."* This is particularly valuable for children with borderline or narcissistic disorders who have suffered very early developmental failures (See Chapter 8). For them life is chaotic and unpredictable and they have no feeling of control. Part of the unpredictability stems from their inability to predict their own responses, as well as those of others. In this modality, the major task for the therapist is to be a stable object that the child can slowly incorporate. For some time the therapist fills the role of a nurturant parent, mirroring both the child's pleasures as well as anxieties. This is a lengthy process (probably 2 or more years) because the therapist is filling a major gap in early development and helping the child to establish self/nonself boundaries, a task normally accomplished during the first 3 years of life.

The third form, *insight-oriented therapy,* more closely parallels cognitive behavior therapy although there are important differences in philosophy and technique. In the first place, in psychodynamic therapy the therapist does more listening than directing and the pace is slower. More emphasis is placed on the identification of feelings that may be disguised or even warded off with various defenses. From a theoretical standpoint, one expects that the troublesome feelings will have to do with showing, receiving, or losing love (with or without sexual overtones), anger and ambivalence, and guilt. Anxiety about losing control of oneself, or helplessness, often underlies many defensive maladaptive maneuvers.

Only after getting to the bedrock of the feelings does the therapist offer explanations in terms of past or present experiences as perceived by the child. One tries to help the child distinguish between reality and fantasy, past and present, and between thought and action, thereby negating "irrational" feelings. In addition, one suggests alternative ways of expressing one's feelings in real life in order to achieve some real objective. All of this has little meaning unless the therapist has become an important person to the child. Almost invariably, some concomitant work is going on with the parents, so that the child's efforts to express feelings more effectively are well received.

There has been considerable debate as to the place of insight in child psychotherapy. Hobbs (1962) suggested that insight was unusual and an "epiphenomenon" of little consequence in achieving change with children, but Wilson (1981) argued that insight in terms of understanding the reasons for feelings and actions gives the child an objective way of thinking of him or herself. With insight, the child feels much less guilty, better able to make "sense" of feelings, and able to see connections between thoughts, feelings, and actions. Insight gives a child new data to work with in solving problems.

Carek (1979) suggested that the therapist's verbalizations can be viewed on a continuum ranging from those that simply clarify the situation to those that will help the child integrate and utilize the newly acquired information. Although the beginner therapist worries about what to say and when,

if he closely follows the child's productions, he will move on naturally from one intervention to another. If he stays in tune with the child and deals with the material at hand, he will automatically encourage the progressive expansion of awareness. Experience teaches that it is wise to nudge but not to push. Furthermore, he does not have to reach for content so much as he needs to be in position to help the child unwrap it. (Carek, 1979, p. 41)

In child psychotherapy one tries to create an inner conflict where the child is striving to overcome some part of his or her self and where the therapist is aligned with the "grown-up" part trying to get control over the "baby" part. This means, of course, that the therapist does "take sides," not so much with the parents as with the part of the child trying to achieve mastery.

With regard to effectiveness, early reports were very negative (Levitt, 1957; 1963) and subsequent reviewers continued to reserve judgment (Barrett, Hampe, & Miller, 1978; Hartmann, Roper, & Gelfand, 1977). In contrast, recently Casey and Berman reviewed 75 psychotherapy outcome studies spanning the period from 1952 to 1983 and concluded that children receiving treatment demonstrated greater improvement than untreated children and "that previous doubts about the overall efficacy of psychotherapy with children can be laid to rest" (1985, p. 388). They included all forms of treatment in their review and found that the behavioral approaches reported more change than nonbehavioral treatments, but they attributed this superiority to differences in the children selected for treatment and differences in the outcome measures used. Typically, parents and therapists give the most positive reports while teachers and peers report little change, and the children themselves do not seem to change in self-report measures. These observations suggest that all the therapies tend to focus on specific symptoms and family relationships and slight other important domains of the child's adjustment and self-esteem.

Future outcome studies will need to be specific as to the nature of the children and families, the diagnostic classification, the particular interventions used with both child and parents, and the measurement of results if they are to provide a sound empirical basis for further development. As mentioned before, the form of therapy is usually based more on therapist's preference than on child characteristics, and we should be moving toward more selectivity. In the author's opinion, psychotherapy is most appropriately employed with children who are fearful or inhibited, so-called personality problems, while acting-out or conduct disorder children, at least in the initial stages, need the structure of the behavioral therapy approach.

Play Therapy

This is more a technique than an approach since play is used in many forms of therapy. Work with children invariably involves play, but therapists make different uses of it. Kleinian psychoanalysts use it for symbolic interpretations of unconscious conflicts, but psychoanalysts following Anna Freud use it more as a way of helping the child to feel at ease and are more conservative in their interpretation of content. Virginia Axline (1947) wrote about play therapy in the context of nondirective, client-centered therapy which stresses empathic acceptance of the child rather than interpretation of psychological content. Play then serves as a liberating force. Structured techniques have evolved using a "play" or make-believe format such as the mutual story-telling technique (Gardner, 1971) where the therapist initiates, intervenes, or completes stories with themes analogous to the child's problem. In Gardner's approach, the therapist completes the child's story with a deliberately contrived, "healthier" solution and he does not feel that it is necessary to make an explicit connection with real life events.

Others have used play almost as a training tool. Meichenbaum (1979) suggested that imagery and fantasy procedures be used in teaching children self-control (cognitive behavior therapy). He quoted Smilansky (1968) who found that as a result of role playing in sociodramatic play, children were less aggressive and impulsive. Freyberg (1973) also noted that enhanced fantasy play was associated with greater verbal communication, more sensitive responding to the cues of other children, increased attention span, and more positive expression of emotions. "Such internal representations (i.e., in play) free the child from the control of external stimulation and permit thinking about objects and events that are not immediately present" (Meichenbaum, 1979, pp. 24–25).

Since play is used in such a wide variety of treatment situations, it is impossible to consider the results out of context. Any child therapist must be comfortable with playing, well-acquainted with useful toys and materials, and familiar with themes that children borrow from television or books. It is advisable to avoid activities requiring intense concentration (like model building, playing chess or checkers) and elaborate creations that cannot remain intact from one session to the next. Dismantling and putting toys away should be part of the session; if the child has some favorites, they may be kept in a special place. The therapist should be interested and helpful in the child's play, but not too expert nor too involved. Above all, the therapist should accede to the natural interest of the child in order to establish a relaxed situation in which the child can use the materials expressively. Any observations the therapist wishes to make regarding reactions of frustration if the game or activity does not work out well, or comments about the relationship of the fantasy to real life should be carefully considered so that the child does not become self-conscious and inhibited. The therapist may serve a useful function in helping the child learn to play, but he or she should not simply become a "playmate."

Group Therapy

Group therapy also is not strictly speaking an "approach," because many therapies may be done using groups. Slavson (1943, 1952) distinguished four categories: activity group psychotherapy, transitional groups, play group psychotherapy, and activity-interview group psychotherapy. The difference between activity-interview group psychotherapy and activity group psychotherapy is similar to that between psychodynamically oriented therapy and relationship psychotherapy. Schiffer (1969) described the "therapeutic play group" as a form of activity group therapy appropriate for youngsters of between 6 and 9 years.

The practice is predicated on the premise that many problems can be completely or partially resolved in the play group through a sustained, rehabilitative experience with an adult who functions as an optimal parent surrogate in relationships with the children. The therapeutic outcome derives from a process of undoing within the family ana-log—the play group—some of the psycholog-ical trauma which occurred during earlier development. (p. 1)

This approach is in marked contrast to Rose's description of the behavioral ap-proach for treating children in groups (1973). Most of the approaches used in individual therapy are mirrored in group therapies (Slavson & Schiffer, 1975).

Abramowitz (1976) concluded that empirical outcome research on chil-dren's activity, behavior modification, play, and verbal therapy groups yielded unconvincing evidence of their effective-ness with an approximately equal num-ber reporting positive, mixed, or null results. Thirty-one of the 42 studies reviewed involved elementary school groups referred by teachers for a variety of reasons including poor academic per-formance. It is not easy to assemble and maintain an appropriate group outside an institution or school setting. Further-more, it is difficult to include the "nor-mal" models one would like, so the group therapist usually must take an ac-tive role. Perhaps because of the practi-cal problems of organization, group therapy for children from 6 to 12 years seems to have faded somewhat and to have been replaced by psychoeduca-tional programs of "social skills train-ing." These programs vary in format and emphasis but have generally shown indi-cation of positive change (Pellegrini & Urbain, 1985). However, improved social behavior does not guarantee greater peer acceptance for any given child, and the problem of modifying perceptions and attitudes of the peer groups re-mains.

Family Therapy

In contrast, family therapy, which might be considered a kind of "mini-group" therapy, has flourished in the past 20 years. Ackerman was perhaps the first to take the leap from one-to-one psycho-therapy to family therapy. His proce-dures were flexible, with separate ses-sions with the child being interspersed with interviews in which the child was seen jointly with other family members.

Because the primary patient is viewed both as an individual in distress and as a symp-tomatic expression of family pathology, the disturbance of this patient becomes the ful-crum or entering wedge for the appropriate levels of intervention into the disorder of the family relations. (Ackerman, 1958, p. 305)

In the early days the field of family ther-apy was very much shaped by observa-tions of families with a schizophrenic member (see the discussion of the men-tally ill parent in Chapter 2) but it soon widened to look at all families as sys-tems in which change in any one part changes the entire system. The referral problems of the identified patient were downgraded in importance compared to the family structures, processes, and re-lationships.

Erickson and Hogan (1981) suggested a threefold classification of family treat-ment approaches, namely, psychody-namically based, behaviorally based, or systems based. The systems-based ap-proaches cover a wide spectrum. The so-called communication theorists within this spectrum include Jackson (1965), Haley (1971), and Satir (1967). Jackson emphasized the cognitive aspects of communication; Haley emphasized the power struggles; and Satir (1967) focused on acceptance versus rejection. Structural family therapy, also a systems approach, was developed by Minuchin (1974).

The structuralists adopt a more holistic view, observing the activities and functions of the family as a clue to how the family is organized or structured. Put another way, the focus here is on using the content of a transaction in the service of understanding how the family organizes itself; the structuralists in general are more concerned with how family members communicate than what they communicate. (Goldenberg & Goldenberg, 1980, p. 119)

Alexander and Malouf (1983) described three major components of family intervention: entering or joining the family, therapeutically modifying the family's sets, attributions, and expectations, and educating the family in order to change their behavior sequences. These authors commented on the demands on the family therapist for two classes of behavior: structuring skills and relationship skills.

Structuring skills include such attributes as directiveness, clarity, and self-confidence, all of which are necessary for the therapist to "take charge" of the therapeutic encounter, provide the family with a sense of hope and direction. . . . Relationship skills include sensitivity to affect, an ability to relate family members' experiential reality and affect to overt behavior, and sufficient warmth and humor that family members can feel less trapped by their existing circular and problematic interactions. (p. 944)

What makes this a difficult order to deliver is that the therapist must juggle the concerns of each member and the fractured parts of the family system, keep from becoming enmeshed in one part or another, and still act forcefully and quickly.

For an outsider it is difficult to understand the fine points of difference in the theoretical models and techniques of the various family therapy "schools," and it is probable that many therapists do not have the necessary disposition to practice family therapy. However, the family therapists have contributed a whole new vocabulary which captures important dynamic features. Minuchin described family structures as ranging from the "enmeshed" family with "tight interlocking" to the "disengaged" family with each member moving in "isolated orbits" (1967). The concepts of alignments, splits in families, and "triangulation" (i.e., two people who are not relating bring in a third party to reestablish homeostasis) go far beyond the dyadic relationships usually considered in working with parents and children. The notion of roles that members play in maintaining the family structure is very important when one is focused on bringing about significant change in one of these members. For example, a handicapped child may serve the function of keeping the parents together, or fulfilling the mother's wish to feel needed, and these purposes, more than the handicap per se, may interfere with the child's becoming independent.

Although the concepts may be borrowed by anyone, the choice of family therapy will very much depend on the therapist's own predilections. Also, one encounters families who are so disengaged that it is impossible to get all, or any, members to participate on behalf of the child. Empirical demonstrations of the efficacy of systems therapies with children are few (Stanton, 1980). Reports by Minuchin, Rosman, and Baker (1978) on anorexia nervosa indicated an 86% complete recovery rate in follow-up; the review of over 200 outcome studies reported by Gurman and Kniskern (1978) are encouraging for psychophysiological disorders in general. It is interesting that family therapy gained its popularity during a time of erosion of the nuclear family institution. In family therapy, "the family has been at least implicitly convened to bring its individually anomic members back home again and to reassert its solvency from a nearly bankrupt situation" (Brodkin, 1980, p. 14). The battle cry to "save the family" has given this form of therapy the significance of a mental health movement.

Special Education

During this same period of time another development has shown equal vigor in the institution of the school, quite apart from the institution of the family. Prior to the 1960's, seriously disturbed or handicapped children were regularly excluded from school, with or without provision for teaching at home. Educators were all too familiar with the role of the family and tended to absolve themselves from responsibility. Hewett's book on the emotionally disturbed child in the classroom (1968) was one of the first to argue that teachers should be prepared to help children modify behavior and that "the emotionally disturbed child must be helped to get ready for school while he is in school." He proposed specific strategies whereby the teacher pre-

sents developmentally relevant tasks, structure, and appropriate rewards to teach the most basic kinds of adaptive behaviors such as attention, responding, following directions, and social skills. From his frame of reference, an educational program could be devised for any child, no matter how immature or nonresponsive.

The increased responsibility of the public school system was made official when the the Education for All Handicapped Children Act (P.L. 94-142) was signed into law in 1975. This law required that by 1980 a "free appropriate public education" must be available to all handicapped children aged 3 through 21 years, unless state law set a different, older age for entry into public schools. According to the child count figures published by the U.S. Department of Education as of December, 1982, a total of 4,285,606 handicapped children were served in the United States and its territories. The educational developments for learning disabled and mentally retarded children are discussed at length in Chapters 11 and 12. Here mention will be made only of educational programs for "emotionally disturbed" children, representing about 7% of the total number of educationally handicapped.

The problem of definition is a major one, as shown by a longitudinal study reported by Rubin and Balow (1978). For 1,586 children followed from kindergarten through the sixth grade, more than half (58.6%) were identified as exhibiting behavior problems by at least one teacher, but only 3% were consistently identified on all six of the annual teacher ratings. Identification under P.L. 94-142 is restricted to severe and chronic emotional problems which result in academic difficulties or major classroom management difficulties, with a specific exclusion for children who are "socially maladjusted," which apparently had reference to delinquent children (Raiser & Van Nagel, 1980). Educators much prefer the term "behaviorally disturbed" because it fits better with the behavioral treatment strategies typically employed and it seems to carry less stigma. The public school programs for the severely behaviorally disordered serve a heterogeneous group of autistic, psychotic, and very aggressive children. These are children who by and large would have been excluded in years past.

Most of the special education programs follow the operant model in behavior modification, although cognitive elements have been added (Fagen & Long, 1979). However, an important variation was developed by Nicholas Hobbs in the early 1960's. *Project Re-ED* began in two residential sites for children between 6 and 12 years old. Since then it has been adopted in many other locations, frequently in day treatment rather than residential programs. Hobbs took the position that emotional disturbance is a symptom not of individual pathology "but of a malfunctioning human ecosystem" (1982, p. 14). In brief, this means that the trouble lies in the transactions between the child and his environment, not in the child. The intervention is primarily a major change in the environment, individually designed to fit the child's needs. In Hobbs's view,

Behavior modification, powerful as it is, is not a sufficient theoretical base for helping disturbed children and adolescents. It pays insufficient attention to the evocative power of identification with an admired adult, to the rigorous demands of expectancies stated and implicit in situations, and to the fulfillment that comes from the exercise of competence. (1982, p. 327)

The 12 principles of Project Re-ED (p. 22) include the importance of trust and also the experience of "joy." He suggested that feelings should be nurtured and shared spontaneously, but not probed or suggested. The importance of group and community life and some ceremonious celebrations is stressed. The idea of learning competence, self-control, and management of one's body are also incorporated. The therapist is the "teacher-counselor" who is like the "psychoeducateur" described by Guindon (1973). After school hours, the "night teacher-counselor" continues in the same vein and the "liaison teacher-counselor" works to effect "ecological" changes in the family, regular school, and community in the interests of the child. Although programs vary, Re-ED consistently tried to keep length of stay as short as possible and introduced the idea of 5-day-a-week residential care to avoid disruption in family relationships. Hobbs estimated the cost of residential programs to be between $80 and $100 a day; day-care programs, following the Re-ED model, were estimated to be between $35 to $50 per day (in 1980 dollars).

Weinstein (1974) evaluated the effectiveness of one of the original programs at Cumberland House in Tennessee. Most of the data indicated improvement in the treated group lasting over 18 months. However, in contrast to the generally positive ratings from adults, sociometric data from classmates indicated no improvement as a result of

Re-ED in relationships with peers, and after Re-ED, these children, though doing better than the untreated children, continued to differ on most measures from a group of children defined by their schools as not having behavior problems. With refreshing candor, Hobbs presented case examples of both successes and failures. Of the two reported failures, one was an 11-year-old boy, a good academic student presenting no problems to teachers, described by his parents as "a pain." He had many compulsive behaviors and was extremely involved emotionally with his mother. During his brief stay in residence, his behavior deteriorated, almost in a conscious effort to return home. From the material presented, one would judge him to be a "borderline psychotic" child who was not ready to take advantage of the nurturance in the new environment. Although Project Re-ED eschews the use of diagnostic categories, in this instance, understanding the internal structures of this child would predict a catastrophic reaction to separation. In contrast, the child described as the "most successful" was clearly reacting to an abusing mother and flourished in a rational and supportive environment.

In some ways the ecological view of the child's behavior as the outcome of external influences in the social system of the family, school, neighborhood, and community is like the family therapy approach. But here the locus of intervention is the school and the therapist— a specially trained educator who also acts as the child's advocate in altering the system. The work of Hobbs reminds us that children behave differently in different settings, and it behooves us to provide the best possible circumstances even if they do not bring about miraculous cures for all.

Placement Away from Home

If the child's home is found seriously wanting, and unmodifiable, placement out of the home may be in order. In the past 20 years there has been a strong movement to "deinstitutionalize" mentally ill or mentally retarded adults and this has had its effect on children's services as well. Child welfare institutions for dependent and neglected, unwanted children have been criticized on the basis of regimentation and lack of long-term emotional ties (Bush, 1980), and there has been a concerted effort to find other kinds of surrogate care.

Foster home placement, which would seem an obvious alternative, has its problems, including the likelihood that the child will be replaced more often than not (Fashel & Shinn, 1978). The continuing dissatisfaction with all the temporary care alternatives led to a strong push for "permanency planning" through adoption or efforts to support remaining with the biological parents. However, such efforts, although laudable in intent, are often difficult to maintain over time. Maluccio (in press) warned

In our eagerness to achieve permanency planning at all costs, we sometimes run the risk of doing further damage to the child and—in some cases—the parents. Research shows, for example, that a substantial proportion of permanent plans do not work out, particularly those of children who are reunited with their biological families. (Fein, Maluccio, Hamilton, & Ward, 1983)

As for "special" adoptions:

Too many severely disturbed children and emotionally limited adoptive parents have been linked in the legalities of adoption, which then are disrupted by the need for separation and placement of the children in residential treatment facilities. In "deinstitutionalization" and "permanency planning," the reality fit of adoptive home and child is often overlooked, as is the inability of some children to relate to the intimacy of family life. (Mishne, 1983, p. 208)

In some fashion, we must face the fact that there are children who are too disturbed to adapt to a family living situation. Some of these children have their problems as a result of previous neglect and abuse which have distorted their development, and some have problems which are more reflective of biological/genetic factors. No matter the cause, these children need treatment and an environment which can tolerate their behavior and work towards gradual amelioration.

At present, the recommendation of residential treatment is often one of last resort, so that the child has already endured multiple placements and many failure experiences. The majority of children in residential treatment are adolescents. In a survey of the child residents in the State of Alabama (Wurtele, Wilson, & Prentice-Dunn, 1983), only 30% were under 13 years of age. In this age group, residential treatment should be reserved for those who need 24-hour care beyond that which could be considered reasonable for any family. The children are characterized by extreme and frequent out-of-control behavior which requires close supervision for the safety of themselves and others, or they place exceptional demands on other family members because of their bizarre and inappropriate behaviors. In some measure this is a judgment of the family's ability to be helpful to the child, but the belief that home is the best place for a child must be tempered by what one can reasonably expect from even the best of parents.

For these children, residential care is likely to be fairly lengthy, ranging from 2 to 4 years, and expensive. There are many models of residential treatment (Wilson & Lyman, 1983), but they are all "labor-intensive." An adequate number of child-care staff are needed around the clock and there must be time to coordinate the therapy, schooling, cottage life, group programs, and contacts with family members so that there is sense, consistency, structure, security, and compassion in the real world of the child. Although we are dealing with a small minority of "emotionally disturbed" children, the interests of the many should not blind us to the desperate needs of the few.

Psychopharmacologic Treatment

For elementary-school-age children, the most common drug treatment is stimulants for those with attentional deficit disorders; this is discussed in detail in Chapter 10. Recently there has been some exploration with antidepressants for depressed children. Psychotic adolescents are usually treated with the same drugs used for psychotic adult patients. Rarely would one follow the diagnostic assessment immediately with a drug treatment. It is equally unusual for drug treatment to be sufficient by itself, but it may be an adjunct to any one of the psychological treatment approaches which have been described.

SUMMARY

In this chapter we have followed a tortuous path from referral, through assessment and diagnosis, to the choice of treatment. The focus has been on the age group between 6 and 12 years because both younger and older children present somewhat different problems. Unfortunately the relationship between diagnosis and choice of treatment is murky, partly because therapists often select what they have "ready" to offer rather than selecting on an empirical basis. But there is another problem, namely, that children do not come in simple categories; more often than not there is a multiplicity of possible diagnoses. The importance of moving back and forth from treatment to diagnosis was stressed in recognition of this fact.

On the other hand, totally discarding diagnostic classifications would not be helpful because we would lose our frame of reference for considering effectiveness of interventions. Standardized but comprehensive descriptions of child and family, including but not limited to diagnostic classification, should be a first requirement of an intervention effort. If this were put together with a good description of the intervention, beyond simple labeling, and an honest appraisal of results achieved in individual cases, we should know better what approach works best with what children. In such a venture, careful study of those who drop out or who are considered failures is as important as the study of the successes.

With all the differences, there seem to be some converging themes and increasing overlap between treatment approaches. It is generally accepted that rarely, if ever, can any therapy be successful with a child unless the parents support the process of change. The crucial importance of flexibility and ability to maintain a positive relationship with the child is also stressed by most therapists. All therapies include some components of "play" and "work" and try to teach new strategies for solving problems. Outcome studies indicate that children treated by all the current methods show measurable improvement, at least as judged by parents and therapists. It is equally clear that teachers and peers perceive less improvement, which may mean that the treated child's improvement does not generalize to all situations, or that teachers and peers retain their attitudes and expectations regardless of change. Although techniques for changing home environments abound, much less is done to change school and recreational environments. In the future, one can hope for a generic "child and family therapist" who can move around comfortably from one intervention to another and perhaps have an even wider range of influence in the life space of the child.

REFERENCES

AARONSON, L. J., & KESSLER, J. W. (1968). Point:Counter Point on minimal brain dysfunction. *The Clinical Psychologist, 21,* 125–8.

ABRAMOWITZ, C. V. (1976). The effectiveness of

group psychotherapy with children. *Archives of General Psychiatry, 33*, 320–326.

ACHENBACH, T. M. (1966). The classification of children's psychiatric symptoms: A factor analytic study. *Psychological Monographs, 80.*

ACHENBACH, T. M. (1978). Psychopathology of childhood: Research problems and issues. *Journal of Consulting and Clinical Psychology, 46,* 759–776.

ACHENBACH, T. M., & EDELBROCK, C. (1983). *Manual for the Child Behavior Checklist and Rev. Child Behavior Profile.* Burlington, VT: University of Vermont, Queen City Printers, Inc.

ACHENBACH, T. M., & LEWIS, M. (1971). A proposed model for clinical research and its application to encopresis and enuresis. *Journal of American Academy of Child Psychiatry, 10,* 535–554.

ACKERMAN, N. W. (1958). *The psychodynamics of family life.* New York: Basic Books.

ALEXANDER, J. F., & MALOUF, R. E. (1983). Problems in personality and social development. In P. H. Mussen & E. M. Hetherington (Eds.), *Handbook of child psychology* (4th ed., Vol. 4). New York: John Wiley.

ALLEN, D. (1948). *Three Dimensional Apperception Test.* New York: The Psychological Corporation.

American Psychiatric Association. (1980). *Diagnostic and statistical manual of mental disorders* (3rd ed.), DSM-III. Washington, DC: Author.

ANDERSON, D. V., & HIGHAM, E. (1956). The use of the Rorschach technique in child guidance clinics. In B. Klopfer (Ed.), *Developments in the Rorschach technique. (Vol. 2) Fields of application* (pp. 177–194). New York: Harcourt, Brace, Jovanovich.

ANTHONY, E. J., & BENE, E. J. (1957). A technique for the objective assessment of the child's family relationships. *Journal of Mental Science, 103,* 541–555.

ARNOLD, L. E. (1978). *Helping parents help their children.* New York: Brunner/Mazel.

AXLINE, V. (1947). *Play therapy.* Boston: Houghton Mifflin.

BARRETT, C., HAMPE, T. E. & MILLER, L. (1978). Research on child psychotherapy. In S. Garfield & A. Bergin (Eds.), *Handbook of psychotherapy and behavior change* (pp. 411–436). New York: Wiley.

BECK, S. J. (1931). The Rorschach Test in problem children. *American Journal of Orthopsychiatry, 1,* 501–9.

BEITCHMAN, J. H., DIELMAN, T. E., LANDIS, J. R., BENSON, R. M., & KEMP, P. L. (1978). Reliability of the Group for the Advancement of Psychiatry diagnostic categories in child psychiatry. *Archives of General Psychiatry, 35,* 1461–1468.

BELLAK, L. (1986). *The T.A.T., C.A.T., and S.A.T. in clinical use* (4th ed.). New York: Grune & Stratton.

BERGMAN, A., & SCHUBERT, J. (1974). The Rorschachs of normal and emotionally disturbed children: A review of the literature. *British Journal of Projective Psychology and Personality Studies, 19,* 7–13.

BERNAL, M. E., KLINNERT, M. D., & SCHULTZ, L. A. (1980). Outcome evaluation of behavioral parent training and client-centered parent counseling for children with conduct problems. *Journal of Applied Behavior Analysis, 13,* 677–691.

BREIDENBAUGH, B., BROZOVICH, R. I., & MATHESON, K. (1974). The Hand Test and other aggression indicators in emotionally disturbed children. *Journal of Personality Assessment, 38,* 332–334.

BRICKLIN, B., PIOTROWSKI, Z. A., & WAGNER, E. E. (1970). *The Hand Test.* Springfield, IL: Charles C Thomas.

BRODKIN, A. M. (1980). Family Therapy: The making of a mental health movement. *American Journal of Orthopsychiatry, 50,* 4–17.

BUCK, J. N. (1948). The H-T-P Technique: A qualitative and quantitative scoring manual. *Journal of Clinical Psychology, 4,* 317–396.

BUHLER, C. (1951). The World Test. *Journal of Child Psychiatry, 2,* 69–81.

BUSH, M. (1980). Institutions for dependent and neglected children. Therapeutic option of choice or last resort? *American Journal of Orthopsychiatry, 50,* 239–255.

CAREK, D. J. (1979). Individual psychodynamically oriented therapy. In J. D. Noshpitz & S. I. Harrison (Eds.), *Basic handbook of child psychiatry* (Vol. 3, pp. 35–56). New York: Basic Books.

CASEY, R. J., & BERMAN, J. S. (1985). The outcome of psychotherapy with children. *Psychological Bulletin, 98,* 388–400.

CHETHIK, M. (1976). Work with parents: Treatment of the parent-child relationship. *Journal of the American Academy of Child Psychiatry, 15,* 453–463.

CLEMENTS, S. D., & PETERS, J. E. (1965). The diagnostic dilemma in child guidance. In B. Straub & J. Hellmuth (Eds.), *Learning disorders* (Vol. 1, pp. 197–218). Seattle: Special Child Publications.

CONNERS, C. K. (1973). Rating scales for use in drug studies with children. *Psychopharmacology Bulletin: Pharmacotherapy with children.* Washington, DC: U.S. Gov. Printing Office.

COSTELLO, A. J., EDELBROCK, C. S., DULCAN, M. K., & KALAS, R. (1984). *Testing of the NIMH Diagnostic Interview Schedule for Children (DISC) in a clinical population.* Final Report (Contract No. DB-81-0027. Rockville, MD: Center for Epidemiological Studies, National Institute of Mental Health.

CROMWELL, R. L., BLASHFIELD, R. K., & STRAUSS, J. S. (1975). Criteria for classification systems. In N. Hobbs (Ed.), *Issues in the classification of children* (Vol. 1 pp. 4–25). San Francisco: Jossey-Bass.

DAVIDS, A. (1973). Aggression in thought and action of emotionally disturbed boys. *Journal of Counseling and Clinical Psychology, 40,* 322–327.

DI GIUSEPPE, R. A. (1981). Cognitive therapy with children. In G. Emery, S. D. Hollon, & R. C. Bedrosian (Eds.), *New directions in cognitive therapy* (pp. 50–65). New York: The Guilford Press.

EDELBROCK, C., COSTELLO, A. J., DULCAN, M. K., KALAS, R., & CONOVER, N. C. (1985). Age differences in the reliability of the psychiatric interview of the child. *Child Development, 56,* 265–275.

ELLIS, A. (1962). *Reason and emotion in psychotherapy.* New York: Lyle Stuart.

ELLIS, A. (1978). Rational-emotive guidance. In L. E. Arnold (Ed.), *Helping parents help their children* (pp. 91–101). New York: Brunner/Mazel.

ERICKSON, G. D., & HOGAN, T. P. (Eds). (1981). *Family therapy. An introduction to theory and technique* (2nd ed). Monterey, CA: Brooks/Cole.

EXNER, J. E., & WEINER, I. B. (1982). *The Rorschach: Assessment of children and adolescents* (Vol. 3). New York: John Wiley.

FAGEN, S. A., & LONG, N. J. (1979). A psychoeducational curriculum approach to teaching self-control. *Behavioral Disorders, 4,* 68–83.

FANSHEL, D., & SHINN, E. B. (1978). *Children in foster care—A longitudinal investigation.* New York: Columbia University Press.

FEIN, E., MALUCCIO, A. N., HAMILTON, V. J., & WARD, D. (1983). After foster care: outcomes of permanency planning for children. *Child Welfare, 62,* 485–558.

FERSTER, C. B., & DEMYER, M. K. (1962). A method for the experimental analysis of the behavior of autistic children. *American Journal of Orthopsychiatry, 32,* 89–98.

FREEDHEIM, D. K., & RUSS, S. W. (1983). Psychotherapy with children. In C. E. Walker & M. C. Roberts (Eds.), *Handbook of clinical child psychology* (pp. 978–994). Somerset, NJ: John Wiley.

FREUD, A. (1954, May). *Diagnosis and assessment of early childhood difficulties.* Paper presented at Philadelphia Association for Psychoanalysis, Philadelphia, PA.

FREUD, A. (1965). *Normality and pathology in childhood. Assessments of development.* New York: International Universities Press.

FREUD, S. (1955). Analysis of a phobia in a

five-year-old boy. In J. Strachey (Ed. and Trans.), *The standard edition of the complete psychological works of Sigmund Freud* (Vol. 10). London: Hogarth Press. (Original work published 1909)

FREYBERG, J. (1973). Increasing imaginative play of urban disadvantaged kindergarten children through systematic training. In J. Singer (Ed.) *The child's world of make believe* (pp. 129–154). New York: Academic Press.

FRIEDMAN, H. (1952). Perceptual regression schizophrenia: An hypothesis suggested by the use of the Rorschach Test. *Journal of Genetic Psychology, 81,* 63–98.

FROST, B. P. (1969). The Family Relations Test, a normative study. *Journal of Projective Techniques, 33,* 403–413.

FURMAN, E. (1979). Filial therapy. In J. D. Noshpitz & S. I. Harrison (Eds.), *Basic handbook of child psychiatry* (Vol. 3, pp. 149–158). New York: Basic Books.

GARDNER, R. (1971) *Therapeutic communication with children: The Mutual Storytelling Technique.* New York: Science House.

GELFAND, D. M., & HARTMANN, D. P. (1968). Behavior therapy with children: A review and evaluation of research methodology. *Psychological Bulletin, 69,* 204–215.

GITTELMAN-KLEIN, R. (1978). Validity of projective tests. In R. I. Spitzer & D. F. Klein (Eds.), *Critical issues in psychiatric diagnosis.* New York: Raven Press.

GOLDENBERG, I., & GOLDENBERG, H. (1980). *Family therapy: An overview.* Monterey, CA: Brooks/Cole.

GOLDFRIED, M. R., STRICKER, G., & WEINER, I. B. (1971). *Rorschach handbook of clinical and research applications.* Englewood Cliffs, NJ: Prentice-Hall.

GOODMAN, J. F. (1987). Diagnosis and intervention in young children: The continuing gap. *Journal of Psychology, 121,* 21–36.

GOULD, M. S., WUNSCH-WITZIK, R., & DOHRENWEND, B. (1981). Estimating the prevalence of childhood psychopathology: A critical review. *Journal of the American*

Academy of Child Psychiatry, 20, 462–476.

GRAHAM, P. (1979). Epidemiological studies. In H. C. Quay & J. S. Werry (Eds.), *Psychopathological disorders of childhood* (2nd ed.) (pp. 185–209). New York: John Wiley.

GRAHAM, P., & RUTTER, M. (1973). Psychiatric disorder in the young adolescent: A follow-up study. *Proceedings of the Royal Society of Medicine, 66,* 1226–1229.

Group for the Advancement of Psychiatry (GAP). (1966). *Psychopathological disorders in childhood: Theoretical considerations and a proposed classification.* GAP Report No. 62.

GUERNEY, B. (1964). Filial therapy: Description and rationale. *Journal of Consulting Psychology, 28,* 450–460.

GUINDON, J. (1973). (1) The Re-education Process and (2) The psychoeducateur training program. *International Journal of Mental Health, 2,* 15–26, 27–32.

GURMAN, A. S., & KNISKERN, D. P. (1978). Research on marital and family therapy: Progress, perspective and prospect. In S. L. Garfield & A. E. Bergin (Eds.), *Handbook of psychotherapy and behavior change: An empirical analysis* (pp. 817–902). New York: Wiley.

HALEY, J. (1971). Family therapy: A radical change. In J. Haley (Ed.), *Changing families: A family therapy reader* (pp. 272–284). New York: Grune and Stratton.

HARRIS, D. B. (1963). *Children's drawings as measures of intellectual maturity.* New York: Harcourt, Brace and World.

HARTMANN, D. P., ROPER, B. L., & GELFAND, D. M. (1977). An evaluation of alternative modes of child psychotherapy. In B. Lahey & A. E. Kazdin (Eds.), *Advances in clinical child psychology* (Vol. 1, pp. 1–46). New York: Plenum Press.

HAWORTH, M. R. (1986). Children's Apperception Test. In A. I. Rabin (Ed.), *Projective techniques for adolescents and children* (pp. 37–72). New York: Springer.

HERJANIC, B., HERJANIC, M., BROWN, F., & WHEATT, T. (1975). Are children reliable reporters? *Journal of Abnormal Child Psychology, 3,* 41–48.

HERJANIC, B., & CAMPBELL, W. (1977). Differentiating psychiatrically disturbed children on the basis of a structured interview. *Journal of Abnormal Child Psychology, 5,* 127–134.

HERJANIC, B., & REICH, W. (1982). Development of a structured psychiatric interview for children: Agreement between child and parent on individual symptoms. *Journal of Abnormal Child Psychology, 10,* 307–324.

HEWETT, E. F. (1968). *The emotionally disturbed child in the classroom: A developmental strategy for educating children with maladaptive behavior.* Boston: Allyn and Bacon.

HOBBS, N. (1962). Sources of gain in psychotherapy. *American Psychologist, 17,* 741–747.

HOBBS, N. (1982). *The troubled and troubling child.* San Francisco: Jossey-Bass.

HODGES, K., McKNEW, D., CYTRYN, L., STERN, L., & KLINE, J. (1982). The Child Assessment Schedule (CAS) Diagnostic Interview: A report on reliability and validity. *Journal of the American Academy of Child Psychiatry, 21,* 468–473.

HOLT, R. R., & HAVEL, J. (1977). A method for assessing primary and secondary process in the Rorschach. In M. Rickers-Ovsiankina (Ed.), *Rorschach psychology* (2nd ed.) (pp. 375–420). Huntington, NY: Robert E. Krieger.

HORNSBY, L. G., & APPELBAUM, A. S. (1978). Parents as primary therapists: Filial therapy. In L. E. Arnold (Ed.), *Helping parents to help their children* (pp. 126–134). New York: Brunner/Mazel.

HUMPHREYS, L. E., & CIMINERO, A. R. (1979). Parent report measures of child behavior: A review. *Journal of Clinical Child Psychology, 8,* 56–63.

HUTT, M. L. (1980). *The Michigan Picture Test Revised.* New York: Grune and Stratton.

JACKSON, D. D. (1965). Family rules: Marital quid pro quo. *Archives of General Psychiatry, 12,* 589–594.

JONES, M. C. (1924). The elimination of children's fears. *Journal of Experimental Psychology, 7,* 383–390.

KAL, E. F. (1969). Organic versus functional diagnoses. *American Journal of Psychiatry, 125,* 164.

KENDALL, P. C. (1981). Cognitive-behavioral interventions with children. In B. B. Lahey & A. E. Kazdin (Eds.), *Advances in clinical child psychology* (Vol. 4, pp. 53–90). New York: Plenum Press.

KESSLER, J. W. (1971). Nosology in child psychopathology. In H. E. Rie (Ed.), *Perspectives in child psychopathology* (pp. 85–129). Chicago, IL: Aldine/Atherton.

KESSLER, J. W., & WOLFENSTEIN, C. M. (1953). A comparison of Rorschach retests with behavior changes in a group of emotionally disturbed children. *American Journal of Orthopsychiatry, 23,* 740–754.

KOPPITZ, E. M. (1968). *Psychological evaluation of children's human figure drawings.* New York: Grune and Stratton.

KOVACS, M. (1985). The Interview Schedule for Children (ISC). *Psychopharmacology Bulletin, 21,* 991–994.

KRUGMAN, J. I. (1942). A clinical validation of the Rorschach with problem children. *Rorschach Research Exchange, 6,* 61–70.

LACHAR, D., & GDOWSKI, C. L. (1979). *Actuarial assessment of child and adolescent personality: An interpretive guide for the Personality Inventory for Children Profile.* Los Angeles, CA: Western Psychological Services.

LEVITT, E. E. (1957). Results of psychotherapy with children: An evaluation. *Journal of Counseling Psychology, 21,* 189–196.

LEVITT, E. E. (1963). Psychotherapy with children: A further evaluation. *Behaviour Research and Therapy, 60,* 326–329.

LINDSLEY, O. (1978). Teaching parents to modify their children's behavior. In L. E. Arnold (Ed.), *Helping parents help their children* (pp. 83–90). New York: Brunner/Mazel.

LINKS, P. S. (1983). Community surveys of the prevalence of childhood psychiatric disorders: A review. *Child Development, 54,* 531–548.

LOBITZ, G. K., & JOHNSON, S. M. (1975). Normal versus deviant children: A multimethod comparison. *Journal of Abnormal Child Psychology, 3,* 353–374.

MACHOVER, K. (1949). *Personality projection in the drawing of the human figure.* Springfield, IL: Charles C Thomas.

MACHOVER, K. (1960). Sex differences in the developmental pattern of children as seen in the Human Figure Drawings. In R. A. Rubin & M. R. Haworth (Eds.), *Projective techniques with children* (pp. 238–257). New York: Grune and Stratton.

MALUCCIO, A. N. (in press). The role of group child care in permanency planning. G. C. Carman (Ed.), *Prevention, permanence, and family support.* New York: Child Welfare League of America.

MASH, E. J., & TERDAL, L. G. (1981). Behavioral assessment of childhood disturbance. In E. J. Mash & L. G. Terdal (Eds.), *Behavioral assessment of childhood disorders* (pp. 3–78). New York: The Guilford Press.

MATTISON, R., CANTWELL, D. P., RUSSELL, A. T. & WILL, L. (1979). A comparison of DSM II and DSM III in the diagnosis of childhood psychiatric disorders. *Archives of General Psychiatry, 36,* 1217–1228.

MCDERMOTT, J. F., JR., HARRISON, S. I., SCHRAGER, J., WILSON, P., KILINS, E., LINDY, J., & WAGGONER, R. W. (1968). Social class and mental illness in children: The diagnosis of organicity and mental retardation. In S. Chess & A. Thomas (Eds.), *Annual progress in child psychiatry and child development* (pp. 437–448). New York: Brunner/Mazel.

MEICHENBAUM, D. (1979). Teaching children self-control. In B. Lahey & A. Kazdin (Eds.), *Advances in clinical child psychology* (Vol. 2, pp. 1–35). New York: Plenum Press.

MEICHENBAUM, D., & GOODMAN, J. (1971). Training impulsive children to talk to themselves: A means of developing self-control. *Journal of Abnormal Psychology, 77,* 115–126.

MELAMED, B. G., & SIEGEL, L. J. (1975). Reduction of anxiety in children facing hospitalization and surgery by use of filmed modeling. *Journal of Consulting and Clinical Psychology, 43,* 511–521.

MILLER, L. C. (1967). Louisville Behavior Checklist for males, 6–12 years of age. *Psychological Reports, 21,* 885–896.

MINUCHIN, S. (1967). *Families of the slums: An exploration of their structure and treatment.* New York: Basic Books.

MINUCHIN, S. (1974). *Families and family therapy.* Cambridge, MA: Harvard University Press.

MINUCHIN, S., ROSMAN, B. L., & BAKER, L. (1978). *Psychosomatic families: Anorexia nervosa in context.* Cambridge MA: Harvard University Press.

MISHNE, J. (1983). *Clinical work with children.* New York: Free Press.

MORGAN, C. D., & MURRAY, H. A. (1935). A method for investigating fantasies: The Thematic Apperception Test. *Archives of Neurological Psychiatry, 34,* 289–306.

MUNDY, J. (1972). The use of projective techniques with children. In B. B. Wolman (Ed.), *Manual of child psychopathology* (pp. 791–819). New York: McGraw-Hill.

O'LEARY, K. D., & JOHNSON, S. B. (1979). Psychological assessment. In H. C. Quay & J. S. Werry (Eds.), *Psychopathological disorders of childhood* (2nd ed.) (pp. 210–246). New York: John Wiley.

PALMER, J. O. (1983). *The psychological assessment of children* (2nd ed.). New York: John Wiley.

PEED, S., ROBERTS, & FOREHAND, R. (1977). Evaluation of the effectiveness of a standardized parent training program in altering the interaction of mothers and their noncompliant children. *Behavior Modification, 1,* 323–350.

PELLEGRINI, D. S., & URBAIN, E. S. (1985). An evaluation of interpersonal cognitive problem solving training with children. *Journal of Child Psychology and Psychiatry, 26,* 17–41.

PEREZ-REYES, M., & LANSING, C. (1967). The diagnostic evaluation process. *Archives of General Psychiatry, 16,* 609–620.

PETERSON, D. R. (1961). Behavior problems of middle childhood. *Journal of Consulting Psychology, 25,* 205–209.

QUAY, H. C. (1979). Classification. In H. C. Quay & J. S. Werry (Eds.), *Psychopathological disorders of childhood* (2nd ed.) (pp. 1–42). New York: John Wiley.

QUAY, H. C., & PETERSON, D. R. (1983). *Interim manual for the Revised Problem Checklist.* Coral Gables, FL: Applied Social Sciences, University of Miami.

RACHMAN, S. (1972). Clinical applications of observational learning, imitation and modeling. *Behavior Therapy, 3,* 379–397.

RAISER, L., & VAN NAGEL, C. (1980). The loophole in Public Law 94-142. *Exceptional Children, 46,* 516–520.

RORSCHACH, H. (1921). *Psychodiagnostik.* Bern:Bircher. [Translation: *Psychodiagnostics.* (1951)]. New York: Grune and Stratton.

ROSE, S. D. (1973). *Treating children in groups. A behavioral approach.* San Francisco: Jossey-Bass.

ROSENZWEIG, S. (1978). *Aggressive Behavior and the Rosenzweig Picture-Frustration Study.* New York: Praeger Special Studies, Praeger.

ROSENZWEIG, S., FLEMING, E. D., & ROSENZWEIG, L. (1948). The children's form of the Rosenzweig Picture-Frustration Study. *Journal of Psychology, 26,* 141–191.

ROSENZWEIG, S., & ROSENZWEIG, L. (1952). Aggression in problem children and normals as evaluated by the Rosenzweig-P-F Study. *Journal of Abnormal and Social Psychology, 47,* 141–191.

ROSS, A. O. (1959). *The practice of clinical child psychology.* New York: Grune and Stratton.

ROSS, A. O. (1974). *Psychological disorders of children. A behavioral approach to theory,* *research and therapy.* New York: McGraw-Hill.

ROTTER, J. B., & WILLERMAN, B. (1947). The incomplete sentence test as a method of studying personality. *Journal of Consulting Psychology, 2,* 43–48.

RUBIN, R. A., & BALOW, B. (1978). Prevalence of teacher identified behavior problems: A longitudinal study. *Exceptional Children, 45,* 102–114.

RUTTER, M., & GRAHAM, P. (1966). Psychiatric disorder in 10- and 11-year-old children. *Proceedings of the Royal Society of Medicine, 59,* 382–387.

RUTTER, M., & GRAHAM, P. (1968). The reliability and validity of the psychiatric assessment of the child: Interview with the child. *British Journal of Psychiatry, 11,* 563–579.

SATIR, V. (1967). *Conjoint family therapy* (2nd ed). Palo Alto, CA: Science and Behavior Books.

SCHIFFER, M. (1969). *The therapeutic play group.* New York: Grune and Stratton.

SEIGEL, M. (1948). The diagnostic and prognostic validity of the Rorschach test in a child guidance clinic. *American Journal of Orthopsychiatry, 18,* 119–133.

SHECHTMAN, A. (1970). Age patterns in children's psychiatric symptoms. *Child Development, 4,* 683–693.

SHNEIDMAN, E. S. (1952). Manual for the Make a Picture-Story Method. *Journal of Projective Techniques Monograph, No 2.*

SHURE, M. B., & SPIVACK, G. (1984). Interpersonal problem solving as a mediator of behavior adjustment in preschool and kindergarten children. *Journal of Applied Developmental Psychology, 1,* 29–43.

SINES, J. O., PAUKER, J. D., SINES, L. K., & OWEN, D. R. (1969). Identification of clinically relevant dimensions of children's behavior. *Journal of Consulting and Clinical Psychology, 33,* 728–734.

SLAVSON, S. R. (1943). *An introduction to group therapy.* New York: International Universities Press.

SLAVSON, S. R. (1952). *Child psychotherapy.* New York: Columbia University Press.

SLAVSON, S. R., & SCHIFFER, M. (1975). *Group psychotherapies for children.* New York: International Universities Press.

SMILANSKY, S. (1968). *The effects of sociodramatic play on disadvantaged children.* New York: John Wiley.

STANTON, M. D. (1980). Family therapy: Systems approaches. In G. P. Sholevar, R. M. Benson, & B. J. Blinder (Eds.), *Handbook of emotional disorders in children and adolescents: Medical and psychological approaches to treatment.* Jamaica, NY: Spectrum.

STOLZ, S. B., WIENCKOWSHI, L. A., & BROWN, B. S. (1975). Behavior modification. A perspective on critical issues. *American Psychologist, 30,* 1027–1048.

TAVORMINA, J. B. (1974). Basic models of parent counseling: A critical review. *Psychological Bulletin, 81,* 827–836.

URBAIN, E. D., & KENDALL, P. C. (1980). Review of social-cognitive problem-solving interventions with children. *Psychological Bulletin, 88,* 109–143.

WAGNER, E. E. (1986). Hand Test interpretation for children and adolescents. In A. I. Rabin (Ed.), *Projective techniques for adolescents and children* (pp. 279–305). New York: Springer.

WEINSTEIN, L. (1974). *Evaluation of a program for re-educating disturbed children: A follow-up comparison with untreated children.* Washington, DC: U.S. Department of Health, Education and Welfare. (Available through ERIC Document Reproduction Service, ED-141-966.)

WERRY, J. S., & WOLLERSHEIM, J. (1967). Behavior therapy with children: A broad overview. *Journal of American Academy of Child Psychiatry, 6,* 346–370.

WILSON, D. R., & LYMAN, R. D. (1983). Residential treatment of emotionally disturbed children. In C. E. Walker & M. C. Roberts (Eds.), *Handbook of clinical child psychology* (pp. 1069–1088). New York: John Wiley.

WILSON, S. J. (1981). A Piagetian-based analysis of insight and the interpretive process. *American Journal of Orthopsychiatry, 51,* 626–635.

WINNICOTT, D. W. (1971). *Therapeutic consultations in child psychiatry.* New York: Basic Books.

WIRT, R. D., LACHAR, D., KLINEDINST, J. K., & SEAT, P. D. (1977). *Multidimensional description of child personality: A manual for the Personality Inventory for Children.* Los Angeles: Western Psychological Services.

WOLFENSBERGER, W. (1965). Embarrassments in the diagnostic process. *Mental Retardation, 3,* 29–31.

WURTELE, S. K., WILSON, D. R., & PRENTICE-DUNN, S. (1983). Characteristics of children in residential treatment programs: Findings and clinical implications. *Journal of Clinical Child Psychology, 12,* 137–144.

ZUBIN, J. (1969). Cross national study of diagnosis of the mental disorders: Methodology and planning. *American Journal of Psychiatry (Suppl.), 125,* 12–21.

CHAPTER 8

ANXIETY DISORDERS

In this chapter we examine the characteristics and treatment of a group of problems which fall into the cluster called "personality problems" by Peterson (1961), "internalizers" by Achenbach (1966), or "anxiety-withdrawal pattern" by Quay and Werry (1979). Many of these problems were subsumed under the old diagnosis of "neurosis" that was deleted from DSM III. These disorders represent one of the two most prominent forms of psychological disability, second only to the conduct disorders. Trying to estimate their prevalence is particularly difficult because there is so much variation in diagnostic thinking.

Some professional workers use these diagnoses only when anxiety is obvious in the presenting symptoms or when the child scores "high" on some report measure. Others consider the possibilities of "latent anxiety" as an underlying cause

for behavior or learning problems. In the chicken-egg relationship between feelings and behavior, behavior therapists and dynamic therapists will disagree as to which (i.e., feelings or overt behavior) should constitute the primary diagnosis. A survey of 1,568 child patients referred to the Child Psychiatric Services at the University of Louisville School of Medicine over a 2-year period showed that 42% were given diagnoses of anxiety as the primary disability (Miller, 1983). In sharp contrast, in a survey of behavior therapists only 7% of their child patients were diagnosed as "fear or phobia" (Graziano & DeGiovanni, 1979). The discrepancy may be partly because of selection factors influencing where people go for help, but probably child psychiatric services use a broader definition of "anxiety" than do the behavior therapists.

THE CONCEPT OF NEUROSIS

Although this diagnosis is no longer included in the official nomenclature, there are many clinicians who use the concept, if not the term. Clinicians with a psychodynamically oriented background use the term "neurosis" to refer to a special form of emotional disturbance where there is an internalized, partially unconscious conflict, as opposed to those disorders that result from a conflict between the child and his environment or those that are a direct reaction to environmental conditions. Dichotomizing causes into simple internal or external sources presents difficulties, and there is always need for external support in the treatment of the most "internalized" disorder. But the distinction makes a difference in treatment emphasis.

The essential ingredients of the psychoanalytic theory of neurosis have changed little since Freud's original exposition at the beginning of this century. One of his first contentions was that neurotic behavior is similar in kind to normal behavior, which was the major reason for his great interest in the psychology of dreams. He saw neurotic symptoms, like dreams, as a compromise formation between a repressed element and the defenses of the ego. A second contention was his belief that there is a universal application of determinism to mental life and that it should be possible, in theory, to discover the psychological determinants of the smallest detail of the mind's processes. In understanding the relationship between present behavior and past events, Freud introduced the concept of the unconscious, declaring "The theory of repression is the cornerstone on which the whole structure of psychoanalysis rests" (1914/1957, p. 16). Initially Freud related the etiology of adult symptoms to real-life experiences, although he realized that the long-lasting reaction was disproportionate to the actual event and suggested that the connection was often a "symbolic relation between the precipitating cause and the pathological phenomenon, a relation such as healthy people form in dreams" (1893/1955, p. 5). Later on, Freud was to pay less attention to reality events and more attention to inner events, that is, fantasies and affects aroused as much by inner drives as by external circumstances.

In the evolution of theory, Freud suggested various combinations of drives as the basic, biological "givens." In his early expository lectures at Clark University, he asserted that the origin of neuroses was predominantly of a sexual nature:

The imperishable, repressed wishful impulses of childhood have alone provided the power for the construction of symptoms, and without them, the reaction to later traumas would have taken a normal course. But these powerful wishful impulses of childhood may without exception be described as sexual. (1910/1957, p. 41)

This was the period when he was concerned with establishing the fact of infantile sexuality, its "polymorphous perverse nature" and the complications of the Oedipal complex. Much later, Freud modified his theory of drives to include aggression as the second basic drive: "In all that follows I adopt the standpoint therefore that the inclination to aggression is an original, self-subsisting instinctual disposition in man, and I return to my view that it constitutes the greatest impediment to civilization" (1930/1961, p. 122). Validation of this or any theory of basic drives depends more on neurophysiology than psychology, but it is nonetheless useful because one soon discovers that love-sexual and hate-aggressive feelings can be very troublesome indeed and represent a potent source of anxiety.

PSYCHOANALYTIC THEORY OF ANXIETY AND THE MECHANISMS OF DEFENSE

It is important to keep in mind that the fear response is essential in development. Quoting Ann Freud:

Archaic fears make the infant cling more closely to the protecting mother, thereby increasing object relatedness; fear of loss of love, of criticism or punishment, is the well-known incentive for compliance with educational demands; anxiety aroused by the strength of the id impulses furthers the construction of effective defenses; fear of the superego, guilt, leads to drive modification and social adaptation. In short, the same unpleasant affects which are the direct cause of neurotic symptom formation are known to be indispensable assets for normal character building. (1977, p. 89)

In Chapter 5, we discussed the difficulties in distinguishing between fear, justified by external circumstances, and anxiety, emanating from internal sources. Particularly with children under 5 years, their perception of external reality is easily distorted by their cognitive immaturity and egocentricism as well as by the strength of their drives, or

feelings. However, even with older children, their fears contain a mix of reality and fantasy. It is usually within the realm of possibility that their fears could be realized, but if the fears have a phobic character, the outside possibility is taken as a probability. Something within the child leads them to expect the worst.

To understand how a child, old enough to "know better," can persistently misconstrue reality, it is necessary to review the mechanisms used to defend against the experience of anxiety. The term *defense* was first used by Freud in 1894 to describe the ego's struggle against painful or unendurable ideas or affects. For a long time, he concentrated on the part played by *repression*. In *Inhibitions, Symptoms, and Anxiety* (1926/1959), he remarked on the concept of defense and suggested that repression was only one example of a defense mechanism, but it was only with Anna Freud's *The Ego and Mechanisms of Defense* (1936/1946) that these mechanisms achieved the importance they deserve in both theory and therapy. This was the real beginning of what is loosely called "ego psychology." Psychoanalysts no longer concentrated solely on making "the unconscious conscious," but equal concern was given to discovering and interpreting the various maneuvers the child uses to avoid the feeling of anxiety, no matter what its specific source. The following is a description of the basic defenses.

Introjection and Identification

Introjection and identification belong together because they are operative from a very early age and continue, to some extent, throughout life. Both have to do with incorporating something from the environment into the self. Both are basic ingredients of the learning process and an essential part of normal development. Introjection is a kind of piecemeal identification where a child takes in a part of someone else's personality, for instance, the "scolding mother." It is somewhat related to the mechanism of "splitting," where the child perceives the "mother who scolds" and the "mother who loves" as two different people. Ordinarily these perceptions are fused into one person with whom the child makes an identification. This brings pleasure and security to the child who feels closer to the grownups. But it is pathological when identification goes so far that the child's identity is lost, when the child's personality melts into that of another. Such total fusion renders the child helpless, totally dependent, unable to tolerate separation from his or her other half. Fear of loss of the other person is the particular kind of anxiety which would ordinarily lead to pathological identification.

Turning Passive into Active

Turning passive into active is an essential principle of normal development and social learning. In part, identification is an example of doing unto others as one has been done to. However, in what is known as the "repetition compulsion," it takes a strange twist. A child may behave in a way that is almost guaranteed to elicit a bad reaction—with full knowledge of the probable conse-

quences. For example, an abused child may provoke further incidents. One might interpret the behavior as simple attention-seeking, but there often seems to be a deliberate choice for negative rather than positive attention. To understand such paradoxical behavior, which seems to defy the basic law of effect, it helps to think of the child as trying to exert control. Having experienced negative responses unexpectedly in the past, the child now brings them about voluntarily and predictably. "Bad" things which happen expectably are less frightening than those which occur as a surprise.

Denial and Repression

Denial and repression are alike in that they both serve to make something unconscious. Denial is perhaps the more primitive of the two. It is related to faith in the magical power of thoughts and words. The child acts as if wishes could change reality; that which he or she does not want to see or acknowledge ceases to exist. This is normal in the very young child, but if it is not outgrown, it can become a serious handicap. Internal feelings as well as external events may be denied. For instance, an 8-year-old girl in obvious emotional difficulty was talking with her mother, sobbing all the while, and saying "I am not happy." At no time was this obviously unhappy girl able to admit her feelings, despite encouragement to do so.

Repression, a derivative of denial, is more complex. Assume that our sobbing 8-year-old girl admits her sadness (i.e., no denial) but is unable, 15 minutes later, to recall either her tears or her admission (i.e., repression). Repressing is making unconscious an unwanted feeling, memory, or fantasy. A repressed memory is a forgotten one, but it can return when the guard is down, as in illness, fatigue, intoxication, or sleep.

A rather special mechanism, which is halfway between denial and repression, was termed *negation* by Freud. Here the person makes a special point of saying that something is not so. A child who was consistently losing in a game suddenly remarked "Don't think I am angry that you are winning all the time." He felt in danger of expressing anger (and perhaps losing a friend), so he made a conciliatory gesture in advance of the actual danger. Negation is a kind of compromise between repression and denial. In this example, the child brought up the possibility of feeling angry—so repression was not yet operative—but denied the affect in advance. This does not mean that children always mean the opposite of what they say, but it does require empathy and intuition to detect their true meaning. One has to think, "If I were in the child's place, how would I be feeling?" and be ready to question gratuitous statements which are contrary to what one would expect.

Projection and Displacement

Projection and displacement are both mechanisms which alter the source of danger. The affect is acknowledged, but is attributed to someone else (i.e., projection) or to some other cause (i.e., displacement). In projection, the child says in effect "I am not angry; the teacher is angry," or "It is not I who doesn't like the other children; they don't like me." However, if the other people are viewed as hostile (by projection), then the child's angry feelings are justified and become self-perpetuating. Projection is derived from the primitive thought processes previously described as egocentric. The very young child does not distinguish between his or her thoughts and the thoughts of others. In projection, the child gets rid of anxiety-provoking affects by giving them to someone else: "Let him worry, not me." This may be carried so far as to distort the person's perception of reality. Paranoid patients interpret ordinary events personally, ascribing all kinds of malicious purpose to the most innocent circumstances.

A certain measure of projection is involved in a special kind of identification, namely, *identification with the aggressor.* "By impersonating the aggressor, assuming his attributes, or imitating his aggression, the child transforms himself from the person threatened into the person who makes the threat" (A. Freud, 1946, p. 121). The child makes this transformation as a prophylactic measure on the basis that the best defense is a good offense. Sometimes, however, the aggressiveness of others is more assumed than real. Still the child expects attack; he has, by projection, attributed his own hostile intention to the other person. The operation of these mental processes can be seen in the typical Oedipal conflict situation. Identification with the aggressor is an extremely important mechanism for the clinician to recognize. Aggressive behavior may be a cover-up for anxiety. If so, the first step in helping is to assure the child: "You may be angry with me, but I am not angry with you. I will not fight you or hurt you." This puts the feeling back where it belongs and eliminates the child's need for counterattack.

In displacement, the child feels the affect about the wrong thing. One idea or image may be substituted for another which is associated with it, or one source of anxiety may be substituted for another. For instance, a child who is afraid of his mother's disapproval may be unaware of this fear (repression) and may replace it with a morbid fear of the teacher's disapproval. Projection and displacement go hand-in-hand in the formation of phobias. Displacement is the same kind of behavior as that described by the learning term "generalization"; the tendency to make the response learned in connection with stimulus to another similar stimulus. However, displacement is a defensive substitution. By simple generalization, the child might be angry at mother and every other woman as well; if displacement has occurred, the child is angry at the teacher instead of the mother.

Reaction Formation, Undoing, and Isolation

Reaction formation, undoing, and isolation are considered together because they so often occur in conjunction, particularly in obsessional-compulsive disorders. They are directed against internal feelings that are repressed initially. Then an additional defense is constructed in order to guard against the return of the repressed. In reaction forma-

tion, an attitude is taken that counters the original desire. This may be observed during toilet training when the child is more offended by dirt and messiness than the parents, outdoing them in fastidiousness in order to ward off temptation. This same mechanism may be invoked against other unwelcome impulses. An impulse to hurt others may be warded off by excessive sympathy and gentleness, to the point that a child cannot bear to have a housefly destroyed.

In undoing, still another defensive step is taken. Something positive is done which, actually or by magic, is the opposite of something that was done before. The child who has renounced pleasure in messing and set up a reaction formation of great cleanliness may find that this is not enough. The child may still feel "dirty" and get relief only by constant hand washing. A formerly aggressive person may find that excessive sympathy for others is not enough and go to unreasonable lengths to perform kind acts, acts which may even be undesirable to the recipient.

Isolation is a rather specialized mechanism of defense and difficult to detect. It may be manifested as compartmentalized thinking. The person fails to see obvious connections; he or she keeps things apart, separated. Feelings may be separated from the actual event. Such a child may recall an emotional experience in detail, but feel no emotion about it. It is discussed as if it happened to someone else.

Other children try to resolve conflicts by isolating certain spheres of their lives from one another. They may think of themselves as two people. Perhaps the good one goes to school and the bad one stays at home, or vice versa. Children may worry that they have bad thoughts or think bad words, and they may disown the part that does such things. Sometimes they even have a name for the other self for which they feel no responsibility. The phenomenon of isolation is related to anxieties about touching.

Regression and Fixation

Regression and fixation are alike in having a pervasive effect on development. In fixation, a child does not move ahead because something about the forward step causes anxiety. In regression, the child moves backward, giving up something which has proven painful and regressing to an earlier stage. Whenever a person feels frustrated, he or she tends to long for "the good old days," the easier times before trouble set in. Both of these mechanisms have the common effect of causing "immaturity," that is, maintaining behavior patterns which belong to a younger age.

All these defenses can be adaptive at times; they become pathological only when they are overworked. Then they may produce any combination of the following: (a) restricting the freedom of the child to learn or try new things; (b) alienating the child from other people; or (c) seriously distorting reality awareness. The whole field of psychopathology, including the formation of symptoms, is greatly illuminated by an understanding of the value of defenses in warding off anxiety. Despite their possible long-range disadvantages, defenses immediately reduce anxiety. Because of this, they tend to persist and become more and more ingrained until they are second nature.

OTHER THEORIES OF ANXIETY

For this author, it is surprising to read that "despite some sixty years of psychological research in children's fears, little is known in any systematic way about the development, response characteristics, maintenance and reduction of children's fears and phobias" (Graziano & DeGiovanni, 1979, p. 161). Behaviorists readily see that children have many fears and that the character of these fears change with age. Their puzzlement seems to be about why children should have so much anxiety and how they overcome these fears on their own. Anxiety can be learned by association (classical conditioning); anxiety-avoidant responses can be reinforced by parental sympathy or by the mere fact that arousal of anxiety is reduced by avoidance (operant conditioning). Although these learning mechanisms are certainly valid, they do not sufficiently account for the initial experience of anxiety—in other words, they explain the maintenance but not the acquisition. To quote Miller:

Social learning theories explain an individual's stimulus perceptions on the basis of his or her unique conditioning history, but clinical evidence suggests that conditioning does not occur on the basis of a simple stimulus-response model. Very seldom does a clinician obtain a history of a uniquely painful situation associated with the onset of an anxiety. More typically, the child reports events at onset that have no deleterious effects on many other children who are equally exposed. But the anxious child sees as dangerous a stimulus that most children disregard even though there may be some potential unpleasantness or a low probability of danger (e.g., wind noise and thunderstorms). (1983, p. 348)

Following this observation, Miller continues with a discussion of the child's different view of the world because of cognitive immaturity (see Chapter 5). What is missing, however, is the impact that events may have because of the affective state of the child. Similar to the cognitive stages outlined by Piaget, there are emotional stages where the child is preternaturally sensitive to certain possibilities. Although one might take issue with the specifics, psychoanalytic theory has offered a sequence of "basic danger situations" (i.e., fear of helplessness, fear of loss of loved person, fear of loss of love, fear of bodily injury, fear of guilt or loss of self-esteem). As the child wrestles with these "dangers," outside reality is interpreted as a "signal" of safety or danger. The important point is that the child see reality in the light of his or her cognitive understanding but with further distortion because of basic and universal insecurities. Perception of reality is even further confounded by inner impulses which create affective states of strong feeling (excitement, love, or anger). Thus, memories of a past event are tangled with the associated feelings, the spontaneous causal explanations, and the special significance given to the event because of its meaning in the context of the child's ongoing developmental agenda. All of

this constitutes the child's private fantasy, which exerts an influence far beyond that justified by the original event alone.

ASSESSMENT AND DIAGNOSIS OF ANXIETY DISORDERS

There are self-report instruments developed for children which are used predominantly to survey general child populations rather than for individual clinical diagnosis. The Fear Survey Schedule for Children (Scherer & Nakamura, 1968) and the Louisville Fear Survey Schedule (Miller, Barrett, Hampe, & Noble, 1972) list specific objects or events with the "fearfulness" of each to be rated by the child or parent (see Appendix). Parent and child ratings show substantial inconsistency (Miller, Barrett, Hampe, & Noble, 1971), suggesting that parents may be quite out of touch with their children's fears. Other instruments are designed to get more global indices of anxiety, for example the State-Trait Inventory for Children (Spielberger, 1973) and the revised version of the Children's Manifest Anxiety Scale (Reynolds & Richmond, 1978). These measures inquire more about feelings than about specific items or situations with items such as "I often worry about something bad happening to me."

In selecting a diagnosis and making the decision to treat or not to treat, *duration* of the fears or phobias is an important diagnostic consideration because so many show spontaneous remission (Miller, Barrett, & Hampe, 1974). Graziano, DeGiovanni, and Garcia (1979) suggested that clinical level fears be defined as those with a duration of over 2 years or an intensity that is debilitating for the child. Miller (1983) remarked that 2 years can be a long time and proposed a 3-month period of observation, which seems more reasonable. In addition to duration, the *impact* of the phobia on the child's life should be considered. For instance, if a child is out of school for 3 months because of anxiety, a good deal is missed. Also, generally anxiety is not restricted to a single item or place; if there is a well-established pattern of avoidance, the effect is widespread restriction of activities. As mentioned many times, fears are common in young children. Eme and Schmidt (1978) found that an unidentified group of fourth graders reported an average number of 4.8 fears in personal interview and further, that these fears remained relatively stable over a period of a year. The mere presence of one or more stated fears is not diagnostically significant; one must also assess the total context of the child's functioning.

Classification

In the section on "Disorders Usually First Evident in Infancy, Childhood or Adolescence," The DSM-III has three relevant categories: Separation Anxiety Disorder; Avoidant Disorder of Childhood; and Overanxious Disorder. The first is concerned with separation from the adult attachment figure and includes specific phobic reactions. The description of Avoidant Disorder reads more like a pervasive personality disorder, where the child is generally clinging, dependent, and fearful; the child avoids strangers, new situations, and

peers. Children fitting the Overanxious Disorder are less immature and do a lot of worrying about themselves, often with perfectionistic or obsessional traits. They do not avoid situations but are uncomfortable and may show nervous tension symptoms such as persistent nail biting or occasional stuttering. These children have more anxiety from guilt or fear of failure than about loss of a loved person. This is similar to the distinction between "anaclitic" and "introjective" disorders proposed by Blatt:

Anaclitic psychopathologies (e.g., Separation Anxiety and Avoidant Disorders) are distorted and exaggerated attempts to maintain satisfying interpersonal experiences; introjective psychopathologies (e.g., Overanxious Disorder) are distorted and exaggerated attempts to establish an effective concept of the self. (1983, p. 188)

Also, children are frequently diagnosed as "Adjustment Disorder, with Depressed or Anxious Mood," where the problem is considered to be a response to a specific life event, such as divorce, major illness, family move and so on. It is also possible to use an adult diagnosis from the group of Anxiety Disorders, namely, phobic disorders, panic disorder, or obsessive-compulsive disorder. To date there is no data to indicate the prevalence of DSM-III diagnoses; one suspects that Separation Anxiety Disorder and Adjustment Disorder with Anxious Mood are by far the most commonly used.

Treatment of "Simple" Phobias

In consort with the major differences in explanatory theories, the two major therapeutic approaches for the anxiety disorders are behavioral and psychodynamic. Behaviorists are consistent in their concentration on the symptom itself; psychodynamic therapists focus much more on the child's fantasies. In a well-designed study comparing treatment effectiveness for "clinical level" phobic children, Miller et al. (1972) found that about 80% of the children aged 6 to 10 years improved considerably over a 3-month period whether they were in behavior therapy (reciprocal inhibition), in psychotherapy, or on the waiting list. Although there was no treatment effect for either approach according to the "objective evaluator," parents of both treatment groups reported more positive changes than the parents of the waiting list children. The children were not asked for their opinion. A very interesting, and unexpected, finding was that 80% of the older phobic children, ages 11 to 15, did *not* show improvement—whether on the waiting list or in either treatment program.

Therapy Procedures. Behavior therapy for phobias, other than school phobias, follows a classical conditioning model, that is, it is assumed that avoidance behavior has been learned from the association of anxiety with a specific object or event. The goal then is to break the association either by counterconditioning or extinction. Although there is some overlapping, Graziano, DeGiovanni and Garcia (1979) described four categories: reciprocal inhibition, contact desensitization, implosion/flooding and in vivo desensitization plus guided practice.

Reciprocal inhibition is a form of counterconditioning where the feared stimulus is paired with a "safe, happy" situation. For instance, in the Miller project mentioned before, the technique involved "emotive imagery" where the child was asked to imagine first the feared object and then a happy scene in quick alternation. The various forms of desensitization are similar in that there is a systematic exposure to graded stimuli, such as pictures, models, and real objects with positive reinforcement for progressing through the sequence. In contrast with reciprocal inhibition, there is no particular effort to pair the feared stimulus with a relaxation stimulus.

"Implosive therapy" is quite different because the child is exposed immediately to extremely anxiety-provoking imaginary scenes presented by the therapist. No matter how upset the child becomes, no escape is allowed. It is assumed that the child will soon "habituate," that is, that the anxious feelings will "wear off" so that the connection between stimulus and response will disappear. However, there have been criticisms of this technique.

There are obvious ethical and humanitarian issues involved in deliberately, maximally and repeatedly frightening children, whatever the therapeutic goals might be. After all, the child client is not allowed the option of walking out of a session or of summarily disengaging the therapists, options that are routinely available to adults. . . . We submit, then, that there are good reasons for not using implosive techniques with children, and we strongly urge that their use be discontinued. (Graziano, 1975, p. 286)

A variant on the desensitization model is teaching children to "talk themselves down" by self-statements such as "I am a brave boy (girl). I can take care of myself in the dark" (Kanfer, Karoly, & Newman, 1975). In their review of behavioral treatments, Graziano, DeGiovanni, and Garcia (1979) concluded that this cognitive, verbal mediation approach "is promising," that "modeling is the most frequently used and reliably effective fear-reduction strategy," and "that there is little evidence that systematic desensitization or contingency management are effective" (p. 804). It should be noted that in clinical practice, one rarely relies on a single approach. In any treatment, the child has to approach the feared object, mentally if not in fact, thereby involving some desensitization; approach behavior is applauded and avoidant behavior ignored (contingency management), and the child is encouraged to talk to him or her self about the realities (verbal mediation). Despite the common features, however, there are striking differences between behavioral and psychodynamic approaches.

Psychodynamic Therapy. Unfortunately there is no "treatment package" which outlines precisely what to do in psychodynamic therapy. The psychodynamic therapist tries to elicit the child's fantasies gradually, weaving through the defenses in search of the basic anxicty which is probably related to a wish the child deems unspeakably dangerous. The therapist asks the child to imagine the actual occurrence of the conscious fear with questions like "what if such-and-such came true, what would happen after that?" Although there is some desensitization involved in this form of emotive imagery, there also may be an increase in the child's anxiety as one probes for the imagined consequences to follow the conscious fear. Unless this is done cautiously, the child may even become phobic about the therapist.

The horse phobia of 5-year-old Hans, reported by Freud (1909/1955), is the classic case in child literature. Hans's phobia was not derived directly from the frightfulness of the horse, but from his own frightening impulses that were first projected and then displaced. Hans's repressed wish was to attack his father, but this was handled with projection: It is not he who wishes to attack the father, but the father who will attack him. The next step is the displacement: It is not the father who is dangerous; it is the horse. Fearing the horse instead of the father is a way of solving the internal conflict. The hatred is displaced onto the horse, which can be avoided much more easily than the father; also, the father who has been loved and hated simultaneously can now be loved completely. Features of the home life that contributed to Hans's anxiety included the father's frequent absence from the home, rather open sexual stimulation (which in those days was not recognized as such), and a lot of fictional nonsense regarding sexual differences and origin of babies which now would be atypical. Also, in present-day circumstances, a horse would be an unlikely phobic object, but the mechanisms of repression, projection and displacement could apply equally well to another choice.

The following case examples illustrate different levels of intervention, although both follow a psychodynamic approach. Shapiro (1983) described in detail a single interview with a 5-year-old girl with a sleep disturbance which she explained as a fear that she or someone in the family would die. He used

Winnicott's "Squiggle Game" (1971), where the therapist starts a drawing with any kind of "squiggle" and asks the child to finish it. In the hour, Emily drew and talked about her father operating on children who were "asleep"; her mother's appendectomy scar; the sudden death of two cousins from a house fire; some fun she had when she was very young (age 2 years); various comparisons between herself, her mother, and her brother; her plans to be a nurse and work with her father (cutting up people?); and finally a story about a toad. She and her brother made it a special bed and "put it to sleep one night." The next day, the toad couldn't get up and her father declared that it was dead. The therapist then suggested that "it was a hard thing for children to tell the difference between sleeping and dying and that makes going to sleep very worrisome. I then added that even though children sometimes get confused, grownups know the difference very well" (p. 560). Following this, the parents reported that Emily was sleeping well and treatment was concluded.

Emily was very clear in providing all the many good reasons to fear mortal danger during sleep, not only the fire but her vivid imaginings regarding surgical mutilation and the mystery of the toad. The therapist listened carefully, with occasional empathic remarks, and made the final statement regarding her confusion about sleep and death. For this intelligent girl in a supportive family, hearing her out was enough. Shapiro reiterates Winnicott's statement that a prime goal is to give children a feeling that they are truly understood; only with that conviction does reassurance really help.

The second example is far more complicated in the treatment, but it represents a more usual clinical situation. Tyson (1978) described the 28-month analysis of a boy who developed a dog phobia at age 5 years. However, he might better be described as having an "avoidant disorder of childhood," as he seemed immature in all respects. His speech development was slow; he made peculiar grimaces and screaming noises at home and in public; he had frequent temper tantrums; cried long and often; had difficulty in sleeping; and did not mix or play with other children. His early care had been shared with a succession of domestic helpers who had unrealistic expectations for him. The birth of a brother followed by a serious and frightening accident occurred shortly before his third birthday. The fear of dogs appeared around 3 years of age and was minimized by the mother as a presenting problem, perhaps because she also had an animal phobia and thus served as a "model." His multiple fears had led to frequent co-sleeping, facilitated by the father's frequent absences, thereby, of course, lending credibility to the Oedipal wishes.

The treatment report covers a wide field of anxieties, fears of abandonment, fear of injury, concerns about parental relationships (both sexual and aggressive), fears about parental retaliation for his messing or his rage against his brother, worries about making babies, and also fears that he was not as competent as others (partly true). Tyson described the threatening external symbol of the dog as combining the various constituents of the boy's conflicts and highlighted the evolution of his fear, which was expressed in a variety of ways at different times and included fear of the sight of a dog; fear of large but not small dogs; fear of being bitten by a dog; fear of a dog's angry bark, a dog's erect tail, and a dog's messing. From a different frame of reference, Miller et al. (1972) made a similar observation: "A childhood phobia is a varying response to a stimulus whose properties may also vary" (p. 278). In other words, a "simple" phobia may be far from "simple"; one has to look at the attributes of the feared object and the situational context in which it strikes fear.

Before leaving the subject of phobia, it should be noted that a phobia may appear disguised as an inordinate fascination. On the surface, the counterphobic child vigorously denies any fear and actively seeks the object or situation to prove the denial. The anxiety is betrayed only by the excitement and repeated statements about the "scary" properties of the object, for everyone else, that is! Up to a point, active exploration is a good coping mechanism, but when it persists, because the underlying fear does not change, the denial may lead to dangerous risk-taking behavior. In their description of children showing counterphobic defense, Poznanski and Arthur (1971) particularly stressed the parents' encouragement of "toughness." The case histories showed that these children had been expected to "tough out" some very frightening family events, including child abuse.

School Phobia: Definitional Issues

This term is still difficult to define even after many years of attention to the fact that some children are very anxious about attending school and avoid it if at all possible. It is relatively easy to distinguish between truancy and school phobia. In the latter, the child usually remains at home with the parents' knowledge and tacit consent whereas in truancy, the parents are unaware of the child's whereabouts and the child is usually in the company of his or her peers. Broadwin (1932) first suggested that some truant children stayed away from school because of obsessional anxieties that something would happen at home in their absence. Johnson, Falstein, Szurek, and Svendsen (1941) provided the name "school phobia" and observed that the child's anxieties were matched by anxieties in the mother. Estes, Haylett, and Johnson (1956) designated school phobia as a particular form of separation anxiety.

The DSM-III (1980) differentiates between "separation anxiety disorder" and "school phobia" on the basis that in the latter, the child fears the school situation, whether or not he or she is accompanied by the parent. In practice, however, this distinction is seldom checked out since parents rarely "come" to school. Many writers use the term "school refusal" as a synonym for school phobia and consider separation anxiety as only one possible cause. Berg (1980) commented on the peak incidence at around age 11 years, at least in Great Britain, and the fact that maternal attitudes of overprotectiveness supporting the child's dependency have not always been found in the mothers of school-phobic children over the age of 10 years. He suggested that other causative factors must be looked for in school refusal in early adolescence. Hersov concluded that school refusal is "not a true clinical entity with a uniform etiology, psychopathology, course, prognosis, and treatment, but rather a collection of symptoms or a syndrome occurring against a background of a variety of psychiatric disorders" (1977).

Reluctance to Go to School: Normal and Pathological. In a British survey of parents of children between 5 and 12 years of age, 5% of the boys and 3% of the girls were said to dislike school; the percentage said to like school very much peaked at age 5 years with a steady decline thereafter, reaching a low of 20% for boys at age 13 (Mitchell & Shephard, 1980). An earlier parent survey of a sample of London children (Moore, 1966) was more discouraging, in that "18% never became thoroughly reconciled to school" during the 6-year period from 5 to 11 years. Moore found that with regard to specific aspects of school life, difficulties with teachers and with work were relatively frequent, as were dislike of school meals and objections to the toilets. Studies restricted to truants and phobics may not sufficiently examine the many reasons that children are reluctant to go to school.

In an interesting study of developmental changes in school-related fears and perceptions, Bauer (1980) found that, "when contrasted with younger children, the majority of older ones appeared to be alienated from adulthood and reluctant to use the distant future for fulfillment in imagination of personal wishes and desires" (p. 204). This confirms the findings of Minuchin et al. (1969) that only 25% of fourth-graders felt it would be "wonderful to be all grown up." Although going to school starts off as a separation from home, a problem for some children, continuing in school represents moving toward adulthood, which does not seem attractive to a good many children. Apparently many children protest without success, perhaps because their parents are more firm or perhaps because the children feel less strongly than those who stay away from school.

School refusal has been estimated at about 5% of child psychiatric referrals but represents about two-thirds of those identified as "phobic." In a survey of about 2,200 10- and 11-year-old children, 118 psychiatric disorders were identified of which only 3 had a clinically significant fear of school (Rutter, Tizard, & Whitmore, 1970). But the same group of children produced 15 cases of school phobia at age 14 (Rutter, Graham, Chadwick, & Yule, 1976). The overall prevalence rate for the general population has been estimated at about 1% (Berg, 1980). There are no consistent sex differences and interestingly, educational achievement does *not* seem to be impaired in school phobics. That is not to say that some do not have real academic difficulties, but such problems do not distinguish this group.

Manifestations of School Phobia: The "Masquerade Syndrome." The degree of reluctance to go to school varies along a spectrum from a mere statement, to oversleeping, dawdling, missing the bus, or being late, to crying and refusing to leave the house, to a real panic reaction when taken to school. Often the reluctance is expressed in somatic complaints, particularly abdominal pain and nausea or even vomiting. The child who has been legitimately absent because of a minor illness may stretch out the convalescence as long as possible.

Waller and Eisenberg (1980) coined the term "masquerade syndrome" to describe children who have persistent and mysterious somatic complaints which result in prolonged absence even though school refusal is not the presenting problem. In fact, the mother may aver that the child "loves school." Waller and Eisenberg describe the emergence of the typical and recognizable features of the school refusal syndrome when return to school was advised by the attending physician. Both mother and child maintained that the physical symptom made it impossible for the child to attend, or they predicted that the symptom would recur, necessitating return home. In an extreme case known to this author, a child who had a convulsion at age 5 years remained at home on home instruction until the mother's death when he was 15 years old! For this period of 10 years, the child lived according to the mother's schedule, and the two remained as a psychological unit with serious consequences for the boy. It was extraordinary that this had been allowed on a "medical excuse" with no one questioning the wisdom of such a restricted childhood.

School Phobia: Etiology. As mentioned before, school phobia does not have a unitary cause. To choose the most likely explanation for a single case, it is necessary to examine the child's history, the specific fears involved, the relationship to other aspects of the child's functioning, and the family history. The following list comprises the causes which, acting singly or together, have been found important in clinical cases.

1. Separation anxiety as the core problem is perhaps the predominant explanation. This is usually presented as a mutual dependency of mother and child with the parent almost a co-conspirator in the child's remaining at home. However, this deserves further analysis. The child may be afraid of something happening to him or her—or the fear may involve something happening to the mother. In the latter instance, there is probably some unconscious aggression which the child fears will be fulfilled. On the mother's side, it may be that she enjoys the child's company and gets some satisfaction from the child's continuing dependency, or it may be that she is frightened by the child's anxiety and believes she should spare the child from such unhappiness.

2. Fear of failure keeps some children away from school. Although on the surface it may look like separation anxiety, the source of fear is different (Lachenmeyer, 1982). The child is not anxious about the mother's well-being nor is he, or she, anxious about personal safety away from home. Rather it is more a question of self-esteem and anxiety about the competitive demands made in the school situation. Leventhal and Sills (1964) proposed that school-phobic children overvalue themselves and their achievements and try to maintain their unrealistic self-image. In the author's extreme case cited earlier, the mother perceived her son to be a genius, and he shared her opinion. At age 15 years, efforts to return to school failed utterly, at least partly because his exalted ideas of his ability far exceeded the reality; he was

enraged at the teachers who failed to appreciate his "genius."

3. For the older child or young adolescent, the fears may focus more around peer relationships than those with the mother. The child may feel like a rejected outcast, or possibly even be afraid of sexual feelings stimulated by the close presence of both same sex or opposite sex classmates. There does seem to be consensus that school phobia in older children has a different structure and is more resistant to treatment. Older children tend to develop a fear of school which comes on more insidiously as a symptom of a general personality disorder (Berg, 1980).

4. In learning theory terms, the possibility of "traumatic conditioning" at school has also been considered, generally in the light of previous overprotection at home. Bolman (1970), in a systems analysis of school phobia, called for serious examination of the role of schools. Gordon and Young suggested that "an acceptance of the separation model has led to a neglect of the possibility that in some cases at least the school plays a major role" (1977, p. 421). The previous comments regarding "normal" reluctance to attend school would suggest that indeed external reality factors play a contributory role.

5. Kelly stated the two-part learning theory explanation as follows:

The child fears loss of his mother as a result of comments about leaving by the mother, who is usually disturbed. This fear becomes verbally conditioned to ideas about going to school, where he would "lose" his mother. As the fear of school becomes intense, he finally refuses to go. Staying at home has reinforcing properties in that it reduces fear and usually offers other rewards, such as toys and affection. (1973, p. 36)

Clearly in this formulation, the mother's actions represent the original "cause" and there is little room for the contribution from the child's fantasies (projection, displacement, etc.).

Considering the emphasis that has been placed on the causative role of the parents, it should be noted that the same kind of psychopathology has been observed in mothers of children with very different problems (e.g., psychosis or psychosomatic diseases). Also, we have no way of knowing how many other mothers have the same problems since the information is gathered after the children's symptoms are reported; it is hard to tell which came first, the child's distress or the mother's overprotectiveness. It would be interesting to know the incidence of school phobia in the homes of working mothers where the secondary gains would be minimal. However, whatever the origin of the child's phobia, an anxious mother will have a more difficult time in coping with the child's anxiety and so may unintentionally prolong it. Maintenance factors may be quite different from those involved in acquisition of the phobia.

Another dimension, in addition to the source of fear, which needs to be included in subtyping of school-refusal children, is the extensiveness of disturbance (Atkinson, Quarrington, & Cyr, 1985). In some children fear of school is only one manifestation of an all-pervasive disturbance. These children are generally phobic, approach everything with reluctance and fear, and are often distrustful, hypersensitive, and generally depressed. Many authors have suggested a two-part classification based on the circumscribed versus pervasive nature of the symptom (Coolidge, Hahn, & Peck, 1957; Kennedy, 1965; Hersov, 1960).

Treatment Approaches. The treatment reports contain the variety one would expect. All report success in fairly short order, at least with preadolescent children, and are unanimous in recommending that the child return to school at the earliest moment, at any level of school participation that she can tolerate. The choice of treatment seems to depend more on the theoretical preference of the therapist rather than the individual clinical assessment.

In behavior therapy, the gradual return to school is systematically programmed with varied application of classical and operant conditioning methods. Garvey and Hegrenes (1966) provided a straightforward account of the small steps by which 10-year-old Jimmy was "desensitized to school." The therapist and Jimmy began by coming to school early in the morning, and Jimmy was told to report any uncomfortable feelings. When he said he was feeling afraid, the therapist immediately indicated that it was time to leave and generously praised him for what he had accomplished. After a period of 20 days, he returned to school completely. The authors explained the success on the basis of counterconditioning, or reciprocal inhibition. "Since Jimmy and the therapist had a good relationship, the presence of the therapist may be considered as a relatively strong stimulus evoking a positive affective response in the pa-

tient," and this inhibited the anxiety response associated with school.

Others have involved the parents in reinforcement procedures. Patterson (1965) described the treatment of 7-year-old Karl in which desensitization was started by doll play structured in the office to reproduce the situation of going to school. Reinforcement consisted of both praise and candy, given whenever Karl reported that the boy doll was not afraid—in marked contrast to the Garvey and Hegrenes treatment where the child was permitted to express anxiety. After 23 15-minute sessions, four times a week, Karl returned to school. Patterson concluded that ". . . one of the crucial variables involved in this procedure is the reinforcement contingencies being used by social agents other than the experimenter" and felt that ". . . the highly structured interviews with the parents are of particular importance in insuring generalization of the conditioning effects from the laboratory to the home."

Lazarus and Abramovitz (1965) modified these procedures by the use of "emotive imagery" for the anxiety-inhibiting response. Lazarus, Davison, and Polefka (1965) described this with 9-year-old Paul. The application of numerous techniques in the consulting room was abandoned because "It was obvious that his verbal reports were aimed at eliciting approval rather than describing his true feelings," and the therapist and Paul started going to school in fact. In the company of the therapist, "Paul's feelings of anxiety were reduced by means of coaxing, encouragement, relaxation and the use of emotive imagery, i.e., the deliberate picturing of subjectively pleasant images such as Christmas and a visit to Disneyland, while relating them to the school situation." For the parents, "A long list of do's and don'ts was drawn up and discussed"; for instance, the mother was instructed not to allow him in the house during school hours. A mild tranquilizer was also prescribed. In the later stages, when anxiety was less but avoidant behavior continued, operant conditioning was used with tokens and rewards contingent upon his entering school and remaining there alone. The authors comment that the presence of the therapist (although several were involved) seemed to have as much reward value as the comic books and tokens. This treatment extended over 4½ months and required the therapist to make a lot of on-the-spot judgments. For instance, when Paul left the classroom to seek out the therapist because he was scared, the therapist had to decide whether to reassure him or urge him to return. The critical factor in determining the appropriate procedure was in the degree of anxiety as judged by the therapist (Lazarus et al., 1965).

Kennedy (1965) "treated" school phobics by instructing the parents to force the child to return to school no matter how intense his anxiety responses might be, which might be considered a kind of implosive therapy in vivo. In contrast, Smith and Sharpe (1970) used implosive therapy to extinguish the anxiety response by having the child picture the most frightening possibilities in the office; they suggest that this might be preferable since the child's fear remains a private matter, thereby avoiding any ridicule from classmates.

Drugs have been used as an adjunct to behavior treatment. Gittelman-Klein and Klein (1980) reported a double-blind study investigating the efficacy of imipramine (a trycyclic antidepressant drug) with 45 children with an average age of 10 years, 7 months. Of the placebo-treated children, 44% were back in school within 6 weeks compared to 70% of the drug-treated group. Also, the drug-treated group reported feeling more comfortable than those receiving the placebo. Cautiously, the authors recommend drug therapy only as a last resort when other interventions have failed. In such instances, one can presume that the symptom was part of a pervasive disturbance, quite possibly of a depressive nature.

Review of these reports and the many others reported in the literature shows significant variation in technique included in the category of "behavior therapy." For instance, emotive imagery involves happy scenes to divert or neutralize the anxiety; implosive therapy starts with frightening thoughts to extinguish the anxiety. Some behavior therapists reward verbal statements of "not being afraid" and others allow the child some control over what happens on the basis of statements of fear. The nature of the rewards varies as well as the instructions to the parents. Yule, Hersov, and Treseder (1980) offered four steps in overall behavioral treatment approach:

(i) establishing a good, trusting relationship with the child and family; (ii) clarifying the stimulus situations which give rise to anxiety; (iii) desensitizing the child to the feared situations by using imagination, relaxation or merely talking, whichever is appropriate; and (iv) confronting the feared situations. We prefer, when we have a choice, to adopt a gradual rather than a sudden approach to the latter. Nevertheless, we try to remain firm and we have learned that in most cases the fears and tantrums which destroy the resolve of many parents soon subside when the child makes progress. The art is to know what is progress in the eyes of the child. (1980, p. 299)

Behavioral reports, however, are similar in that there is no attempt to probe further as to why the child is afraid; the goal is the behavioral one of immediate return to school. One might ask whether a real change results or merely suppression of affect. Behavior therapists say that the proof is in the overt behavior change of the child: If he does not act on his fear, then it is not important.

Review of "psychodynamic" treatment reports of school phobics reveals a diversity in philosophy and techniques almost equaling that found in the behavioral literature. For a number of years, the staff at Judge Baker Guidance Center in Boston conducted a clinical investigation into the causes and treatment of school phobia. They reported a close relationship between prompt therapeutic intervention and remission of symptoms: 20 out of 21 children treated during the same semester in which the symptom appeared returned to school within 3 months (Waldfogel, Tessman, & Hahn, 1959). In view of this experience, they undertook a project of early intervention at the first signs of an incipient school phobia. A total of 36 children were referred to the unit during its 2 years of operation in the Newton public school system. Sixteen of these were treated successfully in the school with 10 or fewer half-hour interviews. Four others were referred to the clinic for treatment; 5 recovered spontaneously; and 11 were not treated because of staff time or refusal by the parents.

The authors made a special point of the advantages of treating in the school, where ". . . the therapist can offer direct support to the child in the feared situation," which sounds very much like "reciprocal inhibition" by another name. In explaining their treatment philosophy, reference was made to the concept of the "corrective emotional experience" advanced some years ago by Alexander and French (1946). Although Alexander and French were psychoanalysts, their statements emphasized the role of learning and the subordinate role of such factors as intellectual insight, abreaction, recollection of the past, and so on.

In their case reports, Waldfogel, Tessman, and Hahn did more than encourage the mother and child to master the anxiety by keeping the child in school. They considered the phobic reaction as a crisis situation which made internal conflicts more accessible to brief psychotherapy. In the case of Sue, age 5, 14 interviews elicited a good deal of material about her fears for her mother and her fantasies about her mother's pending operation for ear trouble. The mother clarified the real situation for the child and the therapist relieved Sue's guilt about her hostile wishes.

Sperling (1967) made a distinction between "induced school phobia" where there is a long-standing symbiotic relationship between mother and child and "acute school phobia" which starts suddenly. She reported success after relatively brief psychotherapy in cases of acute phobia (1961) such as that of 7-year-old Peter, who had been out of school for 3 weeks following a sudden panic while listening to a teacher play the piano in assembly. He associated the music with the funeral of a neighbor who had committed suicide while her child was in school.

For the purpose of bringing him back to school, it was sufficient to make him aware of his fear that this could happen to his mother and to link it with the unconscious wish by remarking casually that boys sometimes have such wishes when they are angry and are afraid that they might come true. His phobia cleared up immediately. (Sperling, 1967, p. 379)

Staying at home was Peter's way of protecting his mother from the fantasized consequences of his anger. He would not have been so torn if he had not at the same time loved her very much.

Family Therapy Approaches. Malmquist (1965) was one of the first to suggest focusing on family dynamics in a "phobogenic" family, although not to the extent of ignoring the internalized conflicts of the school phobic child. Miller (1983) reported treatment for the mother of an 8-year-old girl who periodically refused to go to school. In 12 hours of therapy, the mother painfully reexperienced events of her own life, particularly in school, and connected them to her current inability to let her daughter work out her own problems with her peers and teachers.

Behind it all was a conflict between the ideal mother of her dreams and the woman and mother she now realized she must be to help her child. The dream mother that she had tried to be was the all-giving, self-sacrificing, fiercely protective mother: the opposite of her own self-pitying, sickly and exploitive mother. The real mother had been an efficient and highly respected career woman, who, now, as a housewife, was resentful

when her husband and child went into the exciting world. Moreover, she was afraid to stay alone in the house. She usually finished her work by 10:00 A.M. and then had nothing to do with her energy and talents except to worry about her daughter and mull over her past rejections. As she faced this conflict and released the past, she decided to go back to work and let her daughter fight her own battles. Almost like magic, when mother decided she no longer needed the daughter, the daughter decided she no longer needed mother. (p. 372)

Skynner (1976) described another family approach to the treatment of school phobia which emphasized marital therapy. In his view, the usual emphasis on the role of the mother neglects the unintentional collusion of the father. He suggested that in school-phobic families, the marital relationship is weak; the father is either a peripheral figure or a dependent child who fails to intervene in the mother-child attachment. In other words, the father does not take his part as an active rival for the mother's attention, and the child does not relinquish omnipotent demands for exclusive possession of the mother. In his treatment strategy, Skynner first attempts to enable the family to move forward, but if this fails, the therapist takes an authoritative role in insisting on return to school.

Outcome Evaluation. In trying to compare the validity of different treatment philosophies, the crucial question is not so much whether the psychodynamic explanations are correct, but whether it is necessary to "detoxify" unconscious wishes in order to (a) cure the phobia and (b) prevent later neurotic difficulties. Davison made the astute observation that " . . . from evidence regarding efficacy in changing behavior, one cannot claim to have demonstrated that the problem evolved in an analogous fashion" (1968, p. 98). The converse may also be true. Although phobia may well start by touching off an unconscious wish (which was obviously latent before the phobia), it may not be necessary for the child to recognize the wish in order to regain equilibrium. All treatment approaches agree on the importance of the child's continued exposure to school, however brief, and most agree in opposing coercive measures. They all capitalize on the child-therapist relationship and with few exceptions, encourage the child's expression of feelings and fantasies. The rate of recovery seems to be related more to promptness of intervention, age of child, associated personality problems, and family cooperation than to the form of treatment, so therapists have an option of choosing for themselves what they consider the most important factor in success.

Berg, Marks, McGuire, and Lipsedge (1974) provided some interesting retrospective data from a group of women who were members of a nationwide correspondence club for people with agoraphobia and a small group of nonagoraphobic psychiatric outpatient clients. About one-fifth of these respondents, in both groups, indicated that they had had a school phobia defined as staying out at least 2 weeks, with a great fear of returning. This suggests that anxiety and unhappiness in school may be a predictor of adult unhappiness. For the children of the agoraphobic mothers, the overall incidence of school phobia was 7% with higher percentages for the ado-lescents, particularly for daughters. It is not surprising of course to find that phobic mothers are more likely to have phobic children, but the indication of continuity from childhood to adulthood suggests that the mere physical return to school may not be a sufficient treatment goal.

Although follow-up reports indicate a high percentage of success using return to school as the criterion, very few researchers have considered more general features of the child's adjustment as part of the follow-up information. Coolidge, Brodie, and Feeney (1964) and Coolidge (1979) reported 10-year and 21-year follow-up studies of the original 66 school-phobic children. Of the 49 located during adolescence, only 13 were doing well, and 14 were at a "severe impasse." Almost half of the children reevaluated were performing below what would have been expected from IQ test scores. Those studies 21 years later were described as constricted by separation difficulties and dependency issues, showing as an overly cautious obsessional approach to life with difficulty in assertiveness. From a research point of view, these studies are deficient because they include no control group and because of attrition of the original sample, but nonetheless the results constitute a warning. If the school phobia has been replaced by depression, or a generalized learning difficulty, not much has been gained. It would be unfortunate to discontinue therapy abruptly on return to school simply in the interest of "cost-effectiveness." In many instances, continuing supportive therapy can assist the child to cope with feelings in constructive ways and thereby enjoy a freer, fuller life.

Avoidant and Overanxious Disorders

These two DSM III categories share common characteristics of diffuse anxieties attached to varying situations, as opposed to phobias which are of a specific nature. In the DSM III description, avoidant disorder describes a generally immature and inhibited child, and overanxious disorder relates more to excessive anticipatory worrying almost of an obsessional nature. The avoidant child refuses to engage in some age-appropriate behaviors (like sleep-overs, going to camp, joining recreational groups, etc.) whereas the over-anxious might partake in such activities but at great emotional cost. In real life, however, the same child might well move back and forth from one category to the other.

Poznanski (1973) studied 28 children, under 12 years of age, who were identified from a much larger patient sample on the basis of multiple, unrealistic fears. The great majority of the children had a marked increase of fear at night, and 10 of the children occasionally or consistently slept with their parents in contrast to only 3 in the patient group used for comparison. She categorized the fears according to the possible *effect* of the external object or situation, i.e., fears of abandonment, fears of mutilation, and sexualized fears, with the first category the most common. Fear of abandonment occurred equally in the boys and girls whereas sexualized fears and fears of mutilation were more frequent in the girls. Fear of abandonment was usually directly expressed in contrast to the more symbolic expression of sexualized anxiety, for instance, the fear of a 10-year-old girl that a cobra would find its way into her bedroom while she was sleeping.

Poznanski stressed the ubiquity of fear and the necessity for every child to find ways to master anxiety.

It would appear that the ability of the child to handle fear producing stimuli . . . was a highly important aspect in the development of excessive fears. . . . In epidemiological studies, the older child has fewer fears than the younger child, which would suggest that ego development in general tends to help the child master fear. As the child becomes older this mastery occurs without direct reference to the mother. The excessively fearful children alleviate the immediate anxiety by close proximity to the adults, but at the expense of lessening the opportunity for an age appropriate behavior of handling fearful situations independently. (p. 436)

It is important to note that these excessively fearful children showed other behavioral problems such as hyperactivity, somatic complaints, and obsessive-compulsive traits, as well as encopresis, enuresis, learning difficulties, and obesity. Three were diagnosed as "borderline" and one child as psychotic. These concurrent problems contribute quantitatively to the experience of anxiety at the same time that they reduce the child's ability to cope. This indicates the necessity for a total diagnostic frame of reference in which to consider the significance and the treatment for specific behavioral symptoms.

In this heterogeneous group, those who have mainly social anxieties interfering with peer relationships constitute an important subset. Good peer relationships reduce the child's need for parental support; peer bonds permit a shared mastery of everyday fears and worries.

Conversely, there is some evidence that childhood social incompetence is related to adult mental health problems (Cowen, Pederson, Babigian, Izzo, & Trost, 1973). Many of these children are reasonably comfortable with an adult and it is difficult for the therapist to work with the anxieties that surface only when they are with their peers. This is an ideal situation for group therapy, not only to confront the feared situation but also to have the opportunity to practice social interaction in a "safe" situation and to observe "models" in action.

The group program may be structured in the form of social skills training, for instance in assertiveness (Combs & Slaby, 1977; Michelson & Wood, 1980), or it may be more "therapy-oriented," relying on the therapist to take advantage of spontaneous interactions to stimulate discussion on understanding one anothers' feelings and intentions and to try out conflict-resolution tactics. In the partial hospitalization program at the Louisville Medical School, the staff has reported impressive beneficial effects of group therapy with overly anxious and socially inhibited children which have generalized to the home and neighborhood settings (Miller, 1983, p. 371). Outside hospital, school or institutional settings, there are often logistical problems in assembling an appropriate group, but where feasible, it is a preferred treatment mode for social anxieties.

Obsessive-Compulsive Disorders. Although the DSM-III describes "perfectionistic tendencies, with obsessional self-doubt, and excessive conformity and seeking of approval" as associated features in the "Overanxious" classification, one would use the label of "obsessive-compulsive" only when the obsessions or compulsions are fixed patterns which intrude in everyday life and cause the child great discomfort. At that stage, the symptoms which originally served to reduce anxiety are themselves anxiety-provoking. This is a low incidence problem; no cases at all were identified in the epidemiological survey of all 10- and 11-year-olds on the Isle of Wight (Rutter et al., 1970). The rate of occurrence in child psychiatric populations has been estimated from 1% (Judd, 1965) to 2% (Adams, 1973). Nonetheless, obsessive-compulsive disorder deserves attention because it can be severely crippling and also because it is of considerable theoretical interest. It is different from most childhood disorders in that the clinical picture in childhood is virtually identical to the adult form, and one-third of adult cases have been reported to begin before age 15 (Rapoport, Elkins, Langer et al., 1981).

Differential Diagnosis. There are normal variants of compulsive behavior, with peaks around the age of 2 years, at 7 to 8 years, and in early adolescence. The 2-year-old tends to be very upset with any change in his physical surroundings or daily routines and clings tenaciously to established habits. Custom becomes law, and any departure from the usual routines is regarded with suspicion and alarm. Part of the rigidity of this age is the 2-year-old's attempt to control his environment in his search for autonomy, and part of it reflects his magical thinking (see Chapter 5).

Around the age of 7 or 8 years, a variety of compulsive rituals are sometimes observed in children who seem generally happy and well adjusted. These may be related to the harshness of conscience and "moral absolutism" characteristic of this age. The child is venturing out in new social situations and is faced with many temptations. The realization that "bad things" may escape detection leaves one dependent on the dictates of conscience for self-control. Benjamin Spock used the example of stepping over sidewalk cracks with the accompanying rhyme "Step on a crack, break your grandmother's back" to show how a compulsion can be related to unconscious aggression (1957). In her discussion of play, Peller pointed out that one feature of school-age games is the strictness of the rules, which are regarded as absolute by the players. "Their meticulous observance gives independence from external superego figures . . . the plot is codified, and the roles, too, are frozen and conventional. Rules, ceremonies, rituals are essential elements of all games" (1954, p. 192).

The common compulsions are like games which the child enjoys playing by himself or with others, and there is no feeling of inner coercion. In the pathological form, the compulsion is unique to the child and there is no pleasure or social benefit. Obsessional manifestations which occur as part of the child's effort to control his behavior through thought and deliberate action appear normally as part of the forward thrust of development. It is only when these defenses escalate, or when the child continues to use them to control external reality events according to the magical thinking of the very young child that one considers the diagnosis of "obsessional neurosis" (Sandler & Joffe, 1965).

Adams (1973) identified *circumscribed interests* as another "station on the obsessive spectrum in childhood." These are children who become totally involved, "obsessed," with very specialized, narrow activities which set them apart from other children. The possible interests vary widely, for example, television, cars, space, etc. Such children acquire a phenomenal amount of knowledge on their topic which may look like "genius." Although such preoccupations are restricting and may serve to avoid anxiety-causing situations, particularly social interactions, they are not properly called "obsessional" if the child retains an intellectual interest. If the child starts to ascribe protective significance to some aspect of these special interests, it may well be an obsession. For example, a little girl interested in a special make of car (the "Gremlin") felt safe if she counted an even number of them on the road but endangered if she arrived at an odd number.

Turning to the action side of this disorder, namely, the compulsions, there are some important distinctions to be made. Some people include any kind of repetitious behavior which the person cannot control under the umbrella of "compulsion." Glue sniffers, drug users, and so on, give themselves some pleasure even if it goes against their judgment; the same can be said about transvestites, fetishists, exhibitionists, and so on. In this context, however, compulsion refers to out-of-control behavior which brings no pleasure other than the reduction of anxiety. Behavior of which the child is unaware, such as tics, also needs to be separated from compulsions.

Gilles de la Tourette syndrome, characterized by tics and verbal outbursts of swearing and "dirty words," may look on the surface like an obsessive-compulsive disorder, but its involuntary and sporadic nature establishes the neurological diagnosis. The compulsive person knows what he or she is going to do before doing it although there is a feeling of coercion.

Finally, compulsive behavior can be associated with other more serious conditions such as brain damage or psychosis. The perseveration of a severely retarded or neurologically impaired child is in a sense compulsive but without any subjective awareness of being forced to do something. Severely obsessive-compulsive neurotic children may be diagnosed as having childhood schizophrenia (Despert, 1968) and vice versa. Again, it is a matter of awareness. The schizophrenic child feels no sense of inner conflict whereas the obsessive-compulsive child views his thoughts and actions as unwanted.

Clinical Picture. Obsessional ideas often start with a phobia, but when avoidance of the external object does not suffice, the person becomes obsessed with the idea of it. It is like a continuous self-torture in which the person has to think about the very thing which is most frightening or upsetting. In general, there seem to be two types of obsessional preoccupations: those which are precautionary; for instance, ideas about safeguarding health and cleanliness, and those which are repugnant; for instance, obsessive fantasies about hurting someone, sexual perversions, or doing something shocking.

Usually compulsions have been preceded by obsessions: the person can no longer control his anxiety by selected thoughts but has to do something in addition. Again, compulsive acts seem to fall into two major categories: those which serve as restrictions, prohibitions, or precautions (such as wiping doorknobs free of germs or repeated checking of locks and gas jets) and those which symbolize penances, atonements, and punishments (such as ritualistic counting). Ordinary everyday activities such as eating, dressing, washing, etc., may be elaborated into highly complicated rituals, sometimes caricaturing parental demands for care and cleanliness. All of this leads to a great problem in time management so that the child is always late, keeping others waiting and failing to complete necessary tasks. In their aggravation with these consequences, it may take parents a while to realize that the child has lost control.

It should be clear that the obsessive-compulsive person is in an unhappy state of conflict, constantly being forced to consider unwelcome thoughts or perform "ridiculous" actions. There is little relief from the pervading sense of self-doubt. This contrasts with the typical anxiety disorder, where some peace of mind can be obtained by avoidance. The mental processes involved in this condition include displacement by magnification of small details, reaction formation, undoing, and isolation. The obsessive-compulsive is usually hopelessly "virtuous," refusing to accept any infraction, in thought or deed, of impossible standards of propriety. The obsessional neurotic behaves as if he were divided into both the bad child and the stern parent. Various "undoing" mechanisms serve as the self-punitive devices for bad thoughts.

The mechanism of isolation is prominent in common compulsions about touching and not touching. The patient tries to put things into tight categories (e.g., dirty or clean, nice or not nice, feminine or masculine). The slightest suggestion of contact contaminates the object or thoughts belonging to the desired category. Zetzel (1966) proposed that the obsessive-compulsive thinks in terms of inexorable either-or categories as a result of failure to integrate emotions which are initially experienced as mutually exclusive, such as love and hate. One of the developmental tasks is to learn to tolerate ambivalence and to fuse contradictory emotions so that there is some constancy which cannot be destroyed by a momentary anger. The obsessive-compulsive, in some of the defenses, tries to establish the simplistic state of affairs obtaining for the very young child.

Isolation also occurs in the separation of thought and feeling. Obsessive-compulsive individuals strive to control their feelings by mental exercise, and words come to have a life of their own. Great stress is put on the "right" word and general context dwindles in significance. It is not what you mean that counts but what you say. Often these children are impressive in their intellectual prowess and do well academically.

However, the condition does not require a high IQ. The author was acquainted with a mildly retarded adolescent boy who spontaneously asked his teacher for help with classical compulsions—repeated hand washing, checking and rechecking, and indecisiveness to the point of physical immobility at times. The problem had an insidious onset several years before when his parents noted that he required an inordinate amount of time for his newspaper route because he had to place and replace the newspapers in a "just-so" position. He was considered a model child because of conscientiousness, politeness, neatness, etc., which the parents felt would go a long way to compensate for his mental retardation. In therapy one learned that he was tremendously preoccupied with fantasies about girls which he was totally unable to verbalize or to find outlets for in social relationships. The crucial factor does not seem to be IQ but whether the child has an internalized conscience.

Loneliness and tremendous anxiety are easily perceptible behind the defenses.

The obsessive child, therefore, lives as if extermination were impending. He fears for his existence, for his autonomy, and he doubts his worth. His adaptive devices are sick ones: compulsions to act out rituals lest panic wipe him out; doubting, and the impossible combination of halfhearted commitment and striving for superhuman performance. (Adams, 1973, p. 92)

Somehow there is no one or nothing in the outside world which provides a sense of security and safety. Feeling totally unprotected, the obsessive child tries every device to anticipate and control every eventuality, leaving nothing to chance.

Etiology. Explanations for the origin of obsessive-compulsive symptoms vary in the expected way according to theoretical orientation. Behavioral theorists look at the symptoms as learned ways to avoid anxiety, but have little explanation for the overpowering nature of the anxiety. In the psychoanalytic view, the anxiety belongs to the anal-sadistic phase of development—between 1 and 3 years. Indeed, these children typically show the triad of characteristics which Freud identified as the "anal character" (1908/1955), namely, obstinacy, miserliness, and orderliness. Also, many of the typical defenses and modes of thinking are characteristic of this age. For these reasons, many therapists have assumed that toilet training must have been coercive or traumatic in some way.

Attractive as this hypothesis may be, clinical data does not seem to validate it. In Adams's careful review (1973), only 20 of the 49 child cases had a history of rigid, punitive, or prolonged toilet training. He agreed with Rado (1959) in suggesting that it is the general onrush of social demands which the child defied, not solely the toilet discipline. The obsessive is typically concerned with power and control issues and sets great store on autonomy, but the original battle of wills could take in the gamut of parental demands which are typically imposed on the toddler. And, of course, at that young age, the toddler is indeed helpless in his rage and defiance—as well as terrified by the possible consequences of these feelings on others.

Recasting the explanation in terms of interpersonal relations, the role of the mother looms very large. The parents are generally described as overcontrolling and lacking in empathy and furthermore very pleased with themselves.

Indeed, the parents are downright smug in their being effective, productive, verbose and conventional adult North Americans.

They are inclined to see themselves as exemplary models for all humanity to copy and they are more than impatient with rebellion; they cannot "feel for it" at all. So from an early age, they categorize all of the child's defiance as wicked, and all of his conformity to parental wishes as the index of goodness. (Adams, 1973, p. 223)

They also serve as "successful" obsessional models. Although it is hard to establish as a primary cause, parental rage seems to be easily aroused but usually covered by a thin veneer of sweet solicitude in the classical "double bind" mode of communication. It is conceivable that the obsessive-compulsive child's extreme anxiety comes from a partially justified fear that he or she will be abandoned as the result of angry feelings—the child's and those of his or her parents.

Certainly *after* the obsessive compulsive disorder is established, the parental message is perplexing. Up to a point, the behavior is praised and wins love, but the same behavior, carried to an extreme, becomes the target of sharp criticism. The balance of power shifts, and the parents feel enslaved and helpless in the face of their child's obsessive-compulsive disorder which usually requires something from them—their physcial presence or at least their indulgence.

Treatment and Outcome. Obsessive-compulsive disorder has baffled those seeking a cure as much as those seeking a cause. A review of follow-up studies (Elkins, Rapoport, & Lipsky, 1980) found that as many as half of the children fail to respond to treatment. As an approach to adult obsessive-compulsive persons, Meyer (1966) presented the behavioral technique of "response inhibition" where the compulsive individual is forced to remain in a feared situation and to abstain from the compulsive behavior. Meyer suggested that if the patient's fearful expectations could be disproved in this manner, new expectancies would evolve which would lead to new behaviors, hopefully not compulsive.

Response inhibition was reported successful in eliminating ritualistic behavior in an 8-year-old girl (Stanley, 1980). Amanda's rituals, which involved only activities in her home, had started about 6 months before treatment. Amanda herself was very distressed and embarrassed, particularly upset about having to do everything three times over. After the details were identified, the first step was for the family to "treat Amanda as a girl who did not have compulsive urges," that is, to behave as they did with her sister. The program of response prevention was explained to Amanda and the various situations involving rituals were graded as to their "upset value." Starting with the mildest, the parents systematically prevented her from carrying out the rituals. They did this by talking to her and sometimes physically removing her from the situation. After 2 weeks the symptoms disappeared; at a 2-year follow-up, no symptoms were reported.

The successful treatment ws undoubtedly facilitated by the fact that it was instituted relatively soon after the appearance of the symptoms. Also, the author remarked on the sensitivity and support provided by the parents and the child's high motivation to regain her "carefree attitude to life." It boded well for treatment that her compulsions were limited to scope and that she was "normally" a happy person with lots of friends, eager to be rid of her "fussiness."

A youngster of the author's acquaintance showed equally rapid improvement without benefit of specific therapy. He first came at the age of 5 years because of anxiety about separation from his mother which abated with brief therapy and suggestions to the parents. A few years later, the parents returned because of their concern about his grumpiness and negative attitude, particularly around the restrictions imposed by their religion. He was frank in his envy of the freedom and material possessions of other children, which the mother particularly found hard to tolerate. He returned yet a third time because of ritualistic behavior which developed shortly after his Bar Mitzvah. Most of his compulsions involved repeating prayers, but he had other concerns, such as fear of spitting or spraying when talking. He was embarrassed and annoyed by all of this, feeling that these extra obligations were real impediments to him. To the author, it appeared that he was almost mocking the religious observances by outdoing everyone with his care and precision. Considering his previous resentment, this seemed like a classical reaction formation. He was going to be beyond any possible reproach, from himself or anyone else; at the same time, he was quite reproachful and critical of what he viewed as the hypocrisy of his teachers (one of whom was his father).

The symptoms dramatically disappeared after his parents arranged a personal interview with a very famous rabbi who simply told him that on a religious basis, his anxieties were not justified. Somehow he could use these authoritative words from someone both remote and exalted to curb his compulsions. Again we have a favorable situation in that this boy was certainly capable of having "fun" and good peer relationships, and his compulsive symptoms were circumscribed in scope.

The special issues with regard to psychotherapeutic techniques concern matters of style and matters of content. With regard to the former, in the words of Adams (1973), "Keep it clean." With an obsessional child, one tries to keep all verbal communication simple and straightforward, avoiding long-winded or metaphorical comparisons on one's own part and restating simply what the child has said in many words. It is even possible to interrupt, not to criticize the circumlocution or repetition, but to find a simple statement. With these children who are so inhibited, one can safely encourage action and play—avoiding intellectual games like chess and checkers and utilizing more primitive, unstructured materials such as clay and fingerpaints. These children have great difficulty with spontaneous or make-believe play, and the therapist may be helpful as a participant-facilitator. Often they are deadly serious and remark reproachfully, "We are here to talk about my problems," to which one can reply, "Exactly, one of your problems is that you cannot have any fun, so let's find out why."

With regard to content, the focus is always on feelings and feelings in the context of here and now. The whys and wherefores are not nearly as important as the basic affects of rage, sadness, and panic. These are often glossed over with mild statements, like "I am a little disappointed in you" and need to be acknowledged in a bolder form in order to dis-cover that even strong feelings are not dangerous. These children need more "real world" reassurance than most. They are particularly concerned about "what people would think" and see themselves as exceptional, both positively and negatively. They are ambivalent about discovering the fact that they are not so different from other children, but mainly it is reassuring. The therapist's judgments need to be clearly stated, in part to counteract the vague, mixed messages received from their parents. They need the active support of the therapist to take risks.

With respect to gaining insight, the most important thing is the identification of defenses and trying to show that their original "value" has been lost. This will entail some reconstruction of the past when the child felt endangered and helpless and tried to regain control by magic, "leaning over backwards," or whatever. In such reconstructions, the therapist may have to elucidate the actual mistakes made by parents (in terms of their expectations, etc.); it is very helpful if the concurrent work with the parents has reached the point where they can confirm with the child that they were in error. Often the parents know vaguely that they "wronged" the child, but their guilt is expressed by inconsistency and their own form of undoing. To be really helpful, the specific "mistake" needs to be labeled, regretted and put in the past.

Even more than in the case of phobia, early intervention is important for obsessive-compulsive children. At the onset, the symptoms are still "ego-alien" and one can engage in a treatment contract with the child, offering rewards for giving up the symptoms. When the obsessive-compulsive disorder is widespread and interferes with the capacity for pleasure or satisfactory interpersonal relationships, treatment is very difficult. It is doubtful that the child would agree to a response inhibition program because the rewards would seem so much less than the pain. Also, insight-oriented therapy has little to build on. In long-term outcome study of 17 obsessive-compulsive cases, from the records of a child psychiatric clinic over a 16-year period, Hollingsworth, Tanguay, Grossman, and Pabst (1980) found that the 10 who agreed to an evaluation interview had serious problems with social life and peer relationships. Of these 10, 7 still suffered from obsessive-compulsive symptoms. The area of greatest strength for most was pursuit of higher education. The authors also noted that the parents of 14 of the total sample of 17 had significant serious mental illness before or at the time of onset of symptoms of obsessive-compulsive neurosis in the child. Undoubtedly this factor complicated the course of the children's individual therapy.

Borderline Disorders of Childhood: Differential Diagnosis

In recent years, the diagnosis "borderline disorder" has attracted a great deal of attention. It is a new diagnosis, even for adult patients, and appeared for the first time in the DSM-III classification. Like depression (see Chapter 9), borderline disorder does not appear in the section on childhood disorders, but nonetheless clinicians apply it to children. What are now called "borderline chil-

dren" used to be labeled "psychotic" or "schizophrenic"; indeed, there is a continuum with no sharp dividing line. It has become customary to reserve the diagnosis of schizophrenia for those who have had a period of normal or near-normal development with a marked regression in functioning, including a loss of reality testing with hallucinations or delusions. Borderline children, in contrast, have no such marked personality change and their psychotic symptoms come and go in brief periods of time. It is still such a new diagnosis that it is impossible to estimate the true incidence.

The origins of the term "borderline personality" come from psychoanalytic case reports describing adult patients who did not present typical psychotic symptoms but on the other hand showed a readiness to regress to confused thinking and out-of-control behavior under stress. There are significant differences in the conceptualization of this diagnosis. Those with a psychodynamic orientation consider borderline personality as a particular personality structure which may be manifest in a variety of behavioral symptoms, whereas those trying to avoid a particular theoretical position have developed behavioral checklists with specific diagnostic criteria. In reviewing the salient characteristics of borderline conditions in children, Leichtman and Shapiro (1980) commented that

Particular attention has been given to the experience of anxiety, which (1) frequently centers upon concerns about separation, survival, and annihilation, (2) may be both diffuse and intense, (3) tends to rapidly escalate into panic rather than serve a signal function, and (4) typically gives rise to regression and desperate actions rather than to the mobilization of higher-level defenses. (p. 348)

Vela, Gottlieb, and Gottlieb (1983) developed a list of six "consensus symptoms" for borderline conditions in children which included the following:

1. Excessive, intense anxiety
2. Disturbed interpersonal relationships manifested by clinging and demandingness alternating with withdrawal or outbursts of rage
3. Disturbances in reality testing with magical thinking, omnipotent fantasies, and conviction of unfair treatment
4. Excessive and severe impulsive behavior
5. "Neurotic-like symptoms" such as rituals, obsessions, multiple phobias, and somatic concerns
6. Early developmental delays or obvious deviations.

Almost every other diagnosis in the childhood section has some features in common with borderline conditions but they are less pervasive and less severe in character.

In contrast to the conditions already covered, the early history of these children is usually marked by many irregularities and delays in maturational patterns and physiological functioning, suggestive of a strong constitutional component. In that sense it comes close to a "developmental disability." In fact, Leichtman and Shapiro make the important point that in the preschool age period, "psychotic children, borderline children, children with severe charac-

terological problems and those manifesting various kinds of organic problems and retardation behave in much more similar ways than they will as they get older" (1980, p. 344). Since it is the affective rather than the cognitive disturbances which have been the target of study and treatment with borderline children, they are more appropriately discussed in the context of this chapter.

Clinical Features. Borderline children are under constant threat of being overwhelmed by anxiety; the perceived dangers are everywhere in the outside world. The projection is so great that it borders on the paranoid. Faced with all these externalized dangers, the child is likely to live a very restricted life, clinging to a "protector" and sometimes constructing a compensatory fantasy world where everything is different and the child is the master. Although this might look a little like the "circumscribed interest patterns" described by Adams (1973), the borderline child's fantasies are much more elaborated and "far out," animated with magical, surreal characters who ward off all kinds of terrible threats. In contrast with obsessive-compulsive anxieties, there is relatively little concern about shame or guilt. In contrast with phobics, the fear of abandonment seems to be based on the fear of being totally "wiped out" and ceasing to exist.

Repression is notably deficient with borderline children; their aggressive-sadistic wishes are little, if at all, disguised. Often their fantasy "heroes" are as aggressive as they are aggressed against. The failure of repression is particularly manifest in responses to projective tests where primitive impulses are directly expressed without regard for the reality limits suggested by the form of the inkblots or the features of the characters in stimulus pictures (Leichtman & Shapiro, 1980). In real life, borderline children may show impulsive outbursts of rage, quickly followed by abject terror. It is the strength and the suddenness of these affective responses which distinguish the borderline child. With emotional arousal, borderline children may become confused about what is "real" and "not-real" so that they appear to be psychotic. They are readily recognized by their peers and by adults as being very different.

Etiology. There are probably several paths which can lead to similar pathology. As mentioned before, many of these children were "difficult" infants who were not easily comforted or soothed. Some seemed to be in a perpetual state of agitation and over-stimulation, perhaps deficient in the "protective barrier" described by Freud (1920) or "stimulus-augmenters" as described by Petrie (1967). Rosenfeld and Sprince (1965) described these children as being "swamped" by stimuli and unselective in their choice of what is relevant and what is irrelevant. Some show behavior at the other extreme of apathy. One way or the other,

A borderline infant may not respond to mother's face for months, may react negatively to cuddling, may mold poorly, and may fail to make anticipatory gestures when picked up. This poor foundation often disturbs later communication between mother and child, and the child will not develop an adequate system for signaling his needs to the environment. (Chethik, 1979, p. 308)

Chethik also mentioned early motoric peculiarities in the form of hyperactivity, body rigidities, and peculiar gaits or postures. They do not seem able to regulate and master arousal from within so they cannot relieve their own discomfort.

The inability of some children to modify early pain experiences (due either to defective physiology or inadequate care-taking) produces a number of fundamental problems. One notes an easy disruption in the normal function of physiological systems and the continued presence of a high level of primary anxiety. Another major effect is that the growing child "learns" that the outside world is painful and ungratifying, and that one can expect little pleasure from it. (1979, pp. 312–313)

With this inauspicious beginning, it is not surprising that development goes awry in the second year. The clinging behavior of the toddler is intensified, and the children do not take the usual steps in separation-individuation. They do not tolerate normal frustration well; anger is tantamount to the destruction of the outer object, so they cannot achieve object constancy (see Chapter 1), nor do they manage to combine (fuse) anger and love in the realization that both can exist without fatal results. Lacking a sense of the fundamental stability in the love of the parent, they do not feel safe in venturing on their own. At a later stage, this takes the form of "splitting" everything "good" to one person or place, and everything "bad" to another person or place. The mother may emerge as the only "good" safe person who cares, denying any fact to the contrary. This unrealistic image leads to clutching the mother for a very shaky form of security.

Although a biological vulnerability is probably more often the case than not, sufficient pathological parenting can also result in a borderline child. In a well-documented case report, Olesker (1980) demonstrated the devastating effects of a mother who persistently clung to her son throughout infancy and his early years, not so much from anxiety as from depression. As an example, he was almost forced to sleep in the parents' bed with them, holding onto her hair as a kind of transitional object. Under such circumstances, the son did not develop a sense of autonomy and later on he seemed to cling to people whom he could mirror and follow as if they were a part of himself rather than separate personalities. The final result was similar. The borderline child has little concept of self-efficacy and is dependent on external persons for security; these external persons are contaminated by the child's projections. As Kohut (1971) described it, people are seen as "self-objects," experienced as part of the self, their independent needs and feelings disregarded.

Treatment Approaches. Usually these children require an intensive, lengthy, and comprehensive treatment which involves a total milieu, either in residential or day treatment programs. Chethik described the special problems stemming from (1) the child's attachment to the narcissistic fantasy world, (b) the primitive level of relationship with the therapist, and (c) the deficits in coping evident in the borderline child's daily interaction with reality. In his opinion, the therapist must first become part of the gratifying fantasy world and only slowly intrude with reality elements. These

children will often attach to the therapist but only on their own terms. The therapist may feel like a fantasy figure as the child manipulates the conditions, but after a time, the therapist may introduce some reality-based "conditions" and thus start to bridge the gap between fantasy and reality. If this is done prematurely, the child will take flight. Finally, Chethik emphasized that as borderline children attempt to cope with reality, "treatment techniques should be ego supportive and interpretations should be related directly to building up defenses" (1979, p. 320). Thus, the treatment is unique in trying to establish defenses where there have been none in contrast to modifying maladaptive, existent defenses.

Some writers have suggested that therapy moves the borderline child to a neurotic structure (Ekstein, 1966; Rosenfeld, & Sprince, 1965), but Chethik expressed a contrary opinion.

The child's adaptation to the reality world may improve markedly; he may establish much better control of the severe regressive trends in his personality; and he may develop and maximize the healthier aspects of his defenses and his ego functioning. We have not experienced, through therapy, the marked changes in synthetic function, in the ability to neutralize energy, in the capacity for repression as a major defense, and in libidinal object relations that are necessary for the development of a neurotic personality structure. (1979, p. 318)

Kestenbaum (1983) re-evaluated seven cases diagnosed as borderline in childhood, using the consensus symptoms mentioned before. The adult diagnoses were varied, with only one fitting the adult borderline classification. One young man had had several hospitalizations for paranoid schizophrenia, and two had developed affective disorders. Overall, the adult adjustment of these seven treated cases was better than one might have hoped from the childhood picture. Four had completed college, were working in professional fields, and reported satisfactory personal relationships. The schizophrenic adult was obviously seriously disturbed, and the other two cases had achieved only a marginal adjustment. Although this is a small and select sample, the findings suggest that a borderline condition in childhood does not predict a similar status in adulthood. There is general agreement that treatment for these children is particularly taxing for the therapist; fortunately it is a relatively rare condition.

SUMMARY

In this chapter we have reviewed some theoretical considerations regarding the nature of anxiety and defenses and childhood disorders, progressing from the less to the more pathological forms. The major emphasis has been on psychodynamic theory and treatment approaches, although behavior therapies for phobias were presented. Important differences between these two approaches are very evident in the importance assigned to internal versus external factors. However, behavior therapists and psychodynamically oriented practitioners are alike in stressing the role of the parents in modeling and reinforcing phobic and/or obsessive-compulsive behavior. The borderline condition is different in that the contri-

bution from the child makes the parenting task extraordinarily difficult.

It is important to note that children with any one of these diagnoses are different one from another despite the commonalities. They will have differences in intellectual ability, social skills, family supports, physical health, and real traumatic life events which limit generalization regarding treatment recommendations and expected outcomes. A good therapist relates to each child as unique and seeks to understand the presenting problems in the total context of that child's life experience. However, there are some general developmental principles which greatly facilitate one's understanding of the common sources of anxiety and the ways in which children try to handle this uncomfortable feeling. In treating a child, one tries to convey a sense of understanding and acceptance so that treatment does not come across as coercive or unfriendly. Naturally the therapist is gratified by positive results, but the child's perception should be positive as well.

REFERENCES

ACHENBACH, T. M. (1966). The classification of children's psychiatric symptoms: A factor analytic study. *Psychological Monographs, 80,* 1–37.

ADAMS, P. (1973). *Obsessive children.* New York: Penguin Books.

ALEXANDER, F., & FRENCH, T. M. (1946). *Psychoanalytic therapy.* New York: Ronald Press.

ATKINSON, L., QUARRINGTON, B., & CYR, J. J. (1985). School refusal: The heterogeneity of a concept. *American Journal of Orthopsychiatry, 55,* 83–101.

BAUER, D. (1980). Childhood fears in developmental perspective. In L. Hersov & I. Berg (Eds.), *Out of school* (pp. 189–208). New York: John Wiley & Sons.

BERG, I. (1980). School refusal in early adolescence. In L. Hersov & I. Berg (Eds.), *Out of school* (pp. 137–148). New York: John Wiley & Sons.

BERG, I., MARKS, I., McGUIRE, R., & LIPSEDGE, M. (1974). School phobia and agoraphobia. *Psychological Medicine, 4,* 428–434.

BLATT, S. J., & SHICHMAN, S. (1983). Two primary configurations of psychopathology. *Psychoanalysis & Contemporary Thought, 6,* 187–254.

BOLMAN, W. M. (1970). Systems theory, psychiatry, and school phobia. *American Journal of Psychiatry, 127,* 25–32.

BROADWIN, I. A. (1932). A contribution to the study of truancy. *American Journal of Orthopsychiatry, 2,* 253–257.

CHETHIK, M. (1979). The borderline child. In J. D. Noshpitz (Ed.), *Basic handbook on child psychiatry* (Vol. 2, pp. 304–320). New York: Basic Books.

COMBS, M. L., & SLABY, D. A. (1977). Social skills training with children. In B. B. Lahey & A. E. Kazdin (Eds.), *Advances in clinical child psychology* (Vol. 1, pp. 161–203). New York: Plenum.

COOLIDGE, J. C. (1979). School phobia. In J. D. Noshpitz (Ed.), *Basic handbook of child psychiatry* (Vol. 2, pp. 453–463). New York: Basic Books.

COOLIDGE, J. C., BRODIE, R. D., & FEENEY, B. A. (1964). 10-year follow-up study of 66 school phobic children. *American Journal of Orthopsychiatry, 34,* 675–695.

COOLIDGE, J., HAHN, P., & PECK, A. (1957). School phobia: Neurotic crisis or way of life. *American Journal of Orthopsychiatry, 27,* 296–306.

COWEN, E. L., PEDERSON, A., BABIGIAN, II., IZZO, L. D., & TROST, M. A. (1973). Long-term follow-up of early detected vulnerable children. *Journal of Consulting and Clinical Psychology, 41,* 438–446.

DAVISON, G. C. (1968). Systematic desensitization as a counter-conditioning process. *Journal of Abnormal and Social Psychology, 73,* 91–100.

DESPÈRT, J. L. (1968). *Schizophrenia in children.* New York: Robert Brunner.

EKSTEIN, R. (1966). *Children of time and space, of action and impulse.* New York: Appleton-Century-Crofts.

ELKINS, R., RAPOPORT, J. L., & LIPSKY, A. (1980). Obsessive-compulsive disorder of childhood and adolescence. A neurobiological viewpoint. *Journal of the American Academy of Child Psychiatry, 19,* 511–524.

EME, R., & SCHMIDT, D. (1978). The stability of children's fears. *Child Development, 49,* 1277–1279.

ESTES, H. R., HAYLETT, C. H., & JOHNSON, A. M. (1956). Separation anxiety. *American Journal of Psychotherapy, 10,* 682–695.

FREUD, A. (1936/1946). *The ego and the mechanisms of defense* (Cecil Baines, Trans.). New York: International Universities Press.

FREUD, A. (1977). Fears, anxieties and phobic phenomena. In R. S. Eissler, A. Freud, M. Kris, P. B. Neubauer, & A. J. Solnit (Eds.), *Psychoanalytic study of the child* (Vol. 32, pp. 85–90). New Haven: Yale University Press.

FREUD, S. (1955). On the psychical mechanism of hysterical phenomena: Preliminary communication. In J. Strachey (Ed. and Trans.), *The standard edition of the complete psychological works of Sigmund Freud* (Vol. 2, pp. 1–18). London: Hogarth Press. (Original work published 1893)

FREUD, S. (1959). Character and anal erotism. In J. Strachey (Ed. and Trans.), *The standard edition of the complete psychological works of Sigmund Freud* (Vol. 9, pp. 167–176). London: Hogarth Press. (Original work published 1908)

FREUD, S. (1955). Analysis of a phobia in a five-year-old boy. In J. Strachey (Ed. and Trans.), *The standard edition of the complete psychological works of Sigmund Freud* (Vol. 10, pp. 5–148). London: Hogarth Press. (Original work published 1909)

FREUD, S. (1957). Five lectures on psychoanalysis. In J. Strachey (Ed. and Trans.), *The standard edition of the complete psychological works of Sigmund Freud* (Vol. 11, pp. 3–55). London: Hogarth Press. (Original work published 1909)

FREUD, S. (1957). On the history of the psychoanalytic movement. In J. Strachey (Ed. and Trans.), *The standard edition of the complete psychological works of Sigmund Freud* (Vol. 14, pp. 7–66). London: Hogarth Press. (Original work published 1914)

FREUD, S. (1959). Inhibitions, symptoms and anxiety. In J. Strachy (Ed. and Trans.), *The standard edition of the complete psychological works of Sigmund Freud* (Vol. 20, pp. 75–176). London: Hogarth Press. (Original work published 1926)

FREUD, S. (1961). Civilization and its discontents. In J. Strachey (Ed. and Trans.), *The standard edition of the complete psychological works of Sigmund Freud* (Vol. 21, pp. 64–145). London: Hogarth Press. (Original work published 1930)

GARVEY, W. P., & HEGRENES, J. R. (1966). Desensitization techniques in the treatment of school phobia. *American Journal of Orthopsychiatry, 36*, 147–252.

GITTELMAN-KLEIN, R., & KLEIN, D. (1980). Separation anxiety in school refusal and its treatment with drugs. In L. Hersov & I. Berg (Eds.), *Out of school* (pp. 321–342). New York: John Wiley.

GORDON, D. A., & YOUNG, R. D. (1977). School phobia: a discussion of etiology, treatment and evaluation. In S. Chess & A. Thomas (Eds.), *Annual progress in child psychiatry and child development* (pp. 409–434). New York: Brunner/Mazel.

GRAZIANO, A. M. (1975). *Behavior therapy with children* (Vol. 2.) Chicago: Aldine.

GRAZIANO, A. M., & DeGIOVANNI, I. S. (1979). The clinical significance of childhood phobias: A note on the proportion of child-clinical referrals for the treatment of children's fears. *Behavior Research and Therapy, 16*, 161–162.

GRAZIANO, A. M., DeGIOVANNI, I. S., & GARCIA, D. A. (1979). Behavioral treatment of children's fears: A review. *Psychological Bulletin, 86*, 804–830.

HERSOV, L. (1960). Refusal to go to school. *Journal of Child Psychology and Psychiatry, 1*, 137–145.

HOLLINGSWORTH, C. E., TANGUAY, P. E., GROSSMAN, L., & PABST, P. (1980). Long-term outcome of obsessive disorder in childhood. *Journal of the American Academy of Child Psychiatry, 19*, 134–144.

JOHNSON, A. M., FALSTEIN, E. I., SZUREK, S. A., & SVENDSEN, M. (1941). School phobia. *American Journal of Orthopsychiatry, 11*, 702–711.

JUDD, L. (1965). Obsessive-compulsive neurosis in children. *Archives of General Psychiatry, 12*, 136–146.

KANFER, F. H., KAROLY, P., & NEWMAN, A. (1975). Reduction of children's fear of the dark by competence-related and situational threat-related verbal cues. *Journal of Consulting and Clinical Psychology, 43*, 251–258.

KELLY, E. (1973). School phobia: A review of theory and treatment. *Psychology in the Schools, 10*, 33–42.

KENNEDY, W. A. (1965). School phobia: Rapid treatment of fifty cases. *Journal of Abnormal Psychology, 70*, 285–289.

KESTENBAUM, C. J. (1983). The borderline child at risk for major psychiatric disorder in adult life. In K. S. Robson (Ed.), *The borderline child* (pp. 49–82). New York: McGraw-Hill.

KOHUT, H. (1971). *The analysis of the self.* New York: International Universities Press.

LACHENMEYER, J. R. (1982). Special disorders of childhood: Depression, school phobia and anorexia nervosa. In J. R. Lachenmeyer & M. S. Gibbs (Eds.), *Psychopathology in childhood* (pp. 53–89). New York: Gardner Press.

LAZARUS, A. A., & ABRAMOVITZ, A. (1965). The use of "emotive imagery" in the treatment of children's phobias. In L. P. Ullman & L. Krasner (Eds.), *Case studies in behavior modification* (pp. 300–304). New York: Holt.

LAZARUS, A. A., DAVISON, G. C., & POLEFKA, D. A. (1965). Classical and operant factors in the treatment of a school phobia. *Journal of Abnormal Psychology, 70,* 225–230.

LEICHTMAN, M., & SHAPIRO, S. (1980). An introduction to the psychological assessment of borderline conditions in children: borderline children and the test process. In J. S. Kwawer, H. D. Lerner, P. M. Lerner, & A. Sugarman (Eds.), *Borderline phenomena and the Rorschach Test* (pp. 343–366). New York: International Universities Press.

LEVENTHAL, T., & SILLS, M. (1964). Self-image in school phobia. *American Journal of Orthopsychiatry, 34,* 685–695.

MALMQUIST, C. P. (1965). School phobia: A problem in family neurosis. *Journal of the American Academy of Child Psychiatry, 4,* 293–319.

MEYER, V. (1966). Modifications of expectations of cases with obsessional rituals. *Behavior Research and Therapy, 4,* 273–280.

MICHELSON, L., & WOOD, R. (1980). A group assertiveness training program for elementary school children. *Child Behavior Therapy, 2,* 1–9.

MILLER, L. C. (1983). Fears and anxieties in children. In C. E. Walker & M. C. Roberts (Eds.), *Handbook of clinical psychology* (pp. 337–380). New York: John Wiley.

MILLER, L. C., BARRETT, C. L., & HAMPE, E. (1974). Phobias of childhood in a prescientific era. In A. Davids (Ed.), *Child personality & psychopathology: Current topics* (Vol. 1, pp. 89–137). New York: John Wiley.

MILLER, L. C., BARRETT, C. L., HAMPE, E., & NOBLE, H. (1971). Revised anxiety scales for the Louisville Behavior Checklist. *Psychological Reports, 29,* 503–511.

MILLER, L. C., BARRETT, C. L., HAMPE, E., & NOBLE, H. (1972). Comparison of reciprocal inhibition, psychotherapy and waiting list control for phobic children. *Journal of Abnormal Psychology, 79,* 269–279.

MINUCHIN, P., BIBER, B., SHAPIRO, R., & ZIMILES H. (1969). *The psychological impact of school experience.* New York: Basic Books.

MITCHELL, S., & SHEPHERD, M. (1980). Reluctance to go to school. In L. Hersov & I. Berg (Eds.), *Out of school* (pp. 7–24). New York: John Wiley.

MOORE, T. (1966). Difficulties of the ordinary child in adjusting to primary school. *Journal of Child Psychology and Psychiatry, 7,* 17–38.

OLESKER, W. (1980). Early life experience and the development of borderline pathology. In J. S. Kwawer, H. D. Lerner, P. M. Lerner, & A. Sugarman (Eds.), *Borderline phenomena and the Roschach Test* (pp. 279–284). New York: International Universities Press.

PATTERSON, G. R. (1965). A learning theory approach to the treatment of the school phobic child. In L. P. Ullman & L. Krasner (Eds.), *Case studies in behavior modification* (pp. 279–284). New York: Holt.

PELLER, L. (1954). Libidinal phases, ego development and play. In R. S. Eissler, A. Freud, H. Hartmann, & E. Kris (Eds.), *Psychoanalytic study of the child* (Vol. 9, pp. 178–198). New York: International Universities Press.

PETERSON, D. R. (1961). Behavior problems of middle childhood. *Journal of Consulting Psychology, 25,* 205–209.

PETRIE, A. (1967). *Individuality in pain and suffering.* Chicago: University of Chicago Press.

POZNANSKI, E. (1973). Children with excessive fears. *American Journal of Orthopsychiatry, 43,* 428–438.

POZNANSKI, E., & ARTHUR, B. (1971). The counterphobic defense in children. *Child Psychiatry & Human Development, 1,* 178–191.

Quay, H. C., & Werry, J. S. (1979). *Psycho-pathological Disorders of Childhood* (2nd ed.). New York: Wiley.

RADO, S. (1959). Obsessive behavior: So-called obsessive-compulsive neurosis. In S. Arieti (Ed.), *American handbook of psychiatry* (Vol. 1, pp. 324–334). New York: Basic Books.

RAPOPORT, J., ELKINS, R., LANGER, D. H., SCEERY, W. BUCHSBAUM, M. S., GILLIN, J. C., MURPHY, D. L., ZAHN, T. P., LAKE, R., LUDLOW, C., & MENDELSON, W. (1981). Childhood obsessive-compulsive disorder. *American Journal of Psychiatry, 138,* 1545–1554.

REYNOLDS, C. R., & RICHMOND, B. O. (1978). What I think and feel. A revised measure of children's manifest anxiety. *Journal of Abnormal Child Psychology, 6,* 271–280.

ROSENFELD, S., & SPRINCE, M. (1965). Some thoughts on the technical handling of borderline children. In R. S. Eissler, A. Freud, H. Hartmann, & E. Kris (Eds.), *Psychoanalytic study of the child* (Vol. 20, pp. 495–517). New York: International Universities Press.

RUTTER, M., GRAHAM, P., CHADWICK, O. F. D., & YULE, W. (1976). Adolescent turmoil: Fact or fiction. *Journal of Child Psychology and Psychiatry, 17,* 35–56.

RUTTER, M., TIZARD, J., & WHITMORE, K. (1970). *Education, health and behavior.* London: Longman.

SANDLER, J., & JOFFE, W. G. (1965). Notes on obsessional manifestations in children. In R. S. Eissler, A. Freud, H. Hartmann, & M. Kris (Eds.), *Psychoanalytic study of the child* (Vol. 20, pp. 425–440). New York: International Universities Press.

SCHERER, M. W., & NAKAMURA, C. Y. (1968). A fear survey schedule for children (FSS-FC): A factor analytic comparison with manifest anxiety (CMAS). *Behaviour Research and Therapy, 6,* 173–182.

SHAPIRO, T. (1983). The unconscious still occupies us. In A. J. Solnit, R. S. Eissler, & P. B. Neubauer (Eds.), *Psychoanalytic study of the child* (Vol. 38, pp. 547–568). New Haven: Yale University Press.

SKYNNER, A. C. R. (1976). Applications of family techniques to the study of a syndrome: School phobia. In A. C. R. Skynner, *Systems of family and marital psychotherapy* (pp. 306–326). New York: Brunner/Mazel.

SMITH, R. E., & SHARPE, T. M. (1970). Treatment of a school phobia with implosive therapy. *Journal of Consulting and Clinical Psychology, 35,* 239–243.

SPERLING, M. (1967). School phobias: Classification, dynamics, and treatment. In R. S. Eissler, A Freud, H. Hartmann, & M. Kris (Eds.), *Psychoanalytic study of the child* (Vol. 22, pp. 375–401). New York: International Universities Press.

SPIELBERGER, C. D. (1973). *Manual for the State-Trait Anxiety Inventory of Children.* Palo Alto: Consulting Psychologists Press.

SPOCK, B. (1957). *Baby and child care.* New York: Pocket Books.

STANLEY, L. (1980). Treatment of ritualistic behavior in an eight-year-old girl by response prevention: A case report. *Journal of Child Psychology and Psychiatry, 21,* 85–91.

TYSON, R. L. (1978). Notes on the analysis of a prelatency boy with a dog phobia. In A. J. Solnit, R. S. Eissler, A. Freud, M. Kris, & P. B. Neubauer (Eds.), *Psychoanalytic study of the child* (Vol. 33, pp. 427–460). New Haven: Yale University Press.

VELA, R., GOTTLIEB, H., & GOTTLIEB, E. (1983). Borderline syndromes in childhood: A critical review. In K. S. Robson (Ed.), *The borderline child* (pp. 31–48). New York: McGraw-Hill.

WALDFOGEL, S., TESSMAN, E., & HAHN, P. B. (1959). A program for early intervention in school phobia. *American Journal of Orthopsychiatry, 29,* 324–333.

WALLER, D., & EISENBERG, L. (1980). School refusal in childhood—A psychiatric-paediatric perspective. In L. Hersov & I. Berg (Eds.), *Out of school* (pp. 209–230). New York: John Wiley.

WINNICOTT, D. W. (1971). *Therapeutic consul-*

tation in child psychiatry. New York: Basic Books.

YULE, W., HERSOV, L., & TRESEDER, J. (1980). Behavioral treatment in school refusal. In L. Hersov & I. Berg (Eds.), *Out of school* (pp. 267–302). New York: John Wiley.

ZETZEL, E. R. (1966). 1965: Additional notes upon a case of obsessional neurosis: Freud 1909. *International Journal of Psychoanalysis, 47,* 123–129.

CHAPTER 9

DEPRESSION AND BEREAVEMENT

RESURGENCE OF INTEREST

In 1946 Rene Spitz introduced the term "anaclitic depression" to identify the response of some infants after lengthy separation from their mothers during the second 6 months of life. These infants developed weepy behavior, withdrawal, weight loss, psychomotor retardation, sleeplessness, and somatic illness. The only effective intervention was reunion with the mother. This response to separation was considered an example of the effects of "maternal deprivation," and although it had a major influence in the area of infant care (see Chapter 1), the condition was not observed or considered applicable to older children. Although there were occasional articles on the subject of depression in childhood, it

was not of general concern. Malmquist's chapter in Wolman's *Manual of Child Psychopathology* (1972) was perhaps the first instance of inclusion in a basic review text.

Since 1972, a great deal of attention has been directed to depression in childhood. The National Institute of Mental Health convened a conference on childhood depression in 1975 (Schulterbrandt & Raskin, 1977) and there has been a continuous outpouring of publications since that time. Review of four journals in the field (*American Academy of Child Psychiatry, Abnormal Child Psychology, Clinical Child Psychology*, and *Child Psychiatry and Psychology*) for the period from 1979 through 1983 identified 31 papers on the topic of childhood depression compared with only 7 articles that included the word "anxiety" in the title. There are a number of reasons for this quickening of interest, including the possibility that there is an actual increase in childhood depression. Achenbach (1978) found a syndrome of depression in his 1978 report on behavior problems of boys aged 6 through 11 which he had not found in 1966; this led him to suggest that cultural changes may be leading to increased incidence. But one reason stands out clearly and that is the reversal of an earlier position that children were considered incapable of a true depressive disorder equivalent to that experienced by adults.

There has been a similar heightened interest in adult depression, in part derived from the success of drug therapies and the search for biological factors. Since the late 1950's, the effectiveness of antidepressant drugs (tricyclics, monoamine oxidase inhibitors, and lithium) has been documented in a considerable number of clinical studies although the mechanism of this therapeutic result has not been satisfactorily elucidated. A biomedical concept of depression leads to investigation of genetic factors and utilization of drug therapy for childhood forms of depressive disorder. Throughout the literature there is a latent disagreement as to the relative importance of psychological and biological factors. This is confounded, particularly for children, by the difficulty in distinguishing between depression as an affect or feeling which is at least in part justified by external reality, and depression as a disorder or "disease" with little external justification. Traditionally, the former has been termed "reactive" and the latter has been called "endogenous."

PSYCHODYNAMIC MODELS OF DEPRESSION

To understand the controversy as to the existence or nonexistence of depressive disorder in childhood, it is helpful to review some of the landmark articles. Freud's article on *Mourning and Melancholia* (1917/1957) represents the first effort to explain melancholia, or depression, from a psychodynamic standpoint. He cautioned against over-generalization of his conclusions in the statement that

Melancholia, whose definition fluctuates even in descriptive psychiatry, takes on various clinical forms the grouping together of which into a single unity does not seem to be established with certainty; and some of these forms suggest somatic rather than psychogenic affections. (p. 243)

He observed many similarities in "normal" mourning and "abnormal" melancholia except that in the latter, the person suffers from a loss of self-regard, with many self-reproaches and expectations of punishment.

Freud was intrigued by the source of these self-recriminations which have little reality justification. For the first time, he introduced the idea of a "critical agency" which is split off from the ego and commonly called the conscience. Further, he suggested that the self-reproaches were a substitution for reproaches directed against a loved person. The dynamic process started with a disappointment or loss in a significant relationship, but the relationship was not relinquished, nor was the aggression expressed against the offending person, but instead the melancholic identified in part with this person and turned the aggression against the self. "The narcissistic identification with the object then becomes a substitute for the erotic cathexis, the result of which is that in spite of the conflict with the loved person the love-relation need not be given up" (p. 249).

Both mourning and melancholia begin with a loss—in the former the loss is real and in the latter the loss is psychological. In both instances there is an identification with the lost object, but in melancholia it is the negative aspects of the loved person which are incorporated into the identification. Freud also appreciated the secondary gains, in that melancholic patients "torment their loved one through their illness, having resorted to it in order to avoid the need to express their hostility to him openly" (p. 251). It is also possible for a bereaved person to develop melancholia if the previous relationship was a particularly ambivalent one. This formulation pivots on the twin concepts of identification with a loved person who is in some way lost and the turning of aggression against the self which has incorporated this person.

Bibring (1953) offered a major revision by minimizing the importance of aggression turned against self and emphasizing the loss of self-esteem and feeling of total helplessness. He suggested that the expectation of failure to live up to important narcissistic aspirations was the common denominator. He suggested three groups of "such persisting aspirations":

(1) the wish to be worthy, to be loved, to be appreciated, not to be inferior or unworthy;

(2) the wish to be strong, superior, great, secure, not to be weak and insecure; and (3) the wish to be good, to be loving, not to be aggressive, hateful and destructive. (1953, p. 24)

Briefly, the basic mechanism of depression was conceptualized as the awareness of helplessness vis-a-vis the outside world, and the turning of aggressive impulses against the self was seen as secondary to the breakdown in self-esteem. In many respects, this is the model used in rational emotive therapy, which is designed to modify unrealistic narcissistic aspirations, or irrational beliefs in Ellis' terms (1962).

In 1966, Rie examined these psychodynamic considerations to determine the implications for depression in childhood. He questioned the validity of the diagnosis for children on three grounds. First, with regard to the role of the conscience, or superego, he suggested that in childhood it could not function in the self-punitive manner ascribed to it in adult depressives. Second, he considered the Bibring hypothesis and suggested that self-esteem is a function of ego identity or self-representation and that these personality constructs fail to achieve stability until the late childhood years. Therefore, it is hard to imagine that a child would feel excruciating helplessness to achieve ego ideals which have not been truly articulated as personal goals. His final point had to do with the child's sense of a future. He doubted that a child had a sufficient time perspective to experience despair. "One wonders, finally, whether this development does not also demand some grasp of what is meant by infinity, for does not pervasive and enduring 'hopelessness' imply an abiding, generalized expectation of failure to gain gratification for all time?" (1966, p. 682). This article is frequently cited as a disclaimer of the existence of childhood depression, but in fact Rie was questioning the relevance of the psychodynamic explanations when considering depressed children.

There is no doubt in anyone's mind that children of all ages can be very sad and miserable. In fact, Lefkowitz and Burton (1978) objected to the diagnostic construct of "childhood depression" for the very reason that the symptoms of depression occur so frequently in "normal" children that they cannot be considered statistically deviant. There are two debatable questions. First, if the sadness is an immediate response to a real-life situation should it be called "depression," which implies a degree of permanence and self-perpetuation? Second, what are the necessary cognitive components of depression? Does the experience of depression require a certain degree of self-awareness and expectations of the future? These questions illustrate the continuing difficulty of distinguishing between depression as a pathological state and depression as a basic affect.

Anxiety and Depression Compared

Bibring (1953) suggested that depression and anxiety are "basic ego responses" which are diametrically opposed. Anxiety arouses the urge to action, fight or flight, but depression stimulates passivity, or inaction. Depression may well follow anxiety when action proves fruit-

less, but depression may be primary when there has been no time for the "signal function" of anxiety. In distinguishing between anxiety and depression, Dorpat emphasized the degree of certainty: "One feels anxiety over something painful that might happen, but one experiences depressive affect about something painful which has happened or that one has some certainty will happen" (1977, p. 5).

After careful study of the treatment records of some 100 children treated by psychoanalysis at the Hampstead Clinic in London, Sandler and Joffe (1965) found that a large number showed depressive reactions at one time or another. The common factor eliciting the depressive reaction was "the feeling of having lost, or of being unable to attain, something which was essential to his narcissistic integrity. Coupled with this was the feeling of being helpless and unable to undo the loss" (p. 91). This may take the form of an actual object loss, a major change in status (as after the birth of a sibling), or a significant disappointment.

Following Bibring's lead, they identified depression as a "basic psycho-biological affective reaction."

Like anxiety, the depressive reaction is, in certain circumstances, a normal and appropriate affective response, and it appears to be largely a quantitative factor which determines its intensity and duration. The healthy capacity to tolerate depression also plays a part in determining the extent to which this affect can be endured without the ego's abandoning its role in progressive adaptation. (1965, p. 90)

Clinically, depression and anxiety are closely associated. In a pilot study of major depressive disorders on an inpatient child psychiatric service, Puig-Antich, Blau, Marx, Greenhill, and Chambers (1978) noted that all had pathological levels of separation anxiety and conversely, Gittelman-Klein and Klein (1971) reported that 35% of children with separation anxiety disorder (specifically school phobia) presented depressive affect. In the particular case of separation anxiety (i.e., fear of object loss), the link with depressive disorder is very close.

DEPRESSION AND DEVELOPMENT

Bemporad (1978) discussed the role of cognitive and affective limitations at different stages of childhood in modifying the experience and expression of emotions in general. Because of the cognitive limitations of the infant, he would not classify "anaclitic depression" as a form of depression. In the next stage, toddlers may become overly inhibited and unable to engage in spontaneous play; they may forego the normal exuberance of the age if the parents are overly restrictive. Although this response may lay the groundwork for future depression, the fact that the toddler's mood state shifts with different persons suggests that it is not internalized. The young school-age child shows longer periods of sadness generalizing from experiences with parents to others. Such children may feel hopeless and resigned to disappointment, but like Rie, Bemporad suggested that this age child is incapable of sustaining a consistent and continued low estimation of himself. He felt that the child does not per-

petuate a depressive mood in the absence of an external cause.

In late childhood (8 years and older), "the child's cognitive abilities appear to allow for a system of thought that includes the sense of responsibility toward others, the internalization of values and rules, and a budding sense of one's self" (1978, p. 195). More chronic states of depression may emerge, partly because the child is less susceptible to external influences.

The affect state is not an automatic consequence of experience as in younger children; rather, it is a personal logical evaluation of the experience . . . older, repeatedly rejected children are reacting to their own belief that they are unlovable rather than only to the immediate pain of the rejection. (p. 196)

At this point, Bemporad stated that an actual depressive illness is possible. The depressions of adolescence equal the adult forms in severity, and may even be intensified by the adolescent's characteristic view that his future is now.

Sandler and Joffe (1965) emphasized that in the normal process of development, every child must relinquish previous satisfactions and become increasingly independent from the objects of early childhood. In the process of individuation (see Chapter 1), there is a gradual development of more reality-adapted ideals and giving up of ideal states of infantile satisfaction. These authors remarked that "It not infrequently happens that the child's parents are in unconscious opposition to progressive individuation and the influence of the parents may be perpetuated in their successor, the superego" (1965, p. 94). From their clinical experience, they concluded that "the outlook becomes progressively bleaker for children (and adults) who repeatedly react with a depressive response to disappointment, who fail to individuate and who cannot withdraw their attachment from infantile ideals" (p. 95). One valuable "defense" against depression is aggression, which is a natural response to frustration or pain and leads to action rather than passive resignation. When anxiety blocks the expression of aggression, even as a feeling state, the child in "mental pain" has no recourse except helpless resignation.

Symptomatic Manifestations of Depression in Childhood

Although much of the depression in childhood may well be of a reactive nature and thus have a different structure than adult depression, children show behavior which is readily recognizable as "depressed." The symptoms include feelings of apprehension, sadness, helplessness; self-judgments of being bad, dumb, or unlovable; withdrawal and inability to enjoy play or success; disturbances in appetite and sleep; moodiness and crying; and often problems in concentration leading to poor academic performance. These have been included in the various inventories to be discussed shortly.

Malmquist (1983), however, pointed out that dysphoria (sadness) is not as prominent a presenting symptom in allegedly depressed children as it is in depressed adults. Children do not spontaneously complain of "feeling sad"; they are much more likely to deny such feelings vigorously. Developmentally, children are more prone to action than to introspective thought. The childhood propensity for acting out was picked up in the concept of "masked depression." Cytryn and McKnew (1972) suggested that more often than not, childhood depression was "masked" by such disorders as hyperactivity, aggressive behavior, psychosomatic illness, hypochondriasis, and delinquency. Aggressive behavior, for example, could serve to ward off feelings of helplessness so that the child would not be depressed in mood. The suggestion of "depressive equivalents" is somewhat similar in concept. Sperling (1959) described loss of appetite and sleep disturbances (related to separation anxiety) as the somatic equivalents of depression in children. More recently, Hughes (1984) reported on 23 children hospitalized for recurrent abdominal pain. Although the presenting problem was a physical one, these children met the criteria for a major depressive episode with depressed affect, inability to enjoy anything (anhedonia), and morbid preoccupation that they and their parents would die. It was Hughes' contention that the abdominal pain did not truly hide the depression, except perhaps to the parents who persisted in their search for physical explanations and medical-surgical relief.

The concept of "masked depression" or "depressive equivalents" unique to children has been virtually rejected. Clearly it widened the scope of what might constitute depression to include almost every kind of childhood problem and left much room for clinical inference. The "masks" are little more than the presenting complaints and many writers have pointd out that careful interviews of parents and child will elicit clear evidence of depression in many instances (Carlson & Cantwell, 1980a; Cytryn, McKnew, & Bunney, 1980; Kovacs & Beck, 1977). Although it may not be in the foreground of presenting complaints, the presence of depression can be clinically determined without recourse to inference that particular behaviors always signify depression. However, it is entirely possible for a genuine depression to be associated with other conditions. In a comprehensive clinical study of 43 prepubertal boys at the Child Depression Clinic at the New York State Psychiatric Institute, Puig-Antich (1982) found that one-third were concurrently diagnosed as "depressed" and "conduct disorders." Thus we see that depression usually co-exists with other conditions, e.g. anxiety disorder, somatic complaints, conduct disorders, and learning disabilities. As an interesting sidelight, Kashani, Cantwell, Shekim, and Reid (1982) found that those depressed children with somatic complaints did not have a conduct disorder, and vice versa, suggesting different channels for expressing aggressive feelings—a hypothesis which might well be checked with nondepressed populations as well.

ASSESSMENT TECHNIQUES

A lot of effort has been made to operationalize "depression" by developing self-report measures and interview schedules. For young children, these two approaches merge because so often the self-report questionnaires are read to the children and their responses recorded by the interviewer, who may then ask for clarification and elabora-

tion on the child's replies. Kazdin and Petti (1982) looked at the psychometric properties of eight self-report inventories, two of which are described in the Appendix (Children's Depression Inventory (CDI), Kovacs & Beck, 1977; the Children's Depression Scale (CDS), Tisher & Lang, 1983). Of the five measures derived from interviews, most are restricted to the evaluation of depression (e.g. Bellevue Index of Depression (BID), Petti, 1978; Children's Depression Rating Scale, Poznanski, Cook, & Carroll, 1979) but a few are more inclusive (Interview Schedule for Children, Kovacs, 1978 and Kiddie-SADS, Chambers, Puig-Antich, & Tabrizi, 1978). Also, as mentioned earlier, the Achenbach Child Behavior Checklist (Achenbach & Edelbrock, 1978) includes a depression subscale.

Published reports indicate that different measures of depression completed by the same person are highly intercorrelated (Kazdin, French, Unis, & Esveldt-Dawson, 1983; Weissman, Orvaschel, & Padian, 1980), but there are surprisingly low correlations between parent and child measures. Thus in the diagnostic process, it is imperative to consider the source of information. Apparently, parents are better reporters of their children's behavior than of their children's feelings. In the extensive study of Kazdin et al. (1983), test-retest data indicated high reliability correlations but a significant decrease of depression during a 6-week period of hospitalization, especially as seen by the mothers. The various depression measures successfully discriminated between the 20 children who were clinically, and independently, diagnosed as depressed and the 84 who received other psychiatric diagnoses. In this regard, the parents' measures were more discriminating than those provided by the children, probably because outward behavior counted heavily in both clinician's and parents' judgments.

A very different approach, called the Peer Nomination Inventory of Depression, was developed by Lefkowitz and Tesiny (1980) with a nonclinical population. Subjects were nearly a thousand children in the fourth and fifth grades in a New York City school. The children were asked to identify "who" fit 13 depression, 4 happiness, and 2 popularity items. Interestingly, no sex differences were found. Analysis of the intercorrelations indicated that

Children who received higher total scores by their peers on the 13 items were also viewed as depressed by their teachers and tended to rate themselves as depressed. Intellectual functioning was reduced as indicated by lower scores on standardized achievement tests. . . . Viewed by their peers as generally unhappy and unpopular, these children tended to possess low self-esteem and to view events in their environment as externally controlled. They were absent from school significantly more often than were children less frequently nominated and tended to come from low-income families. (1980, pp. 48–49)

There is no way of determining the causal relationships; as mentioned before, the depression may be a reaction to poor school performance or unpopularity rather than the cause.

Lefkowitz and Tesiny (1981, 1985) used the PNID with 3,020 children in grades 3, 4, and 5 and identified 5.2% as "depressed" on the basis of scoring 2 standard deviations or more above the mean. A subsample of subjects were evaluated with additional depression measures and reassessed after a 6-month interval (Tesiny & Lefkowitz, 1982). The peer nominations had the highest correlation over time (.70), followed by teacher ratings (.60) and self-ratings (.44). Such data are of considerable interest since they are derived from nonidentified populations and provide yet another perspective on the subject. Potentially, over time, such data could provide a kind of natural history of childhood depression, telling us the fate of such symptoms as the child grows up. However, the requirement that each child be evaluated by peers who are well acquainted with him or her imposes a limitation and makes it impractical in clinic settings.

Diagnostic Criteria and Prevalence

Considering the ambiguity inherent in the word "depression," it is not surprising that prevalence estimates vary widely depending on definition. In the major epidemiological study on the Isle of Wight (1970), Rutter, Tizard, and Whitmore identified depression only if subjective sadness were associated with apathy, loss of appetite and weight, and sleep disturbance. Using this relatively conservative definition, the problem was found in only 3 out of about 2,000 "non-referred" 10- and 11-year-old children. But in follow-up when the children were 14 to 15 years old, about 36 (10 times the original) had a diagnosis of depression (Rutter, Graham, Chadwick, & Yale, 1976). Even though the diagnosis is now made with more frequency for prepubertal children, there is no doubt that depression is still far more common in adolescence.

In recent years, many investigators have surveyed clinical populations in the age range from 6 to 14 years. From interviews with parent and child, Weinberg, Rutman, Sullivan, Penick, and Dietz (1973) identified 62% of children aged 6 to 12 referred to an educational diagnostic clinic (in a medical setting) as depressed. Using the Bellevue Index of Depression with criteria modified from Weinberg, Petti (1978) diagnosed depression in about 60% of hospitalized child psychiatry patients aged 6 to 12 years. Clearly the majority of children in these populations were unhappy and understandably so. It is "no fun" to have a severe and chronic learning problem nor to be in a child psychiatry hospital ward! The unanswered question is whether the depression was a primary cause or a secondary result.

The DSM III now provides a common reference point for clinical investigators. Essentially the same diagnostic criteria are used for establishing depressive disorder in adults and children. The primary symptoms include dysphoric mood or loss of interest in usual pastimes with at least four of the following present for a minimum of 2 weeks: change in appetite; sleep difficulty; psychomotor retardation or agitation; loss of pleasure; loss of energy; feelings of self-reproach or guilt; diminished ability to concentrate; and recurrent thoughts of death or suicide. Some authors use the Research Diagnostic Criteria proposed earlier by Spitzer, Endicott, and Robins (1978), which are virtually the same. The DSM III also includes a category of Dysthymic Disorder

(or Depressive Neurosis) to describe a more chronic disturbance of mood which for children must be present for 1 year's duration.

Carlson and Cantwell (1980b) pointed out that the more rigorous and systematic the definition of depression, the less frequent it becomes. They illustrated this fact in a study sample of 210 psychiatrically referred children with a mean age of 11 years, 6 months. Depression as one of the presenting symptoms was very common (again about 60% of the total); depression as measured by a self-report inventory was somewhat less common (49%), and depression as a disorder using the DSM III diagnostic criteria was still less (27% of the interview sample). Looking at the congruence of self-report depression scores and psychiatric diagnosis, these authors found that 75% of the clinically diagnosed depressed children had elevated scores, but there were 39% "false positives" in children with a variety of conduct and physical disorders who complained of unhappiness, low self-esteem and poor school performance on the inventory.

Kashani and Simonds (1979) made a similar distinction between "symptom" and "disorder" in a study of nonreferred children between 7 and 12. The symptom of sadness was present in 17%, whereas only about 2% met the DSM III criteria of depression. The importance of sample selection is shown by a 7% prevalence rate for depressive disorder for children admitted to a pediatric ward (Kashani, Barbero, & Bolander, 1981).

As Freud remarked many years ago, depression means many things. Children can be depressed for present and sufficient reasons; they may be overreacting to stress or disappointment; or they can be chronically or periodically depressed with little basis in current reality. It is difficult to see how these important distinctions can be made without a total history which takes into account past history, present life circumstances, and family relationships. But these figures in their aggregate make it very clear that many children are profoundly unhappy, whether for short times or long, for a wide variety of reasons.

Relationships between Parent and Child Depressive Disorders

These have been examined from two directions, that is, proceeding from the depressed parent to the children and from depressed children to their parents. Also, there have been two reasons for these examinations—one, to establish underlying genetic connections and two, to consider interactive phenomena between parent and child when one or the other is depressed. There is clear evidence of genetic factors when one examines incidence of affective disorders in adults. For example, the overall monozygotic twin concordance rate is 76%, opposed to an overall dizygotic twin concordance rate of 19%, monozygotic twins reared apart still have a concordance rate of 67% (Cantwell, 1983).

Clinical studies of the parents of depressed children have indicated considerable parental psychopathology of various forms. The high prevalence rates of depression in the parents (Brumback, Dietz-Schmidt, & Weinberg, 1977; Kashani et al., 1982) does not establish the genetic base, since these children were raised in the homes of their biological parents and were therefore subject to the environmental consequences. However, two adoption studies (Cadoret, 1978; Mendlewicz & Rainer, 1977) demonstrated an increased prevalence rate for depression in adoptees whose biological parents had a major affective disorder, suggesting a genetic factor. One would like to know more about the age and reasons for adoptive placement, because the depressed mother's influence may be great even in the first few months of a child's life. Puig-Antich (1986) found a 50% occurrence of depressive disorder in the first-degree biological relatives (over 16 years of age) of prepubertal children with depression. When alcoholism and antisocial personality were added to major affective disorder, 55% of the biological relatives were affected by at least one of these conditions. These figures are higher than the reported risk figures for relatives of adults with depressive disorder which suggests that both genetic and environmental factors are involved for children.

In contrast to the limited number of studies looking at the parents of depressed children, there are many which have studied the offspring of depressed parents. As mentioned in Chapter 2, the depressed mother is an "exceptional parent" and her children can be considered "at risk." Typically the depressed mother is withdrawn and nonresponsive, or unpredictably intrusive when she tries to assuage her guilt and "make up" to the child with bursts of energy. If the mother has a bipolar depressive disorder (i.e., manic-depressive), the contrasts in her behavior are even more startling and unrelated to the needs of the child. Beardslee, Bemporad, Keller, and Klerman (1983) reviewed 24 studies of children of a parent with an affective illness and found a 40 to 45% rate of psychiatric disorder in the children, with a large percentage of depression diagnoses. The results in some studies are confounded by the special issue of separation caused by the parent's hospitalization (McKnew, Cytryn, & Effron, 1979; Welner, Welner, & McCrary, 1977). As mentioned in Chapter 6, mothers of preschool children with problems are identified as more depressed than mothers of "normal" preschoolers. Although it is difficult to determine the cause-and-effect relationships, Ghodsian, Zajicek, and Wolkind (1984) confirmed the interrelationship between child problems at 27 and 42 months with maternal depression and found little indication of behavior problems preceding maternal depression.

An experimental program at the National Institute of Mental Health utilizes standardized laboratory situations to examine the responses of 2-year-old children of both bipolar and unipolar depressed mothers, who have not been hospitalized during the life of the child (Zahn-Waxler, Cummings, Iannoti, & Radke-Yarrow, 1984). Both groups of children, when compared to controls, showed signs of preoccupation or hypersensitivity toward distress of others (in simulated situations) and exhibited signs of emotional disturbance following psychological stress; however, children of bipolar parents seemed more upset. The heightened sensitivity to stress could, of course, reflect a genetic-biological difference as well as reaction to features of the home environment. These authors emphasized the individual vari-

ation, finding that some children with depressed mothers handled the situations as well as the control children, and some control children showed problems. This report is the beginning of an important longitudinal study; follow-up studies will tell us if these deviations in social and emotional functioning are precursors of later depression.

Continuity of Depression from Childhood to Adulthood

The question of continuity between childhood and adult depression is as yet unresolved. Zeitlin (1985) examined the records of patients who had been seen in the child and adult psychiatry services at Maudsley Hospital, London, England. Two findings emerged. First, nearly all those who were diagnosed "depressed" in childhood had recurrent depressed episodes as adults. But the converse did not hold. The latter finding is not surprising since depression is a common diagnosis in adulthood and still rare in childhood. Most depressed adults had not shown psychiatric problems in childhood, and of those depressed adults with a history of childhood problems, the childhood difficulties were as often "antisocial" as "affective."

Clearly the continuity issue is confounded by the fact that depression in childhood is usually associated with other problems which traditionally assume primacy (e.g., conduct disorders, learning problems, phobias, social difficulties, etc.). Sroufe and Rutter (1984) suggest that when these maladapative difficulties which "belong" to the childhood period as associated with depressive affect, the adult disorder of depression may be predictable. This line of logic would give a great deal of weight to the presence of depressive phenomena in children and minimize the behavioral symptoms for diagnostic purposes. If indeed, it can be established that there is a predictable connection between childhood and adult depression, despite the surface behavior differences, it would go a long way to confirm the medical disease model. In the past there has been a similar argument about whether childhood schizophrenia is the same "disease" as schizophrenia in adults. Briefly, the answer in that case seems to be negative (see Chapters 8 and 13).

DRUG THERAPY

Since the fortuitous discovery of the benefits of chlorpromazine (Thorazine) with schizophrenic adult patients in the early 1950's, there has been steady progress in the development of psychopharmacological therapy. This has been an important development not only because of clinical benefits but also for theoretical reasons. Putting together the known facts about the neurophysiological action of the drugs and the accompanying behavior change has generated hypotheses about the biological nature of the psychiatric condition. Although these connections are better developed in the case of schizophrenia, a linkage has been suggested between depression and a "functional deficit of one or more neurotransmitter amines at critial synapses in the central nervous system" (Zis & Goodwin, 1982, p. 175) from the fact that drugs that increase the func-

tional output of catecholamine systems act as antidepressants. If indeed depressive disorder in childhood is the same as that occurring in adulthood, drug therapy should be carefully considered. However, Puig-Antich and Gittelman (1982) warned that similarities in drug response are at best suggestive.

As has often been noted, the assumption that two disorders share a common pathophysiological defect if they both respond to the same pharmacological intervention is unwarranted . . . Tricyclics have multiple action patterns and different mechanisms may account for the modification of clinical states. (p. 388)

The major antidepressants used to date have been the so-called tricyclic drugs, e.g., imipramine (Tofranil) and amitriptyline (Elavil). These same drugs have been tried for a variety of childhood problems including enuresis, school phobia, and hyperactive-conduct disorders as well as depression. Sometimes the diagnosis of depression has been inferred from the fact of improvement of any kind of problem, assuming that if a drug called "antidepressant" works, then there was a depression causing the symptom! This assumption verges on "word magic" and is unjustified by what is really known about the "pharmacological bridge" to behavior or feelings.

Clinical reports indicate that imipramine is effective in relieving depressive symptoms (Petti, 1983a) although well-controlled, double-blind studies are few. There is a tendency for professionals to be "believers" or "nonbelievers" so that those who support the idea of a biological or "endogenous" origin to depression rely on medication. This is apparent in Ossofsky's conclusion that "All children treated under the age of 5 years have required continued drug maintenance, which suggests that the younger the child, the more severe the illness and the greater the necessity for continued treatment with relatively high doses of imipramine" (1974, p. 24). It would be equally logical to conclude that the medication was inappropriate for the problems of these young children. Rapoport and Mikkelsen (1978) commented that there are occasional side effects for the tricyclics such as dryness of mouth, drowsiness, tremors, nausea, and sweating, which are viewed as "minor annoyances." There are more serious possibilities with increased dosages, such as seizures, cardiotoxicity, and even fatal poisoning, and nothing is known about long-term effects of chronic administration. Weighing the risk-benefit balance is clearly important in prescribing antidepressants.

Paralleling the interest in medication has been the search for independent biological "markers" for diagnosing depressive disorder. A major research area with adult patients is the use of the so-called DST (dexamethasone suppression test) in identifying major depression (Leckman, 1983). An abnormal test indicates a failure of suppression, or hypersecretion of cortisol, from activation of the hypothalamic-anterior pituitary-adrenocortical axis. Puig-Antich, Chambers, Halpern, Hanlon, and Sachar (1979) were among the first to demonstrate that prepubertal children with major depressive illness showed a pattern of cortisol excretion similar to that of depressed adults. Poznanski, Carroll, Banegas, Cook, and Grossman (1982) applied this test with 18 6- to 12-year-olds

and found that of the 6 children with abnormal DST's, 5 had major depressive disorder (one false positive), although there were 4 false negatives. Other studies of prepubertal children hospitalized because of "substantial emotional disturbance" confirmed the sensitivity of the DST for depressive disorder but also found that a significant number of children with other serious disorders showed the same phenomenon (Livingston, Reis, & Ringdahl, 1984; Petty, Asarnow, Carlson, & Lesser, 1985). This area of investigation is still controversial and inconclusive, but it suggests a physiological link with psychological experience. The "trigger mechanism" which initiates these biochemical changes has not been identified, leaving us very much in the dark as to primary causes. There have been reports of some normal subjects showing similar changes under psychological stress (Leckman, 1983), so the biochemical alterations may serve both as a cause and as a result.

PSYCHOLOGICAL TREATMENT OF DEPRESSION

In a psychological approach, one would take a more comprehensive view of the child and his environment, carefully considering the possibility that the depression is a response rather than a cause. One must keep in mind that depression is frequently associated with other conditions, and the reactions of discouragement and helplessness may be secondary, thereby perpetuating a vicious circle where the response aggravates the initial problem, for example school failure. In multiple problem cases, the diagnostic process is crucial in identifying basic reasons for the various difficulties and selecting targets for intervention.

Behavioral approaches have been derived from two major etiological constructs: (a) loss of reinforcement, chronic frustration, and lack of control over interpersonal relationships, and (b) negative cognitive set, hopelessness, and helplessness (Petti, 1983b). The first set of constructs emphasizes external reinforcers which result in "learned helplessness," and the second set focuses more on internal characteristics of the child which lead him or her to interpret reality in a certain way—or to behave in a way which has foreseeable negative results. Accordingly, the first order of business is to modify the environment so that the child can legitimately expect positive reinforcement as a consequence of his or her efforts. It is, of course, easier to direct the significant adults in the child's environment than it is to persuade the child's peers to be encouraging in the face of the depressed child's grouchiness or withdrawal. Research with adults has provided some evidence that the depressed person does not behave towards others in a way that is favorably received, leading to the suggestion that environmental response may play an important role in the maintenance of depressed behavior (Coyne, 1976). The depressed person expects to be rejected and behaves in such a way as to fulfill this prophecy. In order to change the picture for children, it may be appropriate to utilize techniques for development of self-control and social skill training so the child can "win friends and influence people," thereby

reducing the secondary effects of depression.

The second order of business would be modifying the child's assumptions and beliefs. Emery, Bedrosian, and Garber (1983) reviewed some techniques of cognitive therapy which are specific to depression, such as self-monitoring to disprove the belief that "nothing is any good"; activity scheduling to include pleasurable activities; graded task assignments to ensure experiences of success; and cognitive change strategies.

The core of cognitive therapy involves examining the validity of the patient's beliefs. In order to challenge their beliefs, patients need to distance themselves from them and to learn that believing something doesn't necessarily make it so.... The therapist's job is to teach children strategies for subjecting their beliefs to critical scrutiny. Once children have learned to identify their thoughts and record them, they should learn the three methods of challenging these beliefs: 1) looking at the evidence, 2) exploring alternative explanations, and 3) examining the consequences if what they believe turns out to be true. (1983, p. 456)

Cognitive therapy tends to be quite structured, analyzing the child's reactions into component parts and tackling one after the other in a sequential fashion. Although it is mentioned in passing, the importance of the relationship with the therapist is not highlighted. However, it is clear that to convince the child that what he has been told, or what he has concluded on his own, is in substantial error requires that the child have considerable faith and trust in the therapist.

As one would expect, child-therapist relationship is emphasized in psychotherapeutic approaches. Bemporad (1978) discusses psychotherapy with depressed children as a developmental experience rather than a discovery, or insight-oriented process.

In brief, therapy with children is much less artificial than with adults; for the child, it is a living relationship with another adult and is treated as part of the totality of the experience. This impiles that the therapist does not spend a great deal of time correcting the child's distortions by verbal interpretations; rather, the therapist demonstrates by his very behavior that he does not accept the child's mistaken estimation of himself and others. (1978, p. 346)

However, the therapist alone cannot do the job; the positive opinions must be validated by the parents as well.

Bemporad described the home atmosphere of the depressed child as frequently "depressing," with a lack of spontaneity, joy, and laughter and a feeling of deadly seriousness. This may bring about a "stifling network of extreme interdependence" in which the child feels part of the parents' mood and burdened with an undue sense of responsibility. This may well explain what Cytryn and McKnew described as a fascinating and unexpected finding that almost all acutely depressed children and even some chronically depressed children improved promptly when admitted to an inpatient service despite the absence of any formal treatment (1979). The "contagion" of depression is neatly confirmed by the laboratory findings with 2-year-olds previously described in the NIMH research project where the children of depressed mothers were un-

duly disturbed by the simulated distress of adults in the situation. Although it may be difficult to change the life-style of the parents, it is imperative to help the child get some psychological distance from their problems and achieve some psychological separation. Considering the crucial importance of the parents in shaping the child's negative self-concept, it is somewhat surprising that family therapy has not been widely used. In part, this may be because family therapy reports are not indexed according to the child's diagnosis, so that such cases are difficult to locate.

TREATMENT EFFICACY

In one sense, treatment outcomes for childhood depression are generally positive, but the effect of any treatment per se is difficult to evaluate because depression usually remits spontaneously at some time or other, with a good chance of recurrence. In a 5-year longitudinal study of 65 children meeting the DSM III criteria for Major Depressive Disorder, Dysthymic Disorder, or Adjustment Disorder with Depressed mood (Kovacs et al., 1984), 92% of the children with major depressive disorder had "recovered" within 18 months of time of onset. As one would expect, the recovery rate was much less impressive for the more chronic dysthymic disorder and much better for those diagnosed as "Adjustment Disorder with Depressed Mood." For those with major depressive disorder, there was a 40% recurrence rate within a 2-year period of "recovery." This study was restricted to statistical analysis of diagnostic information from structured interviews with no control over the therapies received in the participating child psychiatric services. About two-thirds of the depressed cohort had some type of therapy, mainly "some type of conventional psychosocial care" and apparently all on an outpatient basis. Briefly, Kovacs and her colleagues found no clinical advantage for the treated group.

In reviewing the child treatment reports, there are few which combine drug and psychological therapy. Those who report on drug efficacy refer vaguely to some "psychosocial" therapy, usually to indicate that it was not successful, and those who offer psychological case descriptions often fail to distinguish between depression as an affect and depression as a unique disorder. Looking to the adult treatment reports for possible guidelines, combined drug and psychotherapy seems to be more effective than either alone, at least for outpatient populations. Klerman and Schechter (1982) pointed out that drugs and psychotherapy have a different action, operating at different points in the recovery process. Drugs were most helpful early in symptom alleviation, whereas psychotherapy was effective later in areas related to problems in living, social functioning, and interpersonal relationships.

It seems likely that a similar situation holds for children. Puig-Antich and Gittelman (1982) reported on 14 depressed children 3 to 4 months after clinical recovery and discontinuance of antidepressant medication. In comparison with nondepressed emotionally disturbed children, the formerly depressed group showed impaired peer relation-

ships, almost as restricted as during their illness. Also, although the mother-child relationship had improved, it was not considered to be as satisfactory as that demonstrated by the normal or nondepressed, emotionally disturbed groups. This is a very important study, suggesting as it does that vulnerability to depression is linked with special impairment in social relationships—in contrast to the hypothesis that the person has social difficulties because of the depression. From the standpoint of good treatment, it is important to offer continuing psychologically based help after the relief of the acute phase of the depression. The current interest in the biological features of depression should not blind us to the psychological concomitants. Also, both drug therapists and psychotherapists see the problem as essentially coming from within the child (mind or body); we must take care not to overlook real environmental stresses, such as the presence of a depressed or ill parent.

SUICIDAL BEHAVIOR

Completed suicide is extremely unusual before the age of 12 years. In fact, in the period between 1962 and 1968, Shaffer (1974) found that 31 verdicts of suicide in children under 15 years but none under 12 years. The most frequent precipitating cause was a disciplinary crisis (11 cases). There were 3 cases that were directly related to living with a psychotic parent. Almost half of the children had previously discussed, threatened, or attempted suicide, 8 within 24 hours of their death. It is interesting to note that many of these children presented antisocial symptoms rather than "emotional" problems of depressed mood, excessive fears, etc. In discussing the rarity of suicide before 12 years, Shaffer suggested two possibilities, one, that there are changes in the phenomenology of depression at the time of puberty with intensification of feelings of hopelessness, and two, that younger children simply do not have access to or mastery over the means of successful suicide. To carry a suicidal intent to completion requires knowing what will be fatal, obtaining the necessary materials, and selecting a time and place where no one will be watching.

Two recent studies of children between the ages of 5 and 14 hospitalized because of suicidal attempts, by chance 20 in each sample, have emerged with remarkably similar findings. Compared with other child psychiatric populations, the suicidal children had suffered more losses, usually within a year of the suicide attempt. Cohen-Sandler, Berman, and King (1982) found that even compared with a depressed, nonsuicidal group, the suicidal children were confronted more frequently with both temporary and permanent losses of a parent or grandparent due to illness, death, or divorce as well as the stress of a remarriage of one or both parents in the 12 months prior to admission. The idea that suicide could be a road to reunion was expressed by a 5-year-old who tried to hang himself, giving as his reason "to be with my dead brother so my mother will love me like she (still) loves him" (Kosky, 1983, p. 459). One wonders whether this child understood the irreversibility of death, but the poignancy of his statement remains. A 12-year-old explained his three suicidal attempts as an effort to impress upon his mother how much he wanted to return to his grandmother in another state with whom he had lived all his life (Cohen-Sandler et al., 1982), attesting to the fact that a psychological mother may not be the biological one.

Although the majority were recorded in interview as "unhappy" or diagnosed as depressed, the suicidal children were more likely to be angry and hostile rather than withdrawn. Several researchers have noted that depression and conduct disorder may occur concomitantly (Chiles, Miller, & Cox, 1980; Marriage, Fine, Moretti, & Haley, 1986). Hawton, Osborn and O'Grady (1982) noted that adolescents who made repeated suicide attempts were characterized by behavioral disturbances such as truancy, stealing, drug taking, heavy drinking, fighting, and difficulties with the police. Cohen-Sandler et al. reported that nearly two-thirds of the suicidal children also made homicidal threats, gestures, or attempts in contrast to around 10% in the comparison groups. The suicidal children were still enmeshed in love-hate struggles in a no-win situation, sometimes using suicidal behavior to gain revenge or to punish parents who had disciplined them. The transparent motivation sometimes leads to minimization of the behavior, writing off the attempt as "he is just mad" or "she is just trying to get attention." Depression linked with a pattern of acting-out behavior is hard to detect.

Compared to his psychiatrically ill but nonsuicidal group, Kosky found a significantly greater amount of physical violence in the homes of the suicidal group. Two-thirds had witnessed physical fights between their parents and two-thirds had themselves been the target of physical abuse. Similarly, Cohen-Sandler et al. observed that the "parents of suicidal children we studied seemed to have more impulsive coping styles than those of other children; they abused alcohol and/or drugs more often and engaged in earlier and more frequent marital unions and separations" (p. 184). Clearly the suicidal children had parental models for acting on feelings, but it is not so clear why they chose to act against themselves. It is possible that they might have been frightened by the dire consequences or the total uselessness of aggression against others, or there may have been more complex reasons for choosing themselves as victims.

One is left with the distinct impression that the rarity of completed suicide before age 12 reflects problems of execution rather than differences in aim. In Kosky's words,

The suicidal children in this study were serious in intent, they wished to die and they were secretive in their purpose. After surviving their attempt a quarter exhibited a classical picture of depressive illness and were so diagnosed, but the majority of the others were angry, frightened and unhappy children. (1983, p. 465)

A suicidal attempt, no matter how poorly conceived, sends a clear message of desperation.

BEREAVEMENT IN CHILDHOOD

The following discussion is restricted to children's responses to loss through death. Many writers combine bereavement responses with the grieving which may follow losses through desertion and divorce or any kind of separation, but we have chosen to consider many of these other topics as "stressors" (see Chapter 13). Loss through death is unique in its finality and also because it forces one to think about one's own mortality. Loss through death is a great deal more than loss by physical distance or absence of communication. The chief concern will be the effect of the loss of a parent, which is not as uncommon as one might think. Witmer (1965) reported that as of 1961, 4.3% of children up to age 18 years had lost one parent by death, and Furman (1974) cited a 4.7% figure from the 1971 Statistical Abstract of the U.S. The major issues have to do with (a) the process of affective detachment, and (b) the child's cognitive understanding of death.

What Is Mourning?

Just as Rie wrote that children were incapable of a "true" depression of the same structure as an adult depression, Wolfenstein (1966) concluded that children were developmentally incapable of "true" mourning before adolescence. In the Wolfenstein argument, major assumptions are made with regard to the process of mourning in adult persons, whereas in fact adults show more variation in response than would be expected from Freud's original description. From her observations of a sizable number of bereaved children, Furman (1974) concluded that "no parent who had lost his spouse fully conformed to the model of adult mourning portrayed by Freud (1915). Those parents who bore the pain of mourning or who could be helped to do so did not altogether withdraw into their grief" (p. 58).

It is surprising that there are so few firsthand accounts of bereavement responses written by psychologists, considering that most of us have had some experience with personal loss. It is relatively easy to communicate and empathize with the initial stage of sorrow, but there are so many other delayed reactions. In her insightful description of her responses to the death of her husband, Helen Hayes explained

It wasn't just grief. It was total confusion. . . . That's a time I look back on and flinch to think of, because I was most unattractive. Unreliable and erratic, I squabbled with directors—I had never squabbled before. I took umbrage at nothing at all. I gave rather pompous and silly statements to the press. I was nutty, and that's the truth. How did I come out of it? I don't know, because I didn't know when I was in it that I was in it. (O'Brien, 1973, p. 234)

The feelings of being betrayed, deserted, and alone make children of us all. Then there are delayed reactions of painful flashbacks, guilt about "forgetting" or making significant changes which would be unrecognizable or unacceptable to the person who died which seem to go on indefinitely. For some bereaved persons, recovery may involve a willingness to look for new relationships. But "some cultivation of the sense of the deceased and continued emotional involvement with the deceased are common and should not be viewed as pathological even if continued for years" (Clayton, 1982, p. 403). Chronological age is one important factor in shaping the process of mourning, but other important factors include the rela-

tionship with the person who died, the availability of other significant relationships, the circumstances of the death, and the patterns which one has developed for handling feelings. It is a mistake to use a single model to represent "normal mourning." For varying periods of time, there will be more or less obvious disruptions in "normal" behavior until a new equilibrium is achieved.

Bereavement Responses in Children

Compared with adults, children are more likely to hide their feelings and to seek a semblance of everything being the same as quickly as possible. Part of this is in the nature of children, and part of it comes from adults' reluctance to see a child grieve. Wolfenstein (1966) observed that with children, sad feelings were curtailed; there was little weeping, and involvement in the activities of everyday life continued. The child did not appear to engage in reminiscing about the lost person, a process which serves to underscore the permanence of the loss for adult persons and to pave the way for detachment. In her treatment cases, the children continued in various ways to deny the irrevocability of the loss. She acknowledged the fact that her cases might represent exceptions, but even in an instance of what she termed an "adaptive reaction," she observed an immediate attachment to the available substitute parent without evidence of mourning. However, this might have been deceiving, as this boy's mother had been seriously ill for some time and there had been a gradual transfer of care prior to her death. His mother, a psychologist, had invested a good deal in helping him to separate from her so that much of the loss and mourning had already taken place when she died. Adults also show a different pattern of reaction if there has been a debilitating illness with suffering and major changes in the person who died.

Since Wolfenstein's paper there has been a growing consensus that children, at least by 5 years, are capable of mourning. In addition to clinical case reports, there have been investigations of bereavement responses in "normal" children. In a longitudinal study of 25 preadolescent kibbutz children who lost their fathers in the Israeli war of 1973, Kaffman and Elizur (1983) found that about half exhibited severe and persistent behavior problems as long as 42 months after the death. When compared with a sample of bereaved children living in urban settings, there was little difference in the overall prevalence of continued disturbance. They reported that younger children were more spontaneous in their expression of feelings and memories and more frequently denied the finality of death. The responses of the city children compared with the kibbutz children were more like the preschoolers (e.g., more sleeping problems and separation difficulties). But despite the variety of affective grief responses and reactive behavior problems, the loss of the father was a major traumatic event for the majority. Particularly with regard to the kibbutz children, whom they regarded as having so many social supports, the authors expressed surprise about "the high incidence, severity and persistence of clinical manifestations in a sample of normal children with no special problems before the loss" (Kaffman & Elizur, 1983, p. 435).

There are two necessary conditions for mourning. The first is that the child has achieved object constancy (see Chapter 1) because "In order to remember with longing that he experienced the loss of a love object, a child must have reached the beginning of the stage of object constancy" (Furman, 1974, p. 41). The second condition, which would follow the first by a matter of years, is the understanding that death is final. "We concluded that the reality of death was the sine qua non of mourning because this reality implied a special finality. For the bereaved person the full work of mourning became possible only when such a reality could be perceived, comprehended and acknowledged" (Furman, 1974, p. 49). To appreciate "forever," the young child must have some notion of the future. Allowing for individual variation, by 4 or 5 years, children meet these two conditions.

Children's Conceptions of Death

Without reference to the affective aspects of bereavement, we discussed children's concerns about death as an abstract concept in Chapter 5. With few exceptions, by the age of 6, children "know" that death is permanent although they may wish otherwise. For example, the author's granddaughter, at age 6 years, surprised her family by starting her Christmas list with a wish that her grandfather, who had died when she was 4, would be alive again. This was not so much a reflection of her personal loss as a wish to be rid of what she called her "horrified feeling" when he died. Of greatest interest to the young child is what happens to the body.

Whether it is disposed of by cremation or burial, this is hard to explain without "horror." The disposal of the body makes it very clear something momentous has occurred which is like nothing else.

However, there are exceptions to the rule. In Koocher's study of "normal" children between the ages of 6 to 15 years, he found that 8 of the 75 thought that dead things could be brought back to life; he related this to their general cognitive level, which was "preoperational" as defined by failure on conservation tasks (1973). Also, there are religious differences. Kaffman and Elizur found that about half of the city children denied the finality of death, relying on ideas about the coming of the Messiah and resurrection of the dead (1983). One mother did not tell her child that the father's body was buried in a grave. "These examples clearly demonstrate how religious belief, or the adult's difficulty in coping with the finality of death, strengthens the child's tendency to denial and makes it difficult for him to understand the concept of irreversibility and the full meaning of death" (Kaffman & Elizur, p. 440).

Children also formulate reasons for the occurrence of death, usually in terms of illness or advanced age. The concept of "old" is, of course, a relative one and the children in Koocher's study suggested everything from 7 years (offered by a 6-year-old) to a high of 300 years (suggested by a 9-year-old). However, in some manner children seek an explanation which gives the problem some predictability. Despite one's knowledge of the inevitability of death, everyone cherishes the notion that at least it can be postponed by taking precautions.

This may lead to assignment of personal responsibility—the doctor overlooked something, or the patient did not take the right care in some respect. It is not surprising that in the special instance of sibling death, children frequently feel guilty not only because of something they did or didn't do, but also because they are still alive. The guilt reactions can take many forms—accident-prone behavior, provocative acting out, avoidance of success, or even "super-good" behavior (Cain, Fast, & Erickson, 1964). There is always something to feel guilty about, whether it be a real act of meanness, an omission rather than a commission, or simply feelings of resentment which are always present to some degree in close relationships. The therapeutic task is to recognize the source of guilt and to discover that it was irrelevant to the fact of dying.

Special Role of Identification

One way of keeping a person alive is by doing the same things and acting in the same way so that the dead person leaves less of a void. With an adult person, this identification is probably a useful part of mourning, but with bereaved children it may be less useful and stand in the way of forming new relationships. The child may identify with the ill parent whom they may recall more vividly than they do the well parent. This identification leads directly to the possibility of their own death with all the ensuing fears. Or the child may "freeze time" by identifying with the nurturance that a parent would give a very young child, thus inhibiting further growth and development. If the child can be helped to identify with the healthy parent with some flexibility, the result can be adaptive. It is also true that the child will make a lot of comparisons as other people attempt to take over the parental role, resenting both similarities and differences. Although the child must be assured that he will get continuing love and care, no one should try to offer a carbon copy. There are different ways to love and different people to love, and new love does not destroy an old one. One has only to recall the feelings of deprivation experienced by a young child after the birth of a sibling to appreciate the child's doubts on this score, however.

Cain, Fast and Erickson (1964) observed that about 40% of the children with siblings who had died showed either immediate, prolonged, or "anniversary" identifications with the dead child's prominent symptoms. It is clear that the parents should avoid comparisons and make it clear that the surviving child is loved for him or herself and is in no way expected to be a replacement. Surprisingly, some parents are quite insensitive to this issue, even to the extent of changing a child's name to that of the one who died!

Helping the Child to Cope

The bereaved child needs both to know the facts and to share the feelings. Information about the cause of death helps to counteract guilty feelings, and information about the nature of death works against fantasies of ghostly beings or future reunion. Religious explanations of the "hereafter" which may comfort the adult who recognizes the spiritual meaning of the concept, probably will confuse the child who thinks in concrete terms and expects a body that eats, sleeps, talks, and so on. Many questions are asked about having the child attend funeral services. Except for very young children, this is usually a good idea if others are able to pay some attention to the child's feelings at the time.

The young child needs to be assured that his or her life will continue and that food, clothes, bedtime, school, holidays, and so on will be provided. Despite this necessary reassurance, the child's doubts and fears should be acknowledged with the sadness. The remaining parent or grandparents should share their sorrow with the child even as they pick up the pieces and try to reestablish a pattern of family life. As Brice said,

It is important to remember that familial stability is the bedrock of the latency child's self-esteem. Here again, the tendency to personalize the death is an issue. The child needs help in understanding that mommy didn't die because she didn't love him/her. (1982, p. 318)

It is particularly important for the adults to avoid their own self-recriminations or specific regrets and to acknowledge their helplessness in the face of death in contrast to their ability to cope with living.

The Relationship of Parental Loss and Adult Adjustment

Numerous studies have investigated the association of parental death during childhood and risk of adult depressive disorders. One review led to the conclusion that parental death during childhood has not been proven to be a special cause of adult depression (Crook &

Eliot, 1980) whereas Tennant, Bebbington, and Hurry, reviewing virtually the same material, concluded that "parental death in childhood has some effect, albeit weak, upon risk of adult depression" (1980, p. 297). In most reports, the risk of illness in bereaved subjects was less than twice that in nonbereaved. The weakness of these retrospective findings by no means trivializes the experience of parental loss; it simply means that there are many interacting causes for adult depressive disorders, and no single biographical event suffices to explain depression. There is evidence that risk of adult illness varies with the subject's age at parental death; Birtchnell (1970) found a difference for those whose parents died when the child was between 0 and 9 years and no difference for those whose parents died between 10 and 19 years. Similarly, Caplan and Douglas (1969) found that 11.3% of depressive children compared to 3.8% of nondepressed neurotic children had lost a parent by death before the child reached age 8, which lends support to the relationship between early object loss and later depression. However, experiences that follow parental loss also play an important role, as witness the larger number of depressive children who had been placed in a foster home. Clearly, early object loss followed by object replacement has much less permanent impact than early object loss followed by continuing disruptions in relationships.

SUMMARY

After years of denial and neglect, depression in childhood has become a topic of great interest. Methods of operationalizing definitions of depression as an affect (mainly measured by self-report inventories) and as a disorder (following the DSM III criteria) have been developed and are widely used for standardization. In the medical literature, there have been many comparisons between childhood and adult depression with studies of drug responses, remission and recurrence patterns, family factors, and psychophysiological findings. Much of this has been dominated by the question of whether depression in these two periods of life are basically the same illness. An affirmative answer would seem to support a biogenetic explanation.

However, there are significant differences in presentation if not in cause between adult and childhood depression. Typically, children do not describe themselves as "feeling sad," and parents often fail to recognize this emotional response, so it is elicited only by careful inquiry. Depressed children usually have other serious presenting symptoms, and it is difficult to determine what is primary and what is secondary. With children, guilt seems to play a lesser role than the loss of self-esteem. Preschoolers become depressed when they feel unloved and school-age children when they feel inferior. Older children approaching adolescence begin to blame themselves for what they perceive as the appraisal of others and at that point project a hopeless future.

Evaluation of treatment effectiveness is confounded by the naturally episodic nature of depression. Although drug therapy has proven useful for some and probably should be considered in the acute phase, exclusive reliance on this mode of treatment is unwarranted and one should keep in mind the possible toxicity of the drugs in common use. Even if there is a constitutional vulnerability, the actual emergence of a depressive reaction has other important parameters such as "joyless" home atmosphere and unsatisfying peer relationships. Also, there are internal parameters of fantasies and expectations which color the child's perception of reality. A comprehensive diagnosis of depression should include more than the presenting symptoms in order to formulate a treatment plan which focuses on the features specific to the situation.

The topic of depression naturally brings up the subject of death and dying. Although depressed children often think of dying, rarely are they successful in taking their lives prior to adolescence, partly because they lack the necessary know-how. Suicidal children are not simply more depressed; they have some special characteristics and family background factors which promote acting out feelings in behavior. These children have experienced relatively more chaotic and unpredictable life events, including loss of a parent and parental models for acting out. It is commonly observed that these children are as much enraged as they are depressed by the situations in which they find themselves.

Bereavement occupies a central place in a discussion of depression, and some have taken it as the prototype. Children and adults alike feel unhappy following a significant loss, although the manifestations of mourning vary with age, the nature of the relationship, and the available emotional supports. Helping children to cope requires realistic explana-

tions of the nature and cause of the death, reassurance that the child will continue to be loved and taken care of, disentanglement from morbid identifications, relief from guilt and responsibility, and the opportunity to share sadness with others. Some significant losses (not necessariy from death) are inevitable in the process of growing up and the child who does not feel sad as a consequence is unlikely to feel joy on other occasions. In a predictable life situation where one can reasonably expect affection and personal gratifications, one recovers from the sadness elicited by a specific event.

REFERENCES

ACHENBACH, T. M. (1978). The Child Behavior Profile: I. Boys aged 6–11. *Journal of Consulting and Clinical Psychology, 46*, 478–488.

BEARDSLEE, W. R., BEMPORAD, J., KELLER, M. B., & KLERMAN, G. L. (1983). Children of parents with major affective disorder: A review. *American Journal of Psychiatry, 140*, 825–832.

BEMPORAD, J. (1978). Psychodynamics of depression and suicide in children and adolescents. In S. Arieti & J. Bemporad (Eds.), *Severe and mild depression* (pp. 185–207). New York: Basic Books.

BIBRING, E. (1953). The mechanism of depression. In P. Greenacre (Ed.), *Affective disorders* (pp. 13–49). New York: International Universities Press.

BIRTCHNELL, J. (1970). The relationship between attempted suicide, depression and parent death. *British Journal of Psychiatry, 116*, 307–313.

BRICE, C. W. (1982). Mourning throughout the life cycle. *American Journal of Psychoanalysis, 42*, 315–324.

BRUMBACK, R. A., DIETZ-SCHMIDT, S. G., & WEINBERG, W. A. (1977). Depression in children referred to an educational diagnostic center: Diagnosis and treatment and analysis of criteria and literature review. *Diseases of the Nervous System, 38,* 529–535.

CADORET, R. J. (1978). Evidence for genetic inheritance of primary affective disorder in adoptees. *American Journal of Psychiatry, 135,* 463–466.

CAIN, A. C., FAST, I., & ERICKSON, M. E. (1964). Children's disturbed reactions to the death of a sibling. *American Journal of Orthopsychiatry, 34,* 741–752.

CANTWELL, D. P. (1983). Family genetic factors. In E. P. Cantwell & G. A. Carlson (Eds.), *Affective disorders in childhood and adolescence: An update* (pp. 249–265). New York: Spectrum.

CAPLAN, M. G., & DOUGLAS, V. I. (1969). Incidence of parental loss in children with depressed mood. *Journal of Child Psychology and Psychiatry, 10,* 225–232.

CARLSON, G. A., & CANTWELL, D. P. (1980a). Unmasking masked depression in children and adolescents. *American Journal of Psychiatry, 137,* 445–449.

CARLSON, G. A., & CANTWELL, D. P. (1980b). A survey of depressive symptoms, syndrome and disorder in a child psychiatric population. *Journal of Child Psychology and Psychiatry, 21,* 19–25.

CHAMBERS, W., PUIG-ANTICH, J., & TABRIZI, M. A. (1978). *The on-going development of the Kiddie-SADS (Schedule for Affective Disorders and Schizophrenia for School-Age Children).* Presented at the American Academy of Child Psychiatry, San Diego, California.

CHILES, J., MILLER, M., & COX, G. (1980). Depression in an adolescent delinquent population. *Archives of General Psychiatry, 37,* 179–183.

CLAYTON, P. J. (1982). Bereavement. In E. S. Paykel (Ed.), *Handbook of Affective Disorders* (pp. 403–415). New York: Guilford Press.

COHEN-SANDLER, R., BERMAN, A. L., & KING, R. A. (1982). Life stress and symptomatology: Determinants of suicidal behavior in children. *Journal of the American Academy of Child Psychiatry, 21,* 178–186.

COYNE, J. C. (1976). Depression and the response of others. *Journal of Abnormal Psychology, 85,* 186–193.

CROOK, T., & ELIOT, J. (1980). Parental death during childhood and adult depression: a critical review of the literature. *Psychological Bulletin, 87,* 252–260.

CYTRYN, L., & MCKNEW, D. H. (1972). Proposed classification of childhood depression. *American Journal of Psychiatry, 129,* 149–155.

CYTRYN, L., & MCKNEW, D. H. (1979). Affective disorders. In J. D. Noshpitz (Ed.), *Basic handbook of child psychiatry* (pp. 321–340). New York: Basic Books.

CYTRYN, L., MCKNEW, D. H., & BUNNEY, W. E. (1980). Diagnosis of depression in children: A reassessment. *American Journal of Psychiatry, 137,* 22–25.

DORPAT, T. L. (1977). Depressive affect. In R. S. Eissler, A. Freud, M. Kris, P. B. Neubauer, & A. J. Solnit (Eds.), *Psychoanalytic study of the child* (Vol. 32, pp. 3–28). New Haven: Yale University Press.

ELIZUR, E., & KAFFMAN, M. (1983). Factors influencing the severity of childhood bereavement reactions. *American Journal of Orthopsychiatry, 53,* 668–676.

ELLIS, N. (1962). *Reason and emotion in psychotherapy.* New York: Lyle Stuart.

EMERY, G., BEDROSIAN, R., & GARBER, J. (1983). Cognitive therapy with depressed children and adolescents. In D. P. Cantwell & G. A. Carlson (Eds.), *Affective disorders in childhood and adolescence* (pp. 445–472). Jamaica, NY: Spectrum.

FREUD, S. (1957). *Mourning and melancholia.* In L. Strachey (Ed. and Trans.), *The Standard edition of the complete psychological works of Sigmund Freud* (Vol. 14, pp. 243–260). London: Hogarth Press. (Original work published 1917)

FURMAN, E. (1974). *A child's parent dies.* New Haven: Yale University Press.

GHODSIAN, M., ZAJICEK, E., & WOLKIND, S. (1984). A longitudinal study of maternal depression and child behaviour problems. *Journal of Child Psychology and Psychiatry, 25,* 91–111.

GITTELMAN-KLEIN, R., & KLEIN, D. F. (1971). Controlled imipramine treatment of school phobia. *Archives of General Psychiatry, 25,* 204–207.

HAWTON, K., OSBORN, M., & O'GRADY, J. (1982). Classification of adolescents who take overdoses. *British Journal of Psychiatry, 140,* 124–141.

HUGHES, M. C. (1984). Recurrent abdominal pain and childhood depression: Clinical observations of 23 children and their families. *American Journal of Orthopsychiatry, 54,* 146–156.

KAFFMAN, M., & ELIZUR, E. (1983). Bereavement responses of kibbutz and non-kibbutz children following the death of the father. *Journal of Child Psychology and Psychiatry, 24,* 435–442.

KASHANI, J. H., BARBERO, G. T., & BOLANDER, F. D. (1981). Depression in hospitalized pediatric patients. *Journal of the American Academy of Child Psychiatry, 20,* 123–134.

KASHANI, J. H., CANTWELL, D. P., SHEKIM, W. O., & REID, J. C. (1982). Major depressive disorder in children admitted to an inpatient community mental health center. *American Journal of Psychiatry, 139,* 671–672.

KASHANI, J. H., & SIMONDS, J. F. (1979). The incidence of depression in children. *American Journal of Psychiatry, 136,* 1203–1205.

KAZDIN, A. E., FRENCH, N. H., UNIS, A. S., & ESVELDT-DAWSON, K. (1983). Assessment of childhood depression: Correspondence of child and parent ratings. *Journal of the American Academy of Child Psychiatry, 22,* 157–164.

KAZDIN, A. E., & PETTI, T. A. (1982). Self-report and interview measures of childhood and adolescent depression. *Journal of*

Child Psychology and Psychiatry, 23, 437–457.

KLERMAN, G. L., & SCHECHTER, G. (1982). Drugs and psychotherapy. In E. S. Paykel (Ed.), *Handbook of affective disorders* (pp. 329–337). New York: Guilford Press.

KOOCHER, G. P. (1973). Childhood, death and cognitive development. *Developmental Psychology, 9,* 369–375.

KOSKY, R. (1983). Childhood suicidal behaviour. *Journal of Child Psychology and Psychiatry, 24,* 457–469.

KOVACS, M. (1978). *Interview Schedule for Children (ISC)* (19th revision). Pittsburgh, PA: University of Pittsburgh School of Medicine.

KOVACS, M., & BECK, A. T. (1977). An empirical clinical approach toward the definition of childhood depression. In J. G. Schulterbrandt & A. Raskin (Eds.), *Depression in childhood* (pp. 1–25). New York: Raven Press.

KOVACS, M., FEINBERG, T. L., CROUSE-NOVAK, M., PAULAUSKAS, S. L., POLLOCK, M., & FINKELSTEIN, R. (1984). Depressive disorders in childhood: II. A longitudinal study of the risk for a subsequent major depression. *Archives of General Psychiatry, 41,* 643–650.

LECKMAN, J. F. (1983). Editorial: The Dexamethasone Suppression Test. *Journal of the American Academy of Child Psychiatry, 22,* 477–479.

LEFKOWITZ, M. M., & BURTON, N. (1978). Childhood depression: A critique of the concept. *Psychological Bulletin, 85,* 716–726.

LEFKOWITZ, M., & TESINY, E. P. (1980). Assessment of childhood depression. *Journal of Consulting Clinical Psychologists, 48,* 43–51.

LEFKOWITZ, M. M., & TESINY, E. P. (1981). *The epidemiology of depression in normal children.* Presented at the American Association for the Advancement of Science, Toronto.

LEFKOWITZ, M. M., & TESINY, E. P. (1985). Depression in children: Prevalence and correlates. *Journal of Consulting and Clinical Psychology, 53,* 647–657.

LIVINGSTON, R., REIS, C. J., & RINGDAHL, I. C. (1984). Abnormal dexamethasone suppression test results in depressed and nondepressed children. *American Journal of Psychiatry, 141,* 106–107.

MALMQUIST, C. P. (1972). Depressive phenomena in children. In B. B. Wolman (Ed.), *Manual of Child Psychopathology* (pp. 497–540). New York: McGraw-Hill.

MALMQUIST, C. P. (1983). Major depression in childhood: Why don't we know more? *American Journal of Orthopsychiatry, 53,* 262–268.

MARRIAGE, K., FINE, S., MORETTI, M., & HALEY, G. (1986). Relationship between depression and conduct disorder in children and adolescents. *Journal of the American Academy of Child Psychiatry, 25,* 687–691.

McKNEW, D. H., CYTRYN, L., & EFFRON, A. M. (1979). Offspring of patients with affective disorders. *British Journal of Psychiatry, 134,* 140–152.

MENDLEWICZ, J., & RAINER, J. D. (1977). Adoption study supporting genetic transmission in manic-depressive illness. *Nature, 268,* 327–329.

O'BRIEN, P. (1973). *The woman alone.* New York: Quadrangle.

OSSOFSKY, H. J. (1974). Endogenous depression in infancy and childhood. *Comprehensive Psychiatry, 15,* 19–25.

PETTI, T. A. (1978). Depression in hospitalized child psychiatry patients. *Journal of the American Academy of Child Psychiatry, 176,* 49–58.

PETTI, T. A. (1983a). Imipramine in the treatment of depressed children. In D. P. Cantwell & G. A. Carlson (Eds.), *Affective disorders in childhood and adolescence* (pp. 375–416). New York: Spectrum.

PETTI, T. A. (1983b). Behavioral approaches in the treatment of depressed children. In D. P. Cantwell & G. A. Carlson (Eds.), *Affective disorders in childhood and adolescence* (pp. 417–444). New York: Spectrum.

PETTI, L. K., ASARNOW, J. R., CARLSON, G. A., & LESSER, L. (1985). The dexamethasone suppression test in depressed, dysthymic and nondepressed children. *American Journal of Psychiatry, 142,* 631–633.

POZNANSKI, E. O., CARROLL, B. J., BANEGAS, M. D., COOK, S. C., & GROSSMAN, J. A. (1982). The dexamethasone suppression test in prepubertal depressed children. *American Journal of Psychiatry, 139,* 321–324.

POZNANSKI, E. O., COOK, S. C., & CARROLL, B. J. (1979). A depression rating scale for children. *Pediatrics, 64,* 442–450.

PUIG-ANTICH, J. (1982). Major depression and conduct disorder in prepuberty. *Journal of the American Academy of Child Psychiatry, 21,* 118–128.

PUIG-ANTICH, J. (1986). Psychobiological markers: Effects of age and puberty. In M. Rutter, C. E. Izard, & P. B. Read (Eds.), *Depression in young people: Developmental and clinical perspectives* (pp. 341–382). New York: Guilford Press.

PUIG-ANTICH, J., BLAU, S., MARX, N., GREENHILL, L. L., & CHAMBERS, W. (1978). Prepubertal major depressive disorder: A pilot study. *Journal of the American Academy of Child Psychiatry, 17,* 695–707.

PUIG-ANTICH, J., CHAMBERS, W., HALPERN, F., HANLON, C., & SACHAR, E. J. (1979). Cortisol hypersecretion in prepubertal depressive illness. *Psychoneuroendocrinology, 4,* 191–197.

PUIG-ANTICH, J., & GITTELMAN, R. (1982). Depression in childhood and adolescence. In E. S. Paykel (Ed.), *Handbook of affective disorders* (pp. 379–392). New York: Guilford Press.

RAPOPORT, J. L., & MIKKELSEN, E. J. (1978). Antidepressants. In J. Werry (Ed.), *Pediatric psychopharmacology: The use of behavior modifying drugs in children* (pp. 208–233). New York: Brunner/Mazel.

RIE, H. E. (1966). Depression in childhood: A survey of some pertinent contributions. *Journal of the American Academy of Child Psychiatry, 5,* 653–685.

RUTTER, M., GRAHAM, P., CHADWICK, O., &

YULE, W. (1976). Adolescent turmoil, fact or fiction? *Journal of Child Psychology and Psychiatry, 17,* 35–56.

RUTTER, M., TIZARD, J., & WHITMORE, K. (1970). *Education, health, and behavior: Psychological and medical study of childhood development.* New York: Wiley.

SANDLER, J., & JOFFE, W. G. (1965). Notes on childhood depression. *International Journal of Psychoanalysis, 46,* 88–96.

SCHULTERBRANDT, J. G., & RASKIN, A. (Eds.). (1977). *Depression in children: Diagnosis, treatment and conceptual models.* New York: Raven Press.

SHAFFER, D. (1974). Suicide in childhood and early adolescence. *Journal of Child Psychology and Psychiatry, 15,* 275–291.

SPERLING, M. (1959). Equivalents of depression in children. *Journal of Hillside Hospital, 8,* 138–148.

SPITZ, R., & WOLF, K. M. (1946). Anaclitic depression: An inquiry into the genesis of psychiatric conditions in early childhood. In A. Freud, H. Hartmann, & E. Kris (Eds.), *Psychoanalytic study of the child* (Vol. 2, pp. 313–342). New York: International Universities Press.

SPITZER, R. L., ENDICOTT, J., & ROBINS, E. (1978). Research diagnostic criteria: Rationale and reliability. *Archives of General Psychiatry, 35,* 773–779.

SROUFE, L. A., & RUTTER, M. (1984). The domain of developmental psychopathology. *Child Development, 55,* 17–30.

TENNANT, C., BEBBINGTON, P., & HURRY, J. (1980). Parental death in childhood and risk of adult depressive disorders: A review. *Psychological Medicine, 10,* 289–299.

TESINY, E. P., & LEFKOWITZ, M. M. (1982). Childhood and depression: A 6-month follow-up study. *Journal of Consulting and Clinical Psychology, 50,* 778–780.

TISHER, M., & LANG, M. (1983). The Children's Depression Scale: Review and further developments. In D. P. Cantwell & G. A. Carlson (Eds.), *Affective disorders in childhood and adolescence* (pp. 181–205). New York: Spectrum.

WEINBERG, W. A., RUTMAN, J., SULLIVAN, L., PENICK, E. C., & DIETZ, S. G. (1973). Depression in children referred to an educational diagnostic center: Diagnosis and treatment. *Behavioral Pediatrics, 83,* 1065–1072.

WESSMAN, M. M., ORVASCHEL, H., & PADIAN, N. (1980). Children's symptoms and social functioning self-report scales: Comparison of mothers' and children's reports. *Journal of Nervous and Mental Disorders, 168,* 736–740.

WELNER, Z., WELNER, A., & McCRARY, M. D. (1977). Psychopathology in children of inpatients with depression: A controlled study. *Journal of Nervous and Mental Disorders, 164,* 408–413.

WITMER, H. L. (1965). National facts and figures about children without families. *Journal of the American Academy of Child Psychiatry, 4,* 249–253.

WOLFENSTEIN, M. (1966). How is mourning possible? In R. S. Eissler, A. Freud, H. Hartmann, & M. Kris (Eds.), *Psychoanalytic study of the child* (Vol. 21, pp. 93–104). New York: International Universities Press.

ZAHN-WAXLER, C., CUMMINGS, E. M., IANNOTTI, R. J., & RADKE-YARROW, M. (1984). Young offspring of depressed parents: A population at risk for affective problems. In D. Cicchetti & K. Schneider-Rosen (Eds.), *New directions for child development: Childhood depression.* San Francisco: Jossey Bass.

ZEITLIN, H. (1985). *The natural history of psychiatric disorder in childhood.* Institute of Psychiatry/Maudsley Monograph. London: Oxford University Press.

ZIS, A. P., & GOODWIN, F. K. (1982). The amine hypothesis. In E. S. Paykel (Ed.), *Handbook of affective disorders* (pp. 175–187). New York: Guilford Press.

CHAPTER 10

CONDUCT DISORDERS

DEFINITION

It is difficult to draw the boundary lines for all the diagnostic categories of childhood problems, but "conduct disorders" is perhaps the worst offender. The term is used to cover all kinds of behaviors which are unacceptable to others, from simple defiance and noncompliance to aggressive assaults. Such children have always been with us but under different names. Some of the terms were frankly pejorative. In statutes originating in 1654, The Commonwealth of Massachusetts identified "the stubborn child" and permitted the courts to commit such children, along with various other kinds of "undesirables," to imprisonment for no more than 6 months. It was not until 1974 that the law was changed and the classifications of Stubborn Child, Runaway, Truant, and Habitual School Of-

fender were changed from "criminal" to "Children in Need of Services" (Devlin, 1985).

Bernal, Duryee, Pruett, and Burns (1968) coined the term "brat syndrome" to describe a child who often engages in tantrums, assaultiveness, threats, and other aversive behavior. Other terms, such as antisocial personality, psychopathic, or sociopathic personality, have been used as diagnostic categories. Although they appear less judgmental, the inclusion of the word "personality" implied a pervasive and serious defect of conscience. The current term of "conduct disorders" was chosen for the DSM III as part of the intent to be atheoretical and descriptive. Conduct disorder children do "bad" things but it is not satisfactory to explain this on the basis of an inherent "badness" in the child.

In 1931, Ackerson differentiated between "personality problems" and "conduct problems" on the basis that the former causes internal discomfort and the latter creates discomfort for others. Without reference to this early work, some 30 years later, Peterson suggested the term "conduct problem" for "a tendency to express impulses against society" (1961, p. 208). These distinctions parallel the two principal factors which invariably emerge from factorial analyses of symptom behavior, namely, outer-directedness or undercontrolled type and inner-directedness or the overcontrolled type (see Chapter 7).

The DSM-III describes the essential feature of conduct disorder as "a repetitive and persistent pattern of conduct in which either the basic rights of others or major age-appropriate societal norms or rules are violated." In DSM-III-R (APA, 1987), the diagnostic criteria specify that at least 3 of a list of 13 antisocial acts must have occurred in the past 6 months. Isolated acts may be coded as Childhood Antisocial Behavior in the supplementary "V Code" covering conditions that are a focus of treatment but are not attributable to a mental disorder. There is an overlap with "oppositional disorder," defined as "a pattern of disobedient, negativistic, and provocative opposition to authority figures" but where less real harm is done to others. Also, attention deficit disorder with hyperactivity is a common associated diagnosis since it almost always gets the child into difficulties. For example, in a population referred to as a child psychiatry clinic, 61% were diagnosed as either hyperactive, unsocialized aggressive, or both. Three out of four children with an aggressive conduct disorder were also hyperactive, and two out of

three hyperactive children also had conduct disorder (Stewart, Cummings, Singer, & DeBlois, 1981). DSM-III-R includes Attention-deficit Hyperactivity Disorder, Oppositional Defiant Disorder, and Conduct Disorder under the rubric of "Disruptive Behavior Disorders."

SUBCLASSIFICATION OF CONDUCT DISORDERS

The DSM III proposes four subclassifications on the basis of the presence or absence of serious aggressive behavior and whether or not the general personality can be veiwed as "undersocialized" or "socialized." DSM-III-R retains the distinction between "isolated aggressive type" ("undersocialized") and the "group type" ("socialized") but drops the second distinction between "aggressive" and "nonaggressive," adding a catch-all "undifferentiated type."

The difference between isolated and group conduct disorders refers to the presence or absence of significant social attachments, particularly with peers. Much has been made of this in considering causes of delinquency. The child who is a loyal member of a delinquent gang may be following the patterns of behavior highly regarded in a subculture of his neighborhood. In contrast, the undersocialized conduct disorder child has no close friends and obeys no rules so that the resultant behavior is much more unpredictable and erratic. Henn, Bardwell, and Jenkins (1980) used this subclassification in their 12-year follow-up study of institutionalized delinquents and found, as one would expect, that the socialized group had a better outcome in terms of later confrontations with the law.

Other investigators have attempted to classify conduct disorders in terms of the nature of the misconduct. The symptom list includes such behaviors as running away, truancy, lying, stealing, fire-setting, physical cruelty, and initiating fights. Although they are all violations of societal rules, these behaviors may be quite different in psychological structure. Aggression is an immediate, overt response against some person, usually unpremeditated and impulsive. Running away or lying, on the other hand, may represent ways of avoiding aggressive confrontation. Stealing is still another matter. It may be an impulsive reaction to opportunity; it may have some symbolic significance as in kleptomania; or it may be carefully planned with a definite purpose in mind. In every case, however, it is covert and some planning is required in the cover-up. From the analysis of the combined results of 22 studies which reported child behavior ratings, Loeber and Schmaling (1985) confirmed the overt-covert distinction in antisocial behaviors and suggested that treatment approaches should be equally distinctive.

In a follow-up study, Moore, Chamberlain, and Mukai (1979) found that stealing was far more predictive of later adolescent delinquency (77%) than aggression at home without stealing (13%). Patterson (1982) reported significant differences in parental characteristics. The parents of boys who stole tended to be more distant and uninvolved in comparison to the punitive environment of the families of aggressive boys. Also, these parents tended to be casual about property rights and to overlook incidents in

the home or incidents involving objects of little monetary value. All of this suggests that conduct disorders constitute a heterogeneous group of behaviors which defy simple generalizations.

Prevalence and Prognosis

It is clear that those behaviors which disturb adults are the most frequent reasons for referral. Aggressiveness, conduct disorder, and antisocial behavior account for one-third to one-half of referrals (Gilbert, 1957; Herbert, 1978; Robins, 1981). Prevalence estimates in nonidentified populations has varied from 4% in children ages 10–11 years in a rural area (Isle of Wight) to 8% in a London urban area (Rutter, Cox, Tupling, Berger, & Yule, 1975).

The general belief that there has been more leniency in child rearing and at the same time more violence in society raises the possibility of increased prevalence of conduct disorders in the past few decades. Historical comparisons are always difficult because of changes in definition and reporting practices, but the data from the Uniform Crime Reports maintained by the FBI suggest little change in age-specific arrest rates between 1974 and 1983.

Many dire statements have been made about the future for conduct-disordered children, particularly for those with aggressive behavior.

It is from the population who show antisocial behavior disorders of childhood that apparently virtually all adult sociopaths derive. It is from this group that a very high proportion of the prisoner population comes as do many of our vagrants, our skid row inhabitants, those drug addicts who resort to crime to support their habits, and even substantial proportions of those psychotic adults who require restraint because of their aggressive and combative behavior. (Robins, 1974, p. 450)

Looking at the continuity problem from a prospective rather than a retrospective point of view, Robins (1966) examined the adult outcomes of children referred for antisocial behavior to a St. Louis child guidance clinic. About half of this sample were court referrals so the group was biased toward serious antisocial behavior. When interviewed at an average age of 43 years, more than 25% had continued to be severely antisocial, in marked contrast to comparison groups of clinic children referred for reasons other than antisocial behavior and a group of normal school children. She also reviewed 23 follow-up studies of antisocial children and concluded that antisocial children were found to have worse adult outcomes than normals and than neurotic children, second only to the outcome findings for psychotic children (Robins, 1970).

These studies included adolescent populations; for instance, the median age at the time of referral in the St. Louis clinic study was 13 years (Robins, 1966). Cass and Thomas (1979) reported similar findings in a follow-up study of a younger group (median age of 9 years) who had been seen at the Washington University Child Guidance Clinic between 1961 and 1965. As adults, slightly more than half were rated as functioning adequately, about one-fourth showed considerable difficulty, and one-fifth had major problems.

The types of behavior prevalent in the persistently "most disturbed" group were generally antisocial. In addition, this group tended to externalize anxiety, were more likely to show extreme emotionality, and were more often diagnosed as character disorders, borderline, or brain syndromes; while those with least disturbance at both time points were diagnosed neurotic or showed transient or developmental difficulties. (Cass & Thomas, p. 111)

Although many statistically significant correlations between demographic variables and childhood assessment status with adult functioning measures have been reported, none is of sufficient magnitude to be useful for *individual* prediction. About all one can conclude is that antisocial adults were almost always antisocial children, and antisocial children seem to have about one chance in four of continuing this pattern into adulthood, particularly if their problems are multiple and severe.

Developmental Considerations

It is imperative to use appropriate age norms in judging a child's conduct. In a way of speaking, the majority of 2-year-olds could be said to have a "conduct disorder" in that they tend to be very active, to resist directions, to express their emotions impulsively, and to be uninhibited in their aggressive reactions. Friedlander offered the following description of the normal toddler:

Feelings of shame, disgust or pity seem to be wholly absent; the toddlers are intent only on doing what gives them the greatest pleasure for the moment. And this pleasure is gained by activities which, if present in the adult, would be classified as criminal, insane or perverse ... They certainly are not socially adapted, for they have no regard for the desires of other people and do not submit of their own free will to demands made upon them. Looked at from another angle, we might say that they do not yet show any signs of conscience ... It seems really much more astonishing that so many of these little "savages" develop into socially adapted human beings than that some of them do not reach that stage. (1947, p. 13)

Herbert presented the developmental hypothesis succinctly in his statement that "I maintain that the concept of conduct disorder broadly defines phenomena that represent a persistence of normal behaviors beyond the normal time span, rather than the equivalent (as they are sometimes made to appear) of medical disorders" (1982, p. 102).

Developmentally, a great deal takes place between ages 2 and 5 years (see Chapter 5) both affectively and cognitively. Briefly, the immediate response of aggression to frustration is tempered by the wish to please. The child holds back, partly for fear of punishment, but mainly for the positive consequences of keeping the love of important people. This does not happen if (a) the child has no "important people" to care about, or (b) the child has not been successful in winning their expressed approval. From the cognitive standpoint, the child starts to use cognitive mediators and to direct herself by words which remind the child of previous consequences and also serve to delay immediate action, thereby providing alternative modes of action.

Origins of Conscience. A giant step in self-control occurs around the age of 5 years with the development of an inter-

nal conscience. Both Piaget and Freud described the development of conscience as a two-stage process. In Piaget's description, the first stage is characterized by heteronomy, literalness, and lack of regard for motivation. Heteronomy gives way to autonomy only through cooperation, which forces the individual to become interested in the point of view of other people so as to compare it with his own. The genesis of personal conscience is the result of "spiritualization of filial respect and a liberation of individual minds" (1932, p. 385). "The quasi-physical element of fear which plays a part in unilateral respect gradually begins to disappear in favour of the purely moral fear of falling in the esteem of the respected person" (1932, p. 387).

Similarly, Freud perceived the source of behavior control as first external to the child, to be internalized into the personality structure known as the superego or conscience. Freud was not interested in what behavior caused a person to feel guilt or pride; he was concerned with the source of such feelings and the resultant capacity for self-control in the absence of external detection, reward, or punishment. He saw the force of the conscience as directly related to the affective ties with the parents. The formation of the conscience was explained as the introjection of the parents' attitudes, loving and otherwise, as experienced by the child in fact or imagined in fantasy. In his theory, the forcefulness of the self-control mechanism derives from the resolution of the Oedipal complex, with the defensive identification with the same-sexed parent, and turning the aggression originally directed against this parent against the self. Although Freud examined the affective component and Piaget studied the cognitive aspects, both agreed that around 5 years the child takes on some of the monitoring and enforcement responsibilities which previously belonged to the parents. Every serious type of education tries to induce in the child the desire to adapt to social standards, not because of rewards and punishments but because they are accepted as "the right thing to do."

Psychologists operationalized the general concept of conscience in order to study its relationship to child rearing. Sears, Maccoby, and Levin (1957) contrived situations with 4- and 5-year-old children which measured resistance to temptation, instruction to others, and reactions after transgression, and found "lowly positive" intercorrelations (around .40) in these conscience measures. Grinder (1962) reported a follow-up study on 140 sixth graders who had been part of the original sample. This involved a situation testing the child's ability to resist the temptation to cheat for a game prize. Interestingly, about 30% of the children resisted. There was strong evidence of stability in character, in that those children who had been reported high in conscience development at age 5 years were able to resist temptation at age 11 or 12 years. However, the relationships with child rearing practices were unclear and probably obscured by the relative homogeneity of the population studied.

In the past 20 years or so, there has been a real bifurcation of interest in moral development. Kohlberg (1976) expanded Piaget's work into six-stage cognitive developmental theory of moral reasoning. Others investigated moral behavior by examining the conditions which elicit altruism (Bryan & London, 1970), sharing, helping (Yarrow, Scott, & Waxler, 1973), compliance, and so on. Efforts to relate these behaviors to early child rearing fell by the wayside. This does not mean that earlier concepts are invalidated but only that defining the relationships proved very difficult.

Developmental Failures. Conduct disorder children have failed to develop an adequate system of self-control and are much more dependent on external structures than the normal school-age child. This may come about for any number of reasons. The social environment may have been deficient in not offering sufficient guidance, incentive, and support to make the effort to please worthwhile. The children may not have learned alternative ways of coping with frustration. Adult models of self-control may have been lacking.

Also, one must consider the innate or biological nature of the individual child. In an interesting research study with first- and sixth-grade children, Grim, Kohlberg, and White (1968) found significant relationships between measures of attention and resistance to temptation. The authors discussed moral behavior as a product of the development of attention-volition factors rather than as a product of internalized moral values and concluded with a quotation from James (1890): "The essential achievement of will is to attend to a difficult object" (p. 540). Children who have an attention deficit disorder thus are much more likely to act impulsively, even if the result violates their stated beliefs of right and wrong. Temperamental characteristics such as high activity level, intense reactivity, and low threshold of responsiveness are likely to increase the areas of parent-child conflict and at the same time increase the child's resistance to parental influence (see Chapter 1). When the temperamental differences are extreme, one invokes the notion of something "organic" or "neurological." This concept will be discussed in some detail in relation to hyperactivity.

Before assigning a diagnostic label to a child, the child's behavior must be evaluated not only from a developmental standpoint but also in a situational context. It is probable that there is some external justification for some of the child's behavior, and these antecedent conditions must be taken into account. Usually the aggressiveness seen in conduct-disordered children is an overreaction to an external frustration; the child's perception of such events must be included in assessment and treatment planning. All too often, these children have developed a "bad" reputation, so that they encounter more than their fair share of negative responses from peers and adult authorities. The tolerance level for misbehavior varies widely among parents and teachers, thus it is imperative to get very specific information in support of their judgments, which are invariably negative with regard to a conduct disordered child.

PARENT MANAGEMENT TRAINING

Assuming that a major cause of conduct disorder is a failure in learning, a logical locus of treatment is the home, with the parents as the therapeutic agents.

Planned or unplanned, the parents act to modify behavior; clearly, they cannot stand on the sidelines with a conduct disordered child. Although psychodynamically oriented psychotherapists refer briefly to the importance of parents "setting limits," the behaviorally oriented therapists have developed the "know-how" to accomplish this.

Reference was made earlier (see Chapter 6) to the work of Forehand and his colleagues at the University of Georgia in training parents to handle noncompliant behavior, particularly in preschool children. Treatment is on an individual basis and carried out in clinic playrooms equipped with one-way mirrors, sound systems, and bug-in-the-ear devices by which the therapist can communicate with the parent. By means of modeling by the therapist and role playing, as well as direct instruction, the parent is trained to attend to and reinforce all positive behaviors (which are often overlooked) and to interact positively on the child's level in the "Child's Game" time.

In the second phase, "Compliance Training," one moves to a direct attack on the problem behavior. Here the setting of priorities, the giving of commands, and the execution of consequences for noncompliance are explicated. Although the idea of "time-out" (e.g. sitting in a chair for 3 minutes) is a familiar one to parents and teachers, it is often used in isolation without regard to the other elements in the Forehand training program (Forehand & McMahon, 1981). The parents are taught how to give "alpha commands" which are direct, concise, and one-at-a-time in contrast to "beta" commands which are multiple, vague, or even contradictory.

It is also important to note that the criterion for success is taken at a 75% compliance rate, so the parents' expectations must be adjusted accordingly. If they expect too much, they give up too soon, viewing themselves as helpless and the child as hopelessly recalcitrant.

With continued experience, Forehand, Middlebrook, Rogerts, and Steffe (1983) added some elements to the basic treatment program, particularly in recognition of parental maladjustment. They suggested that parental adjustment must be assessed as well as parent perception of the child and that in some cases, treatment may need to focus on the parents' maladjustment rather than, or in addition to, the remediation of ineffective parenting skills. This recommendation would be heartily endorsed by family therapists who assert that child mental health professionals join a family conspiracy in "blaming the child" for what is often a breakdown in family systems.

Patterson (1982) has made this point even more cogently. Working with a greater diversity of aggressive conduct disorders from varied socioeconomic backgrounds at the Oregon Social Learning Center, he has spent years analyzing family social interaction patterns. Patterson refers to his view as coercion theory, where the deviant behavior is reinforced by the parent by attention to aggression and compliance, with increasingly severe child coercive behaviors in order to terminate the confrontation. He also examined the antecedents of aggressive behavior with the goal of "precursor intervention." In between confrontation, the conduct disordered child is often subjected to family experience which leave him feeling powerless and like the "low man on the totem pole." The aggressive behavior may be an immediate consequence or a delayed effort to establish a sense of power.

Patterson (1982) offered some valuable descriptions of parents in difficulty. Compared to Forehand, who viewed the parental maladjustment as a separate although contributory phenomenon, Patterson's view is more interactional and focuses on disturbances in parental role. The "parent-sibling" mother functions as an equal, a friend, and gives up the disciplinarian role. She fears rejection and buys friendship with indulgence. Somewhat similar are the parents who want to be perfect and are wide open for the "guilt trip" or "guilt induction" at which children are adept. The tactics vary from "You don't really love me" to "You're not fair" to "I'll run away," which may paralyze the over-anxious parent. This is an example of role reversal, where the child is doing to the parent what the parent should be doing to or for the child. At another extreme, the "unattached parent" is disengaged and has little motivation, resenting demands made by therapist and child alike. This may also show in a very subtle form where the parent gives lip service to therapy but then "proves" that it won't work, justifying continued rejection of the child and taking steps to place the child outside the home.

Still another situation arises when parents are overwhelmed by outside pressures so that there is little time or energy for parenting. They want to do right but they haven't the time. There are also parents who are confused in terms of expectations. This may come about because the child has been identified as "special" in some way (for instance, mentally retarded), or it may be more deep-seated. As mentioned in the discussion of child-abusing parents (see Chapter 2), some parents expect far too much from young children and attribute malevolent intentions. They take aspects of even normal child behavior as a personal affront and respond as if to an equal.

A more complicated situation involving a triad rather than a dyad was labeled the "sadomasochistic arabesque" (Patterson, 1982, p. 299) with the parents following different programs. Usually one parent takes the role of the harsh martinet and the other attempts to mitigate the perceived severity of the other by being supportive and subtly sabotaging the position of the absent partner. This can be quite devastating as each partner pushes the other into more extreme positions. The child becomes an active participant in the arabesque and knows just how to exploit the rift between the parents. In cases of divorce or stepfamilies, the situation can become absurd, with only one parent allowed to punish; children can turn the situation into one of punishing the "bad" parent who steps out of line with the other parent.

These parental types are familiar to every clinician, and other variations will be discussed in the later section on psychodynamic approaches. These parents can upset the best laid plans of any therapist. Patterson himself said that there was more to treatment than the technology described in the manual (Patterson, Reid, Jones, & Conger, 1975) and talked about the need for warmth, humor, and good timing (Patterson, 1982). He briefly mentioned "the intricacies of working through resistance" which is the core of many therapies. Clinical skills provide

the ability to adapt to the individual situation, but social learning theory provides techniques which are generally applicable—once the treatment alliance has been established.

The Question of Punishment

Even using all of the skills in prevention, positive reinforcement for prosocial behavior, setting priorities, and making clear demands, it is impossible to escape the necessity of punishment in dealing with aggressive, conduct-disordered children. Although some undesirable behavior will extinguish by the tactic of ignoring, other behaviors cannot be ignored and require effective action. The key issues become what to punish and how to punish effectively. From his studies, Patterson concluded that

Parents of normal children tend to ignore most coercive child behavior; as a result, the episodes tend to be of short duration. When they want to, these parents are able to use punishment to stop or suppress these behaviors. Parents of antisocial children ignore less and natter more. (1982, p. 136)

The term "nattering" was coined to describe parental rebukes, exhortations, and threats which either cannot or will not be acted on. The parents seem to be talking in order to relieve their own tension, but what they say has no meaning. Children quickly learn to ignore "nattering." Coercive behavior continues, parental frustration grows, and the final outcome is likely to be extreme and uncontrolled on the parents' side.

The question of physical punishment must be addressed by any therapist working with parents of conduct-disordered children. Physical punishment is certainly a common practice although perhaps somewhat less now than before. Stark and McEvoy (1970) found that 84% of middle-class parents had spanked their children, compared with 98% reported by Sears, Maccoby, and Levin (1957). However, spanking is ordinarily a rare occurrence for any given child and it cannot be the mainstay of a treatment program for a child who is in frequent conflict. Unless it is truly painful to the point of physical endangerment, the child becomes immune.

There are many reports demonstrating a relationship between the degree of physical punishment imposed by parents on their children and subsequent criminal and otherwise destructive behavior on the part of these children (Buttons, 1973; Feshbach & Feshbach, 1973). Welsh (1976) cited studies documenting the frequency with which extreme physical punishment is reported by male delinquents. Welsh suggested that this physical aggression might be a primary cause of the child's aggressive behavior, the so-called "belt theory" of juvenile delinquency. Apparently the modeling effect of the physically punitive parent is very strong.

Patterson reported that roughly one-third of the parents in antisocial children referred to the Oregon Social Learning Center had physically abused their children (1982). The physical abuse may in part represent a reaction to the child as an escalation from the failure of less violent punishment to have an influence. However, whichever comes first, parental aggression and child aggression occur in tandem. It is a pattern that is hard to change. Time-out procedures, loss of privileges, and extra work assignments have proven effective in bringing about behavior change, but these procedures do take time and patient repetition. The parents must see them through each and every time. For parents who are themselves impulsive it is difficult to muster the self-discipline to persist in implementing the consequences.

Evaluation of Parent Management Therapies

The programs have many commonalities, such as detailed behavior observations and recording, systematic positive reinforcement for prosocial behavior, implementation of punishing consequences, and didactic instruction in learning principles. The therapist models the behaviors but the burden of therapeutic change falls on the parents. Although most behavior therapists use frequency counts of observed behavior to judge progress, an inventory of child conduct problem behaviors has been developed (see Appendix for ECBI) which permits comparison across studies (Eyberg & Ross, 1978; Robinson, Eyberg, & Ross, 1980).

After a comprehensive review, Kazdin concluded that "No other intervention for antisocial children has been investigated so thoroughly as parent management training and has shown as favorable results" (1984, p. 14). McMahon and Forehand (1984) concluded that treatment gains endure up to 4 years after treatment and that parents maintain their satisfaction with the parent training program well after treatment termination. However, the positive results did not persist in a small, but well-controlled, study reported by Bernal, Klinnert, and Schultz (1980). This study was designed to compare behavioral training for parents with a client-centered treatment which emphasized feelings, attitudes, communication and family experiences. Immediately after 10 weeks of parent training, the behavioral group was most positive. However, home observers failed to find significant differences and in a 2-year follow-up, there were no differences in parents' reports about their children's deviance. Even more surprising, those parents on the waiting list who simply provided telephone reports of child problems to staff over an 8-week period indicated improvement equal to that reported by the treatment groups. It seems that the improvement was related more to an attention placebo effect than a specific treatment technique. It should be noted that the children in this study were recruited by general advertising which attracted a group of college-educated parents. They probably were not as disturbed as children coming through the usual clinical referral sources. Therefore, there might not have been as much room for improvement—or as much need for treatment.

There are recognized limitations to parent management therapies. With regard to generalization, McMahon and Forehand found that the treatment results seemed to spread to nontargeted behavior and even to the siblings, but they found little evidence of generalization to the school setting. Also, there are self-selection factors. As indicated, the time and energy involvement for parents is considerable, and this doubtlessly influences who agrees to participate.

There is no data to show what percentage of parents accept the idea in the first place. In some instances, there is no parent available or accessible to even entertain the recommendation. The figures for dropping out averaged 28% in a review of 22 studies of parent training (Forehand, Middlebrook, Rogers, & Steffe, 1983). Dropout and failure rates are higher for families in low socioeconomic circumstances, particularly for single-parent families (Webster-Stratton, 1985).

Therapists have tried to increase parental cooperation by using refundable deposits or modifying the regimen to make parents feel more comfortable, but for some parents the program is just too much. Of course, the ability to make the necessary commitment is an indication of parental strength, and for those who can engage, the parent training therapists have a lot to offer.

COGNITIVE-BEHAVIORAL TREATMENTS

Although these therapies are also "behavioral," the focus is more on the child than on the parent. The cognitive approaches are usually considered supplemental to the operant approaches which involve changing the environment. There are many variations, partly depending on the nature of the child's problems and partly on the theoretical preferences of the therapist. However, all the strategies involve the child "thinking through" situations and practicing new solutions to conflicts. A first step is to help the child see situations realistically and to correct "irrational beliefs." Di-

Giuseppe gave two straightforward examples. One was a 12-year-old boy who reacted with fighting when teased, which he interpreted as "This kid doesn't like me—no one likes me—it's terrible not to have any friends" (1981, p. 64). When this over-generalization was corrected, he was helped to consider other responses and to imagine other consequences. The other example involved a 10-year-old who became out of control whenever his parents argued, behavior he interpreted as the first sign of a divorce. This was corrected by proving to him that disagreements were common in marriage and that his fears were groundless. Although no harm would be done in starting with this approach, it probably is successful only if the aggressive problems are circumscribed and one can identify the antecedent conditions with some precision.

Most conduct-disordered children have pervasive difficulties in self-control and react impulsively to all sorts of situations. Meichenbaum and Goodman (1971) developed a self-instructional training regimen using a variety of cognitive tasks. The program starts with an adult model performing the task and talking out loud, with the child following suit and proceeding through successive stages to the point where the child performs the task using "private speech," i.e., silent self-instruction. This paradigm for developing inner speech control has been used for hyperactive children (Douglas, Parry, Marton, & Garson, 1976) and aggressive children (Camp, Blom, Hebert, & van Doorninck, 1977). It seems to serve to create a capability, a cognitive "structure," which is then available for use in problem situations involving other people rather than impersonal tasks.

Kendall's cognitive-behavioral therapy for impulsive children shares many of the same features. The manual (Kendall & Braswell, 1985) describes a basic program of 12 sessions (extended if necessary), in which the first 8 sessions concentrate on self-instructional strategies for psychoeducational tasks and game playing. The ninth session focuses on "affective education," or labeling emotions, and the last three deal with interpersonal problem solving, first to consider causes and consequences of action and then role playing in hypothetical and real-life situations. Although the procedures are presented in specific detail, mention is also made that the therapist must be "active, alive and animated" in order to involve the child. In all of these programs, there is room for social skills training in appropriate assertiveness, understanding the point of view of others, increasing the child's ability for self-evaluation and self-reward, and branching out in different directions. There is an assumption, of course, that the environment is prepared to respond positively to the child's efforts. Essentially the therapist takes the role of an expert teacher in problem-solving strategies.

Another approach which derives from a very different theory deserves mention, although it is more involved and difficult to pick up simply from reading about it. Santostefano (1971; Santostefano & Reider, 1984) looked at the question of cognitive controls as related to perceptual processes rather than verbal mediators. Following earlier suggestions of George Klein (Klein & Schlesinger, 1949), he looked at cognitive controls as part of the information processing input system. One such cognitive control principle is labeled "Leveling/ Sharpening" which involves comparing memory images with present perceptions. Working with high-aggressive children in an inpatient psychiatric unit at McLean Hospital, Santostefano found that they were more observant ("sharp") to changes in aggressive stimuli in comparison with the low-aggressive group who perceived the same stimuli in a more neutral (levelized) fashion. Santostefano has developed an elaborate diagnostic and treatment scheme which attempts to change the cognitive control processes, first using neutral tasks and then moving to affective situations. His study population seems to be much more disturbed in general than the client populations of Meichenbaum or Kendall. Such children are probably more confused about external reality, and the idea of tapping into preverbal processes so that they can "see" more clearly is attractive. It seems to be effective in its place of origin, i.e. McLean Hospital, but little use of it has been made elsewhere.

Evaluation of Cognitive-Behavioral Treatments

Cognitive behavior therapy has its origins in the field of developmental psychology, and many of the outcome studies have used cognitive measures such as the Matching Familiar Figures Test (Kagan, 1966) or the Porteus Mazes (Palkes, Stewart, & Kahana, 1968). The studies have usually found that training modified impulsivity, but it is not at all clear that those children who showed the most change on cognitive skills or tasks showed the most behavioral change. Kendall and Wilcox (1979) developed a self-control rating scale (see appendix) as a measure of assessing impulsivity in "natural" settings. In two stuides, teachers' blind ratings of self-control and hyperactivity evidenced significant change for the treatment groups compared to control groups for periods up to 2 months after termination. This is particularly impressive when one considers that in one study there were only 6 treatment sessions (Kendall & Wilcox, 1980) and in the other, 12 sessions (Kendall & Zupan, 1981). They concluded that there is evidence for generalization to the classroom (from the teachers' ratings) but that the long-term effects (1 year later) were weak.

Relatively few studies have evaluated cognitive therapy with clinical child populations referred to standard psychiatric settings. "Investigations have generally been restricted to a narrow range of responses of nonclinic populations studied in laboratory settings" (Hobbs, Moguin, Tyroler, & Lahey, 1980, pg. 164). Attempts at replication have generally been less successful than the prototypical programs (Billings & Wasik, 1985). Bornstein (1985) suggested that there may be important therapist variables which have been overlooked. Kendall and Braswell (1985) tried to identify critical treatment variables, but admitted that much depends on the nature of the child's problem. Their comment that "It seems that as the child's level of aggression increases so does the difficulty of achieving a positive outcome" (p. 63), suggests that this is a treatment approach suitable for a less disturbed population.

PSYCHODYNAMIC APPROACHES

Therapists approaching the problem from a psychoanalytic background have emphasized the internal structure of the child, particularly in terms of superego or conscience, and ego controls or cognitive controls. They categorize conduct disorders roughly in three levels. The most serious are those who seem to be without conscience, the "unsocialized aggressive child." The next are those who have conscience gaps, or "lacunae" which may well follow the parental models (Johnson, 1949). Finally, there are those who have poor controls and act in an unsocial way although they experience remorse after the fact, similar to the impulsive children described by Kendall and Braswell (1985). Although many of the psychoanalysts in this field were writing in the 1930's and 1940's, the principles have not changed and are worth reiteration.

One of the early pioneers was August Aichorn, a teacher in the Viennese elementary schools, who became interested in "wayward children" and was made superintendent of a reformatory in Vienna. The emphasis on identification (and modeling) arising from positive relationships is well summarized in the closing remarks of his study, *Wayward Youth*:

You have seen that a character change in the delinquent means a change in his ego ideal. This occurs when new traits are taken over by the individual. The source of these traits is the worker. He is the important object with whom the dissocial child or youth can retrieve the defective or non-existent identification and with whom he can experience all the things in which his father failed him. With the worker's help, the youth acquires the necessary feeling relation to his companions which enables him to overcome the dissocial traits. The word "father substitute," so often used in connection with remedial education, receives its rightful connotations in this conception of the task.

What helps the worker most in therapy with the dissocial? The transference! And especially what we recognize as the positive transference. It is above all the tender feeling for the teacher that gives the pupil the incentive to do what is prescribed and not to do what is forbidden. The teacher, as a libidinally-charged object for the pupil, offers traits for identification that bring about a lasting change in the structure of the ego ideal. (1935, pp. 235–36)

Redl and Wineman (1951, 1957) elaborated on the specifics of residential treatment for severely aggressive children and described in detail what is meant by "milieu therapy." They started with a description of "ego tasks" in which the severely delinquent child was deficient. Listed as the first task, and perhaps the most encompassing one, was "frustration tolerance." The second item on their list was coping with insecurity, anxiety and fear. Closely related to this was disorganization in the face of guilt, one reason to avoid any such feeling. They also mentioned "sublimation deafness":

With our children, it was easy to see how often the "natural voice" of situations and things would be out-yelled by the screams of their inside urges and impulses. It seems that they were "deaf" to the natural challenge of life around them, while sensitively geared to the push of their impulsivity from within. (1951, p. 93)

With all this in mind, Redl and Wineman organized a residential treatment environment which provided for positive identifications but also programmed for ego support. With great care, they described arranging for play to provide opportunities for mastery with a minimum of frustration and over-stimulation. The surface management of the child's behavior entailed ignoring, setting limits, circumventing and forestalling difficulties, treating difficult situations with humor, using rewards and punishments, and so on. Although a well-planned (and expensive) therapeutic residential environment changes behavior, it is a question whether the change will survive when the child returns to a destructive home life. The memoir of Mark Devlin (1985) gives pathetic testimony to this problem. Repeatedly he was discharged from residential placements, beginning at age 7 years, only to return to a chaotic and hostile family situation, apparently without any continuing psychological support. It was observations of this phenomenon which prompted Hobbs to introduce "Project Re-Ed" with its combined residential and home-school treatment (see Chapter 7).

Willock (1983) provided a contemporary account of individual, psychodynamically oriented therapy with aggressive, acting-out children. Although brief mention is made of the "ego-supportive" measures provided by the residential environment of the Children's Psychiatric Hospital at the University of Michigan and the work with the families, Willock

focused on the role of the individual therapist with children who are characteristically provocative and acting out to a dangerous degree. They firmly reject friendly overtures and task the patience of the most seasoned therapist. Willock suggested that

Much of the explosive behavior which typifies the hyperaggressive child can be understood in terms of the underlying narcissistic vulnerability. In order to ward off the anxiety, the anger, and the depression which are associated with the disregarded and the devalued self, these children adopt an angrily alienated, "I don't care" attitude (I don't care about you. I don't care what you think about me.)—a posture which they may reinforce by indulging in blatantly antisocial activities. (1983, p. 389)

In a perverse way, the child tries to turn the tables so that the therapist is in danger of losing control—which then constitutes a victory for the child. The therapist's task is to persist and to interpret the defensive nature of the behavior. As treatment progresses, the therapist helps the child to label feelings and identify warning signals before all is lost.

The cases described by Willock are indeed extreme and had defeated more moderate measures. The "success" case, Sean, age 10 years, was in residence for a year and his thrice-weekly appointments continued for some time after discharge. His early life prior to treatment was characterized by many separations and losses, harsh physical punishment, and inadequate parenting from an immature, overwhelmed mother. He thus accumulated plenty of evidence that he was a "bother to the whole world" and that he wasn't "worth shit." The therapist (as well as the entire residential staff it is assumed) managed to convince him otherwise.

Thus, Sean's belief that he would necessarily be disregarded and devalued by any important adult was challenged and he began to understand something of the origins of these negative convictions, all of which made his antisocial stance less necessary and freed up his potential for developing a more positive relationship with his therapist (and others). (Willock, 1983, p. 406)

Reading the case history, however, helps one to appreciate the necessity for the residential setting because there were many stormy sessions! And although he did well for some time after leaving the hospital, it is sad to read that his mother terminated treatment for her own personal reasons. Perhaps the most frustrating thing for therapists, and for the children, is the fact that one has limited jurisdiction over parental authority.

Individual therapy with an antisocial child introduces role problems for the therapist. On one hand the therapist is aligned with parents, teachers and other authorities against the antisocial behavior and yet she must persuade the child that she is acting in his best interest and really "on his side." A behavior therapist does this by ensuring that a system of immediate rewards is forthcoming and that the child is treated with fairness and consistency. Even so, the child patient will probably show some negative feelings in therapy. DiGuiseppe (1983) recommended that one "ride this through," maintaining both individual therapy and the behavioral components without radical change. Also, a therapist should be prepared for the feelings which an aggressive child is likely to

evoke. An aggressive child can test unmercifully and sometimes with great skill to try and get the therapist to lose control or to give up. Acting-out children would far prefer to have a fight with someone outside than to struggle with inner conflicts. Preserving one's calm (at least on the surface), while maintaining the safety of the child and one's self can be very difficult. Besides the natural reaction of anger, the therapist becomes very anxious that the treatment is doomed to failure. In a lengthy case report of the psychoanalysis of an aggressive boy in a residential setting, Crocker (1955) described some of the errors he made in trying to placate and reassure. His statement that it "takes a certain kind of ability on the analyst's part to maintain a quiet, firm attitude of evaluation of the situation when the necessity to defend oneself emotionally and physically is a prominent part of the picture" (1955, p. 312) is equally true for any therapist.

The concept of "superego lacunae" introduced by Johnson (1949) applies to children with more circumscribed behavior problems which are unconsciously sanctioned by the parents. Some fathers will approve of their son's aggressiveness as evidence of "manly toughness," although the conditions for "approved aggressiveness" may be ambiguous to say the least. Rexford remarked that

The overwhelmingly predominant character structure of fathers of antisocial young children we have seen over the past eleven years is that of a passive, restricted and hostile man, strongly allied with his obstreperous son, firm in his belief that aggressive behavior of whatever kind or degree is evidence of desirable masculine self-assertion and is not to be curbed. (1959, p. 215)

Similar conclusions were reached by Bandura and Walters from their study of aggressive adolescent boys (1959). Patterson's observations of parental acceptance of child stealing is another such example. Such parents are ambivalent partners at best in a parent management training program and a more dynamic family therapy approach is necessary to identify the parents' contribution to the child's antisocial behavior (Perez, 1978). One way to detect this situation is if the parents seem other than pleased by improvement in the child's behavior.

Finally, there are some children who exhibit antisocial behavior, usually sporadic and circumscribed, on the basis of an internal conflict. Friedlander (1947) labeled these as "neurotic delinquents." Generally the behavior has a compulsive nature and is alien to the usual behavior of the child. The particular behavior may be stealing (kleptomania), firesetting, lying, exhibitionism, or whatever, but the hallmark is that it does not "fit" with the child's everyday actions. Such children are not impulsive or noncompliant except in isolated situations where an impulse "breaks through" their normal patterns. When the antisocial behavior is of low frequency, it is probably better approached through individual psychotherapy rather than parent management or cognitive behavioral approaches.

RELATIONSHIP OF ASSESSMENT AND TREATMENT

There really is no fundamental incompatibility among these different approaches to the treatment of aggressive/impulsive children. The choice of treatment should depend on the seriousness of the problem and the resources available. Assessment cannot rely solely on behavioral manifestations, even including duration, severity, and frequency. One must also consider the general personality structure of the child and the complex motivations which go into aggressiveness. It may be simple manipulation (getting one's way); it may be a way of asserting one's power and position; it may be purely impulsive and a matter of the moment; it may be a defense against overwhelming anxiety and depression; or it may be some combination of all of these.

If the parents are able to participate, parent management training seems like a good beginning. Self-instructional training, or cognitive behavior therapy, may be a useful adjunct, again assuming that the child has some motivation for change. These approaches are predicted on the hypothesis of some failure in social learning which can be remedied by supplying the missing ingredients of good models, clear communication, consistent positive and negative consequences, and verbal-cognitive self-control strategies. But some children are so traumatized (conditioned) that past experiences cannot easily be erased by new experiences. They have been rejected; they expect to be rejected; and they make it happen on their terms rather than waiting for the inevitable. It probably requires a well-planned and well-structured residential treatment setting, identification with a therapist, and some insight into their fears and where they came from to give them the motivation to try to change. Then, and only then, might one introduce the cognitive behavior strategies for self-instruction. Given the usual history of rejection and separation, one would hope that there would be some consistent caring person to see them through the ups and downs of finding a new identity.

HYPERACTIVITY

Definition and Prevalence

In the past two decades, hyperactivity has attracted a great deal of attention both in the public at large and in the professional community. It has been estimated as accounting for up to half of all diagnosed psychiatric disorders in school-age children (Safer & Allen, 1976). DSM-III introduced a significant change by subsuming "hyperactivity" under the general classification of "Attention Deficit Disorder." The diagnostic criteria for Attention Deficit Disorder with Hyperactivity include behavioral signs of (a) inattention, (b) impulsivity, and (c) hyperactivity, all with onset before age 7 years. Attention Deficit Without Hyperactivity was so rarely diagnosed that it was dropped in DSM-III-R. The following discussion is restricted to the first type and, for sake of brevity, the umbrella term "attention deficit disorder" is not repeated.

It is deceptively easy to describe the hyperactive child. However, at times, and in some settings, even the best of children will be inattentive, impulsive, distractible, and more active than one would like. In surveys of "normal" child populations, anywhere from a sixth to a half are reported by their parents or teachers to be overactive or inattentive (Lapouse & Monk, 1958; Rutter, Tizard, & Whitmore, 1970/1981; Werry & Quay, 1971). A number of rating scales have been developed in an effort to get some quantitative measure of hyperactivity and norms to use in identifying a "pathological" degree. Some are designed for teachers (Abbreviated Teacher Questionnaire, Conners, 1973; Rating Scales for Hyperkinesis, Davids, 1971; Hyperactivity Rating Scales, Spring, Blunden, Greenberg, & Yellin, 1977) and others are prepared for parents (Conners, 1973; see appendix). Different cutoff scores have been used for the clinical determination of hyperactivity, which of course results in different prevalence figures.

Another important diagnostic issue has to do with the pervasiveness of the problem. The correlations of hyperactivity ratings between parents and teachers have ranged from .18 to .36 (Sandberg, 1981), indicating a low level of agreement. The figures in the Isle of Wight study indicated that only 2% were assessed "high" on the Rutter scales by both parents and teachers (Schachar, Rutter, & Smith, 1981). This is reasonably close to the findings of Lambert, Sandoval, and Sassone (1978), namely that 1.2% of children in kindergarten through fifth grade in a representative sample in the San Francisco Bay Area were judged hyperactive by parents, teachers, and physicians. The difference in ratings could reflect differences in adult tolerance and perceptions, or real differences in child behavior in different situations.

Clearly with such variation in parent-teacher ratings, there is much latitude for individual clinical judgment in making the diagnosis. Rutter (1983) pointed out that the diagnosis is diagnosed nearly 50 times as often in North America (up to half of all children referred to psychiatric clinics) as in Great Britain (1 to 2% of child patients). Rutter went on to say that this huge cross-national difference could reflect real differences in the child populations but that the evidence suggests otherwise. Average scores on the hyperactivity factor on the Conners scale are just as high, or higher, for nonidentified child populations in Britain as in the United States. Rutter suggested that the frequency difference reflected a difference in diagnostic usage.

While good empirical data on diagnostic practice are lacking, it would seem from a reading of clinical papers that clinicians in the United Kingdom tend to reserve the diagnosis for the very few children who are markedly overactive and inattentive in nearly all situations whereas, as is evident from the DSM-III criteria, the U.S. practice does not demand that the behavior be pervasive. (Rutter, 1983, p. 261)

In reading the vast literature on this subject, it is imperative to keep in mind the specific diagnostic criteria used in each instance. The clinical picture of children labeled hyperactive "varies from the little boy who is silly, immature and not performing academically up to expected standards to the markedly active, aggressive, and anti-social child who is unable to be managed in a regular classroom setting" (Cantwell, 1977, p. 525). Many writers have felt that the DSM III criteria are too vague and liberal and have suggested modifications. For instance, Barkley (1981) developed a Home Situations Questionnaire and a School Situations Questionnaire

and required that the child have problems in at least half of these situations as a measure of pervasiveness. Although the children identified by any behavioral measurement standards will still be heterogeneous, such measures restrict the facile use of the word "hyperactive."

Factor analytic studies have demonstrated clearly that hyperactive behavior is highly correlated with conduct disorder (Cantwell, 1978; Conners, 1969; Goyette, Conners, & Ulrich, 1978; Quay, 1979). Case example 10.1 illustrates the overlap between these two diagnoses.

The "Organic" versus "Functional" Debate

Originally hyperkinesis, or hyperactivity, was considered in the context of neurological disease. In 1934 Kahn and Cohen described some cases in which hyperkinesis was the predominating feature. They called this "organic driveness" and considered it to be referable to the brain stem. This was followed shortly by a number of papers contributed by the staff of the Emma Pendleton Bradley Home (established in 1931 as a memorial to a post-encephalitic child). The pediatrician-director wrote the first article on the use of amphetamines with children's behavioral problems (Bradley, 1937). There was a series of papers defining the hyperkinetic impulse disorder (Laufer, Denhoff, & Solomons, 1957) and attempting to understand the neurological mechanisms involved. These writers were emphasizing the organic factors in child psychopathology in opposition to the prevailing psychody-

Case Example 10.1   Ben

Ben was the third of four children with three sisters all doing well at school and at home. His parents were ambitious, hardworking, conservative people with high expectations for all their children. They first came for help when Ben was 4 years old because of his out-of-control behavior, which took various forms including daytime wetting, property destruction, hitting others, and noncompliance. The mother was concerned about Ben's lack of remorse and feared that he would grow up to be a juvenile delinquent.

He had always presented difficulties, starting with neonatal jaundice. He was a fretful infant and was switched from breast to bottle feeding because of poor weight gain. A pediatric neurologist diagnosed neurofibromatosis (a genetic neurological disease) and concluded that "although a higher percentage of children with this have difficulties with learning, the difficulties which they have are no different than those seen in the 'usual' child with disorders of behavior and learning." Because of his hyperactivity, Ritalin was prescribed; it had an obvious quietening effect.

During the next few years, Ben had many individual intelligence tests because of his poor academic performance. The results ranged from a low of IQ 85 to a high of 100 (obtained under rather special conditions) but always showing a significant discrepancy (more than 15 IQ points) between verbal and performance abilities. Perceptual motor tests such as the Bender Gestalt were consistently scored about 1 standard deviation below his chronological age expectancy. Despite special educational help, at the age of 10 years, Ben's scores on academic achievement tests were about 1 year below his grade level. Clearly he could achieve lit-

tle success or satisfaction from school work.

Ben was regularly in difficulty at home as well. With therapy, he was able to become dry and develop improved personal habits of cleanliness. The property destruction and hitting others diminished considerably but was replaced with using bad language and verbal insults. The family conflicts were particularly acute at bedtime and getting up in the morning. Although these were better during vacation time and in some periods of treatment, the probems never disappeared. Occasionally he would admit his fear of nightmares (usually about monsters) and assert his conviction that dreams really come true, but usually he vigorously denied any problems. Both psychotherapy and behavior therapy (parent management training) were tried but with limited success. Both therapists discovered that the parents, although very involved, found little opportunity to relate positively and were in a state of constant disappointment and frustration. So here too Ben had little opportunity to feel successful.

With his peers, Ben was likely to be ignored, although he had a few casual friendships, with "undesirables" in the parents' opinion. He had almost as much difficulty in playing games as he did with school work. His ability to pretend was very limited; he was quickly put off by any failure; and he could not sustain any kind of "game plan" for a reasonable period of time. His favorite activities were television and listening to tapes. One of these tapes, which he brought to his therapist, told the story of a "star prince" who lived on a far-off planet and was totally rejected because he was "mentally retarded." His father rescued him from extermination by taking him to another planet where he was highly regarded because he could read minds (not books). Although Ben said little about the tape, his absorption showed his identification with a rejected, endangered character in an alien world.

Prognostically, it is unlikely that Ben will ever be a juvenile delinquent. His learning problems will probably become even more obvious and he and his parents will continue their struggles. A possible outcome in ado-lescence would be depression or school phobia unless he finds a support system—teachers or friends who also can comfort the parents. His behavior arises from a combination of constitutional inadequacies, a school and home environment which is "deprived" in the sense of providing sufficient positive reinforcements, and developmental-emotional conflicts which he is unable to master by "thinking through."

---

namic emphasis. As Laufer remarked in his personal reminiscences: "This was a very uncomfortable situation in which to be. Even to hint to fellow candidates (in psychoanalysis) that there might be an organic component of significance in some of the children under discussion was an invitation to be dealt with in a manner remarkably close to ostracism" (1975, p. 110).

The debate about organic versus functional causes continued for some time. In a landmark publication, Strauss and Lehtinen (1947) suggested that the diagnosis of "brain injury" could be made on the basis of psychological characteristics alone, with distractibility, or hyperactivity, a cardinal sign. There were objections to this line of reasoning and to the use of the word "brain injury" in the absence of clear-cut neurological evidence. Birch (1964), for one, pointed out that many children with known and independently verified brain damage did not exhibit the patterns of behavior presumably characteristic of "brain damage." Rapin (1964) suggested that the same behavior could result from either "damage" or emotional arousal, via the same neurological system:

The point which the author wishes to make is that hyperactivity, distractibility and forced responsiveness are not pathognomic of brain damage, but that they may be seen just as well in functional derangements of the subcortical mechanisms which influence the activity of the reticular formation. In other words, cortical damage with decreased cortico-fugal control of sensory inputs is only one possible explanation for the observed behavior. Increased activity in the reticular formation secondary to anxiety is another. (p. 23)

This high-level criticism brought about a change in terminology. "Minimal brain dysfunction" was used by Clements in an important monograph published by the National Institute of Neurological Diseases and Blindness (1966). The possible causes for this syndrome (which included a great variety of symptoms as well as hyperactivity) were

Genetic variations, biochemical irregularities, perinatal brain insults, or the results of illnesses and injuries sustained during the years critical for the normal development and maturation of the central nervous system. The definition also allows for the possibility that early severe sensory deprivation could result in central nervous system alterations which may be permanent. (Clements, 1966, p. 10)

The alternative explanation was seen as parental mishandling, and the dichotomy between "organic" and "functional" etiologies remained. This argumentation is further developed in the discussion of learning disabilities (see Chapter 11).

Implication of Organic Factors

Attention shifted from trying to identify a specific locus of disturbance to a more diffuse aspect of neurological functioning, namely, the biochemistry of the neurotransmitters. Like the biochemical research in schizophrenia and depression, a good deal of the evidence is indirectly derived from drug effects. Particularly implicated are the catecholamines (dopamine and norepinephrine). Numerous studies have confirmed the fact that stimulants (amphetamines) reduce anxiety and improve attention, at least for some hyperactive children (Barkley, 1977; Whalen & Henker, 1976). Since it is known that these stimulants act directly on catecholaminergic mechanisms, it is a logical next step to conclude that brain catecholamines are influential in the cause of hyperactivity (Wender, 1971, 1978).

At first it was thought that these drugs had a "paradoxical effect," that is, that they acted as "downers" for hyperactive children only as contrasted with the stimulating effect on "normal" children. For ethical reasons, drug research with normal children is limited. However, Rapoport et al. (1978) studied the effects of a single dose with normal prepubertal boys and found that these children too showed short-term improvements in attention and learning, reduced rates of task-irrelevant verbalization and less movement during structured task activity. Other evidence was also served to refute the idea of a "paradoxical effect" (Taylor, 1983). A favorable drug response cannot be used to "validate" the organicity of the hyperactivity. In reviewing this subject, Whalen (1982) also pointed out that the danger of reasoning backward from treatment to etiology, i.e., assuming that a positive medication response confirms a physiological defect.

The numerous psychophysiological studies have yielded equivocal results. Quite often a statistically significant difference will be found for the "average" score in the hyperactive group compared to a normal sample, but there will be many individual exceptions. Some of the findings suggest that the hyperactive is like a normal but younger child. For instance, as a group they show electroencephalographic differences (patterns of underarousal) and neurologic "soft signs" (e.g., visual-motor problems and motor incoordination) interpreted as indications of neurologic immaturity. On the other hand, some of the findings suggest a difference which is not readily attributable to immaturity. A fair percentage seem to be underreactive to stimulation, that is, their psychophysiologic responses appear to be smaller in amplitude, slower to occur, faster to habituate (discontinue) and more variable from moment to moment than the responses of normal children (Hastings & Barkley, 1978). Finally, Barkley (1981) pointed out that hyperactive children show a higher number of physical ailments (for instance, serious allergies) and anomalies than normal children. It is clear that there are subgroups in the hyperactive population, some of which show other indications of neurologic vulnerability.

Etiology

In 1974, Feingold, an allergist, proposed that salicylates, artificial flavors, and food-coloring caused hyperactivity and accordingly suggested a special diet. This hypothesis has been subjected to considerable investigation and numerous reviews have been published (Conners, 1980; Stare, Whelan, & Sheridan, 1980; Taylor, 1979). Briefly, the data from double-blind studies offer little, if any, support for Feingold's hypothesis. Swanson and Kinsbourne (1980) did find some deterioration on a learning task when a large amount of artificial food color was administered, but this far exceeded the level of additives in a normal diet. It seems probable that the success Feingold observed with the dietary restriction stemmed from parental expectations or other alterations in the child's environment secondary to the diet regimen.

Some consideration has been given to sugar intake in relationship to hyperactivity. Prinz, Roberts, and Hantman (1980) found a significant positive association between consumption of sugar products and observation of playroom behavior in a group of 28 hyperactive children 4 to 7 years of age. They did not find the same relationships between behavior and ingestion of additives or salicylates. However, there is some overlap and it is likely that a child on the Feingold diet might also experience a significant reduction in sugar consumption. This lead has not been subjected to the rigorous investigation of the Feingold diet, but it warrants further study. The authors are rightfully cautious in attributing a cause-and-effect relationship but suggest simply that "sucrose in high amounts might aggravate hyperactive children."

One other environmental toxin deserves mention, namely, lead. Elevated blood lead levels seems to cause a fair number of children to become hyperactive (David, Hoffman, Sverd, & Clark, 1977) but the majority of hyperactive children do not have elevated blood levels. In his critical review of research on organic factors in hyperactivity, Dubey (1976) remarked that no particular organic agent has emerged as a ubiquitous etiological factor and further noted that some observed differences in organic indicators between hyperactive and normal subjects might be a result rather than a cause of the behavioral differences. The fact that neurological disorders can cause hyperactivity is not in dispute; the controversy is whether organic disorders are in fact a primary cause in the majority of children identified as hyperactive.

The search for a biological basis of hyperactivity has taken a different tack in genetic studies. Study of parents alone does not separate environmental from biological factors, but there have been several studies of the biological parents of adopted-away offspring. In two such studies (Cantwell, 1975; Morrison & Stewart, 1973) biological fathers had higher rates of alcoholism and sociopathy and biological mothers had higher rates of hysteria compared with adoptive and control fathers and mothers. Alberts-Corush, Firestone, and Goodman (1986) compared the biological parents of adopted-away hyperactive children with the adoptive parents and found slower reaction times and other differences on attentional measures which mirrored the findings of studies with hyperactive children. On the other hand, the biological parents of normal control children and the adoptive parents for both hyperactive and normal control children did not differ on these measures. This study provides strong evidence for a genetic link between childhood hyperactivity and attentional deficits in the biological parents.

Another line of evidence suggesting a genetic link comes from differential concordance rates for twins. Willerman (1973) studied 93 pairs of same-sexed twins from a normal population and found that correlations for activity level ratings in monozygotic twins were substantially higher than those for dizygotic twins. In their review, Ferguson and Rapoport (1983) concluded that family studies suggest a genetic link for problem behavior "but implicate a general hyperactive-conduct disorder entity, rather than a hyperactivity syndrome" (p. 375).

The key question seems to be "what is it that is inherited?" Kinsbourne (1977) suggested that hyperactive children merely represent the extreme ends of the normal distribution for characteristics related to temperament. Using retrospective parent interview data, Lambert (1982) found that the primary hyperactive children were remembered as different in the first year of life because of low threshold level (hypersensitivity), difficulties in staying on schedule, adjusting slowly to changes, and being very active and not persistent. It seems probable that a larger number of hyperactive children represent the interaction of temperamental extremes and environmental conditions which do not facilitate the development of self-control. Some of these children could also be vulnerable to dietary excesses. Since all behavior is mediated through the nervous system, this does not minimize biological (organic) variations but suggests rather that the functioning of the central nervous system is developed through experience as well as through primary biological factors.

Underlying Psychological Mechanisms

Changing the name to "attention deficit disorder" was in part a recognition that hyperactive behavior was secondary to a more basic cognitive process, namely, attention. Douglas, psychologist at McGill University who has devoted many years to the study of cognitive processes of hyperactive children, recently suggested that the list of defective processes includes "(1) the investment, organization, and maintenance of attention and effort; (2) the inhibition of impulsive responding; (3) the modulation of arousal levels to meet situational demands; and (4) an unusually strong inclination to seek immediate reinforcement" (Douglas, 1983, p. 280).

It is difficult indeed to find any kind of cognitive task where hyperactive children perform as well as normal control children! Even on simple reaction time tasks, they tend to be slower to respond; where the task is complicated by delay or choice, hyperactive children make more errors (Douglas, 1983). Hyperactive children perform poorly on complex cognitive tasks requiring scanning or looking for common features of task stimuli. There seems to be no difference in their perceptual discrimination ability nor in short-term memory. It appears rather that the hyperactive child is unable to keep an idea sufficiently in mind (for instance, the directions for the particular task) to avoid response errors. As one would expect, hyperactive children encounter difficulty in concept discovery and rule learning tasks which require sustained attention to the material presented and the feedback from correct and incorrect responses.

It is not surprising that these cognitive differences add up to significant IQ differences (Palkes & Stewart, 1972) which seem to increase with age (Loney, 1974). In evaluating the reasons for the difficulties experienced by hyperactive children even when they are compared with matched IQ "normal" children, the question of motivation comes up. Is it that they "can't" or "just don't care to"? Efforts to manipulate motivation by positive or negative consequences have suggested that hyperactive children are unusually sensitive to rewards, and consequently particularly frustrated by failure. The need for immediate reward

could go a long way toward accounting for the phenomena reviewed in the chapter, including the children's vulnerability to re-ward-associated distractors, their faiulre to invest attention and effort to nonrewarding situations, their failure to modulate arousal levels in keeping with task demands, and their impulsive behavior on the DRL Task. (Douglas, 1983, pp. 321–2)

An example of a DRL, differential reinforcement for low-rate responding, task is given by Gordon (1979), where children were required to withhold responding for brief time intervals (6 seconds) in order to obtain a candy reward. If they were too quick, they had to wait another 6 seconds before getting the candy. The hyperactive boys responded more frequently but obtained fewer rewards than the normals, and this in a situation requiring a delay of only 6 seconds! From this experiment, one can appreciate the dilemma of motivating a hyperactive child. The prospect of the reward can itself be overpowering and distracting.

In a recent presentation, Douglas (1985) suggested that the core problem explaining the cognitive defects in hyperactive children is a deficiency in self-regulation and pointed out parallels with the cognitive performance typical of frontal lobe patients, fatigued individuals, and younger children. These parallels do not offer any support, one way or the other, in the old "organic" versus "functional" debate but simply highlight the fact that some organic conditions have a regressive effect, thereby reducing performance to a level "normal" for younger individuals. Further, Douglas suggested that because of the central importance of self-regulation, cognitive training offers considerable promise.

Drug Management

Even in the context of psychosocial treatments, most children diagnosed hyperactive probably receive psychostimulant therapy at some time during their school years. It has been estimated that about 1.5 to 2% of school-aged children take psychostimulants (Sprague & Gadow, 1976), and in most cases the drug is either Ritalin (methylphenidate) or Dexedrine (dextroamphetamine). There is abundant research investigating the effects using a variety of measures, including parent-teacher ratings (Barkley, 1977) and performance on laboratory tasks (Solanto, 1984). It is estimated that some 60 to 90% of hyperactive children show improvement, not so much in a general reduction of motor activity but more in terms of better control and attention so that the child adapts better to environmental demands (Whalen, 1982). Studies suggest that hyperactive behavior may be worsened in some 12% (Barkley, 1977).

In view of the well-documented short-term benefits of medication, it is suprising that they do not translate into evidence of long-term improvement in academic progress. Even though the child may get better school grades, achievement test scores show no improvement (Gittelman-Klein & Klein, 1975). Rie and Rie (1977) had children learn a story and tested their recall 2 hours and again 2 days later. Ritalin enhanced story recall in the first instance, but there were no medication-related differences 2 days later. Follow-up studies indicate that the academic difficulties of hyperactive children persist regardless of type, intensity, and duration of treatment. These results are as perplexing as they are disappointing beause it is usually assumed that the poor academic performance is a direct result of poor attention.

On the other hand, there have been reported improvement in the domain of social behavior. In studies of mother-child interactions, the improved responsiveness of the child with medication was reflected in more praise and less criticism from the mothers (Barkley & Cunningham, 1979; Humphries, Kinsbourne, & Swanson, 1978). Although the children seem to get along better with authority figures, it is not so clear what the effect is on peer relationships. Whalen, Henker, Collins, McAuliffe, and Vaux (1979) devised an interesting "astronaut game" to study referential communication and found that hyperactive boys were less efficient in their communications, with higher rates of task-irrelevant chatter and disagreement and less ability to shift from "command" to "follow." Medication had the effect of changing style but not of changing content. In other words, they did not have a better understanding of the problems involved but they were more agreeable in "playing the game."

The use of any drug demands careful consideration of side effects. The two most common side effects of stimulants are decreased appetite and insomnia. These usually respond to dosage adjustments, but there has been some concern about depression of growth rate (Safer & Allen, 1973). In a review of this literature, Roche, Lipman, Overall, and Hung (1979) reported evidence of temporary growth retardation, more apparent at high dosage levels and in children who take medication continuously (without "drug holidays"). There has also been some evidence of increases in heart rate and blood pressure, generally considered so small as to pose no health hazard (Whalen, 1982), but this serves to emphasize the importance of careful monitoring and using the minimum dose. "Over-dosing" may also be immediately apparent in behavioral changes which bear some resemblance to schizophrenia. Wender (1971) cited the case of a hyperactive child who persisted in writing a repetitive "punishment lesson" for 5 hours; Solanto and Conners (1982) described a child who became obsessively preoccupied and withdrew into a corner to read the same story over and over; and Young (1981) described an instance where methylphenidate precipitated visual hallucinations in a hyperactive child.

Whalen (1982) discussed the unintended consequences of psychostimulant medication other than physical. One is the child's view of the medication as perhaps "magic" for making him "smart" or "good." This suggests an external locus of control and might diminish the child's efforts to work on his own behalf. With all the research that has been done in this field it is surprising that there has been no systematic investigation of the child's perceptions of "the pill." The possibility that children accustomed to medication might turn to drugs of a different kind has been considered, but to date there is no evidence to suggest that these children are at risk for later substance abuse (Henker, Whalen, Bugental, & Barker, 1981). As Whalen said, drug treatment is seductive. It is quick, inexpensive, and has an immediately visible effect. However, when one looks at the picture as a whole, drug therapy does not cure the situation and one should not lose sight of the other treatment needs.

Multiple Interventions

Historically, treatment efforts focused on one or another single approach. In their early work with brain-injured children, Strauss and Lehtinen (1947) proposed various environmental manipulations to reduce external distractions— for example, placing a hyperactive child in an individual study cubicle with no windows or decorations. These procedures were widely adopted in public schools but proved less successful than was hoped (Cruickshank, Bentzen, Ratzeburg, & Tannhauser, 1961; Zentall & Zentall, 1976). Containment is not so easy, and even in this stripped-down environment, the hyperactive child does not stay "on task." With the advent of operant behavioral techniques in the early 1960's, case reports of success with hyperactive children appeared. Patterson, Jones, Whittier, and Wright (1965) described the conditioning of a neurologically damaged, mildly mentally retarded boy who was outfitted with earphones and a radio receiving unit. If he remained still and continued with his assignment task, a buzzer sounded every 10 seconds and he was given a piece of candy. Compared to a control subject, he showed significantly fewer nonattending behaviors and the effects persisted, without the apparatus, over a 4-week period. However, the improvement was not dramatic and even in the short follow-up, there was some regression. It was enough at that time to prove that hyperactive behavior, presumably of an organic origin, could be altered by operant methods.

Behavior therapists often decried the use of drugs (Brundage-Aguar, Forehand, & Ciminero, 1977; Mash & Dalby, 1979), citing the evidence of good results with behavior therapy alone. Wolraich (1979) reviewed 157 studies where this was the only treatment and found that the majority yielded positive results. Interestingly, and in contrast to the drug therapy studies, 36 of 39 studies which reported academic achievement found postitive changes. A major limitation of operant behavior therapy is the frequent regression when the reinforcement schedule is discontinued. Kent and O'Leary (1976) found that the beneficial treatment effects disappeared in a 9 months' follow-up. Another limitation is the practical one of dispensing the reinforcements on a consistent basis (even though on a variable schedule) and with sufficient frequency.

Gradually, professional workers of various persuasions became more tolerant of the use of drugs as the results of comparative studies became available. For example, Gittelman-Klein et al. (1980) studied 61 hyperactive children randomly assigned to (a) Ritalin only, (b) behavior therapy with a placebo, and (c) behavior therapy with Ritalin. Teacher ratings, direct classroom observations, and global ratings of improvement by parents, teachers, and physicians served as the outcome measures. On all measures, the combined program of drugs and behavior therapy was the best, but only slightly better than medication used alone. Most behavior therapists now feel comfortable with a combined approach (Pelham & Murphy, 1986).

Further, there has been a trend away from reliance on operant methods only. Certainly positive rewards must be forthcoming as a result of appropriate behavior, but as mentioned before, the prospect of the reward may in itself be distracting and evoke impulsive reactions. And it is difficult to use negative reinforcement (punishment) consistently for something as nebulous and yet continuous as "not paying attention." A frequent negative consequence is "response cost," that is, losing out on the positive reward, but unless this is carefully calibrated, the child becomes discouraged and stops making an effort. So, in tune with the times, cognitive-behavioral techniques have been developed specifically to help hyperactive children manage their own behavior.

Douglas developed a program of this type in an educational setting (1980). She starts with helping children to understand the nature of their deficits and ways in which training can help them. This is like establishing a "treatment alliance" where the child understands what is going to happen and for what purpose so that he can actively participate. This is followed by teaching general rules for approaching tasks and specific techniques for scanning, focusing, checking, careful listening, considering alternatives, organizing materials and schedules, rehearsal strategies and memory aids, etc. Also, the child is assisted in labeling his behavior and his feelings, in using verbal self-commands, in differentiating careless errors from errors of misunderstanding, and in setting goals which are neither too high nor too low. This is a mix of "metacognition strategies" (Ryan, Short, & Weed, 1986), and the procedures developed by

Meichenbaum, Kendall, and others described earlier.

In any intervention program, it is essential to tailor the teaching material and expectations to the child's individual capacities. There is no magic transformation with either drug therapy or behavior therapy, and one cannot expect that a child who is behind in academic skills will suddenly "catch up" without remedial educational help. At the very least this means presenting academic material which is below the child's level of frustration and proceeding with a gradually increasing order of difficulty. At most it means the use of special methods and materials which circumvent specific deficiencies (for example, visual-motor problems). Simply sitting still, holding the pencil, or looking fixedly at the book or blackboard does not mean that the child is learning. Sprague (1983) pointed out that teaching techniques and the cirriculum have been ignored in the vast literature concerning psychoactive drug treatments, behavior modification, and other treatments. This is amazing in view of the fact that school is a major problem situation for these children, and teacher rating scales are often the standards used to judge treatment effects.

Another problem area is peer relationships, and one of the very few studies of social behavior compared cognitive-behavioral and drug interventions (Hinshaw, Henker, & Whalen, 1984). The outcome measures were playground behavior observations obtained during a summer school program for hyperactive boys. The basic program included daily training in self-instructional procedures with academic tasks, intervention focused on anger control in peer provocative situations, and instruction in self-evaluation skills. The comparative experiment was conducted in the fourth week of summer school with the boys equally divided between combinations of treatment conditions. Medication (compared with placebo) reduced negative social behavior significantly; augmented reinforcement which included rewards for accurate self-evaluation had more effect than simple external rewards for cooperative behavior; and the combination of drug and augmented reinforcement had the most effect. It is noteworthy that the older children (ages 10.8 to 13.2 years) did not show the medication-placebo differences found with the younger children (ages 7.9 to 10.8 years). Also, 4 of the 12 boys in the older group received primary diagnoses of conduct disorder as compared to none in the younger group. There is not enough clinical information to attempt an explanation, but it fits with the common experience of discontinuing drug medication around the age of 12 years, at least in part because the beneficial effects are less obvious.

In the vast treatment literature on hyperactive children, there is very little which might be called "psychodynamic" in orientation. Although individual child psychotherapy by itself would probably be of little help with a pervasively hyperactive child, there are some relevant principles which can be "borrowed" by others. The fact that anxiety increases hyperactivity leads one to consider possible sources of anxiety. Hyperactive children respond poorly to new situations or "wide-open" situations where anything goes, or seems to. Offering suggestions, preparation for what is to come, and explanations even when no question is asked may dilute the anxiety. Also, much anxiety has a fantasy basis rather than a basis in reality. Hyperactive children are no better in processing their inner mental life than they are in processing external stimuli. Fantasies seem to pop into their heads, cause a stir, and disappear as quick as a flash. They do not take, or have, the time to clearly distinguish real from unreal, so they are poor at "pretend games" and are often confused by "dream monsters."

Anxiety may be masked by activity or anger so that one does not consider the possibility. Even more confusing are those children who develop counter-phobic mechanisms where they not only deny anxiety but are compulsively drawn to scary things or risky activities in order to prove again and again that there is nothing to be afraid of. Although these children score low on behavioral anxiety measures, this does not mean that they have no anxiety. Freeman and Cornwall (1980) gave brief case summaries of the psychotherapy of five hyperactive children which illustrate the diverse nature of hyperactivity and the improvement which came about from uncovering their fears and defensive maneuvers. This report serves to remind us that all children face common problems in growing up, and it is not surprising that hyperactive children have more difficulty in finding adaptive solutions.

Helping the Parents to Cope

Barkley selected this as a chapter title in order to emphasize "coping" rather than "curing": "While improvements may be made in the child's behavior problems, some problems are likely to remain, or others are more likely to develop in the future (1981, p. 363). Principles and techniques are borrowed from the parent training already discussed in relation to child aggressive and noncompliant behavior and do not need further elaboration in this context. What is special in working with parents of hyperactive children is a shift in expectations, described by Barkley as "half the battle." On the basis of much less specialized experience, this author would concur. Barkley remarked that "In my opinion, this new attitude will often help parents who tend to drift from one therapist to another, always seeking the quick fix or elusive cure for their hyperactive children while never being satisfied with those services that are delivered, even if these are helpful" (1981, p. 281).

The parents get a lot of professional support for their optimism. As long as the child is not mentally retarded, educators, psychologists, pediatricians, and psychiatrists tend to minimize the problems, ascribing them to immaturity (which supposedly will be outgrown), or poor home discipline (curable by greater parental strictness), or simple frustration from external causes. The dilemma is that these factors do explain some instances of hyperactivity, and we do not have sufficiently sensitive diagnostic tools to identify pervasive and persistent hyperactivity. The tendency in the United States to over-use the diagnosis makes it more benign since the serious cases are outnumbered by those who are "too active" for one person's liking or only in occasional situations.

Developmental Course and Outcome

Laufer and Denhoff (1957), pioneers in this field, suggested that hyperactivity spontaneously lessened with age and disappeared by adulthood. Further studies have been far less optimistic. The symptom picture changes with less reported hyperactivity, but distractibility, immaturity, poor school performance, and social maladjustment persist (Weiss, 1983). It is not surprising that as adolescents, hyperactive children show more depression and self-denigration than matched controls.

Thorley (1984) reviewed 24 long-term outcome studies published since 1967. In general, the studies do not include any psychiatric comparison group, so one cannot say if hyperactive children fare better or worse than any other group identified in childhood as having a problem. Compared to "matched controls" (without psychiatric history), they do not fare so well. Also, the follow-up investigators do not describe the characteristics of the 20% or so that are "lost" in the follow-up, a group that might possibly be doing better than those who are relocated. With these limitations in mind, the overall conclusion is that performance and social difficulties persist into adulthood. Major psychiatric problems are not likely but the impulsive personality style continues. As mentioned earlier, conduct disorder and hyperactivity are often associated diagnoses but they need to be separated in considering outcomes. In a 4-year follow-up, August, Stewart, and Holmes (1983) found that the "pure" hyperactive group did not show aggressive and antisocial problems but only a continuance of the original inattentiveness and impulsivity.

Weiss, after reviewing the negative findings in follow-up studies of hyperactive children treated with stimulant medication, asked "how are clinicians to modify or prevent the poor self-esteem, poor socialization, lower educational level and impulsivity which are seen in most hyperactives even in adulthood?" (1983, p. 428). She concluded that "a condition with such a broad spectrum of difficulties as the hyperactive child syndrome requires a wide range of therapeutic input and can only rarely be managed by medication alone" (1983, p. 431). Even with the best and most comprehensive of treatment programs, we will probably be able to recognize the hyperactive child in the adult. We should be helping the child to feel "OK" about himself and to be proud of what he has achieved against obstacles rather than trying to transform the child into an idealized version of "normal."

SUMMARY

This chapter has dealt with two conditions, conduct disorders and hyperactivity, which bring the child into serious conflict with parents and teachers alike. Both categories encompass a wide diversity of problems and need to be subdivided for proper understanding and consideration of treatment choice. Although hypersensitivity is usually associated with conduct problems, the reverse is not necessarily the case. Conduct disorders are generally regarded as a failure in social learning and the most successful treatments to date have followed a behavioral approach, either directly with the child or in parent management training programs. The positive evaluation of success of such treatments should be tempered by the fact that many families cannot be engaged in these programs. The theoretical question involved has to do mainly with the modification of aggression through identification, modulation by desire to please, and learning constructive methods of dealing with frustration.

Hyperactivity is distinguished by the historical emphasis on organic factors and its modifiability by drug therapy. However, the absence of long-term effects (particularly in academic learning) strongly suggests that reliance on drug therapy alone is unwise. In all probability, a multifactor etiology should be considered with genetic vulnerability given considerable weight but with subsequent environmental stresses playing a part. These children need direct help in the way of special education and strategies to control their impulsivity and to focus attention. Cognitive behavior therapy programs have been outlined but little is known about their long-term effects.

In both conditions, it is easy to lose sight of the fact that these children experience all the conflicts faced by all children in growing up. They are not reflective children who readily talk about their fears and fantasies; on the contrary, they tend to discharge tension by immediate action. Although psychotherapy is not the main treatment of choice in most instances, it can serve an important supplemental role.

REFERENCES

ACKERSON, L. (1931). *Children's behavior problems*. Chicago: The University of Chicago Press.

AICHORN, A. (1935). *Wayward youth*. New York: Viking.

ALBERTS-CORUSH, J., FIRESTONE, P., & GOODMAN, J. T. (1986). Attention and impulsivity characteristics of the biological and adoptive parents of hyperactive and normal control children. *American Journal of Orthopsychiatry, 56*, 413–424.

APA. (1987). *Diagnostic and statistical manual of mental disorders* (DSM-III-R). Washington, DC: American Psychiatric Association.

AUGUST, G. J., STEWART, M. A., & HOLMES, C. S. (1983). A four year follow-up of hyperactive boys with and without conduct disorders. *British Journal of Psychiatry, 143*, 192–198.

BANDURA, A., & WALTERS, R. H. (1959). *Adolescent aggression*. New York: Ronald Press.

BARKLEY, R. A. (1977). A review of stimulant drug research with hyperactive children. *Journal of Child Psychology and Psychiatry, 18*, 137–165.

BARKLEY, R. A. (1981). *Hyperative children: A handbook for diagnosis and treatment*. New York: Guilford Press.

BARKLEY, R., & CUNNINGHAM, C. (1979). The effect of methylphenidate on the mother-child interaction and hyperactive children. *Archives of General Psychiatry, 36*, 201–208.

BERNAL, M. E., DURYEE, J. S., PRUETT, H. L., & BURNS, B. J. (1968). Behavior modification and the brat syndrome. *Journal of Consulting and Clinical Psychology, 32*(4), 447–455.

BERNAL, M. E., KLINNERT, M. D., & SCHULTZ, L. A. (1980). Outcome evaluation of behavioral parent training and client-centered parent counseling for children with conduct problems. *Journal of Applied Behavior Analysis, 13*, 677–691.

BILLINGS, D. C., & WASIK, B. H. (1985). Self-instructional training with preschoolers: An attempt to replicate. *Journal of Applied Behavioral Analysis, 18*(1), 61–67.

BIRCH, H. G. (1964). *Brain damage in children: The biological and social aspects*. Baltimore: Williams & Wilkins.

BORNSTEIN, P. H. (1985). Self-instructional

training: A commentary and state-of-the-art. *Journal of Applied Behavioral Analysis, 18*(1), 69–72.

BRADLEY, C. (1937). The behavior of children receiving benzedrine. *American Journal of Psychiatry, 94,* 577–585.

BRUNDAGE-AGUAR, D., FOREHAND, R., & CIMINERO, A. (1977). A review of treatment approaches for hyperactive behavior. *Journal of Clinical Child Psychology, 3,* 3–9.

BRYAN, J. H., & LONDON, P. (1970). Altruistic behavior by children. *Psychological Bulletin, 73,* 200–211.

BUTTONS, A. (1973). Some antecedents of felonies and delinquent behavior. *Journal of Clinical Child Psychology, 2,* 35–37.

CAMP, B., BLOM, G., HEBERT, F., & VAN DOORNINCK, W. (1977). "Think Aloud": A program for developing self-control in young aggressive boys. *Journal of Abnormal Child Psychology, 5,* 157–169.

CANTWELL, D. (1975). Genetic studies of hyperactive children: Psychiatric illness in biological and adopting parents. In R. Fieve, D. Rosenthal, & H. Brill (Eds.), *Genetic research in psychiatry* (pp. 273–282). Baltimore: Johns Hopkins University Press.

CANTWELL, D. (1977). Hyperkinetic syndrome. In M. Rutter & L. Hersov (Eds.), *Child psychiatry: Modern approaches* (pp. 524–555). London: Blackwell.

CANTWELL, D. (1978). Hyperactivity and antisocial behaviour. *Journal of the American Academy of Child Psychiatry, 17,* 252–262.

CASS, L. K., & THOMAS, C. B. (1979). *Childhood pathology and later adjustment.* New York: Wiley.

CLEMENTS, S. D. (1966). Minimal brain dysfunction in children—Terminology and identification. *National Institute of Neurological Diseases and Blindness Monographs, 3,* Washington, DC.

CONNERS, C. K. (1969). A teacher rating scale for use in drug studies with children. *American Journal of Psychiatry, 126,* 884–888.

CONNERS, C. K. (1973). Rating scales for use in drug studies with children. *Psychopharmacology Bulletin* (Special Issue—Pharmacotherapy with children), 24–84.

CONNERS, C. K. (1980). *Food additives and hyperactive children.* New York: Plenum.

CROCKER, D. (1955). The study of a problem of aggression. In R. S. Eissler, A. Freud, H. Hartmann, & E. Kris (Eds.), *Psychoanalytic study of the child* (Vol. 10, pp. 300–335). New York: International Universities Press.

CRUICKSHANK, W. M., BENTZEN, F. A., RATZEBURG, F. H., & TANNAHUSEER, M. (1961). *A teaching method for brain-injured and hyperactive children.* Syracuse: Syracuse University Press.

DAVID, O. J., HOFFMAN, S. P., SVERD, J., & CLARK, J. (1977). Lead and hyperactivity: Lead levels among hyperactive children. *Journal of Abnormal Child Psychology, 5,* 405–416.

DAVIDS, A. (1971). An objective instrument for assessing hyperkinesis in children. *Journal of Learning Disabilities, 4,* 35–37.

DEVLIN, M. (1985). *The stubborn child.* New York: Atheneum.

DiGIUSEPPE, R. (1981). Cognitive therapy with children. In G. Emery, S. D. Hollon, & R. C. Bedrosian (Eds.), *New directions in cognitive therapy* (pp. 50–67). New York: Guilford Press.

DiGIUSEPPE, R. (1983). Rational-emotive therapy and conduct disorders. In A. Ellis & M. E. Bernard (Eds.), *Rational-emotive approaches to the problems of childhood* (pp. 111–138). New York: Plenum Press.

DOUGLAS, V. I. (1980). Treatment and training approaches to hyperactivity: Establishing internal or external control. In C. Whalen & B. Henker (Eds.), *Hyperactive children: The social ecology of identification and treatment* (pp. 283–317). New York: Academic Press.

DOUGLAS, V. I. (1983). Attentional and cognitive problems. In M. Rutter (Ed.), *Developmental neuropsychiatry* (pp. 280–239). New York: Guilford Press.

DOUGLAS, V. I. (1985, April). *Cognitive deficits*

in children with attention deficit disorder with hyperactivity. Paper presented to Society for Research in Child Development, Toronto, Canada.

DOUGLAS, V., PARRY, P., MARTON, P., & GARSON, C. (1976). Assessment of a cognitive training program for hyperactive children. *Journal of Abnormal Child Psychology, 4,* 389–410.

DUBEY, D. R. (1976). Organic factors in hyperkinesis: A critical evaluation. *American Journal of Orthopsychiatry, 46,* 353–366.

EYBERG, S. M., & ROSS, A. W. (1978). Assessment of child behavior problems: The validation of a new inventory. *Journal of Clinical Child Psychology, 7,* 113–116.

FEINGOLD, B. F. (1974). *Why your child is hyperactive.* New York: Random House.

FERGUSON, H. B., & RAPOPORT, J. L. (1983). Nosological issues and biological validation. In M. Rutter (Ed.), *Developmental neuropsychiatry* (pp. 369–384). New York: Guilford Press.

FESHBACH, S., & FESHBACH, N. (1973). Alternatives to corporal punishment. *Journal of Clinical Child Psychology, 2,* 46–49.

FOREHAND, R. L., & MCMAHON, R. J. (1981). *Helping the noncompliant child. A clinician's guide to parent training.* New York: Guilford Press.

FOREHAND, R., MIDDLEBROOK, J., ROGERTS, T., & STEFFE, M. (1983). Dropping out of parent training. *Behaviour Research and Therapy, 21,* 663–668.

FREEMAN, D. F., & CORNWALL, T. P. (1980). Hyperactivity and neurosis. *American Journal of Orthopsychiatry, 50,* 704–711.

FRIEDLANDER, K. (1947). *The psychoanalytic approach to juvenile delinquency.* New York: International Universities Press.

GILBERT, G. M. (1957). A survey of "referral problems" in metropolitan child guidance centers. *Journal of Clinical Psychology, 13,* 37–42.

GITTELMAN-KLEIN, R., & KLEIN, D. F. (1975). Are behavioral and psychometric changes related in methylphenidate-treated hyperactive children? *International Journal of Mental Health, 4,* 182–198.

GITTELMAN-KLEIN, R., ABIKOFF, H., POLLACK, E., KLEIN, D. F., KATZ, S., & MATTES, J. (1980). A controlled trial of behavior modification and methylphenidate in hyperactive children. In C. K. Whalen & B. Henker (Eds.), *Hyperactive children: The social ecology of identification and treatment* (pp. 221–243). New York: Academic Press.

GORDON, M. (1979). The assessment of impulsivity and mediating behaviors in hyperactive and non-hyperactive boys. *Journal of Abnormal Child Psychology, 7,* 317–326.

GRIM, P. F., KOHLBERG, L., & WHITE, S. H. (1968). Some relationships between conscience and attentional processes. *Journal of Personality and Social Psychology, 8,* 239–252.

GRINDER, R. E. (1962). Parental childrearing practices, conscience and resistance to temptation of sixth grade children. *Child Development, 33,* 803–820.

HASTINGS, J. E., & BARKLEY, R. A. (1978). A review of psychophysiological research with hyperactive children. *Journal of Abnormal Child Psychology, 7,* 413–447.

HENKER, B., WHALEN, C. K., BUGENTAL, D. B., & BARKER, C. (1981). Licit and illicit drug use patterns in stimulant treated children and their peers. In K. D. Gadow & J. Loney (Eds.), *Psychosocial aspects of drug treatment for hyperactivity* (pp. 443–462). Boulder, CO: Westview Press.

HENN, F. A., BARDWELL, R., & JENKINS, R. L. (1980). Juvenile delinquents revisited: Adult criminal activity. *Archives of General Psychiatry, 37,* 1160–1163.

HERBERT, M. (1978). *Conduct disorders of childhood and adolescence: A behavioural approach to assessment and treatment.* Chichester, England: Wiley.

HERBERT, M. (1982). Conduct disorders. In A. E. Kazdin & B. B. Lahey (Eds.), *Advances in clinical child psychology* (Vol. 5, pp. 95–136). New York: Plenum Press.

HINSHAW, S. P., HENKER, B., & WHALEN, C. K.

(1984). Cognitive-behavioral and pharmacologic intervention for hyperactive boys: Comparative and combined effects. *Journal of Consulting and Clinical Psychology, 52,* 739–749.

HOBBS, S. A., MOGUIN, L. E., TYROLER, M., & LAHEY, B. B. (1980). Cognitive behavior therapy with children: Has clinical utility been demonstrated? *Psychological Bulletin, 87,* 147–165.

HUMPHRIES, T., KINSBOURNE, M., & SWANSON, J. (1978). Stimulant effects on cooperation and social interaction between hyperactive children and their mothers. *Journal of Child Psychology and Psychiatry, 19,* 13–22.

JOHNSON, A. (1949). Sanctions for super-ego lacunae of adolescents. In K. R. Eissler, (Ed.), *Searchlights on delinquency* (pp. 225–245). New York: International Universities Press.

KAGAN, J. (1966). Reflection-impulsivity: The generality and dynamics of conceptual tempo. *Journal of Abnormal Psychology, 71,* 17–24.

KAHN, E., & COHEN, L. H. (1934). Organic driveness: A brain stem syndrome and an experience. *New England Journal of Medicine, 210,* 748–756.

KAZDIN, A. E. (1984). Treatment of conduct disorders. In J. B. Williams & R. L. Spitzer (Eds.), *Psychotherapy research: Where are we and where should we go?* (pp. 3–28). New York: Guilford Press.

KENDALL, P. C., & BRASWELL, L. (1985). *Cognitive-behavioral therapy for impulsive children.* New York: Guilford Press.

KENDALL, P. C., & WILCOX, L. E. (1979). Self-control in children: Development of a rating scale. *Journal of Consulting and Clinical Psychology, 47,* 1020–29.

KENDALL, P. C., & WILCOX, L. E. (1980). A cognitive-behavioral treatment for impulsivity: Concrete versus conceptual training with non-self-controlled problem children. *Journal of Consulting and Clinical Psychology, 48,* 80–91.

KENDALL, P. C., & ZUPAN, B. A. (1981). Individ-

ual versus group application of cognitive-behavioral self-control procedures with children. *Behavior Therapy, 12,* 344–359.

KENT, R. N., & O'LEARY, K. D. (1976). A controlled evaluation of behavior modification with conduct problem children. *Journal of Consulting and Clinical Psychology, 44,* 586–596.

KINSBOURNE, M. (1977). The mechanism of hyperactivity. In M. Blaw, I. Rapin, & M. Kinsbourne (Eds.), *Topics in child neurology.* New York: Spectrum.

KLEIN, G. S., & SCHLESINGER, H. J. (1949). Where is the perceiver in perceptual theory? *Journal of Personality, 18,* 32–47.

KOHLBERG, L. (1976). Moral stages and moralization: The cognitive-developmental approach. In T. Lickona (Ed.), *Moral development and behavior: Theory, research and social issues* (pp. 31–53). New York: Holt, Rinehart & Winston.

LAMBERT, N. M. (1982). Temperament profiles of hyperactive children. *American Journal Orthopsychiatry, 52,* 458–467.

LAMBERT, N. M., SANDOVAL, J., & SASSONE, D. (1978). Prevalence of hyperactivity in elementary school children as a function of social system definers. *American Journal Orthopsychiatry, 18*(3), 446–463.

LAPOUSE, R., & MONK, M. A. (1958). An epidemiologic study of behavior characteristics in children. *American Journal of Public Health, 48,* 1134–44.

LAUFER, M. W. (1975). In Osler's day it was syphilis. In E. J. Anthony (Ed.), *Explorations in child psychiatry* (pp. 105–126). New York: Plenum.

LAUFER, M. W., & DENHOFF, E. (1957). Hyperkinetic behavior syndrome in children. *Journal of Pediatrics, 50,* 463–474.

LAUFER, M. W., DENHOFF, E., & SOLOMONS, G. (1957). Hyperkinetic impulse disorder in children's behavior problems. *Psychosomatic Medicine, 19,* 39–49.

LOEBER, R., & SCHMALING, K. (1985). Empirical evidence for overt and covert patterns of antisocial conduct problems: A meta-analysis. *Journal of Abnormal Child Psychology, 13,* 337–352.

LONEY, J. (1974). The intellectual functioning of hyperactive elementary school boys. A cross-sectional investigation. *American Journal of Orthopsychiatry, 44,* 754–762.

MASH, E. J., & DALBY, J. T. (1979). Behavioral interventions for hyperactive. In R. L. Trites (Ed.), *Hyperactivity in children: Etiology, measurement and treatment implications* (pp. 161–216). Baltimore: University Park Press.

McMAHON, R. J., & FOREHAND, R. (1984). Parent training for the noncompliant child. In R. E. Dangel & R. A. Polster (Eds.), *Parent training* (pp. 298–328). New York: Guilford Press.

MEICHENBAUM, D. H., & GOODMAN, J. (1971). Training impulsive children to talk to themselves: A means of developing self-control. *Journal of Abnormal Psychology, 77,* 115–126.

MOORE, D., CHAMBERLAIN, P., & MUKAI, L. (1979). Children at risk for delinquency. A follow-up comparison of aggressive children and children who steal. *Journal of Abnormal Child Psychology, 7,* 345–355.

MORRIS, J. R., & STEWART, M. A. (1973). The psychiatric status of the legal families of adopted hyperactive children. *Archives of General Psychiatry, 23,* 888–891.

PALKES, H., STEWART, M., & KAHAN, A. B. (1968). Porteus Maze performance of hyperactive boys after training in self-directed verbal commands. *Child Development, 39,* 817–826.

PALKES, H., & STEWART, M. (1972). Intellectual ability and performance of hyperactive children. *American Journal of Orthopsychiatry, 42,* 35–39.

PATTERSON, G. F. (1982). *A social learning approach: Vol. 3. Coercive family process.* Eugene, OR: Castalia.

PATTERSON, G. R., JONES, R., WHITTIER, J., & WRIGHT, M. A. (1965). A behavior modification technique for the hyperactive child. *Behaviour Research and Therapy, 2,* 217–226.

PATTERSON, G. R., REID, J. B., JONES, R. R., & CONGER, R. E. (1975). *A social learning approach to family intervention: Vol. 1. Families with aggressive children.* Eugene, OR: Castalia.

PELHAM, W. E., & MURPHY, H. A. (1986). Behavioral and pharmacological treatment of hyperactivity and attention deficit disorders. In M. Hersen (Ed.), *Pharmacological and behavioral treatment: An integrative approach.* New York: Wiley.

PEREZ, J. F. (1978). *The family roots of adolescent delinquency.* New York: Van Nostrand Reinhold.

PETERSON, D. R. (1961). Behavior problems of middle childhood. *Journal of Consulting Psychology, 25,* 205–9.

PIAGET, J. (1932). *The moral judgment of the child* (M. Gabain, Trans.). London: Kegan Paul.

PRINZ, R. J., ROBERTS, W. A., & HANTMAN, E. (1980). Dietary correlates of hyperactive behavior in children. *Journal of Consulting and Clinical Psychology, 48,* 760–769.

QUAY, H. C. (1979). Classification. In H. C. Quay & J. S. Werry (Eds.), *Psychopathological disorders of childhood* (2nd ed., pp. 1–42). New York: Wiley.

RAPIN, I. (1968). Brain damage in children. In J. Brennemann (Ed.), *Practice of pediatrics* (Vol. 4, pp. 1–58). Hagerstown, MD: Prior Publications.

RAPOPORT, J., BUCHSBAUM, M., ZAHN, T., WEINGARTNER, H., LUDLOW, L., & MIKKELSEN, E. (1978). Dextroamphetamine: Behavioral and cognitive effects in normal prepubertal boys. *Science, 199,* 560–563.

REDL, F., & WINEMAN, D. (1951). *Children who hate.* New York: Free Press.

REDL, F., & WINEMAN, D. (1957). *The aggressive child.* New York: Free Press.

REXFORD, E. N. (1959). Anti-social young children and their families. In L. Jessner & E. Pavenstedt (Eds.), *Dynamic psychopathology in childhood* (pp. 186–220). New York: Grune & Stratton.

RIE, E. D., & RIE, H. E. (1977). Recall, retention and Ritalin. *Journal of Consulting and Clinical Psychology, 45*, 967–972.

ROBINS, L. N. (1966). *Deviant children grown up: A sociological and psychiatric study of sociopathic personality.* Baltimore, MD: Williams & Wilkins.

ROBINS, L. N. (1970). The adult development of the antisocial child. *Seminars in Psychiatry, 2*, 420–435.

ROBINS, L. N. (1974). Antisocial behavior disturbances in childhood: Prevalence, prognosis and prospects. In E. J. Anthony & C. Koupernik (Eds.), *The child in his family: Children at psychiatric risk.* (pp. 447–460). New York: Wiley.

ROBINS, L. N. (1981). Epidemiological approaches to natural history research: Antisocial disorders in children. *Journal of the American Academy of Child Psychiatry, 20*, 566–580.

ROBINSON, E. A., EYBERG, S. M., & ROSS, A. W. (1980). Inventory of Child Problem Behaviors. The standardization of an inventory of child conduct problem behaviors. *Journal of Clinical Child Psychology, 7*, 22–28.

ROCHE, A. F., LIPMAN, R. S., OVERALL, J. E., & HUNG, W. (1979). The effects of stimulant medication on the growth of hyperkinetic children. *Pediatrics, 63*, 847–850.

RUTTER, M. (1983). Behavioral studies: Questions and findings on the concept of a distinctive syndrome. In M. Rutter (Ed.), *Developmental neuropsychiatry* (pp. 259–279). New York: Guilford Press.

RUTTER, M., COX, A., TUPLING, C., BERGER, M., & YULE, W. (1975). Attainment and adjustment in two geographical areas: I. The prevalence of psychiatric disorder. *British Journal of Psychiatry, 126*, 493–509.

RUTTER, M., TIZARD, J., & WHITMORE, K. (Eds.). (1981). *Education, health and behaviour.* Huntington, NY: Krieger. (Original work published 1970).

RYAN, E. B., SHORT, E. J., & WEED, K. A. (1986). The role of cognitive strategy training in improving the academic performance of learning disabled children.

Journal of Learning Disabilities, 19, 521–529.

SAFER, D. J., & ALLEN, R. P. (1973). Factors influencing the suppressant effects of two stimulant drugs on the growth of hyperactive children. *Pediatrics, 51*, 660–667.

SAFER, D. J., & ALLEN, R. P. (1976). *Hyperactive children: Diagnosis and management.* Baltimore, MD: University Park Press.

SANDBERG, S. (1981). On the overinclusiveness of the diagnosis of the hyperkinetic syndrome. In M. Gittelman (Ed.), *Strategic interventions for hyperactive children* (pp. 8–38). New York: Sharpe.

SANTOSTEFANO, S. (1971). Beyond nosology: Diagnosis from the viewpoint of development. In H. E. Rie (Ed.), *Perspectives in child psychopathology* (pp. 130–177). Chicago, IL: Aldine–Atherton.

SANTOSTEFANO, S., & RIEDER, C. (1984). Cognitive controls and aggression in children: The concept of cognitive-affective balance. *Journal of Consulting and Clinical Psychology, 52*, 46–56.

SCHACHAR, R., RUTTER, M., & SMITH, A. (1981). The characteristics of situationally and pervasively hyperactive children: Implications for syndrome definition. *Journal of Child Psychology and Psychiatry, 22*, 375–392.

SEARS, R. R., MACCOBY, E., & LEVIN, H. (1957). *Patterns of child rearing.* New York: Harper & Row.

SOLANTO, M. V. (1984). Neuropharmacological basis of stimulant drug action in attention deficit disorder with hyperactivity: A review and synthesis. *Psychological Bulletin, 95*, 387–410.

SOLANTO, M. V., & CONNERS, C. K. (1982). A dose-response and time-action analysis of automatic and behavioral effects of methylphenidate in attention deficit disorder with hyperactivity. *Psychophysiology, 19*, 658–667.

SPRAGUE, R. L., & GADOW, K. D. (1976). The role of the teacher in drug treatment. *School Review, 85*, 109–140.

SPRAGUE, R. L. (1983). Behavior modification

and educational techniques. In M. Rutter (Ed.), *Developmental neuropsychiatry* (pp. 404–421). New York: Guilford Press.

SPRING, C., BLUNDEN, D., GREENBERG, L. W., & YELLIN, A. M. (1977). Validity and norms of a hyperactivity rating scale. *Journal of Special Education, 11,* 313–321.

STARE, F. J., WHELAN, E. M., & SHERIDAN, M. (1980). Diet and hyperactivity: Is there a relationship? *Pediatrics, 66,* 521–525.

STARK, R., & McEVOY, J. (1970). Middle class violence. *Psychology Today, 4,* 52–57.

STEWART, M. A., CUMMINGS, C., SINGER, S., & DE BLOIS, C. S. (1981). The overlap between hyperative and unsocialized aggressive children. *Journal of Child Psychology and Psychiatry, 22,* 35–45.

STRAUSS, A. A., & LEHTINEN, L. E. (1947). *Psychopathology and education of the brain-injured child.* New York: Grune & Stratton.

SWANSON, J. M., & KINSBOURNE, M. (1980). Food dyes impair performance of hyperactive children on a laboratory learning test. *Science, 207,* 1485–1486.

TAYLOR, E. (1979). Food additives, allergy and hyperactivity. *Journal of Child Psychology and Psychiatry, 20,* 357–363.

TAYLOR, E. (1983). Drug response and diagnostic validation. In M. Rutter (Ed.), *Developmental neuropsychiatry* (pp. 348–368). New York: Guilford Press.

THORLEY, G. (1984). Review of follow-up and follow-back studies of childhood hyperactivity. *Psychological Bulletin, 96,* 116–132.

WEBSTER-STRATTON, C. (1985). Predictors of treatment outcome in parent training for conduct disordered children. *Behavior Therapy, 16,* 223–243.

WEISS, G. (1983). Long-term outcome: Findings, concepts and practical implications. In M. Rutter (Ed.), *Developmental neuropsychiatry* (pp. 422–436). New York: Guilford Press.

WELSH, R. S. (1976). Severe parental punishment and delinquency: A developmental theory. *Journal of Clinical Child Psychology, 5,* 17–21.

WENDER, P. H. (1971). *Minimal brain dysfunction in children.* New York: Wiley-Interscience.

WENDER, P. H. (1978). Minimal brain dysfunction: Overview. In M. A. Lipton, A. DiMascio, & K. F. Killam (Eds.), *Psychopharmacology: A generation of progress* (pp. 1429–1435). New York: Raven Press.

WERRY, J., & QUAY, H. (1971). The prevalence of behavior symptoms in younger elementary school children. *American Journal of Orthopsychiatry, 41,* 136–143.

WHALEN, C. K. (1982). Hyperactivity and psychostimulant treatment. In J. R. Lachenmeyer & M. S. Gibbs (Eds.), *Psychopathology in childhood* (pp. 375–402). New York: Gardner Press.

WHALEN, C. K., & HENKER, B. (1976). Psychostimulants and children: A review and analysis. *Psychological Bulletin, 83,* 1113–1130.

WHALEN, C. K., HENKER, B., COLLINS, B. E., McAULIFFE, S., & VAUX, A. (1979). Peer interaction in a structured communication task: Comparisons of normal and hyperactive boys and of methylphenidate (Ritalin) and placebo effects. *Child Development, 50,* 388–401.

WILLERMAN, L. (1973). Activity level and hyperactivity in twins. *Child Development, 44,* 288–293.

WILLOCK, B. (1983). Play therapy with the aggressive, acting-out child. In C. E. Schaefer & K. J. O'Connor (Eds.), *Handbook of play therapy* (pp. 387–411). New York: John Wiley.

WOLRAICH, M. L. (1979). Behavior modification therapy in hyperactive children. *Clinical Pediatrics, 18,* 563–569.

YARROW, M. R., SCOTT, P. M., & WAXLER, C. Z. (1973). Learning concern for others. *Developmental Psychology, 8,* 240–260.

YOUNG, J. G. (1981). Methyphenidate-induced hallucinosis: Case histories and possible mechanisms of action. *Developmental and Behavioral Pediatrics, 2,* 35–38.

ZENTALL, S., & ZENTALL, T. R. (1976). Activity and task performance of hyperactive children as a function of environmental stimulation. *Journal of Consulting and Clinical Psychology, 44,* 693–697.

CHAPTER 11

LEARNING PROBLEMS IN SCHOOL-AGE CHILDREN

OVERVIEW

Education is regarded as the key to occupational success, so parents and teachers are naturally alarmed when a child fails in school or consistently falls short of his or her potential; this means future livelihood is threatened. Also, school performance constitutes an important component in a child's self-concept, whether it is based on report card grades or visible evidence of poor mastery of basic academic skills. There has always been a great deal of attention paid to academic difficulties of children, but the focus shifted noticeably in the period between 1965 and 1985. Prior to 1965, "underachievement" was the popular term, freely used to describe a child who was not doing as well as expected from ability measures. There were countless investigations of the psychosocial characteristics of underachievers as a group, suggesting differences in home background and parental demands, lower self-concept and more unrealistic levels of aspiration, but most of these studies were descriptive rather than explanatory. Individual case studies emphasized motivational problems, family relationships, inhibitions, and defenses against anxiety. The recommended treatments were usually psychotherapy or group or family counseling, with little direction for educational personnel (Kessler, 1966).

Although the research investigators studied underachievers as if they were a single group, educators and clinicians were well aware of the fact that there were some children with special learning problems referred to as "dyslexics" or "brain-injured." It was presumed that they accounted for a very small number of the very large number of "underachievers." But many factors coalesced to change the focus of attention. Parents who keenly felt the frustration of schools "doing nothing" for their children pushed for more individualized assessments and special education programs. "Brain injury" (or some variation like "neurologically handicapped") was the only diagnostic category which offered special educational services, but this presented many definitional problems for pediatric neurologists who had to certify the diagnosis. Alternatives such as "minimal brain damage" or "minimal cerebral dysfunction" were suggested to modify the diagnosis, but the debate continued as to what the criteria should be and who should make the diagnostic determination.

In a presentation at the 1963 conference sponsored by the Fund for Perceptually Handicapped Children, Inc., Kirk stated that the medical labels then in current usage to describe children with educational deficits simply were not useful and proposed the term "learning disability." At that conference the group voted to organize itself as the Association for Children with Learning Disabilities (ACLD) and a new special education category was born. This quickly became the generic term to describe the population formerly called "underachievers." Learning disability was included in the 1975 Education for All Handicapped Children Act (P.L. 94-142), which mandated that the schools provide special services for children so designated.

Paralleling this development, which was largely spearheaded by parent advocacy groups, professional workers were shifting their attention from the emotional aspects of learning to the cognitive factors. New tests and measures were developed which offered more analysis of cognitive processing functions than the traditional global IQ tests and which seemed more directly relevant to the academic learning situation. There was less concern about the etiology of cognitive differences and much more concern about the modification of such differences for academic improvement. A significant byproduct of this shift in attention is the fact that most of the action for these children, both diagnostic and therapeutic, now takes place within the school system rather than in an outside child psychiatry or mental health clinic. Nonetheless, a good understanding of the complex issues involved in assessing a learning problem and carrying out a comprehensive treatment program is essential for all professionals working with children because the majority of children treated in any clinic have some degree of academic difficulty, either primary or secondary to their other problems. This chapter covers the wide spectrum of academic difficulties which may occur with children of normal intelligence.

MEASUREMENT OF INTELLIGENCE

Academic difficulties are identified either by the child's failure to master the material of his or her grade level or by mediocre performance when compared with ability. Group tests of ability are routinely administered and used for comparison purposes, but identification of a learning problem requires an individually administered test as a first step. The original test was the Stanford-Binet, based on a mental age scale. Stern (1914) introduced the ratio score obtained by dividing the mental age score by the chronological age (with provisions for changing the denominator at older ages) and multiplying by a factor of 100. Although the Binet used a variety of intellectual tasks, it was highly verbal and dependent on vocabulary at the older age levels. In 1944 Wechsler introduced a new intelligence scale for adults, which was shortly followed by the Wechsler Intelligence Scale for Children (Wechsler, 1949). The WISC substituted 10 subtests, divided evenly into verbal and performance scales, for the single mental age scale. The ratio method of calculating IQ was replaced by the "deviation IQ," a standardized way of expressing the difference from the average score (usually but not always 100) of children of the same age. This became the standard way of expressing test scores, also adopted in the second major revision of the Stanford-Binet in 1960. Given a large representative sample population, roughly 68% fall within the limits of plus and minus 1 standard deviation from the mean; that is, 16% will be below 85 and above 115 on the WISC, and about 2% will be below 70 and above 130.

The variety of scores available with the WISC provided the opportunity for factor analysis and pattern profiles. Verbal-Performance IQ differences were the subject of much investigation, sometimes failing to take into account that differences less than 12 points are probably not significant. There has also been a tendency to over-interpret differences in subtests. Kaufman analyzed the data from the standardization sample of sup-

posedly "normal" children and found that the average difference between the highest and lowest subtest score was 7 points (1976). By and large, efforts to identify "profiles" characteristic of particular groups have not been productive. Verbal-Performance discrepancies did not distinguish children diagnosed as "minimal brain dysfunction" from "normals" (Hartlage, 1970; Paine, Werry, & Quay, 1968). On the other hand, if one selects only those few children who show extreme variation, there are usually important correlates. Holroyd and Wright (1965) found that children whose Verbal IQ was at least 25 points higher than their Performance IQ had significantly more medical diagnoses of brain damage. Although there are no templates which one can routinely use for clinical diagnosis, an individual child may show variability of a degree and kind which is helpful in understanding the academic problems.

For many years, the Stanford-Binet and the WISC were the standards for measuring ability. But there was a growing feeling that these tests did not "get down to basics" or provide a useful analysis of cognitive functioning. Some tried to solve the problem by suggesting a "dynamic assessment of learning potential" whereby one systematically evaluated the amount of instruction a child required to learn a task (Feuerstein, 1979). Others created new scales with different theoretical models and organizational structures. Most of the new scales simplified administration procedures by using an easel format. Generally, the test authors substituted some kind of "composite score" for "IQ," which has been the target of much political controversy. In fact, "intelligence quotient" is now semantically obsolete since there is no quotient involved in getting the scores.

The recent developments in ability measurement show a concerted effort to modernize the structure of tests. The dissatisfaction with the undefined mixture of items which made up the single score of "mental age" on the Stanford-Binet brought about a radical change in the fourth edition (Thorndike, Hagen, & Sattler, 1986) which completely dropped the mental age concept for a point scale. The 15 subtests are divided into clusters of "verbal reasoning," "abstract/visual reasoning," "quantitative reasoning," and "short-term memory." In explaining the theoretical model for this edition the authors put "g" (a general reasoning factor cutting across all kinds of tasks) in first position, but at the next level, they distinguished between "crystallized abilities" (verbal and quantitative reasoning), "fluid-analytic abilities" (visual-perceptual reasoning), and short-term memory. Although it is true that mental age has little meaning for older children, it is a useful concept in the range between 2 and 6 years if one thinks in terms of Piagetian stages, and it is perhaps a loss in the zeal for modernization.

The Kaufman Assessment Battery for Children (K-ABC; Kaufman & Kaufman, 1983) introduced another way of looking at intelligence. Briefly, the "general ability" subtests are divided into "sequential processing" and "simultaneous processing" scales. The sequential scale tests memory for sequences of presented stimuli (numbers, words, or hand movements). The simultaneous scale, which is twice the length of the sequencing scale, consists of visual-performance

tasks, some of which involve memory as well. One of the "simultaneous" subtests, placing pictures in an appropriate chronological order, is similar to the WISC Picture Arrangement which is traditionally described as measuring "sequencing ability," but in the Kaufman sense, sequencing processes refer to memory for order rather than arranging things in order by logical reasoning.

The sequential-simultaneous scales of the K-ABC were designed to relate to the current theories about hemisphere lateralization with the right cerebral hemisphere processing information in a holistic or simultaneous fashion and the left cerebral hemisphere more prepared to process in a logical or sequential fashion. However, it would be a gross oversimplification to conclude that these tests are direct measures of right brain and left brain functioning. There is much disagreement among theorists about the neurological location of sequential versus simultaneous information-processing strategies, but general agreement is that mental activities depend on the coordinated action of both cerebral hemispheres. With regard to the K-ABC tests, several authors have commented that they are not "pure" measures and that a child could employ different strategies for their solution (Das, 1984). Nevertheless, the K-ABC introduced a new way of looking at the old subject of intelligence.

To date, there is not enough experience to know which of all the new scales will prove most useful and for what purposes. Each has some unique advantage. The K-ABC incorporates an achievement measure which allows for within-scale comparison; the fourth edition of the Stanford-Binet has the widest age coverage, allowing for comparison over time; and the WISC (Revised) has an established track record. Test administration has been simplified so that one can administer and score the new tests with relatively little training, but interpretation of the results remains as difficult as ever. The options which are now available make the diagnosticians think more carefully about what they are testing for and about choosing scales (or subtests) to check out particular hypotheses which might explain the difficulties in an individual case. The next question, of course, is whether this leads to more effective modes of intervention.

RELATIONSHIP OF ABILITY AND ACHIEVEMENT MEASURES

At the present time, eligibility for special educational services requires some discrepancy between intellectual ability and achievement. Typical correlations between aptitude and achievement are in the .50–.60 range for all kinds of populations, including minority groups as well as handicapped children (Kaufman, 1979). Although the relationship is statistically a strong one, the magnitude is such that only about 25% of the variation in achievement can be accounted for by differences in ability, which leaves a lot of room for other considerations. There is no more justification for expecting an exact correspondence between academic achievement and scholastic aptitude than for expecting a perfect correspondence between height and weight (which also tend to vary directly with one another). Because of a statistical phenomenon known as "regression

toward the mean," children who are exceptionally low or high in intelligence tend to be "more average" in achievement, so that more underachievers will be identified in the high ability group and more overachievers in the low ability group. One can predict the percentage of underachievers who will be identified in large group surveys; about 17% will have lower-than-expected achievement scores, using 1 standard error of estimate, and about 2% if one uses a more stringent criterion of 2 standard errors of estimate. Some of these children will change classification in another test comparison, but others retain their "substandard" position.

At first glance the difference between ability and achievement seems simple. Ability is one's "natural" aptitude and achievement is what one has done with it. This implies that ability is a stable characteristic with limits set from a very early age, if not from birth. The studies of the environmental effects on intelligence (Kessler, 1966) and the cultural influences related to IQ measures suggested that ability is not simply an inborn characteristic. The types of tasks used to measure ability clearly involve acquired information, which is a kind of "achievement," so there is increasing recognition that these two are interdependent. The more intelligent child learns facts which are helpful in solving new problems.

The confounding of these two variables is obvious when one examines the composition of test items. Although achievement is still assessed by evaluating reading, arithmetic, and knowledge of specific academic subject matter, some arbitrary decisions are made as to the classification of particular skills as representative of "ability" or "achievement." Tasks which have traditionally been considered as "general ability" are included in "achievement" scale; for instance, Expressive Vocabulary, Information, and Verbal Reasoning are combined with Arithmetic and Reading in the K-ABC achievement scale. On the other hand, "Blending," closely related to phonics in reading, is included in the "General Cognitive Ability Scale" in the Woodcock-Johnson Psychoeducational Test Battery (1977). Also, educational curricula more and more include instruction in skills such as finding synonyms or categorizing objects (usually found in "ability" scales), which further blurs a distinction between "natural aptitude" and "learned information." This has no important consequence except for the peculiarities which ensue when one rigidly defines a learning problem only in terms of a statistical difference between some selected measures of ability and achievement.

DEFINITIONS OF LEARNING DISABILITY

Definition of learning disability has always been the province of educators rather than psychiatrists or mental health professionals, and the DSM III only makes mention of specific reading and arithmetic disorders under the category of "specific developmental disorders" where the respective impairment "is not accounted for by chronological age, mental age, or inadequate schooling." Initially, the identification of learning disability depended more on discrepancies between specific abilities

rather than between general ability and achievement. In the federal legislation known as the Children with Specific Learning Disabilities Act of 1969, the target population was defined as follows:

Those children who have a disorder in one or more of the basic psychological processes involved in the understanding or in using language (spoken or written), which disorder may manifest itself in an imperfect ability to learn, think, read, write, spell, or do mathematical calculations. These disorders include such conditions as perceptual handicaps, brain injury, minimal brain dysfuction, dyslexia, and developmental dysphasia.

This definition was incorporated in P.L. 94-142 (Education for All Handicapped Children Act, 1975) with the additional proviso that there be a "severe discrepancy between achievement and intellectual ability in one or more of the following areas: oral expression, listening comprehension; written expression; mathematical calculations; or mathematics reasoning." It is curious that reading is not included in this list although dyslexia, which is a severe form of reading disability, is mentioned as one of the disorders subsumed under the classification of "learning disability." Learning disability is an educationally defined category and there are at least 60 different definitions used by schools (Sabbatino & Miller, 1980), which, of course, results in a lot of confusion for the consumer public as well as difficulty in comparing published studies.

In practice, identification procedures became more inclusive and less specific. Quite often, some "rule of thumb" procedure was used; for instance, academic level 1 year below expected grade level achievement for the early grades and 2 years' retardation in the upper primary grades, presuming always that intellectual ability was normal. School systems witnessed a tremendous increase in the numbers of children identified. Nationally, the number of learning-disabled children increased 119% between 1976 and 1982 and in some states much more. For instance, in California, the "learning-disabled" population increased by about 167% to a total of almost 5% of the kindergarten through twelfth grade population (Boyan, 1985).

Partly because of the high cost involved in providing for such large numbers, states began to set a funding cap on special education services. By setting more stringent criteria for discrepancy, the number identified as "learning disabled" can be reduced. Different formulas will change who and how many are identified, accounting for the widely varying estimates of the prevalence rates of learning disability, anywhere from 1% to 30% (Epstein, Cullinan, Lessen, & Lloyd, 1980).

The definition of learning disability specifically excludes visual, hearing, or motor handicaps, mental retardation, and environmental, cultural or economic disadvantages as a primary cause of the achievement discrepancy. For some, this part of the definition has been interpreted to mean that a mentally retarded child, for example, could never be classified as learning disabled. It is indeed more difficult for a child scoring low in mental ability to have as much discrepancy with achievement as a child who scores high. In a lawsuit filed against the California system, it

was alleged that this results in discrimination (Boyan, 1985).

The use of standardized tests can also discriminate against children from economically deprived backgrounds because ability measures are depressed by cultural factors. In 1971, Franks found that 34% of children in classes for the educable mentally retarded were Afro-American compared with only 3% in the learning-disabled classes. In 1975, Burke also found a disproportionate number of Afro-American students in mentally retarded classes with less than expected numbers in the learning disability classes; at the elementary school level, however, there were equal numbers of black and white students, suggesting a trend toward increased placement in learning disability classes for black students. And, indeed, national figures for 1984 indicate proportionate enrollment of blacks, hispanics, and whites in learning disability classes (Chinn & Hughes, 1987). The diagnostician has to look beyond the obvious factors to determine whether the mental retardation or deprived background is indeed the primary cause for the low achievement or whether several factors are operating concurrently.

The federal mandate for special services was postulated on the assumption that a learning disabled child is failing in school because of some pre-existing handicappng condition and not that the child is handicapped because of the fact of school failure (Lieberman, 1980). But as Senf pointed out, "Failure at school is relatively easy to determine, whereas being handicapped (as the presumed cause of that failure) is anything but obvious" (1986, p. 35). The question has been raised as to whether the "net" of learning disability simply identifies a group of low-achieving children who have very little in common beyond the mere fact of poor achievement. Algozzine and Ysseldyke (1983) expressed the opinion that educators should give up the effort to define a subcategory of "specific learning disabilities" and concentrate their efforts on remediation of low achievement per se. Others feel that there is a "true" learning-disabled child who can be distinguished from other low achievers (Wilson, 1985). At best, the distinction is an elusive one and diagnostic decisions are often made on the basis of eligibility for services rather than "true" psychological differences.

HISTORICAL EXPLANATIONS: NEUROLOGICAL ABNORMALITY

Considering the fact that the term "learning disability" evolved from the diagnosis of "brain injury," it is not surprising that neurological factors are often presumed to be primary. To quote Myklebust:

To have a learning disability is to have one of the conditions which lead to underachievement; there is a discrepancy between potential and actual success in learning. A learning disability, however, differs from other types of involvement in that the deficiency can be attributed to neurogenicity, to a dysfunction in the brain. (1968, p. 4)

Recently, the ACLD introduced a definition which re-emphasized this distinction: "Specific learning disabilities is a chronic condition of presumed neurologic origin which selectively interferes with the development, integration, and/or demonstration of verbal and/or non-verbal abilities" (ACLD, 1985). In acknowledgment of the chronicity of the handicap, the ACLD changed its name to the Association for Children and Adults with Learning Disabilities.

Efforts to pinpoint the neurologic base for learning disability have been legion. Many of these explanations have been discarded by research evidence from comparative group studies, but nonetheless the old ideas resurface from time to time. Probably all the theories, with their recommended treatments, are effective for *some* learning disabled children, which accounts for their remarkable durability. If a particular observation applies only to a few in the learning disabled group, it is lost in group comparisons.

Historically, the first neurological explanations were attempts to localize the underlying brain pathology in specific conditions like dyslexia. From post-mortem study, Dejerine (1892) identified the neuropathology in a well-studied case of a 68-year-old man who had suddenly lost the ability to read. The anatomical lesions in the occipital part of the brain explained his blindness for stimuli coming from the right side of his visual field (right hemianopia), but in addition there were lesions in the corpus callosum, the structure of the brain which connects the two cerebral hemispheres. Apparently the visual stimuli which the patient could see normally were not transmitted to the language areas in the left cerebral hemisphere and so the patient could not translate the visual symbols into words. This study, confirmed by others, indicated that reading function was not localized in a single part of the brain but depended on interactional communication between parts of the brain.

In 1917 a Scottish opthalmologist, Hinshelwood, described a number of children who were "congenitally word blind." They had no trouble seeing lines and forms and recognizing numbers, and were fluent talkers. Hinshelwood compared them to Dejerine's case and suggested that they lacked the necessary connections between the visual and speech centers of their brains.

Evidence from adults who lose an ability is probably not relevant for the understanding of developmental failure to acquire an ability because of the greater plasticity of the developing nervous system. As Geschwind (1962) pointed out, even total destruction of the left hemisphere in early childhood ordinarily does not prevent the acquisition of language, so the neuropathology in developmental failures must involve something other than what is involved in dyslexia or aphasia of adults. The idea of some neurological abnormality was not relinquished, but investigators looked for signs of diffuse dysfunction rather than indications of localized damage.

Studies looking for evidence of neurological impairment independent of the specific learning problem yielded equivocal results. Belmont's review (1980) found that where neurologic and/or medical data were reported, the learning disabled groups had a higher proportion of children with some kind of neurologic abnormality than was found in control groups; none of these differences were reported to be statistically significant, however. In a study of fourth-graders, Adams, Kocsis, and Estes (1974) found that of the various neurological functions tested, only two (difference in tapping speeds between the two hands and recognition of numbers drawn on the skin of the hand) had a significantly greater frequency in the learning-disabled group (about 14%).

It is clear that neurologic involvement is not a necessary concomitant of learning disability, although it is manifestly present in a small minority. But it is virtually impossible to disprove a neurological cause because one can always argue that the detection methods are at fault. The organic hypothesis, vague as it may be, seems to offer an explanation and take the onus of responsibility off the parents. Very few people have any conception of how the brain structures work and think of the brain as a single organ which is either "all right" or "broken." Because efforts to separate "brain-damaged" from "normal" children proved so difficult (Herbert, 1964; Rapin, 1968) and because there were no practical treatment consequences emanating from the distinction, this line of investigation was dropped.

LATERALIZATION OF BRAIN FUNCTION

Although the idea that learning disability may arise from a failure to establish dominant functions in the respective cerebral hemispheres is not new, it still receives serious consideration. Normally, language functions are strongly lateralized in the left hemisphere; other functions such as spatial orientation and visual recognition of complex forms appear to be more effectively mediated by the right or nondominant hemisphere (Gazzaniga, Bogen, & Sperry, 1965). As far back as 1928, Orton coined the phrase "strephosymbolia," meaning "twisted symbols," to explain reading disability on the basis of mixed cerebral dominance. His reasoning was as follows: In learning to read, engrams, or traces, of the printed words are registered in both cerebral hemispheres. Those in the nondominant hemisphere are normally suppressed, but when dominance is not completely established, there is confusion between the engrams of the dominant hemisphere and the unsuppressed engrams of the nondominant hemisphere which are their mirror images. This he used to explain mirror writing and mirror reversal of words and letters in reading. In later years, he restated his position: "In skeleton, then, my theory of the obstacle to the acquisition of reading in children of normal intelligence which results in the varying grades of reading disability is a failure to establish the physiological habit of working exclusively from the engrams of one hemisphere" (1966, p. 96).

Other than the learning disability itself, evidence of mixed cerebral dominance was mixed handedness or crossed hand and eye preference, but reviews of the literature failed to find significant differences between normal and reading-disabled children in mixed handedness and crossed hand and eye preferences (Benton, 1975). In a study of a nonidentified population of 648 elementary school-age children, Ullman (1977) found that almost 60% of the younger children and 35% of the older children demonstrated either mixed or inconsistent lateral preference patterns in different hand, eye, and foot tasks. Further, there were no differences in IQ or academic achievement scores among the various groups. Even more sophisticated and direct methods of assessing hemispheric dominance, such as visual half-field recognition and differential recall for digits spoken into both ears simultaneously, have given little evidence for the hypothesis of lateral asymmetry or mixed dominance in reading-disabled children (Naylor, 1980). Although the reading-disabled children invariably performed poorly, Naylor suggested that cognitive processes such as short-term memory, sequencing, and attention (which may or may not be lateralized) were more likely explanations.

Despite equivocal research evidence, investigators continue to suggest neuropsychological models related to hemispheric dominance to explain reading problems (Masland, 1975; Satz & van Nostrand, 1973). Bakker (1979) did an interesting developmental study of nonidentified children using the dichotic listening technique. Kindergarten children who showed a left-ear preference had higher reading scores in the fifth grade than those with right-ear preference, and children who shifted from left- to right-ear preference in the first grade were the best readers of all. He used these findings to support the idea that in the initial stages of learning to read, decoding the perceptual symbols is best served by right hemisphere strategies. When this becomes automatized, the further development of speed and comprehension is dependent on the left hemisphere. It is possible that failure to consider developmental differences accounts for some of the inconsistency in the research. A learning disability that is identified in the early grades is probably different in structure than a disability which becomes evident at a later time when reasoning and comprehension are necessary. Finally, we cannot ascertain whether the difference in hemispheric functioning indicates some innate deficit or whether it is a result of whatever causes the learning problem itself. Rourke (1976) and others have suggested that reading-disabled children have a developmental lag in brain maturation and that this could be as much a result of learning failure as a cause.

MOTOR ACTIVITY TREATMENT METHODS

Many diverse approaches have been developed to train basic functions which are assumed to be prerequisite for academic learning. Although these methods emphasize different basic functions, they are alike in that they do not offer any direct remediation of academic subject matter. Some programs were designed to establish hemispheric dominance, for example, the extensive "patterning" program developed by Doman, a physical therapist, and Delacato, an educational psychologist. Delacato postulated that the development of neurological functioning progresses systematically from the most primitive to the most complex. For remediation even of a cognitive defect, one must start by perfecting the most primitive activities such as creeping and crawling (1963; 1966). Training in the use of one hand and one eye and restrictions on listening

to music (presumably stimulating to the nondominant hemisphere) were prescribed to develop dominance. Controlled studies failed to show any evidence of significant change, but even more serious, the program was harshly criticized because of the unrealistic demands placed on families and the possible side effects of the restrictions and manipulations inflicted on the children. With remarkable unanimity, 12 major medical and health organizations condemned both the theory and methods and declared that the Doman-Delacato treatment was "not recommended" ("Official Statement," 1968). None of the programs to be discussed has been so harshly criticized but none has equalled this program in promises or demands.

There were other motor activity programs, but with the child as an active participant rather than a passive participant. Kephart, a special educator, focused on posture and general movement patterns which he felt preceded perceptual development (1964; 1971). In his view, the body is the zero point, or point of origin, for all movements, and perceptual understanding of outside objects will be disturbed if the body image is disturbed. Laterality, the ability to distinguish the left from the right side of the body and to control these individually or simultaneously, was considered prerequisite to the differentiation of left and right and space. According to this theory, letter and word reversals would reflect an absence of a proper kinesthetic, body reference point.

Getman, an optometrist, collaborated with Kephart and proposed a comprehensive program for the development of perceptual-motor skills which included practice in general coordination, balance (walking beam), eye-hand coordination, eye movements, form recognition (templates), and visual memory (Getman, 1962). The American Academy of Pediatrics, the American Academy of Opthalmology and Otolaryngology, and the American Association of Opthalmalogy issued a joint statement critical of the visual or neurological organizational training proposed by optometrists (American Academy of Pediatrics, 1972). This continuing controversy between opthalmologists and optometrists often puts the parents in the middle as they try to decide what is best for their child.

Barsch, who also worked with Getman, developed a program known as "movigenics" built around 12 components of motor movement and spatial awareness (1967). Superficially, this has some resemblance to the sensory integration therapy developed by Ayres (1963), an occupational therapist. She stressed the importance of both tactile and vestibular stimuli for basic sensory integration and prescribed specific activities (such as brushing the child's skin with soft brushes to reduce tactile defensiveness and rolling in a carpeted barrel for both vestibular and tactile stimulation) on the basis of the child's status on her "Southern California Sensory Integration Tests" (Ayres, 1972a). She suggested that this graded stimulation program would improve interconnections between sensory modalities and visual and auditory inputs and that normalization of postural mechanisms organized in the midbrain would enable better communication between the two hemispheres and consequently improve academic learning (Ayres, 1972b).

Visual-Motor Training Programs

Although some of the previously mentioned therapies included visual tracking or other exercises, the major emphasis was on motor rather than perceptual functions. But dating back to the original work of Strauss and Lehtinen (see Chapter 10) there has been concern about the ability of the learning disabled child to "see" patterns and extract figures from their background. The Bender-Gestalt Test has been, and still is, a standard assessment tool. It consists of nine cards, each with a design adapted from the figures Wertheimer (1923) used in gestalt perceptual experiments. The child is asked to copy these designs, one at a time, with as much time as needed. It is appropriate for children between the ages of 5 and 12. The Bender scores for learning-disabled children of average intelligence characteristically show a lag in visual-motor integration. Koppitz, one of the leading contributors to the Bender-Gestalt research, felt that the solution was allowing more time for maturation. "To date, efforts to speed up the rate of development of a slowly maturing child have produced, at best, only some immediate short-lived improvements; they have failed to result in any permanent increase in the rate of maturation" (Koppitz, 1975, p. 68).

Nonetheless, many programs were marketed to foster figure perception, usually involving some kind of drawing, tracing, or block design assembly. Frostig, an educational psychologist, developed a five-part visual-motor test with specific educational materials to train visual perception via eye-hand coordination exercises and training in form discrimination and spatial orientation (Frostig, 1968; Frostig, Lefever, & Whittlesey, 1964).

There have been other variations, but one way or another, all such programs offer remedial exercises based on the theory that learning problems result from inadequate development of the neurophysiological substrates regulating perceptual and motor functions viewed as cornerstones for the evolution of high-level cognitive functions. The evidence for improvement of academic learning by perceptual-motor training is generally viewed as negative by reviewers (Hammill, 1972; Hirsch & Anderson, 1976; Keogh, 1974; Lyon, 1977; Mann, 1970). Cruickshank, a staunch defender of "deficit-oriented teaching," explained the generally negative results on the basis of poor "prescriptions," that is, failure to match the remediation to the specific deficits of the individual child.

Without the detailed and often qualitatively determined understanding of deficits, the obtaining of a perceptual-motor match, as described by Kephart, will be possible only rarely. If achieved without analysis, it will have been accomplished by the teacher on a trial-and-error basis long after the time when she should have had the information and should have begun a program of true educational development for the child. For children with specific learning disability, every learning activity, whether it be gross-motor or fine-motor in nature, or whether it be of a nature not usually seen as "motor," must be complementary to the psychomotor deficit or psychopathology observed in the child. (Hallahan & Cruickshank, 1973, p. 262)

Some of these procedures may be of value for certain children and at certain stages in their development. Probably such procedures are justifiable only for preschoolers or kindergartners as a preliminary to the serious business of teaching reading, writing, and arithmetic. It is quite possible that current educational practices start formal reading instruction prematurely, so that some children experience failure and become "disabled" out of sheer discouragement.

Other "Deficit-Oriented" Treatment Methods

The visual perceptual-motor programs were one-sided in that they did not address the fact that learning-disabled children often had an antecedent delay in the development of spoken language. In language-delayed children, deficits of auditory perception, temporal sequencing, or auditory memory might well be of equal or more importance than visual perceptual deficits. There were some remedial programs developed from the Illinois Test of Psycholinguistic Abilities (Kirk, McCarthy, & Kirk, 1968). This is a battery of 12 subtests utilizing the Osgood model of communication to assess reception and expression, automatic versus representational levels of meaning in both auditory-vocal and visual-motor channels. Although the test is directed toward assessment of psycholinguistic abilities, five of the items involve visual-motor functioning. The remedial programs were developed on the assumption that language behavior is composed of discrete components, that these components are prerequisite for learning, and that they are amenable to remedial activities.

In their review of some 39 studies that attempted to train psycholinguistic abilities, Hammill and Larsen (1974) concluded that the effectiveness had not been conclusively demonstated. Kavale (1981) re-analyzed these data using a meta-analysis and concluded that the findings were more positive. The average child receiving training performed better than 65% of untrained children, with the greatest improvement evident on the measure of verbal expression. Although this would seem encouraging, the outcome measure was scores on the ITPA, and the relationship with academic progress is unclear. By and large, these techniques were used with culturally deprived, educable mentally retarded or preschool children rather than with the typical "learning-disabled" population. Again, it seems that these programs are useful in establishing a readiness for academic learning but do not guarantee subsequent success.

We conclude this section with a relative newcomer, namely, the "Tomatis program" developed by a French otolaryngologist (Tomatis, 1978) and first transplanted in Canada. Briefly, this is an audiological program designed to "organize" the left hemisphere by stimulating the right ear. Various tapes are played through earphones for some 200 hours, starting with a tape of the mother's voice. There is even some thought that the special mother tapes will correct what might have gone wrong in utero. The program has been recommended for all ages and all types of disabilities. No research has been reported and it has not been accepted by professional organizations. On the other hand, it has an enthusiastic following. Participants report general improvement in all areas of functioning, and one is left to speculate as to the reasons. Perhaps it

serves to improve listening skills, to focus attention, to provide relaxation, or simply to give a feeling that "something important is happening" (placebo effect). All we can be sure of is that techniques like this will come and go, only to reappear because they seem so simple and promise so much.

Attention Deficit Hypothesis

Dykman, Ackerman, Clements, and Peters (1971) first proposed that the variety of auditory-visual-kinesthetic-expressive defects might be surface expressions of a deficit in attention. In their view, attention was a unitary trait consisting of the components of alertness, stimulus selection, focusing, and vigilance. In one of several studies, 82 boys with learning disabilities were contrasted with 34 academically adequate boys. The experimental procedures included a variety of conditioning and impulsivity testing as well as physiological and EEG measures. The learning-disabled children made more errors in following instructions, were slower in responding, and showed decreased physiological activity in learning situations when compared with the controls.

Dykman et al. (1971) explained these results in terms of organically based deficiencies in attention related to the brain stem reticular formation and its antagonist, the forebrain inhibitory system, which are known to play important roles in attention and physiological excitation. Like Koppitz, they saw the cause as a "lag in neurological maturation" and made the very important point that neural maturation depends to some degree on life experiences. They concluded that:

The significant task is to develop educational programs that will help the presumably neurologically immature child to develop to his full capacity with a minimum of frustration-induced anxiety. It is unlikely that this can be accomplished in a fixed age-grade system or indeed by any one technique of special education. More importantly, many of our present educational efforts may be misplaced if the most critical defect of learning disability children is faulty attention. (1971, p. 89)

This research confirmed other studies (McGrady & Olson, 1970; Rugel & Rosenthal, 1974) which showed that learning-disabled children (including but not restricted to those who are also hyperactive) are slower in responding than normal control subjects. This is a finding of potential significance to teachers because it suggests that they should speak more slowly, repeat their instructions, and not be deceived by the apparent quickness of even the hyperactive child.

Other measures of attention also show deficits in learning-disabled children. Sroufe, Sonies, West, and Wright (1973) found less anticipatory cardiac deceleration to the appearance of novel stimuli than with normal students. On vigilance or continuous performance tasks, learning disability children usually do less well (Ackerman, Dykman, & Peters, 1977; Anderson, Halcomb, & Doyle, 1973; Keogh & Donlan, 1972). However, as seems to be the inevitable fate of group comparisons, there are some studies reporting no differences on measures of attention. From the reports it is hard to reconcile the inconsistencies, but there are differences in sample selection which may affect the results. For instance, in a recent study reporting "no difference," Samuels and Miller (1985) identified boys in the third grade as learning disabled on the basis of IQ-achievement score discrepancies; nonetheless, they had a reading grade equivalent score of 4.0. Although this was a lower score than the "normals," these were not seriously handicapped children. This illustrates the importance of a complete description of the children labeled "learning disabled" in any study. It is probable that real "nonlearners" will perform differently than children who are learning, but more slowly than expected.

An impulsive style of responding, resulting in many errors, has also been observed in many learning disabled children (Douglas, 1972). It is quite possible that this is more a result than a cause of learning problems. Ross (1980) suggested that repeated failure experiences make cognitive tasks unpleasant and anxiety-provoking so that the child uses an avoidant defense to get the situation over with as quickly as possible. "Better to give a wrong answer quickly than to struggle for a long time only to find that the answer is wrong anyway," might be the operative logic for such children. Or it may be that such a child has concluded that "being fast" is a virtue and "looking good" covers up for other deficiencies.

SUBTYPING LEARNING DISABILITIES

Faced with the great diversity both in degree and in kind of handicap presented by learning-disabled children in the public schools, a number of investigators have abandoned the search for a single syndrome (with a single deficit) in favor of a multiple syndrome point of view. Subclassifications have been developed on the basis of grouping children who have similar profiles of strengths and weaknesses on psychometric tests, a procedure known as cluster analysis (Rourke, 1985). However, as mentioned by Fletcher (1985), the fact that different subtypes emerge by cluster analysis does not establish the validity of the subtypes. The particular clusters identified may vary according to the subjects selected, the variety of measures used, and, to some extent, the particular statistical procedures followed. In the final stage, hypotheses concerning subtype differences must be systematically evaluated against external criteria not involved in deriving the subtypes. To date, there is no consensus on just which clusters are sufficiently independent and yet consistent enough to be considered "syndromes," but some of them seem to appear in many studies and make sense from one's knowledge of individual cases.

Several studies have been reported from the Carolina Longitudinal Learning Disabilities Project (Frank Porter Graham Child Development Center in Chapel Hill). McKinney, Short and Feagans (1985) followed 55 children who had been identified by the school system in the first or second grade as learning disabled. Six perceptual and linguistic tasks were used to provide the data for subgrouping. About half of the LD children did not exhibit uneven profiles or significant deficits, but the others clustered into three subtypes that repre-

sented significant perceptual or linguistic processing problems. Consistent with previous evidence (McKinney, 1984; Satz & Morris, 1981), the most common subtype (27%) presented a pattern of severe to mild linguistic deficits combined with adequate perceptual skills. There was no subtype of "pure" perceptual deficit (i.e., without linguistic deficiency) although it has been found in other studies (Satz, Morris, & Fletcher, 1985).

Short (1986) used the cluster analysis procedure to identify cognitive motivational subtypes in a group of low-achieving children compared with normal achievers and found that about two-thirds of the low-achieving group showed a "maladaptive classroom orientation style." For example, one of the identified clusters (with the largest number) resembled the classic learned helplessness pattern. These children appeared to lack self-esteem overall, they preferred easy tasks, were not curious, lacked independent judgment, and were very reliant on teacher's perceptions regarding performance. The educational implications of these subtypes (and others) are being explored by some researchers through training studies, but so far there is no evidence that intervention specifically designed for particular subtypes has specific effects.

Efficacy of Special Education

Despite the initial optimism for the "treatability" of learning disabled children, results, when they are examined "across the board," have not been encouraging. Koppitz (1971) found that only 25% of the LD children returned to regular classes in a 5-year follow-up period. Her description indicated a great variety of problems, suggesting that placement policies in the mid-1960s when these special education programs first got started were even more inclusive than they are presently. The first programs were self-contained classrooms. In a sample of 62 LD children restudied at age 14 years (Ackerman, Dykman, and Peters, 1977), only 9 had moved comfortably into the academic mainstream and there had been little significant change for the LD groups tested at about the 20th percentile on basic skills when first seen and when followed up. Level of intelligence and degree of initial academic retardation were the most predictive variables.

With the mandate to provide "the least restrictive alternative" contained in PL 94-142, the special programs shifted to the use of "resource rooms" for varying periods of the school day. Even with the new policies, the outcome data are not significantly better. Short, Feagans, McKinney, and Applebaum (in press) found that LD children tended to become more disabled over a 3-year period in terms of the IQ-achievement discrepancy despite the special program. Within the group, there were individual differences with some doing much better than others. Looking at the academic differences in the third grade, all the original LD children were still behind their matched "controls," but the children in the "normal-appearing" clusters had progressed in a straight line and the difference was proportionately less. On the other hand, the children in the "atypical" clusters showed much less learning, and the gap had widened (McKinney et al., 1985). It seems apparent that a special education program which treats all learning-disabled children as a homogeneous group is bound to fail with some.

With the greater numbers of children identified as LD and the fact that perhaps only half of these present specific perceptual-motor or linguistic deficiencies (coupled with the discouraging results of deficit-oriented teaching), there has been a shift toward more generalized remedial programs. The idea of operant conditioning was readily adopted by special educators, and these principles of behavior modification were employed to reduce concurrent problems such as poor attention span, conduct disorder, and hyperactivity. But again the results were not impressive. Decreasing disruptive behavior and/or increasing the rate of attending (often called "time-on-task") did not consistently result in increased academic performance (Ayllon, Layman, & Kandel, 1975; Ferritor, Buckholdt, Hamblin, & Smith, 1972).

Some behavior therapists recommended targeting academic performance with reinforcement only for "getting the answer right" in the hopes that other behaviors would drop out (Broughton & Lahey, 1978). Neeper and Lahey suggested that this "enables the child to make the final decision as to what behaviors actually are incompatible with learning" (1983, p. 690). For example, the child may find it easier to work standing rather than sitting, or to work in spurts with interruptions, but only the results would matter.

Although this behavioral approach seems logical, successful application depends on the teacher's skill in choosing and presenting the educational targets.

In the literature, there is surprisingly little discussion of this aspect of intervention. Although a great deal has been done in the area of child assessment, there is little thought given to assessing the learning task, beyond assigning it to a certain grade level expectancy.

Early Detection

There have been many efforts to predict learning disabilities before a pattern of school failure has been established. A review of representative studies in this area indicated considerable variation in predictive accuracy. At best, about 75% of those predicted to have later learning problems in fact did and about 25% did not, but the "hit rates" in other studies were much lower (Jason, Durlak, & Holton-Walker, 1984). Although one would expect that early identification and early treatment would improve the prognosis, the evidence is evenly divided between positive and negative on this point (Schonhaut & Satz, 1983). Early intervention probably works most effectively when there is a major environmental component or when the cause is "simple" developmental immaturity. If, on the other hand, the learning problem results from an intrinsic specific cognitive deficit which is of sufficient magnitude to be obvious in the preschool years, the effects probably cannot be obviated by early intervention.

Reconsideration of Psychodynamic Factors

In the past 10 years or so, learning disabilities have been studied as psychoneurological or cognitive dysfunctions, ignoring more general personality issues. This is probably a mistake. Although psychotherapy was no more successful than special education with the treatment of learning problems, the answer probably lies in some combination which is as yet undefined. Anna Freud described the possible complexities in the following remarks:

Where cognitive development and mastery of the inner and outer world are concerned, the indispensable elements include a large number of factors such as: the intactness of organic and sensory equipment; its environmental stimulation at appropriate periods; on the ego side, the smooth progress from primary to secondary functioning, i.e. from the pleasure principle to the reality principle; on the side of the drives, the transfer of energy from sexual curiosity and scoptophilia (love of looking) to neutralized pursuits; on the superego side, the absence of inhibiting and limiting prohibitions; on the parental side, the presence of positive responses to every forward step. The very multiplicity of factors needed to ensure progress is reflected in the multiplicity of disorders affecting orientation, active mastery, intellectual growth, including the various learning disturbances and school failures. (1975, p. 280)

Sometimes in the concern about the learning problem, other emotional problems are overlooked. The emotional problems which are associated with learning difficulties are usually both pervasive and chronic and have become an integral part of the child's personality. For example, conflicts around early functions such as eating and toileting may be displaced, or generalized, to learning activities. The child with a long history of picky appetite and struggles over eating may come to associate the intake of knowledge and the intake of food and how poor absorption, appearing not to understand what they are taught, not remembering from one time to the next; they can, however, often retain knowledge acquired on their own, knowledge which has not been "fed" to them through instruction. Such children can even appear mentally retarded (Sperry, Staver, & Mann, 1952).

A more common displacement is from conflicts belonging to the second year. These children are more likely to have difficulty in producing rather than taking in. Withholding may take the form of refusal to participate orally or to do any written work (in a timely fashion). This may be associated with a history of toilet training struggles or even with continuing soiling. These children are particularly frustrating to parents and teachers because they can demonstrate that they "know" basic facts, but they simply do not comply with school requirements. Every once in a while, under great pressure, they submit and perform adequately, but with great resistance. The stubbornness and argumentativeness displayed by these "non-producers" is truly awesome, as they manage to nullify all teacher-parent inducements with their passive aggression.

A specific symptom commonly found with learning-disabled children is enuresis (Katan, 1946). This association could be explained in a number of ways including a neurological immaturity as the reason for both problems (see Chapter 6). However, there may be a cogent psychological connection as well. At the simplest level, a child who considers his genitals to be "defective" may assume that his mind is defective as well. The feeling of genital inadequacy may be displaced to specific learning functions like "looking" or "showing." There is a certain amount of exhibitionism involved in showing what one can do or what one knows, and the child may fear that in displaying his knowledge, he is displaying something else at the same time. If he has a deep conviction that his genitals are not right, he may be equally convinced that his knowledge is not right.

An obsession with damaged genitals may come from a confusion about the reason for sexual differences, obvious malfunctioning (e.g., enuresis), or guilt about masturbation. Young children commonly believe that masturbation is injurious to the genitalia, and adolescents usually think it is injurious to the mind, an example of the close association between genital and mental functioning in the unconscious. What the child may demonstrate in class is his own idea of himself, derived from his idea of his genitals. His behavior may be foolish and out of control, making him an object of ridicule and earning him the title of "class clown." Such a child is constantly on exhibition, demanding attention from everyone, but in silly ways. Usually he is restless and overactive and resembles the organically hyperactive child, but the reason for his activity is different. It keeps him too busy to think about masturbatory fantasies and at the same time is an unconscious confession. Many children think of masturbation as "goofy," not unlike the exhibitionist clowning in school which usually brings the punishment that the child thinks is deserved by someone who indulges in masturbation.

It is important to keep in mind that

learning difficulties may arise as a by-product of conflicts within the child as a result of displacement from activities not obviously connected with school learning. Parents and teachers may fail to see any connection and focus on the single fact of school failure. At the very least, assessment of children with chronic learning difficulties should include a careful review of associated symptomatology.

PARENTAL ROLES IN THE FACILITATION OR IMPEDANCE OF LEARNING

In some cases it is probable that parents make a genetic contribution to their child's learning problems. Childs and Finucci (1983) concluded that "the evidence favoring the familial nature of dyslexia is overwhelming" but warned that imprecision of the diagnosis and the failure to distinguish between different forms of reading disability make it difficult to understand the genetic mechanisms involved. These difficulties are even greater when trying to understand parent-child or sibling-sibling resemblances in the more diffuse area of learning disability. It is difficult to separate the role of identification or environmental influences from heredity, so the following discussion minimizes the genetic aspects.

Before starting any litany of how parents can go wrong in fostering optimum development for their children, it is important to remind the reader that this does not depend on single events but persistent parental attitudes. Also, these attitudes must interact with tempera-mental or constitutional characteristics of the child in order to produce serious learning problems. These problems are almost always "over-determined"; one rarely finds a simple single factor to be the cause. There was a major shift in emphasis from home to school with the enactment of P.L. 94-142 which spelled out educational responsibilities, but what parents do or don't do still can make a difference in the child's academic progress.

The prototype for school learning begins in the second year of life when the toddler learns to be clean, to heed verbal commands, and to inhibit raw aggression. At the same time that the child is learning compliance, he or she is turning from passive to active through imitation and identification. The toddler wants to do those things that he or she has experienced passively. Ambitions far exceed ability, and the drive for autonomy is likely to cause mother-child conflict; nonetheless, the ambition to gain active control, to do instead of being done to, gives tremendous impetus to the learning process.

Parents can err in either of two directions, that is, by over-zealous education which squelches the drive for independence and autonomy or by infantilization of the child. A parent who systematically attempts to avoid all conflicts and who takes a passive role as a teacher in these matters does not prepare a child for the rigors and inevitable frustrations of school. Of course, some children "beat this out" by virtue of some natural assertiveness in their personality, but others feel unloved and inadequate. In some instances, there is a more profound parental disturbance where a parent almost forces the child to be "backward" and inept.

Berger and Kennedy (1975) described some clinical case histories of children who appeared to be retarded in their early years because "there was no parental pride and pleasure in the child; accordingly, there was a complete lack of admiring approval from the parents' side which acts simultaneously as a reward for achievement and as a powerful spur and encouragement toward further efforts in the same progressive direction" (1975, p. 280). These mothers perceived their children from earliest infancy as damaged or inadequate, and they seized on any unusual aspect in their children as evidence. This denigration was limited to one child who for some reason was selected as being most like themselves or whose birth circumstances were complicated. Thus this child came to receive differential treatment based on a special set of parental expectations.

One can imagine how complicated it becomes, even for a relatively normal parent, after the child is formally labeled "learning disabled." Research by Chapman and Boersma (1979) showed that mothers of learning-disabled children reported less positive and more negative reactions to their children's achievement experiences than did mothers of control children; Pearl and Bryan (1982) also reported that mothers of learning-disabled children attributed successes less to ability and more to luck, and failures more to lack of ability, than did mothers of nondisabled children. As the authors remark, the attributions of the mothers of learning-disabled children could be either the cause of or the result of their children's perform-

ances, but the fact remains that both the mothers and the children themselves have little confidence. The persistence of this pessimism was shown in a referral to the author by the parents of a learning-disabled boy when he was a freshman in college. Despite his B-C grades in a regular curriculum, they felt that somehow he must need "special help," or that he was working too hard. They were more worried than pleased by his college success.

Returning to developmental issues, another natural impetus for learning is the child's curiosity. From the age of 2 years or so, the child's curiosity becomes increasingly intellectual. Again, ambitions exceed ability and the child's questions are hard to answer in a way that is comprehensible. Still, the curiosity must be rewarded if it is to stay alive. During this stage, the child learns that curiosity is useful, that his or her questions interest the parents, and that their answers help to allay anxieties and feelings of impotence. At the same time, the child is learning to express thoughts and feelings verbally; the facility with language, so important in school, is crucially affected by the early verbal interchanges with the parents.

There is clinical evidence that maternal secretiveness can have a ripple effect, spilling over into the domain of school learning (Brodie & Winterbottom, 1967). In a study of mothers of children with intellectual inhibitions, Hellman (1954) discussed the burden of family secrets in inhibiting the expression of the child's curiosity. In her cases, the mothers were entangled in extramarital affairs that necessitated the child "not seeing" the obvious, but there are many kinds of family secrets that require the child to be "stupid" on some counts. It is difficult to compartmentalize "knowing" and "not knowing," so a general attitude that ignorance is a virtue may result. An open family atmosphere where parents encourage and answer questions, even of a personal nature, reinforces the child's efforts to gain knowledge.

EMOTIONAL READINESS FOR SCHOOL

Some critical changes in personality occur normally in the years between 4 and 6, enabling the child to learn in the group situation of school. The 4-year-old is a natural "show-off" and regales parents and visitors alike with tricks and clever sayings. But this exhibitionism has to be toned down so that the child finds satisfaction in playing without continual adult attention or praise. If the child remains dependent on the mother's attention and has no interests of his or her own, the child is ill-prepared for the impersonality of school.

Acceptance of reality and responsibility is a quantum leap, usually taken in the period between 4 and 6 years. The child must master the distinction between make-believe and reality, relinquish belief in magic, and shift from primary to secondary thinking processes (see Chapter 5). As long as the child thinks anything is possible, or that a wish or thought is tantamount to an act, there is no need for real knowledge.

The growing ability to distinguish fantasy from reality brings an appreciation of limitations. Some children, boys in particular, wrestle with this downgrading process. They may resist being shown or taught anything, feeling that an admission of ignorance is an admission of inferiority. Until they accept reality limitations, no one can teach them anything. On the other hand, the child must not degrade himself mentally so much that he gives up. The ideal is a middle course which helps him or her to understand that although there are many things he or she cannot do yet, the situation will soon change. The child must see the limitations as temporary rather than permanent, so that, in spite of the inevitable delays and detours in store, the child retains the ambition to grow up.

A corollary to the child's acceptance of reality limitations is the increasing sense of identity with other children of the same age. The realization that they share problems is a boon and the child gains psychological strength from a friend with whom to identify. But then the child must also be able to tolerate competition and comparison, because there will be inequalities in abilities and achievements even with peers.

PARENTAL ROLE MODELS

A parent who enjoys active learning and feels confident in his or her mental abilities may provide an example for imitation and identification if not intimidating. If the parent is very outstanding, exhibitionistic, or intolerant, the child may feel that it is impossible to measure up to parental standards. But more often, the parental models are discouraging because the parents have little confidence in themselves. Grunebaum, Hurwit, Prentice, and Sperry (1962) brought the role of the father into sharp focus in a study of elementary school boys with learning problems. The fathers, although all of middle class, regarded their own achievements as below standard and considered their work unimportant and tedious. "The readiness of these men to accept a self-derogatory role with an attitude of helpless resignation was impressive" (1962, p. 464).

A family situation of this kind is conducive to the formation of a learning problem, as the parents tacitly expect the child to fail also. Also, the possibility of his actually succeeding, in a way the father could not, may expose the child to paternal jealousy, his own Oedipal guilt, or excessive admiration or resentment from the mother, depending on her neurotic structure. These reactions to a child's superior achievements do not occur, however, if a father's failure has been determined by outside events. An immigrant father, one who had to start work at an early age, or one who never had a chance to attend college, can enjoy his son's success and believe that the same success could have been his had he had the proper opportunities. The father who considers himself a failure despite opportunities to succeed has more conflicts about his son's achievements.

In this sort of family, the child's school performance is affected by his identification with his father. The boy's view of achievement, competition, and masculinity is distorted; achievement and competitiveness are equated with femininity. The life of a grown man has

no appeal. If the father dislikes his work, there is nothing for the boy to anticipate except more tedium and onerous responsibility. The child is faced with a dilemma; should he imitate the passive, weak, but so-called masculine role of his father, or should he try to be active, competitive, and successful in the aggressive style of the mother? When there is such a conflict, passivity is the easier alternative.

In other instances, the family constellation is quite different. Buxbaum (1964) described some clinical cases where the fathers were outstandingly successful and the sons were so intimidated that they did not even try to compete. The passive withdrawal may serve as a covert way of expressing aggression in a family which prizes competitive success. Usually these children do not show an all-pervasive learning inhibition but rather a selective and intermittent failure pattern.

This brings us to further consideration of the role of aggression in learning. Learning is work which requires the expenditure of energy. There is some evidence to suggest that the overly aggressive child has a better intellectual outcome when compared with the passive-dependent child (Harris, 1961; Sontag, Baker, & Nelson, 1955; Sperry, Ulrich, & Staver, 1958). Study of a group of adolescent underachievers revealed that in comparison with the normal achievers, the underachievers had great difficulty dealing with their aggression and presented a "good child facade" (Dudek & Lester, 1968). If the parents generally foster passive-dependent compliance and actively discourage assertiveness, this can lead to an inhibition of learning.

CASE 11.1   Henry

Henry was 10 at the time of referral, and in the third grade, but achieving at a first grade level. Everyone was baffled because Henry appeared so eager to do well and had no other difficulties.

Exploration of the living situation indicated some crowding. Henry and his sister shared a small bedroom and for an extraordinary reason. Some years before, a friend of the mother's had come for a weekend and never departed. She paid no room or board, had no job, and constantly criticized and nagged Henry's parents. They didn't

like her but could not face asking her to leave. The father was also passive at work. He worked at the same place for 12 years without a vacation. The parents recognized the injustice of these situations but were powerless to do anything.

Henry displayed the same compliance and inhibition of aggression. For example, his teacher repeatedly mispronounced his last name so that it lent itself to ridicule by his classmates, but he had never been able to correct her and was shocked when the possibility was suggested.

Case 11.1, the case of Henry, is an illustration.

Defensive Inhibitions

In Henry's case, he was clearly following the extraordinary example set by his parents in overall passivity, but many other learning-disabled children develop more specific inhibitions directly related to learning and less imitative of their parents. These children do not have other obvious emotional problems, but they have developed patterns of behavior which, if not the cause, at least perpetuate the learning difficulties.

One characteristic that has been frequently noted is *passivity;* the learning-disabled child seems to do little to help him or herself do better. It has been suggested that this might be in part due to "metacognitive deficits," for example, failure to utilize rehearsal strategies for memory storage (Douglas, 1981) and de-

ficiencies in task approach skills which help to select the most relevant and important features (Hallahan & Kneedler, 1979). In the reading domain, poor readers manifest less awareness of the informational functions of reading, an overemphasis on decoding, less knowledge concerning appropriate processing strategies, and less sensitivity to their own level of comprehension (Short & Ryan, 1984). Briefly, the evidence shows that children with learning problems do not use systematic problem solving to try and overcome their difficulties, but it is not at all clear why this is so.

One explanation is that they are conditioned to expect failure, so that the mere presentation of learning tasks arouses anxiety and avoidant defenses (such as impulsive responding). One is often struck with how quickly the learning-disabled child gives up and accepts failure as an inevitable consequence. Ryna, Weed, & Short (1986) suggested that the apparent lack of motivation on the part of many LD children can be understood in terms of their habitual attributions of success to external causes rather than to their own effort. It has been well established that high school achievers tend to perceive an internal "locus of control" (Messer, 1972), although it might follow rather than precede the fact of school success. It is easy to understand that children with difficulties might increasingly adopt an external "locus of control" explanation. External causes may be something about the teacher ("she's not fair"; "he never explains anything") or something vague about the brain where even the diagnosis can be used as an external reason ("my brain doesn't work right"). As mentioned before, these external attributions are often reinforced by parents and teachers who believe that the child needs something very special in the way of educational presentation. In the process of relieving the child of responsibility or guilt about the poor school performance, it is not surprising that the child concludes that his or her actions are of little avail.

This kind of passive learning-disabled child is very dependent on external reinforcement, like a much younger child. Friebergs and Douglas (1969) contrasted the performance of 65 hyperactive learning-disabled and 99 control subjects of elementary-school age in concept learning. Briefly, the only significant difference was in the condition of partial reinforcement (when every second correct response was reinforced). The authors described the extreme frustration experienced by the learning-disabled children when no reinforcement was given. Short (1986) found that about 24% of a group of learning disabled showed the "classic learned helpless

pattern," lacking self-esteem, preferring easy tasks, lacking curiosity, and relying on teacher's perceptions for judging performance, whereas none of the normally achieving children showed this motivational subtype cluster.

However, learning-disabled children are heterogeneous in regard to personality-motivational variables as well as cognitive variables. For some children, the reasons for the apparent passivity are more complicated. One can readily sympathize with the child who is afraid of failure even if an inordinate amount of praise and support is necessary. Other children, however, make it difficult for educators because they never do enough to achieve an honest, successful experience, and one failure or near-failure brings on another. In some instances, such children will not exert any effort because they prefer to fail as a result of not trying, rather than risk the disappointment of failure after they have made a genuine effort. It is face-saving to think "it doesn't matter because I didn't really put much into it." By assuming an I-don't-care attitude, one is protected in advance against embarrassment or disappointment. The failure which is "feared" is failure to meet one's own expectations rather than a fear of objective failure. Despite appearing "stupid," it is possible for the child to retain a narcissistic fantasy of limitless potential. After all, the LD child is reassured many times that he or she is *not* "stupid" and could do "much better," and the child is free to imagine any possibility. It is unrewarding to some children to work diligently only to reach a mediocre level.

Many years ago, Sears (1940) investigated the question of "levels of aspiration" in academically successful and unsuccessful children ages 9 to 12 years. She found that the children with a history of school success were consistent in setting their performance goals slightly above their scores (in a special laboratory task) but that the children with a history of school failure had varied reactions, shooting very high or very low. The child who set himself or herself an easy target derived pleasure from doing better, but the child who fell short of a totally unrealistic goal also seemed to derive pleasure from the mere verbal statement of ambition. Although they are relatively few, one does encounter LD children who appear blissfully unaware of their real difficulties and seem to have substituted wishful intentions for real achievement. These children are hard to work with because when the defense of denial is relinquished, they are likely to be abjectly despairing, and the therapist or teacher must be able to provide a basis for comfort in reality.

After all is said and done, the LD child discovers the injustice of individual differences and the fact that amount of effort does not directly match up with level of accomplishment as it is judged by the outside world. Only the individual person knows what he or she wants to accomplish and how much it costs to do so. An 18-year-old girl, about to graduate from high school, described it well:

People say I worry a lot and yet they do not know how hard I have to work in order to keep up with them. I probably work twice as hard at one thing and twice as long as it takes them to do it, at least this is the way I feel. Not only do I spend a lot of time and energy but if something goes wrong, then I just feel even more discouraged. To keep this motivation and ambition up at the rate I am

doing is quite hard and I do not seem to be getting the backing I usually got from the teachers. In fact, I still wonder sometimes if it is worth it for my parents to spend so much money on education when I just learn about three-fourths of it. For all of my time and effort, I wish I got a lot more out of it. I am totally exhausted by the time I get home. It is a miracle if I do not cut down my parents, complain and criticize. The reason why I pick on my parents is because it seems to me that they are the only ones who understand what I seem to have to go through. This makes them the nearest target and the hardest. For they understand what I go through and yet I pick on them. I try to plan fun things for myself but by the time I am done with all the crap I have to do, I do not have the time or the energy.

Although the cognitive difficulties of most learning-disabled individuals result in a somewhat lower than average IQ, there is an occasional child who scores in the superior range on individual intelligence tests but still has persistent academic difficulties. Characteristically these children are very verbal and have picked up a lot of general information by listening, or watching TV. Often these children are good readers but poor in writing and mathematics. For these children, their self-concept seesaws between the extreme of "genius" and "idiot," and to some extent their confusion is shared by parents and teachers. Parents, teachers, and therapists alike may come to the simple conclusion that "he can, but he won't," a title aptly chosen by Newman, Dember, and Krug (1973) for a clinical report of 15 boys with IQ's above 130 and school grade scores of C or below. Although these children may seem like "walking encyclopedias," lengthy discussion reveals that their knowledge is fragmented, with inadequate comprehension of the underlying concepts. These authors emphasized the role of enhancement or reinforcement of precocious verbal skills by the mother's delight in the preschool period and suggested that

Precocious intelligence may also lead to tendencies in the child to force hasty premature closure in his thinking, as he anxiously avoids trial and error while he strains to maintain the appearance of superior competence. He uses his intelligence for quick solutions, he seeks problems which have flash-answers, not daring to show uncertainty, anxiety, ignorance, and searching behavior, which are a necessary part of larger tasks. (Newman et al., p. 113)

By the time these children are identified as having serious learning problems (usually around 8 or 9 years of age), it is impossible to ascertain whether the difficulties are the end-result of years of systematically avoiding certain tasks and practicing others or whether the learning problems reflect some neurologically based difference. In any case, treatment requires simultaneous attention to family attitudes, educational deficiencies, and emotional responses and is nowhere near as simple as it might appear from the mere fact of the high IQ.

The most paradoxical situation is when the child's learning inhibition is based on a fear of success rather than the more usual fear of failure. Success in school may be tied to anxieties about growing up or perhaps anxieties about increased responsibilities and expectations. Once in a while a child actually fears that others will be jealous or dislike him or her. Edith Weiskopf (1951) pointed out that the desire to succeed and the desire to be liked by one's fel-

lows are frequently incompatible. The beloved fool of legend and literature is the classic illustration of an intellectual blocking to ward off hostility. He is an innocent, appealing, and harmless figure, protected by all and envied by none. He may know more than he admits, but he makes everyone feel superior.

Peer Relationships

Although intelligence and academic performance are generally found to be positively correlated with peer acceptance, the magnitude of this relationship (average around .35) accounts for no more than about 10% of the variance in peer popularity. Although it has not been systematically investigated, one would suspect a curvilinear relationship, with extremely intelligent children no more popular in general than children of average abilities. In a survey of teasing (Shapiro, Baumeister, & Kessler, in press), physical differences were most commonly targeted and academic performance was second, with attention given to either being "stupid" or "too smart."

With regard to the social status of learning-disabled children, they are usually less well-accepted than their regular classmates (Bruininks, 1978; Bryan, 1974a). One might conclude that this is the result of the stigma attached to special school programming, except that even when LD children are transferred to new classrooms and new teachers, the situation does not change (Bryan, 1976). It is not altogether clear why this is the case. It does not seem to be the direct result of academic performance, as indicated by McMichael's study showing that poor readers who conformed to classroom requirements were no more rejected than good readers (1980). But it is not clear what it is about their behavior which causes peer rejection. Hartup remarked that "It is also known that LD children are less accurate in self-perceptions of peer status, believe themselves to be no different from their classmates, and are more intrusive in their social interactions than other children" (1983, p. 130). On the other hand, others have reported that LD children are not more intrusive, but in fact initiate fewer comments to others (Bryan, 1974b; Bryan & Wheeler, 1972). This is reflected in the experimental task of "referential communication" where one child instructs another child in how to do a particular task "unseen" (Feagans & Short, 1986). Although the LD child's communication deficiency in this situation might be regarded as another sign of the basic cognitive problem, it is an impedance in social relations as well.

In general, LD children seem to have a poor sense of social context so that their timing is off, they don't know when to start or stop a social interaction, they have little awareness of the social conventions in their group, and they tend to interpret events in a literal and personal way without recognizing "in-house jokes" or exaggerated statements. In a social sense, they continue to be egocentric; that is, they have difficulty taking the perspective of another person. As an example, one LD child expressed great puzzlement to his therapist because his junior-high classmates were angry with him when he correctly predicted that the home team would lose the next game. This lack of awareness of what is expected of a teenager was reflected in his mother's comment that they were going to vacation at an ocean beach so that "Paul could have fun digging in the sand." Some years later (and after some more psychotherapy) Paul said "I try to get psyched before sports events," showing that he now appreciated what was expected although he did not really "feel it."

Psychological Interventions

There has been a move toward "cognitive strategy training" to "promote active, self-regulatory learning styles" (Ryan, Weed, & Short, 1986). Ross discussed various strategies for controlling impulsive responding (1980) and pointed out that simple instruction to "stop, look, and think" was not effective unless it was combined with some suggestions as to what to think about. The LD child typically has difficulty in defining the central problem, scanning the material presented, storing and retrieving the facts relative to the presented task, and planning what he or she will do. These so-called "metacognitive deficits" have been investigated particularly with regard to memory strategies, but there has also been some work with reading comprehension. For example, Wong and Jones (1982) used a five-step self-questioning training procedure with junior-high LD students. The five steps taught were:

1. What are you studying this passage for?
2. Find the main ideas in the passage and underline them.

3. Think of a question about the main idea you underlined.
4. Learn the answers to your questions.
5. Always look back at your questions and answers to see how each successive question and answer provides you with more information.

Briefly, this five-step self-questioning training procedure was helpful for the LD students but did not change the performance of a group of non-LD children. Other self-instructional programs have been successful with teaching arithmetic.

The cognitive strategy training programs are designed not only to accomplish a specific educational goal but to give the LD student some autonomy in considering problems of all types. By stressing the "how" of problem solving, one takes out some of the mystery. The child may not know the answer, but he or she knows that there is a way of finding it. So far, cognitive interventions have been research-oriented, brief programs apart from the classroom. Adaptation to the classroom would require considerable modification of standards teaching materials such as workbooks and so on, but it seems entirely compatible with general goals of teaching. Most of this work has been done with upper elementary and older children, which is interesting in view of the discouraging plateau effect for LD children as they progress into the higher grades. It may be that the educational methods useful at the beginning stage of learning basic academic skills are not appropriate at later stages, so that one must shift gears in order to prevent stagnation.

There are other psychological approaches described in individual case reports which seem to hold promise for more than the individual case. Harter (1977, 1982) treated a 6-year-old child who was having school learning problems. The child had arrived at the simple conclusion that she was "all dumb," whereupon Harter drew a circle with a line down the middle of it with "S" for "smart" on one side and "D" for "dumb" on the other. After a period of treatment (both in play therapy and in school), she made further differentiations in this picture of herself so that "D" regions became much smaller. This case is particularly interesting because Harter did not fall into the all-or-none trap of reassuring the little girl by saying "oh no, you are smart" but rather helped her to differentiate those areas where she was in reality "smart" and those where she was "dumb." This process of differentiation is a dynamic one where the classifications can change, as compared to a static, overall trait label.

Play therapy is a psychological intervention far removed from the serious, task-oriented behavioral therapies or cognitive strategy training procedures. One might think that such an approach would be frivolous for a child who has academic problems, except that there is increasing evidence that a child who can be creative in play tends to be more intellectually competent as well (Russ, in press). Saltz, Dixon, and Johnson (1977) speculated that fantasy play was positively related to cognitive development because of the involvement of representational skills and concept formation, but fantasy play also carries an important affective component. Russ (1980) found a substantial relationship (correlation of .54) between reading achievement in second grade children and a measure of affective response on the Rorschach. This work suggests that children who are impoverished in affective expression, or who are overwhelmed by affects, are both handicapped in an academic learning situation.

Play therapy provides a safe, nonjudgmental situation where a child can discuss feelings and fantasies indirectly; also, there are forms of play which involve strategy planning, not unlike what is needed in academic situations. Guerney (1983) described a case with the mother as the play therapist (filial therapy, see Chapter 7).

At first the child demonstrated an enormous amount of helplessness and dependency which the mother reinforced by having wonderful ideas for him. The play session rules required her to permit him to lead the way, and over a period of time, he learned to make decisions for himself and to dare to take some modest risks. When the mother could see that he was capable of moving on his own, she pulled back in real life and the child became willing to try new tasks, did not give up at the slightest obstacle, persevered and got up to grade level in arithmetic. He became less clinging and fearful so that he was willing to join other children in the neighborhood for games—except baseball. (1983, p. 430)

It is ironic that it is often the very best of mothers who unwittingly encourage dependence and "learned helplessness" in their efforts to be helpful.

The LD Child as an Adult

As mentioned before, the problems of the LD child may persist into adulthood. Cato and Rice (1982) described the learning-disabled adult as follows:

Among the common characteristics of the adult population found in the literature are a basic impairment in the ability to focus attention; a history of early learning disabilities; current complaints of diffuse symptoms with elements of anxiety and depression; reported feelings of inadequacy and low self-esteem; continued difficulty with basic academic skills, which limits vocational opportunities; a variety of negative consequences in daily living as a result of behavior disorganization; attention deficits; poor impulse control; and self-reported difficulty in developing sensitive and lasting relationships with others. As with any listing of common characteristics, individual differences will be found in this population. (p. 18)

Discussing the psychotherapeutic issues for the learning-disabled adult, Schulman (1984) talked about the importance of identifying the effect of the disability, but at the same time remarked that

Were therapy to stop without analyzing the defenses—with focus only having been placed on the disability and its "evil" influence on the patient—the therapy would be giving the patient permission to feel sorry for himself or herself and to develop a sense of hopelessness about trying to change. The truth about many disabilities, though, is that with the proper attitude, their severely limiting effect on the patient's life can be drastically minimized. (p. 864)

This double-edged approach is just as important for children as for adults. It is important to "see" the child as a unique person and not just as a "learning disability."

SUMMARY AND PERSONAL PERSPECTIVE

The vast amount of literature which has been accumulated on the subject of learning difficulties defies brief summary and in any case is disappointing because it has not evolved into any kind of consensus about definition or intervention. What follows is a composite of highlights and opinions developed from the author's experience with many cases.

Children judge themselves and are judged by their success in school; achievement failure is and always has been a frequent reason for referral for special attention. With poor grades, the first step is a determination of the ability-achievement discrepancy, and there has been a great change in the methods of measuring both these factors.

In recent years, the term "underachievement" has been replaced by "learning disability," which is the fastest-growing category of educational handicap. Different measures are used to define this category, depending often on the limits set by financial resources since all children so identified are eligible for "free and appropriate educational services" under P.L. 94-142. More and more of these services are provided on a part-time basis in resource rooms rather than separate full-time classroom programs.

But learning disability is not a diagnosis; in fact, it does not appear as such in DSM III, although there are relevant diagnoses such as Developmental Reading Disorder and Developmental Arithmetic Disorder. A learning disability may co-exist with any of the standard diagnostic categories. There is agreement that the LD category is heterogeneous and there have been efforts to identify meaningful subtypes. The specific perceptual and linguistic deficiencies which were formerly identified with "brain-injury" or "minimal cerebral dysfunction" do exist but are relatively rare. There is growing interest in motivational problems, particularly as reflected in the passivity frequently observed in LD children of all types. Despite extensive amounts of research on attention deficits, slow cognitive processing, poor cognitive strategies, etc., there has been relatively little impact on techniques of intervention, and special education has not been particularly effective for these children. Doubtlessly, one reason for this indifferent record is the failure to match the specific intervention to the specific problems presented by an individual child. In the real world, assessment is used more to determine eligibility for services than to establish causation, and the mandated individual education plans place more stress on individual target goals than on the methods and materials to be used to reach these goals.

The Education for All Handicapped Children Act (P.L. 94-142) gave the public school system a tremendous responsibility and opened up opportunities for many children, particularly in the category of severely handicapped children who were previously excluded. However, it had some secondary consequences, perhaps disadvantageous to the less handicapped. By stipulating that the "supportive services" deemed necessary for promoting education must also be provided by the public schools, there has been an understandable reluctance to recommend psychotherapy because of economic liability. As a consequence, there has been a growing separation between public schools and child mental health facilities.

On their part, psychotherapists seem

to stand in awe of the diagnostic label "learning disability" and view the problems of these children as the business of the educator. They are dismayed by the multitude of tests and constructs used by educators and the suggestion that the problem may be "organic" after all. In fact, however, psychotherapy has a great deal to contribute to the enterprise. Helping the child to understand the problem, to set realistic goals and to work on his or her own behalf towards such goals, and to accept some responsibility for success or failure requires the sustained relationship inherent in psychotherapy. Common obstacles are anxieties about success and failure, inhibitions of aggression, and confusion in self-concept. The task of looking at oneself is peculiarly difficult for the LD child, who is not at all sure of what he or she sees; the perspective of the therapist can help in distinguishing what is "real" and what is "not real." It is likely, although not inevitable, that the LD child still uses egocentric modes of communication and encounters social problems as well as academic problems. The psychotherapy situation provides an opportunity to practice taking other points of view and to consider alternative strategies for coping with social encounters.

Looking at these tasks suggested for the psychotherapists, one might argue that teachers share a concern for the same issues. But the psychotherapy situation offers a nonjudgmental one-to-one relationship, with a guarantee of privacy and confidentiality. Given time to build some trust, the child can express feelings and fantasies—about self, family members, and teachers—which he may know only dimly. It is the therapist's special task then to connect these with the learning problem so that the learning situation can be "neutralized" and seen for what it is rather than what it might stand for symbolically. The therapist has advantages in the opportunity to focus exclusively on one child for some period of time and also in the access to family information normally not shared with public school personnel.

On the other hand, the teacher sees the child in the all-important arena of school where the problems are manifest. It is essential to integrate the educational and therapeutic efforts, but this is not easy since these are usually going on under different auspices and with different expectations. The teacher wants to know on a session-by-session basis what is happening and expects short-term tangible results. On the other hand, the therapist may expect that the teacher has some "magic methods" of instruction or that she can make individual allowances which are incompatible with usual classroom practices. Sometimes the collaboration is an uneasy one, with each partner a little suspicious of the other, or even blaming the other for what is, after all, the child's difficulty. Occasionally the therapist and teacher find themselves competing for the child's affection and ascribing differences in behavior to the child's preference for the one or the other. Although a therapist may sometimes teach, and a teacher may sometimes talk about feelings and fantasies, their central roles are different and should be complementary.

REFERENCES

ACKERMAN, P. T., DYKMAN, R. A., & PETERS, J. E. (1977). Teenage status of hyperactive and nonhyperactive learning disabled boys. *American Journal of Orthopsychiatry, 47*, 577–596.

ADAMS, R. M., KOCSIS, J. J., & ESTES, R. E. (1974). Soft neurological signs in learning-disabled children and controls. *American Journal of Diseases of Children, 128*, 614–618.

ALGOZZINE, R., & YSSELDYKE, J. (1983). Learning disabilities as a subset of school failure: The over-sophistication of a concept. *Exceptional Children, 50*, 242–246.

American Academy of Pediatrics. (1972). Statement of the Executive Board: The Eye and Learning Disabilities. *Pediatrics, 49*, 454–455.

ANDERSON, R. P., HALCOMB, C. G., & DOYLE, R. B. (1973). The measurement of attentional deficits. *Exceptional Children, 39*, 534–539.

Association for Children with Learning Disabilities (ACLD). (1985). Definition. *Special Education Today, 2*, 1.

AYLLON, T., LAYMAN, D., & KANDEL, H. J. (1975). A behavioral-educational alternative to drug control of hyperactive children. *Journal of Applied Behavior Analysis, 8*, 137–146.

AYRES, A. J. (1963). The development of perceptual-motor abilities: A theoretical basis for treatment of dysfunction. *American Journal of Occupational Therapy, 17*, 221–225.

AYRES, A. J. (1972a). Southern California Sensory Integration Tests (SCSIT). Los Angeles: Western Psychological Services.

AYERS, A. J. (1972b). Improving academic scores through sensory integration. *Journal of Learning Disabilities, 5*, 339–345.

BAKKER, D. J. (1979). Hemispheric differences and reading strategies. *Bulletin of the Orton Society, 29*, 84–100.

BARSCH, R. H. (1967). *Achieving perceptual-motor efficiency.* Seattle, WA: Special Child Publications.

BELMONT, L. (1980). Epidemiology. In H. E. Rie & E. D. Rie (Eds.), *Handbook of minimal brain dysfunctions: A critical view* (pp. 55–74). New York: John Wiley.

BENTON, A. L. (1975). Developmental dyslexia: Neurological aspects. In W. J. Friedlander (Ed.), *Advances in neurology: Vol. 7 Current review of higher nervous system dysfunction* (pp. 1–47). NY: Raven Press.

BERGER, M., & KENNEDY, H. (1975). Pseudobackwardness in children: Maternal attitudes as an etiological factor. In R. S. Eissler, A. Freud, M. Kris, & A. J. Solnit (Eds.), *The psychoanalytic study of the child* (Vol. 30, pp. 279–306). New Haven: Yale University Press.

BOYAN, C. (1985). California's new eligibility criteria: Legal and program implications. *Exceptional Children, 52*, 131–141.

BRODIE, R. D., & WINTERBOTTOM, M. R. (1967). Failure in elementary school boys as a function of traumata, secrecy and derogation. *Child Development, 38*, 701–711.

BROUGHTON, S. F., & LAHEY, B. B. (1978). Direct and collateral effects of positive reinforcement, response cost, and mixed contingencies for academic performance. *Journal of School Psychology, 16*, 126–136.

BRUININKS, V. L. (1978). Peer status and personality of learning disabled and nondisabled students. *Journal of Learning Disabilities, 11*, 29–34.

BRYAN, T. H. (1974a). Peer popularity of learning disabled children. *Journal of Learning Disabilities, 7*, 621–625.

BRYAN, T. H. (1974b). An observational analysis of classroom behaviors of children with learning disabilities. *Journal of Learning Disabilities, 7*, 26–34.

BRYAN, T. H. (1976). Peer popularity of learning disabled children: A replication. *Journal of Learning Disabilities, 9*, 307–311.

BRYAN, T., & WHEELER, R. (1972). Perception of learning disabled children: The eye of the observer. *Journal of Learning Disabilities, 5*, 484–488.

BURKE, A. A. (1975). Placement of Black and White children in educable mentally handicapped classes and learning disability classes. *Exceptional Children, 41*, 438–439.

BUXBAUM, E. (1964). The parents' role in the etiology of learning disabilities. In R. S. Eissler, A. Freud, H. Hartmann, & M. Kris (Eds.), *Psychoanalytic Study of the Child* (Vol. 19, pp. 421–447). New York: International University Press.

CATO, C., & RICE, B. D. (1982). Report from the study group on rehabilitation of clients with specific learning disabilities. St. Louis, MO: National Institute of Handicapped Research.

CHAPMAN, J. W., & BOERSMA, F. J. (1979). Learning disabilities, locus of control and mother attitudes. *Journal of Educational Psychology, 71*, 250–258.

CHILDS, B., & FINUCCI, J. M. (1983). Genetics, epidemiology and specific reading disability. In M. Rutter (Ed.), *Developmental neuropsychiatry* (pp. 507–519). New York: The Guilford Press.

CHINN, P. C., & HUGHES, S. (1987). Representation of minority students in special education classes. *Remedial and Special Education, 8*, 41–46.

DAS, J. P. (1984). Review of the Kaufman Assessment Battery for Children (K-ABC). *Journal of Psychoeducational Assessment, 2*, 83–88.

DEJERINE, J. (1892). Contribution a l'étude anatomo-pathologique et clinique des differentes varietés de cecite verbale. *Memoire de la Societé de Biologie, 4.*

DELACATO, C. H. (1963). *The diagnosis and treatment of speech and reading problems.* Springfield, IL: Charles C Thomas.

DELACATO, C. H. (1966). *Neurological organization and reading.* Springfield, IL: Charles C Thomas.

DOUGLAS, L. C. (1981). *Metamemory in learning-disabled children: A clue to memory deficiencies.* Paper presented to the Society for Research on Child Development, Boston.

DOUGLAS, V. I. (1972). Stop, look and listen: The problem of sustained attention and impulse control in hyperactive and nor-mal children. *Canadian Journal of Behavioral Science, 4*, 259–281.

DUDEK, S. Z., & MESTER, E. P. (1968). The good child facade in chronic underachievers. *American Journal of Orthopsychiatry, 38*, 153–160.

DYKMAN, R. A., ACKERMAN, P. T., CLEMENTS, S. D., & PETERS, J. E. (1971). Specific learning disabilities: An attentional deficit syndrome. In H. R. Myklebust (Ed.), *Progress in Learning Disabilities* (Vol. 2, pp. 56–93). New York: Grune & Stratton.

EPSTEIN, M. H., CULLINAN, D., LESSEN, E. I., & LLOYD, J. (1980). Understanding children with learning disabilities. *Child Welfare, 59.*

FEAGANS, L., & SHORT, E. J. (1986). Longitudinal assessment of referential communication skills in normally achieving and learning disabled children. *Developmental Psychology, 22*, 177–183.

FERRITOR, D. E., BUCKHOLDT, D., HAMBLIN, R. L., & SMITH, L. (1972). The noneffects of contingent reinforcement for attending behavior on work accomplished. *Journal of Applied Behavior Analysis, 5*, 7–17.

FEUERSTEIN, R. (1979). *The dynamic assessment of retarded performers.* Baltimore, MD: University Park Press.

FLETCHER, J. M. (1985). External validation of learning disabilities typologies. In B. P. Rourke (Ed.), *Neuropsychology of learning disabilities.* (pp. 187–225). New York: The Guilford Press.

FRANKS, D. J. (1971). Ethnic and social status characteristics of children in EMR and LD classes. *Exceptional Children, 37*, 537–538.

FREUD, A. (1975). Foreword for M. Berger & H. Kennedy. Pseudobackwardness in Children. In R. S. Eissler, A. Freud, M. Kris, & A. J. Solnit (Eds.), *The psychoanalytic study of the child* (Vol. 30, pp. 279–280). New Haven: Yale University Press.

FRIEBERGS, V., & DOUGLAS, V. I. (1969). Concept learning in hyperactive and normal children. *Journal of Abnormal Psychology, 74*, 388–396.

FROSTIG, M. (1968). Education for children with learning disabilities. In H. Myklebust (Ed.), *Progress in learning disabilities* (Vol. 1, pp. 234–266). New York: Grune & Stratton.

FROSTIG, M., LEFEVER, D. W., & WHITTLESEY, J. R. B. (1964). *The Marianne Frostig developmental test of visual perception.* Palo Alto: Consulting Psychology Press.

GAZZANIGA, M. S., BOGEN, J. E., & SPERRY, R. W. (1965). Observations on visual perception after disconnexion of the cerebral hemispheres in man. *Brain, 88,* 221–236.

GESCHWIND, N. (1962). The anatomy of acquired disorders of reading. In J. Money (Ed.), *Reading disability* (pp. 115–130). Baltimore, MD: The Johns Hopkins Press.

GETMAN, G. N. (1962). *How to develop your child's intelligence. A research publication.* Luverne, MN: G. N. Getman.

GRUNEBAUM, M. G., HURWITZ, I., PRENTICE, N. M., & SPERRY, B. M. (1962). Fathers of sons with primary neurotic learning inhibition. *American Journal of Orthopsychiatry, 33,* 462–473, 1962.

GUERNEY, L. F. (1983). Play therapy with learning disabled children. In C. E. Schaefer & K. J. O'Connor (Eds.) *Handbook of play therapy* (pp. 419–435). New York: John Wiley.

HALLAHAN, D. P., & CRUICKSHANK, W. M. (1973). *Psycho-educational foundations of learning disabilities.* Englewood Cliffs, NJ: Prentice-Hall.

HALLAHAN, D. P., & KNEEDLER, R. D. (1979). *Strategy deficits in the information-processing of learning-disabled children.* Charlottesville, VA: University of Virginia Learning Disabilities Research Institute, Technical Report, #6.

HAMMILL, D. (1972). Training visual-perceptual processes. *Journal of Learning Disabilities, 5,* 552–559.

HAMMILL, D. D., & LARSEN, S. C. (1974). The effectiveness of psycholinguistic training. *Exceptional Children, 41,* 5–14.

HARRIS, I. D. (1961). *Emotional blocks to learning.* New York: Free Press of Glencoe.

HARTER, S. (1977). A cognitive-developmental approach to children's expressions of conflicting feelings and a technique to facilitate such expressions in play therapy. *Journal of Consulting and Clinical Psychology, 45,* 417–432.

HARTER, S. (1982). A cognitive-developmental approach to children's understanding of affect and trait labels. In F. C. Serafica (Ed.), *Social-cognitive development in context* (pp. 27–61). New York: The Guilford Press.

HARTLAGE, L. C. (1970). Differential diagnosis of dyslexia, minimal brain damage and emotional disturbances in children. *Psychology in the Schools, 7,* 403–406.

HARTUP, W. (1983). Peer relations. In P. H. Mussen & E. M. Hetherington (Eds.), *Handbook of child psychology* (Vol. 4, pp. 103–196). New York: John Wiley.

HELLMAN, I. (1954). Some observations on mothers of children with intellectual inhibition. In R. S. Eissler, A. Freud, H. Hartmann, & E. Kris (Eds.), *Psychoanalytic study of the child* (Vol. 9, pp. 259–273). New York: International Universities Press.

HERBERT, M. (1964). The concept and testing of brain damage in children. A review. *Journal of Child Psychology and Psychiatry, 5,* 197–217.

HINSHELWOOD, J. (1917). *Congenital word blindness.* London: H. K. Lewis.

HIRSCH, S. M., & ANDERSON, R. P. (1976). The effects of perceptual motor training on reading achievement. In R. P. Anderson & C. G. Halcomb (Eds.), *Learning disability/ minimal brain dysfunction syndrome* (pp. 162–181). Springfield, IL: Charles C Thomas.

HOLROYD, J., & WRIGHT, F. (1965). Neurological implications of WISC Verbal-Performance discrepancies in a psychiatric setting. *Journal of Consulting Psychology, 29,* 206–212.

JASON, L. A., DURLAK, J. A., & HOLTON-

WALKER, E. (1984). Prevention of child problems in the schools. In M. C. Roberts & L. Peterson (Eds.), *Prevention of problems in childhood: Psychological research and applications* (pp. 311–341). New York: John Wiley.

KATAN, A. (1946). Experiences with enuretics. In A. Freud, H. Hartmann, & E. Kris (Eds.), *The psychoanalytic study of the child* (Vol. 2, pp. 241–256). New York: International Universities Press.

KAUFMAN, A. S. (1976). Verbal-Performance IQ discrepancies on the WISC-R. *Journal of Consulting and Clinical Psychology, 44,* 739–744.

KAUFMAN, A. S. (1979). *Intelligent testing with the WISC-R.* New York: John Wiley.

KAUFMAN, A., & KAUFMAN, N. (1983). *Kaufman Assessment Battery for Children.* Circle Pines, MN: American Guidance Services.

KAVALE, K. (1981). Functions of the ITPA: Are they trainable? *Exceptional Children, 47,* 496–510.

KEOGH, B. K. (1974). Optometric vision training programs for children with learning disabilities: Review of issues and research. *Journal of Learning Disabilities, 7,* 36–48.

KEOGH, B. K., & DONLAN, G. (1972). Field independence, impulsivity, and learning disabilities. *Journal of Learning Disabilities, 5,* 331–336.

KEPHART, N. C. (1964). Perceptual-motor aspects of learning disabilities. *Exceptional Child, 31,* 201–206.

KEPHART, N. C. (1971). *The slow learner in the classroom* (2nd ed.). Columbus, OH: Charles C. Merrill.

KESSLER, J. W. (1966). Learning disorders in school-age children. In *Psychopathology of childhood.* Englewood Cliffs, NJ: Prentice-Hall.

KIRK, S. (1963). Behavioral diagnosis and remediation of learning disabilities. In *Conference on the exploration into the problems of the perceptually handicapped child.* Evanston, IL: Fund for the Perceptually Handicapped Child.

KIRK, S. A., MCCARTHY, J. J., & KIRK, W. D. (1968). *Illinois Test of Psycholinguistic Abilities.* Urbana: University of Illinois Press.

KOPPITZ, E. M. (1975). *The Bender Gestalt Test for young children* (Vol. 2). New York: Grune & Stratton.

KOPPITZ, E. M. (1971). *Children with learning disabilities: A five-year follow-up study.* New York: Grune & Stratton.

LIEBERMAN, L. M. (1980). The implications of noncategorical special education. *Journal of Learning Disabilities, 13,* p. 65–68.

LYON, R. (1977). Auditory-perceptual training: The state of the art. *Journal of Learning Disabilities, 10,* 564–572.

MANN, L. (1970). Perceptual training: Misdirections and redirections. *American Journal of Orthopsychiatry, 40,* 30–39.

MASLAND, R. L. (1975). Neurological bases and correlates of language disabilities: Diagnostic implications. *Acta Symbolica, 6,* 1–34.

MCGRADY, H. J., & OLSON, D. A. (1970). Visual and auditory learning processes in normal children and children with specific learning disabilities. *Exceptional Children, 35,* 581–591.

MCKINNEY, J. D. (1984). The search for subtypes of learning disabilities. *Journal of Learning Disabilities, 17,* 43–50.

MCKINNEY, J. D., SHORT, E. J., & FEAGANS, L. (1985). Academic consequences of perceptual-linguistic subtypes of learning disabled children. *Learning Disabilities Review, 1,* 6–17.

MCMICHAEL, P. (1980). Reading difficulties, behavior and social status. *Journal of Educational Psychology, 72,* 76–86.

MESSER, S. B. (1972). The relation of internal-external control to academic performance. *Child Development, 43,* 1456–1462.

MYKLEBUST, H. R. (1968). Learning disabilities: Definition and overview. In H. R. Myklebust (Ed.), *Progress in learning disabilities* (Vol. 1, pp. 1–15). New York: Grune & Stratton.

NAYLOR, H. (1980). Reading disability and lateral asymmetry: An information processing analysis. *Psychological Bulletin, 87,* 531–545.

NEEPER, R., & LAHEY, B. B. (1983). Learning disabilities of children. In C. E. Walker & M. C. Roberts (Eds.), *Handbook of clinical child psychology* (pp. 680–696). New York: John Wiley.

NEWMAN, C. J., DEMBER, C. F., & KRUG, O. (1973). "He can but he won't": A psychodynamic study of so-called "gifted underachievers." In R. S. Eissler, A. Freud, M. Kris, & A. J. Solnit (Eds.), *Psychoanalytic study of the child* (Vol. 28, pp. 83–130). New Haven: Yale University Press.

"Official Statement." (1968). The Doman-Delacoto treatment of neurologically handicapped children. *Archives of Physical Medicine and Rehabilitation, 49,* 183–186.

ORTON, S. T. (1928). An impediment to learning to read: A neurological explanation of the reading disability. *School and Society, 28,* 286–296.

ORTON, S. T. (1966). "Word-blindness" in school children and other papers on strephosymbolia (Specific Language Disability—Dyslexia). Orton Society Monograph, No. 2.

PAINE, R. S., WERRY, J. S., & QUAY, H. C. (1968). A study of "minimal cerebral dysfunction." *Developmental Medicine and Child Neurology, 10,* 505–520.

PEARL, R., & BRYAN, T. (1982). Mothers' attributions for success and failure: A replication with a labeled learning disabled sample. *Learning Disability Quarterly, 5,* 183–186.

RAPIN, I. (1968). Brain damage in children. In J. Brennemann (Ed.), *Practice of pediatrics* (Vol. 4, pp. 1–57). Hagerstown, MD: Prior Publications.

ROSS, A. O. *Psychological disorders of children. A behavioral approach to theory, research and therapy.* New York: McGraw-Hill, 1980.

ROURKE, B. P. (1976). Reading retardation in children: Developmental lag or deficit? In R. M. Knights & D. J. Bakker (Eds.), *The neuropsychology of learning disorders* (pp. 125–137). Baltimore, MD: University Park Press.

ROURKE, B. P. (Ed.) (1985). *Neuropsychology of learning disabilities: Essentials of subtype analysis.* New York: The Guilford Press.

RUGEL, R. P., & ROSENTHAL, R. (1974). Skin conductance, reaction time and observational ratings in learning-disabled children. *Journal of Abnormal Child Psychology, 2,* 183–192.

RUSS, S. W. (1980). Primary process integration on the Rorschach and achievement in children. *Journal of Personality Assessment, 44,* 338–344.

RUSS, S. W. (1987). Assessment of cognitive affective interaction in children: Creativity, fantasy and play research. In C. Spielberger & J. Butcher (Eds.), *Advances in personality assessment* (Vol. 6, pp. 141–155). Hillsdale, NJ: L. Erlbaum.

RYAN, E. B., WEED, K. A., & SHORT, E. J. (1986). Cognitive behavior modification: Promoting active, self-regulatory learning styles. In J. Torgeson & B. Wong (Eds.), *Psychological and educational perspectives on learning disabilities* (pp. 367–397). New York: Academic Press.

SABBATINO, D. A., & MILLER, T. L. (1980). The dilemma of diagnosis in learning disabilities: Problems and potential directions. *Psychology in the Schools, 17,* 76–86.

SALTZ, E., DIXON, D., & JOHNSON, J. (1977). Training disadvantaged preschoolers on various fantasy activities: Effects on cognitive functioning and impulse control. *Child Development, 48,* 367–380.

SAMUELS, S. J., & MILLER, N. L. (1985). Failure to find attention differences between learning disabled and normal children on classroom and laboratory tasks. *Exceptional Children, 51,* 358–375.

SATZ, P., & MORRIS, R. (1981). Learning disabilities subtypes: A review. In F. J. Pirozzolo & M. C. Wittrock (Eds.), *Neuropsychological and cognitive processes in reading* (pp. 109–141). New York: Academic Press.

SATZ, P., & VAN NOSTRAND, G. K. (1973). Developmental dyslexia: An evaluation of a theory. In P. Satz & J. J. Ross (Eds.), *The disabled learner* (pp. 121–148). Rotterdam: Rotterdam University Press.

SATZ, P., MORRIS, R., & FLETCHER, J. M. (1985). Hypotheses, subtypes and individual differences in dyslexia: Some reflections. In D. Gray & J. Kavanagh (Eds.), *Biobehavioral measures of dyslexia* (pp. 25–40). Parkton, MD: York Press.

SCHONHAUT, S., & SATZ, P. (1983). Prognosis for children with learning disabilities: A review of follow-up studies. In M. Rutter (Ed.), *Developmental neuropsychiatry* (pp. 542–563). New York: Guilford Press.

SCHULMAN, S. S. (1984). Psychotherapeutic issues for the learning disabled adult. *Professional Psychology, 15,* 856–867.

SEARS, P. S. (1940). Levels of aspiration in academically successful and unsuccessful children. *Journal of Abnormal and Social Psychology, 35,* 498–536.

SENF, G. M. (1986). LD research in sociological and scientific perspective. In J. K. Torgesen & B. Wong (Eds.), *Psychological and educational perspectives on learning disabilities* (pp. 27–54). New York: Academic Press.

SHAPIRO, J., BAUMEISTER, R. F., & KESSLER, J. W. (1987). Children's awareness of themselves as teasers and their value judgments of teasing. *Perceptual and Motor Skills, 64,* 1102.

SHORT, E. J. (1986, March). *The educational implications of cognitive motivational subtypes.* Paper presented at the 19th Annual Gatlinburg Conference in Mental Retardation and Developmental Disabilities, Gatlinburg, TN.

SHORT, E. J., & RYAN, E. B. (1984). Metacognitive differences between skilled and less skilled readers: Remediating deficits through story grammar and attribution training. *Journal of Educational Psychology, 76,* 225–235.

SHORT, E. J., FEAGANS, L., MCKINNEY, J. D., & APPLEBAUM, M. I. (1986). Longitudinal stability of LD subtypes based on age- and IQ-achievement discrepancies. *Learning Disability Quarterly, 9,* 214–225.

SONTAG, L. S., BAKER, C. T., & NELSON, V. P. (1955). Personality as a determinant of performance. *American Journal of Orthopsychiatry, 25,* 552–562.

SPERRY, B. D., STAVER, N., & MANN, H. E. (1952). Destructive fantasies in certain learning difficulties. *American Journal of Orthopsychiatry, 22,* 356–366.

SPERRY, B. D., ULRICH, D. N., & STAVER, N. (1958). The relation of motility to boys' learning problems. *American Journal of Orthopsychiatry, 28,* 98–111.

SROUFE, L. A., SONIES, B. C., WEST, W. D., & WRIGHT, F. S. (1973). Anticipatory heart rate deceleration and reaction time in children with and without referral for learning disability. *Child Development, 44,* 267–273.

STERN, W. (1914). *The psychological methods of testing intelligence.* Baltimore, MD: Warwick & York.

THORNDIKE, R. L., HAGEN, E. P., & SATTLER, J. M. (1986). *The Stanford-Binet Intelligence Scale: 4th Ed. Guide for administering and scoring.* Chicago, IL: Riverside.

TOMATIS, A. A. (1978). *Education and dyslexia.* Switzerland: Association Internationale D'Audio-psychophonologie. Montreal: Les Edicion France-Quebec.

ULLMAN, D. G. (1977). Children's lateral preference patterns: Frequency and relationships with achievement and intelligence. *Journal of School Psychology, 15,* 36–43.

WECHSLER, D. (1949). *Manual for the Wechsler Intelligence Scale for Children.* New York: Psychological Corporation.

WEISKOPF, E. A. (1951). Intellectual malfunctioning and personality. *Journal of Abnormal and Social Psychology, 46,* 410–423.

WERTHEIMER, W. (1923). Studies in the theory of Gestalt psychology. *Psychologische Forschung, 4,* 301–350.

WILSON, L. R. (1985). Large-scale learning disability identification: The reprieve of a concept. *Exceptional Children, 52,* 44–51.

WONG, B., & JONES, W. (1982). Increasing metacomprehension in learning-disabled and normally achieving students through self-questioning training. *Learning Disabilities Quarterly, 5,* 228–240.

WOODCOCK, R. W., & JOHNSON, M. B. (1977). *Woodcock-Johnson Psycho-Educational Battery.* Allen, TX: DLM Teaching Resources.

CHAPTER 12

MENTAL RETARDATION

HISTORICAL REVIEW

As mentioned in the discussion of the exceptional infant in Chapter 3, mental retardation is probably the most dreaded of all possible handicaps. It has been difficult indeed to agree on a term to encompass the whole range of "incomplete development of the mind" or "subaverage intellectual functioning." The fashions of the past century are shown in the changes of name of the professional organization first organized in 1877 as the Association of Medical Officers of American Institutions for Idiotic and Feebleminded Persons. It was known as the American Association for the Study of the Feebleminded from 1918 to 1940 at which time it adopted the name, The American Association on Mental Deficiency. In October 1987, the name was changed to the American Association on Mental Retardation.

In the past there have been efforts to differentiate between mental deficiency and mental retardation (Sarason & Gladwin, 1958) on the basis of the presence or absence of central nervous system pathology, but this proved to be not only a difficult but also a rather meaningless distinction. Mental retardation became the commonly accepted generic term. The impetus for the change from mental deficiency to mental retardation came mainly from parents' associations (e.g., the National Association for Retarded Children, established in 1950) which found the older term distasteful. Already "retarded" has taken on negative connotations and many are using "developmental disability" as a generic label. One of the motivations in the "developmental disabilities movement" was to reduce the stigma attached to categorical labels by coining a new, more neutral term (Breen & Richman, 1979). It is hard to escape the unhappy fact, however, that any term which indicates that a child is stupid or slow is insulting and inevitably becomes undesirable.

For many years, the definition proposed by Edgar Doll (1941) was generally applied. He suggested six criteria: (1) social incompetence, which is (2) due to mental subnormality, which (3) has been developmentally arrested, which (4) obtains at maturity, (5) is of constitutional origin, and (6) is essentially incurable. This definition includes two inferences which present difficulties. First, one must determine that the child was "born retarded," and in the absence of positive organic findings, there is no satisfactory way of proving that a particular child had a specific IQ potential from the time of birth. There are many known instances where life circumstances seriously impaired intellectual development. In 1948, Kanner proposed a formal classification of feeblemindedness as "absolute," "relative," or "pseudo." The prefix "pseudo" indicated that the child had not been born retarded and need not necessarily remain retarded. Although Kanner included psychometric errors ("tester's clumsiness"), the classification generally was used in reference to retardation resulting from conflict or deprivation.

Clinicians welcomed the dynamic view that intelligence is a function of personality rather than a fixed, inborn quantity. A number of clinical papers and case histories reported instances in which pseudo-retardation served the same defensive purposes as a neurotic symptom. In other words, the child remained stupid and did not learn, in order to obtain some surreptitious instinctual gratification (Mahler, 1942; Staver, 1953) or to ward off some anxiety which would arise if he or she were more knowledgeable. The term "pseudo-retardation" was also used where the developmental failure seemed to be the result of early deprivation and neglect. The author (Kessler, 1966) presented the case history of Susan who had a history of early neglect followed by three changes of foster home in her first year of life. At age 13 months, she functioned like a 6-month-old, but with placement in a specially chosen foster home, she blossomed quickly and by the time she was 5 years of age, her IQ tested 100. In this case, thanks to the enterprise of the social agency and the excellence of the foster home, the deleterious effects of the early deprivation were reversed. However, it was not possible to predict this result—Susan might have had some form of retardation which the best environment in the world could not completely undo.

There was a tendency to overemphasize the difference between "pseudo-retardation" and "true retardation." If a child were diagnosed as pseudo-retarded, the intellectual deficiencies were sometimes unrealistically ignored. Even if the intellectual arrest was originally caused by conflict or deprivation, remediation of the cause did not thereby catapult the child into a more advanced intellectual state. Remediation could do no more than permit resumption of the normal learning process, starting from the point where the child was arrested. On the other hand, those children with "real retardation" could usually be helped far more than one would expect from Doll's rather nihilistic definition, which included "hopelessness."

This brings us to the other problem in Doll's definition, namely, that the social incompetence prevailed throughout life. Follow-up studies of the adult adjustment of mentally retarded children proved that many achieved independence in adulthood (Charles, 1953; Windle, 1962). Such studies compelled serious reconsideration of the criteria to be used in establishing the diagnosis of mental retardation.

AAMD DEFINITION AND SUBSEQUENT REVISIONS

In 1960, the American Association on Mental Deficiency adopted the definition that "mental retardation refers to subaverage intellectual functioning which originates during the developmental period and is associated with impairment of adaptive behavior" (Heber, 1961, p. 499). This definition stressed the idea of *current* functioning level and completely discarded the concepts of constitutional origin and permanence of handicap. Thus, it rendered the distinction of "pseudo-retardation" obsolete. At that time "subaverage" was defined as more than 1 standard deviation below the mean in IQ, or below 85. This had the effect of broadening the population to include marginal groups with relatively subtle intellectual handicaps, so that as many as 15% of the population could be classified as retarded, if they also had associated social impairment.

Although the intent was to enable more persons to receive special services, the development of special services categorically designed for the mentally retarded went counter to the principle of normalization (Wolfensberger, 1972, 1980). Another reaction against the expanded definition was the untoward effect of labeling too many children and adults who might otherwise blend unnoticed into the lower social, economic, and educational ranges of society (Mercer, 1973). In 1973, the definition was narrowed to the "significantly subaverage," specified as more than 2 standard deviations below the mean, or below IQ 70; the category of "borderline retardation" was deleted (Grossman, 1973).

The definition as it stands in the latest revision (Grossman, 1983) retains the emphasis on current functioning level. An individual may meet the criteria of mental retardation at one time in life and not at some other time. This allows for the possibility of significant change in IQ, adaptive functioning, or societal expectations (which might increase or decrease the degree of social impairment). The importance of the dual criteria of intellectual and social impairment is also firm. Intellectual impairment is assessed by one of the individual tests discussed in Chapter 11, and some allowance in setting cutoff points is made for the standard error of measurement. Considering the 3- or 4-point error of measurement in the WISC-R or Stanford-Binet, a child might score as high as 78 and be classified as retarded if there was sufficient evidence of adaptive impairment.

The wide range of possible intellectual impairment necessitates differentiation by degree. The AAMD classification is as follows:

MILD	52–67 (Binet)	55–69 (WISC-R)
MODERATE	36–51	40–54
SEVERE	20–35	
PROFOUND	Below 20	

The category of mild mental retardation is roughly equivalent to what was formerly termed the "educable retarded," and moderate mental retardation is synonymous with what was called "trainable retarded." These terms have been discontinued because they suggest a significant difference between those who are to be in educational programs and those who are relegated to "training" programs. Before the enactment of the Education for All Handicapped Children Act (P.L. 94-142), public schools used the IQ of 50 as the basis for exclusion, since these chidren were deemed "uneducable." Now all children are to be "educated" under the aegis of local school authorities.

Assessment of Adaptive Functioning

Some of the problems in evaluating intelligence were discussed in Chapter 11 and will be discussed further in considering social-cultural factors in retardation. The focus here is on the assessment of social impairment which is part of the two-dimensional definition. The 1973 AAMD Revised Manual defined adaptive behavior as "the effectiveness or degree with which the individual meets the standards of personal independence and social responsibility expected of his age and cultural group." Since it is so inti-

mately bound with this particular diagnosis, it is not surprising that techniques for assessing social competence were first developed by people working with the mentally retarded. Edgar Doll developed the Vineland Social Maturity Scale in 1935, which paralleled the structure of the Binet, yielding a social age and social quotient. For many years, this was the only instrument available. Although the social age was useful in differentiating beginning stages of self-care (i.e., dressing, bathing, toileting, feeding, etc.), the scale did not discriminate well with older, or less handicapped, individuals.

In 1965 work was begun at Parsons State Hospital (for the retarded) which culminated in the AAMD Adaptive Behavior Scale. The current edition of the Adaptive Behavior Scale (Nihira, Foster, Shellhaas, and Leland, 1975) is in two parts. The first part of the scale "is organized along developmental lines, and is designed to evaluate an individual's skills and habits in ten behavioral domains considered important to the development of personal independence in daily living" (Nihira et al., 1975, p. 1). The second part is "designed to provide measures of maladaptive behavior related to personality and behavior disorders" (Nihira et al., 1975, p. 7) and gives scores in 14 areas. More recently, Sparrow, Balla, and Cicchetti (1984) published a new edition of the Vineland which departs from the unitary concept of social competence and instead provides standard scores (mean is 100) for four adaptive behavior scales and one maladaptive scale. (See Appendix for further details on the ABS and the Vineland.)

The Vineland and ABS rely on information provided by caregiver, teacher, or parent and score the child's typical behavior in his or her natural environment rather than "testing" for ability to perform a particular act. Thus, a scored "failure" may represent a basic inability, no opportunity to acquire a skill, or even disinterest or lack of motivation. The adaptive measures have been widely used (particularly with adults) in making recommendations for residential placement and as the basis for developing individual habilitation plans. Adaptive behavior is in part a function of environmental supports and demands. Obviously, a person may function well in a sheltered workshop but be at a loss in competitive employment, but there may be more subtle personal relationships which make one workshop, or job setting, more stressful than another. Unfortunately there is no reliable way of assessing the person's social context in relation to performance, so there is a tendency to look at the adpative scores as the product of the person rather than the person-environment interaction.

With the requirement to include an adaptive measure in determining educational placement for the mildly retarded child, new instruments appeared designed for this population. Lambert, Windmiller, Cole, and Figueroa (1975) published a public school version of the AAMD adaptive behavior scale using teacher ratings of a sample of 2,618 public school children in California. As expected, class placement correlated significantly with ABS scores. However, at the 12- to 13-year-old level, the mildly retarded pupils seemed to be functioning as well as regular class subjects. With the perspective of public school educators, the authors commented that: "the

behaviors included in the entire Adaptive Behavior spectrum are those which ultimately can be achieved by nearly all children" (Lambert et al., 1975, p. 40). This observation refers to the ceiling effect of the ABS, which like other adaptive behavior measures seeks to identify minimally adequate social functioning. Individuals may well develop higher level skills than those represented by the items in these scales, but the objective is to assess social adequacy rather than the entire range of individual differences in social functioning.

One other system of assessment deserves mention because it proceeds from a different theoretical base. The Adaptive Behavior Inventory for Children (ABIC) was developed by Mercer and Lewis (1977) as part of their System of Multicultural Pluralistic Assessment (SOMPA). The impetus for the development of the SOMPA arose from their data in the University of California-Riverside project demonstrating that minority group children and those from lower socioeconomic backgrounds were overrepresented in public school programs for the retarded (Mercer, 1973). For Mercer, the central issue in adaptive behavior measurement is its inclusion as part of a system for the least-biased assessment for labeling and placement rather than for intervention planning.

In the ABIC, adaptive behavior is defined in terms of the child's ability to perform the social roles appropriate for persons of his/her age in a manner which meets the expectations of the surrounding social systems. The inventory includes six subscales covering family role performance, peer group role performance, and student role performance (Mercer & Lewis, 1977). The information is obtained from parent interview, in contrast to the Public School Version of the AAMD ABS, which relies on teacher judgments. Not unexpectedly, it has been found that parents and teachers do not always agree on the child's level of adaptive behavior (Mealor & Richmond, 1980), partly because a child behaves differently in different situations and also because parents and teachers will use different bases of comparisons.

There are many other measures of adaptive behavior (Coulter & Morrow, 1978; Grossman, 1983). There has been little comparison of results from different measures and none has emerged as preeminent in the field. Overall, there is a moderately high correlation with measured intelligence, especially at the lower end of the scales. The degree of overlap between "adaptive behavior" and "intelligence" from birth to 5 years has been noted and questions have been raised as to the justification of a two-dimensional definition at these early ages. On the other hand, at older ages, with mild to moderate intellectual retardation, adaptive functioning can vary independently.

The assessment of maladaptive behavior introduces problems of a different sort. The ABS items are not weighted as to frequency (beyond the difference of "occasionally" and "frequently"), provocation, or degree of seriousness. For instance, scores on "Runs away from hospital, home, or school ground"; "takes others' belongings by opening or breaking locks"; "lies on the floor all day" are quantitatively equal to "Is late to required places or activities"; "Has been suspected of stealing"; and "Drums fingers." Also, no distinction is made between "Uses threatening gestures" and actually carrying out aggressive threats. A suggestion has been made for rescoring according to relative seriousness or importance of the various behaviors, but it has not been widely adopted (Clements, Bost, DuBois, & Turpin, 1980). The items are not arranged in any particular sequence so that the scales emerge as a "laundry list" of complaints that others may have about a retarded person. No reference is made to the possibility of fears or anxieties, fantasies, sleep problems, depression, suspiciousness, or any kind of psychological data that might be provided by the retarded person directly.

In general, the scales suffer from a disregard of environmental or motivational factors. The emphasis is placed on compliance with authority and socially acceptable behavior. Maladaptive behaviors are viewed simplistically as behavior to be extinguished with no regard to the underlying reasons. Here there is a real gap between the treatment approach of the mental health professional and the training/education approach of those who work with the mentally retarded.

Prevalence. Three percent is the prevalence figure that is traditionally quoted. This is derived theoretically from the normal distribution curve of measured intelligence. Since intelligence tests are constructed to yield a normal distribution, one would expect approximately 2.5% to fall 2 standard deviations below the mean, i.e., below IQ of 70, with .5% added to account for biomedical "accidents" which increase the lower end more than would be expected from "natural" causes. However, survey figures show considerable variation according to geographic region and age and also are generally lower than 3% (Robinson & Robinson, 1976). For example, Rantakallio and Von Wendt (1986) followed all children born in 1966 in northern Finland, and at age 14 years identified about 1.2% as mentally retarded, which is close to Mercer's report in California (1973). The surprising finding in the Finnish study was the larger number of moderately and severely retarded. Their figure of 6.3 per 1,000 exceeded the average of 4 per 1,000 reported by Abramowicz and Richardson (1975) from a review of 27 epidemiological studies. Rantakallio and Von Wendt noted the excess number of Down syndrome children in their population but otherwise could not account for the high figure. This study is cited simply to show the need for local prevalence rates against which to compare the results of preventive efforts. The rule-of-thumb figure of 3% has little justification in reality.

Prevalence figures can, of course, be altered by the simple expedient of changing the upper IQ limit, as was done in 1973. Since schools do most of the labeling, variations in definitional practices result in different numbers. Discrepancies in eligibility guidelines have resulted in large differences among states in the percentages of students classified as mildly mentally retarded, from .49% in Alaska to 4.14% in Alabama (Morsink, Thomas, & Smith-Davis, in press). Some schools rely more heavily on cutoff scores in cognitive and achievement test scores whereas others give more weight to social adaptive measures or interpret the cutoff scores more generously, which often results in the classification of learning disability. The slippery criteria for defining mental retardation give us a range of prevalence figures anywhere from 1 to 3%.

Etiologic Classification: Medical Causes. Mental retardation is more of a symptom than a diagnosis and once identified, every effort should be made to establish cause. It is estimated that specific organic causes can be identified in about one-fourth of the retarded population as a whole (Grossman, 1983) and in about half of the moderately and severely retarded. By and large, individuals who are "organically retarded" are more severely disabled and have more associated physical handicaps, but there are many exceptions to this general rule. The following discussion is by no means comprehensive but uses illustrative examples of the various medical categories.

Perhaps the greatest advance in the past decade or so has been in the identification of chromosomal defects. Down syndrome, or trisomy 21, remains the most common and accounts for about one-third of the mentally handicapped population with IQ's below 50. The special problems of this group, which is almost always identified at the time of birth, was discussed in Chapter 3. Other chromosomal anomalies involving chromosomes 13 and 18 have also been identified. Children with chromosomal defects show characteristic physical differences which are usually the clue to the very early prenatal timing of the developmental aberration. Although neurological textbooks (Farmer, 1983) may include "severe and profound mental retardation" as part of the syndrome, in fact, there may be considerable variation in the degree of intellectual handicap.

A relative newcomer to the list of chromosomal anomalies is the "Fragile X syndrome" (De la Cruz, 1985). Fragile X derives its name from the fragility of a specific region of the distal end of the long arm of the X chromosome where there is constriction or breaking off. Diagnosis is complicated by the fact that the "marker X" appears in only about half of the tissue samples so it can easily be missed. The physical symptoms include enlarged testes (after puberty), low-set ears, and some minor differences in facial features. The effect on males is much greater than on females. Fragile X males show a range of intellectual ability but are reported to average around 40 IQ, whereas carrier females are usually "normal" although Turner, Brookwell, Daniel, Selikowitz, and Zilibowitz (1980) reported that about one-third showed some cognitive deficit. It has been estimated that Fragile X syndrome is second only to Down syndrome in frequency in children with a chromosome abnormality and it may provide a partial explanation for the fact that males are overrepresented in the mentally retarded population.

Another condition which is thought to represent an aberration in a portion of chromosome 15 (Ledbetter et al., 1981) is Prader-Willi syndrome. This syndrome is characterized by hypotonia, hypogonadism, short stature for genetic background, and obesity (Zellweger & Schneider, 1968). One reason for the obesity is excessive appetite, which leads to incessant eating of practically anything available. Before this condition was identified, the craving for food was interpreted as a "bad habit" or as an indi-

cator of very early insecurity, depending on one's theoretical orientation. In the author's experience with a limited number of cases, these children also showed constant skin-picking to the extent of almost self-injurious behavior. Further adding to the obesity, Prader-Willi children are often described as lethargic and tiring easily (Hanson, 1981; Herrmann, 1981). Management of the behavioral and physical components of this syndrome greatly complicates the problems of the retardation which is often "mild" in degree.

Other causes of genetic origin involve single gene defects transmitted according to the usual pattern for recessive genes. The best-known example is phenylketonuria (PKU) which is now routinely tested for by urinalysis in infancy. This is one example where early detection leads directly to prevention because a special diet eliminating phenylalanine saves the child from mental retardation. However, new complications have arisen because "treated" individuals are likely to produce offspring with severe defects unless the pregnancy is handled with special care.

Another metabolic disorder is Lesch-Nyhan syndrome which, although rare, is extremely handicapping. In addition to the mental retardation, these individuals show unusually severe, compulsive self-destructive behavior and self-mutilation. The children do experience pain but it is not effective in stopping their behavior. Physical restraints, positive reinforcement, and medication have all been tried with some limited success (Graham, 1983). This is one condition where genetic engineering seems to hold some promise.

Infections or intoxications in the prenatal period include rubella (German Measles), toxoplasmosis, and fetal alcohol syndrome. These conditions are preventable and much publicity has been directed to this end. They serve to underscore the point that the mother's health during pregnancy is an important factor and that conditions which are not serious for the mother may have serious consequences for the brain development of the fetus.

Although the great majority of biologically based mental retardation is prenatal in origin, there are some perinatal and postnatal factors. Encephalopathy from the ingestion of lead or on rare occasions, following one of the common childhood infectious diseases, has been more common in the past than at present. The role of birth injury or insufficient oxygen has also lessened with advances in neonatal care. Kernicterus, which results from very high levels of bilirubin in the blood ("the jaundiced baby"), is now a very rare cause of mental retardation because of preventive techniques used in pretoxic stages and the techniques for handling mother-infant blood type incompatibilities. As discussed in Chapter 2, very low birth weight is associated with an increased risk for mental retardation although the fact of the premature birth may itself indicate a prenatal disorder. There is still the possibility of severe head injury as a postnatal cause of mental retardation. Perhaps no situation is more tragic than that of children who are retarded as the result of violent child abuse.

Etiologic Classification: Psychosocial Disadvantage. This category is used for those cases in which there are indications of adverse environmental conditions and where there is evidence of subnormal intellectual functioning in at least one of the parents and in one or more of the siblings. This general grouping has gone under many different names in the past, such as "simple amentia" (Tredgold & Soddy, 1956); "subcultural mental deficiency" (Lewis, 1933); "garden-variety mental deficiency" (Sarason, 1953); "endogenous mental deficiency" (Strauss & Lehtinen, 1947); "familial mental deficiency" (Allen, 1958); and "relative mental deficiency" (Kanner, 1948). All of these terms acknowledge the fact that there is a normal distribution of intelligence which is in part determined by inheritance, but, in addition, parents of subnormal intelligence are usually of lower socioeconomic status and provide a less stimulating environment than parents who are more able and have more resources. In Heber's revision of the AAMD manual on terminology (Heber, 1959), the comparable diagnostic classification was "cultural-familial mental retardation" which clearly straddled the dilemma of how much is heredity and how much is environment.

In order to examine these factors more closely, we will consider the evidence of heritability of intelligence, the relation of intelligence and socioeconomic status, and the cultural bias in intelligence tests. There is really no argument that intelligence is in some part determined by genetic inheritance of a polygenic nature (as opposed to single genes). Many reports of people with various degrees of genetic relationship, raised together and raised apart, show an increasing similarity on intelligence tests with increasing closeness of genetic relationship. The crucial question is the weight to be given to the genetic factor. From his review and analysis of the studies, Jensen (1969) concluded that the heritability of IQ was approximately .80; on the basis of a similarly thorough review and analysis, Jencks (1972) arrived at a heritability figure of .45. Nichols (1981) and Vernon (1979) reviewed the methods of analysis and assumptions in the many studies of this issue and concurred in a compromise value of .60 for genetic influence. The heritability issue has been very much confounded by the search for inborn racial differences of intelligence, but except for Jensen's controversial publications, few writers have addressd this hypothesis directly.

There is also a great deal of evidence attesting to environmental influences on intelligence (Kessler, 1965). Tyler (1965) remarked that "the relationship of measured intelligence to socioeconomic level is one of the best documented findings in mental test history" (p. 336) and cited a figure of .70 between intelligence and socioeconomic status. Adoption studies provide evidence that can be used either to demonstrate the hereditary or the environmental contribution to intelligence. In 1949, Skodak and Skeels published the results of a longitudinal study of 100 adopted children which showed that the children scored on the average some 20 points higher than their biological mothers (environmental influence), but the IQ correlations with biological mothers and their children (at age 14 years) was .44, close to the average of about .50 commonly found for children and their parents when the children are raised in their own home (Honzik, 1957). More recent studies have again confirmed the essen-

tial facts that adoptive children score higher on the average than would be expected from the level of their natural parents, but that the rank order of IQ scores in the adopted group bears more resemblance to their biological parents than to their adoptive parents (Scarr & Weinberg, 1979).

With particular reference to mental retardation, Kushlick and Blunden (1974) pointed out that in contrast to severe subnormality, which is divided more or less evenly among all social classes, mild retardation occurs predominantly in the lower social classes. "Indeed, there is evidence that almost no children of higher social class parents have IQ scores of less than 80 unless they have one of the pathological processes . . ." (Kushlick & Blunden, 1974, p. 51).

Prevention. There have been early intervention programs designed to prevent psychosocial retardation, and their results have implications for the nature-nurture controversy. One of the earliest was undertaken in 1957 by the Child Development Clinic at the University of Iowa. The subjects were children between 3 and 6 years of age, scoring between 50 and 84 on IQ tests and with one parent and one sibling in the same IQ range. The children attended a special full-day school and the parents were engaged in a variety of home-making instruction programs and regular social work contacts. It seemed that the workers were discouraged by the parents' lack of progress and they concluded their report by commenting that the primary target for change in familial mental retardation should be the young child. "One must also raise the question as to whether starting to work with these children at age 3 years is not too late. Perhaps efforts to reach the children and their families soon after birth should be considered" (Kugel & Parsons, 1967, p. 57).

And indeed this suggestion was followed in two subsequent experimental preventive programs. In 1966, drawing from poverty areas in Milwaukee, Heber and his colleagues identified 40 pregnant women with IQ's less than 75 and assigned 20 of the newborn children to an experimental group and 20 to a control group. Starting at age 3 months, the experimental children were enrolled in an all-day program, 5 days a week for 12 months a year. The program started with home visits and continued at the learning center with a one staff to one infant ratio until the children were a year old.

Thus, each infant was paired with one consistent mothering figure in an effort to provide an environment that would support the growth of primary social attachments. Care was also taken to establish a relationship with at least one other adult in an attempt to continue to provide a secure environment if a child's teacher became ill or left the program. . . . Feeding and the other caretaking activities for the infants were viewed not only as routine necessities but as soothing experiences that helped to develop the necessary emotional attachment between the child and teacher. (Heber & Garber, 1975)

The teachers truly served as additional caregivers in the most comprehensive sense of the word. After a transition period between ages 15 and 24 months, the children were eased into a more structured program which has been described in detail (Heber & Garber, 1975; Heber, Garber, Harrington, Hoffman, & Falender, 1972) and could serve as a model for any preschool.

As one would expect from the original purpose of this program, the results have been reported mainly in terms of IQ. At age 5½ years, the Experimental group (reduced to 17 in number) had a mean IQ of 122 and the Control group (18) had a mean IQ of 91. At the age of 10 years, 4 years after leaving the program, the Experimental group had a mean IQ of 105 compared with Control group mean of 85 (Garber & Heber, 1981). This study has recently been sharply criticized on the basis of failure to publish in refereed journals and lack of replication (Sommer & Sommer, 1983). Replication would be a very costly proposition, but one would like to see an independent review of the original data considering the weight that this study gives to environmental factors in determining psychosocial retardation.

Like Kugel and Parsons before them, these investigators were disappointed by the family intervention and concluded, "We are rapidly approaching the view that intervention and support for children reared with an intellectually inadequate parent and living in a disrupted family environment must continue throughout the child's school as well as preschool years" (Garber & Heber, 1981, p. 86). Parenthetically, it should be noted that the intervention with the mothers seemed less comprehensive and less sophisticated than the intervention provided for the children; for instance, there was no effort to establish a special relationship between mother and a "therapist" as discussed in Chapter 2.

The second program, the Abecedarian

Project, began in 1972 in North Carolina (Ramey, Holmberg, Sparling, & Collier, 1977). The prospective participants were interviewed in the last trimester of pregnancy and multiple criteria, including maternal IQ, were weighted and combined to yield a single score called the High Risk index. The mean maternal IQ was 84 with an average 10th grade education; the population was poor and almost 100% black. A total number of 112 children were divided between experimental and control groups. The experimental infants began a day-care program by 3 months of age and continued until entry in kindergarten. The child-to-staff ratio was 3 to 1 for the infants, in contrast to the 1 to 1 in the Milwaukee program. The control group was provided some extra nutritional, pediatric, and social work services in order to have the systematic infant curriculum and preschool program the only difference.

From the age of 24 months, the IQ differences were significant, with the experimental group performing near average (mean IQ of 96 at age 4 years) and the control group significantly below average (mean IQ of 84) (Ramey & Haskins, 1981). This is not as dramatic as the Heber early results, and one wonders if this might relate to the major differences in the structure of the infancy day-care program. Also, the intervention efforts with the mother were minimal even compared to the Milwaukee project. It was hypothesized that the combination of relief from child-care responsibilities and the presence of brighter, more responsive children would, by the transactional model, bring about changes in the mothers. Although there was some laboratory evidence that the Experimental children did elicit differ-

ent responses from their mothers (Falender & Heber, 1975; Ramey & Mills, 1977), it is not clear how long-lasting or significant these child-initiated changes might be. It is clear that these intervention programs, where the children were selected in large measure because of the mental subnormality of their mothers, were more successful with the children than with the mothers.

Bold statements have been made about the promise of prevention. The President's Commission on Mental Retardation (PCMR) stated that "Using present knowledge and techniques from the biomedical and behavioral sciences, it is possible to reduce the occurrence of mental retardation by 50 percent before the end of the century" (PCMR, 1972, p. 31), and this figure was adopted as a national goal. In 1976, PCMR significantly modified this goal by restricting the 50% goal to those conditions with biomedical causes. There have been examples where medical knowledge has led to effective prevention, but one must keep in mind that in the largest group of biomedical causes, namely, the chromosomal abnormalities, prevention is essentially a matter of selective abortion.

In the Comptroller General's Report to the Congress in 1977, it was stated that in about ¾ of the diagnosed cases of mental retardation, no organic cause could be identified and that adverse environmental conditions were a major cause. Reviewing the evidence of prevention programs for this group strongly suggests that whatever genetic influences are at work, the developmental course for children at risk can be significantly improved by early intervention which in effect provides surrogate parenting. To do it right is an expensive social undertaking.

CULTURAL BIAS IN TESTING

Some of the reasons for the relationship of socioeconomic status and children's intelligence have already been discussed in Chapter 4. They include nutritional differences, family size, maternal stimulation, value systems, patterns of child rearing, and resources and support systems, as well as some indeterminate genetic factor. Still another consideration is the issue of potential cultural bias in psychological tests. Although this is not a new question, it remained in the arena of academic debate until it was brought to court. Two major federal district courts of equivalent rank handed down diametrically opposite decisions on whether tests are biased against black children.

In the case of *Larry P. et al.* v. *Wilson Riles*, Superintendent of Public Instruction for the State of California (1979), the plaintiffs were the parents of seven black children who had been placed in EMR classes but who, when retested by psychologists who made special attempts to establish rapport, "to overcome plaintiff's defeatism and easy distraction, to reword items in terms more consistent with plaintiff's cultural background, and to give credit for nonstandard answers which nevertheless showed an intelligent approach to the problems," scored above the IQ cutoff for such placement. The court accepted the statistics that blacks comprised 9.1% of all school children in California, but 27.5% of all children in EMR classes, as prima facie evidence of test bias. The judge in the case assumed that there should be a random distribution and ordered that "no black student may be placed in an EMR class on the basis of criteria which rely primarily on the results of IQ tests as they are currently administered." The other case, *Pase* v. *Hannon*, 1980, was decided in the opposite direction by the judge's personal opinion regarding the apparent "fairness" of the test questions which he reviewed. Neither the assumptions of the California judge nor the informal assessment of the second judge in Illinois can be considered to be the final word on this question. As of 1984, black students were still disproportionately represented in classes for mildly retarded although slightly less so than in previous years (Chinn & Hughes, 1987).

In his review, Reynolds (1986) identified the problems most often cited in the use of tests with minorities. First, has the minority child had equal opportunity for exposure to the information tapped by the content of the test items? Second, does the standardization sample represent all groups proportionately? Third, is the examiner able to communicate comfortably with the minority student and establish good rapport? Fourth, do the consequences of test results (e.g., labeling and special class placement) deprive minority students of equal opportunity? Fifth, do the tests have the same predictive validity for white middle-class children and minority group members? Like the judges, psychologists are divided in their opinions. Reynolds remarked that "the empirical evidence regarding test bias does not support the contentions of minority spokespersons; only scattered, inconsistent evidence for bias exists" (1986, p. 128) and added that "the psychologist cannot ignore the data demonstrating that low IQ, ethnic disadvantaged children are just as likely to fail academically as are white middle-class low IQ children, provided that their environmental circumstances remain constant" (p. 129). He would have us consider environmental interventions in tandem with special education resources to "beat" the prediction.

Jane Mercer, the sociologist who first reported the disproportionate number of minority and socially disadvantaged children in the mentally retarded population, took another approach. Her system of evaluating adaptive behavior in terms of social role behavior has already been described, but as another part of the System of MultiPluralistic Assessment (SOMPA), the environment is assessed by parent interview. This score is used to adjust the child's conventional WISC-R IQ to arrive at an Estimated Learning Potential (ELP). The difference between the WISC-R and the ELP can be as high as 12–15 points for some groups and even 30 points for individual children. By this system, one "explains away" the retardation. It is very reminiscent of the diagnosis of "pseudo-retardation" which we struggled with in the 1950's. The addition of IQ points on the basis of evidence of environmental deprivation does not change the presenting educational needs of the child. Wurtz, Sewell, and Manni (1985) found that the ELP did not predict retarded children's ability to learn in a special coaching situation significantly better than the traditional IQ score. It does not follow that self-contained, special classrooms with limited goals (the traditional

model of EMR classes) are the solution, but some kind of accommodation and special help is necessary if the child is consistently slow learning—for whatever reason.

Cognitive Differences

In the "cognitive revolution" which has taken place in the past 20 years, it is not surprising that mentally retarded persons have been the focus of intense research interest in an effort to probe the mysteries of how the mind works. The discussion that follows is concerned with mildly retarded persons who are more obviously on a continuum with normally intelligent persons than the moderately and severely handicapped. Developmental theorists such as Zigler (Zigler, 1982) maintain that retarded persons, without organic impairment, follow the same cognitive path as normally intelligent persons but at a slower rate and with a lower ceiling. Others have taken the position that even when retarded and nonretarded persons are matched for mental age, or level of development, they differ in the cognitive processes used. This "developmental" or "different" controversy has stimulated a great deal of research. Detterman (1987) suggests that both may be correct, depending on the sort of measure which is used for comparison. However, there must be something "different" in the way that the mentally retarded person processes information which makes it less efficient.

There seems to be consensus that at the simplest level, mentally retarded persons are slower to process information whether it is presented visually

(Caruso & Detterman, 1983; Nettelbeck, 1985) or orally (Bilsky, 1985) when compared with nonretarded individuals of comparable mental age. Various explanations have been offered, for instance, a deficit in attention (Zeaman & House, 1979) or a deficit in input organization (Spitz, 1966), but none seems sufficient. Whatever the reason, the slowness of the encoding process contributes to the deficit in short-term memory which has been consistently noted for retarded persons (Ellis & Cavalier, 1982). This may seem to contradict the lay opinion that retarded persons have a good memory, but one needs to distinguish between short-term memory which represents the initial registration of new material, and long-term memory. Indeed, the rate and process of forgetting in long-term memory (Belmont, 1966) seems no different for retarded persons. With regard to differences in forgetting after brief intervals (5 to 30 seconds), the results favor "no difference" (Fagan, 1967), but this may not be true for all kinds of stimuli. For instance, Ellis, Deacon, and Wooldridge (1985) found similar rates of forgetting for pictures with liberal encoding time, but differential rates of forgetting for letters, a finding used to support the "structural defect" position.

A contemporary version of the (physiological) deficit/(motivational) difference distinction is the differentiation between structural features and control processes in cognitive functioning. Using a computer analogy, structural features refer to the physiological hardware, and control processes are like the software, which suggests that the mentally retarded can be "reprogrammed." It seems likely that there is an interaction effect, that is, that the "structural defects" are exacerbated by motivational or "control processes." Justice (1985) commented that retarded children with mental ages of approximately 8 years are aware that they are not good "rememberers" and suggested that their expectation of failure might influence their proficiency. There are strategies such as imagery, rehearsal, grouping, labeling, categorizing, and linking units (perhaps in story form) which can be taught and which facilitate learning and memory (Glidden, 1985).

Although most of this work has been done with laboratory-type tasks, there are implications for real-life learning which will not eliminate the mental retardation but which will improve learning. First, one should allow more time in presentation and identify the particular memory strategy useful for the task. Second, it is easier to remember something which connects with previous information, so it is important to make the connection between the new and the old explicit for the retarded learner. Mechanical rote repetition is not particularly helpful and is probably as boring to the retarded student as to anyone else.

Special Education

What, in fact, is special about special education? One central point is that the objectives for each child are within his or her grasp and do not arise from standard grade expectations. The necessity for developing individual lesson plans for the different levels normally represented in a special class is one reason for a student-teacher ratio which is about half of the ratio obtaining in regular classes. The good intent of guaranteeing success and avoiding failure can be destructive if one sets these goals too low. Another point of general emphasis is that the curriculum should be functional and teach skills that will be needed to manage one's own affairs. Usually the individual education plans for special students stress personal habits and social skills along with academic proficiencies.

Retarded learners present special problems in motivation (MacMillan, 1971). Because they have usually experienced a succession of past failures, they tend to approach problems in a way that avoids failure rather than that achieves success (MacMillan & Keogh, 1971). They have learned that they are often "wrong" and so distrust their own efforts and search instead for cues from the outside, the phenonemon of "outer-directedness" described by Zigler (Zigler & Balla, 1981). Intrinsic motivation stimulated by curiosity and their own questions is not as potent as it is for normally successful children (Harter & Zigler, 1974). The findings in this regard are very much the same as those described for learning-disabled children in Chapter 11.

For all these reasons, special education teachers build in special motivators such as increasing the interest value of the activities, alternating "pleasure" and "work," visible recording of progress, token economies, and so on. Smith, Neisworth, and Hunt urge teachers "to demonstrate immediate approval of even small instances of progress on the part of children. Your approval can take the form of verbal praise, a pat on the back, a smile, or shaking the child's hand" (1983, p. 142). The principles of operant reinforcement are heavily utilized in most special education classrooms. Again, this too can be overdone and increase the child's dependency on the others. The child who continues to expect applause for doing a good job may be very disappointed in the outside world when a "good job" is taken for granted.

All of these features are related to the teaching environment of special education, but when one examines the instructional strategies more carefully, it is hard to see what is so "special." Reading instruction is perhaps an exception, as many special approaches have been developed, such as the language experience method (using chart stories), the kinesthetic or manual tracing method, the Initial Teaching Alphabet, and Peabody Rebus Reading Program utilizing picture symbols, the Distar method, and programmed instruction like the System 80 (Cegelka & Cegelka, 1970). Unfortunately, these techniques, which require special materials and teacher training, are generally adopted for a group of children and none has proved superior. It is entirely possible that on an individual match basis, one could improve reading performance.

It is somewhat surprising that within the restricted range of mild mental retardation, there is a negligible correlation between IQ and achievement scores (Blackman, Bilsky, Burger, & Mar, 1976; Reger, 1966; Wurtz, Sewell, & Manni, 1985). In the Blackman et al. study, memory for digits showed the highest correlation for word recognition and was equal to the IQ in relating to arithmetic computation scores, further evidence of the crucial importance of short-term memory. As things stand now, most mildly retarded students master the decoding or mechanics of reading but have considerable difficulty at the later stages which require comprehension of text (Stanovich, 1985). Here perhaps is one of the greatest weaknesses of special education, namely, that it does not utilize the strategies for problem solving and comprehension which have evolved from modern cognitive science. Generally, special education does well in the initial stages of teaching basic skills, but it does not carry on to the next stage of thinking through problems.

The work of Reuven Feuerstein in Israel is noteworthy because his program carries on where the traditional special education curriculum seems to stop. The program of Instrumental Enrichment (Feuerstein, Rand, Hoffman, & Miller, 1980) consists of some 16 paper and pencil "instruments," so called because each is designed to be instrumental in overcoming one or more cognitive deficiencies. The program is as a supplement to the regular content curriculum in classes ranging from fifth grade through high school and extending over a 2-year period. Many of the exercises involve imposing organization on initially unstructured materials. For example, children practice making comparisons, identifying spatial relationships, identifying temporal relationships, identifying numerical relationships, noticing underlying categories, and so on.

Perhaps more important than the content is the method of instruction. Although the students may work in groups, there is a great deal of individual teacher-student dialogue in which the student is encouraged to put his or her thought processes into words.

Feuerstein referred to this as a "mediated learning experience" which helps the students to become aware of their strategies as thinkers and to be more planful and systematic. There is very little emphasis on "getting the answers right" and much more on "what are you thinking and what are you going to do next." Feuerstein and Jensen (1980) remarked that the Instrumental Enrichment program is designed to produce in the learner an instrinsic need for adequate cognitive functioning so that the person becomes an active problem solver rather than a repository of memorized information.

The program has been employed by now with thousands of adolescents in Israel, Canada, the United States, and Venezuela. Both immediate and long-term effects have been reported for Israeli programs. Rand, Feuerstein, Tannenbaum, Jensen, and Hoffman (1977) compared adolescents receiving general versus instrumental enrichment and found significant differences on standardized cognitive and achievement tests. A follow-up study 2 years later showed an even greater difference on an army test of intelligence in favor of the instrumental enrichment group, suggesting that the program "produces changes of a structural nature. We may assume that IE activates a self-perpetuating process that has a progressive positive effect on the individual's cognitive functioning" (Rand, Mintzker, Miller, Hoffman, & Friedlender, 1981, p. 151). There is still a question of whether the program will be equally successful when it is exported and utilized away from its point of origin. Arbitman-Smith, Haywood, and Bransford (1984) have undertaken a large-scale evaluation and reported "encouraging but not overwhelming" results. After 1 year, students commonly show gains of 5 to 10 IQ points and significant improvement on some standardized achievement tests. Parents and teachers, however, were reported as very enthusiastic and subjectively, the students seemed to have much more interest in school and learning. The authors commented on the commitment that this program involves in terms of teacher training and classroom time, but to this author, at least, it seems to represent teaching at its best and time well spent.

LABELING AND SEGREGATION

Special education can be provided in a variety of settings. After decades of trying to "sell" special classes to public school administrators, this form of delivery of services came under sharp criticism (Dunn, 1968; Johnson, 1962). In his review, Kolstoe (1972) discussed the six allegations made by critics, as follows:

1. That mentally retarded individuals are not noticeably handicapped after school years
2. Labeling harms children
3. Special class placement is damaging to the child's self-concept
4. Segregated classes are not effective
5. Teachers expect less and therefore the children achieve less
6. General education can deal with individual differences in the regular classroom.

With regard to the effectiveness of traditional special class education, one of the few studies utilizing random placement indicated no difference in academic achievement or on a test of social knowledge for those in special classes versus those who remained in regular classes after a 3-year period (Goldstein, Moss, & Jordan, 1965). However, subsequent employment records indicated an advantage for those who attended a special work-study group (Chaffin, Spellman, Regan, & Davison, 1971).

One of the arguments used to persuade parents to accept special class placement was that the child would feel better about him or her self. After reviewing results of questionnaire-type studies of self-concept, Lawrence and Winschel (1973) concluded that "segregated placement patterns are not ordinarily conducive to overall positive concepts of self and cannot be justified on that basis" (p. 316); however, the main effect was the relationship between academic achievement and self-concept— whatever the placement. On the other hand, Schurr, Towne, and Joiner (1972) investigated the self-concept of children prior to placement into EMR classes and found that self-concept improved after placement. In theory, one would like to offer the child an option for mainstreaming or special class. An opinion survey of children in segregated classes indicated that younger children were more positive than those at the high-school level. Younger children believe that they are in the special class "to catch up" but older children apparently no longer expect that to happen. Few of the children, in fact, less than 10%, perceived themselves as being "mentally retarded" (Warner, Thrapp, & Walsh, 1973).

The issue of labeling is a thorny one. The original work on the "Pygmalion Effect" was with "normal" children (Rosenthal & Jacobson, 1968). At random, the children were arbitrarily designated as "bright" or "not so bright" to their teachers at the beginning of the year. Year-end differences in test scores corresponded to the early designations, suggesting that in some fashion the different expectancies of the teachers caused a difference in the children's learning. Subsequent studies, however, failed to replicate these findings in natural classroom settings (Dusek & O'Connell, 1973; Humphreys & Stubbs, 1977). Studies investigating the specific effects of the label of mental retardation on the observer vary according to the sophistication of the observer and the amount of information given in addition to the label (Severance & Gasstrom, 1977). MacMillan, Jones, and Aloia (1974) concluded that there was a "paucity of evidence" to support the belief regarding the negative effects and pointed out that in real-life situations, the label "mental retardation" is used to describe deviant behavior and not arbitrarily assigned to a child.

There is no doubt that a label can lead to stereotyping. There was a time when parents were routinely told that a child with an IQ below 50 "could not learn to read" and that an EMR child "will get as far as the fourth grade level in academic skills." Clearly, if one believed in these absolute ceilings, the self-fulfilling prophecy would operate. The controversy about labeling children reached such proportions in the 1970's that a task force was established by the Secre-

tary of Health, Education and Welfare to study its effects. The final report (Hobbs, 1975) rejected the idea that classification could be abandoned despite the fact that bureaucratic efforts to help children are sometimes detrimental. It addressed the issues of the legal status of exceptional children and the necessity for due process and privacy in classification procedures. The recommendations, some 40 in number, focused on improving classification systems, reducing the harmful effects of categories and labels, and generally improving educational and treatment programs with better coordination, staffing, and funding. A special point was made of the need for more research "since so many policy issues affecting exceptional children rest, at the present time, on a precarious knowledge base" (Hobbs, 1975, p. xvii). Above all, we need the constant reminder that any diagnostic label, including mental retardation, describes only part-features of a child and not the whole child.

The discussion so far has dealt with the influence of labels on adult perceptions, but one should also consider the effect of labels on peer perceptions as well as self-perception. As mentioned earlier, even the child in special classes rejects the label of mental retardation and this feeling is apparently never outgrown. In interviews with adults who had formerly resided in an institution, Edgerton (1967) found that the need to deny to themselves that they were or ever had been "mentally retarded" was a constant preoccupation. Children readily accept the idea that the label has caused their troubles—whatever the research might say. This attitude can be modified to some extent if one can talk with the retarded person at some length about what the label means and does not mean. Counseling on this particular issue is important because some answer to the question "What's wrong with you?" will be required in many situations when they are adult. Also, it is likely that their social life will revolve around other retarded persons, and if they do not accept themselves in this light, neither will they accept these companions as friends.

This prediction of a somewhat segregated social life runs counter to one of the major objectives of mainstreaming, namely, that the retarded person will be integrated into the social world of his or her peers. What we know from sociometric studies and clinical observations suggests, however, that this is not likely. In Chapter 3, we discussed the special efforts which teachers need to make in order to have the retarded preschool child included in the play of the others. It is apparently little different throughout the age span. Under natural circumstances, mildly handicapped youngsters are isolated and rejected. There is even some evidence that when they are mainstreamed, regular class peers are even less accepting of them than when they are enrolled in special classes (Corman & Gottlieb, 1978; Gottlieb, 1975). Rejection by their peers seems to stem from their ineptitude in games and play more than from the label (Taylor, Asher, & Williams, 1987).

Although the empirical evidence could be read in different ways, the belief that segregation and labeling were bad for children crystallized in the provision for the "least restrictive environment" in the Education for All Handicapped Children Act (P.L. 94-142).

Despite the attention accorded to the "mainstreaming movement," the actual effect, 10 years later, is perhaps less than one would have expected. There has been some movement toward class programs in regular public school buildings for moderately and severely mentally handicapped children, a kind of mainstreaming by physical proximity. Learning-disabled children are more often served by a combination of regular class and resource room. Fewer children are identified as EMR or "developmentally handicapped" and these children are usually included in the regular classes and general school activities for art, music, gym, home economics, etc., but self-contained classrooms are maintained for their academic program. There is an in-between group of children, scoring too high for mental retardation classification but too low for learning disability, who are in truth mainstreamed.

Since the data seems to show no significant differences for the individual contingent on special class placement, how does one decide in a particular situation what to do? The present law gives parents the right to choose, and often they seek outside consultation. From the vantage point of an external consultant, one can assess achievement level, personality, and social functioning and determine if it is commensurate with mental age expectancy. As long as this is the case, mainstreaming seems to be a viable choice. However, despite the ideological movement toward mainstreaming, school personnel continue to be frustrated by the "different" child in their midst. The author followed one girl who was "mainstreamed" before it was a legal option. This mildly mentally retarded girl was attractive, and with quiet dignity she did what she could throughout her school career. Because of her obvious effort, she usually received "D's," sometimes with the extra help of outside tutoring. Her parents were supportive and realistic, only grateful that she need not be labeled "retarded." There was a minor crisis in junior high school when it was discovered that she had carefully and neatly copied the jacket blurb for a required book report. Clearly this is not acceptable for a student of normal intelligence, but for a girl consistently testing around 65 IQ, it showed ingenuity and effort. She graduated with a certificate of special education because some of the required high school courses in sciences and mathematics were simply beyond her. She then worked for some time as a salesclerk in a dress shop and married in her early 20's. At the time, and in retrospect, there seemed to be no advantage to special class placement, but there were many factors working in her favor.

EMOTIONAL DISTURBANCE AND MENTAL RETARDATION

All retarded persons have reality adjustment problems as they face some limitation of their vocational aspirations and social opportunities. But there are clearly many who have persistent emotional difficulties which represent an additional handicap on top of the mental retardation. Attempts have been made to identify the secondary or associated emotional difficulties in retarded populations, but the prevalence figures reported from the various studies have varied widely, depending on the nature of population sample and the method of assessment. The assessment of emotional problems in this population is very difficult for the professional who has not had a wide exposure to retarded persons. Chess (1970) warned that deviant behavior may be appropriate for the child's developmental level and so should not be diagnosed as a sign of emotional disturbance. But on the other hand, Reiss, Levitan, and Szyszko (1982) described the phenomenon of "diagnostic overshadowing" where emotional problems are overlooked because of the presence of the mental retardation. With a sufficiently extensive experience with retarded persons, one learns to spot the special problems of some and identify what has been called the "dually diagnosed" child.

In studies of mildly mentally retarded children at home, Chazan (1964), using the Bristol Social Adjustment Inventory, found the rate of maladjustment to be twice that of a control group, whereas Chess and Hassibi (1970), using psychiatric interview, found about 40% to have a psychiatric impairment. Also using psychiatric evaluation methods but with a much wider range of age and IQ, Eaton and Menolascino (1982) reported that 14.3% showed psychiatric impairment, whereas Philips and Williams (1975) reported 87% with some psychiatric disorder. The message is clear that retarded persons have more emotional disturbance, but how much more is open to question. The range of emotional problems is similar to that found in normally intelligent populations but with a higher incidence of psychosis in particular (Philips & Williams, 1975).

Various explanations have been proposed for the greater vulnerability of retarded persons. First, both the retardation and the emotional disturbance may have a common cause, namely, impairment of the central nervous system. For example, in the Isle of Wight studies (Rutter, Graham, & Yule, 1970), the rate of psychiatric disorders was highest in children with neurological disorders accompanied by seizures (58%). We have already mentioned some of the severe behavior problems associated with specific organic syndromes, namely, self-injurious behavior in Lesch-Nyan and compulsive eating in Prader-Willi. However, this hypothesis does not seem so cogent in regard to mildly retarded children. In a British longitudinal study which included a comparison group and a variety of data collected at different points, Richardson, Koller, and Katz (1985) did not find more behavior disturbance for the 30% with identified CNS impairment.

A second suggestion has been adverse home conditions. In the same study, Richardson et al. (1985) found that 45% of the mildly retarded group compared with 5% of the comparison group were reared in homes with patently poor care, disruptions, parental desertion or abuse, and so on. This led them to the conclusion that "the significantly higher rate of behavior disturbance found among the retarded young adults seems therefore to have been due to their more often experiencing unstable conditions of upbringing than did comparison subjects" (1985, p. 6). The third suggestion is somewhat related to the second, namely, that mental retardation causes family stresses which lead to less favorable conditions for the child. This inter-actional hypothesis would require analysis of more subtle factors than the gross social aberrations documented by Richardson et al. (1985), so although it seems reasonable and certainly true in individual clinical cases, it is hard to prove or disprove.

The fourth suggestion is that there are factors intrinsic to the mental retardation. Tarjan remarked that "retarded individuals are highly vulnerable to emotional traumata. Stresses that result in no significant sequelae in an average child can produce overt psychiatric manifestations in retarded persons" (1977, p. 407). Simply put, the retarded child has fewer coping resources and so is less able to anticipate consequences, to ask questions, to articulate feelings, and to call on his or her social environment for support. And given a child who asks no questions and demonstrates distress in a diffuse, delayed way, the parents fail to volunteer the explanations that might dilute the traumatic experience. For example, a mildly retarded 7-year-old boy, with many severe anxieties and compulsions, became wildly agitated when his parents were trying to arrange "an appointment" with the psychologist. The psychologist made a good guess that "appointment" for him meant a doctor's appointment, and when appointment was explained as "only a time for meeting and talking," he calmed down.

Others have looked at the intrinsic factors a little differently. The best example is Webster's notion of "primary psychopathology of the mental retardation syndrome" (1970). He spent a good deal of time in observing 159 children between the ages of 3 and 6 years who attended the Boston Preschool Retarded

Children's Program between 1958 and 1961. He concluded that "even those retarded children who showed the best emotional development were not comparable to nonretarded children of the same mental age" (1970, p. 17). He felt that practically all the children showed poor development in their capacity to make emotionally significant distinctions between the familiar and the unfamiliar, between friends and strangers, between persons and places, and between persons and inanimate objects. He was particularly impressed by the general characteristics of repetitiousness, inflexibility, passivity, and simplicity of emotional life. He rated close to half as moderately emotionally disturbed and 18% as psychotic. Webster did not ascribe all the psychopathology to intrinsic factors but also discussed various secondary influences in terms of parenting and experiences with hospitalization and surgery.

Webster's sample was not representative of the mentally retarded population, because nearly 80% demonstrated fairly clear evidence of brain disease with a high incidence of convulsive disorders. Also, over a third was moderately retarded, twice the proportionate number that one would expect. Even if his observations were based on a special subset, his paper was important in highlighting the spill-over effect from cognitive deficit to emotional development. We have previously discussed the fact that retarded children have difficulty in advancing through the separation-individuation phase to the phase of object constancy and the possibility that the separation in nursery school may add to this difficulty, unless it is handled with great sensitivity (see Chapter 3). It is dif-

ficult, if not impossible, to separate intrinsic and extrinsic factors since so many things that are expected of, or done to, retarded children, are out of synchrony with their internal timetable.

There is a real need for more mental health services for mentally retarded persons, both from a preventive standpoint and for the amelioration of secondary emotional problems. All too often, these problems are looked at simplistically as a failure of training; this view leads to behavior strategies, ignoring the emotional life of the retarded child. The mental health needs receive inadequate professional attention for a number of reasons. As pointed out by Reiss, Levitan, and McNally (1982), mental health agencies and developmental disability programs argue about their responsibilities in this area, and neither clinical psychologists nor psychiatrists have shown much interest in this population.

RANGE OF TREATMENTS

Mentally disturbed, retarded individuals are all too frequently treated with drug therapy. In fact, judging by the numbers reported to be on regular drug therapy, one would conclude that half of the retarded were also emotionally disturbed! Surveys have consistently shown that 40–50% of institutionalized mentally retarded individuals are receiving neuroleptic drugs (major tranquilizers normally used for treating psychotic conditions), but this is not limited to institutionalized populations. Davis, Cullari, and Breuning (1982) found that 58% of a random sample of mentally retarded individuals in community foster and group homes were receiving thioridazine, chlorpormazine, or haloperidol. After reviewing the literature, Breuning and Poling (1982) concluded that the neuroleptics are greatly overused, with very little evidence of therapeutic effect and with considerable evidence of negative side effects in decreased learning and permanent motor disorder (dyskinesia). It is difficult to determine to what extent the drugs are used with disturbed, retarded children but the indiscriminate use of drugs with the retarded population as a whole reflects a double standard, where the retarded are not really expected to "get better" so negative results are tolerated.

Behavior therapy, specifically in the operant model, has been the mainstay of psychological treatments for retarded individuals, and has brought a ray of hope for moderately and severely retarded persons who are unable to participate on a voluntary choice basis. It is unnecessary to recount the documented changes following judicious manipulation of external reinforcement schedules, but there have been problems with the maintenance of changed behavior in different environments and over time (Bornstein, Bach, & Anton, 1982). Behavior is easier to change than people and there is a tendency for the moderately and severely retarded to regress when the treatment program is discontinued.

Psychotherapy

There has been an unwarranted presumption that psychotherapy is not useful with retarded persons. Despite the fact that there are many successful case reports in the literature, mental health professionals usually give a retarded/disturbed child low priority. Sternlicht (1977) suggested that

Most of the professional workers in the field come heavily laden with intellectualized and verbal proficiencies, with an intellectually oriented system of values and beliefs. These individuals generally find it nearly impossible to fully understand the phenomenology of mental retardation, to be able to view the world from the eyes of a retarded individual. (p. 455)

Not only do they have difficulties with empathy, but they find it difficult to accept the fact that at the conclusion of a successful treatment, the individual will still be retarded. This conflicts with their personal values in that they wonder if their investment is worthwhile.

But assuming some commitment to the venture, what can one expect in psychotherapy? First, the child-therapist relationship is of vital importance. The child must be convinced of the therapist's interest and liking, which may require more tangible evidence than is usual in other situations. Second, the therapist will probably take a more active and educational role than that warranted for other children. Explanations will be offered even when not asked for and interpretations of "what most people feel" will be needed to assure the child of the legitimacy of his or her feelings. The therapist needs to be "cognitively flexible" and be able to understand primitive modes of thought which are likely to be retained alongside more sophisticated thought processes which have been "told" to the child. Also, the retarded child needs much more help to play, to imagine, and to ask questions than the child of normal intelligence; the therapist will probably have to initiate these activities. Finally, the therapist can expect to be bored at times, partly in response to the dullness of the child's verbal and play productions, but also perhaps in response to a feeling of helplessness to effect change. Doris and Solnit (1963) suggested that the therapist will be more gratified if he or she adds to the perspective the question of how treatment of the child will enable him or her to advise and collaborate with the parents and teachers. And always, there is plenty to think about in terms of understanding the relation of the cognitive deficit to the presenting emotional problem.

It is instructive to speculate on the possible distortions of normal emotional development which result from cognitive deficit. One such reconstruction was attempted from the therapeutic work with a mildly retarded girl who was referred because of hyperactivity, excitability, bossiness, psoriasis, enuresis, and general difficulties in behavior management at home and at school (Smith, McKinnon, & Kessler, 1976). In common with most mildly retarded children, the first clear indication of obvious divergence appeared in the second year when language was delayed. One might ask what difference it makes if speech is delayed. Does not the normal process occur at a later time? There seem to be several factors that distort further development. First, the delayed speech casts a shadow on the mother's pride and pleasure in her child. Second, in this prolonged verbal period in which they do not have verbal tools of mastery, these physically active children, of normal size and vigor, get into things and

meet innumerable reality frustrations. It is as though they were eternal toddlers, always being controlled and not having the means of turning passivity into activity. They cannot identify with the "talking" mother and say "no" to her, or make verbal demands in response to verbal prohibitions. The only recourse they have is to take flight or to fight.

The issue of who controlled whom was central in the entire course of this girl's psychotherapy. Constantly, Susie demonstrated the process of turning passive into active in a ceaseless effort to assert her independence and autonomy. Susie endeavored to use a form of identification but had difficulty in executing it because of the limitations in her imagination; hence it remained a rather exact reenactment of past experiences with a change in roles. It was difficult to move on from repetitious replay of past events, and perhaps the greatest sign of health and progress in Susie was her fantasy of being a 15-year-old babysitter. For once she was looking ahead with an original fantasy, compounded, of course, of elements from her past, but a far cry from her simple games of doing to others exactly what had been done to her. This fantasy also involved identification with the nurturant aspects of caretakers, in contrast to the simple power axis previously so prominent in Susie's role-reversal play. Of course, there were idiosyncratic features in this case which we have omitted, but the course of treatment suggested that an early point of fixation is around the conflicts of establishing ego autonomy. Trying to find ways by which she could assert her independence, other than simple negativism or "turning the tables," was a pivotal task for the therapist.

Family Adjustment

Clearly, the presence of a mentally retarded child is stressful for a family and the manner of coping affects all members as well as the retarded child. In Chapter 3, we discussed the significance of early mother-child relationships in this context and reviewed common parental reactions when an infant or very young child is first diagnosed as mentally retarded. Support during the diagnostic process is important not only for the parent of an infant but also for the parent of an older child. Parents have written eloquently about their experiences with professional workers (Gorham, 1975; Turnbull & Turnbull, 1979) which have been characterized more by frustration than support. Gorham's suggestion that professional workers provide copies of reports to parents seems eminently worthwhile. It is the parents who need to understand the information and who need the documents on hand as they progress through the maze of services, including establishing eligibility for supplementary social security. It is often good practice to have the parent sit in on the psychological examinations so that they can see the basis for judgment. They also need to understand labels, implicit or explicit, and the consequences for eligibility in educational services. It is also important that they understand their role in facilitating their child's development and do not become overawed by professional expertise of any kind.

Parents expect professional persons to help them with practical questions with regard to expectations, discipline, school placement, baby-sitters, summer programs, special therapies, recreational activities, etc., and one should expect that new questions will arise at various developmental transition points. As Blacher (1984) pointed out, parents' adaptation to having a handicapped child is cyclical and their concerns change with the age of their children. As the children grow older, they encounter less acceptance from neighbors and much more difficulty in finding playmates (Birenbaum, 1970; Suelzle & Keenan, 1981). As parents of adolescents, they focus on sexuality, future living arrangements, job possibilities, and issues of economic security. Also, they have to deal with the adolescent's own reaction to the handicap, which adds a whole new dimension (Zeitlin & Turner, 1985). Parental counseling only starts with the diagnosis; it should be intermittent throughout the life span.

In order to be effective over the long haul, parent counseling must be family oriented, with due consideration of the needs of all the members. Parenting a handicapped child takes its toll, as witness the general finding that both mothers and fathers of retarded children show greater depressive affect and lower self-esteem than parents of nonretarded children (Crnic, Friedrich, & Greenberg, 1983). Studies examining the impact on the marital relationship of parenting developmentally disabled children contradict one another with regard to divorce figures (Bristol & Gallagher, 1986), but it is interesting that marital satisfaction in two-parent families is highly related to effective coping with the child (Friedrich, 1979).

There has been very little attention given to the father's role with the retarded child, but there is some evidence that fathers do affect their children by indirectly affecting the mother's ability to cope (Bristol & Gallagher, 1986). Crnic, Friedrich, and Greenberg (1983) emphasized the variability in family responses to a retarded child and introduced the idea of "buffer variables" such as social networks, financial resources, strong interpersonal relationships, and even religious faith, which moderate the stress inherent in raising a handicapped child—regardless of the specific nature of the handicap.

There has been relatively extensive research on the siblings of handicapped children. One consistent finding is that there is more of an effect on sisters than on brothers (Farber, 1960; Fowle, 1968; Grossman, 1972). Apparently they identified more with their mothers and felt more responsibility for care. In the Grossman study, which was restricted to interviewing college students, those siblings who were interviewed at private universities showed less effect than those who were attending community college, supposedly as the indirect result of the more limited financial resources of these families. In both groups, older siblings exhibited more adaptive coping than did younger siblings, a finding confirmed in many other reports (Simeonsson & Bailey, 1986). Grossman concluded that about half the college subjects seemed more tolerant, compassionate and mature than their peers, but that others had suffered from the experience of a retarded sibling. They tended to feel guilty about the anger they felt at their parents for being neglected or deprived of opportunities and were more fearful of being damaged themselves.

All too often, intervention efforts are directed to the mother-child dyad as a separate system in the family. The mother is often given additional responsibilities as teacher/trainer, which may intensify an already overly enmeshed mother-child relationship (Berger & Foster, 1986) or further restrict her social support system. Deliberate efforts must be made to involve the father and the siblings, not just to share the burden, but so that they have a first-hand understanding of the problem and have some ideas as to what is expected of them. Siblings need reassurance that it is all right to be angry at their retarded brother or sister—sometimes—and that differences in parental treatment do not mean differences in parental love. Finally, time for having fun must not be sacrificed by the constant presence of the handicapped child.

THE MENTALLY RETARDED ADULT

Almost all parents ask for some prediction of the future, and here one must take care to talk in terms of probabilities rather than certainties. The future for a given child may hold surprises which are either better or worse than the probability; it is wise to talk in terms of short-term futures and stress the need for repeated re-evaluation. Nevertheless, the future is very much on the mind of the parents, particularly as the child approaches adolescence, and some general expectations can be presented with caveats about the hazards of prediction. The discussion that follows is limited to mildly and high-moderately retarded persons because they can be expected to find a place in the community with total or partial independence.

Most of the studies which have followed retarded children into adult life have used employment status as a criterion. There are many such reports from different times and places. Results vary widely from a "low" of 40% employed, reported by Keeler (1964) in San Francisco to a "high" of 86% employed, reported by Kidd (1970) in St. Louis, Missouri. Some of the variability in the early studies probably derives from major differences in the populations identified as "retarded."

Since the enactment of the Education for All Handicapped Children Act in 1975 there has been a trend to include children in a lower IQ range in what are now often known as classes for the "developmentally handicapped" students. Recent studies have been more consistent in reporting that about half of former special class students are employed in the competitive labor market (Fardig, Algozzine, Schwartz, Hensel, & Westling, 1985; Hasazi, Gordon, & Roe, 1985). The fact that P.L. 94-142 mandated that public school services be available for handicapped children until their 22nd birthday necessarily involved educators with vocational preparation and initial job placement. But this responsibility ends abruptly at age 22 years, leaving the young adult and his or her family to fend for themselves. The reasons for job change are much the same as for any population, but it is much harder for a retarded adult to get that second job. With realistic anxiety about job security, the parent may influence the young

adult to apply for supplemental social security income which is predicated on "unemployability" and limits one's aspirations to part time or sheltered employment.

With regard to the probabilities of marriage, published follow-up studies have little predictive value since they are based on cohorts who were identified as retarded in a different time. For example, Ross, Begab, Dondis, Giampiccolo, and Meyers (1985) located a group of former EMR students when they were between 45 and 54 years of age. Their marriage rate of 61% was less than the prevailing national average and their divorce rate of 10% was higher than the national average prevailing in 1970 when the follow-up was done. However, this group had an average Stanford-Binet IQ of 68 as children and an average WAIS IQ of 82 as adults. At the present time, perhaps 20% of these same children would not be labeled retarded. For our present special student population, the chances of marriage are perhaps one in three.

The question of living arrangements perplexes parents and their adult children because rarely do they have sufficient economic or personal resources to live on their own. The majority continue to live at home or with a relative. The movement to establish small group homes, which may be used as transition to independent apartment living, has just begun to get under way in many areas, but priority for the economic subsidies are given to retarded adults coming from institutions or where there is dire need because of family emergency. There is a dilemma in the residential area similar to the one described for employment, namely, more resources are made available to the developmentally disabled, or the more seriously handicapped. There are very few services targeted for the in-between needs of the mildly retarded adult.

SUMMARY

With a focus on mental retardation, this chapter has ranged widely from broad social-political issues related to definition and labeling, for instance, to experimental research on information-processing differences related to general intelligence. Consideration of the multiple causation of mental retardation required enumeration of some related medical conditions and an exposition of genetic and environmental contributions. The policies and philosophies of special education were reviewed and the adjustment problems of family members were discussed.

An effort was made to present the frustrations and feelings of the person who is mentally retarded. It is all too easy to lose sight of the individual who is growing up in handicapping circumstances in the face of all the data that has been amassed about the retarded as a population sample. Success in intervention is usually measured by some test score or ability to hold a job, and personal contentment or happiness is assumed to follow. There is abundant evidence that a low IQ need not seal one's fate to a life of dependency and isolation; however, skill training, of any and all forms, is not enough. Personal relationships are as crucial for the retarded child as for the normal child. To be effective in helping the retarded child

with adjustment difficulties, the mental health professional must "know" what it means to be retarded and make the necessary adaptations, but at the same time go beyond this attribute and empathize with the life circumstances and personality of the individual child who is always unique.

REFERENCES

ABRAMOWICZ, H. K., & RICHARDSON, S. A. (1975). Epidemiology of severe mental retardation in children: Community studies. *American Journal of Mental Deficiency, 80,* 18–39.

ALLEN, G. (1958). Patterns of discovery in the genetics of mental deficiency. *American Journal of Mental Deficiency, 62,* 840–849.

ARBITMAN SMITH, R., HAYWOOD, H. C., & BRANSFORD, J. D. (1984). Assessing cognitive change. In P. Brooks, C. M. Sperber, & R. McCauley (Eds.), *Learning and cognition in the mentally retarded* (pp. 433–472). Hillsdale, NJ: L. Erlbaum.

BELMONT, J. M. (1966). Longterm memory in mental retardation. In N. R. Ellis (Ed.), *Research in mental retardation* (Vol. 1, pp. 219–256). New York: Academic Press.

BERGER, M., & FOSTER, M. (1986). Applications of family therapy theory to research and interventions with families with mentally retarded children. In J. J. Gallagher & P. M. Vietze (Eds.), *Families of handicapped persons* (pp. 251–260). Baltimore, MD: Brookes.

BILSKY, L. H. (1985). Comprehension and mental retardation. In N. R. Ellis & N. W. Bray (Eds.), *International review of research in mental retardation* (Vol. 13, pp. 215–246). New York: Academic Press.

BIRENBAUM, A. (1970). On managing courtesy stigma. *Journal of Health and Social Behavior, 11,* 196–206.

BLACHER, J. (1984). Sequential stages of parental adjustment to the birth of a child with handicaps: Fact or artifact. *Mental Retardation, 22,* 550–568.

BLACKMAN, L., BILSKY, L. H., BURGER, A., & MAR, H. (1976). Cognitive processes and academic achievement in EMR adolescents. *American Journal of Mental Deficiency, 81,* 125–134.

BORNSTEIN, P. H., BACH, P. J., & ANTON, B. (1982). Behavioral treatment of psychopathological disorders. In J. L. Matson & R. P. Barrett (Eds.), *Psychopathology in the mentally retarded* (pp. 253–293). New York: Grune & Stratton.

BREEN, P., & RICHMAN, G. (1979). Evaluation of the developmental disabilities concept. In R. Wiegerink & J. W. Pelosi (Eds.), *Developmental disabilities: The DD movement.* Baltimore, MD: Paul H. Brooke.

BREUNING, S. E., & POLING, A. D. (1982). Pharmacotherapy. In J. L. Matson & R. P. Barrett (Eds.), *Psychopathology in the mentally retarded* (pp. 195–251). New York: Grune & Stratton.

BRISTOL, M. M., & GALLAGHER, J. J. (1986). Research on fathers of young handicapped children: Evolution, review and some future directions. In J. J. Gallagher & P. M. Vietze (Eds.), *Families of handicapped persons* (pp. 81–100). Baltimore, MD: Brookes.

CARUSO, D., & DETTERMAN, D. (1983). Stimulus encoding by mentally retarded and nonretarded adults. *American Journal of Mental Deficiency, 87,* 649–655.

CEGELKA, P. A., & CEGELKA, W. J. (1970). A review of research: Reading and the educable mentally handicapped. *Exceptional Children, 37,* 187–201.

CHAFFIN, J. D., SPELLMAN, C. R., REGAN, C. E., & DAVISON, R. (1971). Two follow-up studies of former educable mentally retarded students from the Kansas work-study project. *Exceptional Children, 37,* 733–738.

CHARLES, D. C. (1953). Ability and accomplishment of persons earlier judged mentally deficient. *General Psychological Monographs, 47,* 3–71.

CHAZAN, M. (1964). The incidence and nature of maladjustment among children in schools for the educationally subnormal. *British Journal of Educational Psychology, 34,* 292–304.

CHESS, S. (1970). Emotional problems in mentally retarded children. In F. J. Menolascino (Ed.), *Psychiatric approaches to mental retardation* (pp. 55–67). New York: Basic Books.

CHESS, S., & HASSIBI, M. (1970). Behavior deviations in mentally retarded children. *Journal of the American Academy of Child Psychiatry, 9,* 282–297.

CHINN, P. C., & HUGHES, S. (1987). Representation of minority students in special education classes. *Remedial and Special Education, 8,* 41–46.

CLEMENTS, P. R., BOST, L. W., DUBOIS, Y. G., & TURPIN, W. B. (1980). Adaptive Behavior Scale Part Two: Relative severity of maladaptive behavior. *American Journal of Mental Deficiency, 84,* 465–469.

Comptroller General's Report to the Congress. (1977, Oct. 3). HRD-77-37. Washington, D.C.: U.S. General Accounting Office.

CORMAN, L., & GOTTLIEB, J. (1978). *Mainstreaming mentally retarded children: Review of research in mental retardation* (Vol. 9). New York: Academic Press.

COULTER, W. A., & MORROW, H. W. (1978). *Adaptive behavior: Concepts and measurements.* New York: Grune & Stratton.

CRNIC, K. A., FRIEDRICH, W. N., & GREENBERG, M. T. (1983). Adaptation of families with mentally retarded children: A model of stress, coping and family ecology. *American Journal of Mental Deficiency, 88,* 125–138.

DAVIS, V. J., CULLARI, S., & BREUNING, S. E. (1982). Drug use in community foster-group homes. In S. E. Breuning & A. D. Poling (Eds.), *Drugs and mental retardation.* Springfield, IL: Thomas.

DE LA CRUZ, F. F. (1985). Fragile X syndrome.

American Journal of Mental Deficiency, *90,* 119–123.

DETTERMAN, D. K. (1987). Theoretical notions on intelligence and mental retardation. *American Journal of Mental Deficiency,* *92,* 2–12.

DOLL, E. A. (1936). The Vineland Social Maturity Scale: Rev. condensed manual of directions. Vineland, NJ: The Training School.

DOLL, E. A. (1941). The essentials of an inclusive concept of mental deficiency. *American Journal of Mental Deficiency,* *46,* 214–219.

DORIS, J., & SOLNIT, A. J. (1963). Treatment of children with brain damage and associated school problems. *Journal of the American Academy of Child Psychiatry,* *2,* 618–635.

DUNN, L. M. (1968). Special education for the mildly retarded—Is much of it justifiable? *Exceptional Children,* *35,* 5–22.

DUSEK, J. B., & O'CONNELL, E. J. (1973). Teacher expectancy effects on the achievement test performance of elementary school children. *Journal of Educational Psychology,* *65,* 371–377.

EATON, L., & MENOLASCINO, F. J. (1982). Psychiatric disorders in the mentally retarded: Types, problems and challenges. *American Journal of Psychiatry,* *139,* 1297–1303.

EDGERTON, R. B. (1967). *The Cloak of Competence: Stigma in the lives of the mentally retarded.* Berkeley: University of California Press.

ELLIS, N. R., & CAVALIER, A. R. (1982). Research perspectives in mental retardation. In E. Zigler & D. Balla (Eds.), *Mental Retardation: The developmental-difference controversy* (pp. 121–154). Hillsdale, NJ: L. Erlbaum.

ELLIS, N. R., DEACON, J. R., & WOOLDRIDGE, P. W. (1985). Structural memory deficits of mentally retarded persons. *American Journal of Mental Deficiency,* *89,* 392–402.

FAGAN, J. F. (1968). Short-term memory processes in normal and retarded children. *Journal of Experimental Child Psychology,* *6,* 279–296.

FALENDER, C., & HEBER, R. (1975). Mother-child interaction and participation in a longitudinal intervention program. *Developmental Psychology,* *11,* 830–836.

FARBER, B. (1960). Effects of a severely mentally retarded child on family integration. *Monograph of the Society for Research in Child Development,* *25,* (1, Serial No. 75).

FARDIG, D. B., ALGOZZINE, R. F., SCHWARTZ, S. E., HENSEL, J. W., & WESTLING, D. L. (1985). Postsecondary vocational adjustment of rural, mildly handicapped students. *Exceptional Children,* *52,* 115–121.

FARMER, T. W. (Ed.). (1983). *Pediatric neurology* (3rd ed.). New York: Harper & Row.

FEUERSTEIN, R., & JENSEN, M. R. (1980). Instrumental Enrichment: Theoretical basis, goals, and instruments. *Educational Forum,* *XLIV,* 401–423.

FEUERSTEIN, R., RAND, Y., HOFFMAN, M. B., & MILLER, R. (1980). *Instrumental enrichment: An intervention program for cognitive modifiability.* Baltimore, MD: University Park Press.

FOWLE, C. M. (1968). The effect of the severely mentally retarded child on his family. *American Journal of Mental Deficiency,* *73,* 468–473.

FRIEDRICH, W. N. (1979). Predictors of the coping behavior of mothers of handicapped children. *Journal of Consulting & Clinical Psychology,* *47,* 140–141.

GARBER, H. L., & HEBER, R. (1981). The efficacy of early intervention with family rehabilitation. In M. J. Begab, H. C. Haywood, & H. L. Garber (Eds.), *Psychosocial influences in retarded performance* (Vol. II, pp. 71–88). Baltimore, MD: University Park Press.

GLIDDEN, L. M. (1985). Semantic processing, semantic memory and recall. In N. R. Ellis & N. W. Bray (Eds.), *International review of research in mental retardation* (Vol. 13, pp. 247–278). New York: Academic Press.

GOLDSTEIN, H., MOSS, J., & JORDAN, L. (1965).

A study of the effects of special class placement on educable mentally retarded children. *US Cooperative Research Project No. 619.* University of Illinois.

GORHAM, K. A. (1975). A lost generation of parents. *Exceptional Children, 41,* 521–525.

GOTTLIEB, J. (1975). Public, peer, and professional attitudes toward mentally retarded persons. In M. Begab & S. Richardson (Eds.), *The mentally retarded and society: A social science perspective* (pp. 99–125). Baltimore, MD: University Park Press.

GRAHAM, P. J. (1983). Specific medical syndromes. In M. Rutter (Ed.), *Developmental neuropsychiatry* (pp. 68–82). New York: Guilford.

GROSSMAN, F. K. (1972). *Brothers and sisters of retarded children: An exploratory study.* Syracuse, NY: Syracuse Univeristy Press.

GROSSMAN, H. (Ed.) (1973). *Manual on terminology and classification in mental retardation (1973 revision).* Washington, D.C.: American Association on Mental Deficiency.

GROSSMAN, H. (Ed.) (1983). *Classification in mental retardation (1983 revision).* Washington, D.C.: American Association on Mental Deficiency.

HANSON, J. W. (1981). A review of the etiology and pathogenesis of Prader-Willi syndrome. In V. A. Holm, S. Sulzbacher, & P. L. Pipes (Eds.), *The Prader-Willi syndrome* (pp. 45–55). Baltimore, MD: University Park Press.

HARTER, S., & ZIGLER, E. (1974). The assessment of effectance motivation in normal and retarded children. *Developmental Psychology, 10,* 169–180.

HASAZI, S. B., GORDON, L. R., & ROE, C. A. (1985). Factors associated with the employment status of handicapped youth exiting high school from 1979 to 1983. *Exceptional Children, 51,* 455–469.

HEBER, R. F. (Ed.) (1959). A manual on terminology and classification in mental retardation. *American Journal of Mental Deficiency, 64,* Monograph Supplement.

HEBER, R. F. (1961). Modifications in the manual on terminology and classification in mental retardation. *American Journal of Mental Deficiency, 65,* 499–500.

HEBER, R., & GARBER, H. (1975). The Milwaukee Project: A study of the use of family intervention to prevent cultural-familial mental retardation. In B. Z. Friedlander, G. M. Sterritt, & G. E. Kirk (Eds.), *Exceptional infant* (Vol. 3, pp. 399–433). New York: Brunner/Mazel.

HEBER, R., & GARBER, H., HARRINGTON, W., HOFFMAN, C., & FALENDER, C. (1972). *Rehabilitation of families at risk for mental retardation—Progress report.* Madison, WI: Rehabilitation Research and Training Center in Mental Retardation.

HERRMANN, J. (1981). Implications of the Prader-Willi syndrome for the individual and family. In V. A. Holm, S. Sulzbacher, & P. L. Pipes (Eds.), *The Prader-Willie syndrome* (pp. 229–245). Baltimore, MD: University Park Press.

HOBBS, N. (Ed.) (1975). *The futures of children.* San Francisco: Jossey-Bass.

HONZIK, M. P. (1957). Developmental studies of parent-child resemblances in intelligence. *Child Development, 28,* 216–277.

HUMPHREYS, L. G., & STUBBS, J. (1977). Longitudinal analysis of teacher expectation, student expectation, and student achievement. *Journal of Educational Measures, 14,* 261–270.

JENCKS, S. (1972). *Inequality: A reassessment of the effect of family and schooling in America.* New York: Basic Books.

JENSEN, A. R. (1969). How much can we boost IQ and scholastic achievement? *Harvard Educational Review, 39,* 1–123.

JOHNSON, G. O. (1962). Special education for mentally handicapped—A paradox. *Exceptional Children, 19,* 62–69.

JUSTICE, E. M. (1985). Metamemory: An aspect of metacognition in the mentally retarded. In N. R. Ellis & N. W. Bray (Eds.), *International review of research in mental retardation* (Vol. 13, pp. 79–108). New York: Academic Press.

KANNER, L. (1948). Feeblemindedness, absolute, relative and apparent. *Nervous Child, 7*, 365–397.

KEELER, K. F. (1964). Post-school adjustment of educable mentally retarded youth educated in San Francisco. *Dissertation Abstracts, 25*(2).

KESSLER, J. W. (1965). Environmental components of measured intelligence. *School Review, 73*, 339–358.

KIDD, J. W. (1970). The "adultated" mentally retarded. *Education and Training of the Mentally Retarded, 5*(2), 71–72.

KOLSTOE, O. P. (1972). Programs for the mildly retarded: A reply to the critics. *Exceptional Children, 39*, 51–56.

KUGEL, R. B., & PARSONS, M. H. (1967). Children of deprivation: Changing the course of familial retardation. *Childrens' Bureau (Publication No. 440)*. Washington, D. C.: Superintendent of Documents.

KUSHLICK, A., & BLUNDEN, R. (1974). The epidemiology of mental subnormality. In A. M. Clarke & A. D. B. Clarke (Eds.), *Mental deficiency: The changing outlook* (3rd ed., pp. 31–81). New York: Free Press.

LAMBERT, N. M., WINDMILLER, M., COLE, L., & FIGUEROA, R. A. (1975a). Standardization of a public school version of the AAMD Adaptive Behavior Scale. *Mental Retardation, 13*, 3–7.

LAMBERT, N. M., WINDMILLER, M. B., COLE, L. J., & FIGUEROA, R. A. (1975b). AAMD Adaptive Behavior Scale: Public school version, 1974 revision: Manual. Washington, DC: American Association on Mental Deficiency.

Larry v. *Wilson Riles*. (1972). U.S. District Court for the Northern District of California, No. C-71-2270 RFP.

LAWRENCE, E. A., & WINSCHEL, J. F. (1973). Self concept and the retarded: Research and issues. *Exceptional Children, 39*, 310–321.

LEDBETTER, D. H., RICCARDI, V. M., AIRHART, S. D., STROBEL, R. J., KEENAN, B. S., & CRAWFORD, J. D. (1981). Deletions of chromosome 15 as a cause of the Prader-Willi syndrome. *New England Journal of Medicine, 304*, 325–329.

LEWIS, E. D. (1933). Types of mental deficiency and their social significance. *Journal of Mental Science, 79*, 298–304.

MACMILLAN, D. L. (1971). The problem of motivation in the education of the mentally retarded. *Exceptional Children, 37*, 579–587.

MACMILLAN, D. L., JONES, R. L., & ALOIA, G. P. (1974). The mentally retarded label: A theoretical analysis and review of the research. *American Journal of Mental Deficiency, 79*, 241–261.

MACMILLAN, D. L., & KEOGH, B. K. (1971). Normal and retarded children's expectancy for failure. *Developmental Psychology, 4*, 343–348.

MAHLER, M. S. (1942). Pseudo-imbecility: A magic cap of invisibility. *Psychoanalytic Quarterly, 11*, 49–164.

MEALOR, D. J., & RICHMOND, B. O. (1980). Adaptive behavior: Teachers and parents disagree. *Exceptional Children, 46*, 386–389.

MERCER, J. R. (1973). *Labeling the mentally retarded: Clinical and social system perspectives on mental retardation.* Berkeley: University of California Press.

MERCER, J. R., & LEWIS, J. R. (1977). System of multicultural pluralistic assessment: Parent interview manual. *Student assessment manual.* New York: The Psychological Corporation.

MORSINK, C. V., THOMAS, C. C., & SMITH-DAVIS, J. (in press). Noncategorical special education programs: Process and outcomes. In M. C. Want, M. C. Reynolds, & H. J. Walberg (Eds.), *The handbook of special education: Research and practice.* Oxford, England: Pergamon Press.

NETTELBECK, T. (1985). Inspection time and mild mental retardation. In N. R. Ellis & N. W. Bray (Eds.), *International review of research in mental retardation* (Vol. 13, pp. 109–143). New York: Academic Press.

NICHOLS, R. C. (1981). Origins, nature and determinants of intellectual development.

In M. J. H. Begab, H. C. Haywood, & H. L. Garber (Eds.), *Psychosocial influences in retarded performance* (Vol. I, pp. 127–154). Baltimore, MD: University Park Press.

NIHIRA, K., FOSTER, P., SHELLHAAS, M., & LELAND, H. (1974). *AAMD Adaptive Behavior Scale: Manual* (rev. ed.). Washington, DC: American Association on Mental Deficiency.

PASE: Parents in Action on Special Education v. *Hannon*. (1980, July). United States District Court for the Northern District of Illinois, Eastern Division, No. C-74-3586 RFP. (slip opinion).

PHILLIPS, I., & WILLIAMS, N. (1975). Psychopathology and mental retardation: A study of 100 mentally retarded children: I. Psychopathology. *American Journal of Psychiatry, 132,* 1265–1271.

President's Committee on Mental Retardation (PCMR). (1972). *Entering the era of human ecology.* Washington, D.C.: Department of Health, Education, and Welfare Publication No. (OS) 72-7.

President's Committee on Mental Retardation (PCMR). (1976). *Mental retardation: Century of decision.* Washington, D.C.: Department of Health, Education, and Welfare Publication No. (OHD) 76-21013.

RAMEY, C. T., & HASKINS, R. (1981). The causes and treatment of school failure. Insights from the Carolina Abededarian Project. In M. Begab, H. C. Haywood, and H. L. Garber (Eds.), *Psychosocial influences in retarded performance* (Vol. II, pp. 89–112). Baltimore, MD: University Park Press.

RAMEY, C. T., HOLMBERG, M. C., SPARLING, J. H., & COLLIER, A. M. (1977). An introduction to the Carolina Abecedarian Project. In B. M. Caldwell & D. J. Stedman (Eds.), *Infant education: A guide for helping handicapped children in the first three years* (pp. 101–121). New York: Walker & Company.

RAMEY, C. T., & MILLS, P. J. (1977). Social and intellectual consequences of day care for high risk infants. In R. A. Webb (Ed.), *So-cial development in childhood* (pp. 79–110). Baltimore, MD: Johns Hopkins Press.

RAND, Y., FEUERSTEIN, R., TANNENBAUM, A. J., JENSEN, M. R., & HOFFMAN, M. B. (1977). An analysis of the effects of Instrumental Enrichment on disadvantaged adolescents. In P. Mittler (Ed.), *Research to practice in mental retardation* (Vol. II, pp. 117–128). Baltimore, MD: University Park Press.

RAND, Y., MINTZKER, Y., MILLER, R., HOFFMAN, M. B., & FRIEDLENDER, Y. (1981). The Instrumental Enrichment Program: Intermediate and long-term effects. In P. Mittler (Ed.), *Frontiers of knowledge in mental retardation* (Vol. I, pp. 141–152). Baltimore, MD: University Park Press.

RANTAKALLIO, P., & VON WENDT, L. (1986). Mental retardation and subnormality in a birth cohort of 12,000 children in northern Finland. *American Journal of Mental Deficiency, 90,* 380–388.

REGER, R. (1966). WISC, WRAT and CMAS scores in retarded children. *American Journal of Mental Deficiency, 70,* 717–721.

REISS, S., LEVITAN, G. W., & MCNALLY, R. J. (1982). Emotionally disturbed mentally retarded people: An underserved population. *American Psychologist, 37,* 361–367.

REISS, S., LEVITAN, G. W., & SZYSZKO, J. (1982). Emotional disturbance and mental retardation: Diagnostic overshadowing. *American Journal of Mental Deficiency, 86,* 567–574.

REYNOLDS, C. R. (1986). Measurement and assessment of exceptional children. In R. T. Brown & C. R. Reynolds (Eds.), *Psychological perspectives on childhood exceptionality* (pp. 91–135). New York: Wiley.

RICHARDSON, S. A., KOLLER, H., & KATZ, M. (1985). Relationship of upbringing to later behavior disturbance of mildly mentally retarded young people. *American Journal of Mental Deficiency, 90,* 1–8.

ROBINSON, N. M., & ROBINSON, H. B. (1976). *The mentally retarded child* (2nd ed.). New York: McGraw-Hill.

ROSENTHAL, R., & JACOBSON, L. (1968). *Pygmalion in the classroom.* New York: Holt, Rhinehart & Winston.

ROSS, R. T., BEGA, M. J., DONDIS, E. H., GIAMPICCOLO, J. S., & MEYERS, C. E. (1985). *Lives of the mentally retarded. A forty-year follow-up study.* Stanford, CA: Stanford University Press.

RUTTER, M., GRAHAM, P., & YULE, W. (1970). A neuropsychiatric study in childhood. *Clinics in Developmental Medicine* (Nos. 35/36). London: SIMP/Heinemann.

SARASON, S. B. (1953). *Psychological problems in mental deficiency* (2nd ed.). New York: Harper & Row.

SARASON, S. B., & GLADWIN, T. (1958). Psychological and cultural problems in mental subnormality. In R. L. Masland, S. B. Sarason, & T. Gladwin (Eds.) *Mental subnormality* (pp. 145–400). New York: Basic Books.

SCARR, W., & WEINBERG, R. A. (1979). Nature and nurture strike (out) again. *Intelligence, 3,* 31–39.

SCHURR, K. T., TOWNE, R. C., & JOINER, L. M. (1972). Trends in self concept of ability over 2 years of special placement. *Journal of Special Education, 6,* 161–166.

SEVERANCE, L. J., & GASSTROM, L. L. (1977). Effects of the label "mentally retarded" on causal explanations for success and failure outcomes. *American Journal of Mental Deficiency, 81,* 547–555.

SIMEONSSON, R. J., & BAILEY, D. B. (1986). Siblings of handicapped children. In J. J. Gallagher & P. M. Vietze (Eds.), *Families of handicapped persons* (pp. 67–80). Baltimore, MD: Brookes.

SKODAK, M., & SKEELS, H. M. (1949). A final follow-up study of one hundred adopted children. *Journal of Genetic Psychology, 75,* 85–125.

SMITH, E., MCKINNON, R., & KESSLER, J. W. (1976). Psychotherapy with mentally retarded children. In R. Eissler, A. Freud, M. Kris, & A. J. Solnit (Eds.), *The psychoanalytic study of the child* (Vol. 31, pp. 493–514) New Haven, CT: Yale University Press.

SMITH, R. M., NEISWORTH, J. T., & HUNT, F. M. (1983). *The exceptional child* (2nd ed.). New York: McGraw-Hill.

SOMMER, R., & SOMMER, B. A. (1983). Mystery in Milwaukee: Early intervention, IQ and psychology textbooks. *American Psychologist, 38,* 982–986.

SPARROW, S. S., BALLA, D. A., & CICCHETTI, D. V. (1984). *Vineland Adaptive Behavior Scales: Survey from manual* (interview edition). Circle Pines, MN: American Guidance Services.

SPITZ, H. H. (1966). The role of input organization in the learning and memory of mental retardates. In N. R. Ellis (Ed.), *Research in mental retardation* (Vol. 2, pp. 29–56). New York: Academic Press.

STAVER, N. (1953). The child's learning difficulty as related to the emotional problems of the mother. *American Journal of Orthopsychiatry, 23,* 131–142.

STERNLICHT, M. (1977). Issues in counseling and psychotherapy with mentally retarded. In I. Bialer & M. Sternlicht (Eds.), *The psychology of mental retardation* (pp. 453–492). New York: Psychological Dimensions.

STRAUSS, A. A., & LEHTINEN, L. (1947) *Psychopathology and education of the brain-injured child* (Vol. 1). New York: Grune & Stratton.

SUELZLE, M., & KENNAN, V. (1981). Changes in family support networks over the life cycle of mentally retarded persons. *American Journal of Mental Deficiency, 86,* 267–274.

TARJAN, G. (1977). Mental retardation and clinical psychiatry. In P. Mittler (Ed.), *Research to practice in mental retardation* (Vol. I, pp. 401–408). Baltimore, MD: University Park Press.

TAYLOR, A. R., ASHER, S. R., & WILLIAMS, G. A. (1987). The social adaptation of mainstreamed mildly retarded children. *Child Development, 58,* 1321–1335.

TREDGOLD, R. F., & SODDY, K. (1956). *A text-*

book of mental deficiency (9th ed.) London: Balliere, Tindall & Cox.

TURNBULL, A. P., & TURNBULL, H. R. (1979). *Parents speak out.* Columbus, OH: Charles E. Merrill.

TURNER, G., BROOKWELL, R., DANIEL, A., SELIKOWITZ, M., & ZILIBOWITZ, M. (1980). Heterozygous expression of X-linked mental retardation and the marker X. *New England Journal of Medicine, 303,* 662–664.

TYLER, L. E. (1965). *The psychology of human differences.* New York: Appleton-Century-Crofts.

VERNON, P. E. (1979). *Intelligence: Heredity and environment.* San Francisco: W. H. Freeman.

WARNER, F., THRAPP, R., & WALSH, S. (1973). Attitudes of children toward their special class placement. *Exceptional Children, 40,* 37–38.

WEBSTER, T. G. (1970). Unique aspects of emotional development in mentally retarded children. In F. J. Menolascino (Ed.), *Psychiatric approaches to mental retardation* (pp. 3–54). New York: Basic Books.

WINDLE, C. (1962). Prognosis of mental subnormals. *American Journal of Mental Deficiency, 66* (monograph supplement).

WOLFENSBERGER, W. (1972). *Normalization: The principle of normalization in human services.* Toronto, Canada: National Institute on Mental Retardation.

WOLFENSBERGER, W. (1980). The definition of normalization: Update, problems, disagreements and misunderstanding. In R. J. Flynn & K. E. Nitsch (Eds.), *Normalization, social integration and community services* (pp. 71–115). Baltimore, MD: University Park Press.

WURTZ, R. G., SEWELL, T., & MANNI, J. L. (1985). The relationship of estimated learning potential to performance on a learning task and achievement. *Psychology in the Schools, 22,* 293–402.

ZEAMAN, D., & HOUSE, B. J. (1979). A review of attention theory. In N. R. Ellis (Ed.), *Handbook of mental deficiency, psychological theory and research* (2nd ed., pp. 63–120). Hillsdale, NJ: L. Erlbaum.

ZEITLIN, A. G., & TURNER, J. L. (1985). Transition from adolescence to adulthood: Perspectives of mentally retarded individuals and their families. *American Journal of Mental Deficiency, 89,* 570–579.

ZELLWEGER, H., & SCHNEIDER, H. J. (1968). Syndrome of hypotonia-hypomentia-hypogonadism-obesity (HHHO) or Prader-Willi Syndrome. *American Journal of Diseases of Children, 115,* 588–598.

ZIGLER, E. (1982). Developmental versus difference theories of mental retardation and the problem of motivation. In E. Zigler & D. Balla (Eds.), *Mental retardation: The developmental-difference controversy* (pp. 163–188). Hillsdale, NJ: L. Erlbaum.

ZIGLER, E., & BALLA, D. (1981). Issues in personality and motivation in mentally retarded persons. In M. J. Begab, H. C. Haywood, & H. L. Garber (Eds.), *Psychosocial influences in retarded performance* (Vol. I, pp. 197–218). Baltimore, MD: University Park Press.

ZIGLER, E., & BALLA, D. (1982). Introduction: The developmental approach to mental retardation. In E. Zigler & D. Balla (Eds.), *Mental retardation: The developmental-difference controversy* (pp. 3–8). Hillsdale, NJ: L. Erlbaum.

CHAPTER 13

DEVELOPMENTAL DISORDERS

THE CHOICE OF LABELS

The major problems covered in this chapter—autistic disorder and developmental language delay—have their onset in the preschool years but they were not covered in Chapter 3 because "The Uncommon Infant" was restricted to those conditions where the diagnosis is established at birth or in the first year of life. At young ages, the developmental disorders look very much alike, and differential diagnosis is often made on the basis of subsequent development rather than at the time of onset. In DSM-III-R, "Autistic Disorder" (formerly "Infantile Autism") is identified as a "Pervasive Developmental Disorder" and included with Mental Retardation and Specific Developmental Disorders under the rubric of Developmental Disorders on Axis II. The essential feature of this group of

disorders is that the predominant disturbance is in the acquisition of cognitive, language, motor, or social skills. Specific Developmental Disorders cover particular academic difficulties such as dyslexia, which were presented in Chapter 11, as well as Developmental Expressive Language Disorder and Developmental Receptive Language Disorder which are topics in this chapter.

The term "developmental disorders" is similar to but not the same as the term "developmental disabilities" which causes some confusion. In the Developmental Disabilities Act of 1984 (P.L. 98-1074), "developmental disability" is defined as a severe, chronic disability of a person, attributable to a mental or physical impairment which will continue indefinitely and result in substantial limitation in self-care and economic self-sufficiency. This is assumed to include the more severe forms of mental retardation, but not the mildly retarded population unless there are associated handicaps. Other conditions that may be included are cerebral palsy, epilepsy, and autism if they are sufficiently handicapping in their own right or if they are associated with some degree of mental retardation. "Developmental disability" is a legal definition that entitles the person to various social and habilitation services on the basis of need rather than diagnosis. The "developmental disabled" population contains persons as diverse as able-bodied severely mentally retarded to quadriplegics with IQs of 150!

Developmental disorders are of much lower incidence than such problems as conduct disorders, learning problems, or mental retardation. Nonetheless, these are highly visible problems that usually demand attention throughout childhood, if not throughout the life span. There is a tacit assumption that these problems are neurologically based, but our focus is on the psychological manifestations and needs of these children.

INFANTILE AUTISM

Differential Diagnosis

Infantile autism has a relatively short history, starting with Kanner (1943). He described his observations on 11 children with particular emphasis on their lack of relationships with people, delay in speech and noncommunicative use of speech after its acquisition, obsessive need for sameness, good rote memory,

and normal physical appearance. Other writers confirmed the validity of this clinical syndrome and infantile autism became a legitimate clinical diagnosis. If one judged by the amount of literature that this condition generated, one would assume that it was a common problem. In fact, it is rare with prevalence reports ranging from .02% in a Swedish survey (Gillberg, 1984) to about .05% in an English study (Wing & Gould, 1979), but it captures an inordinate amount of attention because of its mysterious nature. In contrast to other pathological disturbances of childhood, an autistic child shows some unique behavior patterns that have no counterpart in normal development.

In DSM-III-R, the diagnostic criteria for autistic disorder are described in 16 behavioral items in the areas of qualitative impairment in social interaction and both verbal and nonverbal communication, and restrictions in activities and interests. At least 8 of the 16 must be identified for diagnosis with at least 2 in the area of social impairment. The difficulties in social interaction include (a) lack of awareness of the existence or feelings of others, (b) not seeking comfort from others when distressed, (c) failure to imitate, (d) little or no interactive social play, and (d) inability to establish peer friendships. There are always abnormalities in language, sometimes no response to or use of words, or sometimes limited echoing or mechanical repetition. Frequently, the child is unable to use the personal pronoun and shows peculiarities in stress or rhythm in speech. There are other features that are extremely common such as avoidance of eye contact, resistance to change, stereotypic motor movements, e.g., twirling or fingering, and attachments to inanimate objects but these vary according to degree of autism and developmental level.

At the outset, infantile autism was regarded as one form of childhood schizophrenia, but Rutter (1975), amongst others, offered various arguments against this view. There are demographic differences, in that autistic boys outnumber autistic girls by at least 3 to 1, whereas there are no sex differences in the incidence figures for schizophrenia. The major differentiation is that schizophrenic children develop normally up to a point and then regress, in contrast to autistic children who show failure in development rather than regression. A more cogent argument rests on the evidence for or against continuity between infantile autism and adult schizophrenia. The results of early follow-up studies are difficult to evaluate because the diagnostic criteria for both autism and schizophrenia were not well specified, but Petty, Ornitz, Michelman, and Zimmerman (1985) presented three well-documented cases of infantile autistic children who later developed typical schizophrenic symptoms of delusions and hallucinations; this author could cite an equally unequivocal case from her experience. All these cases fit the DMS-III criteria for autism, but they were unusual in that their verbal IQ scores were in the average range and superior to their performance IQ scores. As these authors point out, most autistic children cannot be evaluated for schizophrenia because of limited verbal expression.

Despite the fact that there are both clinical and theoretical reasons to suspect a link between infantile autism and adult schizophrenia, more and more attention was directed to the cognitive deficits of autistic children, which seemed to be biologically determined. Schizophrenia, which has only recently taken its place as a biomedical condition, was vaguely linked with "emotional disorders," and the move to divorce schizophrenia and autism was in part political. The change of heart is reflected in the name change of the *Journal of Autism and Childhood Schizophrenia* which was first issued in 1971 and became the *Journal of Autism and Developmental Disorders* in 1979.

Another break with the past occurred with the discovery that there was overlap between the condition of mental retardation and infantile autism. Kanner ruled out retardation in his cases on the basis of their "intelligent expression," normal milestones in motor development, and precocious skills in limited areas of memory, musical appreciation, etc. Subsequent studies were unanimous in finding a wide range of intelligence, but with a majority testing retarded. The reported distributions vary from 94% below IQ 70 (DeMyer et al., 1974) to 71% (Schopler, 1983). In the previously cited Gillberg study (1984), 27% tested below 50 IQ, 50% in the 50–70 IQ range, and 23% above IQ 70.

For some time, it was believed that the mental retardation was secondary to the primary autism. However, the stability of IQ test results over time was about the same as that found for normal and retarded children (DeMyer, 1975; Lockyer & Rutter, 1969). Furthermore, IQ scores did not change significantly in autistic children who showed significant behavioral and social improvement, either in the natural course of events (Rutter, Greenfield, & Lockyer, 1967) or following specialized treatment (Howlin, 1981; Rutter, 1980). Follow-up studies demonstrated a clear relationship between level of retardation and general adjustment, suggesting that "Autistic children with low IQ's are just as retarded as anyone else with a low IQ and the score meant much the same thing" (Rutter, 1975, p. 335).

However, autism cannot be regarded as simply one form of mental retardation because most equally retarded children are not autistic. Wing and Gould (1979) found that 10% of moderately and severely retarded children were also autistic, and the percentage is considerably less for the mildly retarded. Also, there is more variability in intellectual functioning, with relatively superior scores on perceptual-motor tasks and memory items and relatively inferior scores on verbal items. In a few individuals with "higher-level autism," some skills are at chronological age level or better so that they look like learning-disabled children (Shea & Mesibov, 1985), but their difficulties in relating to others are much greater and they show more disturbance in play interests. Even the high-functioning autistic children get absorbed in simple sensory stimulation (rocking, watching changing patterns of light and shadow), and enjoy repetitive activities (writing or drawing numbers, words, maps, etc.) which are tedious to most other children, learning disabled or not. On a behavioral level, the ritualistic compulsions and obsessional need for sameness of the autistic child resembles the obsessive-compulsive child, but the total personalities are very different.

The overlap between autism and developmental communication disorders has been subjected to particularly close scrutiny. Since language impairment is a universal part of the autistic syndrome, it was reasonable to consider the possibility that a language disorder was the cause of the other social and behavioral difficulties. Bartak, Rutter, and Cox (1975) examined a sample of boys aged 5 to 10 years who exhibited severe deficiency in the understanding of language despite average performance IQ scores. The 19 autistic children were very different from the 23 children with developmental receptive language disorder in terms of gaze aversion, virtually no friends, total lack of participation in group play, few instances of pretend play, and little use of gesture for communication. Interestingly, the two groups shared equally in the attachment to "odd objects" and resistance to changes in home environment. There was a mixed group of 5 children who showed some autistic features, indicating that autism is not an "all-or-none" condition. The authors concluded that a language disability is a necessary but not sufficient condition for the development of autism. In conclusion, although autistic children show some features in common with mentally retarded, learning-disabled, obsessive-compulsive, and language disordered children, they are readily differentiated by their unique deficiency in relating to people.

Etiology

Considering the primacy of the social impairment, it is not surprising that the first explanations were in terms of the social environment. From his original group, Kanner (1943) observed that

There are very few really warmhearted fathers and mothers ... The question arises whether or to what extent this fact has contributed to the condition of the children. The children's aloneness from the beginning of life makes it difficult to attribute the whole picture exclusively to the type of early parental relations with our patients. (Kanner, 1943, p. 250)

Not long after Kanner's initial publications, psychoanalysts published a number of clinical reports on similar children, choosing the classification of "atypical" to avoid comparison with adult schizophrenia. Rank (1949) remarked that one assumed that these atypical children had suffered gross emotional deprivation and that close investigation indicated that the majority of the mothers were immature and narcissistic with precarious social contact. There were many reports in the 1950's which tended to confirm the hypothesis of parental psychopathology on the basis of intensive clinical study, although some suggested it might be reactive to the child's problems rather than causal (Esman, Kohn, & Nyman, 1959).

Mahler (1965) studied the problem of infantile psychosis from the perspective of developmental psychopathology. She acknowledged that only "constitutionally vulnerable" infants developed schizophrenia but suggested that the core deficiency was the infant's lack of, or loss of, the ability to utilize the symbiotic (need satisfying) object of the mother. Simply put, the mother does not serve the usual functions of comfort, reassurance, and organizing the external world for her infant, what Mahler called the

"human beacon of orientation in the world of reality and in the inner world." She described some instances of debilitating emotional unavailability on the part of the mother because of a depression and some instances of a smothering disregard of the child's need to experience gratification and frustration at his own pace. But she added

We have found in our study just as many cases of infantile psychosis in which the mother belonged to Winnicott's group of ordinary, devoted mothers, and we could reconstruct in some cases such extreme, seemingly intrinsic vulnerability on the part of the child which even the most favorable environmental situations could not conceivably have counteracted. (1965, p. 560)

A strong psychogenic position was developed by Bettelheim in his book *The Empty Fortress* (1967) where he concluded that parental behavior is a necessary but not sufficient factor in the etiology of infantile autism. The nucleus of Bettelheim's argument was that from the beginning, the mother failed to respond to the child's cues so that the child did not acquire any sense of control over the external environment. Bettelheim went further to suggest that the mother becomes a threatening object because of her covert destructive wishes so that the infant withdraws out of both frustration and anxiety. From intensive therapeutic work with these children, he interpreted the autism as a way of coping with unbearable anxiety stemming from the child's evaluation of the conditions of his life as being utterly unpredictable and probably destructive.

Although most of this formulation is speculative and untestable, it may contain a germ of truth. Bemporad (1979)

reported the recollections of an adult who had been diagnosed as autistic by Kanner and others. "Jerry remembered a childhood world of painful confusion and almost constant terror in which other individuals, even his mother, offered no haven or security" (1979, p. 194). But, Bemporad added, his mother was described as a warm and loving person who devoted her life to his welfare. Although the reasons are unclear, it is certainly true that many autistic children suffer from fears which reach panic proportions.

Evidence began to mount to show that parents of autistic children were not psychologically different than parents of other groups (Allen, DeMyer, Norton, Pontius, & Yang, 1971; Cox, Rutter, Newman, & Bartak, 1975; Creak & Ini, 1960) and the focus of attention turned to the nature of the "constitutional vulnerability." Some of the change in focus occurred because new knowledge of the competencies of the neonate required reconsideration of normal infant helplessness (Esman, 1983), but also, parents were outraged by the onus of responsibility. Rimland, himself the father of an autistic son, was one of the first to take public issue with the psychogenic hypothesis. After reviewing the considerable negative evidence against the psychogenic hypothesis, he suggested a biological hypothesis, namely, impairment in the function of the reticular formation of the brain stem (1964). He inferred this as the problem site because it is part of the physiological arousal system. His suggestion served to restore parents' self-respect, and the National Society for Autistic Children was established by parents in 1965.

There is no longer any doubt that the major cause of autism is biological, although there is continuing controversy as to whether it represents a single "disease" or the expression of various biological/etiological factors. Ritvo (1976), taking the first position, stated "these patients share a neuropathophysiologic process which interferes with developmental rate, and the modulation or integration of sensory input within the brain" (p. 5). Coleman and Gillberg, on the other hand, declared

Let it be spelled out at once; autism is not a single disease entity in the sense that, for instance, pheylketonuria is. Rather, the concept of autism represents a comprehensive diagnosis, somewhat along the same lines as cerebral palsy or epilepsy. . . . There is now overwhelming evidence that the behavioral syndrome of autism represents the final (common?) expression of various etiological factors. (1985, p. 15)

Biomedical Findings

The biomedical research would seem to support the second position, that autism represents a symptom rather than a unitary disease. Many differences have been reported but nothing has been universal to all instances. The degree of mental retardation is a confounding factor because many of the findings are found in the moderately and severely retarded but not in the less handicapped. One of the striking findings is the fact that about one in five autistic children develop epileptic seizures for the first time during adolescence (Deykin & MacMahon, 1979; Rutter, 1970) but the risk increases with the severity of the mental retardation. Bartak and Rutter (1976) reported that whereas a third of mentally retarded autistic children developed epileptic seizures, only about 1 in 20 of those of normal intelligence did so. In electroencephalographic studies (EEG), significant numbers of autistic children show abnormalities, but there is no consistency pointing to a specific organic dysfunction.

There are specific medical disease entities which are associated with the autistic syndrome, namely, fragile-X chromosomal abnormality, prenatal rubella (German Measles) and phenylketonuria (Coleman & Gillberg, 1985), but this represents a very small proportion of the autistic population. The only finding related to pregnancy and birth history is increased incidence of maternal uterine bleeding (Coleman & Gillberg, 1985), but clearly this is a nonspecific finding.

In an effort to localize the neuroanatomic source, Ornitz and his colleagues have hypothesized that the vestibular nuclei in the brainstem are the site of the primary dysfunction in autistic children. In several experimental studies they showed that certain functions mediated by the vestibular system are diminished in these children, including ocular nystagmus after rotation (Ornitz, Brown, Mason, & Putnam, 1974) and rapid-eye movements associated with dreaming sleep (Ornitz, Forsythe, & de la Pena, 1973). This is an important part of the perceptual inconstancy theory put forward by Ornitz and Ritvo (1968) in which they suggest that autistic children suffer from a defect in the homeostatic regulation of sensory input and motor output, so that they fail to gain a stable inner representation of the environment.

The faulty modulation of incoming stimuli may be manifested as either underreactivity or overreactivity and in self-stimulative behavior such as hand flapping or spinning objects. Ornitz (1985) pointed out that these disturbances of sensory modulation and motility occur predominantly in the 2- to 4-year-old autistic child and frequently disappear with later development. Ornitz cited evidence of increased reactivity of autonomic responses and deficiency in autonomic habituation which "leads to (or perhaps reflects) the autistic inability to 'gate' or 'filter' trivial sensory stimuli, thereby compromising selective attention" (1985, p. 258).

This idea of malfunctioning in a "filter system" had an earlier counterpart in the psychoanalytic literature in discussions of a "constitutional ego defect" predisposing a child to the development of psychosis. Child analysts made use of Freud's comments on the importance of the protective barrier: ". . . protection against stimuli is an almost more important function for the organism than reception of stimuli" (1920/1955, p. 27). He pointed out the importance of being able to sample the outer world in small quantities. Bergmann and Escalona (1949) observed unusual sensitivities in five infants who later became psychotic and discussed this development in terms of "their thin protective barrier." Rosenfeld and Sprince also used the concept of an inadequate protective barrier in relation to the development of borderline psychotic states. ". . . one of the points which has emerged is that our (borderline) children find it difficult to inhibit stimuli. They seem to be swamped by them, and are unselective in their choice of what is relevant and what is irrelevant" (1963, p. 623). These writers did not distinguish between autism and psychosis, nor did they attempt to identify a neurophysiological explanation, but their clinical observations were remarkably similar.

The other major contending point of view is concerned with cortical loci of dysfunction, particularly some underlying neuropathology of the left hemisphere or possible impairments in cerebral lateralization. This speculation is a natural outcome of the fact that in the majority of the normal population linguistic functions are lateralized to the left hemisphere, whereas the right hemisphere appears to be specialized for visuospatial and musical functions which are often relatively advanced in autistic children. Experimental results seem to be contradictory. For example, Arnold and Schwartz (1983) found no evidence of left hemisphere damage whereas Dawson, Warrenburg, and Fuller (1982) and Dawson (1983) found that most autistic subjects showed left hemisphere dysfunction. The contradiction may be attributable to differences in the measures used or the age of the subjects (children in the Arnold and Schwartz study and adults in the Dawson study) but it seems probable that differences in hemispheric lateralization are secondary rather than primary.

Coleman and Gillberg (1985) suggested that the search for an anatomical site may be in vain because of the developing nature of the child's brain, so that what is true at one point of development is no longer true at a more mature stage. Wetherby, Koegel, and Mendel (1981), for instance, showed dysfunction in the left hemisphere (inferred from dichotic tests) only for those subjects who showed echolalia; autistic children who were no longer echolalic had normal test results. Along the same line of argument, Ornitz (1985) discussed the question of developmental shift. "From a developmental perspective, however, the disturbances of sensory modulation and motility appear early, at which time they dominate the clinical scene, and they may have explanatory value in respect to the total behavioral syndrome" (1985, p. 259). The subsequent problems in language and relating would be the consequence of the primary problem of distorted sensory input. The concept that there is a connection between specific symptoms and specific neurophysiological findings may explain the inconsistency of results which are obtained from groups of autistic children who differ in their stage of development.

Biochemical investigations have become increasingly common in all areas of psychopathology and autism is no exception. Several studies have found the neurotransmitter serotonin elevated in about one-third of autistic children, but it is also elevated in about one-third of non-autistic children with severe mental retardation (*British Medical Journal*, 1978) so it does not seem to play a specific role in the genesis of autism. A double-blind study using a drug which lowers blood levels of serotonin (fenfluramine hydrochloride) with 14 autistic children of widely varying ages and IQ's resulted in short-term behavioral improvement (Ritvo, Freeman, Geller, & Yuwiler, 1983) but this awaits further confirmation from a nationwide collaborative study now under way.

Finally, a word should be said about the genetics of autism. The rarity of the condition and the fact that autistic children almost never have children makes it difficult to establish relevant family histories. Nonetheless, Rutter (1985) cited various lines of evidence supporting hereditary influences. About 2% of the siblings of autistic children are also autistic, about 50 times the general prevalence rate (Rutter, 1967). A family history of speech delay is present in about one-quarter of the cases (Bartak, Rutter, & Cox, 1975) and about 15% of the siblings have language disorders, learning disabilities, or mental retardation (August, Stewart, & Tsai, 1981). Folstein and Rutter's (1977) twin study showed a concordance rate of 36% for autism in monozygotic pairs compared with 0% in dizygotic pairs. A later study provided even stronger genetic evidence with a concordance for autism of 95.7% in 23 monozygotic twins and 23.5% in 17 dizygotic twins (Ritvo, Freeman, Mason-Brothers, Mo, & Ritvo, 1985).

Cognitive Characteristics

Quite aside from the general impairment of intelligence, there have been many experimental investigations to fine-tune the nature of the cognitive differences in autistic children. The previously cited work of Ornitz and Ritvo emphasized early differences in perception. Hermelin and O'Connor carried out a number of studies comparing autistic children with other groups and found (a) that the autistic children showed aberrant eye-movement patterns, tending to look more at the background and fixating on stimuli for shorter intervals than either retarded or normal children (O'Connor & Hermelin, 1967) and (b) that autistic children were less responsive to auditory stimuli and more responsive to tactile stimuli (Hermelin & O'Connor, 1970). They concluded that there was impairment of the ability to process and integrate information from various sources. This work ties in with the large body of research concerned with the hypothesis of "stimulus overselectivity." On the basis of a number of learning experiments, Koegel and his colleagues suggested that autistic children respond only to limited cues in a given situation (Lovaas, Koegel, & Schreibman, 1979). Overselectivity is a developmental phenomenon (Hale & Morgan, 1973) and its specificity for autism has been questioned (Prior, 1984). However, the results of a discrimination learning experiment with retarded and autistic groups gave some evidence that autistic children do indeed show more stimulus overselectivity than their retarded counterparts (Frankel, Simmons, Fichter, & Freeman, 1984).

There are parallel difficulties in the interpretation of the linguistic differences. Early research indicated that autistic children memorized random strings of words as effectively as meaningful sentences (Hermelin & O'Connor, 1967, 1970) but in a replication study, Fyffe and Prior (1978) reported that higher functioning autistic children performed at their mental age level in the use of meaning to aid recall. After her review of the experimental cognitive research, Prior suggested

that for very young autistic children basic perceptual processing and organization of input is seriously impaired. For the most severely handicapped these difficulties are never overcome and behaviors remain fixed at a disorganized and immature level. . . .

For the minority, intellectual and language development proceeds quasi-normally, albeit in an idiosyncratic manner, allowing age level achievement in all except key areas of social communicative competence and higher level abstract thinking. (1984, p. 10)

The idiosyncrasies of language usage, for the 50% who gain speech, include I-you pronoun reversal (e.g., "You want candy" meaning "I want candy"), delayed and inappropriate echoing, stereotyped utterances (often some commercial jingles heard on television), and abnormalities of speech rhythm (Fay, 1979; Simmons & Baltaxe, 1975). In their presence, one often feels more like an eavesdropper than a participant. One misses the changes in facial expressions, vocal tone, and gesture which usually accompany social speech (Fay & Schular, 1980; Feldstein, Konstantareas, Oxman, & Webster, 1982). For example, an 8-year-old autistic boy, seemingly totally occupied with writing some numbers, suddenly said "Tie your shoes—tie your shoes—tie your shoes." It took several repetitions before the psychologist understood that he wanted her to tie his shoelaces which were undone, partly because he never once looked down at his shoes. Clearly, in addition to the syntactical problems, there is a serious defect in the pragmatic use of language which reduces its communication values.

Psychosocial Development

The essential mystery of autism has to do with the problem of social relatedness. How do the defects in information processing, even if rooted in one or another biomedical dysfunction, account for the failure in social development? This is apparent at least by the end of the first year of life in the autistic child's failure to imitate or to engage in the common reciprocal games of peek-a-boo and patty-cake, and it is manifest throughout life in the problems of communicating with and understanding others. Here we look at some relatively new experiments in what is often called "social cognition."

One of the most primitive forms of communication is eye contact, and autistic children are commonly described as avoiding eye contact. The normal child uses eye-to-eye gaze as a social signal, looking up at people's faces when he or she wants their attention. Tinbergen and Tinbergen (1972) argued that anxiety and parental pressure resulting in the prevention of social bonding explain the avoidance of eye contact, whereas others have suggested that autistic children avoid mutual gaze to reduce arousal level (Hutt & Ounsted, 1966; Richer & Coss, 1976). If one considers the very early origin of eye-to-eye contact, it seems to evolve from the inborn visual pattern preferences of the infant (See Fagan, Chapter 1). This developmental aberration suggests some support for the perceptual inconstancy hypothesis of Ornitz and Ritvo. If visual inspection of the face yields little information for the child, the child would be expected to look less and less often (O'Connor & Hermelin, 1967). As experimental study with older autistic children adds some corroboration. Langdell (1978) found that both normal and mentally retarded subjects used the upper regions of the face (that is, the eyes) to recognize the faces of their peers, whereas the autistic children found the lower features most helpful and did well or better in recognizing faces which were presented upside down.

Whatever the explanation, therapists have concentrated on eye contact as one of the very first behaviors for intervention (Lovaas, Berberich, Perloff, & Schaeffer, 1966; Risley, 1968). But there is some serious question as to how much eye contact is "normal" in ordinary situations. Close observation of autistic children suggests that they do not avoid eye contact but rather that they do not use it as a social signal, and they do not receive any signals by looking in the eyes (Rutter, 1985). In the observation study of Mirenda, Donellan, and Yoder (1983), they found that the normal and autistic children spent equal time engaged in eye-to-face gaze with an adult, but the autistic children looked more during a monologue than a dialogue interaction. There is no evidence that eye contact is an essential attending behavior for autistic children to learn and therapeutic efforts directed toward a high level of eye contact may be a misguided effort to make these children appear "normal" in the eyes of the beholder.

Looking beyond superficial appearances for evidence of relatedness, Sigman and Ungerer (1984) used Ainsworth's paradigm for studying attachment behaviors (see Chapter 1) to compare 14 autistic children, average age of 52 months, with 14 normal children matched for average mental age (24 months). As a group, the autistic children did show evidence of attachment to their mothers, directing more social behaviors and seeking proximity to their mothers more than to the stranger during the reunion episodes. But, on the other hand, the autistic children showed no obvious distress during separation, so it would be easy to miss the evidence of attachment under ordinary circumstances. With the autistic children, but not with the normal children, there was a relationship between discriminative behavior and representational play with a doll. These authors suggested the possibility that autistic children require more advanced levels of symbolic ability to form attachments to others than is necessary for the development of attachments in normal children, but a case could be made for the reverse relationship, namely, that the presence of selective attachment increased the ability for representational play.

But in any case, it is important for parents to be told that their autistic child does "know" them because it is all too easy for them to feel rejected and meaningless in their child's life. If they then give up trying to engage their child, the autistic child left to his or her own devices becomes even more strange. Several investigators have confirmed the fact that autistic children are more likely to make some sort of social response when social demands on them are increased (Clark & Rutter, 1981; McHale, Simeonsson, Marcus, & Olley, 1980). Some of the differences observed in older autistic children undoubtedly result from differences in parental response.

Many of the autistic symptoms such as pronominal reversal and gaze aversion have been taken as indicating a lack of self-awareness or a failure to distinguish self from nonself. Using the mirror response developed by Lewis and Brooks-Gunn (1979), two separate investigations (Dawson & McKissick, 1984; Ferrari & Matthews, 1983) found that 21 out of a total of 30 autistic children gave evidence of self-recognition by touching their rouge-smeared noses when placed in front of the mirror. Those children who lacked self-recognition showed other developmental deficiencies, such as object permanence, and had mental ages below the developmental level at which self-recognition usually appears. These results suggest that self-recognition deficits are not specific to autism but rather another sign of general developmental delay. There were some qualitative differences, however. The autistic children vocalized less and showed none of the coy self-consciousness frequently seen with normal infants. Apparently seeing themselves in the mirror did not elicit any special affective response. Also, there was no relationship between self-recognition and imitative behavior with 5 of the 13 autistic children performing at the level of 2- to 6-month-old normal infants on the imitative tasks (Dawson & McKissick, 1984). What goes together in normal development seems to be fragmented and separate in autistic children.

This research rules out some simplistic explanations for the social aloofness of retarded children, so there is still no adequate explanation. They see the external figures of people around them and develop preferences, but they do not perceive these people-figures as loving and protecting and they do not incorporate loving behaviors into their own repertoire. Experience teaches them that these people-figures are useful in manipulating the environment (e.g., getting things you want). For some reason, autistic children fail to connect themselves with other people—they do not seem to recognize how they are the same as others and so do not form any identification. This observation explains one useful technique of intervention, namely, that one can often attract the interest of an autistic child by imitating his behavior. They look vaguely surprised to observe the identity of action, look to see who is the agent behind the action, and take cognizance of your presence.

Hobson investigated the autistic child's ability to recognize emotional states (1982). The children (autistic, normal, and mentally retarded) were presented with short videotapes portraying emotions, people, or things and then asked to match these tapes with drawings. Although the groups were the same in matching "things," the autistic children were significantly worse than the normal and retarded children in matching "emotions" and "people." This deserves some further thought for possible intervention. Can autistic children be directed to look at people-figures, study their actions, and find cues for their feelings? Videotaping offers the opportunity to do this at a slow pace, with repetition of the stimuli, and it might be designed as a programmed interactive exercise. This is in contrast to normal living conditions where nothing repeats exactly and autistic children, having once missed the cues, can never catch up.

TREATMENT APPROACHES AND OUTCOME

Follow-up reports are unanimous in finding autistic children continue throughout life to be readily identifiable as "different." But at the same time, there are significant changes in most of them; some improve much more than others, so that as adults there is a wider diversity than as children. All studies have shown that IQ level is the most important single prognostic indicator (Lotter, 1978; Rutter, 1970) and the presence of useful speech by age 5 years augurs well (Eisenberg, 1956).

There have been psychoanalytic reports of individual treatments (Ekstein & Caruth, 1969; Rank, 1955) with definite amelioration of symptoms, usually following intensive work with the parents as well as the child. In contrast, the residential program at the Orthogenic School removes the parents from the therapeutic work and attempts to rebuild the child's personality through "milieu therapy" (Bettelheim, 1979). Bettelheim suggested that the environment should make minimal demands and instead allow the child to regress and express infantile needs so that he or she can discover, at whatever pace he chooses, that he or she is safe and can have an effect on the environment. Bettelheim (1967) reported improvement in 32 of the 40 children he treated at the Orthogenic School, but these reports generated more skepticism than scientific acceptance. Bettelheim offered selected case reports to illustrate treatment, but he did not define the characteristics of his total population and it is a truism to say that the initial characteristics of a group selected for treatment will be a major determinant of the outcome. Nonetheless, these psychodynamically oriented reports illuminate the role played by anxiety in the lives of these children and the need to help them cope with their fears.

Even if one wished to recommend psychoanalysis, the treatment would probably not be available. There are very few trained child psychoanalysts and those few would probably hesitate to devote their limited time to the problematic treatment of an autistic child. Reducing the schedule from daily sessions to weekly sessions, the norm for conventional psychotherapy, would probably reduce the therapeutic value to little or nothing unless it was a part of a comprehensive program. Almost by default, the behavior therapists stepped into the breech.

Ferster (1961) analyzed the behavior of autistic children in terms of deficiencies in reinforcement and demonstrated that autistic children could be taught simple tasks by systematic and meaningful reinforcement (Ferster & DeMyer, 1962). It was a short step from this to the treatment of symptomatic behavior by operant conditioning. In their 1973 review of behavior therapy with autistic children, Lovaas and Koegel stated that every child made measurable progress, even though it was slow and usually not maintained in new situations. The research to that date had focused primarily on the treatment of autistic children in a one-to-one adult-child ratio so that the failure to generalize to other situations was a very limiting feature. The description given by Lovaas and Koegel (1973) of a classroom approach that was instituted at that time illustrates the principles of treatment.

We began working with two children, using one teacher and two teacher aides. The teacher provides commands and instructions and the aides deliver contingent rewards and punishments. As the children become more and more proficient, reinforcement for appropriate behaviors becomes increasingly intermittent and additional children are introduced into the group, one at a time. (Lovaas & Koegel, 1973, p. 254)

Punishment with autistic children has been a controversial topic over the years. Koegel, Rincover, and Egel (1982) defended the use of aversive stimuli such as a sharp slap or electric shock in treating self-injurious or dangerous behavior on the basis of the dire consequences if the behavior continued. On the other hand, there is evidence that the target behavior is suppressed only in the original experimental setting when the therapist is present (Lovaas & Simmons, 1969; Risley, 1968) so it does not help other caretakers. Also, self-injurious behavior may occur in the absence of anything more interesting to do or to avoid excessive external demands. In such cases, it is far preferable, and more effective, to modify the environmental context and thereby reduce the undesired behavior (Carr, Newsom, & Binkoff, 1976). By and large, physical aversive techniques have been employed with nonverbal, retarded autistic children and, of course, coupled with positive primary reinforcers for desirable behaviors. It is obvious that in the hands of untrained persons, aversive techniques have the potential of child abuse, so most institutions and schools have adopted special review procedures for monitoring the rare use of physical or major aversive procedures.

To an ever-increasing extent, special education has assumed the major treatment responsibility. Usually this follows the model described above, although there are differences of opinion as to what behaviors should be targeted for change and what reinforcements are appropriate. Some therapists target deviant behavior which makes the child stand out whereas others ignore such behavior unless it is preventing the acquisition of desired behaviors. Language is a universal goal but techniques vary. Speech therapists have questioned the regular use of primary reinforcers (like food or drink) for speech production, contending that this does not reinforce the communicative use of speech and so has little value outside the speech therapy situation. Particularly with autistic children who have no language, speech therapists have reported success with the use of Total Communication (oral language and manual signed English presented simultaneously). One major advantage to the sign communication system is the feasibility of physically shaping sign responses in a non-imitative child, whereas it is impossible to provide such physical guidance for an oral response (Barrera, Lobato-Barrera, & Sulzer-Azaroff, 1980). There is some controversy as to whether sign language facilitates the further development of speech in autistic children who already have some verbal skills (Carr, 1979).

Rutter and Bartak (1973) made a systematic comparison of the behavioral, social, and scholastic progress of autistic children in three special classes using different methods. There was measurable improvement in behavior and social responsiveness in school and at home with no differences between the groups. For example, initially 40% had been rated as showing "markedly deviant behavior"; 4 years later this was reduced to 20%. Similarly, only 14% initially showed good social responsiveness (as shown by eye-to-eye gaze, play, and facial expression, etc.); in the follow-up, this was increased to 54%. Only those children in the unit with structured cognitive/educational programming showed significantly greater-than-expected scholastic improvement in the 4-year follow-up. Rutter suggested that the beneficial element common to all the programs was the high level of staff-child interaction. Even in the so-called structured unit, it was reported that the Head often took children to the country at weekends, so the teacher's role did not follow the standard classroom mode.

Considering that autistic children characteristically do not generalize from one situation to another, it is not surprising that there has been a steady move towards engaging the parents as cotherapists. Some of these programs have been very demanding of parents' time (Lovaas, 1978) but other programs have been designed to fit into the family's routines. For example, in the Maudsley Hospital home-based treatment project, the parents were asked to spend just 30 minutes per day in individual work with their autistic child. After 18 months, these "experimental" children showed greater all-round improvement than a matched group receiving intermittent outpatient care and whatever was available in the local schools (Hemsley et al., 1978). With few exceptions, the parents adopted the program easily although almost all had difficulty in keeping the daily charts and diaries, and a number complained that workers had too high an expectation of what they could achieve with their child. In the follow-up study, the program mothers felt that their child had improved as a result of the treatment program, but few reported that they were still using the techniques and, in fact, there were no differences between the groups in their perceptions of general improvement after help had ended (Holmes, Hemsley, Rickett, & Likierman, 1982). The authors concluded that the home-based behavioral treatment was far more satisfactory than the usual pattern of help but they recommended that some kind of follow-up support be provided.

A somewhat similar project called TEACCH (Treatment and Education of Autistic and Related Communications Handicapped Children) is a statewide program directed by Schopler and his colleagues at the University of North Carolina School of Medicine. From parent questionnaire responses, Schopler, Mesibov, and Baker (1982) concluded that the parents found the program helpful and that they felt more competent in dealing with their child. It is of interest that reports of improved understanding and enjoyment of the child were more highly correlated with improvement at home than parents' reports that they are learning specific behavior or educational techniques. This is an interesting project from the standpoint of its political-economic base. Autistic children are so few in number that local resources alone generally cannot provide high quality services without a broader base of support. The low incidence also explains why most of the research has been done in a few centers with a concentrated interest.

Many years ago, Eisenberg remarked on the prodigious efforts made both by the school and the parents of those autistic children who had shown the most improvement. "We cannot escape the feeling that the extraordinary consideration extended to these patients was an important factor in the amelioration of their condition" (Eisenberg, 1956, p. 608). Over and over again one is impressed by the ingenuity, devotion, and persistance demonstrated by some parents, and their efforts do have an impact. What autistic children seem to need most of all is someone who keeps trying to connect with them, who responds to their minimal cues, and who continues to act as a bridge to outer reality. The usual candidate for this position is the parent, but it is an unusually demanding job with less than the usual payback. It may well be that the most useful function for the mental health professional is to support and reinforce the parents' efforts rather than to become immersed in direct therapy with the autistic child. However, in order to be truly useful to the parent, one must have an intimate knowledge of the child and maintain some continuity over the years.

DEVELOPMENTAL LANGUAGE DISORDERS

Definition

Primary developmental language disorders should be differentiated from developmental speech disorders which include impairments in the quality, rhythm, and articulation of speech sounds; such common problems as lisp, stuttering, mispronunciations, and so on will not be discussed. Also, we are not considering the kind of relative inferiority in linguistic skills which constitutes a significant subtype in the learning disability category. The focus here is on children whose language delay is of an extreme form and immediately obvious to even a casual observer. These conditions have been called "developmental aphasia," but technically this is not correct since aphasia means loss of language that has already been acquired.

The disorder may be primarily in comprehending oral language (Receptive type) or in expressing verbal language (Expressive type) but these subtypes are not always "pure." Paul and Cohen (1984) reported on 28 children diagnosed with childhood aphasia. At the initial evaluation, when their average age was 6.5 years, most were not speaking at all and the remaining 43% had only one- to two-word sentences. Although the greatest deficit was in expressive language, they all showed 9 months or more delay in receptive language abilities as well, which is more common than not.

Weiner (1986) pointed out that the existence of children with language disorders has been recognized and commented on for over two centuries. His quotation from Coen describes them well:

A child, usually of good, at times blooming appearance, adequate bodily constitution and normal intellectual development, is brought to the speech doctor with the complaint that despite his advanced age (4 to 10 years), he hasn't yet begun to speak. The child hears very well, understands all that is within the scope of his intelligence, complies accurately with instructions that are given to him orally, enjoys excellent health. It is only that he cannot produce any articulated sounds. (Coen, 1886, p. 227)

The assumption of "normal intellectual development" presents some difficulty in definition. In recent years, the general practice has been to set a minimum performance IQ of 85 (Stark & Tallal, 1981), but this seems to be an arbitrary cutoff point. The diagnostic criterion should be a major discrepancy between language level and other intellectual abilities, even if they are below average. For example, the author tested an 8-year-old boy who had never had any speech at all. On the Arthur Performance Test he achieved an IQ of 69 and an IQ of 76 on the Peabody Picture Vocabulary test. At that time he was able to read simple words and understand their meanings; he functioned academically like a first-grader. Clearly the total absence of spoken speech could not be attributed to mental retardation, so the diagnosis of language disorder, expressive type, or developmental apraxia, seemed entirely appropriate. Looking at the problem from the other side, as many as 50% of retarded children show language delays in excess of mental age expectations (Miller, Chapman, & McKenzie, 1981).

However, the lines between developmental language disorder, mental retardation, autism, and learning disability are not finely drawn. In the previously cited study (Paul & Cohen, 1984), half of the childhood aphasics showed social withdrawal, poor or fleeting social relations, and some of the sensory and motor symptoms of autism. In a follow-up study, 8 years later, these "atypical" language development disordered children were indistinguishable from what has been described as "residual autistic states." Although most of the children scored in the retarded range, the four

developmental language disordered children with average IQ's showed the deficits in language organization and word finding which have been described for some learning-disabled children (Wiig & Semel, 1980). Considering the variations in definition, it is not surprising that there are no good figures for prevalence, although DSM III states that preliminary studies indicate a "possible" prevalence rate of .1 to .2% making it a far more common disorder than infantile autism.

John, discussed in Case 13.1, is a good example of the mixed diagnostic picture one frequently encounters. Initially John was considered a case of infantile autism, but a severe language disorder became increasingly evident as he grew older; thus he would be classified as an "atypical developmental language disorder."

Etiology

Language, like all behavior, is a product of brain activity but because of the experience with adult persons who have lost their speech following trauma, the neurological basis has been specified more precisely for language behavior than for social relationships, learning, or general cognitive development. It is assumed that language disorders in normal hearing children are caused by some brain dysfunction. Myklebust (1954) reasoned that childhood aphasia was essentially the same as adult aphasia and resulted from "damage to the brain." However, the "damage" is hard to detect. Standard neurologic examination, including computerized tomography scan and electroencephalogram, rarely yield any

CASE 13.1   John

John's mother initiated the referral when John was 2 years old, stating that since the age of 8 months, he had not progressed emotionally or socially, that he was indifferent to people and did not try to communicate. At 2 years, he would not attempt to feed himself and insisted on baby food. He preferred to be alone, showed no separation distress, and played with cars by the hour, holding them and rocking back and forth. Occasionally he said things like "bye bye," "all gone," and "mama" but out of context. The mother was sure that he was autistic and felt that it happened because she left him in the care of her mother when he was 8 months.

In a special preschool program for atypical children, he showed behavioral changes in having more eye contact, but at the same time becoming more openly negativistic and aggressive. The mother saw these behaviors as signs of progress and accepted them well. The treatment philosophy of the school was essentially developmental, reinforcing his tentative gestures towards relating and communicating with immediacy and warmth. Although he was given a lot of freedom, some of his repetitive behaviors, such as rocking in a play boat, were actively discouraged after due time.

Testing was difficult because he did not imitate nor follow verbal instructions. When he reached 6 years of age, he was at least cooperative. At that time there was a great deal of variation. On the Leiter, he achieved a Performance IQ of 111 and on the Stanford-Binet an IQ of 70. On the Binet, he failed all verbal items at the 7- and 8-year levels but succeeded with copying designs from memory at the 9-year level and counting blocks at the 10-year level.

As time went on, it became clear that John had many fears. For instance, he insisted on sitting in a certain position because "that wall is scary." At a later age, he was obsessed with the idea that all the water in Lake Erie was going to dry up and he was panicked for some time when there was a plumbing leak in his house on the basis that all the water would be gone and everyone would die. Although he remained in regular classes and did average academic work, he suffered a great deal because of teasing from the other children, which peaked during the 10th grade.

As a young adult, John had difficulty holding a job because of the strange things he said and his misinterpretation of what was said to him. For example, in one job application interview, the interviewer stood and said "Thank you for coming," which John did not understand as a signal that he should depart. At age 23, he was given the Wechsler Adult Intelligence Scale where he achieved a Verbal IQ of 93, Performance IQ of 87, and Full Scale IQ of 89. However, within these scales he showed unusual test scatter. He had perfect memory for digits, exceptional skill with block design, and above average arithmetic score, but items requiring some social knowledge (comprehension and picture arrangement) were far below average.

Almost by chance, a modified "happy ending" came about for John. He went to live with his father (divorced) who was a somewhat inept schizoid personality, where he essentially "kept house" and helped his father and brothers by doing odd jobs for them. John was finally content in a situation where he knew what he should do and where he was surrounded by familiar people who understood his limitations.

positive findings. Compared with other language disorders, children with expressive aphasia, or apraxia, show more neurological findings in poor balance, motor coordination, and failure to develop strong laterality (Aram & Glasson, 1979; Marquardt, Dunn, & Davis, 1985).

The attribution of language disorder to brain dysfunction does little to explain the origin. Marquardt, Dunn, and Davis described our state of ignorance as follows: "We do not know whether the disorder is due to early acquired neuropathology or a congenital (developmental) failure in brain maturation. We also do not know whether the neural dysfunction is bilateral or unilateral, focal or diffuse" (1985, p. 118). One would expect that the "problem" would have to be both bilateral and diffuse since normally the infant brain is capable of compensating for impaired function, if it is localized (Hecaen, 1976; Lenneberg, 1967). However, although both hemispheres have the capability to assume language processing functions, they are not equal in their ability to do so and language processing is organized predominantly in the left cerebral hemisphere even in young children. It has been suggested that the greater incidence of language disorders in boys may be because boys have earlier and more confined specialization for language and other higher cortical functions and so less plasticity than girls (Witelson, 1976). There has been some indirect evidence of a genetic basis because of the preponderance of males and the family histories for speech, language and learning disorders (Aram & Glasson, 1979). Despite a lot of theoretical speculation, there is no good answer to the question "why."

Assessment

There is a bewildering array of published tests to measure various aspects of language comprehension and expression; Aram and Nation (1982) listed 60 of these and there are probably more. Most of these measures target isolated segments of language in an effort to pinpoint a specific deficiency for remediation. The very choice of which tests to use indicates some preliminary diagnostic judgment, which in turn must rest on some theoretical model of language development which goes beyond a simple medical disease type label.

Psycholinguistic studies of normal speech development (Chomsky, 1965) provided one such model. With this model, one examines the four major parameters of phonological development in auditory discrimination and articulation, semantic development in understanding meaning, syntactical development in learning the grammatical rules, and finally, the understanding of pragmatics, which is the understanding of the social usage of language in different contexts (Bates, 1976). This was closely followed by an information processing model with particular emphasis on disruption in auditory processing or decoding. Eisenson (1972) considered this to be the major problem for aphasic children.

Many workers in the field of language pathology found this explanation insufficient and offered expanded multistage processing models. One example is the Child Language Processing Model proposed by Aram and Nation (1982). This is composed of three major processing segments, "viewed as a series of continuous and overlapping transductions needed to receive, comprehend, integrate, repeat, formulate and produce messages" (Aram & Nation, 1982, p. 41). The first segment is "Intake," decoding what is heard into meaningful language. The second is central processing of this language with semantic and pragmatic understanding, and the third is "output" or formulating and producing verbal response. Each of these segments can be analyzed into constituent components. For instance, in the intake phase, Aram and Nation identified five basic auditory operations: auditory attention, auditory discrimination, auditory rate, auditory memory, and auditory sequencing.

The second phase involves what is loosely called "comprehension." Some children can understand the object nouns but cannot understand verb forms, or fail to follow the meaning of full sentences particularly if they have a complicated syntax. Further, the child must integrate the meaning of what has been heard with previous experience and with contextual cues. This leads to an interpretation of meaning so that the words are not necessarily taken literally. Aram and Nation (1982) suggested that echolalic children process what they hear at a very low level, so that the resultant production is nothing more than a repetition of the original perception. The final phase of language formulation involves the selection and retrieval of words and the organization of these words into a logically and syntactically acceptable form. This model is attractive because of its comprehensiveness and if nothing else, it indicates there are many points of possible breakdown in the acts of listening, understanding and speaking.

Intervention and Outcome

Language therapies vary along several dimensions such as amount of formal structure and the degree to which the therapy tries to recapitulate normal speech development versus a "difference" approach. One of the earliest therapy programs is the "elements-Association Method" (McGinnis, 1963). This is a highly structured approach which attempted to compensate for deficits thought to be specific to the aphasic child: (a) that there is no general deficiency in integrating sensory experience, particularly visual perception; (b) that the deficiency is primarily restricted to learning "symbolic handles" for naming experiences; and (c) that a deficiency in auditory memory prevents the usual association of sound (the spoken word) with an appropriate object or action.

Accordingly, the McGinnis method starts with written language, broken down into elements of sound which the child learns to say with the help of all kinds of visual clues, such as different colors, exaggerated mouth movements, and hand gestures. After memorizing the sounds that go with letters, they are blended into combinations and words. These words, in turn, are associated with pictures of real objects. Thus, the child learns to talk by first learning to read and then learns to attach meaning to the written words by means of pictures. The sequence is the reverse of the usual acquisition of langauge, in which reading and writing follow speech.

Eisenson's approach was somewhat similar, based on the hypothesis that aphasic children have auditory perceptual problems. Phonemic discrimination and sequencing form the basis of this program (Eisenson, 1972). Sequential activities are provided from first discriminating environmental, mechanical, and animate noises to more and more complex sequences of consonant-vowel combinations. Other quite different programs evolved from the linguistic-psycholinguistic orientation, often emphasizing the syntactical aspects of language (Trantham & Pederson, 1976). The development of the Illinois Test of Psycholinguistic Abilities (Kirk, McCarthy, & Kirk, 1968) led to treatment programs directed to one or another of the processes identified in the ITPA. The meta-analysis of the pooled results of 34 individual training studies indicated modest but significant positive results especially when the ITPA was used as the outcome measure (Kavale, 1981). However, these psycholinguistic therapies are appropriate mainly to expand language for those children who already have some rudiments.

In recent years, interest has shifted to the pragmatics of communication. Miller (1978) presented a program developed from a pragmatic orientation which emphasized child-centered play activities rather than clinician-directed activities. The clinician's goal is to develop an interactive relationship with the child and model communicative behavior within this context. As pointed out by Aram and Nation (1982), this is not unlike the "natural language approach" advanced by Myklebust (1954), which was relatively unstructured and intended to take place in a "natural" situation. Consistent with the trends in dealing with other handicapping conditions, there has been an ever-increasing involvement of parents, teachers, and peers in the therapeutic effort (Berry, 1980; Muma, 1978). All in all, speech therapists have moved to leave the structured office training in favor of language stimulation in natural settings by building on the spontaneous communication efforts of the child.

However, the apraxic child with reasonably good comprehension and no speech utterance still presents special problems requiring special efforts. For this group, one usually starts with drill on imitating tongue and lip movements, repetition of single sounds, associating rhythm, intonation, and stress with motor activity, and proceeding from simple elements to more complex forms (Macaluso-Haynes, 1978). For children who had no speech as well as for those who seem to understand very little, Total Communication represents a useful approach. Total Communication offers an alternate input channel (visual) as well as an alternate output (manual versus vocal).

The evidence on treatment effectiveness indicates that progress following intervention exceeds what would be expected by maturational gains alone (Leonard, 1981). Attempts to compare various treatment strategies have not shown that any one technique is clearly superior (Friedman & Friedman, 1980); Leonard pointed out that the skills necessary for everyday communicative interaction, such as conversational turn taking, have not been the focus of language training studies so it is not clear that language training enhances the language-impaired child's ability to communicate in the world around him. The wise speech therapist chooses from all the suggested programs for intensive training of the individual child and also works to improve communication at home, at school, and with friends. It does not come as any surprise that follow-up studies indicate that those children who are initially the most handicapped are also most deviant at later ages. Aram, Ekelman, and Nation (1984) reported on 20 adolescents who had been diagnosed 10 years earlier as "language disordered." Of these, 4 were in classes for the mildly mentally retarded, 11 had been tutored, retained, or classified as learning disabled, and 5 had progressed through regular education. The majority were rated by their parents as being less socially competent and having more behavioral problems than their peers. The IQ score from the preschool Leiter International Performance Scale was a strong predictor of later academic and intellectual performance (correlation of .50) which again is no surprise. Although the essential relationships will probably stay the same, we do not know if the present state-of-the-art in language therapy will improve the future attainment levels beyond that reported in the past.

ATYPICAL CHILDREN WITH SPECIAL ABILITIES

We conclude this section with some discussion of atypical children who demonstrate special abilities in the context of generally deviant development. There have been well-publicized cases of "calendar calculators" (Smith, 1983) whose ability to give the day of the week for any past or future calendar date cannot be matched by persons of normal intelligence, with or without special math-

ematical skills. Sacks (1985) described his encounter with twins who had been variously diagnosed as autistic, psychotic, or retarded but who could immediately "see" that 111 matches had fallen on the floor without counting! Further, he described their intense pleasure in number games, discovering prime numbers of 6, 7, 8, and 9 digits. In no way could they explain what they were doing or how they accomplished these numerical feats. (John, described in case 13.1, also showed a passion for numbers and could be absorbed writing them, adding them, multiplying, and so on, although he showed no astronomical calculations.) There have also been some recorded instances of exceptional musical and artistic abilities in autistic children (Selfe, 1977; Viscott, 1970).

In a postscript to a case report of an "idiot savant," Scheerer, Rothman, and Goldstein (1945) attempted to explain the existence of such isolated but exceptional talents. Their case, a boy with an IQ of 50, had remarkable musical aptitude and could calculate calendar dates but was "lacking in social awareness" and could not learn in a normal way. After many years of observation and study, the authors concluded that his various deficiencies were the result of a general impairment of abstract capacity. His precocities were interpreted as a result of the channeling of energy and the development of special abilities through extraordinary practice. Having so little outlet for self-expression and a sense of mastery, this child concentrated all his energies on those limited skills which were relatively intact. Although the powers of concrete imagery and memory are undoubtedly enhanced by practice, this does not seem a sufficient explanation for these islands of re-markable abilities.

Hyperlexia, the precocious ability of a child to recognize written words far above his or her language capabilities and reading comprehension, is a special ability which occurs with some frequency in language-disordered and autistic children. From a review of the records of 155 children diagnosed with infantile autism, Whitehouse and Harris (1984) identified 52 as hyperlexic. Silberberg and Silberberg (1967) described 28 children whose ability to recognize words was significantly better than either comprehension of material read or overall verbal functioning and coined the term "hyperlexia." Although there was a wide range of intellectual functioning, half had been diagnosed as retarded or atypical in development. This was followed by other reports of children who spontaneously learned this kind of reading before the age of 5 years (Huttenlocher & Huttenlocher, 1973; Mehegan & Dreifus, 1972).

Needleman (1982) specified the characteristics of the syndrome of hyperlexia as: (a) occurrence in a developmentally disabled population, (b) early manifestation, as early as age 2, but by age 5, (c) self-generated onset in the absence of specific instruction, (d) a driven, compulsive quality, an (e) word recognition ability that is higher than predicted on the basis of intelligence. Of course, by including the criterion of developmental disability as part of the definition, one would expect that further reports will emphasize the co-occurrence of such conditions. The preponderance of boys to girls is in the order of 10 to 1 and this fact, plus the occasional occurrence of two in the same family (one such instance is known to the author), suggests some genetic basis.

Often the child's ability to name letters and call out words at the age of 3 or 4 years is taken as ipso facto evidence that he or she is intellectually gifted despite deficiencies in language usage and reasoning. A follow-up study of 21 hyperlexic children showed that hyperlexia is no respector of intelligence (Graziani, Brodsky, Mason, & Zager, 1983). Eight scored in the average range (mean IQ 92); 7 in the mildly retarded range (mean IQ 65); and 6 in the moderately retarded range (mean IQ 39). Of the average-scoring children, 4 were doing well despite the delayed language and abnormal behavior in the preschool period and 4 showed conspicuously atypical behavior.

Despite offhand comments by observers that the child "must be a genius," most parents of hyperlexic children are uneasy about the precocious reading and recognize it as deviant. In Healy's (1982) report of interviews with parents, the parents described exceptional memory for unusual features of events. One child called people by their street numbers instead of their names; another recited long sections of scripture verbatim, with particular attention to chapter and verse numbers. Several parents were puzzled by inconsistences such as recalling hotel room numbers from 3 years before and lengthy dictionary definitions of animals, but being unable to master the pattern of opening a car door. Characteristically, the children are attracted by numbers and letters to the exclusion of meaning. They would rather read the Yellow Pages than a story book, and pictures are of much less interest than the fine print. It would be a mistake to explain the exceptional reading ability on the basis of parental pressure or reinforcement; the hyperlexic child's motivation to read seems to be intrinsically determined.

Whitehouse and Harris (1984) suggested that hyperlexia results from good audiovisual association and good memory, with a basic compulsion directed toward written material. Closer inspection of the cognitive functioning of 12 hyperlexic children indicated superior skills in verbal and numerical memory, particularly for nonmeaningful strings. Their performance was inferior when required to create organizational patterns or to utilize relational or abstract thinking. Also, they consistently failed to demonstrate age-appropriate solutions of Piagetian tasks involving seriation or conservation (Healy, Aram, Horwitz, & Kessler, 1982). Linguistically, these children had a high degree of phonological and syntactical accuracy in reading and repetition but were severely limited in their ability to understand or generate meaningful language. In reading ability, 7 of the 12 still showed extraordinary ability to decode both familiar and unfamiliar words while 5 were superior only in relation to their other cognitive abilities. And, as expected, their ability to extract any meaning from what they read was very limited.

Apparently, these children process visual stimuli at a very low level, content to translate the visual presentation into an auditory production. From a very early age, letters and words seem to "say" something to them in sounds but not in meaning. Their fascination and absorption in mastering this code may in part stem from the confusion they experience in regard to oral language and the unpredictable, for them, behavior of people, as suggested by Scheerer, Rothman, and Goldstein (1945). Observations of this unusual group confirm the two-stage process of learning to read and give considerable support to the hypothesis that the decoding difficulty of dyslexic children is a specific neurologically based handicap.

Although speech therapists and special educators play the major role in intervention for these children, there is also a place for the psychotherapist. In these cases, psychotherapy is not designed to root out the causes and "cure" the child, but rather to provide someone who understands, cares, and helps the child to understand the perplexities of his world. The psychotherapist not only augments what the parents do but also supports them in living with the child and in their search for appropriate services. Case 13.2 was seen by the author in once-weekly therapy for some 3 years and followed intermittently after the family moved out of town.

OTHER NEUROLOGICAL AND NEUROMUSCULAR HANDICAPS

There are many other neurological conditions, to be mentioned only briefly because the diagnosis and treatment is basically the responsibility of the physician. However, there are adjustment problems associated with neurological handicaps, both as a part of the underlying neurological dysfunction and as a secondary reaction to the handicap. Hartlage and Hartlage (1986) mentioned some of the behavioral concomitants

CASE 13.2.   Donald

Donald was first seen when he was 3½ years old. He was described as having some autistic features such as stereotypic motor behavior and poor communication skills. He showed some minor physical abnormalities, namely, hypospadias and "toe walking" from tight heel cords (later surgically corrected), and a restricted form of hyperactivity (rocking back and forth). At that time his Stanford-Binet IQ was 72 but he clearly demonstrated the ability to read letters, numbers, and some words. For instance, during the neurological examination, he repetitively read the title of a book on the doctor's desk.

Autism was not considered an appropriate diagnosis because he had a strong relationship with his mother. When he started a special preschool, he showed a great deal of separation distress and it was about 2 months before he could comfortably leave his mother who until that time remained in the building. Individual therapy was started when he was 7 years and had been attending public school for 1 year. For some time the focus was on his anxieties and his defense of non-stop talking. He was fearful about any new thing and needed to rehearse in advance for any change in his routine. He was preoccupied with possible dangers (tornados, germs, fires, electric wires, floods) and comforted himself with reiterations of what must be done to "keep safe."

As time went on, Donald's concerns shifted to more realistic events. He was always intent on doing "good" and being "good." He was genuinely puzzled and frightened by the "bad" behavior of other children although he once said he wished he knew "how to be bad." Often he repeated what had happened in school or on television, faithful to every detail. The therapist learned that usually there was a "why" question hidden in these recounts which he did not know how to ask and would try to answer his unspoken question.

As he approached adolescence, his questions became more clear, centering on what was wrong with him and why did children tease him. These questions were very hard to answer to his satisfaction. Particularly, he could not understand why he was the target of so much teasing. One interchange with the therapist provides a good example of his lack of social comprehension. He had told me a joke, I laughed, and then he repeated the joke many times. It was necessary to explain that I did not keep on laughing because I was no longer surprised. His stereotypic motor behaviors continued and often made him conspicuous. He made efforts to control these habits, but when left to his own devices, they returned. At age 14 years, when he made a visit from out of town, I was surprised that he chose to sit in the back seat of my car but then I observed from the rearview mirror that he was "twiddling" with a piece of string. He would no longer do this when he thought I was watching, but the desire was still the same.

Educational placement was a never-ending problem because he did not fit any of the categories. When he was mainstreamed, his behavior made teachers and children nervous, and he was unhappy. In the program for emotionally disturbed children, he was extremely anxious about their behavior. Academically he was too advanced for the retarded classes; his progress in learning disabilities classrooms was not considered sufficient for him to stay. At age 14 years, he achieved a WISC Verbal IQ of 79; a Performance IQ of 71 and a Full Scale IQ of 73, remarkably close to the original Binet IQ of 72. He was "over-achieving" on the Wide

Range Achievement Test with a Reading grade equivalent of 8.7; Spelling Grade Equivalent of 10.5 and Arithmetic Grade Equivalent of 5.7. In high school he was placed in a classroom with mildly retarded children where he seemed most comfortable

and enjoyed his obvious superiority. This was a difficult step for the parents to take because his other problems had always taken priority in their attention and they had never thought of him as "mentally retarded."

---

often associated with epilepsy, such as attention deficit disorders, academic underachievement, and, as adults, a high rate of unemployment which is out of proportion to the severity of the handicap. The possible reasons include overprotectiveness and the fear of others about seizures, the child's own feelings about "brain damage," and possible effects of long-term therapy with anticonvulsant medication.

Data from a large longitudinal study, the Collaborative Perinatal Project of the National Institute of Neurological and Communicative Disorders, confirm the observation that, as a group, children with seizure disorders have lower scores on intelligence tests than other children, but that is because seizures and retardation are often concurrent symptoms of an underlying neurological abnormality. Ellenberg, Hirtz, and Nelson (1986) found that for those children without prior neurological difficulties, the occurrence of seizures did not cause any intellectual change. However, there is evidence that antiepileptic medication can impair cognitive performance (Hirtz & Nelson, 1985; Trimble & Thompson, 1983) so it is important to monitor this medication and maintain as low a dose as possible.

In contrast to the hidden nature of epilepsy, the motor handicaps of children with cerebral palsy are immediately apparent. Although there is a higher incidence of mental retardation in this group, roughly 75% are *not* mentally retarded (Hartlage & Hartlage, 1986). Many special devices have been developed to stimulate normal or inhibit abnormal movements; electronic communicators have been developed for those whose speech muscles are involved. Happily, the incidence of cerebral palsy has diminished. Most of the decrease is due to a diminished incidence of one form, namely spastic diplegia, and this can be explained as the result of improvements in the care of prematurely born infants.

Another very different neuromuscular disease is muscular dystrophy, which typically appears around 5 years and then is progressive. This is a painful situation both for family and child as they battle against the worsening of the handicap. In the most common form (Duchenne type muscular dystrophy), most children are no longer able to walk independently by 10 years. With further weakening, eventually the respiratory muscles become involved and there is a great risk of death from pneumonia. There has been some argument as to whether intellectual impairment is part of the disease, because IQ tests are usually below the scores of their parents and siblings (Dubowitz, 1978). Others have felt that this is an artifact or temporary situation, reflecting the fatiguability and depressed states of these children (Mearig, 1979; 1985). Sollee, Latham, Kindlon, and Bresnan (1985) suggested that boys with Duchenne muscular dystrophy do not suffer from a fixed, global, cognitive deficit since relatively higher language and attention-organizational skills are found in the older boys compared with the younger boys. Longitudinal studies and research exploring the specific nature of the often-cited verbal deficits are needed. Discovery of the pathogenesis of the disease itself also may contribute to the understanding of intellectual functioning. In any event, it is essential that these children participate as fully as possible in school and other normal activities.

Perhaps the most puzzling of these conditions is Gilles de la Tourette's syndrome, which is manifest by involuntary tics like eye blinking, grimacing, or head tossing, usually appearing between the ages of 4 and 10 years. Approximately half will have verbal as well as motor tics, which vary from soft grunts to loud barks, or even swear words and obscenities. The differentiation of this syndrome from a simple tic may be difficult at times because there is no independent test. Childhood tics reported in surveys of "normal" school children have indicated that 10 to 12% have shown tic-like mannerisms at one time or another (Lapouse & Monk, 1958; Macfarlane, Allen, & Honzik, 1954). Generally these are single tics in contrast to the multiple tics of Gilles de la Tourette's syndrome, and they disappear spontaneously in contrast to the persistence into adulthood of Tourette's disease.

The cause of Tourette's disease is not known, although there has been some speculation based on the fact that haloperidol (Haldol) is often effective in ameliorating the symptoms. Since Haldol acts to block dopamine receptors, the condition may be the result of overactivity in the dopaminergic systems. Haldol can have an undesirable sedative effect so physicians try to find the minimum dosage which will bring relief. This is an embarrassing condition, not easily understood by others, and in rare instances it may progress to a psychotic-like condition with little behavioral control. But all Tourette children and their families need support and acceptance so that they can lead a normal life.

SUMMARY AND PERSONAL PERSPECTIVE

This chapter has chiefly dealt with serious and persistent problems which are primarily caused by neurological dysfunctions, but the problems are manifest in the psychological domains of thinking, communicating, relating, and so on. The diagnosis is determined more by observation and psychological assessment than by physical tests. These are truly organic problems, but even with what looks like the same organic difficulty, the children are different, both from one another and at different points in their development. Even the most handicapped child can learn something, and one must take care that the diagnostic label is not used as an excuse for doing nothing.

We have tried to make it clear that the conditions of mental retardation, infantile autism, and developmental language disorder are overlapping and that different diagnoses may be appropriate for the same child at different times in his life. Although these conditions are apparent in the preschool years, often it is only in retrospect that one gets the whole picture. The diagnosis should be a working diagnosis which leads the way for immediate educational or psychological intervention without a long-term commitment to a single mode of treatment.

Rarely is a diagnosis by itself of any help to a parent. Understandably, the parent wants to know what to do and the person interpreting the diagnostic findings must be ready to offer practical suggestions. There are usually specialized resources in the community as well as parent groups who can offer technical support. Faced with any of these handicapping conditions, the parents have to modify their expectations but at the same time maintain their parenting role. The parents have many special decisions to make about discipline, pushing to the next developmental step, trying special therapies, educational placement, social activities, allowance for autonomy and independence, etc. At the same time they have their own needs and usually siblings to consider. The parent counselor should not presume to know all the answers but rather should seek to help the parents find what works best for them in their situation.

Professional workers in the field of rehabilitation have long been aware of the importance of social and psychologic factors in the life adjustment of people with handicaps. In treating, teaching, or rearing handicapped children, one tries constantly to distinguish between the limitations imposed by the reality of the handicap and the functional overlay—often a very difficult task. It is a truism to say that a handicapped child is a child first and handicapped second, but in practice, that means that the child is subject to the same anxieties experienced by any child growing up. These children have special problems in expressing their thoughts or feelings, so one must be particularly sensitive and empathic, perhaps "guessing" more about their feelings than one would with children of normal intelligence and language skills. As these children approach adolescence, they will have many questions about their future, not unlike the questions the parents asked many years earlier.

These children have mental health needs which are all too often overlooked in the concentrated focus on training or educating them in particular behaviors. Mental health professionals do not happily accept such cases for many reasons. Often, they feel ill-informed about the particular condition or feel it is "hopeless." Sometimes one feels that the psychotherapy is essentially the "purchase of friendship," but that is exactly what these children need the most. The case is never closed with handicapped children, not because intervention was a failure, but because they change over time and face new issues in real life.

REFERENCES

ALLEN, J., DeMYER, M., NORTON, J., PONTIUS, W., & YANG, E. (1971). Intellectuality in parents of psychotic, subnormal and normal children. *Journal of Autism and Childhood Schizophrenia, 1,* 311–326.

ARAM, D. M., EKELMAN, B., & NATION, J. (1984). Preschoolers with language disorders: Ten years later. *Journal of Speech and Hearing Research, 18,* 229–241.

ARAM, D. M., & GLASSON, C. (1979). *Developmental apraxia of speech*. Mini-seminar presented at the Annual Convention of the American Speech-Language and Hearing Association, Atlanta, Ga.

ARAM, D. M., & NATION, J. E. (1982). *Child language disorders*. St. Louis, MO: C. V. Mosby.

ARNOLD, G., & SCHWARTZ, S. (1983). Hemispheric lateralization of language in autistic and aphasic children. *Journal of Autism and Developmental Disorders, 13,* 129–139.

AUGUST, G. J., STEWART, M. A., & TSAI, L. (1981). The incidence of cognitive disabilities in the siblings of autistic children. *British Journal of Psychiatry, 138,* 416–422.

BARRERA, R. D., LOBATO-BARRERA, D., & SULZER-AZAROFF, B. (1980). A simultaneous treatment comparison of three expressive language training programs with a mute autistic child. *Journal of Autism and Developmental Disorders, 10,* 21–37.

BARTAK, L., & RUTTER, M. (1976). Differences between mentally retarded and normally intelligent autistic children. *Journal of Autism and Childhood Schizophrenia, 6,* 109–120.

BARTAK, L., RUTTER, M., & COX, A. (1975). A comparative study of infantile autism and specific developmental receptive language disorder: I. The children. *British Journal of Psychiatry, 126,* 127–145.

BATES, E. (1976). *Language and context: The acquisition of pragmatics*. New York: Academic Press.

BEMPORAD, J. R. (1979). Adult recollections of a formerly autistic child. *Journal of Autism and Developmental Disorders, 9,* 179–197.

BERGMAN, P., & ESCALONA, S. K. (1949). Unusual sensitivities in very young children. In A. Freud, H. Hartmann, & E. Kris (Eds.), *The psychoanalytic study of the child* (Vol. 3/4, pp. 333–352). New York: International Universities Press.

BERRY, M. F. (1980). *Teaching linguistically handicapped children*. Englewood Cliffs, NJ: Prentice-Hall.

BETTELHEIM, B. (1967). *The empty fortress*. New York: Free Press.

BETTELHEIM, B., & SANDERS, J. (1979). Milieu Therapy: The Orthogenic School model. In J. D. Noshpitz (Ed.), *Basic handbook of child psychiatry* (Vol. III, pp. 216–230). New York: Basic Books.

British Medical Journal. (1978). Editorial: Serotonin, platelets and autism. *1,* 1651–1652.

CARR, E. G. (1979). Teaching autistic children to use sign language: Some research issues. *Journal of Autism and Developmental Disorders, 9,* 345–360.

CARR, E. G., NEWSOM, C. D., & BINKOFF, J. A. (1978). Stimulus control of self-destructive behavior in a psychotic child. *Journal of Abnormal Child Psychology, 4,* 139–153.

CHOMSKY, N. (1965). *Aspects of the theory of syntax*. Cambridge, MA: MIT Press.

CLARK, P., & RUTTER, M. (1981). Autistic children's responses to structure and to interpersonal demands. *Journal of Autism and Developmental Disorders, 11,* 201–217.

COEN, R. (1886). *Pathologie und Therapie der Sprachanomalien*. Vienna: Urban & Schwarzenberg.

COLEMAN, M., & GILLBERG, C. (1985). *The biology of the autistic syndromes*. New York: Praeger.

COX, A., RUTTER, M., NEWMAN, S., & BARTAK, L. (1975). A comparative study of infantile autism and specific developmental receptive language disorders: II. Parental characteristics. *British Journal of Psychiatry, 126,* 146–159.

CREAK, M. E., & INI, S. (1960). Families of psychotic children. *Journal of Child Psychology and Psychiatry, 1,* 156–175.

DAWSON, G. (1983). Lateralization brain dysfunction in autism: Evidence from the Halstead-Reitan neuropsychological battery. *Journal of Autism and Developmental Disorders, 13,* 269–286.

DAWSON, G., & McKISSICK, F. C. (1984). Self-recognition in autistic children. *Journal* of Autism and Developmental Disorders, 14, 383–394.

DAWSON, G., WARRENBURG, S., & FULLER, P. (1982). Cerebral lateralization in individuals diagnosed as autistic in early childhood. *Brain and Language, 15,* 353–368.

DEYKIN, E. Y., & MACMAHON, B. (1979). The incidence of seizures among children with autistic symptoms. *American Journal of Psychiatry, 136,* 1310–1312.

DEMYER, M. K. (1975). Research in infantile autism: A strategy and its results. *Biological Psychiatry, 10,* 433–452.

DEMYER, M. K., BARTON, U., ALPERN, G. D., KIMBERLIN, C., ALLEN, J., YANG, E., & STEELE, R. (1974). The measured intelligence of autistic children. *Journal of Autism and Childhood Schizophrenia, 4,* 42–60.

Developmental Disabilities Act of 1984. (September 25, 1984). USC Report 98–1074.

DUBOWITZ, V. (1978). *Muscle disorders in childhood.* Philadelphia: Saunders.

EISENBERG, L. (1956). The autistic child in adolescence. *American Journal of Psychiatry, 112,* 607–612.

EISENSON, J. (1972). *Aphasia in children.* New York: Harper & Row.

EKSTEIN, R., & CARUTH, E. (1969). Levels of verbal communication in the schizophrenic child's struggle against, for, and with the world of objects. In R. S. Eissler, H. Hartmann, A. Freud, & M. Kris (Eds.), *The psychoanalytic study of the child* (Vol. 24, pp. 115–137). New York: International Universities Press.

ELLENBERG, J. H., HIRTZ, D. G., & NELSON, K. B. (1986). Do seizures in children cause intellectual deterioration? *New England Journal of Medicine, 314,* 1085–1088.

ESMAN, A. H. (1983). The "stimulus barrier." A review and reconsideration. In A. J. Solnit, R. S. Eissler, & P. B. Neubauer (Eds.), *The psychoanalytic study of the child* (Vol. 38, pp. 193–208). New Haven: Yale University Press.

ESMAN, A., KOHN, M., & NYMAN, L. (1959). The family of the schizophrenic child. *American Journal of Orthopsychiatry, 29,* 455–460.

FAY, W. H. (1979). Personal pronouns and the autistic child. *Journal of Autism and Childhood Schizophrenia, 9,* 247–260.

FAY, W. H., & SCHULAR, A. L. (1980). *Emerging language in autistic children.* London: Arnold.

FELDSTEIN, S., KONSTANTAREAS, M., OXMAN, J., & WEBSTER, C. D. (1982). The chronography of interaction with autistic speakers: An initial report. *Journal of Communication Disorders, 15,* 451–460.

FERRARI, M., & MATTHEWS, W. S. (1983). Self-recognition deficits in autism: Syndrome-specific or general developmental delay? *Journal of Autism and Developmental Disorders, 13,* 317–323.

FERSTER, C. B. (1961). Positive reinforcement and behavioral deficits of autistic children. *Child Development, 32,* 437–456.

FERSTER, C. B., & DEMYER, M. (1962). A method for the experimental analysis of the behavior of autistic children. *American Journal of Orthopsychiatry, 32,* 89–98.

FOLSTEIN, S., & RUTTER, M. (1977). Infantile autism: A genetic study of 21 twin pairs. *Journal of Child Psychology and Psychiatry, 18,* 297–321.

FRANKEL, F., SIMMONS, J. Q., FICHTER, M., & FREEMAN, B. J. (1984). Stimulus overselectivity in autistic and mentally retarded children—a research note. *Journal of Child Psychology and Psychiatry, 25,* 147–155.

FREUD, S. (1920/1955). *Beyond the pleasure principle.* In J. Strachey (Ed.), *Standard edition* (Vol. 18, pp. 7–64). London: The Hogarth Press.

FRIEDMAN, P., & FRIEDMAN, K. (1980). Accounting for individual differences when comparing the effectiveness of remedial language teaching methods. *Applied Psycholinguistics, 1,* 151–170.

FYFFE, C., & PRIOR, M. (1978). Evidence for language encoding in autistic, retarded, and normal children: A re-examination. *British Journal of Psychology, 49,* 393–402.

GILLBERG, C. (1984). Infantile autism and other childhood psychoses in a Swedish urban region: Epidemiological aspects. *Journal of Child Psychology and Psychiatry, 25*, 35–43.

GRAZIANI, L. J., BRODSKY, K., MASON, J. C., & ZAGER, R. P. (1983). Variability in IQ scores and prognosis of children with hyperlexia. *Journal of the American Academy of Child Psychiatry, 22*, 441–443.

HALE, G. A., & MORGAN, J. S. (1973). Developmental trends in children's component selection. *Journal of Experimental Child Psychology, 15*, 302–314.

HARTLAGE, P. L., & HARTLAGE, L. C. (1986). Epilepsy and other neurological and neuromuscular handicaps. In R. T. Brown & C. R. Reynolds (Eds.), *Psychological perspectives on childhood exceptionality* (pp. 640–666). New York: John Wiley.

HEALY, J. M. (1982). The enigma of hyperlexia. *Reading Research Quarterly, 17*, 319–338.

HEALY, J. M., ARAM, D. M., & HURWITZ, S. J., & KESSLER, J. W. (1982). A study of hyperlexia. *Brain and Language, 17*, 1–23.

HECAEN, H. (1976). Acquired aphasia in children and the ontogensis of hemispheric functional specialization. *Brain and Language, 3*, 114–134.

HEMSLEY, R., HOWLIN, P., BERGER, M., HERSOV, L., HOLBROOK, D., RUTTER, M., & YULE, W. (1978). Training autistic children in a family context. In M. Rutter & E. Schopler (Eds.), *Autism: A reappraisal of concepts and treatment* (pp. 378–411). New York: Plenum.

HERMELIN, B., & O'CONNOR, N. (1967). Remembering of words by psychotic and subnormal children. *British Journal of Psychology, 58*, 213–218.

HERMELIN, B., & O'CONNOR, N. (1970). *Psychological experiments with autistic children.* Oxford, England: Pergamon Press.

HIRTZ, D. G., & NELSON, K. B. (1985). Cognitive effects of antiepileptic drugs. In T. A. Pedley & B. S. Meldrum (Eds.), *Recent advances in epilepsy* (pp. 161–181). New York: Churchill Livingstone.

HOBSON, R. P. (1982). *The autistic child's concept of persons.* Proceedings of the 1981 International Conference on Autism, Boston. (D. Park, Ed.). Washington, DC: National Society for Children and Adults with Autism.

HOLMES, N., HEMSLEY, R., RICKETT, J., & LIKIERMAN, H. (1982). Parents as co-therapists: Their perceptions of a home-based behavioral treatment for autistic children. *Journal of Autism and Development Disorders, 12*, 331–342.

HOWLIN, P. (1981). The effectiveness of operant language training with autistic children. *Journal of Autism and Developmental Disorders, 11*, 89–106.

HUTT, C., & OUNSTED, C. (1966). The biological significance of gaze aversion with particular reference to the syndrome of infantile autism. *Behavioral Science, 11*, 346–356.

HUTTENLOCHER, R. R., & HUTTENLOCHER, J. (1973). A study of children with hyperlexia. *Neurology, 23*, 1107–1116.

KANNER, L. (1943). Autistic disturbance of affective contact. *Nervous Child, 2*, 217–250.

KAVALE, K. (1981). Functions of the Illinois Test of Psycholinguistic Abilities (ITPA): Are They Trainable? *Exceptional Children, 47*, 496–510.

KIRK, S. A., McCARTHY, J., & KIRK, W. D. (1968). *Illinois Test of Psycholinguistic Abilities (Rev. Ed.).* Urbana: University of Illinois Press.

KOEGEL, R. L., RINCOVER, A., & EGEL, A. L. (1982). *Educating and understanding autistic children.* San Diego, CA: College-Hill Press.

LANGDELL, T. (1978). Recognition of faces: An approach to the study of autism. *Journal of Child Psychology and Psychiatry, 19*, 255–268.

LAPOUSE, R., & MONK, M. (1958). An epidemiologic study of behvaior characteristic in children. *American Journal of Public Health, 48*, 1134–1144.

LEONARD, L. (1981). Facilitating linguistic skills in children with specific language impairment. *Applied Psycholinguistics, 2,* 89–118.

LENNEBERG, E. (1967). *Biological foundations of language.* New York: John Wiley.

LEWIS, M., & BROOKS-GUNN, J. (1979). *Social cognition and the acquisition of self.* New York: Plenum Press.

LOCKYER, L., & RUTTER, M. (1969). A five-to-fifteen-year-old follow-up study of infantile psychosis: Psychological aspects. *British Journal of Psychiatry, 115,* 865–882.

LOTTER, V. (1978). Follow-up studies. In M. Rutter & E. Schopler (Eds.), *Autism: A reappraisal of concepts and treatment* (pp. 475–495). New York: Plenum Press.

LOVAAS, O. I. (1978). Parents as therapists. In M. Rutter & E. Schopler (Eds.), *Autism: A reappraisal of concepts and treatment.* New York: Plenum Press.

LOVAAS, O. I., BERBERICH, J. P., PERLOFF, B. F., & SCHAEFFER, B. (1966). Acquistion of imitative speech by schizophrenic children. *Science, 151,* 705–707.

LOVAAS, O. I., & KOEGEL, R. L. (1973). Behavior therapy with autistic children. In C. E. Thoresen (Ed.), *Behavior modification in education. 72nd yearbook of the National Society for the Study of Education* (pp. 230–258). Chicago: University of Chicago Press.

LOVAAS, O. I., KOEGEL, R. L., & SCHREIBMAN, L. (1979). Stimulus overselectivity in autism: A review of the research. *Psychological Bulletin, 86,* 1236–1254.

LOVAAS, O. I., & SIMMONS, J. Q. (1969). Manipulation of self-destruction in three retarded children. *Journal of Applied Behavior Analysis, 77,* 211–222.

MACALUSO-HAYNES, S. (1978). Developmental apraxia of speech: Symptoms and treatment. In D. Johns (Ed.), *Clinical management of neurogenic communication disorders* (pp. 243–250). Boston: Little, Brown.

MACFARLANE, J. W., ALLEN, L., & HONZIK, M. P. (1954). *A developmental study of the behavior problems of normal children between 21 months and 14 years.* Berkeley: University of California Press.

MAHLER, M. S. (1965). On early infantile psychosis: The symbiotic and autistic syndrome. *Journal of the American Academy of Child Psychiatry, 4,* 554–568.

MARQUARDT, T. P., DUNN, C., & DAVIS, B. (1985). Apraxia of speech in children. In J. K. Darby (Ed.), *Speech and language evaluation in neurology: Childhood disorders* (pp. 113–132). New York: Grune & Stratton.

McGINNIS, M. A. (1963). *Aphasic children.* Washington, D.C.: Alexander Graham Bell Association for the Deaf.

McHALE, S. M., SIMEONSSON, R. J., MARCUS, L. M., & OLLEY, J. G. (1980). The social and symbolic quality of autistic children's communication. *Journal of Autism and Developmental Disorders, 10,* 299–310.

MEARIG, J. S. (1979). The assessment of intelligence of boys with Duchenne muscular dystrophy. *Rehabilitation Literature, 40,* 262–274.

MEARIG, J. S. (1985). Cognitive development of chronically ill children. In N. Hobbs & J. M. Perrin (Eds.), *Issues in the care of children with chronic illness* (pp. 672–697). San Francisco: Jossey-Bass.

MEHEGAN, C., & DRIEFUS, F. (1972). Hyperlexia. *Neurology, 22,* 1105–111.

MILLER, J., CHAPMAN, R. S., & McKENZIE, H. (1981, August). *Individual differences in the language acquisition of mentally retarded children.* Paper presented at the 2nd International Congress for the Study of Child Language, Vancouver, Canada.

MILLER, L. (1978). Pragmatics and early childhood language disorders: Communication interactions in a half-hour sample. *Journal of Speech and Hearing Disorders, 43,* 419–436.

MIRENDA, P. L., DONNELLAN, A. M., & YODER, D. E. (1983). Gaze behavior: A new look at an old problem. *Journal of Autism and Developmental Disorders, 13,* 397–408.

MUMA, J. R. (1978). *Language handbook: Con-*

cepts, assessment, and intervention. Englewood Cliffs, NJ: Prentice-Hall.

MYKLEBUST, H. (1954). *Auditory disorders in children: A manual for differential diagnosis.* New York: Grune & Stratton.

NEEDLEMAN, R. M. (1982). A linguistic analysis of hyperlexia. In C. Johnson (Ed.), *Proceedings of the 2nd international study of child language.* Washington, D.C.: University Press of America.

O'CONNOR, N., & HERMELIN, B. (1967). The selective visual attention of psychotic children. *Journal of Child Psychology and Psychiatry, 8,* 167–179.

ORNITZ, E. M. (1985). Neurophysiology of infantile autism. *Journal of the American Academy of Child Psychiatry, 24,* 251–263.

ORNITZ, E. M., BROWN, M. B., MASON, A., & PUTNAM, N. H. (1974). Effect of visual input on vestibular nystagmus in autistic children. *Archives of General Psychiatry, 31,* 369–375.

ORNITZ, E. M., FORSYTHE, A. B., & DE LA PENA, A. (1973). The effect of vestibular and auditory stimulation on the rapid eye movements of REM sleep in autistic children. *Archives of General Psychiatry, 29,* 786–791.

ORNITZ, E. M., & RITVO, E. R. (1968). Perceptual inconsistency in early infantile autism. *Archives of General Psychiatry, 18,* 76–98.

PAUL, R., & COHEN, D. J. (1984). Outcomes of severe disorders of language acquisition. *Journal of Autism and Developmental Disorders, 14,* 405–421.

PETTY, L. K., ORNITZ, E. M., MICHELMAN, J. D., & ZIMMERMAN, E. G. (1986). Autistic children who become schizophrenic. In S. Chess & A. Thomas (Eds.), *Annual progress in child psychiatry and child development* (pp. 452–470). New York: Brunner/Mazel.

PRIOR, M. (1984). Developing concepts of childhood autism: The influence of experimental cognitive research. *Journal of Consulting and Clinical Psychology, 52,* 4–16.

RANK, B. (1949). Adaptation of the psychoanalytic technique for the treatment of young children with atypical development. *American Journal of Orthopsychiatry, 19,* 130–139.

RANK, B. (1955). Intensive study and treatment of pre-school children who show marked personality deviations or "atypical development" and their parents. In G. Caplan (Ed.), *Emotional problems of early childhood* (pp. 498–521). New York: Basic Books.

RICHER, J., & COSS, R. (1976). Gaze aversion in autistic and normal children. *Acta Psychiatrica Scandinavica, 53,* 193–210.

RIMLAND, B. (1964). *Infantile autism.* New York: Appleton-Century Crofts.

RIMLAND, B., CALLOWAY, E., & DREYFUS, P. (1978). The effects of high doses of vitamin B6 on autistic children: A double-blind crossover study. *American Journal of Psychiatry, 135,* 472–475.

RISLEY, T. R. (1968). The effects and side effects of punishing the autistic behaviors of a deviant child. *Journal of Applied Behavior Analysis, 1,* 21–35.

RITVO, E. R. (1976). Autism: From adjective to noun. In E. R. Ritvo (Ed.), *Autism: Diagnosis, current research and management* (pp. 3–6). New York: Spectrum Publications.

RITVO, E. R., FREEMAN, B. J., GELLER, E., & YUWILER, A. (1983). Effects of fenfluramine on 14 patients with the syndrome of autism. *Journal of the American Academy of Child Psychiatry, 22,* 1549–1559.

RITVO, E. R., FREEMAN, B. J., MASON-BROTHERS, A., MO, A., & RITVO, A. M. (1985). Concordance for the syndrome of autism in 40 pairs of afflicted twins. *American Journal of Psychiatry, 142,* 74–77.

ROSENFELD, S. K., & SPRINCE, M. P. (1963). An attempt to formulate the meaning of the concept "borderline." In R. S. Eissler, A. Freud, H. Hartmann, & M. Kris (Eds.), *The psychoanalytic study of the child* (Vol. 18, pp. 603–635). New York: International Universities Press.

RUTTER, M. (1967). Psychotic disorders in early childhood. In A. Coppen & A. Walk (Eds.), *Recent developments in schizophrenia. British Journal of Psychiatry,* Special Publication No. 1 (pp. 133–158).

RUTTER, M. (1970). Autistic children: Infancy to adulthood. *Seminars in Psychiatry, 2,* 435–450.

RUTTER, M. (1975). The development of infantile autism. In S. Chess, & A. Thomas (Eds.), *Annual progress in child psychiatry and child development* (pp. 147–172). New York: Brunner/Mazel.

RUTTER, M. (1980). Language training with autistic children: How does it work and what does it achieve? In L. A. Hersov & M. Berger (Eds.), *Language and language disorders in childhood* (pp. 147–172). Oxford, England: Pergamon Press.

RUTTER, M. (1985). Infantile autism and other pervasive developmental disorders. In M. Rutter & L. Hersov (Eds.), *Child and adolescent psychiatry* (2nd ed., pp. 545–566). London: Blackwell Scientific Publications.

RUTTER, M., & BARTAK, L. (1973). Special educational treatment of autistic children: A comparative study. II. Follow-up findings and implications for services. *Journal of Child Psychology and Psychiatry, 14,* 241–270.

RUTTER, M., GREENFIELD, D., & LOCKYER, L. (1967). A 5-to-15 year follow-up study of infantile psychosis. II. Social and behavioral outcome. *British Journal of Psychiatry, 113,* 1183–1199.

SACKS, O. (1985). *The man who mistook his wife for a hat.* New York: Summit Books.

SCHEERER, M., ROTHMANN, E., & GOLDSTEIN, K. (1945). A case of "idiot savant": An experimental study of personality organization. *Psychological Monographs, 58* (4).

SCHOPLER, E. (1983). New developments in the definition and diagnosis of autism. In B. B. Lahey & A. E. Kazdin (Eds.), *Advances in clinical child psychology* (Vol. 6, pp. 93–127). New York: Plenum Press.

SCHOPLER, E., MESIBOV, G., & BAKER, A.

(1982). Evaluation of treatment for autistic children and their parents. *Journal of the American Academy of Child Psychiatry, 21,* 262–267.

SELFE, L. (1977). *Nadia: A case of extraordinary drawing ability in an autistic child.* New York: Academic Press.

SHEA, V., & MESIBOV, G. B. (1985). Brief report: The relationship of learning disabilities and higher-level autism. *Journal of Autism and Developmental Disorders, 13,* 425–435.

SIGMAN, M., & UNGERER, J. A. (1984). Attachment behaviors in autistic children. *Journal of Autism and Developmental Disorders, 14,* 231–244.

SILBERBERG, N., & SILBERBERG, M. (1967). Hyperlexia: Specific word recognition skills in young children. *Exceptional Children, 34,* 41–42.

SIMMONS, J. Q., & BALTAXE, C. (1975). Language patterns of adolescent autistics. *Journal of Autism and Childhood Schizophrenia, 5,* 333–352.

SMITH, S. B. (1983). *The great mental calculators: The psychology, methods and loves of calculating prodigies, past and present.* New York: Columbia University Press.

SOLLEE, N. D., LATHAM, E. E., KINDLON, D. J., & BRESNAN, M. J. (1985). Neuropsychological impairment in Duchenne muscular dystrophy. *Journal of Clinical and Experimental Neurology, 7,* 486–496.

STARK, R. E., & TALLAL, P. (1981). Selection of children with specific language deficits. *Journal of Speech and Hearing Disorders, 46,* 114–122.

TINBERGEN, E., & TINBERGEN, N. (1972). Early childhood autism: An ethological approach. *Advances in Ethology* (19th Supplement to the *Journal of Contemporary Ethology*). Berlin: Verlag Paul Parey.

TRANTHAM, C. R., & PEDERSON, J. K. (1976). *Normal language development: The key to diagnosis and therapy for language-disordered children.* Baltimore: Williams & Wilkins.

TRIMBLE, M. R., & THOMPSON, P. J. (1983).

Anticonvulsant drugs, cognitive function and behavior. *Epilepsia, 24* (Supplement S), 55–63.

VISCOTT, D. (1970). A musical idiot savant: A psychodynamic study and some speculations on the creative process. *Psychiatry, 33,* 494–515.

WEINER, P. S. (1986). The study of childhood language disorders: Nineteenth century perspectives. *Journal of Communication Disorders, 19,* 1–47.

WETHERBY, A. M., KOEGEL, R. L., & MENDEL, M. (1981). Central auditory nervous system dysfunction in echolalic autistic individuals. *Journal of Speech and Hearing Research, 24,* 420–429.

WHITEHOUSE, D., & HARRIS, J. C. (1984). Hyperlexia in infantile autism. *Journal of Autism and Developmental Disorders, 14,* 281–289.

WIIG, E. H., & SEMEL, E. M. (1980). *Language assessment and intervention for the learning disabled.* Columbus, OH: Charles E. Merrill.

WING, L., & GOULD, L. (1979). Severe impairments in social interaction and associated abnormalities in children: Epidemiology and classification. *Journal of Autism and Developmental Disorders, 9,* 11–29.

WITELSON, S. F. (1976). Sex and the single hemisphere. Specialization of the right hemisphere for spatial processing. *Science, 193,* 425–427.

APPENDIX

A PRACTICAL GUIDE TO INSTRUMENTS FOR THE ASSESSMENT OF CHILDREN AND CHILDHOOD DISORDERS

Julia Krevans

INTRODUCTION: METHODS AND ORGANIZATION

This guide presents instruments which assess a number of the childhood disorders and child development variables that were discussed in the text. The guide is "practical" in that cumbersome, expensive, hard-to-obtain and time-consuming instruments have been excluded. The selected instruments form a collection which will be useful to both the research investigator who wants to minimize resources expended on instrumentation and the clinician who wants to collect data in his or her clinical setting.

The text was used to identify characteristics of children, such as depression and adaptive behavior, and characteristics of children's environments, such as parental childrearing attitudes and classroom quality, which are currently the focus of research efforts or clinical concern. Instruments which assess each characteristic were sought in several sources; the text, articles cited in the text, test collections and recent volumes of psychology and psychiatry journals.

Practical criteria were used to make initial selections. Instruments were excluded if they: (a) required any training beyond self-training for proper use; (b) took 1½ hours or more to administer; (c) cost in excess of $60 (as of 1986) for the first 20 administrations; or (d) were difficult to obtain.

More instruments met these practical criteria than could be described. In the final selection some preference was given to those which had a number of uses, had been examined for reliability and had been used in recent published research. The most important consider-

The author would like to thank the authors of the tests discussed in this appendix who graciously responded to requests to review this material.

ation, however, was representativeness. An effort was made to select two or three instruments for each characteristic which were representative of the types of instruments available for the assessment of that characteristic.

The reader should note that the decision to include only easy-to-use instruments eliminated all measures of a number of characteristics which were discussed at length in the text. For example, intelligence, neonatal health, and linguistic development are each assessed by instruments best left to specialists.

Organization. Like the text, the guide is organized by age. Section 1 presents instruments for the assessment of characteristics of infants, toddlers and preschoolers and Section 2 presents instruments that assess the characteristics of their environments. Sections 3 and 4 describe instruments that assess characteristics of school-aged children and their environments. However, there are exceptions to these age separations. Because there are relatively few instruments for preschool children, those which can be used across the full age span are included in the first two sections. Also, there are upward age extensions of several of the instruments presented in Sections 1 and 2 and downward age extensions of several of the instruments presented in Sections 3 and 4.

Each section is divided into subsections. Subsections describe two or three instruments that assess a particular characteristic and, where appropriate, present a bibliography as a guide to additional measures of that characteristic.

Test descriptions are organized as follows:

Test title (abbreviation). Author, years of publication of test.

Description. Describes the purpose, format, number of items, necessary materials, demands on examiners and subjects, and nature of standardization sample.

Administration and scoring. Time required for administration and scoring, form of administration (individual, group, self), special requirements, type of scoring (i.e., summing, coding), and availability of scoring and administration aids.

Variables and score interpretation. Describes the major scores and classifications generated by the instrument and availability of formal norms and cut-off scores.

Reliability. Presents internal consistency, test-retest and interrater reliability findings in terms of ranges or median coefficients. References are given for more details.

Uses and findings. Describes the way that the instrument has been used in recent research, representative findings, and limitations. While the findings bear on validity issues, validity evaluations are beyond the scope of the instrument descriptions.

Where to obtain. Addresses are those used to obtain the instruments for the preparation of this guide. Over time test authors and publishers may move. Professional directories are useful resources for the location of test authors who are no longer at addresses cited. Because prices will vary over time, the only prices quoted are those which as of 1986 were over $60 for special materials.

INFANTS, TODDLERS, AND PRESCHOOLERS: CHILD CHARACTERISTICS

Temperament

Revised Infant Temperament Questionnaire (RITQ), William B. Cary & Sean C. McDevitt, 1977

Toddler Temperament Scale (TTS), William Fullard, Sean C. McDevitt, & William B. Carey, 1978

Behavioral Style Questionnaire (BSQ), Sean S. McDevitt and William B. Carey, 1975

Description. The RITQ, TTS, and BSQ were designed to simplify the assessment of the temperament dimensions or "categories" which were first identified in the New York Longitudinal Study (see Chapter 1). The instruments consist of 95 to 100 items which specify observable child behaviors and the contexts in which they occur. Parents indicate how frequently their child exhibits each behavior in the specified context. The instruments also standardize procedures for the classification of children in terms of temperament types.

The RITQ is designed for children from 4 to 8 months, the TTS for children 1 to 3 years, and the BSQ for children from 3 to 7 years. (See Hegvik, McDevitt, & Carey, 1982 for a Middle Childhood Temperament Questionnaire for 8–12 year old children.) The standardization samples were drawn from private pediatric practices with white, middle- and upper-class mothers predominating.

Administration and scoring. Each instrument can be self-administered in 30 minutes and hand scored in about 15. Scoring forms and profiles facilitate scoring and diagnosis. Information on computer scoring is available from the authors.

Variables and score interpretation. Each instrument assesses nine temperament categories: activity, rhythmicity, distractibility, approach, adaptability, persistence, threshold, intensity, and mood. Children receive a temperament diagnosis on the basis of their standing on category scores with respect to the standardization sample. Diagnostic classifications are: (a) difficult (arrhythmic, withdrawing, unadaptable, intense, and negative in mood); (b) easy; (c) intermediate high; (d) intermediate low; and (e) slow-to-warm-up (inactive, withdrawing, unadaptable, negative, and mild).

Reliability. Median internal consistency of category scores were: RITQ .57; TTS .70; BSQ 70 (*n*'s 142–350). Median test-retest figures with 1-month interval were: RITQ .75; TTS .81; BSQ .81 (*n*'s 41 to 53). Modest relationships were found between infant temperament and toddler and preschool temperament (Fullard, McDevitt, & Carey, 1984; Hubert, Wach, Peters-Martin, & Gandour, 1982).

Uses and findings. Researchers found that scores and diagnoses were related to observed child behaviors and aspects of adjustment. Infants who were easy, or intermediate-low, responded less negatively to strangers than did other infants (Berberian & Snyder, 1982). A difficulty factor, derived from TTS subscores, was strongly related to difficulty scores based on children's laboratory behavior (Matheny, Wilson, & Nuss, 1984). BSQ activity and approach scores were meaningfully related to peer interactions in nursery school (Billman & McDevitt, 1980).

Where to obtain. For the RITQ—William B. Carey, MD, 319 W. Front Street, Media, PA 19063. For the TTS—William Fullard, PhD, Department of Educational Psychology, Temple University, Philadelphia, PA 19122. For the BSQ—Sean C. McDevitt, PhD, Devereux Center, 6436 E. Sweetwater, Scottsdale, AZ 85254.

References

BERBERIAN, K. E., & SNYDER, S. S. (1982). The relationship of temperament and stranger reaction for younger and older infants. *Merrill-Palmer Quarterly, 28,* 79–94.

BILLMAN, J., & McDEVITT, S. C. (1980). Convergence of parent and observer ratings of temperament with observations of peer interactions in a nursery school. *Child Development, 51,* 395–400.

CAREY, W. B. (1983). Some pitfalls of temperament research. *Infant Behavior and Development, 6,* 247–254.

FULLARD, W., McDEVITT, S. C., & CAREY, W. B. (1984). Assessing temperament in one- to three-year-old children. *Journal of Pediatric Psychology 9,* 205–217.

HEGVIK, R. L., McDEVITT, S. C., & CAREY, W. B. (1982). Middle childhood temperament questionnaire. *Developmental and Behavioral Pediatrics, 3,* 197–200.

MATHENY, A. P., JR., WILSON, R. S., & NUSS, S. M. (1984). Toddler temperament: Stability across settings and over ages. *Child Development, 55,* 1200–1211.

Infant Behavior Questionnaire (IBQ), *Mary K. Rothbart, 1978*

Description. In contrast to Carey and his colleagues who define temperament as behavioral style, Rothbart defines temperament as constitutional patterns of reactivity and self-regulation. The IBQ content reflects this alternative conceptualization of temperament and consists of 94 descriptions of observable infant responses to specific situations. Parents indicate whether situations occurred during the past week, and if so, how frequently their child exhibited the response.

The test development sample included Caucasian parents of varied socioeconomic status who responded with respect to 3-, 6-, 9-, and 12-month-old infants.

Administration and scoring. The IBQ is self-administered. It is scored by averaging items scores within subscales.

Variables and score interpretation. The IBQ subscales were derived from theory and refined with item analysis. Subscales assess activity level, smiling and laughter, fear, distress in response to limitations, soothability, and duration of orienting.

Reliability. Internal consistency estimates for subscales, obtained separately for 3-, 6-, 9-, and 12-month-assessments, ranged from .67 to .85. About 70% of correlations between 6- and 9-month

IBQ scores, 6- and 12-month scores and 9- and 12-month scores were above .50 (*n*'s 34 to 36). Three-month subscores were generally less predictive.

Uses and findings. There was moderate agreement between mothers' temperament ratings and those of other caregivers in the home (Rothbart, 1981; Rothbart & Derryberry, 1981). Significant, but moderate, correlations were found between caregiver-based IBQ scores and home-observation measures of IBQ dimensions. The IBQ has also been used in a study of infant sociability. Infants who were relatively more fearful, more easily distressed, more active, and less likely to laugh or smile were less responsive to strangers (Thompson & Lamb, 1982).

Where to obtain. Mary K. Rothbart, PhD, Department of Psychology, University of Oregon, Eugene, OR 97403.

References

ROTHBART, M. K. (1981). Measurement of temperament in infancy. *Child Development, 52,* 569–578.

ROTHBART, M. K., & DERRYBERRY, D. (1981). Development of individual differences in temperament. In M. E. Lamb & A. L. Brown (Eds.), *Advances in Developmental Psychology* (Vol. 1). Hillsdale, NJ: Erlbaum.

THOMPSON, R. A., & LAMB, M. E. (1982). Stranger sociability and its relationship to temperament and social experience during the second year. *Infant Behavior and Development, 5,* 77–287.

For additional instruments see:

HUBERT, N. C., WACHS, T. D., PETERS-MARTIN, P., & GANDOUR, M. J. (1982). The study of early temperament; Measurement and conceptual issues. *Child Development, 53,* 149–159. *Review.*

Developmental Screening

The Denver Developmental Screening Test (DDST), *W. K. Frankenburg and colleagues*

Description. The DDST screens for developmental delays in four areas of functioning: personal-social, fine motor, gross motor, and language. Items include both questions for parents and tasks for children (e.g., hop, stack blocks). Examiners begin with an age-appropriate item in each of the areas. Progressively harder and easier items are administered until the child's consecutive failures and consecutive successes establish the upper and lower limits of his or her performance in each area. Typically, 20 to 25 of the 150 DDST items must be used. There is also a 12-item format called the DDST-Revised for pre-screening (Frankenburg et al., 1981).

The standardization sample of 1,036 children, about 40 at 25 age levels between birth and 6 years, did not include children known to be at risk for developmental abnormalities. Otherwise it was representative of the population of Denver.

Administration and scoring. Examiners may be trained in about 4 hours with workbooks, videos, and/or films. Scoring forms provide the age norms needed for administration decisions. Administration and scoring require 15 to 30 minutes.

Variables and score interpretations. The child's protocol is examined for delays, that is, failures on items which most children younger than the child pass. The child's pattern of passes, refusals, and delays is used to classify the child as normal, abnormal, or questionable. An abnormal classification indicates that the child should be referred for diagnostic assessment.

Reliability. Interscorer agreement was 90% for items (Frankenburg, Dodd, Fandal, Kazuk, & Cohrs, 1975) and 96% for classifications (Strangler, Huber, & Routh, 1980). Test-retest for classifications with different examiners at 1-week intervals was 97% ($n = 186$) (Frankenburg, Goldstein, & Camp, 1971).

Uses and findings. Frankenburg, Camp, and Van Natta (1971) reported "hit rates" between 74% and 84% when DDST classifications were compared with intelligence tests. However, among younger children, an excessive proportion of children with IQs below 70 were classified as normal by the DDST. Similarly, Applebaum (1978) found that 54% to 62% of infants with Bayley Development Quotients of less than 70 were classified normal by the DDST.

Where to obtain. LADOCA Project and Publishing Foundation, E. 51st Avenue and Lincoln Street, Denver, CO 80216. The basic test kit includes manual, 50 scoring forms, and equipment for administration. Training films and videotapes are available for rent.

References

APPLEBAUM, A. S. (1978). Validity of revised Denver Developmental Screening Test for referred and non-referred samples. *Psychology Reports, 43,* 227–233.

FRANKENBURG, W. K., CAMP, B. W., & VAN NATTA, P. A. (1971). Validity of the Denver Developmental Screening Test. *Child Development, 51,* 475–481.

FRANKENBURG, W. K., DODD, J. B., FANDAL, A., KAZUK, E., & COHRS, M. (1975). *Reference Manual* (Rev. ed.). Denver: LADOCA Project and Publishing Foundation.

FRANKENBURG, W. K., FANDAL, A., SCIARILLO, W., & BURGESS, D. (1981). The newly abbreviated and revised Denver Developmental Screening Test. *Journal of Pediatrics, 99,* 995–999.

FRANKENBURG, W. K., GOLDSTEIN, A., & CAMP, B. W. (1971). The revised Denver Developmental Screening Test: Its accuracy as a screening instrument. *Journal of Pediatrics, 79,* 988–989.

Minnesota Child Development Inventory (MCDI), Harold Ireton & Edward Thwing, 1972, 1974

Description. The MCDI uses mothers' reports to assess the development of children's adaptive behavior, chart the progress of healthy children, and detect developmental delays. Its 320 items describe developmental milestones which discriminate between children of different ages. Mothers indicate whether their child has ever exhibited the milestones described.

The 796 families in the standardization sample were all white and disproportionately upper middle class.

Administration and scoring. Mothers with at least an 8th-grade reading level self-administer the MCDI. Others use audiotapes of MCDI questions. Templates simplify hand scoring. Computerized administration and scoring are available.

Variables and score interpretation. The General Development subscale uses the 131 items which discriminate most sharply between different age levels to index overall developmental progress. Other subscales assess the child's functioning in areas of comprehension/conceptualization, expressive language, gross motor skill, fine motor skill, self-help and personal/social adjustment. Raw scores are compared with age norms to determine whether a child shows developmental retardation in any of the areas.

Reliability. The split-half reliability coefficient for each subscale was determined for each of the 15 age groups in the standardization sample. Most coefficients ranged from the mid .60s to the low .90s. The lower coefficients reflected the inadequate number of items in some subscales at some age levels (Ireton & Thwing, 1972a).

Uses and findings. Standardization data indicated that subscale means increased with age and that, as expected in a normal population, very few children were identified as developmentally delayed (Ireton & Thwing, 1972b). Head Start children, in contrast, exhibited relatively high incidence of MCDI-identified delays (Ullman & Kausch, 1979). Researchers (Ireton, see note for review) also found strong relationships between preschool scores on certain MCDI subscales and both preschool intelligence test scores and grade school achievement.

Where to obtain. Behavior Science Systems, Inc., P.O. Box 1108, Minneapolis, MN 55440. Start-up package consists of manual, 10 questionnaires, 25 answer sheets, profile sheets, and templates. Audiotapes of MCDI questions are available. Computerized administration and scoring costs $95 for 50 uses.

References

IRETON, H. R., & THWING, E. J. (1972a). Minnesota Child Development Inventory. Minneapolis: Behavioral Science Systems.

IRETON, H. R., & THWING, E. J. (1972b). *The Minnesota Child Development Inventory in the psychiatric developmental evaluation of the preschool child. Child Psychiatry and Human Development, 3*, 102–114.

ULLMAN, D. C., & KAUSCH, D. F. (1979). Early identification of developmental strengths and weaknesses in preschool children. *Exceptional Children, 46*, 8–13.

Note

IRETON, H. *Involving parents in the assessment of young children. The Minnesota Child Development Inventories.* Undated mimeo, Minneapolis: Behavioral Science Systems.

Early Screening Inventory (ESI), *S. J. Meisels & Martha Stone Wiske, 1983*

Description. The ESI is designed to screen 4- and 5-year-olds for risk of early school failure. It consists of 22 standardized tasks which assess three areas of child development: (a) visual-motor/adaptive; (b) language/cognition, and (c) gross motor skills/body awareness. In addition, there is a Parent Questionnaire regarding the child's developmental, medical, and educational history.

The normative sample of 465 children between 4 and 6 years of age was predominantly white and low to lower middle class. The development of local cut-off scores is recommended. An age expansion of the ESI to include 3-year-olds and a Spanish-American version are currently in preparation.

Administration and scoring. The ESI is individually administered by trained examiners in 15 to 20 minutes. The manual provides detailed instructions for scoring. Parent questionnaires are self-administered.

Variables and score interpretation. The total ESI score, the sum of all task scores, is compared to cutoff scores for provisional classification as "all right" or in need of rescreening or a more complete assessment. The final screening decision is based on the ESI score, Parent Questionnaire, child's level of comfort and cooperativeness, and the child's pattern of success and failure in the three developmental areas.

Reliability. Pairs of scorers who observed the same test sessions agreed on 90% of 18 ESI total scores. Test-retest agreement, with a 1-week interval and different examiners, was 82% (Meisels & Wiske, 1983).

Uses and findings. Meisels and Wiske (1983) found that ESI scores were highly correlated with the General Cognitive Index of the McCarthy Scales. The relationship between early ESI screening classifications and high versus low grade point averages for kindergarten through fourth-grade children ranged from .82 to .60 in specificity and from 1.00 to .50 in sensitivity. ESI scores improved the accuracy of prediction of grade points, use of special services, and on-time promotions beyond the level obtained by use of parent reports, medical data, and sensory tests.

Where to obtain. Teachers College Press, c/o Harper and Row, Keystone Industrial Park, Scranton, PA 18512. The ESI test kit includes a manual, 30 score sheets, 30 Parent Questionnaires and test materials.

References

Meisels, S. J., Wiske, M. S., & Tirnan, T. (1984). Predicting school performance with the Early Screening Inventory. *Psychology in the Schools, 21*, 25–33.

For additional instruments see:

Barnes, K. E. (1982). Preschool screening: The measurement and prediction of children at risk. Springfield, IL: Charles C Thomas.

Goodwin, W. L., & Driscoll, L. A. (1980). Handbook for measurement and evaluation in early childhood education. San Francisco: Jossey-Bass.

Katoff, L., & Reuter, J. (1980). Review of developmental screening tests for infants. *Journal of Clinical Child Psychology* 30–34.

Lichtenstein, R., & Ireton, H. (1984). *Preschool screening: Identifying young children with developmental and educational problems.* Orlando, FL: Grune and Stratton, Inc.

Southworth, L. E., Burr, R. L., & Cox, A. E. (1981). Screening and evaluating the young child: A handbook of instruments for use from infancy to six years. Springfield, IL: Charles C Thomas.

Strangler, S. R., Huber, C. J., & Routh, D. K. (1980). Screening growth and development of preschool children: A guide for test selection. New York: McGraw Hill.

Self-Management

Preschool Interpersonal Problem-Solving Procedure (PIPS), M. B. Shure and G. Spivack, 1974

Description. The PIPS assesses preschoolers' ability to consider alternative solutions to interpersonal problems and identifies their preferred types of solutions. It consists of two sets of stories which are illustrated with pictures. In one set, a child protagonist wants a toy which another child is using. Stories in the other set depict a child who has damaged his or her mother's property. The respondent is asked to explain how the protagonist might solve a minimum of seven peer problems and five mother problems.

A trained examiner administers the PIPS to 4- and 5-year-olds. The normative sample consisted of 469 innter-city 4-year-olds. Spivack, Platt, and Shure (1976) report that validity findings for the high and low SES populations are similar.

Administration and scoring. The PIPS is administered in 30 minutes. The PIPS score is the number of different relevant solutions which the child provides to the entire series of stories. Criteria for relevant solutions are provided. Solutions are coded for content in order to identify repetitions.

Variables and score interpretation. Norms for both maladjusted and well-adjusted preschoolers are provided. In addition to PIPS scores, researchers have constructed scores from content category frequencies which serve as indices of the extent to which children prefer particular types of solutions to interpersonal problems.

Reliability. Interrater agreement was above 90% (Shure & Spivack, 1974). Internal consistency estimates ranged from .51 to .59 (Spivack et al., 1976). The one-week test-retest coefficient was .72 ($n = 57$) and the 3- to 5-month test-retest coefficient ($n = 180$) was .59 (Shure & Spivack, 1974).

Uses and findings. Shure, Spivack, and colleagues found that the number of preschoolers' relevant PIPS solutions was related to teachers' ratings of social adjustment even when IQ was controlled. They also found that training in social problem solving improved both PIPS scores and school adjustment (Shure, 1981; Shure, Spivack, & Jaeger, 1971).

Where to obtain. Myrna B. Shure, Hahnemann University, Broad and Vine Street, Philadelphia, PA 19102 for the manual and story pictures.

References

SHURE, M. B. (1981). Social competence as a problem solving skill. In J. D. Wine & M. D. Smye (Eds.), *Social competence.* New York: Guilford Press.

SHURE, M. B., SPIVACK, G., & JAEGER, M. A. (1971). Problem-solving thinking and adjustment among disadvantaged preschool children. *Child Development, 42,* 1791–1803.

California Child Q-Sort (CCQ), Ego Control and Ego-Resiliency Measures. Jeanne H. Block & Jack Block, 1980

Description. The CCQ provides a standard vocabulary for the description of children and can be used for a variety of more specific purposes. It consists of 100 personality descriptors, each printed on a separate card. Respondents sort cards into nine piles and a specified number of cards must be placed in each category. Placement is determined by the extent to which the descriptor characterizes the child. When used to assess ego-control and ego-resiliency, the sort which describes the child is compared to criterion sorts which describe the prototypically undercontrolled child and the prototypically ego-resilient child, respectively. Ego control refers to the ability to modulate impulses and delay gratification. Ego-resiliency refers to the ability to adjust one's level of self-control to changing situational demands.

Adults who have had ample opportunity for observation (parents, teachers, and therapists) use the CCQ to describe children 3 years and older. Ideally, the average of several observers' sorts should be obtained. Psychometric data about ego-control and ego-resiliency scores are based on a disproportionately upper and middle class sample of 100 children who were followed from the age of 3 years (Block & Block, 1980).

Administration and scoring. The CCQ can be self-administered in 20 to 40 minutes. Ego-control and ego-resiliency scores are the correlations between the placements of descriptors in the testee's protocol and descriptor placements in the criterion sorts.

Variables and score interpretation. High ego-control scores indicate impulsivity, low scores indicate over-control, and moderate scores indicate appropriate self-control. High ego-resilience scores indicate adaptability while low scores indicate inflexibility.

Reliability. Intersorter agreement on the placements of CCQ descriptors, assessed by intraclass correlations between triads of teachers, was .65. Correlations between ego-control and ego-resiliency scores obtained at age 3 years and again at age 4 years ranged from .65 to .82. Correlations between 3rd- and 4th-year scores and 7th-year scores (obtained from a single teacher) were lower (Block & Block, 1980).

Uses and findings. The Blocks (1980) examined relationships between CCQ ego-control and ego-resiliency measures and measures of ego-control and ego-resiliency derived from a battery of laboratory tasks. Relationships between contemporaneous scores and scores obtained at different ages, i.e., between 3rd-year lab-based scores and 4th-year CCQ-based scores, were examined. Eleven of the 12 correlations between the two types of ego-resiliency measures and 7 of the 9 correlations between the two types of ego-control measures were significant. In contrast, correlations between ego-control and ego-resiliency were generally low and nonsignificant. Arend, Grove, and Sroufe (1979) replicated this finding and obtained predicted relationships between 4- and 5-year-olds' resiliency and control scores and their security of attachment and problem-solving behavior at ages 1½ to 2 years. Block, Block, and Morrison (1981) related resiliency and control scores to socialization experiences.

Where to obtain. Consulting Psychologists Press, Inc., 577 College Avenue, Palo Alto, CA 94306 for CCQ card and manual. Write to Dr. Jack Block, Institute of Human Development, 1203

Tolman Hall, University of California, Berkeley, CA 94720 for additional administration instructions and information needed to compute ego-control and ego-resiliency scores.

References

AREND, R., GROVE, F. L., & SROUFE, L. A. (1979). Continuity of individual adaptation from infancy to kindergarten: A predictive study of ego-resiliency and curiosity in preschoolers. *Child Development, 50,* 950–959.

BLOCK, J. H., & BLOCK, J. (1980). The role of ego-control and ego-resiliency in the organization of behavior. In W. A. Collins (Ed.), *Minnesota symposia on child psychology* (Vol. 13, pp. 39–101). Hillsdale, NJ: Lawrence Erlbaum.

BLOCK, J. H., BLOCK, J., & MORRISON, A. (1981). Parental agreement/disagreement on child rearing orientations and gender-related personality correlates in children. *Child Development, 52,* 965–974.

Thoughts About Oneself and Others

The Pictorial Scale of Perceived Competence and Social Acceptance for Young Children, Susan Harter & Robin Pike, 1980.

Description. The Pictorial Scale assesses domain-specific self-evaluations of young children. The scale consists of 24 items. Items are pictures which each depict two children. One child is doing well at a task or is succeeding in a social situation. The second is performing the same task poorly or is not socially successful. Children indicate which of the two characters is most like themselves. Then they refine their answer by indicating whether the chosen character is "a lot" like them or "just a little" like them by pointing to large ("a lot") or small ("just a little") circle.

There are two versions which differ in item content. One is for preschool and kindergarten children and the second is for first and second graders. The standardization sample included 146 preschoolers and kindergartners and 109 first and second graders. Most were white and from middle class families.

Administration and scoring. The Pictorial Scale is administered individually. Responses are assigned points and item scores are averaged within subscales.

Variables and score interpretations. The scale yields four subscores. Two subscores indicate the extent to which children think that they are competent with respect to cognitive and physical skills. The other two subscores index the extent to which the child believes that he is accepted by others. One measures perceived maternal acceptance and the other, perceived acceptance by peers. Subscores may be combined to form total perceived competence and total perceived acceptance scores. Limited normative data are available in Harter and Pike (1984). A parallel teachers' rating scale also provides a perspective for score interpretation (Harter & Pike, 1983).

Reliability. Internal consistency estimates were made for each grade level in the standardization sample (n's 44 to 90). Estimates for subscales ranged from .50 to .85 and from .75 to .89 for total perceived competence and total perceived acceptance scores (Harter & Pike, 1984).

Uses and findings. Harter and Pike (1984) found that children's justifications of their judgments about their competence were appropriate. Also, scores of subgroups of children differed in predicted ways. For example, newcomers to school perceived less peer acceptance than did long-time pupils. Factor anlaysis confirmed the distinction between competence and acceptance judgments. Modest to moderate relationships were found between children's perceived competence and teachers' competence ratings and achievement test scores (Anderson & Adams, 1985; Harter & Pike, 1984).

Where to obtain. Susan Harter, Department of Psychology, University of Denver, 2040 S. York Street, Denver, CO 80208, for manual, record sheets, and booklets of picture plates.

References

ANDERSON, P. L., & ADAMS, P. J. (1985). The relationship of five-year-olds' academic readiness and perceptions of competence and acceptance. *Journal of Educational Research, 79,* 114–118.

HARTER, S., & PIKE, R. (1983). *Procedural manual to accompany the Pictorial Scale of Perceived Competence and Social Acceptance for Young Children.* Denver: University of Denver.

HARTER, S., & PIKE, R. (1984). The Pictorial Scale of Perceived Competence and Social Acceptance for Young Children. *Child Development, 55,* 1969–1982.

Family Relations Test (FRT), Eva Bene & James Anthony, 1957; 1978

Description. The FRT measures the child's emotional attitudes towards family members and the child's perceptions of feelings directed from family members towards him or herself. It consists of 20 cardboard dolls of varied age and sex and "messages" printed on cards. The child selects the dolls to represent his or her family and is given figures which represent the child and Mr. Nobody. Me card messages, which are read to the child, express children's positive and negative feelings for others, desires for dependency on others, and positive and negative feelings of others towards the child. The child indicates who, if anyone, in his or her family might be the object or the sender of each message by placing the card in the "mailbox" attached to the appropriate cardboard doll.

There are several versions of the FRT: a marital relations version, an adult version, a version for 7- to 17-year-olds and a 40-item version for 3- to 7-year-olds. Manual norms and most FRT research are based on the older child version, but means for preschoolers are also available (Turner, 1982).

Administration and scoring. The FRT is administered individually in 20 to 25 minutes. Scores are the numbers of messages and numbers of messages of different types which are placed in each family member's box. Score sheets facilitate record keeping and computation.

Variables and score interpretation. Scores measure (a) degree of involvement with each family member (total number of messages directed toward a given family member); (b) extent to which relations with family members are experienced as positive or negative (number of positive or negative messages to and from each family member);

and (c) more fine-tuned variables such as the extent to which the child holds negative attitudes towards his or her mother. The manual guides clinical interpretation based on complex patterns of test performance and background information.

Reliability. Bene and Anthony (1978) question the appropriateness of evaluating the FRT with available reliability measures but provide data for the older child's version. Internal consistency of positive and negative message scores for mother, father, and siblings ranged from .65 to .90 (n's 11 to 40).

Uses and findings. Bene and Anthony (1978) found that older children's FRT responses corresponded with case history information about their family relationships. Linton, Berle, Grossi, and Jackson (1961), whose sample of pediatric patients included young children, examined effects of child health, parental concern, family health, fathers' success as a provider, and quality of parents' marriage on FRT responses.

Where to obtain. NFER-Nelson Publishing Co., Darville House, 2 Oxford Road East, Windsor, Berkshire, SL 4 1DF (07535)58961, England, for figures, cards, score sheets and manual.

References

BENE, E., & ANTHONY, J. (1978). Family Relations Test, Children's Version. Windsor, Berks, England: NFER-Nelson Publishing.

LINTON, H., BERLE, B., GROSSI, M., & JACKSON, E. (1961). Reactions of children within family groups as measured by the Bene-Anthony Test. *Journal of Mental Science, 107*, 308–325.

TURNER, I. (1982). Preschool children's perceptions of parental attitudes. *School Psychology International, 3*, 137–142.

Identification of Behavior Problems

Preschool Behavior Questionnaire (PBQ), L. B. Behar & S. Stringfield, 1974

Description. The PBQ assists preschool teachers with the preliminary identification of children who have behavior problems. The measure consists of 30 items which are descriptions of behavior problems that have been found to discriminate between healthy and emotionally or behaviorally disturbed preschoolers (Behar & Stringfield, 1977). The teacher indicates the extent to which the child exhibits each problem.

Teachers rate the 3- to 6-year-olds in their classrooms. Teachers' ratings of 496 preschoolers who were representative of the general population and ratings of 102 children in preschools for the emotionally disturbed were used for test construction. While researchers have used the PBQ with other raters, for other age groups, and in non-school settings, this is not recommended (Gray, Clancy, & King, 1981).

Administration and scoring. The PBQ is self-administered. It is scored by summing item scores to form total and subscores.

Variables and score interpretation. The PBQ yields a total score which provides an index of the pervasiveness of behavior problems and three factor scores.

Factor scores indicate the extent to which children exhibit the following problems: (a) hostility and aggression; (b) anxiety and fearfulness; and (c) hyperactivity and distractibility (Behar & Springfield, 1974).

Reliability. Test-retest coefficients, interval of 3–4 months, factor scores: .60 to .94; total score: .87. Contemporaneous interrater coefficients, factor scores: .67 to .81; total score: .84 ($n = 80$ "normal" and 9 "disturbed" preschoolers).

Uses and findings. Research (reviewed by Behar, 1977) demonstrated predicted relationships between the PBQ and other rating-based measures of preschool adjustment (California Preschool Social Competency Questionnaire, the Kohn Social Competence Questionnaire and the Kohn Problem Checklist). Factor interrelationships revealed correspondence between Kohn Apathy/Withdrawal and PBQ Anxious/Fearful and between Kohn Anger/Defiance and PBQ Hostile/Aggressive. Rubin and Clark (1983) found meaningful relationships between PBQ factors and observed social behavior, popularity and interpersonal problem solving strategies.

Where to obtain. Lenore Behar, 1821 Woodburn Road, Durham, NC 27705 for manual, score sheets, and answer sheets.

References

Behar, L. B. (1977). The Preschool Behavior Questionnaire. *Journal of Abnormal Child Psychology, 5,* 265–275.

Behar, L. B., & Stringfield, S. (1974). A behavior rating scale for the preschool child. *Developmental Psychology 10,* 601–610.

Gray, C. A., Clancy, S., & King, L. (1981). Teacher versus parent reports of preschoolers' social competence. *Journal of Personality Assessment, 45,* 488–493.

Rubin, K. H., & Clark, M. L. (1983). Preschool teachers' ratings of behavioral problems: Observation, sociometric and social-cognitive correlates. *Journal of Abnormal Child Psychology, 11,* 273–286.

A Behavioral Screening Questionnaire (BSQ), *N. Richman & P. J. Graham, 1971*

Description. The BSQ is used to identify children who have behavior problems and to determine the prevalence of specific problem behaviors in child populations. It is a semi-structured interview that includes 12 items which form the behavior scale. Parents are asked about the child's functioning during the preceding 4 weeks.

Interviewers use the BSQ to obtain information about children who are 2½ to 4 years of age. The validity of the BSQ has been demonstrated for both black and white lower class Londoners (Earls & Richman, 1980; Richman, Stevenson, & Graham, 1975) and for middle class children in Massachusetts (Earls et al., 1982). However, researchers (Earls et al., 1982) warn that the BSQ's psychometric properties vary with characteristics of interviewer and informant and recommend that local reliability be computed.

Administration and scoring. The BSQ interview takes up to 30 minutes. Interviewers use behaviorally anchored rating scales to score parents' responses. Item scores are summed.

Variables and score interpretation. Item scores indicate to what extent children exhibit specific problems such as eating problems or excessive attention seeking. The total score (sum of item scores) is a screening index. Children who obtain total scores above cutoffs would be likely to receive a diagnosis of severe or at least moderate behavior problems if given full clinical assessments (Earls et al., 1982).

Reliability. Interrater agreement on the total score was .94 ($n = 20$). Test-retest data over a 1-week interval, with different raters, yielded .95 agreement in screening decisions and a .77 correlation between total scores ($n = 57$) (Richman & Graham, 1971).

Uses and findings. BSQ-based classifications identified 75% of psychiatric clinic patients as disturbed and about 87% of non-hospital children as not disturbed (Richman & Graham, 1971). Similar success rates were obtained when BSQ scores were used to identify children whom clinicians regarded as at least moderately disturbed and children regarded as, at most, mildly disturbed (Earls et al., 1982). The BSQ was also used in epidemiological studies (Richman, Stevenson, & Graham, 1975) and in prospective studies of the consequences of preschool behavior problems (Earls & Richman, 1980).

Where to obtain. The BSQ is in the appendix of Richman and Graham (1971). For notes on coding and scoring, write to Naomi Richman, Academic Depart-

ment of Child Psychiatry, Great Ormond Street, London WCIN3JH, Great Britain.

References

EARLS, F., JACOBS, G., GOLDFEIN, D., SILBERT, A., BEARDSLEE, W., & RIVINUS, T. (1982). Concurrent validation of a behavior problem scale to use with 3-year-olds. *Journal of the American Academy of Child Psychiatry, 21,* 47–57.

EARLS, F., & RICHMAN, N. (1980). Behavior problems in preschool children of West-Indian-born parents. *Journal of Child Psychology and Psychiatry 21,* 108–117.

RICHMAN, N., & GRAHAM, P. J. (1971). A behavioral screening questionnaire for use with 3-year-old children, preliminary findings. *Journal of Child Psychology and Psychiatry, 12,* 5–33.

RICHMAN, N., STEVENSON, J. E., & GRAHAM, P. J. (1975). Prevalence of behavior problems in 3-year-old children. An epidemiological study in a London borough. *Journal of Child Psychology and Psychiatry, 16,* 277–287.

For additional instruments see:

JENKINS, S., BAX, M., & HART, H. (1980). Behavior problems in preschool children. *Journal of Child Psychology and Psychiatry, 21,* 5–17.

ROLF, E., & HASAZI, J. (1977). Identification of preschool children at risk and some guidelines for primary prevention. In G. W. Albee & J. M. Joffee (Eds.), *Primary prevention of psychopathology Vol. I. The issues.* Hanover, NH: University Press of New England. Instrument: Vermont Behavior Checklist.

ORVASCHEL, H., SHOLOMSKAS, D., & WEISSMAN, M. M. (1980). *The assessment of psychopathology and behavioral problems in children: A review of scales suitable for epidemiological and clinical research (1967–1979)* (DHHS Publication No. ADM 80-1037). Washington, DC: U.S. Government Printing Office.

Infants, Toddlers, and Preschoolers: Characteristics of Their Environments

Parental Attitudes Toward Childrearing and the Child

Neonatal Perception Inventories (NPI), *Elsie Broussard, 1970*

Description. The NPI assesses mothers' perceptions of their infants along the positive-negative dimension. Mothers use 5-point rating scales to indicate the extent to which their infants display six behaviors which are often sources of concern, e.g., crying, spitting up. Mothers also indicate the extent to which they believe the average infant displays each behavior.

The NPI I is used to assess mothers' expectations 1 to 4 days postpartum. The NPI II is used when infants are 4 to 6 weeks old. It elicits perceptions of infants' behavior during the preceding month. It is most appropriately used with mothers of healthy, full-term, first-born infants.

Administration and scoring. The NPI is a paper-and-pencil measure which is self-administered and can be group-administered. See Broussard (1970) for scoring and administration details.

Variables and score interpretation. Scores are (a) the average baby score; (b) the "your baby" score; and (c) the difference score, or average baby score minus "your baby" score. Scores are assumed to reflect the mothers' attitudes as opposed to their infants' or the average infant's actual behavior. A difference score of zero or lower is interpreted as an indication that the mother does not idealize her child; that is, that she perceives her infant to be, at best, average. If obtained on the NPI II, a difference score of zero or lower suggests that her infant is at risk for later emotional disorder since mothers tend to "idealize" their infants.

Reliability. Internal consistency ($n = 100$ mothers including first and later births and high risk groups) NPI I Average baby score is .63; Your baby score is .74 (Blumberg, 1980). Because first-time mothers' perceptions of their newborns are expected to be highly fluid, the appropriateness of test-retest reliability for NPI I and NPI II has been questioned (Broussard, personal communication).

Uses and findings. Broussard (1984) followed a sample of full-term healthy first-born infants for two decades. She found that those infants who were high risk on the NPI II assessment were 5.62 more likely to have a diagnosis of psychosocial disorder at age 19 years than those who were at low risk.

Where to obtain. Dr. Elsie R. Broussard, 209 Parran Hall, University of Pittsburgh, Pittsburgh, PA 15261 for a copy of the NPI and permission to use it.

References

BLUMBERG, N. L. (1980). Effects of neonatal risk, maternal attitudes and cognitive style on early postpartum adjustment. *Journal of Abnormal Psychology, 89*, 139–150.

BROUSSARD, E. R. (1984). The Pittsburgh first borns at age 19 years. In R. Tyson, J. Call, & E. Galeson (Eds.), *Frontiers of infant psychiatry* (Vol. 2, pp. 522–530). New York: Basic Books.

BROUSSARD, E. R. (1978). Psychosocial disorders in children: Early assessment of infants at risk. *Continuing Education for the Family Physician, 8*(2), 44–57.

Parents' Report (PR), *Eleanor D. Dibble & Donald J. Cohen, 1974*

Description. The PR assesses parents' perceptions of their parenting style with respect to a particular child. Half of the 48 items describe positive parental behaviors and half describe negative behaviors. Parents use rating scales to indicate how frequently they perform each behavior and how frequently they should ideally perform each behavior. A 20-item short form is available (Cohen, Dibble, & Grawe, 1977). The test development samples included parents of over 350 1- to 6-year-old twins and a small sample of parents of singletons.

Administration and scoring. The PR is self-administered. Item points are summed to compute factor scores.

Variables and score interpretation. Analysis of response of parents of 37% of the twins yielded five factors: (a) respect for autonomy; (b) control through guilt and anxiety; (c) consistency; (d) child-centeredness; and (e) parental temper and detachment (Cohen, Dibble, & Grawe, 1977). Indices of parents' perceptions of their own caregiving practices and their belief about ideal practices are computed. Real-ideal comparisons provide indices of parents' satisfaction with their performance as a parent.

Reliability. Few significant differences were found between initial scores and those obtained one month later for either "real" or "ideal" measures (Dibble & Cohen, 1974).

Uses and findings. Ratings of parents based on interviews and longitudinal case records corresponded with parents' PR responses (Dibble & Cohen, 1974). Research indicated that PR responses of preschoolers' parents were related to parent ratings of the children's personalities and mediated the relationship between stress and children's personalities (Dibble & Cohen, 1980). Parental style was, in turn, related to the mothers' prenatal well-being and the children's neonatal health. The PR has also been used in twin studies to detect differential parental treatment of siblings.

Where to obtain. Dr. Donald Cohen, Yale Child Study Center, P.O. Box 333, New Haven, CN 06510.

References

COHEN, D. J., DIBBLE, E., & GRAWE, J. M. (1977). Parental style: Mothers' and fathers' perceptions of their relations with twin children. *Archives of General Psychiatry, 34,* 480–487.

DIBBLE, E., & COHEN, D. J. (1974). Companion instruments for the measurement of children's competence and parental style. *Archives of General Psychiatry, 30,* 805–815.

DIBBLE, E., & COHEN, D. J. (1980). The interplay of biological endowment, early experience and psychosocial influence during the first year of life: An epidemiological twin study. In E. J. Anthony & C. Chiland (Eds.), *The child and his family. Preventative child psychiatry in an age of transition* (Vol. 6). New York: John Wiley.

Child Rearing Practices Report (CRPR), Jeanne H. Block, 1965

Description. The CRPR assesses parents' socialization practices. It is a 91-item Q-sort. Descriptions of childrearing beliefs are printed on 91 separate cards. Respondents sort the descriptions into seven categories on the basis of how well they describe a particular parent's practices. A specified number of cards must be placed in each category. Category 7 is for descriptions which are most descriptive of the parent, category 6 for descriptions which are quite descriptive, and so on.

The CRPR is used to obtain both parents' self-descriptions and older childrens' and adults' retrospective descriptions of their parents' practices. The CRPR research samples have varied in nationality, education, and SES.

Administration and scoring. Self-administration of the CRPR takes 45 minutes or less. Item scores, sums of scores, and correlations between fathers' and mothers' scores serve as indices (Block, Block, & Morrison, 1981). See Block (note) for details and additional types of CRPR scores.

Variables and score interpretation. The CRPR items assess parents' methods of controlling child behavior (e.g., guilt induction), parents' tendencies to encourage or discourage types of child behaviors (e.g., suppress aggression), and the overall quality of family relationships, as well as other variables. It should be noted that CRPR item scores are ipsative, not normative (See Block, 1961, for discussion of logical and statistical issues).

Reliability. Test-retest item scores, self-report ($n = 90$, 1-year interval) averaged .71; item scores, third person version ($n = 66$, 3-year interval) averaged .64 for mothers and .65 for fathers (see note).

Uses and findings. Mothers who differed in their parenting orientation, as determined by observational data, also differed in their CRPR responses (Block, note). For example, mothers characterized by observers as firm, distant, and critical reported that they did not allow their child to get angry at parents or teachers, to keep secrets, to express feelings, or to experience too much tenderness. Other research linked mother-father agreement on the CRPR to young boys' ego-resiliency and ego control (Block, Block, & Morrison, 1981).

Where to obtain. The Block Project, Department of Psychology, University of California, Berkeley, CA 94720 for the original CRPR. A brief manual and items to type onto Q sort cards are provided.

References

BLOCK, J. (1961). The Q-sort method in personality assessment and psychiatric research. Springfield, IL: Charles C Thomas.

BLOCK, J. H., BLOCK, J., & MORRISON, A. (1981). Parental agreement on child-rearing orientation and gender related personality correlates in children. *Child Development, 52,* 965–974.

Note

BLOCK, J. *The child rearing practices report (CRPR): A set of Q items for the description of parent socialization attitudes and values.* Unpublished manuscript, University of California, Institute of Human Development, Berkeley, CA.

Parent Belief Interviews, *Ann V. McGillicuddy-De Lisi and others, 1980 (Brief Report)*

The Parent Belief Interviews include two instruments that assess the constructs about children that parents bring to childrearing. Twelve vignettes describe situations involving a parent and a preschool child. One section of the interview, the Communication Preference Questionnaire, asks parents of preschoolers to indicate how they should and how they would handle each situation. Probes elicit parents' rationales for their strategies. Rationales are coded for parents' developmental goals and for parents' underlying childrearing orientations. The second part of the interview uses issues raised in the vignettes to examine parents' views of preschoolers' competencies and of developmental processes. There are 22 sets of questions. Responses are coded for the presence of 27 child development constructs which range from those that reflect a view of children as passive, i.e., direct instruction, to those that reflect a view of children as actively constructing their knowledge.

Interrater, test-retest, and split-half reliabilities have been reported (McGillicuddy-De Lisi, 1985; McGillicuddy-De Lisi et al., 1980). Interview responses have been related to observations of parents' teaching behavior, family SES and composition, and children's cognitive development (McGillicuddy-De Lisi, 1982; 1985). Where to obtain. Ann McGillicuddy-De Lisi, Department of Psychology, Lafayette College, Easton, PA.

References

McGILLICUDDY-DE LISI, A. V. (1982). The relation between family configuration and parental beliefs about child development. In L. M. Laosa & I. Sigel (Eds.), *Families as learning environments for children.* New York: Plenum.

McGILLICUDDY-DE LISI, A. V. (1985). The relationship between parental beliefs and children's cognitive level. In I. Sigel (Ed.), *Parental belief systems.* Hillsdale, NJ: Lawrence Erlbaum Associates.

McGILLICUDDY-DE LISI, A. V., JOHNSON, J., SIGEL, I., & EPSTEIN, R. (1980). *Communication beliefs questionnaire and interview administration and coding manual.* Princeton, NJ: Educational Testing Service.

Quality of Caregiving

Parent Behavior Progression (PBP), *R. M. Bromwich & others, 1976; 1983*

Description. The PBP is a tool for developmental specialists, to help them optimize the infant's functioning by enhancing desirable parent-infant interactions. The 66 descriptions of desirable parenting behaviors and attitudes serve as a checklist for infant development specialists. Specialists should, ideally, complete the PBP on the basis of two or three 1 to 1½ hour sessions during which they establish rapport, talk informally with the parent, observe parent-infant interactions, and see the home. The instrument is designed to be used repeatedly as an aid in intervention.

The PBP should be used by specialists who are working with the parents. Self-training is needed. Form I is used with parents of immature or infants up to 9 months of age. Form II is used with parents of infants from 9 months to 3 years. PBP research samples have included handicapped and other "at risk" children of varied SES.

Administration and scoring. Scores of the original PBP were tallies of items checked. A graded system for scoring items was introduced in the recent revision (Bromwich et al., 1983) but has not, as of this writing, been evaluated in published research.

Variables and score interpretation. Items are organized into six levels. Level scores indicate the extent to which parents exhibit specific types of competencies. These competencies are theorized to develop in rough sequence through parents' interactions with developing infants and to build upon each other. Competencies at levels 1, 2, and 3 involve the ability to enjoy one's baby, to respond to one's baby's cues and to interact with the baby in a mutually satisfying way. Competencies at levels 4, 5, and 6 involve the internalization, utilization, and elaboration of childrearing principles.

Reliability. Interrater agreement for levels 1, 2, and 3 averaged 94.8% to 96.6% ($n = 5$) (Bromwich et al., 1983). Test-retest correlations (3–4 month interval, $n = 46$ or less) ranged from .31 to .78 but were lower when obtained over longer intervals (Allen, Affleck, McQueeny, & McGrade, 1982).

Uses and findings. The PBP has been used to evaluate both home and center based interventions for handicapped and low-birth-weight infants. PBP assessments were related to staff evaluations of their success or failure with parents (Bromwich & Parmalee, 1979) and to independent assessment of home environments with the Caldwell HOME (Allen et al., 1982).

Where to obtain. The Center for Educational Psychology, California State University, 18111 Nordhoff Street, Northridge, CA 91330.

References

ALLEN, D. A., AFFLECK, C., McQUEENY, M., & McGRADE, B. J. (1982). Validation of the parent behavior progression in an early intervention program. *Mental Retardation, 20,* 159–163.

BROMWICH, R. M., KHOKHA, E., FUST, S., BAXTYER, E., BURGE, D., & KASS, E. W. (1983). Manual for the Parent Behavior Progression. Northridge, CA: Center for Research, Development and Services, California State-Northridge.

BROMWICH, R. M., & PARMALEE, A. H. (1979). An intervention program for preterm infants In T. M. Field (Ed.), *Infants born at risk*. New York: Spectrum.

The Knowledge Scale, Ann S. Epstein, 1980

Description. The Knowledge Scale assesses the appropriateness of adolescents' and adults' expectations about infant abilities during the first 2 years of life. It consists of 73 items, each of which asks when babies begin to perform a behavior or demonstrate an ability, such as sitting without support or gurgling at adults. Respondents indicate when they think each behavior first appears by sorting the individual item cards onto six pieces of construction paper marked 0–1 month, 1–4 months, 4–8 months, and so on up to 24 months.

The scale was used to assess expectations of 98 pregnant teenagers who were heterogeneous with respect to SES, ethnicity, and other demographics (Epstein, 1980).

Administration and scoring. The scale is administered individually. The examiner reads each card out loud before giving it to the respondent. The answers are recorded on a scoring sheet which simplifies computation.

Variables and score interpretation. Total correct, early expectation, and late expectation scores are computed. The total correct score is the number of items placed in the correct age intervals. Responses which place the onset of infant abilities too early are scored in terms of their temporal distance from the correct response. The sum of these scores is the early expectation score; the late expectation score is computed in the same way. Expectation scores for particular classes of infant ability, i.e., motor abilities, can also be computed.

Reliability. None reported.

Uses and findings. Epstein (1980) found that pregnant teenagers, on the average, underestimated the speed of infant development. Examinations of specific expectations indicated that their expectations about basic care, health and nutrition, and perceptual and motor development were accurate. In contrast, their expectations about the speed of linguistic, cognitive, and social development were underestimates. The more they underestimated infants, the less observant they were of infants and parents presented in a videotape. Mothers with late expectations were less likely to talk to their own babies during interactions 6 months postpartum. Teenagers with early expectations were less sharing with their babies during interactions.

Where to obtain. High/Scope Educational Research Foundation, 600 North River Street, Ypsilanti, MI 48198.

References

EPSTEIN, A. S. (1980). *Assessing the child development information needed by adolescent parents with very young children. Final Report.* Washington, DC: Dept. of HEW.

For additional instruments see:

MacPHEE, D. (1984). The pediatrician as a source of information about child development. *Journal of Pediatric Psychology, 9,* 87–101. Instrument: Knowledge of Infant Development Inventory.
STROM, R. D., & SLAUGHTER (1978). Measurement of childrearing expectations using the parent-as-teacher inventory. *Journal of Experimental Education, 47,* 9–16.
VANDIVERE, P., & BAILEY, P. W. (1981). *Gathering information from parents* (Contract #300-80-0752). Washington, DC: Office of Special Education and Rehabilitative Services. (Eric Document Reproduction Service No. ED 222 005)

Parenting Stress

Life Experiences Survey (LES), *Irwin G. Sarason, James H. Johnson, & Judith M. Siegel, 1978*

Description. The LES quantifies stress associated with changes in life circumstances. It includes 47 descriptions of life events (e.g., marriage, illness) and 3 blanks which allow respondents to insert events. Respondents indicate whether they have experienced any of the events during a specified time period, e.g., the preceding year. They rate the impact of each experienced event on a scale ranging from plus 3 (extremely positive) to minus 3 (extremely negative). The LES has been used with college students, middle class adults, and selected parent populations.

Administration and scoring. The LES is self-administered and scored either by summing impact ratings or by counting checked events. Counts and sums are highly correlated.

Variables and score interpretation. Sarason, Johnson, and Siegel (1978) used the LES to generate positive life change scores, negative life change scores, total life change scores and net (negative minus positive) life change scores. Their findings suggest that it is the negative life change score which is most closely related to the decreases in well-being which are theoretically linked to the concept of stress.

Reliability. Test-retest (5–6 week interval, n's = 34–58 students): Negative change .56–.88; Positive Change .19–.33; Total Change .63–.64. Sarason et al. (1978) regarded these coefficients as underestimates because of special circumstances.

Uses and findings. Crnic, Greenberg, Ragozin, Robinson, & Basham (1983) found that mothers of newborns who reported greater negative life change were relatively less satisfied with parenting. During interactions 3 months later, communication between these mothers and their babies was relatively poor.

Where to obtain. Irwin G. Sarason, Department of Psychology NI-25, University of Washington, Seattle, WA 98195.

References

CRNIC, K. A., GREENBERG, M. T., RAGOZIN, A. S., ROBINSON, N. M., & BASHAM, R. B. (1983). Effects of stress and social support on mothers of premature and full term infants. *Child Development, 54,* 209–217.

SARASON, I. G., JOHNSON, J. H., & SIEGEL, J. (1978). Assessing the impact of life change: Development of the Life Experiences Survey. *Journal of Consulting and Clinical Psychology, 46,* 932–946 (sample instrument).

Parenting Stress Index (PSI), Richard R. Abidin, 1983, 1986

Description. The PSI assesses stress in the parent-child system. It includes a 19-item optional scale, which like the LES, assesses life change. The remaining 101 multiple choice and Likert-type items assess the extent to which families experience distressing chronic life circumstances generated by parent, child and environmental characteristics.

Parents repond with respect to themselves and one of their children. A fifth grade level is required. The normative sample included 543 mothers of healthy and clinic-referred children. Caucasians, college graduates, and mothers of children age 3 or younger were overrepresented.

Administration and scoring. The PSI is self-administered in 20 to 30 minutes. Answer sheets are self-scoring.

Variables and score interpretation. Scores are total score, parent characteristic domain score, child characteristic domain score and optional life events score. The parent score indicates the extent to which the parent-child dyad is stressed by the parent's limitations. The child score indexes stress in the dyad due to the child's characteristics. Child and parent scales are divided into subscales: child's adaptability, child's demandingness, parent's health, and parent's sense of competence. Norms are supplemented with means obtained by various homogeneous diagnostic groups (Abidin, 1983).

Reliability. Test-retest coefficients for parent, child, and total scores ranged from .63 to .96 over 1- to 3-month intervals and .55 to .70 over 1-year interval (*n*'s = 75–54). Internal consistency coefficients ranged from .89 to .95 (*n* = 534). Subscale coefficients were lower (Loyd & Abidin, 1985).

Uses and findings. The PSI Manual provides abstracts of over 50 validity research projects which have involved such populations as: normal families, child abuse, Attention Deficit Disorders, and mentally retarded. The PSI can be used as either a screening tool or as part of an individual diagnostic study.

The factor and subscale structure has been replicated in a transcultural study (Abidin, 1986). Discriminant validity has been established for 15 different clinical groups. Its construct and concurrent validity has been examined in relation to transition to parenthood, husband support, difficult child, infant attachment, and development.

Where to obtain. Pediatric Psychology Press, 320 Terrell Road West, Charlottesville, VA 22901 or Clinical Psychology Publishing Co., Brandon, VT 05733.

References

ABIDIN, R. R. (1986). Parenting Stress Index—Manual (2nd ed.). Charlottesville, VA: Pediatric Psychology Press.

LOYD, B. H. (1986). Parenting Stress Index (Form 6): Statistical characteristics. In R. R. Abidin (Ed.), Parenting Stress Index—Manual (2nd ed.). Charlottesville, VA: Pediatric Psychology Press.

LOYD, B. H., & ABIDIN, R. R. (1985). *Revision of the Parenting Stress Index. Journal of Pediatric Psychology, 10*, 169–215.

Questionnaire on Resources and Stress (QRS), Jean Holroyd, 1974; 1987

Description. The QRS examines the distressing experiences and coping resources of those who care for the chronically ill and the disabled. Most of its 285 items are statements which describe a disabled person or describe that person's effect on the well-being of the respondent and other family members, for example, "(insert name of disabled person) puts a strain on me." Caregivers answer *true* or *false*. The four different short forms include between 44 and 66 items.

QRS research samples included parents of both healthy children and children with varied medical and developmental disorders. Parent demographics and children's ages varied widely.

Administration and scoring. The questionnaire is self-administered and requires a reading level of grade 6. Item scores are summed within subscales.

Variables and score interpretation. The 15 QRS subscales include measures of parent problems (e.g., excessive time demands), child problems (e.g., social obtrusiveness), and family problems (e.g., financial difficulties). Short-form subscales were derived from factor analysis. Test construction samples typically included several small, homogeneous clinical and control groups. The number of factor scores varies from form to form. Holroyd (1987) reports short and full form means for samples (*n*'s = 20 to 153) from several diagnostic groups.

Reliability. QRS internal consistency coefficients ranged from .96 for total scores to the .20's for some subscales. Short form findings were similar (Friedrich, Greenberg, & Crnic, 1983).

Uses and findings. Research (Holroyd, 1987) indicates that differences in child's diagnostic status, severity of child's disability, child's placement (institution versus home), parent demographics, and access to community resources were reflected in patterns of QRS scores.

Where to obtain. Clinical Psychology Publishing Co., 4 Conant Square, Brandon, VT 05733.

References

FRIEDRICH, W. N., GREENBERG, M. T., & CRNIC, K. (1983). A short form of the Questionnaire on Resources and Stress. *American Journal of Mental Deficiency, 88,* 41–48.

HOLROYD, J. (1974). The Questionnaire on Resources and Stress: An instrument to measure family response to a handicapped family member. *Journal of Community Psychology 2,* 92–94.

HOLROYD, J., & McARTHUR, D. (1976). Mental retardation and stress on the parents: A contrast between Downs syndrome and childhood autism. *American Journal of Mental Deficiency, 80,* 431–436.

HOLROYD, J. (1987). Questionnaire on Resources and Stress for Families with Chronically Ill or Handicapped Members. Brandon, VT: Clinical Psychology Publishing Co.

For additional instrument see:

CRNIC, K. A., & GREENBERG, M. T. (1985, April). Parenting daily hassles: Relationships among minor stresses, family functioning and child development. Paper presented at meeting of the Society for Research in Child Development, Toronto. Instrument: Parenting Events Scale.

Home Environment

Home Observation for the Measurement of the Environment (HOME), *Bettye Caldwell & R. H. Bradley, 1968, 1984*

Description. The HOME assesses the quality and quantity of emotional, social, and cognitive support provided to children in their homes. Each of the 45 items on Form I and the 55 items on Form II describe a characteristic of the child's home life. Home visitors determine whether characteristics are present in homes on the basis of observations and interviews with caregivers.

Trained or self-trained visitors assess homes of children under 3 years with Form I and the homes of 3- to 6-year-olds with Form II. A school-aged children's form is also available (Bradley & Caldwell, 1984). Families who were low on SES indicators were predominant in the standardization samples, and scoring "ceilings" may be too low for middle class homes (Mitchell & Gray, 1981).

Variables and score interpretation. There are six factor-based subscales on Form I, including measures of caregivers' responsivity, degree of organization, and variety of stimulation. There are eight Form II subscales which include measures of adequacy of language stimulation, amount of play material provided, and degree to which social maturity is modeled for the child. Age norms for total scores and subscores are available (Bradley & Caldwell, 1984).

Reliability. Internal consistency of total scores was .89 for infants ($n = 174$) and .93 for preschoolers ($n = 238$). Test-retest of total scores over a 6-month interval was .57 for infants ($n = 91$) and .76 for preschoolers ($n = 33$). Subscore figures were lower. Simultaneous observers were found to agree on 92% of the HOME items (Ramey, Mills, Campbell, & O'Brien, 1975).

Uses and findings. Bradley, Caldwell, and colleagues (see Bradley & Caldwell, 1984 for review) found that HOME scores were better predictors of later IQ than SES indices. Further, Home I scores were better predictors of preschool IQ than infant intelligence measures. In light of these findings, researchers examined the ability of the HOME to identify children at risk for mental retardation at age 6 months. HOME scores identified 100% of infants who later obtained IQ scores below 70 and 78% of the infants whose later IQ scores were 70 or above. The HOME has also been used to study language delay, child abuse, and home-based early education.

Where to obtain. The Center for Research, University of Arkansas, 33rd and University, Little Rock, AR 72204 for manual, reproducible scoring sheet, and monograph.

References

BRADLEY, R. H., & CALDWELL, B. M. (1984). Home observation for the measurement of the Environment. Little Rock: Center for Child Research, University of Arkansas.

MITCHELL, S. K., & GRAY, C. A. (1981). Developmental generalizability of the HOME inventory. *Education and Psychological Measurement, 41,* 1001–1010.

RAMEY, C. T., MILLS, P. M., CAMPBELL, F. A., & O'BRIEN, C. (1975). Infants' home environments: A comparison of high risk families and families from the general population. *American Journal of Mental Deficiency, 80,* 40–42.

Cognitive Home Environment Scale (CHES), *Norma Radin, 1965*

Description. The CHES assesses the amount of cognitive stimulation which children receive at home. It is a structured interview with 25 items. Items ask parents about materials which are available in the home, activities which involve the child and parents' expectations for the child.

The CHES is administered to parents of preschool children. The same interview is used with both parents but factor scores for mothers differ from those for fathers. A short form of the scale yields the same subscores for both parents (Radin, 1981). The CHES has been used to study lower, working class and middle-class homes.

Administration and scoring. The full interview requires about 30 minutes and the short form takes about 15 minutes. Item-specific criteria are used to score parent responses. Item scores are summed to form factor scores.

Variables and score interpretation. The short form yields three factors: (a) Future Expectations (of the parents); (b) Educational Materials in the home; and (c) Direct Teaching (by parents). Factor analysis of mothers' responses to the full form added two factors: Grades Expected and Educationally oriented activities (Radin & Sonquist, 1968). Analysis of fathers' responses (Radin & Epstein, 1975) yielded a slightly different set of five factors: (a) Future Expectations; (b) Grades Expected; (c) Father Stimulates Child; (d) Mother Stimulates Child; and (e) Use of External Resources.

Reliability. Interrater agreement in scoring of parents' responses was about 91% (Radin & Sonquist, 1968). A second shortened version recently administered to a working-class population (Radin & Greer, see note) yielded the following factors and alpha coefficients: Educational books in the home—.64 for fathers and .72 for mothers; Cognitively stimulating activities and resources—.64 for fathers and .74 for mothers.

Uses and findings. Radin (1972) used the CHES to evaluate the impact of mothers' involvement in compensatory education. She found pre-post increases in some CHES factor scores when compensatory preschools involved mothers in their children's education but no change when opportunities for involvement were not provided. Children of the involved mothers made relatively large cognitive gains during their kindergarten years. Other CHES research (Radin, 1981) examined fathers' contributions to preschoolers' cognitive development related to the sex of the child.

Where to obtain. Dr. Norma Radin, School of Social Work, University of Michigan, Ann Arbor, MI 48109.

References

RADIN, N. (1972). Three degrees of maternal involvement in a preschool program: Impact on mothers and children. *Child Development, 43,* 1355–1364.

RADIN, N. (1981). Childrearing fathers in intact families, I: Some antecedents and consequences. *Merrill-Palmer Quarterly, 27,* 489–514.

RADIN, N., & EPSTEIN, A. S. (1975). *A questionnaire for fathers on home stimulation of preschoolers.* Unpublished manuscript, University of Michigan, School of Social Work, Ann Arbor.

RADIN, N., & SONQUIST, H. (1968). *The Gale preschool program: Final report.* Ypsilanti, MI: Ypsilanti Public Schools.

Note

RADIN, N., & GREER, E. (April, 1987). *Father unemployment and the young child.* Presentation at the Society for Research in Child Development meeting, Baltimore.

Additional instruments:

BRADLEY, R. H., & CALDWELL, B. M. (1978). Screening the environment. *American Journal of Orthopsychiatry, 48,* 114–131. *Review.*

WACHS, T. D., FRANCIS, J., & McQUEEN, S. (1977). Psychological dimensions of the infant's physical environment. *Infant Behavior and Development, 2,* 155–161. Instrument: *Purdue Home Stimulation Inventory.*

DayCare/Preschool Environments

Quality Day Care Checklists, R. C. Endsley & M. R. Bradbard, 1981

Description. The Checklists were designed to help parents choose daycare programs but can be used by anyone to gather data needed to evaluate daycare settings. The 27-item telephone checklist is used for basic information about a program's policies, costs, and services.

The observational checklists list 75 to 90 desirable program features. The features are those which experts agreed discriminated between high- and low-quality daycare and which mothers would find easy to evaluate.

There is an observational checklist for use with infant-toddler programs and another for preschool programs. Each version includes a supplement which helps determine the appropriateness of the program for handicapped children. The field trial of the instruments was conducted by middle class evaluators who observed center-based programs.

Administration and scoring. A well-planned visit of at least 30 minutes is needed, and filed test data suggest that several visits are preferable for completing some of the items. Scores are the numbers of desirable features at the program.

Variables and score interpretation. The purpose of scores is to sharpen observer perceptions. The checklists cover four aspects of daycare settings, namely, (a) health and safety features; (b) physical space and program activities; (c) adult-child-peer interactions; and (d) home-program coordination.

Reliability. Agreement on items between pairs who visited programs together ($n = 29$) averaged 75%. Interrater reliability over a 1-week interval ($n = 12$) averaged 80% (Bradbard & Endsley, 1978a).

Uses and findings. Bradbard and Endsley (1978a) found that 80% of checklist items were more likely to be present in programs which experts rated as high in quality than in those rated as low in quality. Evaluators who recorded program observations on the checklists later made global evaluations of programs which were similar to those of the experts. Evaluators who did not use the checklists at all did not match the experts as closely (Bradbard & Endsley, 1978b).

Where to obtain. The checklists and discussion about the way in which they are used are presented in Endsley and Bradbard (1981). Those who want to use the checklists in research projects should contact Dr. Richard C. Endsley, Department of Home Economics, University of Georgia, Athens, GA 30602.

References

BRADBARD, M. R., & ENDSLEY, R. C. (1978a). Field testing a parent guide to quality day care centers. *Child Care Quarterly, 7,* 289–294.

BRADBARD, M. R., & ENDSLEY, R. C. (1978b). Improving inexperienced raters' evaluations of day care through use of a guide. *Child Care Quarterly, 7,* 295–301.

ENDSLEY, R. C., & BRADBARD, M. R. (1981). Quality of day care: A handbook of choices for parents and caregivers. Englewood Cliffs, NJ: Prentice-Hall, Inc.

SCHOOL-AGED CHILDREN: CHILD CHARACTERISTICS

Diagnostic/Multiproblem Assessment

Child Behavior Checklist (CBCL) and Related Measures, Thomas M. Achenbach & Craig Edelbrock, 1983.

Description. The CBCL assesses the extent to which children exhibit a variety of problems and strengths. It is also used to classify children's problem behaviors in terms of typology of behavior disorders. It consists of 118 descriptions of problem behaviors. Respondents indicate the extent to which the problems have been characteristic of children during the preceding 6 months. An additional 20 items are used to assess the children's social competence.

The CBCL is used with both sexes, aged 4 to 16 years, but there are separate scoring profiles for each sex at each of three age levels: 4–5, 6–11, and 12–16 (Contact Achenbach at address given below regarding the CBCL for ages 2–3). Parents serve as informants. Teacher-report, adolescent self-report, and observational instruments which parallel the CBCL in form and content are available. Large and heterogenous samples provided test development and normative data.

Administration and scoring. The CBCL is either presented as a structured interview or is self-administered. It is completed in 15–20 minutes. Profiles are computed with the aid of either hand-scoring templates or computer programs.

Variables and score interpretation. Behavior problem items were organized into subscales on the basis of factor analytic studies of clinic-referred children (Achenbach & Edelbrock, 1983). One subscale assesses the extent to which the child exhibits internalizing disorders, and a second assesses the extent to which the child exhibits externalizing disorders, disorders which make others uncomfortable. The same items are also organized into subscales which assess specific behavior problems, such as hyperactivity and depression. Social competence items form subscales which assess school performance, interpersonal skills, and involvement in constructive activities. Separate sets of standard scores for each sex and age group are used. Children's disorders may be classified by comparison of their pattern of subscores with CBCL profiles types derived from cluster analysis.

Reliability. For subscale scores, median test-retest, over a 1-week interval (n's = 11 to 16 non-clinic children separated by age and sex), was .89. Test-restest over 6 months (n's = 37 to 135 outpatients separated by age and sex) ranged from .44 to .79 for Behavior Problem subscales and from .47 to .71 for Social Competence subscales. Additional information is available (Achenbach & Edelbrock, 1983).

Uses and findings. Researchers have examined the ability of CBCL subscores and profile classifications to make clinically relevant differentiations. For example, Achenbach (1979) reported that CBCL profile classifications were associated with treatment outcomes. Boys who were classified as hyperactive-delinquent were found to have improved at follow-up, in contrast to socially withdrawn-immature boys, who worsened. The CBCL has also been used to examine the internalizing-externalizing distinction. Fisher, Rolf, Hasazi, and Cummings (1984) found that the tendency toward externalizing disorders during preschool was modestly related to both externalizing and internalizing subscores of the CBCL obtained when children were 9–15 years old. Preschool internalizing disorders were not predictive of later CBCL scores.

Where to obtain. Dr. Thomas Achenbach, University Associates in Psychiatry, 1 South Prospect Street, Burlington, VT 05401 for Checklists, profiles, scoring templates, and manual. Computer scoring programs are available for $70 to $95.

References

ACHENBACH, T. M. (1979). The child behavior profile: An empirically based system for assessing children's behavioral problems and competencies. *International Journal of Mental Health, 7,* 24–42.

ACHENBACH, T. M., & EDELBROCK, C. S. (1983). *Manual for the Child Behavior Checklists and Revised Child Behavior Profile.* Burlington, VT: University of Vermont, Department of Psychiatry.

FISCHER, M., ROLF, J. E., HASAZI, J. E., & CUMMINGS, L. (1984). Follow-up of a preschool epidemiological sample: Cross-age continuities and predictions of later adjustment with internalizing and externalizing dimensions of behavior. *Child Development, 55,* 137–150.

Revised Behavior Problem Checklist (RBPC), *Herbert C. Quay & Donald R. Peterson, 1983*

Description. The Revised Behavior Problem Checklist is briefer than the CBCL. The instrument consists of 89 behavior problem descriptions. Respondents indicate whether any of the behaviors constitute a problem for children and if so, to what extent. Scores provide information about children's standing on various dimensions of psychopathology.

The RBPC is used to describe children of 5 years or older. The rater may be anyone who knows the child well. The revised scale manual includes data from a variety of clinical and nonclinical samples, and a new manual with data from additional groups is in preparation.

Administration and scoring. The RBPC may be self-administered in 10 minutes and scored with the aid of a template in 5 minutes.

Variables and score interpretation. Subscales were identified through factor analysis (Quay & Peterson, 1983) of the ratings of varied raters with respect to clinical and nonclinical samples of children. Two very short scales are considered tentative. The remaining scales assess conduct disorders, socialized aggression, attention problems, immaturity, and anxiety-withdrawal. Norms, some age and sex specific, are presented for test development populations as well for several other clinical groups (Quay & Peterson, 1984). Data from additional clinical populations and T-scores, both for unselected public school children in grades K through 8 and for school-defined seriously emotionally disturbed children, will be provided in a forthcoming revision of the manual.

Reliability. Internal consistency of subscores (*n*'s = 72 diabetic children and 294 school children) ranged from .70 to .95. Interrater reliabilities (*n*'s = 6 to 20 developmentally disabled children rated by teachers) ranged from .52 to .83. Test-retest over 2 months (*n* = 149 school children) ranged from .49 to .83. The two lowest test-retest coefficients, .49 and

.61, reflect attenuation due to limited variance (Quay & Peterson, 1983).

Uses and findings. Quay and Peterson (1983) were able to correctly classify 85.5% of 665 children as psychiatric clinic clients or not with a multiple discriminant function which was composed of RBPC subscales. The researchers also found expected RBPC subscore differences between children who received different DSM III diagnoses. Further, high correlations between corresponding subscales of the BPC, the original instrument, and the RBPC provided some evidence that the extensive validation of the BPC could be generalized to the RBPC. A bibliography of BPC research is presented in the manual (Quay & Peterson, 1983).

Where to obtain. Dr. Herbert Quay, Box 248074, University of Miami, Coral Gables, FL 33124 for instructions on ordering the manual, scoring stencils, and checklists.

References

QUAY, H. C. (1983). A dimensional approach to behavior disorder: The Revised Behavior Problem Checklist. *School Psychology Review, 12,* 244–249.

QUAY, H. C., & PETERSON, D. R. (1983). *Interim manual for the Revised Behavior Problem Checklist.* Coral Gables: University of Miami.

QUAY, H. C., & PETERSON, D. R. (1984). Appendix I to the interim manual for the Revised Behavior Problem Checklist. Coral Gables: University of Miami.

For additional instruments see:

ORVASCHEL, H., SHOLOMSKAS, D., & WEISSMAN, M. M. (1980). The assessment of psychopathology and behavioral problems in children: A review of scales suitable for epidemiological and clinical research (1967–1979). (DHHS Publication No. (ADM)80-1037) Washington, DC: U.S. Government Printing Office.

Anxiety and Related Disorders

Revised Children's Manifest Anxiety Scale (RCMAS), Cecil R. Reynolds & Bert O. Richmond, 1985

Description. The RCMAS assesses the level of trait, or chronic, anxiety experienced by children and identifies the nature of children's anxiety experiences. It consists of 37 self-descriptive statements. For example, included are descriptions of worries and of anxiety-related physiological states. Children circle "yes" if the statement applies to themselves and "no" if the statement does not apply.

The RCMAS is completed by children 6 years old and older. The standardization sample consisted of 4,972 1st through 12th graders from 80 different schools and 13 different states. They were heterogeneous with respect to race, SES, and the urban versus rural nature of their communities. The factor structure of the RCMAS remained stable across gender and race (Reynolds & Richman, 1985).

Administration and scoring. The RCMAS has about a third grade reading level. When used with young children or poor readers, items are read aloud and individual administration is preferable. Older children can complete the RCMAS in groups. Administration time is 10 to

15 minutes. Raw scores are counts of "yes" replies. Templates aid computation of subscores.

Variables and score interpretation. Norms for the total sample and norms for subsamples of specific sex, race, and age are provided. The total anxiety score indicates level of chronic anxiety. Three anxiety subscales, the result of factor analytic studies (Reynolds & Richman, 1985), assess: (a) physiological symptoms; (b) worry and oversensitivity to environmental pressures; (c) social concerns and concentration difficulty. A fifth score, the lie score, indicates the extent to which concerns about social desirability predominate. The validity of high anxiety scores is uncertain when lie scores are high.

Reliability. Internal consistency of the total anxiety scale was low for black girls under age 12. For almost all other age by ethnicity by sex subsamples total anxiety coefficients were near or above .80. Most subscale coefficients were in the .50s, .60s or .70s. Test-retest coefficients for the total anxiety score ranged from .68 for a 9-month interval ($n = 534$ elementary school pupils) to .98 for a 3-week interval ($n = 99$ Nigerian children) (Reynolds & Richman, 1985).

Uses and findings. Reynolds (1982) supported the convergent and divergent validity of the RCMAS. RCMAS anxiety scores and trait anxiety subscores of the State-Trait Anxiety Inventory for Children (STAIC) were highly intercorrelated. RCMAS anxiety was moderately related to teachers' ratings of children's distractibility, acting-out tendencies, and interpersonal problems. RCMAS scores were not related to either state anxiety or intelligence.

Where to obtain. Western Psychological Services, 12031 Wilshire Blvd., Los Angeles, CA 90025 distributes sets which include 100 tests, the manual, and scoring key.

References

REYNOLDS, C. R. (1982) Convergent and divergent validity of the revised children's manifest anxiety scale. *Educational and Psychological Measurement, 42,* 1205–1213.

REYNOLDS, C. R., & RICHMAN, B. O. (1985). Revised children's manifest anxiety scale manual. Los Angeles: Western Psychological Services.

Revised Fear Survey Schedule for Children (FSSC-R), Thomas H. Ollendick, 1983

Description. The Fear Survey Schedule for Children (Scherer & Nakamura, 1968) identified the type and range of stimuli which frightened children. Ollendick's (1983) revision simplifies its response format. The FSSC-R consists of 80 descriptions of objects or situations which might be frightening. Children indicate whether they fear each stimulus "none," "some," or "a lot."

The FSSC-R is for children age 7 years and older. The test development sample included 217 grade school children who were believed to vary widely in SES. The instrument has been used with children as old as 18 and, with changed administration, visually impaired children.

Administration and scoring. The FSSC-R is read aloud to younger children. Older children read the items themselves. It may be group administered. Scores are counts and sums of ratings.

Variables and score interpretation. Five factor scores were offered tentatively on the basis of analysis (Ollendick, 1983) of responses of 217 8- to 11-year-old children: (a) Fear of Failure and Criticism; (b) Fear of the Unknown; (c) Fear of Injury and Small Animals; (d) Fear of Danger and Death; (e) Medical Fears. Prevalence scores, the number of stimuli feared, and Total Fear scores, the sum of item ratings, may be computed. The latter indicate overall intensity of fear. Individual items identify children's specific fear sensitivities. Separate norms for each sex and each of four age groups between 7 years and 18 years were collected (Ollendick, Matson, & Helsel, 1985a).

Reliability. Internal consistencies of Total Fear scores (*n*'s = 99 and 118 third and fourth graders) were .94 and .95. Test-retest for Total Fear was .82 with a 1-week interval (*n* = 50) and .55 with a 3-month interval (*n* = 60). There were no differences between test and retest means (Ollendick, 1983).

Uses and findings. Ollendick (1983) found that FSSC-R scores correlated with trait anxiety scores. Also, children with lower FSSC-R scores obtained relatively high scores on measures of self-concept and internal locus of control, though relationships were weak and nonsignificant for boys. Further, school-phobic children obtained higher Total Fear scores than did matched controls. Other research (see Ollendick, Matson, & Helsel, 1985b) identified qualitative differences between fear patterns of visually impaired and nonimpaired youth and explored age and sex differences in fears.

Where to obtain. Dr. Thomas Ollendick, Department of Psychology, Virginia Polytechnic Institute and State University, Blacksburg, VA 24061 for a copy of the FSSC-R.

References

OLLENDICK, T. H. (1983). Reliability and validity of the revised fear survey schedule. *Behaviour Research and Therapy, 21,* 685–692.

OLLENDICK, T. H., MATSON, J. L., & HELSEL, W. J. (1985a). Fears in children and adolescents: Normative data. *Behaviour Research and Therapy, 23,* 465–468.

OLLENDICK, T. H., MATSON, J. L., & HELSEL, W. J. (1985b). Fears in visually-impaired and normally-sighted youth. *Behaviour Research and Therapy, 23,* 375–378.

SCHERER, M. W., & NAKAMURA, C. Y. (1968). A fear survey schedule for children (FSS-FC): A factor analytic comparison with manifest anxiety. *Behaviour Research and Therapy, 6,* 173–182.

Leyton Obsessional Inventory—Child Version (LOI-CV), Carol J. Berg, Judith L. Rapoport, & Martine Flament, 1986

Description. The LOI-CV assists in the identification of children and adolescents with obsessive-compulsive disorder and quantifies the severity of symptoms. Children are presented with 44 symptoms, each printed on a card. Children indicate whether they experience each symptom by placing each card in either the "yes" or "no" slot of a response box. For those symptoms present, they indicate the extent to which they try to resist symptoms and the extent to which symptoms interfere with daily activities.

Administration and scoring. The LOI-CV is a card sort task and is administered individually. Children with obsessive-compulsive disorders typically are slow in making response choices, which may increase administration time. Scores are the numbers of symptoms reported and sums of resistance and interference weightings of symptoms.

Variables and score interpretation. The yes score indicates the number of symptoms of obsessive-compulsive disorders which the child experiences. The resistance score indicates the extent to which the child reports symptoms which he or she tries to control or avert. The interference score indicates the extent to which the child's daily functioning is disrupted by symptoms.

Reliability. Test-retest coefficients were based on responses of 10 obsessive patients who were retested during each week of a 5-week placebo treatment. Intraclass correlations ranged from .94 to .97 (Berg, Rapoport, & Flament, 1986).

Uses and findings. Berg et al. (1986) found that obsessive psychiatric patients differed from healthy controls in all three LOI-CV scores. When compared to psychiatric controls, obsessive adolescents differed in resistance and interference scores, but not in yes scores. In the authors' words, "The disadvantage of the LOI-CV is the wide range of yes/ no responses obtained in patient populations, with low scores attributable to either denial of symptoms in obsessive

disorder or monosymptomatic clinical pictures" (Berg et al., 1985, p. 1057). Berg et al. (1986) also found that LOI-CV scores did not correlate with scores on several observer-based measures of obsessive-compulsive symptoms. However, changes in LOI-CV scores in response to drug treatment paralleled changes in the other measures of obsessive-compulsive symptoms.

Where to obtain. Carol J. Berg, Child Psychiatry Branch, Building 10, Room 6N-240, NIMH, Bethesda, MD 20205.

References

BERG, C. J., RAPOPORT, J. L., & FLAMENT, M. (1985). The Leyton Obsessional Inventory-Child Version. *Psychopharmacology Bulletin, 21,* 1057.

BERG, C. J., RAPOPORT, J. L., & FLAMENT, M. (1986). The Leyton Obsessional Inventory-Child Version. *Journal of the American Academy of Child Psychiatry, 23,* 84–91.

For additional instruments see:

MILLER, L. C., BARRETT, C. L., HAMPE, E., & NOBLE, H. (1972). Factor structure of childhood fears. *Journal of Consulting and Clinical Psychology, 39,* 264–268. Instrument: The Louisville Fear Survey for Children.

SPIELBERGER, C. D. (1973). *Preliminary manual for the state-trait anxiety inventory for children.* Palo Alto, CA: Consulting Psychologists Press.

Depression

Children's Depression Inventory (CDI), Maria Kovacs, 1982

Description. The CDI assesses the severity of depressive syndromes experienced by children. It consists of 27 sets of three self-descriptive statements. Each set describes a different symptom of depression. Statements within sets vary in the severity of the symptom they describe. Children select the one statement in each set which best describes their own behavior or experience during the preceding 2 weeks.

The CDI can be completed by children age 6 or older. It has been used with a variety of clinical and nonclinical populations. Psychometric properties of the instrument are not stable across populations which vary in clinical status. For example, the instrument's factor structure when used with psychiatric patients differed from the structure found with a public school sample (Kovacs, note).

Administration and scoring. The CDI was designed to be individually administered, with items read aloud as the child follows and responds. Administration takes about 10 to 20 minutes. Statement choices determine item scores. Item scores are summed.

Variables and score interpretation. The CDI score indicates the severity of a depressive syndrome. It can also identify depressed and nondepressed research samples. Kovacs (note) examined tentative, operational cutoff scores. However, CDI-based classifications should not be confused with psychiatric diagnoses of depression. As expected on conceptual grounds, there is a moderate, not strong, empirical correspondence between the two (Kovacs, note).

Reliability. Internal consistency, estimated for several clinical and nonclinical samples ranged from .71 to .94. Test-

retest data were complex. Over intervals of 1 to 4 weeks estimates were in the .80's for patients but low for well children. Over 6- to 13-week intervals, they were moderate, .50 to .72, for patients; high, .84, for well children (Kovacs, note; Saylor, Finch, Spirito, & Bennett, 1984). Note that short-term estimates for patients, arguably the most appropriate, were high.

Uses and findings. The CDI correlated highly with other self-report measures of depression (Kovacs, note) and with theoretically relevant variables, such as self-esteem anxiety and social adjustment. It was also found to be sensitive to clinically noted changes in severity of depression (Kovacs, note). However, like other self-report measures of childhood depression, the CDI is at best moderately related to assessments of child depression based on reports of parents and others (Kazdin et al., 1983).

Where to obtain. Dr. Maria Kovacs, Western Psychiatric Institute and Clinic, 3811 O'Hara Street, Pittsburgh, PA 15213 for a copy of the CDI, permission to photocopy it, scoring key, instructions, and other information. Recipients are asked only to cover processing costs.

References

KAZDIN, A. E., FRENCH, N. H., UNIS, A. S., & ESVELDT-DAWSON, K. (1983). Assessment of childhood depression: Correspondence of child and parent ratings. *Journal of the American Academy of Child Psychiatry, 22*, 157–164.

KOVACS, M. (1985). The Children's Depression Inventory (CDI). *Psychopharmocology Bulletin, 21*(4), 995–999.

SAYLOR, C. F., FINCH, A. J., SPIRITO, A., & BEN-NETT, B. (1984). The children's depression inventory: A systematic evaluation of psychometric properties. *Journal of Consulting and Clinical Psychology, 52,* 955–967.

Reference note

KOVACS, M. (April, 1983). *The children's depression inventory: A self-rated depression scale for school-aged youngsters.* Unpublished manuscript, University of Pittsburgh School of Medicine (available from Dr. Kovacs, see above address).

Children's Depression Rating Scale, revised (CDRS-R), *Elva O. Poznanski & others, 1984*

Description. The instrument measures severity of depressive symptoms in children. Each of its 17 items assesses the severity of one symptom. Symptoms associated with low mood, somatic symptoms, depressive thought patterns such as low self-esteem, and depressive behavior patterns such as social withdrawal are assessed. Items consist of 7-point rating scales, with each point defined by a behavioral description. At one end of the scale are descriptions of normal behavior patterns, at the other, severely disturbed patterns.

Clinicians use the CDRS to rate 6- to 12-year-old children. The instrument has been used with small samples of medical patients, psychiatric admissions, and children referred for possible depression. Normative data have been obtained from a sample of 233 children interviewed in the community.

Administration and scoring. A 20- to 30-minute unstructured interview with the child provides information needed to make ratings. Any other source of information, such as parents' or teachers' reports, may be used in addition to the interview data. Item ratings are summed to compute the score.

Variables and score interpretation. The depression score provides an index of the severity of the depressive syndrome which the child experiences. Means for children diagnosed as depressed and means for other psychiatric samples are available. Tentative cutoffs are available for research purposes (Poznanski, et al., 1984).

Reliability. The correlation between scores obtained with different raters, on two separate occasions, 2 weeks apart, was .86 ($n = 32$ children referred to a clinic for possible depression). When the interval was 4 weeks, ($n = 36$) the coefficient was .82 (Posnanski et al., 1984).

Uses and findings. Research with the CDRS R and with an earlier version of the scale (Poznanski, Cook, & Carroll, 1979; Poznanski et al., 1984) yielded group differences in scores which were in predicted directions: medical patients lowest, psychiatric patients next, and psychiatric patients referred for possible depression highest. Within the latter group, those given a diagnosis of depression obtained higher scores than those who were not. CDRS-R scores were also highly correlated with clinicians' global ratings of the severity of depression in children. At the same time, the CDRS-R scores were better able to predict formal diagnosis than were global ratings.

Where to obtain. Dr. Elva O. Poznanski, Department of Psychiatry, Rush-Presbyterian St. Luke's Medical Center, 1753 West Congress Parkway, Chicago 60612.

References

POZNANSKI, E. O., COOK, S. C., & CARROLL, B. J. (1979). A depression rating scale for children. *Pediatrics, 64,* 442–450.

POZNANSKI, E. O., GROSSMAN, J. A., BUSHS-BAUM, Y., BANEGAS, M., FREEMAN, L., & GIBBONS, R. (1984). Preliminary studies of the reliability and validity of children's depression rating scale. *Journal of the American Academy of Child Psychiatry, 23,* 191–197.

For additional instruments see:

CLARIZIO, H. F. (1984). Childhood depression: Diagnostic considerations. *Psychology in the Schools, 21,* 181–197.

KAZDIN, A. E., & PETTI, T. A. (1982). Self-report interview measures of childhood and adolescent depression. *Journal of Child Psychiatry and Psychology, 23,* 437–457.

Hyperactivity and Conduct Disorders

Conners' Teacher Rating Scale (CTRS), Conners' Parent Rating Scale (CPRS), Conners' Hyperactivity Index (also called the Abbreviated Teacher Rating Scale), C. Keith Conners and others 1969; 1970; 1973; 1978

Description. The Conners' scales identify hyperkinetic children, identify behavior problems of hyperkinetic children, and evaluate treatment effectiveness. There are five instruments: a 93-item CPRS; a revised 48-item version of the CPRS; a 39-item CTRS; a revised 28-item version of the CTRS; and the Hyperactivity Index. All items describe behavior problems. Four-point rating scales are used to indicate the extent to which children exhibited the problems during the previous month. While norms for the revised forms are more detailed, use of the longer and thus more stable original versions is recommended (Conners, note). The Hyperactivity Index is used for repeated assessments over the course of treatment. It consists of 10 items, found on both Parent scales and Teacher scales, which are particularly sensitive to drug-induced effects.

Parents or teachers complete the scales with reference to 3- to 17-year-old children. Normative samples include: (a) for revised scales and the Hyperactivity Index, 570 children, aged 3 to 17, randomly selected from the Pittsburgh City Directory (Goyette, Conners, & Ulrich, 1978); (b) for the 39-item CTRS, a random stratified sample of 9,583 children, aged 4 to 12, from Ottawa, Canada schools (Trites, Blouin, & Laprade, 1982); and (c) for the 93-item CPRS, 683 children, age 6 to 14 (Conners, note). Data from clinical samples and additional nonclinical groups are available (Conners, note).

Administration and scoring. The scales are self-administered. Individual item ratings are summed to yield total scores and factor scores. Computer scoring is available.

Variables and score interpretation. Factor analyses of responses from normative samples (Conners, note; Goyette et al., 1978; Trites et al., 1982) yielded eight CPRS factors, five revised-CPRS factors, six CTRS factors, and three revised-CTRS factors. The CTRS, for example, yields the follow subscores: (a) hyperactivity; (b) conduct problem; (c) emotionally overindulgent; (d) anxious/passive; (e) asocial; and (f) daydream/attendance problem. Separate norms for children of each age and sex were derived from normative samples for all scales except the 93-item CPRS, which has less detailed norms.

Reliability. Test-retest reliability of CTRS factor scores, assessed with a psychiatric sample over a 1-month interval, was .7 to .9. The 2-week test-retest coefficient for the Hyperactivity Index ($n = 30$ school children) was .89 (Conners, note; Zentall & Barack, 1979). As is often the case with scales like the Conners', agreement between parents' and teachers' ratings was low, from .24 to .45. Agreement between parent pairs and between teacher pairs was higher (Conners, note).

Uses and findings. Several studies (Conners, 1970; Zentall & Barack, 1979) demonstrated that the scales could be used to identify hyperactive children for research purposes. Researchers also repeatedly found that the scales were sensitive to the effects of drug treatment of hyperactivity (Conners, 1972). Conners' scales have often served as outcome measures in evaluations of drug treatments.

Where to obtain. Dr. C. Keith Conners, Behavioral Medicine, Children's Hospital, National Medical Center, 111 Michigan Avenue, Washington, DC 20010 for copies of the instruments, norms, and other relevant information.

References

CONNERS, C. K. (1970). Symptom patterns in hyperactive, neurotic and normal children. *Child Development, 41,* 667–682.

CONNERS, C. K. (1972). Pharmacotherapy of psychopathology in children. In H. C. Quay & J. S. Werry (Eds.), *Psychopathological disorders of childhood.* New York: Wiley.

GOYETTE, C. H., CONNERS, C. K., & ULRICH, R. F. (1978). Normative data on the revised Conners' parent and teacher rating scales. *Journal of Abnormal Child Psychology, 6,* 221–236.

TRITES, R. L., BLOUIN, A. G., & LAPRADE, K. (1982). Factor analysis of the Conners teacher rating scale based on a large normative sample. *Journal of Consulting and Clinical Psychology, 50,* 615–623.

ZENTALL, T. S., & BARACK, R. S. (1979). Rating scales for hyperactivity: Concurrent validity, reliabilty and decisions to label for the Conners and Davids abbreviated scales. *Journal of Abnormal Child Psychology, 7,* 179–190.

Reference Note

CONNERS, C. K. *The Conners rating scales: Instruments for the assessment of child psychopathology.* Mimeo. Washington, DC. Behavioral Medicine, Children's Hospital, National Medical Center. (Write to Dr. Conners at the above address.)

Eyberg Child Behavior Inventory (ECBI), *Sheila M. Eyberg*

Description. The ECBI assesses conduct problems, defined as "an excess of behavior that deviates from the social norm with a frequency or intensity that the child's environment deems too high" (Robinson, Eyberg, & Ross, 1980, p. 23). The scale consists of 36 descriptions of problematic behaviors. Behaviors are those most typically mentioned when parents seek help for children's conduct problems; i.e., fighting and lying. Parents indicate whether they find their child's performance of each behavior problematic and use rating scales to indicate how frequently their child performs each behavior.

The ECBI is used to assess 2- to 17-year-old children. Standardization samples included 512 pediatric clinic clients, ages 2 to 12, and 102 adolescents. The child standardization sample was predominantly white and low to lower-middle class. However, at least among adolescents, social class was not found to affect scores. Age differences in scores were too small to be of concern (Robinson et al., 1980).

Administration and scoring. The ECBI is self-administered. The problem score is the number of child behaviors which parents find problematic. Behavior frequency ratings are summed.

Variables and score interpretation. Individual item scores provide information about the child's specific form of misbehavior. Norms for item scores are available (Robinson et al., 1980). The sum of frequency ratings, called the intensity score, indicates parents' overall perceptions of the frequency of their child's behavior problems. The problem score indicates the degree to which parents regard the child's behavior as problematic. Eyberg and Ross (1978) have established intensity and problem score cutoffs which may be used to identify research samples with conduct problems.

Reliability. Test-retest reliability over an average of 21 days was .88 for problem scores, was .86 for intensity scores, and ranged from .49 to .90 for item scores ($n = 17$ pediatric patients). Both internal consistency estimates, in the .90's, and factor analysis results indicated that intensity and problem scales were homogeneous (Robinson et al., 1980).

Uses and findings. Research (Eyberg & Ross, 1978; Robinson et al., 1980) supported the use of the ECBI as a screening device. Researchers found that children referred for treatment of conduct disorder received higher ECBI scores than did psychiatric, medical, and nonclinical controls. Researchers (Eyberg & Ross, 1978; Webster-Stratton, 1984) also found that the ECBI scores reflected changes in children's problematic behaviors which followed treatment for conduct disorders.

Where to obtain. Sheila Eyberg, Ph.D., Department of Clinical Psychology, Box J165 JHMHC, University of Florida, Gainesville, FL 32610 for a copy of the ECBI which can be photocopied.

References

EYBERG, S. M., & ROBINSON, E. A. (1983). Conduct problem behavior: Standardization of a behavioral rating scale with adolescents. *Journal of Child Clinical Psychology, 12,* 347–354.

EYBERG, S. M., & ROSS, A. W. (1978). Assessment of child behavior problems: The validation of a new inventory. *Journal of Child Clinical Psychology, 7,* 113–116.

ROBINSON, E. A., EYBERG, S. M., & ROSS, A. W. (1980). The standardization of an inventory of child conduct problems. *Journal of Child Clinical Psychology, 9,* 22–28.

WEBSTER-STRATTON, C. (1984). Randomization trial of two parent-training programs for families. *Journal of Consulting and Clinical Psychology, 52,* 666–678.

For additional instruments see:

BARKLEY, R. A. (1981). *Hyperactive children: A handbook for diagnosis and treatment.* New York: Guilford Press.

O'LEARY, S. G., & STERN, P. L. (1982). Subcatagorizing hyperactivity: The Stoneybrook scale. *Journal of Consulting and Clinical Psychology, 50,* 433–435. Instrument: The Stoneybrook Hyperactivity Scale

POGGIO, J. P. (1979). A review and appraisal of instruments assessing hyperactivity in children. *Learning Disability Quarterly, 2,* 9–22.

SANDOVAL, J. (1977). The measurement of the hyperactive syndrome in children. *Review of Educational Research, 47,* 293–318.

WERRY, J. S. (1968). Developmental hyperactivity. *Pediatric Clinics of North America, 15,* 581–599. Instrument: Werry-Weiss-Peters Home Activity Rating Scale.

Self-Management

Self-Control Rating Scale (SCRS), Philip C. Kendall and others, 1979

Description. The SCRS measures the extent to which children exhibit self-control. Self-control is conceptualized as both a cognitive skill which includes the ability to plan, deliberate, and solve problems and as a behavioral skill, which involves the ability to execute chosen behaviors and inhibit unchosen behaviors: The SCRS's 33 items tap both skills. Items are questions about the child's interpersonal and task-related behaviors. Teachers or parents use 7-point rating scales to answer. Rating scales are anchored with opposing one-word answers and are centered about the "average child."

SCRS is used to describe elementary school children. Initial validity and reliability studies (Kendall & Wilcox, 1979) were based on teachers' ratings of predominantly white, middle-class children from grades 2 through 6. Other research samples have included lower SES children who were rated by parents (Robins, Fischel, & Brown, 1984).

Administration and scoring. The SCRS is self-administered. Item ratings are summed to yield a total score.

Variables and score interpretation. A high SCRS score indicates that the child is low in self-control as defined above.

Reliability. Test-retest reliability of the total score, over a 3- to 4-week interval ($n = 24$) was .84. Internal consistency ($n = 110$ third to sixth graders) was .98 (Kendall & Wilcox, 1979).

Uses and findings. Researchers (Kendall & Wilcox, 1979; Kendall, Zupan, & Braswell, 1981) found that the SCRS was associated with other indices of a lack of self-control. High scorers exhibited more off-task behavior, performed more impulsively on measures of reflection-impulsivity, and performed more poorly on a perspective-taking task. However, other predicted relationships, negative relationships with delay of gratification and social problem solving, were not found. The findings suggested that self-control might be a multidimensional construct and that the SCRS might not assess all dimensions. Other findings related SCRS scores to the extent to which children used externalizing adjustment for problems at school. The SCRS was also used (Kendall & Wilcox, 1980) as an outcome measure in research which compared the effectiveness of two types of cognitive therapy for children who show low control in school.

Where to obtain. Dr. Philip Kendall, Department of Psychology, Temple University, Philadelphia, PA 19122 for copies of the SCRS.

References

KENDALL, P. C., & WILCOX, L. E. (1979). Self control in children: Development of a rating scale. *Journal of Consulting and Clinical Psychology, 48,* 80–91.

KENDALL, P. C., & WILCOX, L. E. (1980). Cognitive-behavioral treatment for impulsivity: Concrete versus conceptual training in non-self controlled problem children. *Journal of Consulting and Clinical Psychology, 48,* 80–91.

KENDALL, P. C., ZUPAN, B. A., & BRASWELL, L. (1981). Self-control in children: Further analysis of the self-control rating scale. *Behavior Therapy, 12,* 667–681.

ROBIN, A. L., FISCHEL, J. E., & BROWN, K. E. (1984). The measurement of self-control in children: Validation of the control rating scale. *Journal of Pediatric Psychology, 9,* 165–175.

Rosenzweig Picture Frustration (P-F) Study, Children's Form, Saul Rosenzweig, 1948; 1976

Description. The P-F Study is used to determine the way in which children characteristically respond to frustrations. The instrument consists of 24 cartoons, each of which portrays a child involved in a situation which frustrates the satisfaction of a need. The protagonists' speech bubbles are left blank. The testee fills in each blank bubble with what he thinks that the protagonist would say.

The children's version of the P-F Study is for 4- to 13-year-old children. A sample of 256 4- to 13-year-old children provided normative data. Data from smaller clinical samples and a variety of authorized translations of the P-F Study are available (see Rosenzweig, 1960; 1978a). An additional group of 250 children have recently been added to that sample and norms have been recalculated (Rosenzweig, personal communication, 1987).

Administration and scoring. The P-F Study is administered individually to children under 8 years. Part of the administration for older children must be individualized. Scoring and interpretation requires some self-training. Children's responses are coded, the number of each type of reply is determined, and then these counts and sums of these counts serve as scores. Scoring blanks provide a record and facilitate scoring. Administration takes about 20 minutes, scoring about 15.

Variables and score interpretation. The P-F Study yields six main scores. Three indicate the extent to which the child uses particular types of aggression: need-persistent aggression, ego-defensive aggression, and obstacle-dominant aggression, to cope with frustration. The others index the direction of the child's typical response to frustration. They indicate the extent to which aggression is directed toward the self ("intropunitive"); the extent to which aggression is directed toward others ("extrapunitive") and the extent to which responses to frustration are nonaggressive ("impunitive"). Raw scores are interpreted with respect to sex- and age-specific norms. Many additional scores are described by Rosenzweig (1978a; 1978b).

Reliability. Two independent scorers agreed on 80% of the scores which they assigned to 300 children (Rosenzweig,

1960). Test-retest coefficients for 3-month intervals (*n*'s = eighty-nine 10- to 13-year-olds in two subsamples) ranged from .32 to .69 (Rosenzweig, 1978b). Internal consistency estimates were low. However, Rosenzweig argued that as a projective device, the P-F Study was not meaningfully described by internal consistency reliability.

Uses and findings. A guide to studies which were completed prior to 1977 (Rosensweig, 1978a) and a review of P-F Study validity data (Rosenzweig & Adelman, 1977) are available. Among findings reported in these reviews: (a) expected developmental patterns were found in P-F Study normative data; (b) exposure to stress changes (P-F Study scores; (c) scores correlate with other measures of aggression, measures of adjustment, and physiological indices. More recently, the P-F Study has been used to examine the emotional development of battered children (Kinard, 1982).

Where to obtain. Psychological Assessment Resources Inc, P. O. Box 98, Odessa, FL 33556 for basic manual, children's supplement, test booklets and scoring sheets.

References

KINARD, E. M. (1982). Experiencing child abuse: Effects on emotional adjustment. *American Journal of Orthopsychiatry, 52,* 82–91.

ROSENZWEIG, S. (1960). The Rosenzweig Picture-Frustration Study, children's form. In A.I. Rabin & M.R. Haworth (Eds.), *Projective techniques with children* (149–180). New York: Grune & Stratton.

ROSENZWEIG, S. (1978a). *Aggressive behavior and the Rosenzweig Picture-Frustration Study.* New York: Praeger Publishers.

ROSENZWEIG, S. (1978b). *The Rosenzweig Picture-Frustration (P-F) Study basic manual.* St. Louis, MO: Rana House.

ROSENZWEIG, S., & ADELMAN, S. (1977). Construct validity of the Rosenzweig Picture-Frustration Study. *Journal of Personality Assessment, 41,* 578–588.

Matching Familiar Figures Test (MFF), *Jerome Kagan and others, 1966*

Description. The MFF measures reflection-impulsivity. Reflection-impulsivity refers to the tendency to "reflect on the validity of problem solutions ... when several possible alternatives are available and there is some uncertainty over which is most appropriate" (Messer, 1976, p. 1026). The instrument consists of 12 sets of pictures of familiar objects. Each set includes a standard picture and six facsimiles for children between 5 and 10 years of age. Only one facsimile matches the standard exactly and the child's task is to identify that facsimile. For the adolescent version of the test, there are eight facsimiles.

The school-aged form has been used with a variety of clinical and nonclinical samples of 5- to 10-year-old children. Salkind (note) developed age-norms with data solicited from researchers who had used the MFF. Means, medians, and percentiles were based on a total of 2,846 standard administrations of the MFF to middle-class, normal, American, 5- to 12-year-olds.

Administration and scoring. The MFF is individually administered in about 15 minutes. Scores are the child's average response latency to his or her first solution hypothesis and the total number of errors which the child makes.

Variables and score interpretation. Children who are above the median in response latency and below the median in errors are classified as reflective. Children who are below the median in response latency and above the median in errors are classified as impulsive. For some research purposes the remaining children are classified as fast-accurate or as slow-inaccurate. Researchers have typically used sample medians. With recent evidence (Salkind, note) that medians are quite variable from sample to sample, and the availability of normative medians, this practice might change. Alternative scoring procedures are designed to provide continuous rather than categorical data (see Camp, Blum, Herbert, & van Doornick, 1977; Salkind, note).

Reliability. Messer (1976) reported that internal consistency coefficients for response latency scores tend to be close to .90. In contrast, coefficients for error scores tend to be in the .50s. He reported that test-retest coefficients, estimated for 1- to 8-week intervals, ranged from .34 to .98. Coefficients for error scores were generally lower than those for latencies.

Uses and findings. Considerable research supports the validity of the school-aged form. Findings relate the MFF to a variety of cognitive and behavioral variables such as the inability to inhibit motor activity, problem-solving skill, and anxiety (see Duryea & Glover, 1982; Messer, 1976 for reviews). Researchers (Camp et al., 1977) have also used the MFF to examine the effects of treatment programs for children who are too impulsive. However, it should be noted that the issue of the construct validity of the instrument has generated considerable debate.

Where to obtain. Professor Jerome Kagan, Harvard University, 33 Kirkland Street, 1510 William James Hall, Cambridge, MA 02138 for order forms.

References

CAMP, B. W., BLUM, G. E., HERBERT, F., & VAN DOORNICK, W. J. (1977). "Think Aloud," a program for developing self-control in young aggressive boys. *Journal of Abnormal Psychology, 5,* 157–160.

DURYEA, E. J., & GLOVER, J. A. (1982). A review of research on reflection and impulsivity in children. *Genetic Psychology Monographs, 106,* 217–297.

KAGAN, J., & MESSER, S. B. (1975). A reply to "Some misgivings about the Matching Familiar Figures Test as a measure of reflection impulsivity." *Developmental Psychology, 11,* 244–248.

MESSER, S. B. (1976). Reflection-impulsivity: A review. *Psychological Bulletin, 83,* 1026–1052.

Note

SALKIND, N. J. *The development of norms for the Matching Familiar Figure Test.* Unpublished, undated manuscript available from Dr. Kagan, at address given above.

Adaptive Behavior

AAMD Adaptive Behavior Scale (ABS-SE), School Edition, Nadine Lambert, Myra Windmiller, L. J. Cole, & D. Tharinger, 1981

Description. The ABS-SE assesses children's adaptive behavior, defined as the extent to which the individual meets standards of independence and social responsibility expected for his or her age and culture. This information is needed for diagnosis, placement, and educational planning with children suspected of mental retardation. The ABS-SE consists of 95 short-answer items which vary in format. Part One assesses 9 domains of adaptive behaviors such as independent functioning and economic activity. Part Two, which consists of 12 domains, assesses the extent to which children exhibit maladaptive behaviors. Raters base responses to items on their knowledge of the child or on interviews with others who know the child well.

The ABS-SE may be completed by teachers, mental health, or educational professionals who have trained themselves in use of the instrument. Standardization was accomplished with teachers' ratings of 6,523 three- to 17-year-olds drawn from regular, educable mentally retarded (EMR) and trainable mentally retarded (TMR) populations in California and Florida. Sex and ethnicity were found (Lambert, 1981; 1986) to have minimal effects on adaptive behavior scores for all groups with the exceptions 3- to 6-year-olds who differed on factor scores across ethnic groups.

Administration and scoring. Self-administration by a teacher or professional who knows the child takes about 15 to 45 minutes. The other method, an item-by-item interview with a parent or someone else who knows the child well, takes longer. Scoring requires the computation of numerous sums of item scores. Score sheets and precise instructions facilitate hand-scoring.

Variables and score interpretation. The ABS-SE yields a score for each domain. The ABS-SE also yields five factor scores: (a) Personal Self-Sufficiency; (b) Community Self-Sufficiency; (c) Personal Responsibility; (d) Social Responsibility; and (e) Personal Adjustment. Factor scores are interpreted in terms of age norms from appropriate diagnostic groups. Domain scores and factor scores are interpreted in terms of regular, EMR and/or TMR age-norms. Domain scores guide the planning of individualized programs. Factor scores guide diagnosis and placement. A third type of score, the Comparison score, is the weighted sum of three factor scores. Weights were derived from a discriminant analysis (Lambert & Hartsough, 1981) which used factor scores to predict EMR, TMR, and regular class placements. The score is used to help determine the appropriateness of EMR, TMR, or regular class placement for the child.

Reliability. Internal consistency (*n*'s = 20s to above 600, age by classification subsamples of standardization sample) was .46 to .89 for Personal Self-Sufficiency scores; .27 to .82 for Personal Adjustment scores; .71 to .94 for Community Self-Sufficiency; .85 to .94 for Personal Social Responsibility; .77 to .96 for Social Adjustment. Magnitude of the reliabilities reflects sample size, low variance, or the idiosyncratic nature of the maladaptive behavior items (Lambert, 1981).

Uses and findings. Lambert (1981) obtained predicted moderate correlations between IQ and adaptive behavior domain scores. Highest relationships were between IQ and domains closely related to cognitive skills and between IQ and domains which involved application of learned abilities, i.e., Economic Activity. Lambert also reported that children assigned to TMR, EMR, and Regular classrooms differed, in expected directions, on adaptive behavior domain scores. Factor scores, like domain scores, were modestly related to IQ, and in addition, were moderately related to achievement scores. Cross-validation of the comparison scores indicated that they correctly classified an average of 75% of 7- to 16-year-olds with respect to placement in TMR, EMR, and regular classes.

Where to obtain. Publishers Test Service, CTB/McGraw-Hill, 2500 Garden Rd., Monterey, CA 93940, or Consulting Psychologists Press, P.O. Box 60070, Palo Alto, CA 94306 for the Administration and Instructional Planning Manual, the Diagnostic and Technical Manual, assessment booklets, and profiles.

References

LAMBERT, N. M. (1981). *Diagnostic and technical report, AAMD Adaptive Behavior Scale-School Edition*. Monterey, CA: Publishers Test Service, CTB/McGraw-Hill.

LAMBERT, N. M. (1986). Evidence on age and ethnic status bias in factor scores and the comparison score for the AAMD Adaptive Behavior Scale-School Edition. *Journal of School Psychology, 24*, 143–153.

LAMBERT, N. M., & HARTSOUGH, C. S. (1981). Development of a simplified diagnostic scoring method for the school version of the AAMD Adaptive Behavior Scale. *American Journal of Mental Deficiency, 86*, 138–147.

Vineland Adaptive Behavior Scales: Interview Edition, Survey Form, Sara S. Sparrow, David A. Balla, & Domenic V. Cicchetti, 1984

Description. The Vineland Scales assess the extent to which people meet standards of personal and social sufficiency for their age level. There are three editions. The Survey edition, described here, consists of 297 items. Items describe adaptive behaviors from four domains: communication, daily living skills, socialization, and motor skills. A fifth, optional, set of items describes maladaptive behaviors. Examiners rate the extent to which testees typically display adaptive and maladaptive behaviors on the basis of interviews with primary caregivers. Other editions of the Vineland are the 577-item Expanded Form, which is used to guide treatment plans, and the 244-item Classroom Edition, which is self-administered by testees' teachers.

The Survey Form assesses children from birth to adulthood and low functioning adults. Examiners need a general background in assessment and specific self-training in use of the Vineland. There were 3,000 children, 100 from each of 30 age groups between birth and 19 years, in the standardization sample. Demographics closely matched those of the U.S. population according to the 1980 census. A Spanish translation is available.

Administration and scoring. The examiner scores items during the 20- to 60-minute interview. Basal and ceiling rules limit the items which must be scored to those appropriate for the testee's level of maturity. Record forms help sum item scores. Computerized scoring is available.

Variables and score interpretation. The Survey Form yields: (a) four domain scores: communication, socialization, daily living skills, and motor skills; (b) an adaptive behavior composite score; and (c) two maladaptive behavior scores, a total score, and a score (part 1) which assesses the presence of mild forms of maladaptive behavior only. Subdomain scores assess the performance of specific skills within each domain. Scores indicate current level of performance. Extensive and detailed norms include several types of derived scores based on standardization sample data and supplementary norms from mentally retarded adults, emotionally disturbed children, and sensory-impaired children.

Reliability. Internal consistency (n's = 200, subsamples of standardization sample) was .70 to .95 for domain scores; .89 to .98 for the adaptive composite; and .77 to .88 for maladaptive, part 1. Test-retest, over 2 to 4 weeks, ranged from .85 to .99 for domain and adaptive composite standard scores (n = 484); and .87 for maladaptive, part 1, raw scores (n = 340). Interrater reliabilities, obtained from interviews separated by 1 to 14 days, were a bit lower, .93 to .99. See Sparrow, Balla, and Cicchetti (1984) for more.

Uses and findings. Factor analysis, in general, confirmed the organization of subdomains into domains and the organization of domains into the adaptive composite. Findings consistent with the use of scores to assist in placement decisions and the use of scores to identify strengths and weaknesses were also obtained. Mentally retarded adults in residential facilities obtained lower scores than did retarded adults in nonresidential facilities. Hearing impaired children scored lower in the communication do-

main than in other adaptive domains and emotionally disturbed children did worst in the socialization domain. Correlations between the Vineland and other adaptive behavior scales were moderate and correlations with IQ were low (reviewed by Sparrow, Balla, & Cicchetti, 1984).

How to obtain. Write to American Guidance Service, Circle Pines, MN 55014-1796. A Survey Form starter set (10 record booklets, a parent report form, a manual) costs $21.50. Record forms are $13.25 for 25, training audiocassettes are $8 each; and the computer scoring program is $93.

Reference

SPARROW, S., BALLA, D. A., & CICCHETTI, D. V. (1984). *Interview edition survey form manual.* Circle Pines, MN: American Guidance Service.

Autism

Childhood Autism Rating Scale (CARS), Eric Schopler and others, 1980

Description. The CARS is used to identify children who suffer from autism and to determine their symptoms. It consists of 15 rating scales which each assess a symptom of autism. Symptoms from several different sets of diagnostic criteria for autism are included. Rating scale response options range from normal to severely abnormal and are behaviorally defined. Observers make ratings on the basis of the degree, frequency, and/or intensity with which the child displays each symptom.

The CARS is used with children suspected of autism. Observers must be experienced with children since the age-appropriateness of children's behavior must be taken into account. The standardization sample consisted of 537 children who were seen at a center for treatment of autism and communication disorders. Almost all of the children were 10 years old or younger and most had IQ's below 85. SES was varied.

Administration and scoring. The CARS is completed after observing the child's initial diagnostic interview from parents' reports, records, and teacher observations. A total score is computed by summing ratings.

Variables and score interpretation. The CARS assesses the following symptoms: impairment in human relationships, inability to imitate, inappropriate affect, bizarre use of body movements, and persistence of stereotypes, bizarre object use, resistance to change, peculiarities of visual responsiveness, peculiarities of auditory responsiveness, near receptor responsiveness, anxiety reaction, verbal and nonverbal communication deficits, disturbance in activity level, uneven intellectual functioning, and general impressions. Total scores and patterns of ratings (Schopler, Reichler, DeVellis, & Daly, 1980) are used to classify children as not autistic, mild to moderately autistic, and severely autistic for research and administrative purposes.

Reliability. Interrater correlations for individual item ratings ($n = 280$ cases) ranged from .55 to .93. Internal consistency for the total score was .94 (Schopler et al., 1980).

Uses and findings. Schopler et al. (1980) reported that CARS scores were highly correlated with clinicians' ratings of autism and with independent clinical assessments of children by a psychologist and a psychiatrist. They also found modest overlap between children classified as autistic on the basis of CARS scores and children classified as autistic on the basis of two sets of diagnostic criteria, that of Rutter and that of Ritvo and Freeman. The CARS has been used (Lord, Schopler, & Revicki, 1982) in a study of sex differences among children with autism.

Where to obtain. Irvington Publishers, 740 Broadway, New York, NY 10003. Also available for reproduction in an NIMH publication: Schopler, E., Reichler, R. J., & Renner, B. J. (1985). *CARS (Child Autism Rating Scale) Psychopharmacology Bulletin, 21,* 1053.

References

LORD, C., SCHOPLER, E., & REVICKI, D. (1982). Sex differences in autism. *Journal of Autism and Developmental Disorders, 12,* 317–330.

SCHOPLER, E., REICHLER, R. J., DeVELLIS, R. F., & DALY, K. (1980). Toward objective classification of childhood autism: Childhood Autism Rating Scale (CARS). *Journal of Autism and Developmental Disorders, 10,* 91–103.

Behavior Rating Instrument for Autistic and Atypical Children (BRIAAC), Bertram A. Ruttenberg, Charles Wenar, and others, 1966; 1977

Description. The BRIAAC quantifies problems of autistic and other atypical children and monitors the children's progress. Each of its eight scales assesses a specific area of functioning. Each consists of behavioral descriptions of different levels of functioning within the given area. Levels are presented in developmental order, starting with descriptions of the most severe autistic behavior and proceeding to descriptions of behavior expected of normal 4- to 5-year-olds. Observers indicate how frequently the autistic child performs at each level of functioning by assigning points to each level. For each scale, raters are given 10 to 20 points to distribute among levels.

Examiners base ratings of 1½- to 2-hour observations and caregivers' reports or on clinicians' descriptions. Practice in use of the scales is needed. The instrument development sample consisted of twenty-nine 3- to 8-year-olds who were in treatment for autism at a day care center (Ruttenberg, Dratman, Fraknoi, & Wenar, 1966). A minimum of 4 years of observations were available for each child. The BRIAAC has since been used with children from a wide variety of institutional settings and treatment programs. Interrater reliability should be established locally.

Administration and scoring. Scores are computed by multiplying points assigned by developmental level and summing.

Variables and score interpretation. The BRIAAC yields scale scores and a total score. Scale scores assess relatedness to adults, communication, drive for mastery, social responsiveness, vocalization, sound and speech reception, body

movement and psychobiological development. The total score provides an index of overall severity of the disorder.

Reliability. Correlations between scale scores assigned by pairs of raters to 113 children ranged from .85 to .93. The scale's internal consistency was demonstrated by moderate to high intercorrelations among scale scores, .54 to .86, and factor analysis results (Wenar & Ruttenburg, 1976).

Uses and findings. The organization of behaviors into a progression of developmental levels within each scale was based on extensive clinical observation. The validity of the ordering of levels was examined (Wenar & Ruttenburg, 1976) with a form of scalogram analysis. Findings indicated that the observed behavior patterns of autistic children corresponded with progressions of levels for all but one scale. Research also demonstrated that BRIAAC scores differentiated between autistic and mentally retarded children and between autistic and healthy children (Kalish, 1975; Wolf, Wenar, & Ruttenburg, 1972; both cited by Wenar & Ruttenburg, 1976). The BRIAC was used (Wenar & Ruttenburg, 1976) to determine the effect of different treatments and settings on the progress made by autistic children and to identify (Wenar, Ruttenburg, Kalish-Weiss, & Wolf, 1986) qualitative and quantitative differences between autistic and normal children aged 0–3 years in developmental pathways. The latter study indicated that while in some areas of functioning less severely disturbed autistic children were simply much slower in development; in other areas, with more severely disturbed children, autistic behavior was not typical of any level of normal development.

Where to obtain. Stoelting Company, 1350 South Kastner Avenue, Chicago, IL 60623 for manual and scoring forms.

References

RUTTENBERG, B. A., DRATMAN, M. L., FRAKNOI, J., & WENAR, C. (1966). An instrument for evaluating autistic children. *Journal of the Academy of Child Psychiatry, 5,* 453–478.

WENAR, C., & RUTTENBERG, B. A. (1976). The use of the BRIAC for evaluating therapeutic effectiveness. *Journal of Autism and Childhood Schizophrenia, 6,* 175–191.

WENAR, C., RUTTENBERG, B. A., KALISH-WEISS, B., & WOLF, E. G. (1986). The development of normal and autistic children: A comparative study. *Journal of Autism and Developmental Disorders, 16,* 317–333.

For additional instruments see:

PARKS, S. L. (1983). The assessment of autistic children: A selective review of available instruments. *Journal of Autism and Developmental Disorders, 13,* 255–267.

Self-Perceptions

Self-Perception Profile for Children (Revision of the Perceived Competence Scale for Children), Susan Harter, 1985

Description. The Self-Perception Profile quantifies children's domain-specific and global judgments of self-adequacy. Each of its 36 items elicits children's perceptions of their adequacy with respect to a particular criterion, e.g., looks or skills, or perceptions of their general self-worth. Each presents descriptions of two types of children, children who are adequate in the specific domain (or worthy), and children who are inadequate (e.g., some kids are good at X; but some kids are bad at X). Testees first decide which type of child they themselves most resemble. Then testees decide whether they are "sort of" or "really" similar to the chosen type of child.

The instrument is used with children in third though ninth grades. Self-perception measures for adolescents, adults, and preschoolers are also available. Technical data were derived from four samples of between 173 to 748 predominantly Caucasian, lower-middle to upper-middle-class children drawn from grades 3 through 8. The factor-structure of the instrument was stable across grades 5 through 8, but was somewhat less differentiated for grades 3 and 4. Factor structures for special populations, developmentally delayed, and learning disabled were quite different (Renick, cited in Harter, 1985; Silon & Harter, 1985).

Administration and scoring. The instrument may be administered individually or in groups. Item scores are summed to compute factor scores. Data coding sheets aid scoring and maintain records.

Variables and score interpretation. The Self-Perception Profile yields six subscores. Five are indices of perceived adequacy in specific domains: (a) scholastic competence; (b) athletic competence; (c) social acceptance; (d) physical appearance; and (e) behavioral conduct. The sixth score, the global self-worth score, indicates the degree to which the child likes him or herself as a person. Grade-by-grade means and standard deviations are available. Parallel teacher evaluation rating forms and a measure of children's perception of the importance of each self-evaluation domain provide supplementary information.

Reliability. Internal consistency for the six subscores ranged from .71 to .86 (*n*'s = 178 to 748, see above for description). Two items have been replaced to improve reliabilities; thus, these figures may be underestimates (Harter, 1985).

Uses and findings. Much research has been conducted with an earlier version of the instrument. Harter (1982), with the earlier instrument, found that, as expected, children's self-perceptions had some basis in reality. Appropriate subscales correlated with gym teachers' ratings, achievement test scores, and sociometric ratings. Also, as predicted by theory, children higher in perceived cognitive competence were more likely to seek challenging cognitive tasks. More recent work (Harter, 1986), with the current version of the scale, examined W. James's and C. H. Cooley's hypotheses about determinants of global self-worth. Results indicated that the degree to which perceived success occurs in domains which one regards as important and perceptions of significant others' attitudes toward the self influence global self-worth.

Where to obtain. Susan Harter, Department of Psychology, University of Denver, 2040 South York, Denver, CO 80208. Manual includes instruments and record forms for reproduction.

References

HARTER, S. (1982). The perceived competence scale for children. *Child Development, 53,* 87–97.

HARTER, S. (1985). *Manual for the Self-Perception Profile for Children.* Denver: University of Denver.

HARTER, S. (1986). Processes underlying the construction, maintenance, and enhancement of self-concept in children. In J. Suls & A. Greenwald (Eds.), *Psychological perspectives on the self* (Vol. 3). Hillsdale, NJ: Lawrence Erlbaum Associates.

SILON, E., & HARTER, S. (1985). Assessment of perceived competence, motivational orientation, and anxiety in segregated and mainstreamed educable mentally retarded children. *Journal of Educational Psychology, 77,* 217–230.

Nowicki-Strickland Locus of Control Scale, Stephen Nowicki, Jr., & Bonnie R. Strickland, 1973

Description. The Nowicki-Strickland Locus of Control Scale assesses the extent to which children believe that external forces rather than their own actions determine what happens to them. The scale presents 40 beliefs about the causes of positive and negative outcomes both in general and in specific situations: achievement situations, peer interactions, interactions with parents. Children indicate whether they hold each belief. Short forms of the scale have been developed (Nowicki & Strickland, 1973).

The Nowicki-Strickland scale is for children at or above the third grade level. (A downward extension was constructed (Nowicki & Duke, 1974) for use with 4- to 8-year-olds.) The standardization sample included over 1,000 children from grades 3 through 12. Most SES levels were adequately represented.

Administration and scoring. The scale may be group-administered in 10 to 15 minutes. Items are read aloud. A scoring key shows which responses indicate a belief in external control of outcomes, and children receive 1 point for each external response.

Variables and score interpretation. A high Locus of Control score indicates that the child believes that external forces control the outcomes which he or she experiences. Means and standard deviations for each grade from 3rd to 12th are presented in Nowicki and Strickland (1973). The manual (Nowicki, note) provides separate normative data for black and white students and males and females, and reports means and standard deviations for a variety of clinical and ethnic groups.

Reliability. Internal consistency, which Nowicki and Strickland (1973) argued was underestimated, ranged from .63 for children in grades 3 through 5 to .74 for children in grades 9 through 11. Test-retest coefficients, over a 6-week interval, ranged from .63 for 3rd graders (n = 99) to .71 for 10th graders (n = 125) (Nowicki & Strickland, 1973).

Uses and findings. Nowicki and Strickland (1973) reported moderate correlations between their scale and other locus of control measures. They also found little relationship between their scale and intelligence, but a strong relationship between the scale and scholastic achievement. As predicted, children who were more internal were higher in achievement. There were some inconsistencies. For example, many locus of control-achievement relationships held only for boys. However, research with the scale generally supported theoretical predictions. Many studies have used the scale. A review is provided by Nowicki & Duke (1983) and a bibliography is available from Dr. Nowicki. Examples include a comparison of control orientations of latch-key children with those of controls (Rodman, Pratto, & Nelson, 1985) and a study of the effects of social skill training on control orientation and social behavior (McClure, Chinsky, & Larson, 1978).

Where to obtain. Dr. Stephen Nowicki, Jr., Department of Psychology, Emory University, Atlanta, GA 30322.

References

McClure, L. Chinsky, J., & Larcen, S. (1978). Enhancing problem solving performance in an elementary school setting. *Journal of Educational Psychology, 70,* 504–513.

Nowicki, S., Jr., & Duke, M. P. (1983). The Nowicki-Strickland Lifespan Locus of Control Scales: Construct validation. In H. Lefcourt (Ed.), *Research with the locus of control construct* (Vol. 2, 13–43). New York: Academic Press.

Nowicki, S., Jr., & Duke, M. P. (1974). A preschool and primary internal-external control scale. *Developmental Psychology, 10,* 874–880.

Nowicki, S., Jr., & Strickland, B. R. (1973). A locus of control scale for children. *Journal of Consulting and Clinical Psychology, 40,* 148–154.

Rodman, H., Pratto, D., & Nelson, R. (1985). Child care arrangements and children's functioning: A comparison of self-care and adult care children.

Note

Nowicki, S., Jr. *Children's Nowicki-Strickland Internal-External Locus of Control.*

Unpublished manual, Emory University, Atlanta, GA.

For additional instruments see:

CONNELL, J. P. (1976). A new multidimensional measure of children's perception of control. *Child Development, 56,* 1018–1041. Instrument: Multidimensional Measure of Children's Perceptions of Control.

ELIG, T. W., & FRIEZE, I. H. (1979). Measuring causal attributions for success and failure. *Journal of Personality and Social Psychology, 37,* 621–634.

HARTER, S. (1983). Developmental perspectives on the self-system. In E. M. Hetherington (Ed.), *Handbook of child psychology: Vol. 4. Socialization, personality and social development* (pp. 275–386). New York: Wiley.

MARSH, H. W., BARNES, J., CAIRNS, L., & TIDMAN, M. (1984). Self-description questionnaire: Age and sex effects in the structure and level of self-concept for preadolescent children. *Journal of Educational Psychology, 76,* 940–956. Instrument: Self-Description Questionnaire.

Children's Competencies

Health Resources Inventory (HRI), *Ellis Gesten, 1976*

Description. The HRI measures the degree to which children display various social and personal competencies at school. It consists of 54 descriptions of adaptive classroom behaviors and competencies. Teachers indicate the extent to which each description describes a particular child on a 5-point scale.

The HRI assesses 6- to 8-year-olds. Teachers complete the scale with reference to their observations of a child in their classroom. The standardization samples consisted of city and suburban children from 12 different school districts in the Rochester, New York area. Families of city children were of low SES and families of suburban children were of relatively high SES. Sixty-five teachers served as raters. The instrument has been used (Gesten, Scher, & Cowen, 1978) with behaviorally disturbed samples.

Administration and scoring. The HRI is self-administered. Factor scores, the sum of factors, and a total score are computed.

Variables and score interpretation. Factor analysis of data from 298 children and cross-validation with a sample of 294 children (Gesten, 1976) identified five factors: (a) Good Student; (b) Gutsy; (c) Peer Sociability; (d) Rule Conformity; and (e) Frustration Tolerance. The total score and sum of factors both provide overall indices of competence.

Reliability. Test-retest, over a 4- to 6-week interval ($n = 60$ first, second, and third graders from 11 classrooms), was .87 for Total scores and .72 to .91 for Factor scores (Gesten, 1976).

Uses and findings. Gesten (1976) found that boys in treatment for severe emotional problems scored lower than matched, healthy controls on all HRI factor scales. He also compared teachers' classification of students as most, average, or lowest in competence with independently obtained HRI scores. The classifications corresponded with the scores. The HRI has been used in the Primary Health Project, a program for early detection and prevention of school maladjustment, both to identify children's strengths at referral and to assess treatment outcomes (Cowen, Orgal, Gesten, & Wilson, 1979).

Where to obtain. Dr. Ellis Gesten, Department of Psychology, College of Social and Behavioral Sciences, University of South Florida, Tampa, FL 33620.

References

COWEN, E. L., ORGAL, A. R., GESTEN, E. L., & WILSON, A. B. (1979). The evaluation of an intervention program for young school children with acting out problems. *Journal of Abnormal Child Psychology, 7,* 381–396.

GESTEN, E. L. (1976). A Health Resources Inventory: The development of a measure of the personal and social competence of primary grade children. *Journal of Consulting and Clinical Psychology, 44,* 775–786.

GESTEN, E. L., SCHER, K., & COWEN, E. L. (1978). Judged school problems and competencies of referred children with varying family background characteristics. *Journal of Abnormal Child Psychology, 6,* 247–255.

Social Behavior Assessment (SBA),
Thomas M. Stephens, 1979; 1984

Description. The SBA is designed to be used with a program for teaching social skills in schools (Stephens, 1978) but can be used independently. The instrument consists of 136 descriptions of classroom behaviors which represent four areas of skill and 30 specific skills. All behaviors are described in positive terms and most were rated as important for classroom success by 257 teachers (Stephens, 1984). Teachers use either recollections or observations as a basis for rating students on the behaviors. They indicate whether the item applies and if so whether the student demonstrates the behavior at an "acceptable level," demonstrates it at an "unacceptable level," or doesn't demonstrate it at all.

Raters have included regular classroom and special education teachers. Both emotionally disturbed and healthy children drawn from kindergarten, elementary school, and middle school classes have been assessed (LaNunziata, Hill, & Krause, 1981; Strumme, Gresham, & Scott, 1982).

Administration and scoring. An earlier format was completed in an average of 45 minutes when the entire instrument was used. The revised format should take less time. Further, teachers may (and when using the SBA as a guide to instruction, should), rate only those skills which are a source concern. Scoring involves summing ratings within subscales.

Variables and score interpretation. The SBA yields 30 scores, one for each skill. Examples are listed by area: (a) environmental behaviors: care for the environment, dealing with emergencies; (b) interpersonal behaviors: making conversation, helping others, accepting authority; (c) self-related behaviors: ethical behavior, expressing feelings; and (d) task-related behaviors: attending behavior, independent work, classroom discussion. Scores are examined to determine which skills need to be improved.

Reliability. Interrater agreement between four specially trained teachers and two researchers who made repeated observation-based ratings of one or two skills for each of four students ranged from 85 to 100% and averaged 97.6% (LaNunziata et al., 1981).

Uses and findings. LaNunziata et al. (1981) used the SBA, first, to establish baselines in problem areas for behaviorally disordered children. Next, Stephen's (1978) curriculum and behavior-modification types of teaching strategies were implemented, and the SBA was used to monitor the children's progress. Strumme et al. (1982) found that a linear discriminant function derived from the 30 SBS skills correctly classified 84% of 184 kindergarten through eighth-grade students as either emotionally disabled or nondisabled.

Where to obtain. Cedars Press, P.O. Box 29351, Columbus, OH 43229.

References

LaNunziata, L. J., Hill, D. S., & Krause, L. A. (1981). Teaching in classrooms for behaviorally disordered students. *Behavior Disorders, 6,* 238–245.

Stephens, T. M. (1978). *Social skills in the classroom.* Columbus, OH: Cedars Press.

Stephens, T. M. (1984). *Social Behavior Assessment. Technical information.* Columbus, OH: Cedars Press.

Strumme, V. S., Gresham, F. M., & Scott, N. A. (1983). Dimensions of children's social behavior: A factor analytic investigation. *Journal of Behavioral Assessment, 5,* 161–177.

Family Relations

Parent Perception Inventory (PPI), Ann Hazzard, Andrew Christensen, and Gayla Margolin, 1983

Description. The PPI assesses children's perceptions of how their parents treat them. The instrument asks children how frequently their parents perform various classes of friendly/affectionate and hostile/disciplinary behaviors. Concrete examples of behaviors are provided in order to ensure that children understand questions. The child has five response choices which range from "never" to "a lot" and is provided with graphic representations of the quantities. There are 18 items.

Children complete the PPI with reference to either their mother or father and may complete it a second time so that perceptions of both parents are assessed. The scale was administered (Hazzard, Christensen, & Margolin, 1983) to 75 children, aged 5 to 13 years, from both distressed and nondistressed families. Most of the children were Caucasian.

Administration and scoring. The PPI is administered as an interview. Item points are summed to compute scores.

Variables and score interpretation. There are two subscores. One provides an index of the frequency of positive parental activities such as comforting, praising, and helping. The other provides an index of the frequency of negative parental activities, such as nagging and yelling.

Reliability. Internal consistency for positive mother behavior score, positive father behavior score, negative mother behavior score and negative father behavior score ($n = 75$) ranged from .78 to .88. Coefficients for subsamples of older and younger children were also computed (Hazzard et al., 1983).

Uses and findings. Hazzard et al. (1983) obtained predicted convergent relationships between PPI scores, self-esteem, and parents' ratings of child behavior problems. Children who perceived parents as both higher in positive behavior and lower in negative behavior had more self-esteem. Children who perceived parents as lower in negative behavior were seen as less problematic by parents. Hazzard et al. also related PPI scores to measures of child achievement and parents' perceptions of child intelligence in order to assess the PPI's discriminant validity. Only 2 of 8 correlations were significant. In addition, the researchers found that children from troubled families differed from controls in their perceptions of parents.

Where to obtain. Write to Dr. Ann Hazzard, Box 26065, Grady Hospital, 80 Butler Street, Atlanta, GA 30335.

Reference

HAZZARD, A., CHRISTENSEN, A., & MARGOLIN, G. (1983). Children's perceptions of parental behavior. *Journal of Abnormal Child Psychology, 11,* 49–60.

Conflicts Tactics Scales (CTS), *Murray Straus, 1979*

Description. The CTS provide information about the way in which family members respond to conflicts with one another. There are two forms—Form N, an 18-item interview form and Form A, a 14-item self-administered form. There are also several versions of each form. Each version asks a particular family member, e.g., husband, wife, child, to describe the way that one specific family member responds to conflicts with another specific family member. For example, one version asks the mother to describe her husband's response to conflict with children, another, her own response to conflicts with her husband. A third asks the child to describe father's responses to conflicts with mother. In all versions each item describes a tactic, such as reasoning or yelling, which the specified family member might use in a conflict. The respondent indicates how frequently each tactic was used during the preceding year.

Who's assessed; who reports. The scales are completed by adults with reference to husband-wife, parent-child, and/or sibling relationships within their families. Form N has been administered to a national probability sample of 2,143 families (Straus, 1979).

Administration and scoring. The item scores are summed to yield three main subscores. A variety of other scores are detailed by Straus (1979).

Variables and score interpretation. Subscales were first organized on the basis of theory and then verified with factor analyses of 2,143 husbands' and wives' responses to the husband-wife version of Form N and of 384 college students' responses to the mother-father version of Form A (Straus, 1979). Subscales assess the extent to which family members: (a) use rational discussion during disputes; (b) use verbal aggression during disputes; and (c) use physical force or violence during disputes.

There are percentiles derived from the national probability sample for Form N.

Reliability. Item-total correlations for subscales of several versions of Form A (*n* = 384 students) ranged from .47 to .91. Alpha coefficients for Form N scores (*n* = the probability sample) ranged from .56 to .88. Most coefficients below .75 were for the Reasoning subscale. A longer Reasoning subscale is included in Form A (Straus, 1979).

Uses and findings. Straus and Bulcroft (1975, reported in Straus, 1979) found that college students' CTS reports of verbal aggression and violence between parents corresponded with their parents' self-reports to a moderate extent, but that correspondence between students' and parents' reports about use of reasoning was low. Straus (1974) found that, contrary to catharsis theories, couples who were verbally aggressive were also high in violence. The CTS has also been used (Straus, Steinmetz, & Gelles, 1979) to examine patterns of family violence and the factors which promote it.

Where to obtain. Dr. Murray Straus, Family Research Laboratory, 128 Harten Social Science Center, University of New Hampshire, Durham, NH 03824.

References

STRAUS, M. A. (1974). Leveling, civility and violence in the family. *Journal of Marriage and the Family, 36,* 13–29.

STRAUS, M. A. (1979). Measuring intrafamily conflict and violence: The Conflict Tactics (CT) Scale. *Journal of Marriage and the Family, 41,* 75–88.

STRAUS, M. A., STEINMETZ, S. K., & GELLES, R. J. (1979). *Behind closed doors: Violence in the American family.* New York: Doubleday/Anchor.

Family Environment Scale (FES), *Rudolf H. Moos & Bernice S. Moos, 1974; 1981; 1986*

Description. The FES is used to examine adults' and adolescents' perceptions of the interpersonal, organizational, and growth-promoting aspects of their families. Its items are descriptions of family characteristics which were generated from interviews with members of various types of families. Respondents indicate whether each of the 90 FES statements characterizes their families by answering "true" or "false."

There are three forms. Adults use Form R to describe their nuclear families. In Form E, items elicit adults' expectations about family settings. Form I elicits adults' conception of the ideal family. The standardization samples, 1,125 representative and 500 disturbed families, responded to Form R. Representative families were from all areas of the country and varied in type: e.g., multi-generational, minority, single-parent. The reading level of the FES seems to be fairly high.

Administration and scoring. The FES is designed to be self-administered in about 20 minutes. A special Form R answer sheet and score key simplifies computation of subscores.

Variables and score interpretation. The FES yields 10 subscores which represent three domains. Family relationship subscores include indices of cohesion, expressiveness, and conflict. System maintenance scores index degree of family organization and the extent to which the family is controlled or rigid. Personal growth scores each index the extent to which families promote development in one of several directions: achievement orientation, moral-religious, intellectual-cultural, and orientation towards independence. There are norms for the subscores (Moos & Moos, 1986). Subscores may also be used to classify families in terms of a typology (Billings & Moos, 1982) or to compute special indices, such as an index of family support (Holahan & Moos, 1981).

Reliability. Internal consistency estimates for the 10 subscales ranged from .61 to .78. Eight-week test-retest estimates for subscales were obtained from 48 members of 9 families. Coefficients ranged from .68 to .86. Test-retest estimates which were obtained over longer intervals are also available (Moos & Moos, 1986).

Uses and findings. The FES has been used in well over 100 published studies. Initial research, conducted by Moos and colleagues (see Moos & Moos, 1986) indicated that disturbed families differed from representative families on FES subscales in predictable ways. Other research has examined effects of psychopathology and treatment on families. For example, Karoly and Rosenthal (1977) found both pre-post decreases in children's problematic behaviors and pre-post increases in parents' FES cohesion subscores when parents of conduct disordered children attended parent training sessions. Wait-listed families showed no improvement.

Where to obtain. Consulting Psychologists Press, 577 College Avenue, Palo Alto, CA 94306 for Form R tests, answer sheets, scoring key, and manual. Forms I and E are obtained from the publisher and reproduced locally.

References

BILLINGS, A. G., & MOOS, R. H. (1982). Family environments and adaptation: A clinically applicable typology. *American Journal of Family Therapy, 10*(2), 26–38.

KAROLY, P., & ROSENTHAL, M. (1977). Training parents in behavior modification: Effects on perceptions of family interaction deviant child behavior. *Behavior Therapy, 8,* 406–410.

HOLAHAN, C. J., & MOOS, R. H. (1981). Social support and psychological distress: A longitudinal analysis. *Journal of Abnormal Psychology, 90,* 365–370.

MOOS, R. H., & MOOS, B. S. (1986). *The Family Environment Scale Manual* (2nd ed.). Palo Alto, CA: Consulting Psychologists Press.

For additional instruments see:

OLSON, D. H., McCUBBIN, H. I., BARNES, H. L., LARSEN, A., MUXEN, M. J., & WILSON, M. (1982). *Family inventories: Inventories used in a national survey of families across the family life cycle.* St. Paul: Family Social Science, University of Minnesota. Instruments: Family Adaptability and Cohesion Evaluation Scales, Version II; and others.

PINO, C. J., SIMONS, N., & SLAWINOWSKI, M. J. (1984). *Family Environment Scale, Children's Version.* Palo Alto, CA: Consulting Psychologists Press.

STRAUS, M., & BROWN, B. W. (1978). Family measurement technique: Abstracts of published instruments 1935–1974. Minneapolis: University of Minnesota Press.

Home Learning Environment

Family Environment Schedule, Kevin Marjoribanks, 1979

Description. The Schedule assesses aspects of family life which are likely to relate to children's scholastic attitudes, motivation, and performance. It is a 78-item structured interview with parents which elicits information about parents' aspirations for themselves and their child, their involvement in their child's education, their childrearing practices and their demographic characteristics. Items are questions. Interviewers score parents' replies to questions on 5- or 6-point rating scales.

The schedule was used to assess 1,000 Australian families of 11-year-old children. An earlier version was used in Canada. If it were to be used in other countries, modification of some questions would be needed.

Administration and scoring. The interview is individually administered to either mothers, fathers, or both parents together. Scores are sums of item ratings.

Variables and score interpretation. Marjoribanks (1979) described six subscales which were refined through factor scaling techniques. The subscales assessed the following environmental press variables: (a) parents' aspirations for the child; (b) parents' aspirations for themselves; (c) parents' reinforcement of aspirations; (d) concern for proper language use within the family; (e) parents' knowledge of child's educational progress; and (f) parents' involvement in educational activities. An additional subscale assessed the extent to which parents promoted early independence of children. Subscales and subscale composition have varied somewhat from study to study (i.e., Marjoribanks, 1984).

Reliability. Marjoribanks (1979) reported that internal consistency coefficients for measures of the six environmental press variables were all above .75.

Uses and findings. Marjoribanks (1979) used the interview in a longitudinal examination of relationships between family background, socialization practices, teachers' attitudes towards children, children's peer group orientation, and cognitive and affective educational outcomes. He found that parental socialization variables were moderately related to family background. Socialization variables not only affected children's cognitive outcomes but appeared to be influenced by them as well. Relationships between specific variables varied with ethnicity, age, and sex. For example, parents' aspirations for their children and for themselves had strong direct and indirect effects on boys' academic performance once boys reached high school. For girls, previous school achievements were more important predictors.

Where to obtain. Write to Dr. Kevin Marjoribanks, Department of Education, University of Adelaide, Adelaide, Australia.

References

MARJORIBANKS, K. (1979). *Families and their learning environments.* London: Allen & Unwin.

MARJORIBANKS, K. (1984). Occupational status, family environments, and adolescents aspirations: The Laosa model. *Journal of Educational Psychology, 76,* 690–700.

Henderson Environmental Learning Process Scale (HELPS), *Ronald W. Henderson, 1972*

Description. The HELPS is designed to assess the qualities of homes which affect school success. It is a 55-item structured interview which asks parents about their family life. Questions tap variables which previous research has related to school success. Parents indicate their response on rating scales which are anchored with opposing terms or phrases.

HELPS elicits information about the family life of preschool and elementary school children. Standardization was conducted with reports of mothers of first graders in the Tucson area. Samples included 60 low SES Mexican-Americans and 66 mid-SES Anglo-Americans. Both Spanish and English versions of the scale are available. HELPS can be used with illiterate parents.

Administration and scoring. HELPS is administered in 20 minutes. Interviewers read items aloud while parents follow along and mark answers. Factor scores are computed from item scores.

Variables and score interpretation. Two sets of factor scores are available. Henderson, Bergan, and Hunt (1972) used data from the standardization sample to select 25 items most closely correlated with a total score. Scores on those items were adjusted to remove response bias and then factor analyzed. Five factors emerged: (a) Extended Interests and Community Involvement; (b) Valuing Language and School Related Behavior; (c) Intellectual Guidance; (d) Providing a Supportive Environment for Learning; and (e) Attention. Silverstein, Pearson, and Legutki (1982) factor analyzed uncorrected scores obtained by families of children with learning handicaps on all 55 items. While there were similarities, the six-factor solution differed from results obtained by Henderson et al.

Reliability. Johnson (1976) reported that internal consistency estimates which ranged from .71 to .85 were found for various samples of native Americans, Mexican Americans, and Anglo Americans (*n*'s = 27 to 66).

Uses and findings. Henderson et al. (1972) found that SES and ethnicity were related to the extent to which parents valued language and school-related behavior, as measured by the HELPS. They also found that HELPS factor scores predicted contemporaneous performance on achievement tests and measures of cognitive functioning. Valencia et al. (1986) found that quality of proximal home environment, assessed with a total HELPS score, better predicted Mexican-American children's cognitive performance than did distal aspects of background, such as SES and family size. A longitudinal study which used the HELPS (Nihira, Mink, & Meyers, 1985) examined relationships between environments and competencies among the educable mentally retarded. Findings indicated that a HELPS-based measure of parental aspirations for children predicted the degree to which children increased in community self-sufficiency over 4 years.

Where to obtain. Dr. Ronald W. Henderson, 31 Merril College, University of California-Santa Cruz, Santa Cruz, CA 95064.

References

HENDERSON, R. W., BERGAN, J. R., & HURT, JR., M. (1972). Development and validation of the Henderson environmental process learning scale. *Journal of Social Psychology, 88,* 185–196.

JOHNSON, O. (1976). *Handbook of child development measures* (Vol. 2). San Francisco: Jossey-Bass.

NIHIRA, K., MINK, I. T., & MEYERS, C. E. (1985). Home environment and development of slow-learning adolescents: Reciprocal relations. *Developmental Psychology, 21,* 784–794.

SILVERSTEIN, L., PEARSON, L. B., & LEGUTKI, G. (1982). Factor structure of the Henderson environmental learning process scale. *Psychological Reports, 50,* 856–858.

VALENCIA, R. R., HENDERSON, R. W., & RANKIN, R. J. (1986). Family status, family constellation, and home environmental variables as predictors of cognitive performance of Mexican-American children. *Journal of Educational Psychology, 77,* 323–331.

School Environment

SBS Inventory of Teacher's Social Behavior Standards and Expectations (SBS Inventory) and SBS Checklists of Correlates of Child Handicapping Conditions (Correlates Checklists), *Hill M. Walker & Richard Rankin, 1980*

Description. The measures are part of a five-instrument system, the AIMS (Walker, 1986), which determines the appropriateness of mainstream placements for handicapped children. The SBS Inventory and the Correlates Checklist serve by determining the demands which children must meet in particular teachers' classrooms. The SBS Inventory consists of 107 items in two sections. Section I items describe adaptive classroom behaviors and Section II items describe maladaptive behaviors. Teachers indicate the extent to which each adaptive behavior is required in their classrooms and the extent to which they tolerate each maladaptive behavior. The Correlates Checklist asks teachers how they would respond to efforts to place a child with each of 24 different handicaps in their classrooms. Teachers check the handicaps which would lead them to resist the placement. Teachers also indicate whether the provision of special assistance would make resistance-provoking handicaps, untolerable maladaptive behaviors, and deficits in critical adaptive behaviors more acceptable.

Validity and reliability studies were conducted with small samples of regular classroom teachers, education students, and special-education teachers from the United States, Canada, and Australia. There is data for about 2,000 teachers in all.

Administration and scoring. The instruments are self-administered. Response options on SBS Inventory rating scales are "critical," "desirable," and "unimportant" for Section I and "unacceptable," "tolerated," and "acceptable" for Section II. Inventory scores are numbers of responses of each sort. The total score is the number of "critical" plus "unacceptable" responses. Checklist scores are the number of items checked.

Variables and score interpretation. When used clinically, those adaptive behaviors which are "critical" and those problems which are intolerable are noted. Teachers' requirements can then be compared to skills and problems of handicapped children (see Walker, 1986, for a companion instrument for rating children). The total SBS and checklist scores indicate how demanding a teacher is relative to other teachers. Norms are presented in Walker (1986).

Reliability. Test-retest reliability was obtained over 6-week intervals (*n*'s = 50 regular and 22 special education teachers, 6-week interval). Coefficients for total and other Inventory scores ranged from .54 to .87. Those for Checklist scores ranged from .36 to .54. Internal consistency (*n* = 196) was .96 for Inventory Section I, .93 for Inventory Section II, and .82 for the Checklist (Walker & Rankin, 1983).

Uses and findings. Walker and Rankin (1983) found that teachers with higher Inventory and Checklist scores held less favorable attitudes towards mainstreaming. They also found some relationships between teachers' responses to the instrument and teachers' classroom behavior, but significant correlations were low. Walker (1986) demonstrated additional relationships between Inventory and Checklist scores and observations of teachers' classroom behavior. Walker (1986) noted that the ability of the AIMS system to improve mainstreaming outcome remains to be

demonstrated. He also suggested that the instrument may prove to be useful for the examination of a variety of hypotheses about teachers and educational practices.

Where to obtain. SBS Publications, 2nd Floor Clinical Services Building, 901 E. 18th, University of Oregon, Eugene, OR 97403 for instruments. Dr. Walker on the 3rd floor at the same address for permission.

References

WALKER, H. M. (1986). The assessment for integration into mainstream settings (AIMS) assessment system: Rationale instruments, procedures and outcomes. *Journal of Clinical Psychology, 15,* 55–63.

WALKER, H. M., & RANKIN, R. (1983). Assessing the behavioral expectations and demands of less restrictive settings. *School Psychology Review, 12,* 274–283.

My Class Inventory (MCI), Barry J. Fraser, Gary J. Anderson, & Herbert J. Walberg, 1973, 1982

Description. The MCI assesses classroom learning environment via student perceptions. It asks students about the level of student satisfaction, the difficulty of the schoolwork, their classmates, and the nature of the group experiences provided in their classrooms. It consists of 38 statements about classrooms. Students indicate whether they agree or disagree with each.

Children age 8 through 12 (third through seventh grade) complete the scale with respect to their classrooms. The scale was recently modified (Fisher & Fraser, 1981, cited in Fraser, Anderson, & Walberg, 1982) with data collected from 2,305 Australian children from 100 seventh-grade classrooms. Earlier versions have been used with varied large samples, e.g., 2,677 Wisconsin fifth graders (Walberg, Sorenson, & Fischbach, 1972).

Administration and scoring. The MCI may be group-administered. Item scores are summed to yield subscores.

Variables and score interpretation. MCI subscores assess the following variables: (a) satisfaction, how much students like their classrooms; (b) friction, perceived amount of tension or disagreement; (c) competition, perceived degree of competitiveness among classmates; (d) difficulty, perceived difficulty of classwork, and (e) cohesiveness, perceived intimacy of class relations. Individual students' scores index individual student perceptions. Class means for each subscale describe the learning environment for the class as a group.

Reliability. Internal consistency of subscores for individual students ($n = 2,305$ Australian seventh graders) ranged from .62 to .78; of class mean subscores ($n = 100$ Australian seventh grade classes) ranged from .73 to .88 (Fraser et al., 1982).

Uses and findings. Several studies (see Fraser et al., 1982) used the MCI, or a similar earlier version, to determine the effect of classroom environment on student achievement. For example, Talmadge & Walberg (1978) found that students' perceptions of competitiveness in their classrooms were negatively related to the extent to which their class's read-

ing scores improved after one year of a district reading program. The MCI was also used to measure outcomes. Participation in an experimental mathematics program was significantly related to increments in MCI cohesiveness scores Talmadge & Eash, 1978, cited by Fraser et al., 1982). Other research (Walberg et al., 1972) indicated that children's perceptions of the difficulty and competitiveness of their classrooms varied as a function of the demographic composition of their schools and their own socioeconomic status. See Fraser et al. (1982) for more.

Where to obtain. Herbert J. Walberg, College of Education, University of Illinois at Chicago, Chicago, IL 60680 for manual and instrument.

References

FRASER, B. J., ANDERSON, G. J., & WALBERG, H. J. (1982). *Assessment of learning environments: Manual for the Learning Environment Inventory (LEI) and the My Class Inventory (MCI)*. Australia: Western Australia Institute of Technology. (Write to Dr. Walberg or to Dr. Fraser for copies)

TALMADGE, H., & WALBERG, H. J. (1978). Naturalistic, decision-oriented evaluation of a district reading program. *Journal of Reading Behavior, 10*, 185–195.

WALBERG, H. J., SORENSON, J., & FISCHBACH, T. (1972). Ecological correlates of ambience in the learning environment. *American Educational Research Journal, 9*, 139–148.

For additional instruments see:

CHAVEZ, R. C. (1984). The use of high inference measures to study classroom climates: A review. *Review of Educational Research, 54*, 237–261.

EPSTEIN, J. L., & MCPARTLAND, J. M. (1976).

The concept and measurement of the quality of school life. *American Educational Research Journal, 13*, 15–30. Instrument: Quality of School Life Scale.

Environmental Stressors

Life Events Scale (LES), *R. Dean Coddington, 1972; 1984*

Description. The LES is used to quantify the amount of psychological readjustment which children undergo as a result of recent life events. The instrument is a 36-item list of positive and negative life events, such as starting school or becoming ill. Respondents indicate whether the child has experienced each event during a specified time period, preferably (Coddington, 1984) the previous 3 to 6 months.

The instrument is completed by parents with reference to preschool and elementary school children, or by older elementary-school children themselves. Both parents' reports and childrens' self-reports may be obtained and averaged together (Coddington, 1984). There is also a self-report version for use with adolescents. A heterogeneous sample of 3,620 Ohio school children provided norms for slightly different, earlier version of child and adolescent instruments (Coddington, 1972).

Administration and scoring. The instrument may be group-administered. Scores are computed by summing life change units associated with each life event which the child experienced.

Variables and score interpretation. Life change units are weights assigned to each event on the basis of the amount of

readjustment which the events necessitate. Weights used are averages of those assigned by a large panel of child and health care experts. The total LES score indicates the amount of demand for readjustment which the child has faced. A sample of 80 fourth graders and their parents provided limited normative data for the current child version of the LES (Coddington, 1984).

Reliability. Test-retest reliability of the adolescent scale over a 3-month interval was .69 (Coddington, 1984). Reliability of the children's scale was not reported.

Uses and findings. Coddington (1984) reported that correlations between fourth graders' self-reports and their parents' reports on the LES were significant but quite low. Using the average of children's self-reports and parents' reports and a cutoff of 50, Coddington (1984) found that the combination of low aptitude and high readjustment demands increased the likelihood of behavior problems among fourth graders. Children with low aptitude only did not differ significantly from normal ability, low LES controls in likelihood of behavior problems. Other researchers have used the earlier version of the LES and have sought to relate scores to self-concept, frequency of illness (Bedell, Giordani, Amour, Tavormina & Boll, 1977) and psychopathology (Steinhausen, Schindler, & Stephan, 1983).

Where to obtain. Dr. R. Dean Coddington, Box 307, St. Clairsville, OH 43950.

References

Bedell, J. R., Giordani, B., Amour, J. L., Tavormina, J., & Boll, T. (1977). Life stress and the psychological and medical adjustment of chronically ill children. *Journal of Psychosomatic Research, 21,* 237–242.

CODDINGTON, R. D. (1972). The significance of life events as etiologic factors in the diseases of children. I—A survey of professional workers. II—A study of a normal population. *Journal of Psychosomatic Research, 16,* 1–18, 205–213.

CODDINGTON, R. D. (1984). Measuring the stressfulness of a child's environment. In J. H. Humphreys (Ed.), *Stress in childhood* (97–126). New York: AMS Press.

STEINHAUSEN, H., SCHINDLER, H., & STEPHAN, H. (1983). Correlates of psychopathology in sick children: An empirical model. *Journal of the American Academy of Child Psychiatry, 22,* 559–564.

A Stressful Life Events Scale, Kaoru Yamamoto, 1979

Description. Each of the 20 items in Yamamoto's scale (1979) describes a negative life event. Children are asked to indicate how upsetting they find the event of a 7 point scale. They are also asked to indicate whether they ever experienced the event. It should be noted that the items were designed for research on children's perceptions of unpleasant life events, not to assess individual differences in any sort of clinical context, and thus do not constitute a formal assessment instrument. Also, to this writer's knowledge, these are the only life events items which have been "weighted" or evaluated for stressfulness by large samples of grade school children.

The scale has been completed by fifth and sixth graders from Phoenix (Yamamoto, 1979), a New Mexico city (Yamamoto & Byrnes, 1984), and children from a number of other countries, including Japan (Yamamoto & Davis, 1982), Philip-

pines (Yamamoto & Phillips, 1981), and others (Yamamoto, Soliman, & Parsons, in press).

Administration and scoring. The scale has been group-administered.

Variables and score interpretation. The number of stressful events which children experienced were counted and used to assess individual differences (Yamamoto & Davis, 1982). The researchers also summed the locally derived weights associated with personally experienced stressful events to assess overall stressfulness of children's lives.

Reliability. Median test-retest reliabilities of item stressfulness ratings and reports of personal experience, over a 2-month interval ($n = 70$), were .46 and .57 respectively (Yamamoto, 1979).

Uses and findings. Findings (Yamamoto, 1979; Yamamoto & Davis, 1982) indicated that sixth graders experienced more overall stress than did younger children. There were also a number of differences in the frequencies with which children from different nations, from different ethnic groups, of different sex, and of different grade experienced events. For example, Hispanic Americans in a New Mexico city were more likely to experience unpleasant events associated with school difficulties than were Anglo-American children (Yamamoto & Byrnes, 1984). Further, there were some differences in the absolute levels of distress which different groups associated with different events. However, according to the researchers, correlations between the median stress ratings of the various demographic groups indicated that such scale values, as well as their rank order, were extremely stable from culture to culture, ethnic group to ethnic group, grade to grade, etc. These correlations were considerably higher than within-culture correlations between children's ratings and professional's opinions about how children would rate events (Yamamoto & Felsenthal, 1982).

Where to obtain. Dr. Kaoru Yamamoto, College of Education, Arizona State University, Tempe, AZ 85287.

References

YAMAMOTO, K. (1979). Children's ratings of stressfulness of experiences. *Developmental Psychology, 15,* 581–582.

YAMAMOTO, K., & BYRNES, D. A. (1984). Classroom social status, ethnicity and ratings of stressful events. *Journal of Educational Research, 77,* 283–286.

YAMAMOTO, K., & DAVIS, O. L., JR. (1982). Views of Japanese and American children concerning stressful experiences. *Journal of Social Psychology, 116,* 163–171.

YAMAMOTO, K., & FELSENTHAL, H. M. (1982). Stressful experiences of children: Professional judgments. *Psychological Reports, 50,* 1087–1093.

YAMAMOTO, K., & PHILLIPS, J. A. (1981). Filipino children's ratings of the stressfulness of experiences. *Journal of Early Adolescence, 1,* 397–406.

YAMAMOTO, K., SOLIMAN, A., PARSONS, J., & DAVIS, O. L., JR. (in press). The voices in unison: Stressful events in the lives of children in six countries. *Journal of Child Psychology and Psychiatry.*

INDEX

A